G Embassy Phila

RETAIL LISTS & POSTAL AUCTIONS PRODUCED MONTHLY
CATALOGUE SENT FREE ON REQUEST
1000's OF ITEMS TO VIEW AND BUY ON OUR WEBSITE

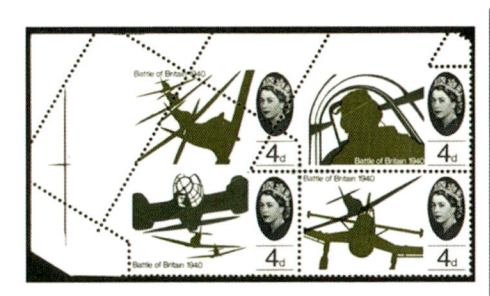

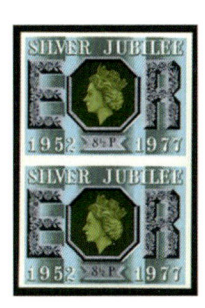

Embassy Philatelists
Est. 30 Years

P.O. BOX 161, CHICHESTER, W.SUSSEX PO19 3SU
Tel: 02392 412 512
Email: info@embassystamps.co.uk

www.embassystamps.co.uk

EBAY SHOP
Submit a 'best offer' today
http://stores.ebay.co.uk/embassy-stamps

BUYING
From single items to major collections, for a fast professional transaction call us today.

We may not be naturalists but we recognise
tadpoles and butterflies when we see them...

We also know that it's the little things that bring a collection to life.

BY APPOINTMENT TO
HER MAJESTY THE QUEEN
PHILATELISTS
STANLEY GIBBONS LTD
LONDON

STANLEY GIBBONS
LONDON 1856

399 Strand, WC2R 0LX, London | Call: 0207 557 4413 | Email: gb@stanleygibbons.com

STANLEY GIBBONS
GREAT BRITAIN SPECIALISED STAMP CATALOGUE

Queen Elizabeth II
Pre-decimal Issues

Volume 3

1964 Tenth International Botanical Congress imperforate imprimatur cylinder blocks of four, from the BPMA archives.

Stanley Gibbons
Great Britain Specialised
Stamp Catalogue

Volume 3

Queen Elizabeth II
Pre-decimal Issues

13th Edition

STANLEY GIBBONS LTD
London and Ringwood

By Appointment to
Her Majesty The Queen
Philatelists
Stanley Gibbons Ltd
London

Published by Stanley Gibbons Ltd
Editorial, Publications Sales Offices
and Distribution Centre:
7 Parkside, Christchurch Road, Ringwood,
Hants BH24 3SH

© Stanley Gibbons Ltd 2019

Copyright Notice

The contents of this Catalogue, including the numbering system and illustrations, are fully protected by copyright. No part of this publication may be reproduced, stored in a retrieval system, or transmitted in any form or by any means, electronic, mechanical, photocopying, recording or otherwise, without the prior permission of Stanley Gibbons Limited. Requests for such permission should be addressed to the Catalogue Editor. This Catalogue is sold on condition that it is not, by way of trade or otherwise, lent, re-sold, hired out, circulated or otherwise disposed of other than in its complete, original and unaltered form and without a similar condition including this condition being imposed on the subsequent purchaser.

1st edition – August 1970
2nd edition – October 1971
3rd edition – February 1976
Reprinted – October 1976
Reprinted – April 1977
4th edition – November 1978
5th edition – November 1980
6th edition – June 1984
7th edition – November 1987
8th edition – September 1990
9th edition – October 1993
10th edition – October 1998
11th edition – March 2006
12th edition – February 2011
Reprinted – July 2015
13th edition – March 2019

British Library Cataloguing in
Publication Data.

A catalogue record for this book is available from the British Library.

Errors and omissions excepted. The colour
reproduction of stamps is only as accurate as
the printing process will allow.

ISBN-13: 978-1-911304-43-2

Item No. R2810-19

Printed by Cambrian Printers, Wales

Contents

Preface vii
Introductory Notes ix

The Wilding Issues (Sections S and T)

General Notes to Section S 1
              Identification Table of Wilding Issues 6
              Index to Wilding Coil Stamps 7
Section SA: Photogravure Low Values (1952–1968) 9
Section SB: Booklet Panes in Photogravure (1952–1968) 58
              Index to Wilding Booklet Panes 59
Section SC: Post Office Booklets of Stamps Containing Wilding Issues (1953–1968) 90
Section T: Recess-printed High Values (1955–1968) 102

The Machin £.s.d. Issues (Section U)

General Notes to Section U 111
              Identification Table to Machin Low Values 116
              Index to Machin Coil Stamps 117
Section UA: Photogravure Low Values (1967–1970) 118
Section UB: Booklet Panes in Photogravure (1967–1970) 131
              Checklist of Machin Booklet Panes 132
Section UC: Post Office Booklets of Stamps Containing Machin Issues (1968–1970) 141
Section UD: Recess-printed High Values (1969) 148

The Special Issues (Section W)

General Notes 151
Design Index 155

The Regional Issues (Section XA)

General Notes on Wilding Regional Issues in Photogravure 260
  A.   Guernsey (1958–1969) 262
  B.   Isle of Man (1958–1969) 264
  C.   Jersey (1958–69) 266
  D.   Northern Ireland (1958–1970) 269
  E.   Scotland (1958–1970) 273
  F.   Wales and Monmouthshire (1958–1970) 279

The Postage Due Stamps (Section ZA)

General Notes 283
The Postage Due Issues (1954–1971) 284

Appendices

Appendix G: Perforators 286
Appendix HB: Postage Rates 294
Further Reading 299

v

WE SPECIALISE IN THE ISSUES OF

GREAT BRITAIN 1840–1970

Including

CYLINDER BLOCKS — VARIETIES

WILDING BOOKLETS — BOOKLET PANES

CYLINDER PANES — COIL LEADERS

Visit our secure website to view our latest stock or send for our FREE illustrated lists, mentioning this advertisement

WANTED
GREAT BRITAIN STAMPS — Mint or Used

CANDLISH McCLEERY LTD

PO BOX 2 HANLEY CASTLE WORCESTER WR8 0ZF
TEL: 01684 311771   FAX: 01684 311778
E-MAIL: ross@candlishmccleery.com

www.candlishmccleery.com

Preface

Compared with earlier and more recent periods of British Philately, it has always seemed that the first two decades of the present reign have been a relatively neglected field of study. True, the 1950s and '60s might not seem to be imbued with the history of the 19th century issues, or even those of the four Kings, neither does it have the current excitement of the decimal Machins, where new releases and discoveries are made almost monthly.

However, the early signs of renewed interest in the pre-decimal issues of Queen Elizabeth referred to in the preface to the last edition of this catalogue, have grown substantially, with many more serious collectors turning to the Wilding issues, in particular, as a field offering opportunities for study.

The reasons for this are not hard to identify; Wilding stamps are getting on for 70 years old now and can be set against a historical background of their own. At the same time this was a period of rapid innovation, with the introduction of new technology in mail handling and sorting, led, as was so often the case, by the British Post Office. The resulting trials of graphite lines and three different phosphor types on top of watermark and paper changes, makes this an area with sufficient complexity to interest the serious philatelist, without, dare we say it, breaking the bank.

The new edition
Against a backdrop of growing interest, it is only right that there should be a new catalogue to meet the needs of the growing body of collectors of the period and, while the gap between publication of this edition and its predecessor has been rather longer than usual, we feel sure that catalogue users will agree that it has been well worth the wait.

The most obvious development, of course, has been the introduction of colour, not only adding to the overall attractiveness of the book but making the plate and cylinder varieties much easier to identify than was possible with the old black and white images. The introduction of colour is an on-going process and, although, with the help of a number of collectors and members of the trade, a good proportion of colour images are now in place, there are still more to find. We therefore request that if you have one of the items still in black and white in this catalogue, you kindly forward a high resolution scan of it to gb@stanleygibbons.com for inclusion in the next edition.

Editorial additions and revisions
New introductions to the Wilding and Machin sections of the catalogue have been written by two of the foremost students of their respective fields, Frank Walton RDP and Douglas Muir RDP, the latter tracing in detail the development of the Machin portrait stamps accompanied by illustrations from the archive of The Postal Museum.

The listings in Section S see a number of improvements with enhanced notes throughout on such subjects as cream and whiter papers and the pricing, for the first time of Wilding coil leaders.

All booklets have been moved forward from Appendix HA, to follow the relevant booklet pane sections. Again, new notes and listings are evident, notably those with date or inscription errors or containing missing phosphor panes. Notes on perforation types have been expanded and Advertiser Voucher Copy (AVC) panes are now fully listed and priced.

Another notable development concerns the expansion of the listings of imprimatur material sold by the National Postal Museum (NPM) and the British Postal Museum and Archive (BPMA). Items from these sources are included in clearly headed entries following the respective issues.

In the commemoratives (Section W) the numbering of the illustrations has been altered to bring them in line with the SG number, as this seems to have caused confusion in the past.

Another previous area of confusion, namely the sideways watermarks on the postage due stamps, has also been eliminated with the addition of clear illustrations of the watermark orientations, as seen from the back of the stamp.

One of the areas of growth in interest from the Wilding period in particular has been a rapid rise in the number of collectors of the postal history of the time. To aid such collectors the appendix on postage rates has been considerably expanded, notably adding listings of Registered Inland and Overseas Surface and Airmail rates.

Prices
Prices have, as always, been very carefully reviewed and revised in line with the current market. Not surprisingly, with eight years having elapsed since the previous edition, changes are widespread, but not necessarily all in the same direction.

The renewed interest in the Wilding issues has resulted in substantial increases to many cylinder blocks and panes, as well as the popular cylinder flaws. However, while demand for the unusual is strong, that for the basic stamps has softened in recent years, resulting in price reductions in the commemorative section in particular, although the out of the ordinary is very clearly still in demand. Some of the more highly priced errors have fallen back from their more speculative peaks of previous years.

Acknowledgements
The catalogue could not be brought to you were it not for the immense amount of help we receive from specialist collectors and members of the trade offering advice and information.

As usual we would particularly like to thank members of the Great Britain Philatelic Society with whom even stronger links have been established in recent years. With a special thank you to Ian Harvey of the GBPS for his untiring assistance throughout.

So many individuals have helped with this edition, either through the GBPS or directly with the editorial team, that we fear it is inevitable that there will be omissions from this list, but, apart from those already mentioned, we would like to thank (in alphabetical order): Eric Abraham, Tony Baker, Tony Bellew, Mark Bloxham, Martin Bomford, David Boyd, Ian de la Rue Browne, Gary Burgess, Ross Candlish, Keith Emerson, Hanns Fasching, John Gledhill, Anthony Hall, John Horsey, Mark Johnson, Ian Lasok Smith, Glenn Morgan, Alan Musry, Tony Pinder, Paul Ramsay, Peter Shaw, Terry Slocket and Stephen Teuma. We apologise to anyone who should have been on this list, but has been missed.

We would also like to thank our colleagues in the Catalogue office and Studio in Ringwood and in the Great Britain Specialist Department at the Strand for their assistance in putting this catalogue to press.

Hugh Jefferies
Vince Cordell
February 2019

Top-rated Internet Stamp Dealers – Galashiels

Buying GB Decimal Collections

Selling Discount GB Postage
for latest prices visit: www.philatelink.co.uk

Buying GB & Commonwealth Collections

We urgently want to buy good GB collections from 1840 to present day, especially Wildings, Machin's and modern postage material. Top prices paid.

We buy and sell almost ANYTHING Philatelic

HOME VALUATION SERVICE
PREPARED TO TRAVEL UK WIDE TO BUY LARGE OR VALUABLE PROPERTIES
WE OFFER BETTER PRICES THAN YOU WOULD GET AT AUCTION

PHILATELINK eBay Shop & Auctions

WE HOLD HUNDREDS OF AUCTIONS EVERY MONTH
often via our CLIENT SELLING SERVICE (ask for Details)

http://stores.ebay.co.uk/PHILATELINK

Auctions start at just £0.99 and P&P is FREE to UK bidders

philatelink
The GB discount postage specialists

Web: www.philatelink.co.uk • Email philatelink@btinternet.com
☎ Landline: 01896 759703 or Mobile 07510 312271
PHILATELINK LTD 13 REDPATH CRESCENT,
GALASHIELS, BORDERS, TD1 2OG, UK

Introductory Notes

The aim of this catalogue is to classify in specialised form the Queen Elizabeth II pre-decimal stamps of Great Britain, to give distinguishing numbers to them and to quote prices which are current with Stanley Gibbons Ltd. at the time of going to press and at which they will supply if in stock.

Detailed Introductory Notes

Before using the catalogue it is important to study the "General Notes" as these explain the technical background of the issues in question. They are to be found at the beginning of the relevant sections.

Arrangement of Lists

The Wilding, Machin £.s.d. and Regional issues are dealt with value by value and Special issues in order of issue. The order of listing is as follows:

A. Basic listing of single stamps from sheets, booklets and coils according to paper, phosphor and gum with errors and varieties.
B. Illustrations of listed cylinder and plate varieties.
C. List of cylinder blocks according to paper, phosphor and gum combinations and priced according to perforation types.
D. Details of constant minor sheet flaws without illustrations and prices but quoting positions on stamps.
E. Information relating to coils.
F. Ancillary data relating to withdrawal dates, and quantities issued or sold.

If there is a deliberate change in the number of phosphor bands this is treated as a separate issue which is then listed in the order shown above.

Booklet panes are listed separately in Sections SB and UB according to paper and gum, with errors and cylinder varieties, and all priced according to perforation types. These are followed by illustrations of cylinder varieties and lists of booklet pane cylinder numbers appear at the end of each listing.

The Special issues (Section W) are listed on the same basis, set by set, with the addition of ancillary information about sheet format, method of printing, a list of the sheet markings, quantities sold and withdrawal dates from information published by the Post Office.

Catalogue Numbering

Users of this Catalogue for the first time will doubtless be familiar with our other Great Britain catalogues, however, in order to understand the unique numbering system used throughout the Specialised catalogues an explanation may help.

The stamps are split up by issue, commencing with the 1840 1d. black as Section A. This volume starts with the Wilding issues as section S and goes on to cover the issues prior to decimalisation on 15 February 1971.

Unlike our other catalogues, the arrangement is by value rather than by set, so all ½d. Wilding stamps are grouped together as numbers S1-12 in chronological order of issue to include watermark and paper changes, graphites and phosphors, etc. Where Specialised Catalogue numbers relate directly to numbers in the current edition of the *Great Britain Concise Stamp Catalogue*, these are clearly shown and the tables at the beginning of each section will also be of consdiderable help. Shades are indicated by a number in brackets and varieties by a letter indication. For example "U18(2)d" indicates "U18" Machin 6d., (2) Bright Magenta, "d" Diadem flaw.

In sections SC and UC the booklets have the same numbers and prefix letters as are used in the *Great Britain Concise Stamp Catalogue*. Varieties of booklets listed in the Specialised Catalogue only are shown with letter in brackets, thus "(a)".

Symbols and Abbreviations

†	(after date of issue) date of issue in sheet format, but available earlier from coil or booklet source. See Dates of Issue, under General Notes
†	(in price column) does not exist
—	(in price column) may exist or is known to exist, but we are unable to quote a price (a blank conveys the same meaning)
*	(against the price of a cylinder block) price includes a listed variety
/	between colours means "on" and the colour following is that of the paper on which the stamp is printed.
Cyl.	Cylinder
Flexo	Flexography
GA	Gum arabic
L/press	Letterpress
mm.	Millimetres
No.	Number
OP	Ordinary and phosphor
Phos.	Phosphor
Photo	Photogravure
Pl.	Plate
PVA	Polyvinyl alcohol (gum)
R.	row (thus "R. 6/4" indicates the fourth stamp from the left in the sixth horizontal row from the top of a sheet of stamps)
Th.	Refers to the Stanley Gibbons "Thirkell" Position Finder. The letters and figures which follow (e.g. Th. E5) pinpoint the position of the flaw on the stamp according to the grid engraved on the Finder
Wmk.	Watermark

Watermark Illustrations

The illustrations show watermarks as seen from the front of the stamp. This is important to remember when classifying sideways watermarks which also exist sideways inverted (i.e. Crown to right).

Quantities Sold

The figures for quantities issued or sold are those published by the Post Office. Some figures for the Regionals, however, came from an article by Mr. E. C. Ehrmann in *Stamp Collecting*.

Items Excluded

In dealing with varieties and minor constant flaws we record only those for which we can vouch, namely items we have seen and verified for ourselves. It should be recognised, however, that some flaws described as constant may be transient: they may develop in size to be sufficiently noticeable to be worth retouching.

Colour shifts due to faulty registration range from minor shifts to quite spectacular varieties. As it is very difficult to draw a line between major and minor shifts we have not listed any. We likewise exclude: doctor blade flaws; paper creases; partially omitted colours; negative offsets: and misplaced perforations.

Ever since the birth of our hobby Stanley Gibbons has been at the forefront of GB philately and we invite collectors access to one of the finest GB stocks in the world by registering for our renowned free Great Britain list.

Please visit www.stanleygibbons.com/gbmailing

BY APPOINTMENT TO
HER MAJESTY THE QUEEN
PHILATELISTS
STANLEY GIBBONS LTD
LONDON

STANLEY GIBBONS
LONDON 1856

Email gb@stanleygibbons.com or phone 020 7557 4413

STANLEY GIBBONS 399 STRAND LONDON WC2R 0LX | WWW.STANLEYGIBBONS.COM

We do not quote for traffic light blocks or positional blocks showing various sheet markings other than cylinder blocks, but when available they will be supplied at appropriate prices.

NPM (National Postal Museum) and BPMA (British Postal Museum and Archive) material

Great Britain material from the NPM archives was sold through three auction sales in 1984-1985, material from the BPMA originates from a direct purchase by Stanley Gibbons Ltd in 2014.

The material involved comprised "SPECIMEN" overprints and imprimaturs from duplicate Post Office registration sheets. These were handstamped "NPM/imprimatur" or "BPMA" on the reverse to indicate their origin. In this catalogue items from these sources are included in special entries under headings clearly indicating this origin.

> **To order from this Catalogue**
> Always quote the Specialised Catalogue number, mentioning Volume 3, 13th Edition, and where necessary specify additionally the precise item wanted.

Prices

Prices quoted in this Catalogue are the selling prices of Stanley Gibbons Ltd., at the time the book went to press. They are for stamps in fine condition for the particular issue, unless otherwise indicated: those of lesser quality may be offered at lower prices. All prices are subject to change without prior notice and no guarantee is given to supply all stamps priced, since it is not possible to keep every catalogued item in stock.

In the case of unused stamps, our prices are for unmounted mint. Prices for used stamps refer to fine postally used examples. Prices are not quoted for used stamps with cylinder flaw varieties and others, such as coil joins and sheet margin narrow phosphor bands, all of which are generally collected unused.

If a variety exists in more than one shade it is priced for the commonest shade and will be worth correspondingly more in a scarcer shade. Except where otherwise stated, varieties are priced for single examples and extra stamps required to make up positional blocks would be valued as normals. All cylinder flaws and other varieties listed under booklet panes are priced for the complete pane.

Cylinder blocks and cylinder booklet panes containing varieties are indicated by an asterisk against the price (which includes the cost of the variety).

Cases can exist where a particular stamp shows more than one listed variety. It might, for example, have an inverted watermark as well as a broad phosphor band, both of which are listed but priced separately. It is not practical to cover every possible combination, but the value of such items may be established by adding the difference between the price of the basic stamp and the dearest variety to the catalogue price of the cheapest variety.

The prices quoted for booklet panes are for panes with good perforations and complete with the binding margin. Prices for complete booklets are for those containing panes with average perforations as it is unusual for all panes in the booklet to show full perforations on the guillotined sides.

Cylinder blocks are priced according to the type of perforator used. This takes account of the state of the perforations on all four sides of the sheet, not just the corner where the cylinder number appears. Note that a full specification of a cylinder block should quote the basic number of the stamp; cylinder number; with or without dot; perforation type; cream or white paper; gum arabic or PVA, wherever such alternatives exist.

Coil leaders are priced as a leader with a single stamp attached or, for the multi-value coil, with five stamps attached.

Guarantee

All stamps supplied by Stanley Gibbons Ltd., are guaranteed originals in the following terms:

If not as described, and returned by the purchaser, we undertake to refund the price paid to us in the original transaction. If any stamp is certified as genuine by the Expert Committee of the Royal Philatelic Society, London, or by B.P.A. Expertising Ltd., the purchaser shall not be entitled to make any claim against us for any error, omission or mistake in such certificate.

Consumers' statutory rights are not affected by the above guarantee.

Expertisation

We do not give opinions as to the genuineness of stamps. Expert Committees exist for this purpose and enquiry can be made of the Royal Philatelic Society, London, 15 Abchurch Lane, London EC4N 7BW, or B.P.A. Expertising Ltd., P.O. Box 1141, Guildford, Surrey GU5 0WR. They do not undertake valuations under any circumstances and fees are payable for their services.

> **Correspondence**
> Letters should be addressed to the Catalogue Editor, Stanley Gibbons Publications, 7 Parkside, Christchurch Road, Ringwood, Hants BH24 3SH, and return postage is appreciated when a reply is sought. New information and unlisted items for consideration are welcomed.
>
> Please note we do not give opinions as to the genuineness of stamps, nor do we identify stamps or number them by our Catalogue.

STANLEY GIBBONS
AUCTIONS

Leading Philatelic Auctioneers Since 1901

Speak to our experts about consigning your material

Entrust your collection to a company with integrity

Reach thousands of potential buyers

Unrivalled expertise

Regular Public and Online Auctions

An internationally recognised and respected brand

To receive our catalogues or to discuss the sale of your stamps contact
Tel: 020 7836 8444 or email: auctions@stanleygibbons.com

STANLEY GIBBONS | 399 Strand | London | WC2R 0LX

www.stanleygibbons.com/auctions

Commemorative Missing Colours.

SG679a 1965 3d Post Office Tower with Olive-yellow (Tower) Omitted

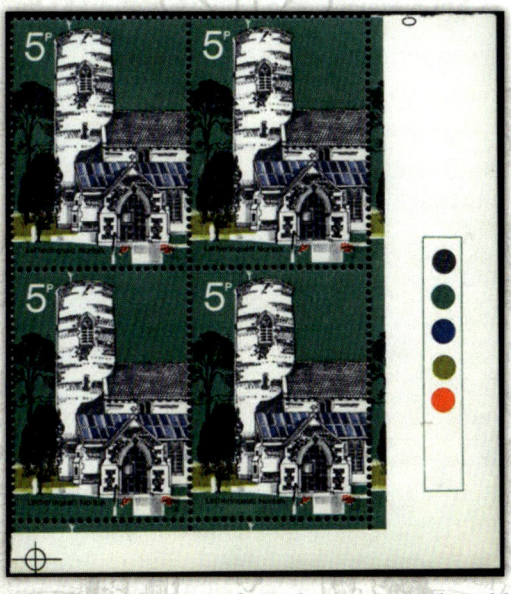

SG906a 1972 3p British Architecture with Gold (Queen's head) Omitted

SG714a 1966 1/6 Christmas with Pink (Hat) Omitted

SG925b 1973 5p Sir Francis Drake (British Explorer) with Grey-black Omitted

SG923/4c 1973 3p British Explorer Turquoise-blue (background & inscription) Omitted.

SG642a 1963 3d Red Cross with Red Omitted

SG624Aa 1961 3d Post Office Savings Bank with Orange-brown Omitted

Est. 1975

MARK BLOXHAM
STAMPS LTD

Proud PTS Member

W: www.philatelic.co.uk   T: +44 (0)1661 871953   E: mark@philatelic.co.uk

Commemorative Errors.

SG637a 1963 3d Yellow Green Brown and Black with Caterpillar Flaw

SG619a 1960 3d Deep Lilac with Broken Mane Flaw

SG632d 1962 3d Light Blue and Violet with Lake in Yorkshire Flaw

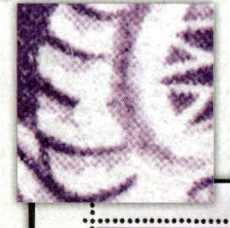

SG567a 1958 3d Deep Lilac with Short Scale Flaw

Mark Bloxham Stamps Ltd

Est. 1975

Proud PTS Member

W: www.philatelic.co.uk   T: +44 (0)1661 871953   E: mark@philatelic.co.uk

Phosphor Bands

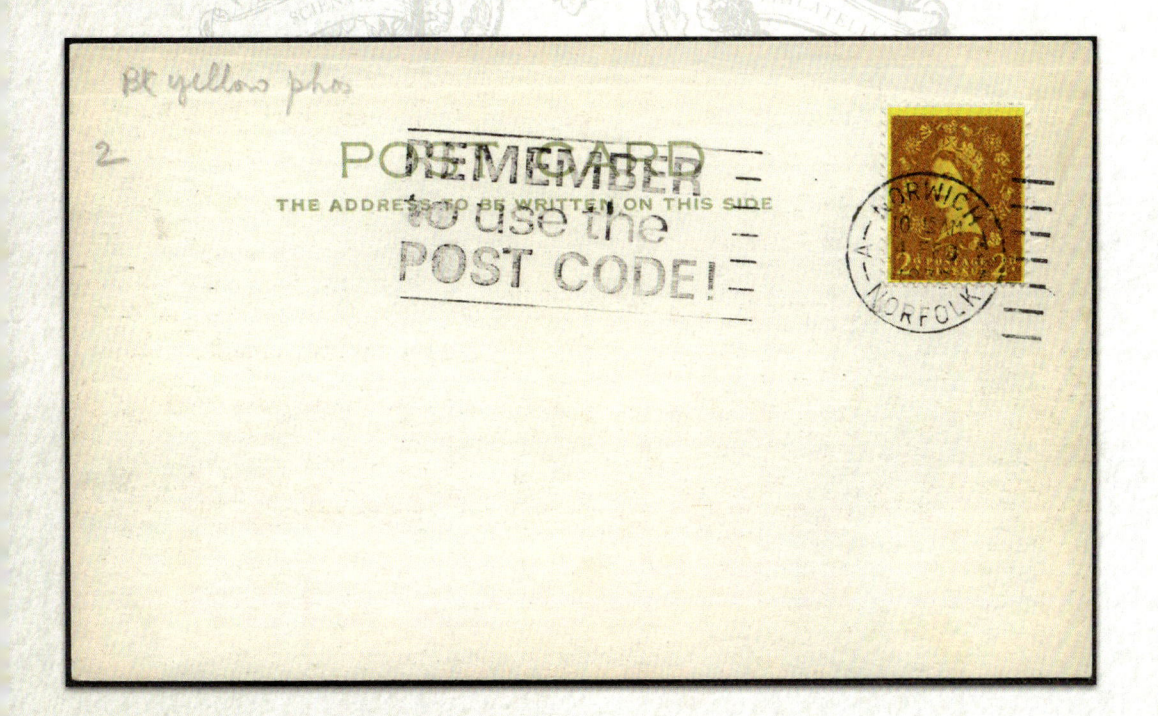

We are looking to buy:

Commemoratives with Missing Colours

Specialised QEII

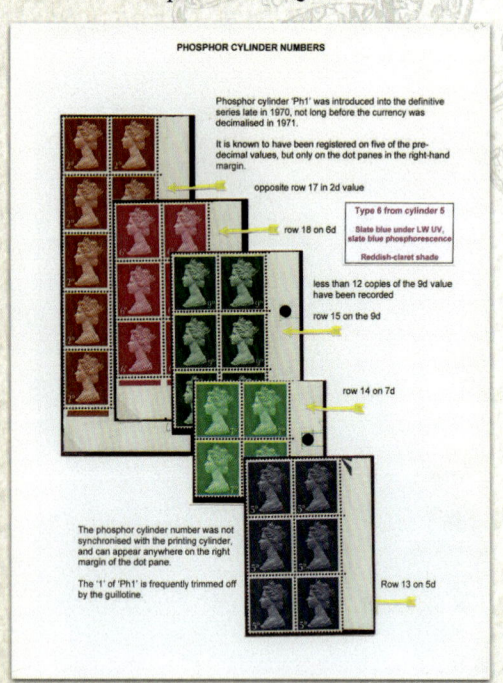

Proofs and Artwork

Specialised Wilding Collections

MARK BLOXHAM
STAMPS LTD

Est. 1975

Proud PTS Member

W: www.philatelic.co.uk   T: +44 (0)1661 871953   E: mark@philatelic.co.uk

Section S
Dorothy Wilding Issues
1952–1968. Sheet, Coil and Booklet Stamps in Photogravure

General Notes

Introduction. The term 'Wildings' has been used by collectors for many decades to describe the British definitive stamps that feature The Queen's portrait that was derived from a series of photographs taken by the famous photographer Dorothy Wilding. The image of Her Majesty's head appeared on a series of small-format definitive stamps from December 1952 until their replacement in 1967 with the first stamps designed by Arnold Machin. The same head design was used on the Castle high value definitive series, regional stamps and also on some commemorative issues.

Background to the issues. In the autumn of 1951, GPO officials started to consider what would happen when King George VI, who had been in ill health, was succeeded by his daughter. This work resulted in a paper entitled 'Initial Steps to be taken in connexion (sic) with new issues of Postage Stamps', written by S W Day. This defined the sequence in which denominations would be issued, how designs would be sought, and also the breadth of products to be created – i.e. coils, booklets, stationery and so on. The document was filed, but was drawn upon rather more quickly than had been anticipated following The King's death on 6 February 1952. As early as 13 February, the Postal Services Department (PSD) approached The Queen's Private Secretary, Sir Alan Lascelles, to commence planning the new stamps. It had already been arranged for Dorothy Wilding, a successful and well-known London photographer, to take a series of portraits of Queen Elizabeth II on 26 February 1952. The PSD had briefed Wilding that it required photographs that could be used for printing by the photogravure process. The instructions were very precise, detailing that 'it was undesirable to have heavy shadows on one side of her face and that top lighting, which threw shadows on the eyes, should be avoided'. A series of review meetings were held, and these resulted in another photographic session by Dorothy Wilding on 15 April 1952. It was images from this session that were used ultimately for the issued stamps.

Development of the Designs. While the central photographic portrait was being perfected, the Post Office established a list of artists to be invited to submit designs for the new stamps. After several iterations, it was finally agreed that designs would be sought from Mary Adshead, Edmund Dulac, John Fairleigh, Abram Games, Joan Hassall, Enid Marx, Percy Metcalfe, Victor Reinganum, John Stobie and Lancelot Thornton. These artists would be paid for their submissions, and it was made clear that any further artists could provide designs, though they would not receive any payment. The design brief insisted that the photographic portrait of The Queen would be the central feature, but also that it was eminently desirable to include the four national floral emblems of rose, shamrock, thistle and daffodil. It was also insisted that the words 'postage' and 'revenue' must feature.

The winning Wilding designs. Ultimately 75 designs were submitted for consideration from the above-named artists, and also from employees of the printers Harrisons, De La Rue, Waterlows and Bradbury Wilkinson. An advisory panel was established to consider all aspects of the designs, including their suitability for production and operational use; after a series of panel meetings the 75 designs were whittled down to 19, then to nine and finally, on 23 July 1952, the final five designs were selected. There was a desire to issue two commonly used values before the end of 1952, so the final choices for the 1½d and 2½d were recommended on 6 October 1952, and received approval from Buckingham Palace the same day. Harrisons had been selected as the printer, and they began work immediately with a target release date of 8 or 12 December 1952 – in time to allow members of the public to use the new stamps on their Christmas mail. In the end, the release deadline was beaten and the two stamps were issued on 5 December 1952. Further consultations were needed to decide which design and colour was to be assigned to which value for the remainder of the series. This took some weeks to conclude, but the final attributions were:

½d, 1d, 1½d, 2d	Marx	No. 35
2½d, 3d, 4d, (later 4½d)	Farrer-Bell	No. 45
5d, 6d, 7d	Knipe (for Harrison & Sons)	No. 39
8d, 9d, 10d, 11d	Adshead	No. 20
1s, 1s 3d, 1s 6d	Dulac	No. 10

Enid Marx photographic essay for the 1½d. with 'POSTAGE' at top and the value in all four corners.

830A - Rejected design by Enid Marx entitled 'Royal Bouquet', dated 25 June 1952

832 - Rejected design by Enid Marx entitled 'Imperial Lace', dated 25 June 1952

S Dorothy Wilding issues *General Notes*

Production. All Wilding small format stamps were printed photogravure by Harrisons and Sons. Harrisons started production in earnest in autumn 1952, but it was not until 8 February 1954 that the final three values of the initial set appeared. The 4½d denomination appeared five years later on 9 February 1959.

Cylinder creation. Each printing cylinder was made by combining an image of the Wilding head with an image of the rest of the design. The two masters were on transparent backgrounds, and overlaid to create the final design ready to be etched onto the cylinder. This was replicated 240 times to complete a sheet in 20 rows of 12 stamps. This combined design was known as a 'multipositive'. For values that required many cylinders to be produced due to the volumes of sheets to be printed, occasionally one master image needed to be replaced. The best-known example of this is the head image for the 2½d where the first image had an imperfect top line to the diadem; this was corrected in the second version. These two head types are known by collectors as Die I and Die II respectively. Die I was used to create the first 45 2½d cylinders, and Die II for Cylinders 46 to 60. Because the head and frame elements of the design were aligned manually, a slightly different orientation can be detected. The records show different multipositives were also used to create the 1½d, 3d, 4d and 6d series of cylinders – but for these cases the differences are minor and beyond the scope of this catalogue.

The stamps were issued value by value over a period, the first being the 1½d. and 2½d. which were placed on sale on the 5 December 1952, but it was not until February 1954 that the series was completed. During this period there was an interesting phase when booklets were issued containing panes of King George VI and Queen Elizabeth II stamps.

Arrangement. This section takes each value in turn and follows its history through the various watermarks, graphite lines, phosphors and papers, taking in the coils and on pages 6 and 7 there are tables setting out which values occurred in each state and quoting their catalogue numbers for easy reference.

The general arrangement of the catalogue is to show first the basic listing with errors and varieties, followed by illustrations of the listed cylinder flaws. These are priced, whereas the minor constant flaws are not, but they are included for reference. The sheet cylinder numbers and a record of the minor flaws follow. Where applicable the description of the coils and Imprimaturs and Specimens that were sold from the then National Postal Museum (NPM), British Postal Museum and Archive (BPMA) and now The Postal Museum archives are dealt with. Quantities sold of the basic issue are included where known at the end of each listing although for the definitives this information was seldom available.

Booklet panes are dealt with in a similar manner in Section SB. For quantities of booklets issued or sold see under Sections SC and UC.

Paper. For the first ten years the definitives were printed on "cream" paper, so all Tudor Crown and St Edward's Crown watermark issues are on cream paper, albeit with some variation in the cream tones. Starting in April 1962 a whiter paper was gradually introduced. It is always a difficult matter to maintain successive supplies of paper in exactly the same colour and so it is not surprising that there is some variation in the degree of whiteness in the whiter paper which sometimes makes it difficult to identify. The terms "cream" and "whiter" papers refer specifically to the appearance from the front in natural daylight. Stamps on cream paper are always opaque, whereas those on whiter paper exhibit a degree of translucence when viewed from the back. In assessing a Crowns watermark stamp, comparison can be made with Tudor or St Edward's Crown examples. Sometimes knowledge of the cylinder used can be decisive. Chalk-surfaced paper was used for the 2s. Holiday Booklet issued in 1963 which affected the ½d. and 2½d. values in the Crowns watermark.

In 1964 an experimental paper was used for the 3d. non-phosphor Crowns watermark which was slightly thicker. It can be distinguished by the fact that an additional watermark letter "T" lying on its side occurred about four times in the sheet margin.

Variations can also be found in the thickness of the paper used, a notable example being the 3d. Tudor Crown watermark (No. S67) on thick paper. As weight standards were applied to complete reels only, such differences on individual stamps were within acceptable tolerances.

Paper Fluorescence. Stamps printed on unsurfaced paper may show varying fluorescence when viewed under a short-wave ultraviolet lamp. This is due to the presence, in the rags used in paper making, of optical brightening agents. Generally, the cream paper does not fluoresce, while the whiter paper does. However, stamps on whiter paper exist, which show no fluorescence. Such fluorescent properties are outside the scope of this catalogue.

Tinted Papers. On some issues the front of the paper appears to be tinted with a light shade of the stamp colour, whereas the gummed side is the same as any other value. This is caused by an intermittent fault of the "doctor blade", failing to fully wipe the surface of the cylinder free of excess ink. Generally, stamps with "tinted paper" are not listed, as most have only slightly shaded paper. However, the 6d. value on St Edward's Crown watermark, S105/6, is known with strongly tinted paper and, exceptionally, is listed in that condition with attached selvedge to illustrate the tint.

Watermarks. The first Queen Elizabeth stamps were printed on Tudor Crown watermarked paper. It is now known that the change to St Edward's Crown paper followed damage to the Tudor Crown dandy roll in early 1955. The change to Multiple Crowns paper followed the decision to isssue regional stamps for Scotland and the possibility that protests could follow the use of the "E2R" cypher on its stamps. In the Crowns watermark differences in the spacing of the Crowns have been noticed, but it is believed that this is due to variations in the dandy roll and does not represent a different version of the watermark.

Errors, or replacement "bits", occur on most dandy rolls. For example during the period 1964 to 1966 the Crowns watermark can be found with one crown inverted. These errors have been seen on various commemoratives.

Watermark Varieties. As the Wilding issues are all printed on continuous reels inverted watermarks cannot occur on the counter sheet stamps, but they do occur on 50% of the booklet panes owing to the manner in which the sheets are arranged with half the columns having the images inverted on the cylinders. The booklets are guillotined before issue resulting in half the panes with the watermark inverted in relation to the image. Booklets are the only source of inverted watermarks in the Wilding issues up to 1s.6d.

Until 1961 all stamps with the watermark sideways came only from coils with left side delivery and these all show the top of the watermark pointing to left *as seen from the front of the stamp*. From 1961 all 2s. booklets on Crowns watermark had the watermark sideways and these, of course, have 50% of the panes with the crowns pointing to left and 50% to right and they are listed both ways.

Sheet Perforators. The perforator types are described and illustrated in Appendix G. Definitive cylinder blocks are from the bottom left corner of the sheet and the following abbreviations relate to the margins at left and the bottom margin. The perforation type is given last and further details on the type of comb and perforation feed are in Appendix G.

(AE/I)   Alternate extension holes in left margin and imperf bottom margin. Perf. Type E no dot pane

(E/I)   One extension hole in left margin, each row and imperf. bottom margin. Perf. Types A both panes, E dot pane and H no dot pane

(E/P)   As last but bottom margin perforated through. Perf. Type C no dot and dot also A(T) dot pane

(I/P)   Imperf. left margin and bottom margin perforated through. Perf. Types B and J no dot panes only

(I/E)   As last but extension holes in bottom margin. Perf. Types F(L) and F(L)* no dot panes

(P/E)   Left margin perforated through and extension holes in bottom margin. Perf. Types F no dot and F(L)* dot panes

(P/I)   Left margin perforated and bottom margin imperf. Perf. Type H dot pane

General Notes **Dorothy Wilding issues**

Experimental Graphite Issues. The first Automatic Letter Facing machine (known as ALF) was introduced experimentally at Southampton on 19 December 1957. The machine, which prepares letters for the sorting process, is fed with letters having their long edges parallel but with stamps in any of four possible positions. The letters are reorientated so that the stamps are in one of two possible positions on one long edge. These two positions, together with First and Second Class mail, are separated into stacks, and the stamps are cancelled. Items which cannot be faced, due for example to the absence of a stamp, are rejected to receive manual treatment.

The prototype facing machine looked in the stamp corner for an area of dense printing ink, having the characteristics of a stamp, as a means of stamp detection. This system was inefficient as the machine's performance was influenced by stamp design and the occasional presence of misleading writing on the envelope. However, facing machines were equipped with this method as a secondary means of stamp detection in order to deal with O.H.M.S. and Business Reply items.

To improve the efficiency of facing it was necessary to give these stamps some unmistakable identity. The first attempt used stamps which were printed with electrically conducting vertical black graphite lines on the back under the gum. One line on the 2d., then the printed paper rate, and two lines on the other values. The use of electrically conducting lines was not a complete success as failures were caused by metallic paper fasteners and damp mail.

There were two graphite issues. The first in November 1957 on the ½d., 1d., 1½d., 2d., 2½d. and 3d. sheet stamps with the St Edward's Crown watermark, all values were also issued in coils. The second issue came out during 1958–1959 on the same values, plus the 4d. and 4½d. in sheets with the Crowns watermark. Here, only the 2d. to 4½d. were issued in sheets, the ½d., 1d., 2d. and 3d. were available from coils and all, bar the 2d., 4d. and the 4½d. in booklets.

Stamps showing faked graphite lines are known, especially on used examples.

Phosphor Trials. As the electrical conductivity of graphite line stamps was not a success, the Post Office decided to experiment with phosphor as the medium to help with letter facing and with sorting stamped mail. These experiments were carried out in the laboratory of the Post Office Research Station located at Dollis Hill, north-west London.

The experiments were started in 1957 by the Chief Chemist, Charles F. Forster, as original research since no other postal authority used phosphorescent materials for this purpose (until the first Canadian issue in 1962). Forster was the inventor of new organic phosphors and his work resulted in a patent, filed in 1959, granted in 1961. Consequently, Forster undertook many short-run experiments with a greater number of phosphor ink mixtures than those which were eventually used on issued stamps and in different formats, some being within the paper. As the Post Office was continually looking for greater efficiency and reduction in cost in the sorting office, the phosphor experiments by Forster and his department were continuous until at least 1972.

Substantially, all the known trial stamps, whether unused or used, derive from the estate of Forster and other material of a similar nature may be assumed to have come from the laboratory. The stamps are listed separately at the end of Section SA, as most were printed by Harrison & Sons, probably in very short runs, on paper or in a format not used for issued stamps. Additionally, whilst some of the trial phosphors react to u.v. in a similar way to those on the issued stamps, others, the result of different experimental mixtures, react slightly differently. The phosphor colour reactions are described.

Apart from some 3d. Deep lilac cylinder 11 blocks, the stamps appear to be low quality printing, probably by Harrison & Sons, and those with phosphor within the paper required hand-made paper for the experiment prior to printing. Even the cylinder blocks do not equate with an issue of stamps as these trials are without graphite lines on the reverse whereas issued cylinder 11 printings were graphite lined stamps only.

Additionally, the cylinder 11 printings used for trials have perf Type B (I/P) selvedges, whereas the contemporary issued sheet stamps printed from other cylinders have Type A (E/I) selvedges, so trial stamps with attached selvedge can be distinguished.

Phosphor-Graphite Issues. In November 1959 existing graphite stamps were overprinted on the face with phosphorescent ink which, when exposed to ultraviolet (u.v.) light, releases energy in the form of visible light. The emission of visible light persists for some time after the exposure to u.v. light has ceased. These stamps were originally issued for further experiments at Southampton, November 1959 to February 1960, when the ALF operated with one electrical scanner and one phosphor scanner. Most countries which handle very large quantities of mail have followed the lead of Great Britain in the use of some form of luminescence on stamps to facilitate automatic facing.

The British Post Office used organic-resin phosphors containing an activator, the choice of activator affecting the optical properties.

Phosphor bands are not always easy to see, especially on used stamps, and it is usually necessary to hold the stamps up to the light at eye level when they become visible as broad bands.

The graphite lined stamps were overprinted with vertical phosphor bands on the face, again one band for the 2d. and two bands for the others. In sheets they appeared on the ½d., 1d., 1½d. and 2d. (in Error) with St Edward's Crown watermark and on the 2d., 2½d., 3d., 4d. and 4½d. with Crowns watermark. The substance used is commercially known as Lettalite B1 (the activator being Parahydroxydiphenyl) and it produces a greenish phosphorescence when reacting with u.v. light in the 2000 to 3000 Ångstrom range.

As the phosphor treatment of stamps at Southampton was successful, residual stocks having graphite lines were distributed as normal stock to other areas and a notice was sent to Post Office clerks to say that they should disregard the black lines. This applied also to the 5s. booklet No. H46g (Sept. 1960).

Phosphor Issues. The Southampton ALF was converted to scan phosphor only on 6 July 1960 and the ½d. to 4d. and 1s.3d. values with Crowns watermark with phosphor bands only were issued on 22 June 1960, the 6d. following on 27 June. Coils and booklets were issued later. The same phosphor reacting green was employed but in 1961 this was replaced as an interim measure by Lettalite B2 (Carbazole sulphonic acid being the activator) which reacts blue to u.v. in the 2000–4000 Ångstrom range. The advantage of this was that it gave a stronger signal.

At this time ALF machines were introduced into other areas and the "blue" phosphor was in use between 1961 and 1966 on the same values as for the "green" phosphor and with the addition of the 4½d. value. This period covered the changeover to the whiter paper and also two changes in postal rates so that the 2d., 2½d. and 3d. were each issued with one and two bands.

With the introduction of address coding and automatic letter sorting, at Norwich in 1965, it became necessary to use a phosphor for stamps which would not interfere with sorting. Thus another change was made, this time to Lettalite B3 (having Terephthalic acid as the activator) which was inert to the u.v. light of wavelength 3650 Ångstroms used in sorting machines but which has a bright visible light output when subjected to 2537 Ångstroms in the facing machine. This reacts violet under the lamp.

Identification of Phosphor Colours. Short wave ultraviolet lamps are available to enable collectors to identify the green, blue and violet phosphors. Please refer to the Stanley Gibbons Accessory list for information on these products currently available. Care should be taken when using such lamps as ultraviolet light can damage the eyes.

Phosphor Band Widths. Both the green and the blue bands measure 8 mm except for the values used for the printed paper rate during the period, which had a single 4 mm side band at left on the 2d. and 2½d. values and alternately at left and right on the 3d. by application of 8 mm. bands across adjacent stamps.

There are two widths of the violet phosphor bands, the

8 mm bands, issued in 1965 (½d., 1d., 1½d., 2d., 4d., 6d. and 1s.3d., plus coils and booklets) and the 9·5 mm bands issued in 1966–1967 (1d., 2d., 4d., 5d., 6d., 7d., 8d., 9d., 10d., 1s., 1s.3d. and 1s.6d. plus coils and booklets). As the bands overlap the stamps it is easier to distinguish these by measuring the space between the bands, this being approximately 12 mm for the 8 mm bands and 10·5 mm for the 9·5 mm bands. As with the "blue" bands the 3d. value has only one band and in the 8 mm band series this is at the left or right of the stamp whilst in the 9·5 mm band series it is a 4 mm. band in the centre.

Letterpress 6 mm and 8 mm Phosphor Bands in Sheets. For values with the phosphor applied by letterpress the bands along the left and right margins were only 6 mm wide, instead of the normal 8 mm. Where these varieties exist they have been listed, the prices being for stamps with the vertical margin attached. Most booklet panes of four from the watermark Crowns sideways issues had the phosphor bands applied by letterpress. Examples with 4 mm. and 5·5 mm. side bands, similar to those on sheets, have been identified on panes also showing shifted phosphor bands.

Phosphor printed on both sides by letterpress. Occasionally, sheets of stamps were printed with phosphor bands on both the front and the back; these result in in phosphor bands on the back showing the same clarity of reaction as on the front and are listed as varieties. Offsets of phosphor on the back from sheet stacking, which appear indistinct and weak are outside the scope of this catalogue.

Application of Phosphor Bands. The choice of method for applying the phosphor bands is a matter for the printer and three different methods have been used: photogravure, letterpress and flexography.

To apply bands by photogravure sometimes an additional printing cylinder is brought into use so that it is done in the same operation as printing the stamps. In the case of multicoloured special issues there may not be a spare cylinder available as this would depend upon the colour capacity of the press and the number of colours to be used. The bands may then be applied by letterpress or photogravure as a separate operation on a sheet-fed press.

Letterpress was used to apply the bands to cut graphite sheets to produce the phosphor-graphite issue; and for various later "emergency" sheet printings and all booklet panes of four except 4d. panes after October 1966.

Flexography is a letterpress process but using a rubber cylinder (which does not indent the paper) to pick up the impression from a photo-etched inking cylinder. The screen pattern is usually blurred, although some traces of it remain. This method was employed for applying bands to stamps already printed "on the web" before being cut into counter sheets.

Photogravure bands do not indent the paper, are screened (either 150 or 250 lines to the inch, but occasionally occur mixed), extend through the top and bottom sheet margins and cause a reflective appearance on the non-phosphor part of the paper, due to the pressure of the cylinder. Bands applied by letterpress often indent the paper, as can be seen from the back, are solid and generally stop short of the edges of the sheet.

It is rather difficult to distinguish flexography phosphor bands from those printed by photogravure, and for this reason they are not listed separately. Flexography is known to have been used to apply phosphor bands to early multicoloured special issues, when all the photogravure cylinders had been used for the colour and a flexographic cylinder was attached to apply the phosphor in the reel. Being a letterpress process the non-phosphor part of the paper is not reflective. Currently, there is no evidence that flexography was used on any other issues.

Phosphor Reaction. The "green" phosphor was overprinted by letterpress on the graphite stamps but by photogravure on the first phosphor only issue. The "blue" phosphor was normally applied by photogravure, but some values also exist with letterpress or flexographic application overprint. The violet 8 mm bands are normally applied by photogravure but again some values exist with them letterpress and the 9·5 mm series exist with them only by photogravure except for the *se-tenant* booklet panes which were letterpress.

Misplaced Bands on Sheets, Coils and Booklet Panes. Phosphor bands frequently appear misplaced but such varieties are outside the scope of this Catalogue, except where the misplacement affects the number of bands, i.e. one band instead of two or two narrow bands over the vertical perforations, instead of one centre or side band.

Cylinder Varieties. Most of the more prominent varieties are listed and illustrated, but we have restricted ourselves to those we have actually seen. Others may be added to future editions as examples become available for illustration.

The position is always indicated by stating first the cylinder number (and where no full stop is shown this means the "no dot" cylinder, whereas a full stop means the "dot" cylinder) followed by the position indicated first by the horizontal row and then the position in it. Thus "Cyl. 15, R. 10/3" means cylinder 15 no dot, the third stamp in the tenth row down. Where the same cylinder is used on stamps with different watermark, paper or type of phosphor, etc. the varieties on that cylinder will recur, unless corrected by retouching, and these are then listed again with footnotes referring back to its first appearance where it is illustrated.

Unless otherwise stated the prices are for single stamps and extra copies needed to make positional blocks will be charged as normals.

Tête-Bêche Errors. These derive from booklets due to faulty making-up; this is described in the introductory notes to Section SC.

Minor Constant Flaws. These are so numerous that they are merely recorded without illustrations. Their location on the stamp is indicated, where helpful, by reference to the SG "Thirkell" Position Finder, an essential tool for identifying flaws. The recording of these flaws, often insignificant in themselves, will prove an aid in identifying a particular cylinder and will also serve to show that the flaw has been considered for listing as a variety but rejected as being too minor. Again we have only recorded what we have actually seen but the picture is necessarily incomplete as we have not been able to view full sheets from every cylinder.

Coils. Vertical delivery coils are generally printed from double-pane cylinders, the exceptions being the ½d. and 1d. with graphite lines, all 6d. Wildings, the 2d. and 6d. Machins and the Scout Jamboree stamps. All sideways delivery coils during this period were single-pane cylinders. In identifying the position of a stamp the roll number is quoted (this is the number printed on the outer wrapper of the coil which corresponds to the row in the sheet before reeling) but where double cylinders are used only half the coils bearing the roll numbers will contain the variety. Hence there are 12 rolls (vertical delivery) and ten rolls (sideways delivery) from every sheet and varieties will be repeated on every 21st stamp on vertical rolls and on every 25th stamp on sideways delivery rolls. Coil leaders are listed with their codes and are priced as a leader with a single stamp attached. No distinction is made for the coil number. Additional stamps are priced as normals.

Shades. Intended changes of colour on the low value Wilding definitives such as the 2d. red-brown and light red-brown, the 6d. reddish purple and deep claret and the 4d. ultramarine and deep ultramarine are given full numbers and some of the more marked shades on other issues which were not made by design are shown as alternatives. In some cases, however, there is a whole range of shades which it would be meaningless to attempt to list. The colour descriptions given are based on the Stanley Gibbons Colour Key. Additionally, some values show a range of shades which may be identified by specialists, but this level of detail is outside the scope of this catalogue.

Dates of Issue. The dates given in bold type in the headings are those on which stamps in normal Post Office *sheets* were first issued, notwithstanding the fact that they may have appeared earlier in booklet form. A dagger is added to the sheet date where stamps were issued at an *earlier* date in booklets or coils. Stamps with inverted or sideways watermarks which appeared either earlier or later than those from ordinary sheets have the dates given after the listing of each item, and for stamps from booklets we have taken the earliest possible dated booklet, i.e. taking into account booklets containing panes with

General Notes **Dorothy Wilding issues** S

mixed watermarks. Where there is a change of watermark or type of phosphor or to the whiter paper, the dates given are generally those on which they were first issued by the Supplies Department to Postmasters.

Withdrawal Date. All the low value Wilding stamps not previously sold out were withdrawn from issue at the Philatelic Bureaux on 27 February 1970, and were invalidated as from 1 March 1972.

Post Office Training School Stamps. Examples of most stamps exist overprinted with two thick vertical bars. Some values are also known overprinted "SCHOOL SPECIMEN" by handstamp. Stamps cancelled with various types of these overprints were used in Post Office Training Schools. Their acquisition by the public was unauthorised, the simplicity of the overprints has resulted in the production of fakes.

Sheet Markings. Compared with the King George VI period a wide variety of markings of various kinds have been introduced in Elizabethan issues to facilitate new elements such as registration of multicoloured stamps, ensuring that the cylinders are applied in the correct sequence, aids to registration of perforation, colour dots to ease checking for omission of colours and so on.

We give below notes and illustrations of the markings which were used in the Wilding issues and those which apply to other issues are described in the General Notes relating to the other Sections. They are particularly helpful in establishing the position of varieties in the case of marginal blocks and can also help in identifying the type of perforator used or the type of machine employed for printing, etc.

Cylinder Number

Cylinder Number. This always occurs in the left-hand margin beside Row 18. In double-pane cylinders the no dot pane is on the left and the dot pane on the right. Booklet cylinder numbers are described in Section SC.

Varieties in Cylinder Blocks. Where a cylinder block contains a listed variety the price is adjusted accordingly and bears an asterisk.

"V" shaped Hand-engraved    "W" shaped Hand-engraved

"W" shaped Photo-etched

Marginal Arrows. These occur against the middle rows of the sheet as an aid to Post Office clerks when breaking up the sheets. They may be hand-engraved or photo-etched. The earlier cylinders were "V" shaped (hand-engraved) at the top and bottom of the sheet and "W" shaped (photo-etched) at both sides. Later cylinders were often "W" shaped (photo-etched) at top, bottom and sides but a number of combinations exist. In some cases they are accidentally missing from the cylinder and where these are known this is stated under the cylinder number listing. The 2½d. on Crowns watermarked paper, cylinder 55, exists with "V" shaped arrow in the correct position below rows 6/7 and a faint outline to the right, below rows 8/9, where the mark had been placed in error.

Narrow Rule   Wide Rule   Damaged Rule

Marginal Rules. These are the solid bands of colour which appear below the bottom row of the sheet and which used to be called "Jubilee Lines" because they were first introduced in the so-called "Jubilee" issue of 1887. These are invariably co-extensive (with breaks between each stamp) and come in various widths.

Unboxed    Boxed

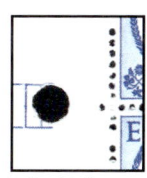

In Double Box    Black Bar

Perforation Guide Holes on Sheets. These large circular punched holes occur on reel-fed printings usually boxed opposite rows 14/15 at left (no dot) or right (dot) or unboxed opposite rows 1 and 7/8 at both sides. They are an indication of the type of perforator used and further reference to these is made in Appendix G. They also occur in double boxes, those illustrated being representative. They are liable to be trimmed off almost completely.

See also General Notes for Section W.

Black Bar. This was used alongside the marginal arrows at left on no dot sheets and at right on dot sheets on "green" and early "blue" phosphor printings. It was intended for easy recognition of phosphor stocks in the Post Office Supplies Department.

Sheet Numbers. Most sheets are serially numbered in black after printing for checking purposes but the numbers are liable to be placed anywhere in the margins and so are of no use for identifying a position. They are not of much help in establishing whether a sheet occurred early or late in a printing either, as a particular printing may not necessarily have been numbered from 1 and several machines may have been used.

Checkers Marks. These are small encircled numbers applied with a rubber stamp in a variety of colours. They are applied by Post Office checkers when counting the sheets delivered by the printer. As with sheet numbers they are liable to be placed anywhere in the sheet margins.

Table of Wilding Issues

References are to Specialised Catalogue Numbers

	½d	1d	1½d	2d Red-brown	2d Light red-brown	2d 2 bands	2½d Type I	2½d Type II	2½d Type II One band	2½d Type II One band	3d	4d Ultramarine	4d Deep Ultramarine	4½d	5d	6d Reddish purple	6d Deep claret	7d	8d	9d	10d	11d	1s.	1s.3d.	1s.6d.
Tudor Crown	S1	S13	S25	S36			S50	S51			S67	S81				S104		S114	S119	S124	S129	S134	S136	S141	S150
St. Edward's Crown	S2	S14	S26	S37	S38		S52	S53			S68	S82				S105		S115	S120	S125	S130	S135	S137	S142	S151
Graphite. St. Edward's Crown	S3	S15	S27		S39			S54			S69														
Crowns. Cream Paper	S4	S16	S28		S40		S56	S55	S56	S64	S70	S83		S93	S100		S107	S116	S121	S126	S131		S138	S143	S152
Crowns. Whiter Paper	S5	S17	S29		S41		S56c	S57		S65	S71	S84	S85	S94	S101		S108	S117	S122	S127	S132		S139	S144	S153
Crowns. Chalky Paper	S6							S58							S102										
Graphite. Crowns	S7	S18	S30		S42			S59			S72	S86		S95											
Phosphor-graphite	S8	S19	S31		S43			S60			S73	S87		S96											
Green Phosphor	S9	S20	S32		S44			S61			S74	S88					S109						S145		
Blue Phosphor. Cream Paper	S10	S21	S33		S45	S46		S62	S63		S75	S89		S97			S110						S146		
Blue Phosphor. Whiter Paper	S11	S22	S34			S47			S66		S76		S90	S98			S111						S147		
Violet Phosphor. 8 mm.	S12	S23	S35			S48							S91				S112						S148		
Violet Phosphor. 9.5 mm.		S24				S49					S80		S92		S103		S113	S118	S123	S128	S133		S140	S149	S154
1 Side Band. Blue Phosphor											S77														
1 Side Band. Violet Phosphor											S78														
1 Centre Band. Violet Phosphor											S79														
Presentation Packs at end of Section SA																									

Table of Wilding Issues **Dorothy Wilding issues**

Index to Coil Stamps

Face Value	Watermark	Further description	Delivery	Stamp No.
½d.	Tudor Crown		V S	S1
½d.	St. Edward's Crown		V S	S2
½d.	St. Edward's Crown	Graphite lines	V	S3
½d.	Crowns	Cream or whiter paper	V S	S6
½d.	Crowns	Graphite lines	V	S7
½d.	Crowns	Green phosphor	V	S9
½d.	Crowns	Blue phosphor, cream or whiter paper	V	S11
½d.	Crowns	Violet phosphor, 8 mm.	V	S12
1d.	Tudor Crown		V S	S13
1d.	St. Edward's Crown		V S	S14
1d.	St. Edward's Crown	Graphite lines	V	S15
1d.	Crowns	Cream or whiter paper	V S	S17
1d.	Crowns	Graphite lines	V	S18
1d.	Crowns	Green phosphor	V	S20
1d.	Crowns	Blue phosphor, cream or whiter paper	V	S22
1d.	Crowns	Violet phosphor, 8 mm.	V	S23
1d.	Crowns	Violet phosphor, 9·5 mm.	V	S24
1½d.	Tudor Crown		V	S25
1½d.	Tudor Crown, sideways		S	S25
1½d.	St. Edward's Crown		V	S26
1½d.	St. Edward's Crown, sideways		S	S26
1½d.	St. Edward's Crown	Graphite lines	V	S27
1½d.	Crowns	Cream paper	V	S29
1½d.	Crowns	Whiter paper	S	S29
2d.	Tudor Crown	Red-brown	V	S36
2d.	Tudor Crown, sideways	Red-brown	S	S36
2d.	St. Edward's Crown	Red-brown	V	S38
2d.	St. Edward's Crown, sideways	Red-brown	S	S38
2d.	St. Edward's Crown	Light red-brown	V	S38
2d.	St. Edward's Crown, sideways	Light red-brown	S	S38
2d.	St. Edward's Crown	Graphite lines	V	S39
2d.	Crowns	Cream or whiter paper	V	S41
2d.	Crowns, sideways	Cream or whiter paper	S	S41
2d.	Crowns	Graphite lines	V	S42
2d.	Crowns	Green phosphor	V	S44
2d.	Crowns	Blue phosphor, 1 left band	V	S45
2d.	Crowns	Blue phosphor, cream or whiter paper, 2 bands	V	S47
2d.	Crowns	Violet phosphor, 8 mm.	V	S48
2d.	Crowns	Violet phosphor, 9·5 mm.	V	S49
2d.	Crowns, sideways	Violet phosphor, 9·5 mm.	S	S49

7

S Dorothy Wilding issues Table of Wilding Issues

Face Value	Watermark	Further description	Delivery	Stamp No.
2½d.	Tudor Crown	Type I	V	S50
2½d.	Tudor Crown, sideways	Type I	S	S50
2½d.	St. Edward's Crown	Type I	V	S52
2½d.	St. Edward's Crown, sideways	Type I	S	S52
2½d.	St. Edward's Crown	Type II, Graphite lines	S	S54
2½d.	Crowns	Type I. Cream or whiter paper	V	S56
2½d.	Crowns, sideways	Type I. Cream or whiter paper	S	S56
2½d.	Crowns, sideways	Type II. Whiter paper	S	S57
3d.	Tudor Crown		V S	S67
3d.	St. Edward's Crown		V S	S68
3d.	St. Edward's Crown, sideways		S	S68
3d.	St. Edward's Crown	Graphite lines	S	S69
3d.	Crowns	Cream or whiter paper	V	S71
3d.	Crowns, sideways	Cream or whiter paper	S	S71
3d.	Crowns	Graphite lines	V S	S72
3d.	Crowns	Blue phosphor, cream or whiter paper, 2 bands	V	S77
3d.	Crowns	Blue phosphor, whiter paper, 1 side band	V	S77
3d.	Crowns	Violet phosphor, 1 side band	V	S80
3d.	Crowns	Violet phosphor, 1 centre band	V	S80
3d.	Crowns, sideways	Violet phosphor, 1 centre band	S	S80
4d.	Tudor Crown	Ultramarine	S	S81
4d.	St. Edward's Crown	Ultramarine	V S	S82
4d.	Crowns	Ultramarine, cream or whiter paper	V S	S85
4d.	Crowns	Deep ultramarine, whiter paper	V	S85
4d.	Crowns, sideways	Deep ultramarine, whiter paper	S	S85
4d.	Crowns, sideways	Violet phosphor, 9·5 mm.	S	S92
6d.	Tudor Crown		V	S104
6d.	St. Edward's Crown	Reddish purple	V	S106
6d.	St. Edward's Crown	Deep claret	V	S106
6d.	Crowns	Cream or whiter paper	V	S108
6d.	Crowns	Violet phosphor, 9·5 mm.	V	S113

General Notes **Dorothy Wilding issues**

Printers. All the Wilding issues were printed by photogravure by Harrison & Sons. They were printed on continuous reels of paper "on the web", generally in double-pane width, i.e. 480 stamps consisting of two panes (no dot and dot) each of 240 stamps arranged in 20 rows of 12 stamps, the panes being guillotined before issue. However, some printings were made from single cylinders printing sheets of 240 stamps (i.e. no dot panes only). For the method of printing booklet panes, see section SB.

Paper and Watermark. All the following issues are printed on unsurfaced paper, except the ½d. and 2½d. values (Nos. S6 and S58) printed on chalk-surfaced paper.

The illustrations of the watermarks are *as seen from the front of the stamp*. The Tudor Crown was in use from 1952 to 1954, the St Edward's Crown from 1955 to 1958 and the Multiple Crowns from 1958 onwards. No pre-decimal Wilding issues appeared on paper without watermark.

Gum. Only gum arabic has been used for the Wilding issues as PVA gum was not introduced until the Machin series.

Perforation. All stamps are comb perforated 15 × 14 as the King George VI issues. However, the horizontal perforation is very close to the three-quarters mark and so is sometimes described as 14½ × 14.

Perforation varieties such as double or misplaced perforations are not listed in this Catalogue.

Tudor Crown **W.22**

St Edward's Crown **W.23**

Crowns **W.24**

Type **SA1**

Type **SA2**

Type **SA3**

Type **SA4**

Type **SA5**

Type **SA6**

Type **SA7**

Portraits of Queen Elizabeth II and National Emblems

Des. Miss Enid Marx (SA1), Michael C. Farrar Bell (SA2/SA3), George T. Knipe (SA4), Miss Mary Adshead (SA5), Edmund Dulac (SA6/SA7)
Portrait by Dorothy Wilding Ltd.

SA Dorothy Wilding issues ½d. Orange-red

½d. Orange-red, Type SA1 (1953–1965)

1953 *(31 August).* **½d.** Wmk Tudor Crown

S1 = SG 515		Mint	Used
½d.	Orange-red	25	15
	a. Watermark inverted *(3.54)*	2·00	2·00
	b. Coil join (horiz. pair)	4·00	
	c. "A" flaw (Vert. coil, Roll 3)	30·00	
	d. Spot on "d" (Vert. coil, Roll 5)	30·00	
	f. Rose flaw (Cyls 1 & 3 Dot, R.19/12)	30·00	

S1c, S2g, S4k

S1d, S2h, S4l

S1f, S2f, S4i Retouched on later Crowns watermark printings

Cylinder Numbers (Blocks of Six)
Perforation Type B (I/P no dot) and C (E/P dot)

Cyl. No.	No dot	Dot
1	35·00	35·00

Perforation Type A (E/I)

Cyl. No.	No dot	Dot
1	10·00	10·00
3	10·00	10·00

Minor Constant Sheet Flaws

Cyl. 1	4/4	White smudge at left of upper left rose (Th. B1)
	5/6	White spot at end of stem of upper right shamrock (Th. C6)
	13/1	Large concealed retouch on Queen's cheek (Th. D3–4)
Cyl. 1.	1/7	Background retouch below upper left rose (Th. B1)
	1/10	Orange spot at top right of centre cross in crown (Th. A–B3–4)
	15/4	Retouched background between "OS" of "POSTAGE"
	18/8	Coloured dot in "P" of "POSTAGE"
Cyl. 3	4/4	As cyl. 1
	5/6	As cyl. 1
Cyl. 3.	18/8	As cyl. 1

Coil Leaders
All coils have the watermark upright and Cylinder A1 or A2 was used.

Sideways delivery made up from sheets with sheet margin joins

Code No.	Number in roll	Face value	
AA	240	10/-	35·00
G	480	£1	25·00
W	960	£2	15·00
D	960	£2	55·00
Y	1920	£4	20·00
P	480	£1	30·00

Imprimaturs from the NPM or BPMA
Imperforate, watermark Type W.22

Watermark upright	£900
Watermark inverted	£900
Tête-bêche pair (Horiz or Vert)	£3250
Cyl. 1 Block of Six	£6250

1955 *(12 December).* **½d.** Wmk St Edward's Crown

S2 = SG 540		Mint	Used
½d.	Orange-red	20	15
	b. Watermark inverted *(9.55)*	45	40
	c. Coil join (horiz. pr.)	3·50	
	d. Flaw on shamrock stem (Cyl. 2 Dot, R. 18/8)	35·00	
	e. Major retouch (Cyl. 2 Dot, R. 19/2)	30·00	
	f. Rose flaw (Cyl. 2 Dot, R. 19/12)	40·00	
	g. "A" flaw (Vert. coil, Roll 3)	35·00	
	h. Spot on "d" (Vert. coil, Roll 5)	35·00	
	i. Shamrock flaw (Vert. coil, Roll 11)	35·00	
	j. "R" flaw (Vert. coil, Roll 11)	35·00	

For illustrations of Nos. S2f/h, see Nos. S1c/d and S1f.

S2d, S4g

S2e, S4h Shows as retouched area to design edge

S2i, S4m, S5g, S9b, S10g, S11f

S2j, S4n, S5i, S9c, S10h, S11g

Cylinder Numbers (Blocks of Six)
Perforation Type B (I/P no dot) and C (E/P dot)

Cyl. No.	No dot	Dot
1	35·00	35·00

Perforation Type A (E/I)

Cyl. No.	No dot	Dot
2	15·00	35·00*
3	10·00	10·00

½d. Orange-red   **Dorothy Wilding issues**   **SA**

Minor Constant Sheet Flaws

Cyl. 1 no dot and dot.	As for No. S1, cyl. 1.
Cyls. 2 and 3 no dot and dot.	As for No. S1, cyl. 3 except that flaw on 4/4 is retouched on cyl. 3 no dot.
Cyl. 2.	20/2	Retouch by lower right thistle and rose (Th. F5–6).

Coil Leaders
All coils have the watermark upright and it is believed that the cylinder numbers used were A3 in double-panes as well as cylinder A1 or A2.

Vertical delivery printed in continuous reels

Code No.	Number in roll	Face value	
AA	240	10/-	25·00
G	480	£1	30·00
W	960	£2	15·00
D	960	£2	85·00
Y	1920	£4	15·00

Sideways delivery made up from sheets with sheet margin joins

| P | 480 | £1 | 25·00 |

Imprimaturs from the NPM or BPMA
Imperforate, watermark Type W.**23**

Watermark upright	£900
Watermark inverted	£900
Tête-bêche pair (Horiz or Vert)	£3250
Cyl. 3 Block of Six	£6250

Graphite-lined Issues

The graphite lines were printed in black on the back, beneath the gum. Two lines per stamp, except for the 2d. value which has one line.

SA8

1957 (19 November). **½d.** with graphite lines, Type **SA8**. Wmk St Edward's Crown

S3 = SG 561	Mint	Used
½d. Orange-red	60	60
a. "E" flaw (Cyl. 5 No dot, R.17/9)	35·00	
b. Extra stem to thistle (Cyl. 5 No dot, R.18/10)	35·00	

S3a, S8b   S3b, S8c

Cylinder Numbers (Blocks of Six)
Single pane cylinders

Cyl. No.		Perforation type	No Dot
4		B (I/P)	12·00
4		C(E/P)	12·00
5		B (I/P)	10·00
5		C(E/P)	10·00

Minor Constant Sheet Flaw

Cyl. 4   12/8   Orange spot in top thistle (Th. A4)

Coil Leaders
All have watermark upright, sheet Cylinder 4 having been converted to a 21-row cylinder.

Vertical delivery printed in continuous reels

Code No.	Number in roll	Face value	
G	480	£1	75·00
W	960	£2	65·00
Y	1920	£4	75·00

Imprimatur from the NPM or BPMA
Imperforate, watermark Type W.**23**

Watermark upright	£2000

Quantity Issued: 22,508,400

1958 (25 November). **½d.** Wmk Crowns

A. Cream Paper

S4 = SG 570	Mint	Used
½d. Orange-red	10	10
c. Watermark inverted (11.58)	40	40
d. Watermark Crown to left (26.5.61)	3·00	3·00
e. Watermark Crown to right	3·00	3·00
f. Coil join (horiz. pair)	3·50	
g. Flaw on shamrock stem (Cyl. 2 Dot, R.18/8)	30·00	
h. Major retouch (Cyl. 2 Dot, R.19/2)	35·00	
i. Rose flaw (Cyl. 2 Dot, R.19/12)	35·00	
k. "A" flaw (Vert. coil, Roll 3)	35·00	
l. Spot on "d" (Vert. coil, Roll 5)	35·00	
m. Shamrock flaw (Vert. coil, Roll 11)	35·00	
n. "R" flaw (Vert. coil, Roll 11)	35·00	

B. Whiter Paper (27 July 1962)†
S5

½d. Orange-red	10	10
a. Watermark Crown to left (5.6.62)	75	75
b. Watermark Crown to right	75	75
c. Watermark inverted (29.7.62)	1·50	1·50
f. Large dot by daffodil (Vert. coil, Roll 4)	35·00	
g. Shamrock flaw (Vert. coil, Roll 11)	35·00	
h. "d" joined to shamrock (Vert. coil, Roll 11)	35·00	
i. "R" flaw (Vert. coil, Roll 11)	35·00	

C. Chalk-surfaced Paper. Booklets only (15 July 1963)
S6 = SG 570k

½d. Orange-red	2·50	2·75
a. Watermark inverted	2·75	3·00

† The earliest issue was in vertical coils on 30 April 1962.
For illustrations of No. S4g, see No. S2d; for No. S4h, see No. S2e; for No. S4k, see No. S1c; for No. S4l, see No. S1d; for Nos. S4m/S4n and S5g, S5i, see Nos. S2i/S2j.

Tête-bêche. No. S5 exists tête-bêche from booklet sheets which were not issued.

11

SA Dorothy Wilding issues ½d. Orange-red

S5f, S12e

S5h, S12f

Cylinder Numbers (Blocks of Six)

A. Cream Paper (No. S4)
Perforation Type B (I/P no dot) and C (E/P dot)

Cyl. No.	No dot	Dot
1	25·00	25·00
3	25·00	25·00

Perforation Type A (E/I)

Cyl. No.	No dot	Dot
2	15·00	40·00*
3	10·00	10·00

B. Whiter Paper (No. S5)
Perforation Type A (E/I)

Cyl. No.	No dot	Dot
1	10·00	10·00
3	10·00	10·00

Minor Constant Sheet Flaws

Cyl. 1	4/4	As for No. S1
	5/6	As for No. S1
	13/1	As for No. S1
Cyl. 1.	1/10	As for No. S1
Cyl. 2.	18/8	Coloured dot in "P" of "POSTAGE" (later retouched)
	20/2	As for No. S2
Cyl. 3	5/6	As for No. S1
Cyl. 3.	18/8	As for No. S1

Coil Leaders
All have watermark upright and cylinder numbers A1, A2 and A3 were used for cream paper printings and numbers A3 and A4 for whiter paper issues.

Vertical delivery printed in continuous reels.
Cream or whiter paper.

Code No.	Number in roll	Face value	
AA	240	10/-	25·00
G	480	£1	30·00
W	960	£2	15·00
D	960	£2	85·00
Y	1920	£4	15·00

Sideways delivery made up from sheets with sheet margin joins. Cream paper

| P | 480 | £1 | 25·00 |

Imprimaturs from the NPM or BPMA
Imperforate, watermark Type W.**24**. Cream or whiter paper

Watermark upright	£900
Watermark inverted	£900
Tête-bêche pair (Horiz or Vert)	£3250
Cyl. 1. (Cream paper) Block of Six	£6250
Cyl. 3. (Whiter paper) Block of Six	£6250
Cyl. A2. (For coils) Block of Six	£6750

1959 *(15 June).* **½d.** With graphite lines, Type **SA8**. Wmk Crowns

S7 = SG 587	Mint	Used
½d. Orange-red	9·00	9·00

1959 *(15 June).* **½d.** With graphite lines, Type **SA8**. Wmk Crowns

S7 = SG 587	Mint	Used
a. Watermark inverted *(4.8.59)*	3·25	4·00

No. S7/a was only issued in booklets and coils. For panes, see Section SB, Nos. SB14/a.

Coil Leaders
All have watermark upright, sheet cylinder 4 having been converted to a 21-row cylinder.

Code No.	Number in roll	Face value	
W	960	£2	75·00
Y	1920	£4	£120

Imprimaturs from the NPM or BPMA
Imperforate, watermark Type W.**24**

Watermark upright	£900
Watermark inverted	£900
Tête-bêche pair	£3250

Quantity Issued: 4,161,840

1959 *(18 November).* **½d.** Phosphor-graphite issue. Wmk St. Edward's Crown

S8 = SG 599	Mint	Used
½d. Orange-red	4·50	4·50
a. Narrow band at left or right (stamp with vert. margin)	30·00	
b. "E" flaw (R. 17/9)	35·00	
c. Extra stem to thistle (R. 18/10)	35·00	

This has two graphite lines, Type **SA8**, on the back and two phosphor bands, applied by letterpress, on the front, which react green under the lamp.

The listed flaws are as illustrated for Nos. S3a/b.

Cylinder Numbers (Blocks of Six)

Single pane cylinder

Cyl. No.	Perf type	No Dot
5	B(I/P)	35·00
5	C(E/P)	45·00

Imprimatur from the NPM or BPMA
Perf. 15 × 14, watermark Type W.**23**

Watermark upright	—

Quantity Issued: 707,040

1960 *(22 June).* **½d.** Two phosphor bands reacting green. Wmk Crowns

S9	Mint	Used
½d. Orange-red	1·75	1·50
a. Watermark inverted *(14.8.60)*	6·00	6·00
b. Shamrock flaw (Coil, Roll 11)	35·00	
c. "R" flaw (Coil, Roll 11)	35·00	
d. Coil join (vert. pair)	4·00	
e. One 8 mm phosphor band	£140	

The bands were applied by photogravure.
For illustrations of Nos. S9b/c see Nos. S2i/j.

Cylinder Numbers (Blocks of Six)
Perforation Type B (I/P no dot) and C (E/P dot)

Cyl. No.	No dot	Dot
1	30·00	30·00

½d. Orange-red **Dorothy Wilding issues** **SA**

Minor Constant Sheet Flaws

Cyl. 1	4/4	As for S1
	5/6	As for S1
	13/1	As for S1
Cyl. 1.	1/10	As for S1
	19/12	White bulge on upper right sepal of lower right rose (Th. E5–6)

Coil Leaders
All have watermark upright and cylinder number A3 was used in double panes.

Vertical delivery printed in continuous reels

Code No.	Number in roll	Face value	
G	480	10s.	60·00
W	960	£2	60·00
Y	1920	£4	85·00

Vertical delivery.
Made up from sheets with sheet margin joins.

Y	1920	£4	£100

Imprimatur from the NPM or BPMA
Imperforate, watermark Type W.**24**

Watermark upright	£900
Watermark inverted	£900
Tête Bêche pair (Horiz)	£3250
Cyl. 1 Block of Six	£6250
Cyl. A2 (for Coils) Block of Six	£6750

●━━━━━━━━━

1961. *(5 June)*†. **½d.** Two phosphor bands reacting blue. Wmk Crowns

A. Cream Paper

S10		Mint	Used
½d.	Orange-red	25	20
a.	Watermark inverted *(3.61)*	1·50	1·50
b.	Watermark Crown to left *(14.7.61)*	15·00	15·00
c.	Watermark Crown to right	15·00	15·00
d.	One band (wmk. sideways)	35·00	
da.	One band (wmk. upright or inverted)	90·00	
g.	Shamrock flaw (Coil, Roll 11)	35·00	
h.	"R" flaw (Coil, Roll 11)	35·00	

B. Whiter Paper *(21 June 1965)*†
S11 = SG 610

½d.	Orange-red	10	15
a.	Watermark Crown to left *(15.8.62)*	15·00	15·00
b.	Watermark Crown to right	15·00	15·00
c.	Watermark inverted *(3.6.63)*	1·50	1·50
f.	Shamrock flaw (Coil, Roll 11)	35·00	
g.	"R" flaw (Coil, Roll 11)	35·00	

The bands were applied by photogravure on the stamps with upright and inverted watermark and by letterpress on those with watermark sideways.
For illustrations of Nos. S10g and S11f see No. S2i and for S10h and S11g see No. S2j.

Cylinder Numbers (Blocks of Six)
Perforation Type A(E/I)

Cream paper (No. S10)

Cyl. No.		No dot	Dot
1		10·00	10·00

Whiter paper (No. S11)

Cyl. No.		No dot	Dot
1		10·00	10·00

Minor Constant Sheet Flaws
As for No. S9

Coil Leaders
All have watermark upright and cylinder number A3 was used in double panes.

Vertical delivery printed in continuous reels.
Cream or whiter paper.

Code No.	Number in roll	Face value	
G	480	10/-	60·00
W	960	£2	45·00

cream paper only

Y	1920	£4	75·00

Imprimaturs from NPM or BPMA
Imperforate, watermark Type W.**24**. Cream or whiter paper

Watermark upright	£900
Watermark upright "Dot on the left Fraction bar" Booklet R. 1/1	£1500
Watermark inverted	£900
Watermark sideways	£900
Tête-bêche pair	£3250
Cyl. 1 Block of Six (Cream paper)	£6250
Cyl. A2 (for Coils) Block of Six	£6750

●━━━━━━━━━

1965 *(13 August)*. **½d.** Two 8 mm. Phosphor bands reacting violet. Wmk Crowns

S12		Mint	Used
½d.	Orange-red	55	45
a.	One 6 mm band at left or right (stamp with vert. margin)	6·00	
b.	L/press. bands omitted*	30·00	
c.	One 8 mm band (l/press.)	20·00	
ca.	As c. but 6 mm band	20·00	
d.	Bands applied photo. *(15.10.65)*	1·25	50
e.	Large dot by daffodil (Coil, Roll 4)	30·00	
f.	"d" joined to shamrock (Coil, Roll 11)	30·00	

The bands were applied by letterpress on the sheets and by photogravure on the coils.
* No S12b can be distinguished from a non-phosphor stamp by the fact that this shows a clear impression of the letterpress. plate with no reaction under the lamp.
For illustrations of Nos. S12e/f, see Nos. S5f/h.

Cylinder Numbers (Blocks of Six)
Perforation Type A(E/I)

Cyl. No.	No dot	Dot
1	25·00	40·00

Minor Constant Sheet Flaws
As for No. S9

Coil Leaders
All have the watermark upright and it is believed a new double-pane cylinder number A4 was used.

Vertical delivery printed in continuous reels

Code No.	Number in roll	Face value	
G	480	10/-	30·00
W	960	£2	50·00
Y	1920	£4	70·00

●━━━━━━━━━

SA   Dorothy Wilding issues   1d. Ultramarine

1d. Ultramarine, Type SA1 (1953–1967)

1953 (31 August). **1d.** Wmk Tudor Crown

S13 = SG 516	Mint	Used
1d. Ultramarine	30	20
a. Watermark inverted (3.54)	6·00	3·00
b. Coil join (horiz. pair)	10·00	
c. Shamrock flaw (Cyl. 2 No dot, R. 18/2)	30·00	

S13c, S14d, also SB22a, see Section SB
White flaw on top shamrock, later retouched on St Edward's Crown watermark

Cylinder Numbers (Blocks of Six)
Perforation Type B (I/P no dot) and C (E/P dot)

Cyl. No.	No dot	Dot
1	25·00	25·00

Perforation Type A (E/I)

Cyl. No.	No dot	Dot
2	35·00*	10·00

Minor Constant Sheet Flaws

Cyl. 2.	19/8	White flaw between thistle stem and lower right rose (Th. E6)

Coil Leaders
Double-pane cylinders B1 or B2 were used for the Tudor Crown watermark. The watermark is always upright.

Vertical delivery printed in continuous reels

Code No.	Number in roll	Face value	
AB	240	£1	£100
E	480	£2	45·00
X	960	£4	20·00
Z	1920	£8	25·00

Sideways delivery made up from sheets with sheet margin joins (as 'vertical delivery coils')

O	480	£2	35·00

Imprimaturs from the NPM or BPMA
Imperforate, watermark Type W.**22**

Watermark upright	£900
Watermark inverted	£900
Tête-bêche pair	£3250
Cyl. 2 Block of Six*	£6750
Cyl. B2 (for Booklets) Block of Four	£4750

1955 (19 September)†. **1d.** Wmk St. Edward's Crown

S14 = SG 541	Mint	Used
1d. Ultramarine	30	15
a. Tête-bêche (horiz. pair)	—	
b. Watermark inverted (8.55)	65	60
c. Coil join (horiz. pair)	10·00	
d. Shamrock flaw (Cyl. 2 No dot, R. 18/2)	30·00	

† The earliest issue was from E coils, released on 23 August 1955.
For illustration of No. S14d see No. S13c.

Cylinder Numbers (Blocks of Six)
Perforation Type A (E/I)

Cyl. No.	No dot	Dot
1	10·00	10·00
2	35·00*	20·00
4	20·00	20·00

Perforation Type B (I/P no dot) and C (E/P dot)

Cyl. No.	No dot	Dot
4	20·00	25·00

Minor Constant Sheet Flaws

Cyl. 2	19/8	As for S13 (Th. E6)
Cyl. 4	11/9	Blue spot in "E" of "POSTAGE"
	19/8	As cyl. 2
Cyl. 4.	14/11	White spur to bottom leaf of shamrock above diadem (Th. A3)

Coil Leaders
Double-pane cylinders B1 or B2 were again used for the St Edward's Crown watermark. The watermark is always upright.

Vertical delivery printed in continuous reels

Code No.	Number in roll	Face value	
AB	240	£1	40·00
E	480	£2	30·00
B	960	£4	85·00
X	960	£4	20·00
Z	1920	£8	20·00

Sideways delivery made up from sheets with sheet margin joins

O	480	£2	35·00

Imprimaturs from the NPM or BPMA
Imperforate, watermark Type W.**23**

Watermark upright	£900
Watermark inverted	£900
Tête-bêche pair	£3250

1957 (19 November). **1d.** With graphite lines, Type **SA8**. Wmk St Edward's Crown

S15 = SG 562	Mint	Used
1d. Ultramarine	80	80
a. Spot on thistle head (Cyls. 7 and 8 No dot, R. 6/1 and Coil, Roll 1)	30·00	
b. Daffodil stem flaw (Cyls. 7 & 8 No dot, R. 15/2 and Coil, Roll 2)	30·00	
c. Extra stop (Coil, Roll 2)	40·00	
d. Stop omitted (Coil, Roll 3)	40·00	
e. White flaw on shamrock leaf (Coil, Roll 8)	35·00	

Spot on thistle head occurs on sheets (Nos. S15a and S19b or coils (Nos. S16n, S18i, S20g and S21g)

14

1d. Ultramarine **Dorothy Wilding issues** **SA**

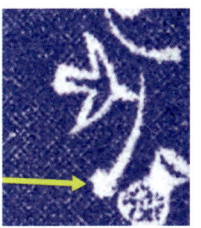

S15b, S19c

S15c Later retouched

S15d White stop omitted

S15e

Cylinder Numbers (Blocks of Six)

Single pane cylinders

Cyl. No.	Perf type	No Dot
7	B(I/P)	15·00
7	C(E/P)	15·00
8	B(I/P)	20·00
8	C(E/P)	20·00

Coil Leaders
Single-pane cylinder B4 and sheet cylinder 7 (converted to 21 rows) were used and all have the watermark upright.

Vertical delivery printed in continuous reels

Code No.	Number in roll	Face value	
E	480	£2	60·00
X	960	£4	50·00
Z	1920	£8	70·00

Imprimaturs from the NPM or BPMA
Imperforate, watermark Type W.**23**

Watermark upright	£900
Cyl. 7 Block of Six	£6250
Cyl. 7 with "Daffodil stem flaw" R.15/2	£1500

Quantity Issued: 29,620,080

1959 *(24 March).* **1d.** Wmk Crowns

A. Cream Paper

S16		Mint	Used
	1d. Ultramarine	25	20
a.	Imperf. (vert. pair from coil)	£4000	
d.	Watermark inverted *(11.58)*	50	50
e.	Watermark Crown to left *(26.5.61)*	1·50	1·50
f.	Watermark Crown to right	1·50	1·50
g.	Coil join (horiz. pair)	6·50	
h.	Daffodil flaw (Cyl. 5 No dot, R.10/11)	30·00	
n.	Spot on thistle head (Coil, Roll 1)	30·00	

B. Whiter Paper *(7 May 1962)*

S17 = SG 571

	1d. Ultramarine	10	10
a.	Watermark Crown to left *(5.6.62)*	1·50	1·50
b.	Watermark Crown to right	1·50	1·50
c.	Watermark inverted *(29.7.62)*	50	50
d.	Coil join (horiz. pair)	3·00	
e.	Daffodil flaw (Cyl. 5 No dot, R.10/11)	30·00	
f.	*Tête-bêche* (horiz. pair)	£2500	

For illustration of No. S16n, see No. S15a.

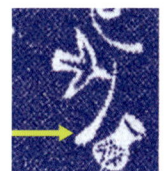

S17f

S16h, S17e, S20c, S21e
Later retouched

Cylinder Numbers (Blocks of Six)

A. Cream Paper (No. S16)
Perforation Type A (E/I)

Cyl. No.	No dot	Dot
4	10·00	10·00
5	10·00	10·00

Perforation Type B (I/P no dot) and C (E/P dot)

Cyl. No.	No dot	Dot
4	20·00	20·00

B. Whiter Paper (No. S17)
Perforation Type A (E/I)

Cyl. No.	No dot	Dot
4	10·00	10·00
5	10·00	10·00

Minor Constant Sheet Flaws

Cyl. 4	11/9	As for S14
	19/8	As for S14
Cyl. 4.	14/11	As for S14
Cyl. 5	3/5	Dark patch below bottom right rose (Th. E5)
	19/8	White flaw between thistle stem and lower right rose (Th. E6)
Cyl. 5.	1/12	Small white flaw on top of top left daffodil (Th. A2)

Coil Leaders
Double-pane cylinder B1 was used for cream paper printings and cylinder B3 was used for both cream and whiter paper issues with the watermark always upright.

Vertical delivery printed in continuous reels.
Cream or whiter paper

Code No.	Number in roll	Face value	
AB	240	£1	25·00
E	480	£2	35·00
B	960	£4	85·00
X	960	£4	15·00
Z	1920	£8	20·00

Sideways delivery made up from sheets with sheet margin joins. Cream or whiter paper.

O	480	£2	30.00

SA Dorothy Wilding issues *1d. Ultramarine*

Imprimaturs from the NPM or BPMA
Imperforate, watermark Type W.**24**. Cream or whiter paper

Watermark upright	£900
Watermark inverted	£900
Tête-bêche pair (Horiz or Vert)	£3250
Cyl. **4.** Block of Six (Whiter paper)	£6250

1958 *(18 December).* **1d.** With graphite lines, Type **SA8**. Wmk Crowns

S18 = SG 588	Mint	Used
1d. (1) Ultramarine (coils)	2·00	1·50
(2) Bright ultramarine (booklets)	3·00	2·00
a. Watermark inverted *(4.8.59)*	3·00	2·00
b. Two lines at left or right *(7.61)*	1·00	1·20
c. One line at left or right	1·00	1·20
d. Three lines	65·00	60·00
i. Spot on thistle head (Coil, Roll 1)	40·00	

No. S18 was only issued in booklets and coils. For panes see Section SB, Nos. SB39/a.

The misplaced graphite lines (varieties b/d) came from Z coils. They were printed after the graphite line experiment had ended to use up residual stock of graphite-lined paper which had been prepared for booklets.

For illustration of No. S18i, see No. S15a.

Coil Leaders
Double-pane cylinder B3 was used only for the Z coils with misplaced lines (issued July 1961); other coils were from cylinder B4. The watermark is always upright.

Vertical delivery printed in continuous reels

Code No.	Number in roll	Face value	
E	480	£2	£100
X	960	£4	85·00
Z	1920	£8	35·00

Imprimaturs from the NPM or BPMA
Imperforate, watermark Type W.**24**

Watermark upright	£900
Watermark inverted	£900
Tête-bêche pair	£3250

Quantity Issued: 12,428,880 including 3,400 Z coils with misplaced lines

1959 *(18 November).* **1d.** Phosphor-graphite issue. Wmk St Edward's Crown

S19 = SG 600	Mint	Used
1d. Ultramarine	12·00	12·00
a. One 6 mm band at left or right (stamp with vert. margin)	20·00	
b. Spot on thistle head (Cyl. 8, R. 6/1)	50·00	
c. Daffodil stem flaw (Cyl. 8, R.15/2)	50·00	

This has two graphite lines, Type **SA8**, on the back and two phosphor bands on the front, (applied letterpress.), which react green under the lamp.

For illustrations of Nos. S19b/c, see Nos. S15a/b.

Cylinder Numbers (Blocks of Six)

Single pane cylinder

Cyl. No.	Perf type	No Dot
8	B (I/P)	£100
8	C (E/P)	£100

Imprimatur from the NPM or BPMA
Perf. 15 × 14, watermark Type W.**23**

Watermark upright	—

Quantity Issued: 709,680

1960 *(June 22).* **1d.** Two phosphor bands reacting green. Wmk Crowns

S20	Mint	Used
1d. Ultramarine	1·50	1·50
a. Watermark inverted *(14.8.60)*	5·50	5·50
b. Single 8 mm band (wmk. upright or inverted)	30·00	
ba. As b but 6 mm band	40·00	
c. Daffodil flaw (Cyl. 5 No dot, R. 10/11	35·00	
g. Spot on thistle head (Coil, Roll i)	35·00	

The bands were applied by photogravure.
For illustrations of No. S20c, see No. S16h and for No. S20g, see No. S15a.

Cylinder Numbers (Blocks of Six)
Perforation Type B (I/P no dot) and C (E/P dot)

Cyl. No.	No dot	Dot
5		11·00 11·00

Minor Constant Sheet Flaws

Cyl. 5	3/5	As for S17
	19/8	As for S17
Cyl. 5**.**	1/12	As for S17

Coil Leaders
Double-pane cylinder B3 was used with the watermark always upright.

Vertical delivery printed in continuous reels

Code No.	Number in roll	Face value	
E	480	£2	65·00
X	960	£4	65·00
Z	1920	£8	90·00

Imprimaturs from the NPM or BPMA
Imperforate, watermark Type W.**24**

Watermark upright	£900
Watermark inverted	£900
Tête Bêche pair	£3250
Cyl. **5.** Block of Six	£6250
Cyl. **B3.** (Coils) Block of Six	£6750

1961 *(5 June)*†. **1d.** Two phosphor bands reacting blue. Wmk Crowns

A. Cream Paper

S21	Mint	Used
1d. Ultramarine	90	90
a. Watermark inverted *(3.61)*	90	90
b. Watermark Crown to left *(14.7.61)*	3·00	3·00
c. Watermark Crown to right	3·00	3·00
d. One band (wmk. sideways)	25·00	
e. Daffodil flaw (Cyl. 5 No dot, R. 10/11)	30·00	
g. Spot on thistle head (Coil, Roll i)	30·00	

B. Whiter Paper *(21 June 1965)* †

S22	Mint	Used
1d. Ultramarine	80	80
a. Watermark Crown to left *(15.8.62)*	3·00	3·00
b. Watermark Crown to right	2·75	2·75
c. Watermark inverted *(3.6.63)*	90	90
d. One band (wmk. sideways)	35·00	
da. One band (wmk. upright or inverted)	45·00	

The bands were applied by photogravure on the stamps with upright and inverted watermark and by letterpress on those with watermark sideways.

For illustrations of No. S21e, see No. S16h and for No. S21g, see No. S15a.

16

1d. Ultramarine   Dorothy Wilding issues   SA

Cylinder Numbers (Blocks of Six)

A. Cream paper (No. S21)
Perforation Type B (I/P no dot) and C (E/P dot)

Cyl. No.	No dot	Dot
5	12·00	12·00

B. Whiter paper (No. S22)
Perforation Type A (E/I)

Cyl. No.	No dot	Dot
4	10·00	10·00

Minor Constant Sheet Flaws

Cyl. 4	11/9	As for S14
	19/8	As for S14
Cyl. 5	3/5	As for S17
	19/8	As for S17
Cyl. 5.	1/12	As for S17

Coil Leaders
Double-pane cylinder B3 was used with the watermark always upright.

Vertical delivery printed in continuous reels.
Cream or whiter paper

Code No.	Number in roll	Face value	
E	480	£2	40·00
X	960	£4	50·00
Z	1920	£8	60·00

Imprimaturs from the NPM or BPMA
Imperforate, watermark Type W.**24**. Cream or whiter paper

Watermark upright	£900
Watermark inverted	£900
Watermark sideways	£900
Tête-bêche pair (Horiz or Vert)	£3250
Cyl. B1. (Coils) Block of Six (Cream paper)	£6750

1965 (13 August). **1d.** Two 8 mm. Phosphor bands reacting violet. Wmk Crowns

S23		Mint	Used
	1d. Ultramarine	22·00	12·00
a.	One 6 mm band at left or right (stamp with vert. margin)	£100	
b.	Bands applied photo. (1966)	50	50
c.	Watermark inverted (9.65)	65	65
ca.	One 8 mm band (wmk. inverted)		
d.	Watermark Crown to left (10.65)	1·50	1·50
e.	Watermark Crown to right	1·50	1·50
f.	One band (wmk. sideways)	20·00	

The bands were originally applied by letterpress on sheets and 2s. Booklets with sideways watermark and later by photogravure on sheets, coils and booklets.

Cylinder Numbers (Blocks of Six)
Perforation Type A (E/I)

Bands letterpress (No. S23)

Cyl. No.	No dot	Dot
5	£375	£475

Bands photo (No. S23b)

Cyl. No.	No dot	Dot
5	10·00	10·00

Minor Constant Sheet Flaws

Cyl. 5	3/5	Dark patch below bottom right rose (Th. E5)
	19/8	White flaw between thistle stem and lower right rose (Th. E6)
Cyl. 5.	1/12	Small white flaw on top of top left daffodil (Th. A2)

Coil Leaders
Double-pane cylinder B3 was used with the watermark always upright. Bands by photogravure.

Vertical delivery printed in continuous reels

Code No.	Number in roll	Face value	
E	480	£2	75·00
X	960	£4	50·00
Z	1920	£8	50·00

1967 (Early). **1d.** Two 9·5 mm. Phosphor bands reacting violet. Wmk Crowns

S24 = SG 611		Mint	Used
	1d. Ultramarine	10	10
a.	Watermark inverted (2.67)	65	65
b.	Watermark Crown to left (4.67)	1·10	1·10
c.	Watermark Crown to right	1·10	1·10
e.	One 9·5 mm band (wmk. sideways)	25·00	

The bands were applied by photogravure, but the 2s. Booklets with sideways watermark had the bands applied by letterpress.

Cylinder Numbers (Blocks of Six)
Perforation Type F (L)*

Cyl. No.	No dot (I/E)	Dot (P/E)
4	10·00	10·00

Perforation Type A (E/I)

Cyl. No.	No dot	Dot
5	10·00	10·00

Minor Constant Sheet Flaws

Cyl. 4	11/9	As for S14
	19/8	As for S14
Cyl. 5	3/5	As for S17
	19/8	As for S17
Cyl. 5.	1/12	As for S17

Coil Leaders
Double-pane cylinder B3 was used with the watermark always upright.

Vertical delivery printed in continuous reels

Code No.	Number in roll	Face value	
E	480	£2	45·00
X	960	£4	45·00
Z	1920	£8	45·00

SA Dorothy Wilding issues 1d. Ultramarine

1½d. Green, Type SA1 (1952–1965)

1952 (5 December). **1½d.** Wmk Tudor Crown

S25 = SG 517		Mint	Used
1½d.	Green	25	20
b.	Imperf. between stamp and top margin	£750	
c.	Watermark inverted (5.53)	1·25	1·25
d.	Watermark sideways (15.10.54)	1·25	1·25
e.	Butterfly flaw (Cyl. 6 Dot, R.19/1) (Cyl. block of 6)	£800	
f.	Flaw on daffodil stem (Cyl. 9 Dot, R.18/1)	30·00	
g.	Extra dot (Cyl. 13 No dot, R.17/10)	30·00	
h.	Rose and thistle joined at right (Cyl. 13 Dot, R.19/1)	35·00	
i.	Scratch on neck (Cyl. 13 No Dot, R.20/3)	35·00	
m.	Flaw over "O" of "POSTAGE" (Sideways coil, Roll 2)	30·00	
n.	Dot over rose (Sideways coil, Roll 10)	30·00	
o.	Daffodil flaw (Sideways coil, Roll 8)	30·00	

Stamps with sideways watermark are from N coils with sideways delivery.

S25e (Cyl. 6)   S26g (Cyl. 14)   S26i (Cyl. 15)

The first and later states of the butterfly flaw. All on dot panes only.

Of the first 13 cylinders, all of which were prepared using multipositive 359 and numbered 1 to 15 (with the exception of Nos. 3 and 7 which were not used), the following is a record of the development of the above illustrated flaws:

Cyl. 1.	No flaws
Cyls. 2, 4 and 5.	Disturbed background
Cyls. 6.	This is found in two states. One with disturbed background and the other with a short white flaw as illustrated, the latter being the first of the clear defects in this position
Cyls. 8 to 13.	Disturbed background
Cyl. 14.	Found in two states, one with disturbed background and the other with a long white flaw as illustrated
Cyl. 15.	Also found in two states, one with disturbed background and the other with a larger white flaw as illustrated, the latter only occurring on the St Edward's Crown watermark

The most plausible explanation of the development of this flaw is that prior to the making of cylinder 2, the multipositive was damaged and imperfectly retouched with the result that cylinders 2, 4 and 5 show an uneven background. Before the making of cylinder 6 the opaque retouching medium appears to have partly peeled off from the multipositive leaving a transparent area which produced the small white flaw on the stamp. This was evidently discovered during the run and the cylinder retouched with the result that we have cylinder 6 with uneven background.

The multipositive was again retouched and this time continued to be used uneventfully for cylinders 8 to 13. After this the retouching medium appears to have peeled off again before making cylinders 14 and 15, each time being discovered and retouched during the printing run. As cylinders 21 and 22 were prepared using a new multipositive 482, they do not show any of these flaws or retouches.

Prices are for cylinder blocks of six. The cylinder blocks showing the disturbed background are priced without an asterisk.

S25f, SB61a

S25g, S26d Later retouched on St Edward's Crown watermark

S25h, S26e

S25i, S26f White vertical line from ear to shoulder

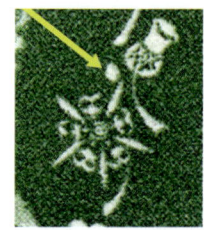

S25m, S26q

S25n, S26r From sideways delivery N Coils

S25o, S26s

Cylinder Numbers (Blocks of Six)
Perforation Type A (E/I)

Cyl. No.	No dot	Dot
1	10·00	10·00
2	10·00	10·00
4	10·00	10·00
5	15·00	15·00
6	20·00	20·00
8	15·00	15·00
9	25·00	35·00*
10	15·00	15·00
11	10·00	10·00
12	15·00	10·00
13	15·00	45·00*

Perforation Type B (I/P no dot) and C (E/P dot)

Cyl. No.	No dot	Dot
1	50·00	50·00
2	50·00	50·00
6	75·00	£100
9	75·00	£100

1d. Ultramarine   Dorothy Wilding issues   SA

Coil Leaders
Printed in continuous reels
Double-pane cylinder C1 was used for the vertical delivery coils and single-pane cylinder C3 for the sideways delivery coils.

(a) Vertical delivery. Watermark upright

Code No.	Number in roll	Face value	
L	480	£3	45·00
K	960	£6	45·00

(b) Sideways delivery. Watermark sideways

N	480	£3	20·00

Imprimaturs from the NPM or BPMA
Imperforate, watermark Type W.**22**

Watermark upright	£900
Watermark inverted	£900
Watermark sideways	£900
Tête-bêche pair (Horiz or Vert)	£3250
Cyl. 1 Block of Six	£6250

1955 *(11 October)*†. **1½d.** Wmk St Edward's Crown

S26 = SG 542		Mint	Used
1½d. Green		25	30
a.	Tête-bêche (horiz. pair)	£3750	
b.	Watermark inverted *(8.55)*	75	70
c.	Watermark sideways *(7.3.56)*	35	70
d.	Extra dot (Cyl. 13 Dot, R. 17/10)	30·00	
e.	Rose and thistle joined at right (Cyl. 13 Dot, R. 19/1)	30·00	
f.	Scratch on neck (Cyl. 13 No dot, R. 20/3)	35·00	
g.	Butterfly flaw (Cyl. 14 Dot, R. 19/1) *(cyl. block of 6)*	90·00	
h.	Bud on shamrock stem (Cyl. 14) No dot, R. 8/6)	35·00	
i.	Butterfly flaw (Cyl. 15 Dot, R. 19/1) *(cyl. block of 6)*	75·00	
j.	Spot between rose and shamrock (Cyl. 15 No dot, R. 20/3)	30·00	
q.	Flaw over "O" of "POSTAGE" (Sideways coil, Roll 2)	30·00	
r.	Dot over rose (Sideways coil, Roll 10)	30·00	
s.	Daffodil flaw (Sideways coil, Roll 8)	30·00	

Stamps with sideways watermark are from N coils with sideways delivery.

For illustrations of Nos. S26d/f see Nos. S25g/i; for Nos. S26g and S26i see No. S25e; and for Nos. S26q/s see Nos. S25m/o.

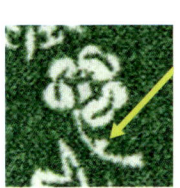

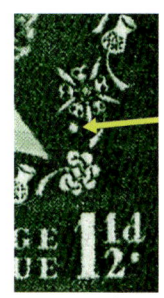

S26h

S26j, S28e, S32b Later retouched on whiter paper with Crowns watermark

Cylinder Numbers (Blocks of Six)
Perforation Type A(E/I)

Cyl. No.	No dot	Dot
11	15·00	15·00
13	10·00	40·00
14	10·00	10·00
15	10·00	10·00

See note below No. S25 on the butterfly flaw which occurs on some examples of cylinders 14 and 15 dot. Prices are for normals with disturbed background.

Minor Constant Sheet Flaws

Cyl. 15	17/9	Nick in frame bottom right (Th. G6)
	20/9	Speck opposite left "1" (Th. G1)
Cyl. 15.	1/4	Green dot in lower half of "1" of left "½" (Th. G1)

Coil Leaders
Printed in continuous reels
Double-pane cylinder C1 was again used for the vertical delivery coils and single-pane cylinder C3 for the sideways delivery coil.

(a) Vertical delivery. Watermark upright

Code No.	Number in roll	Face value	
L	480	£3	50·00
K	960	£6	75·00

(b) Sideways delivery. Watermark sideways

N	480	£3	15·00

Imprimaturs from the NPM or BPMA
Imperforate, watermark Type W.**23**

Watermark upright	£900
Watermark upright with "Extra dot" variety R.17/10	£1500
Watermark inverted	£900
Watermark sideways	£900
Tête-bêche pair (Horiz or Vert)	£3250
Watermark upright with Daffodil flaw Row 8	£1500
Cyl. 13. Block of Six with Rose & Thistle variety R.19/1	£6750
Cyl. C3 (coil) Watermark Sideways Block of Six	£6750

1957 *(19 November)*. **1½d.** With graphite lines, Type **SA8**. Wmk St Edward's Crown

S27 = SG 563		Mint	Used
1½d. Green		2·00	1·75
a.	Both lines at left	£1800	£600
b.	Horiz. pair, one stamp with only one line	£1500	
c.	Coil join (horiz. pair)	15·00	
d.	Green stroke below "E" (Cyl. 21 No dot, R. 13/8)	45·00	

Nos. S27a/b result from a misplacement of the graphite lines.

S27d, S31b Diagonal green stroke below middle "E" of "REVENUE" in bottom margin of stamp

SA Dorothy Wilding issues *1d. Ultramarine*

Cylinder Numbers (Blocks of Six)
Single pane cylinder

Cyl. No.	Perf. Type	No dot
21	B (I/P)	15·00
21	C (E/P)	15·00

Coil Leader
Sideways delivery
made up from sheets with sheet margin joins

Code No.	Number in roll	Face value	
N	480	£3	85·00

Quantity Issued: 10,506,720

Imprimaturs from the NPM or BPMA
Imperforate, watermark Type W.**23**

Watermark upright	£900
Cyl. 21 Block of Six	£6250

1960 *(30 August)*†. **1½d.** Wmk Crowns

A. Cream Paper

S28		Mint	Used
1½d.	Green	40	25
a.	Watermark inverted *(12.58)*	1·50	1.25
b.	Watermark Crown to left *(26.5.61)*	9·00	9·00
c.	Watermark Crown to right	9·00	9·00
d.	Coil join (vert. pair)	6·00	
e.	Spot between rose and shamrock (Cyl. 15 No dot, R. 20/3)	35·00	

B. Whiter Paper *(7 May 1962)*

S29 = SG 572			
1½d.	Green	10	15
a.	Imperf. three sides (horiz, strip of 3)	£8500	
b.	Watermark Crown to left *(5.6.62)*	9·00	9·00
c.	Watermark Crown to right	9·00	9·00
d.	Watermark inverted *(18.9.62)*	4·00	4·00
e.	Coil join (horiz. pair)	5·00	
g.	Thistle flaws (Cyl. 22 Dot, R. 12/1)	35·00	
h.	Daffodil flaw (Cyl. 22 Dot, R. 1/12)	35·00	
i.	Tête-bêche (horiz. pair)	£2500	

For illustration of No. S28e see No. S26j.

S29g, S34f White flaws in and around thistle at upper left

S29h, S34g White spot by upper left daffodil

Cylinder Numbers (Blocks of Six)
A. Cream paper (No. S28)
Perforation Type A (E/I)

Cyl. No.•	No dot	Dot
15	10·00	10·00

B. Whiter paper (No. S29)
Perforation Type A (E/I)

Cyl. No.	No dot	Dot
15	10·00	10·00
22	12·00	12·00

Marginal arrows:
Cylinder 15 "V" shaped, hand-engraved,
Cylinder 22 "W" shaped, hand-engraved at top; "W" shaped, photo-etched, at bottom and at both sides

Marginal rule:
Cylinder 15 At bottom of sheet (1½ mm wide)
Cylinder 22 At bottom of sheet (2 mm wide)

Minor Constant Sheet Flaws

Cyl. 15	13/9	White spur on top left daffodil stem (Th. A2)
Cyl. 15.	1/4	As for S26

Coil Leaders
Made up from sheets with sheet margin joins.
Watermark upright

Code No.	Number in roll	Face value		
L	480	£3 Vertical delivery (Cream paper)		55·00
N	480	£3 Sideways delivery (Whiter paper)		40·00

Imprimaturs from the NPM or BPMA
Imperforate, watermark Type W.**24**. Cream or whiter paper

Watermark upright	£900
Watermark upright with Spot between Rose and Shamrock R.20/3	£1500
Watermark inverted	£900
Tête-bêche pair (Horiz or Vert)	£3250
Cyl. 15 Block of Six (Cream paper)	£6250
Cyl. 15 Block of Six (Whiter paper)	£6250

1959 *(4 August)*. **1½d.** With graphite lines, Type **SA8**.
Wmk Crowns

S30 = SG 589		Mint	Used
1½d.	Green	90·00	80·00
a.	Watermark inverted *(4.8.59)*	75·00	60·00

This was only issued in 3s. Booklets. See Section SB, Nos. SB70/a.

Imprimaturs from the NPM or BPMA
Imperforate, watermark Type W.**24**

Watermark upright	£900
Watermark inverted	£900
Tête-bêche pair (Horiz)	£3250

Quantity Issued: 1,862,400

1959 *(18 November)*. **1½d.** Phosphor-graphite issue.
Wmk St Edward's Crown

S31 = SG 601		Mint	Used
1½d.	Green	5·25	5·25
a.	One 6 mm band at left or right (stamp with vert. margin)	30·00	

1959 *(18 November).* **1½d.** Phosphor-graphite issue. Wmk St Edward's Crown

S31 = SG 601	Mint	Used
b. Green stroke below "E" (Cyl. 21 No dot, R. 13/8)	45·00	

No. S31 has two graphite lines, Type **SA8**, on the back and two phosphor bands on the front, applied letterpress., which react green under the lamp.

For illustration of No. S31b see No. S27d.

Cylinder Numbers (Blocks of Six)
Single pane cylinder

Cyl. No.	Perf Type	No Dot
21	B (I/P)	50·00
21	C (E/P)	50·00

Imprimatur from the NPM or BPMA
Perf. 15 × 14, watermark Type W.**23**

Watermark inverted	—

Quantity Issued: 704,160

1960 *(22 June).* **1½d.** Two phosphor bands reacting green. Wmk Crowns

S32	Mint	Used
1½d. Green	2·00	1·50
a. Watermark inverted *(14.8.60)*	12·00	9·50
b. Spot between rose and shamrock (Cyl. 15 No dot, R. 20/3)	40·00	

The bands were applied by photogravure.
For illustration of No. S32b see No. S26j.

Cylinder Numbers (Blocks of Six)
Perforation Type B (I/P no dot) and C (E/P dot)

Cyl. No.	No dot	Dot
15	25·00	25·00

Minor Constant Sheet Flaws

Cyl. 15	13/9	As for S29
Cyl. 15.	1/4	As for S26

Imprimaturs from the NPM or BPMA
Imperforate, watermark Type W.**24**

Watermark upright	£900
Watermark inverted	£900
Tête-bêche pair (Horiz)	£3250
Cyl 15. Block of Six	£6250

1961 *(5 June)*†. **1½d.** Two phosphor bands reacting blue. Wmk Crowns

A. Cream Paper

S33	Mint	Used
1½d. Green	85	85
a. Watermark inverted *(4.61)*	25·00	22·00
b. Watermark Crown to left *(14.7.61)*	20·00	20·00
c. Watermark Crown to right	20·00	20·00
d. One broad band (wmk. sideways)	25·00	
da. One broad band (wmk. upright or inverted)	40·00	

B. Whiter Paper *(Sept. 1964)*†

S34 = SG 612		
1½d. Green	15	15
a. Watermark Crown to left *(15.8.62)*	22·00	22·00
b. Watermark Crown to right	22·00	22·00
c. Watermark inverted *(7.64)*	25·00	22·00
d. One broad band (wmk. upright or inverted)	75·00	
f. Thistle flaws (Cyl. 22 Dot, R. 12/1)	35·00	
g. Daffodil flaw (Cyl. 22 Dot, R. 1/12)	35·00	
h. White bulge on shamrock (Cyl. 22 No dot, R. 7/2)	40·00	

The bands were applied by photogravure on the stamps with upright and inverted watermark and by letterpress on those with watermark sideways.
For illustrations of Nos. S34f/g, see Nos. S29g/h.

S34h

Cylinder Numbers (Blocks of Six)

A. Cream paper (No. S33)
Perforation Type B (I/P no dot) and C (E/P dot)

Cyl. No.	No dot	Dot
15	35·00	35·00

B. Whiter paper (No. S34)
Perforation Type A (E/I)

Cyl. No.	No dot	Dot
15	10·00	10·00
22	12·00	12·00

The notes on the marginal arrows below No. S29 also apply here.

Minor Constant Sheet Flaws

Cyl. 15	13/9	As for S29
Cyl. 15.	1/4	As for S26

Imprimaturs from the NPM or BPMA
Imperforate, watermark Type W.**24**. Cream or whiter paper

Watermark upright	£900
Watermark inverted	£900
Watermark sideways	£900
Tête-bêche pair (Horiz or Vert)	£3250

1965 *(13 August).* **1½d.** Two 8 mm. Phosphor bands reacting violet. Wmk Crowns

S35	Mint	Used
1½d. Green	1·50	1·50
a. One 6 mm band at left or right (stamp with vert. margin)	20·00	
b. One 8 mm band	30·00	
ba. As b but 6 mm band	25·00	

The bands were applied by Letterpress.

Cylinder Numbers (Blocks of Six)
Perforation Type A (E/I)

Cyl. No.	No dot	Dot
15	45·00	45·00

Marginal arrows as for Cylinder 15 under Nos. S28/9.

SA Dorothy Wilding issues *2d. Red-brown*

2d. Red-brown, Type SA1 (1953–1967)

1953 *(31 August).* **2d.** Wmk Tudor Crown
S36 = SG 518

		Mint	Used
	2d. Red-brown	30	20
a.	Watermark inverted *(3.54)*	30·00	22·00
b.	Watermark sideways *(8.10.54)*	2·00	2·00
c.	Rose petal flaw (Cyl. 3 No dot, R. 4/8)	40·00	
d.	Tadpole flaw (Cyl. 4 Dot, R. 17/6)	55·00	
e.	Retouched (Cyl. 3 Dot, R. 17/6)	40·00	
g.	Extra leg to "R" (Sideways coil, Roll 2)	30·00	
h.	Retouched left "2" (Sideways coil, Roll 5)	30·00	
i.	Dot on rose (Sideways coil, Roll 1)	30·00	

Stamps with sideways watermark are from T coils with sideways delivery.

S36c, S37e

S36d, S37f, S38f White flaw resembles a tadpole below thistle

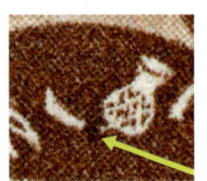

S36e, S37g, S38g, S40d
Later retouched state of the tadpole flaw

S36g, S37l, S38s, S40i, S41b, S49c

Normal

S36h, S37m, S38t, S40j, S41c, S49d

S36i, S37k, S38w

From sideways delivery T Coils

Cylinder Numbers (Blocks of Six)
Perforation Type A(E/I)

Cyl. No.	No dot	Dot
1	10·00	10·00
2	10·00	10·00
3	20·00	20·00

Cyl. No.	No dot	Dot
4	15·00	15·00

Sheets from cylinder 2 No dot are known with the marginal arrows omitted from top and bottom selvedge.

Coil Leaders
Double-pane cylinder number D1 was used for vertical delivery coils and single-pane cylinder D3 for sideways delivery coils.

Printed in continuous reels
(a) Vertical delivery. Watermark upright

Code No.	Number in roll	Face value	
R	480	£4	60·00
Q	960	£8	—
V	960	£8	50·00

(b) Sideways delivery. Watermark sideways

T	480	£4	15·00

Imprimaturs from the NPM or BPMA
Imperforate, watermark Type W.**22**

Watermark upright	£900
Watermark inverted	£900
Watermark sideways	£900
Tête-bêche pair (Horiz)	£3250
Cyl. 1 Block of Six	£6250

2d. Red-brown Dorothy Wilding issues

1955 (6 September). **2d.** Wmk St Edward's Crown

A. Red-brown

S37 = SG 543

		Mint	Used
	2d. Red-brown	25	35
a.	Imperf. between pair (from vert. coil)	£4750	
aa.	Imperf. between pair (from sdwys. wmk. horiz. coil)	£4750	
ad.	Imperf. between vert. pair (from sheet)		
c.	Watermark inverted (9.55)	11·00	9·00
d.	Watermark sideways (31.7.56)	55	70
e.	Rose petal flaw (Cyl. 3 No dot, R. 4/8)	40·00	
f.	Tadpole flaw (Cyl. 4 No Dot, R. 17/6)	50·00	
g.	Retouched (R. 17/6 on Cyls. 3, 6, 7 all Dot. Vertical coil, Roll 6)	30·00	
h.	Tadpole flaw with shamrock flaw (Cyl. 9 Dot, R. 17/6)	35·00	
i.	Flaw between shamrock and diadem (Cyl. 7 Dot, R. 1/6)	45·00	
j.	White spot by daffodil (Cyl. 9 Dot, R. 18/8)	40·00	
k.	Dot on rose (Sideways coil, Roll 1)	30·00	
l.	Extra leg to "R" (Sideways coil, Roll 2)	30·00	
m.	Retouched left "2" (Sideways coil, Roll 5)	30·00	
n.	Extended stem on daffodil (Sideways coil, Roll 9)	30·00	

Stamps with sideways watermark are from T coils with sideways delivery.

No. S37ad came from the second vertical row of a sheet affected by a paper fold. One pair exists from this source being in a perforated block of 18 (6×3) with left sheet margin. Perforations at left and right of the vertical rows were severed during perforating when several stamps were folded under the sheet.

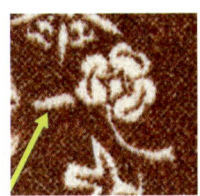

S37aa

S37i, S38j This was a multipositive flaw which was retouched on other cylinders

S37j, S38k

S37n, S38u, S40k, S41d

For illustrations of Nos. S37e/g, see Nos. S36c/e and for Nos. S37k/m, see Nos. S36g/i. No. S37h comprises the variety shown for No. S36d but in addition there is a white flaw to the left of the adjoining shamrock; see also Nos. S40f, S41e and S49e.

B. Light red-brown (17 October 1956)

S38 = SG 543b

		Mint	Used
	2d. Light red-brown	30	20
a.	Tête-bêche (horiz pair)	£3250	

B. Light red-brown (17 October 1956)

S38 = SG 543b

		Mint	Used
c.	Imperf. between stamp and top margin	£750	
d.	Watermark inverted (1.57)	9·00	7·00
e.	Watermark sideways (5.3.57)	8·00	7·00
f.	Tadpole flaw (R. 17/6 on Cyls. 8, 10, 11 and 12 Dot)	35·00	
g.	Retouched (R. 17/6 on Cyls. 6, 7, 8, 11, 12, 13 & 15 all dot, Vertical coil, Row 6)	30·00	
h.	Tadpole and shamrock flaws (R. 17/6 on Cyls. 9 & 12 Dot)	35·00	
i.	Tadpole flaw retouched with shamrock flaw (R. 17/6 on Cyls. 14 and 16 Dot)	30·00	
j.	Flaw between shamrock and diadem (Cyl. 7 Dot, R. 1/6)	35·00	
k.	White spot by daffodil (Cyl. 9 Dot, R. 18/8)	35·00	
l.	Extended leaf on shamrock (Cyl. 10 No dot, R. 8/6)	35·00	
m.	Double trumpet flaw (Cyl. 10 No dot, R. 11/1)	40·00	
n.	Dot on shamrock (Cyl. 10 No dot, R. 20/1)	30·00	
o.	White flaw on crown (Cyl. 11 No dot, R. 9/11)	40·00	
p.	White flaw on shamrock (Cyl. 12 Dot, R. 20/3)	30·00	
q.	White spot by right thistle (Cyl. 14 Dot, R. 11/10)	40·00	
r.	Dot over rose stem (Cyl. 14 No dot, R. 1/1)	40·00	
ra	Dot over rose stem retouched	35·00	
s.	Extra leg to "R" (Sideways coil, Roll 2)	30·00	
t.	Retouched left "2" (Sideways coil, Roll 5)	30·00	
u.	Extended stem on daffodil (Sideways coil, Roll 9)	30·00	
w.	Dot on rose (Sideways coil, Roll 1)	30·00	

Stamps with sideways watermark are from T coils with sideways delivery.

In December 1956 a completely imperforate sheet was noticed by clerks in a Kent post office, one of whom purchased it against P.O. regulations. (*Price £375 pair.*)

Tadpole flaws: Nos. S38f/h are as Nos. S37f/h. The first printings from Cylinder 12 show No. S38h larger, but on later printings both flaws appear to have been retouched. No. S38i is a fourth state which combines the shamrock flaw (small on Cyl. 14, larger on Cyl. 16) with the retouched state of the tadpole flaw.

For illustrations of Nos. S38j/k, see Nos. S37i/j, and for Nos. S38s/w, see Nos. S36g/i and S37n.

S38l

S38m

SA Dorothy Wilding issues *2d. Red-brown*

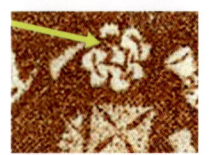

S38n

S38o Later retouched

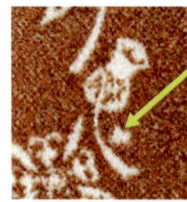

S38p Later retouched

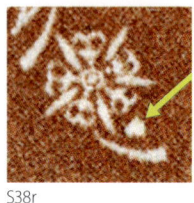

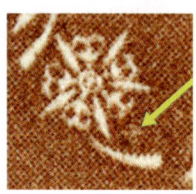

S38q

S38r

S38ra

Cylinder Numbers (Blocks of Six)

A. Red-brown (No. S37)
Perforation Type A (E/I)

Cyl. No.	No dot	Dot
3	10·00	10·00
4	10·00	15·00
6	15·00	10·00
7	12·00	12·00
9	25·00	25·00

B. Light red-brown (No. S38)
Perforation Type A (E/I)

Cyl. No.	No dot	Dot
6	12·00	12·00
7	12·00	12·00
8	10·00	10·00
9	10·00	10·00
10	40·00	10·00
11	10·00	10·00
12	10·00	10·00
13	12·00	12·00
14	12·00	12·00
15	10·00	10·00
16	10·00	10·00

Perforation Type E Cyl. No.	No dot (AE/I)	Dot (E/I)
7	85·00	**
9	£100	**

** Both light red-brown of same appearance and same prices as perforation type A with extension holes in left margin.

Minor Constant Sheet Flaws

Cyl. 7	14/8	White dot above "T" of "POSTAGE"
Cyl. 9	20/1	White spur on lower daffodil (Th. G3)
Cyl. 10	14/12	Nick in "R" of "REVENUE"
Cyl. 10.	9/6	Dark spot on necklace (Th. E–F3)
Cyl. 16.	20/12	"REVENUE" retouched (Th. G2–5)

Coil Leaders
Double-pane cylinder number D1 was used for vertical delivery coils of Nos. S37 and S38; single-pane cylinder D3 was used for the sideways delivery coils of No. S37d and cylinders D3 or D4 for No. S38e.

Printed in continuous reels
(a) Vertical delivery. Watermark upright

Code No.	Cat. No.	Number in roll	Face value	
R	S37	480	£4	70·00
Q	S37	960	£8	90·00
V	S37	960	£8	35·00
R	S38	480	£4	50·00
Q	S38	960	£8	70·00
V	S38	960	£8	30·00

(b) Sideways delivery. Watermark sideways

T	S37d	480	£4	20·00
T	S38e	480	£4	30·00

Imprimaturs from the NPM or BPMA

A. Red-brown. Imperforate, watermark Type W.23

Watermark upright	£900
Watermark upright with Rose Petal Flaw R.4/8	£1500
Watermark inverted	£900
Watermark inverted with Dot on Rose variety Coil 1	£1500
Watermark sideways	£900
Tête-bêche pair (Horiz)	£3250
Cyl. 3 Block of Six	£6250

B. Light red-brown. Imperforate, watermark Type W.23

Watermark upright	£900
Watermark upright with Flaw between Shamrock and Diadem R.1/6	£1500
Watermark inverted	£900
Watermark sideways	£900
Tête-bêche pair (Horiz)	£3250
Cyl. 7. Block of Six	£6250
Cyl. D3 (coil) Watermark sideways Block of Six	£6750
Cyl. D3 (coil) Watermark sideways with Tadpole Flaw Retouch R.17/6	£1250

Graphite-lined Issues

SA9

On the 2d. value, Nos. S39, S42/3 the single graphite line normally appeared at the right when viewed from the back. It was printed in black under the gum.

1957 (19 November). **2d.** With graphite line, Type **SA9**. Wmk St Edward's Crown

S39 = SG 564 Mint Used

2d. Light red-brown		2·40	2·40
a. Line at left (as seen from back)		£850	£300
b. Horiz. pair, one with line omitted		£1500	
c. Coil join (vert. pair)		15·00	
d. Coil join (horiz. pair)		15·00	

Nos. S39a/b result from a misplacement of the line.

2d. Red-brown — Dorothy Wilding issues — SA

Cylinder Numbers (Blocks of Six)
Single pane cylinder

Cyl. No.	Perf Type	No Dot
17	B (I/P)	25·00
17	C (E/P)	25·00

Minor Constant Sheet Flaws

| Cyl. 17 | 11/2 | White flaw on tail of left "d" |
| | 16/1 | White flaw in centre of upper left rose (Th. B1) |

Coil Leaders
Made up from sheets with sheet margin joins

Code No.	Number in roll	Face value	
V	960	£8 Vertical delivery	£150
T	480	£4 Sideways delivery	£120

Imprimatur from the NPM or BPMA
Imperforate, watermark Type W.**23**

Watermark upright	£900
Cyl. 17 Block of Six	£6250

Quantity Issued: 37,686,480

1958 *(4 December)*†. **2d.** Wmk Crowns.
A. Cream Paper
S40

		Mint	Used
2d.	Light red-brown	40	25
a.	Imperf. between stamp and top margin	£850	
b.	Watermark sideways *(3.4.59)*	1·25	1·25
c.	Watermark inverted *(10.4.61)*	£140	70·00
d.	Tadpole retouch (R.17/6 on Cyls. 15 Dot and others)	35·00	
e.	Swan's head flaw (Cyl. 24 Dot, R.19/10)	35·00	
f.	Tadpole flaw retouched with shamrock flaw (Cyl. 27, 29 and 30 Dot, R.17/6)	30·00	
i.	Extra leg to "R" (Sideways coil, Roll 2)	30·00	
j.	Retouched left "2" (Sideways coil, Roll 5)	30·00	
k.	Extended stem on daffodil (Sideways coil, Roll 9)	30·00	

B. Whiter Paper *(5 September 1963)*†
S41 = SG S73

		Mint	Used
2d.	Light red-brown	10	10
a.	Watermark sideways *(27.7.62)*	1·00	1·00
b.	Extra leg to "R" (Sideways coil, Roll 2)	30·00	
c.	Retouched left "2" (Sideways coil, Roll 5)	30·00	
d.	Extended stem on daffodil (Sideways coil, Roll 9)	30·00	
e.	Tadpole flaw retouched with shamrock flaw (Cyl. 27 Dot, R.17/6)	30·00	

† No. S40 was issued in November 1958 in V coils and No. S41 appeared on 20 September 1962 in V coils. Stamps with sideways watermark are from T coils with sideways delivery. Tadpole flaw: No. S40d is as No. S38g. For illustrations of Nos. S40i/j and S41b/c, see Nos. S36g/h; for Nos. S40k and S41d, see No. S37n. For description of Nos. S40f and S41e see below No. S37.

S40e

Cylinder Numbers (Blocks of Six)
A. Cream paper. (No. S40)
Perforation Type A (E/I)

Cyl. No.	No dot	Dot
15	25·00	25·00
19	12·00	12·00
20	12·00	12·00
21	12·00	12·00
22	12·00	12·00
23	10·00	10·00
24	10·00	10·00
25	10·00	10·00
27	10·00	10·00
29	15·00	15·00
30	10·00	10·00

SA Dorothy Wilding issues   2d. Red-brown

B. Whiter paper. (No. S41)
Perforation Type A (E/I)

Cyl. No.	No dot	Dot
23	10·00	10·00
25	10·00	10·00
27	10·00	10·00
30	10·00	10·00

Coil Leaders
Double-pane cylinder D1 was used for vertical delivery coils and cylinders D3 and D4 (single-pane) for sideways delivery coils.

Printed in continuous reels. Cream or whiter paper
(a) Vertical delivery. Watermark upright

Code No.	Number in roll	Face value	
R	480	£4	45·00
Q	960	£8	55·00
V	960	£8	20·00

(b) Sideways delivery. Watermark sideways

T	480	£4	15·00

Imprimaturs from the NPM or BPMA
Imperforate, watermark Type W.**24**. Cream or whiter paper

Watermark upright	£900
Watermark upright wth "Bud on Thistle stem" Booklets R. 2/3	£1500
Watermark inverted	£900
Watermark sideways	£900
Tête-bêche pair (Horiz)	£3250
Cyl. 20 Block of Six (Cream paper)	£6250
Cyl. 25 Block of Six (Whiter paper)	£6250
Cyl. 27 Block of Six (Whiter paper)	£6250
Cyl. D1 (coils) (Block of Six)	£6750

1958 *(24 November).* **2d.** With graphite line, Wmk Crowns

S42 = SG 590

	Mint	Used
2d. Light red-brown	10·00	3·50
a. Line at extreme left (as seen from back)	£1250	
ab. Horizontal pair, one stamp as S42a and one without line	£2500	
b. Coil join (vert. pair)	30·00	

Cylinder Numbers (Blocks of Six)

Single pane cylinder

Cyl. No.	Perf type	No Dot
17	B (I/P)	75·00
17	C (E/P)	75·00

Minor Constant Sheet Flaw
Cyl. 17   11/2   As for S39

Coil Leader
Vertical delivery.
Made up from sheets with sheet margin joins

Code No.	Number in roll	Face value	
V	960	£8	£175

Imprimatur from the NPM or BPMA
Imperforate, watermark Type W.**24**

Watermark upright	£900

Quantity Issued: 48,419,520

1959 *(18 November).* **2d.** Phosphor-graphite issue. Wmk Crowns

S43 = SG 605

	Mint	Used
2d. Light red-brown	6·00	5·00
a. Error. Watermark St Edward's Crown Type W.**23** *(3.60)*	£200	£175

This has one graphite line (Type **SA9**), on the back and one phosphor band on the front, applied letterpress, which reacts green under the lamp.

Cylinder Numbers (Blocks of Six)

Single pane cylinder
Watermark Crowns (No. S43)

Cyl. No.	Perf type	No Dot
17	B (I/P)	75·00
17	C (E/P)	65·00

Watermark St Edward's Crown (No. S43a)

Cyl. No.	Perf type	No Dot
17	B (I/P)	£1500
17	C (E/P)	£1500

Minor Constant Sheet Flaws

Cyl. 17	11/2	As for S39
	16/1	As for S39

Imprimatur from the NPM or BPMA
Perf. 15 × 14, watermark Type W.**24**

Watermark upright	—

Quantity Issued: 4,509,120 (including both watermarks)

1960 *(22 June).* **2d.** One phosphor band at left reacting green. Wmk Crowns

S44 = SG 613

	Mint	Used
2d. Light red-brown	22·00	22·00
a. Coil join (vert. pair)	45·00	

The band was applied by photogravure.

Cylinder Numbers (Blocks of Six)

Single pane cylinder

Cyl. No.	Perf Type	No Dot
17	B (I/P)	£175
17	C (E/P)	£190

Minor Constant Sheet Flaw
Cyl. 17   11/21   As for S39

Coil Leader
Vertical delivery.
Made up from sheets with sheet margin joins

Code No.	Number in roll	Face value	
V	960	£8	£150

Imprimatur from the NPM or BPMA
Imperforate, watermark Type W.**24**

Watermark upright	£900
Cyl. 17 block of six	£6250

26

2d. Red-brown Dorothy Wilding issues SA

1961 *(5 June).* **2d.** One phosphor band at left reacting blue. Wmk Crowns

S45
	Mint	Used
2d. Light red-brown	35·00	28·00

This exists on cream paper only and the phosphor band was applied by photogravure.

Cylinder Numbers (Blocks of Six)
Perforation Type A (E/I)

Cyl. No.	No dot	Dot
29	£300	£300

Perforation Type B (I/P no dot) and C (E/P dot)

Cyl. No.	No dot	Dot
29	£300	£300

Minor Constant Sheet Flaw
Cyl. 29. 17/6   See 540f

Coil Leader
Double-pane cylinder D1 was used.

Printed in continuous reels.
Vertical delivery with watermark upright

Code No.	Number in roll	Face value	
V	960	£8	85·00

Imprimaturs from the NPM or BPMA
Imperforate, watermark Type W.**24**

Watermark upright	£900
Cyl 29 Block of Six	£6250
Cyl D1. (coil) Strip of Five	£5250

1961 *(4 October).* **2d.** Two phosphor bands reacting blue. Wmk Crowns

A. Cream Paper Bands Letterpress

S46
	Mint	Used
2d. Light red-brown	10·00	7·00
a. Imperf. three sides	£4500	
b. One 6 mm band at left or right (stamp with vert. margin)	25·00	
c. Error. One 8 mm band (l/press)	20·00	
ca. As c. but 6 mm band	25·00	
d. Bands applied photo. *(3.4.62)*	2·00	2·00
da. Error. One 8 mm band (photo)	25·00	

S46a This comes from Cyl. 29 no dot with bands applied by photogravure.

B. Whiter Paper *(5 November 1964)*†
Bands applied by photogravure

S47
2d. Light red-brown	7·00	7·00
a. Error. Single 8 mm band	£110	

† No. S47 appeared earlier from V coils on 21 January 1963.

Cylinder Numbers (Blocks of Six)

Cream paper
Two bands applied by letterpress (No. S46)
Perforation Type A (E/I)

Cyl. No.	No dot	Dot
25	£150	†
27	†	£150
29	£150	£150
30	£150	£150

Two bands applied by photogravure (No. S46d)
Perforation Type B (I/P no dot) and C (E/P dot)

Cyl. No.	No dot	Dot
29	25·00	25·00

Whiter paper
Two bands applied by photogravure (No. S47)
Perforation Type A (E/I)

Cyl. No.	No dot	Dot
25	75·00	75·00

As the letterpress bands were applied on individual sheets and not in the reel, it is possible that the items marked with a dagger may exist.

Minor Constant Sheet Flaw
Dot cyls. 17/6   See S40

Coil Leader
Double-pane cylinder D1 was used.

Printed in continuous reels.
Vertical delivery with watermark upright.
Cream or whiter paper.

Code No.	Number in roll	Face value	
V	960	£8	75·00

Imprimaturs from the NPM or BPMA
Imperforate, watermark Type W.**24**. Cream or whiter paper

Watermark upright	£900
Cyl. 29 Block of Six (Cream paper)	£6250
Cyl. 25 Block of Six (Whiter paper)	£6250

1965 *(17 August).* **2d.** Two 8 mm. Phosphor bands reacting violet. Wmk Crowns

S48
	Mint	Used
2d. Light red-brown	90	60

The bands were applied by photogravure only.

Cylinder Numbers (Blocks of Six)
Perforation Type A (E/I)

Cyl. No.	No dot	Dot
27	†	£2000
30	12·00	12·00

Minor Constant Sheet Flaw
Cyl. 30. 17/6   See S41e

Coil Leader
Double-pane cylinder D1 was used.

Printed in continuous reels.
Vertical delivery with watermark upright

Code No.	Number in roll	Face value	
V	960	£8	45·00

27

SA Dorothy Wilding issues   2d. Red-brown, 2½d. Carmine-red

1967 *(September).* **2d.** Two 9·5 mm phosphor bands reacting violet. Wmk Crowns

S49 = SG 613a	Mint	Used
2d. Light red-brown	10	15
a. Watermark Crown to left *(6.4.67)*	30	60
b. One band (wmk. sideways, ex coil)	1·00	1·00
c. Extra leg to "R" (Sideways coil, Roll 2)	30·00	
d. Retouched left "2" (Sideways coil, Roll 5)	30·00	
e. Tadpole flaw retouched with shamrock flaw (Cyl. 27 Dot, R. 17/6)	30·00	

The bands were applied by photogravure only.

Stamps with sideways watermark are from coils with sideways delivery.

For illustrations of Nos. S49c/d, see Nos. S36g/h. No. S49e is described below No. S37.

Cylinder Numbers (Blocks of Six)
Perforation Type F (L) *

Cyl. No.	No dot (I/E)	Dot (P/E)
25	10·00	10·00

Perforation Type A (E/I)

Cyl. No.	No dot	Dot
27	10·00	10·00

Minor Constant Sheet Flaw

Cyl 27. 17/6   See S41e

Coil Leaders
Double-pane cylinder D1 was used for the vertical delivery coils and cylinder D3 (single pane) for sideways delivery coils.

Printed in continuous reels
(a) Vertical delivery. Watermark upright

Code No.	Number in roll	Face value	
R	480	£4	45·00
V	960	£8	40·00

(b) Sideways delivery. Watermark sideways

| T | 480 | £4 | 35·00 |

2½d. Carmine-red, Type SA2 (1952–1965)

Two Types

Type I   In the frontal cross of the diadem, the top line is only half the width of the cross.
Type II The top line extends to the full width of the cross and there are signs of strengthening in other parts of the diadem.

I   II

Variations in the Multipositives

The original multipositive (No. MP358) became damaged and had to be replaced. The original negative consisted of two negatives placed in contact against each other, one for the frame and one for the Queen's head and oval setting. When these two pieces of glass were placed together the position of the two was not exactly the same as when the first multipositive was made, resulting in a slight tilting of the portrait.

The second multipositive (Type B, No. MP460) was used for making cylinder 46 which was employed for No. S53 and the third multipositive (Type C, No. MP474) was used for all later cylinder numbers, i.e. Nos. 49 onwards.

Multipositive A was used for the booklets listed under Nos. S53, S55, S57, S59, S61/2 and S65 and, in consequence, stamps from these sections showing multipositive A and upright watermark are worth the same as inverted watermark varieties from booklets

A   B

C

Type A. At the shoulder lines above "E" of "POSTAGE" the line dividing the light from the dark material of the dress, if projected, runs level with the top of the two diagonal lines of the ribbon on the wreath.
Type B. The line runs between the first and second diagonal line of the ribbon.
Type C. The line runs level with the first diagonal line of the ribbon.

These are not listed as separate varieties because the stamps printed from the cylinders made from the three variations in the multipositives differed in other respects. It was, however, a most interesting development which also applied to the 3d. value.

2½d. Carmine-red   Dorothy Wilding issues   **SA**

1952 *(5 December).* **2½d.**, Type I. Wmk Tudor Crown

S50 = SG 519	Mint	Used
2½d. Carmine-red	30	15
a. Watermark sideways *(15.11.54)*	12·00	12·00
b. Broken value circle (Cyl. 8 No dot, R. 20/2)	30·00	
c. Extended broken top of diadem (Cyl. 16 Dot, R. 20/5)	35·00	
d. Frame retouch (Sideways coil, Roll 7)	35·00	

Stamps with sideways watermark are from M coils with sideways delivery.

S50b   S50c

S50d, S52e, S56ba, S56da

Cylinder Numbers (Blocks of Six)
Perforation Type A (E/I)

Cyl. No.	No dot	Dot
2	10·00	10·00
4	10·00	10·00
5	10·00	10·00
6	12·00	12·00
7	10·00	10·00
8	40·00*	10·00
9	15·00	15·00
10	10·00	10·00
11	10·00	10·00
12	10·00	10·00
13	15·00	15·00
14	15·00	15·00
15	15·00	15·00
16	10·00	15·00
17	15·00	15·00
18	10·00	15·00
19	15·00	15·00
22	10·00	10·00
23	15·00	15·00
24	15·00	15·00
25	15·00	15·00
27	25·00	25·00

Perforation Type B (I/P no dot) and C (E/P dot)

Cyl. No.	No dot	Dot
14	75·00	50·00
24	75·00	50·00

Minor Constant Sheet Flaws
Multipositive flaws on all cylinders

No dot	1/4	Red dot over left of crown (Th. A3)
	12/4	Red spot in leaf of shamrock (Th. G1)
	18/1	Diagonal scratch from chin to neck (Th. E3–F4)
Dot	11/9	White spot in "R" of "E R" (Cyls. 23, onwards)

Cylinder flaws

Cyl. 2	16/1	Smudge line across top of "REVENUE"
Cyl. 8.	19/1	Red spot in "1" of fraction
Cyl. 10.	20/1	Extended top of "2" in value

Coil Leaders
Double-pane cylinder L1 was used for the vertical delivery coils and L3 for the sideways delivery coils.

Printed in continuous reels
(a) Vertical delivery. Watermark upright

Code No.	Number in roll	Face value	
F	960	£10	65·00
U	1920	£20	—

(b) Sideways delivery. Watermark sideways

| M | 480 | £5 | 35·00 |

Imprimaturs from the NPM or BPMA
Imperforate, watermark Type W.**22**

Watermark upright	£900
Watermark inverted	£900
Watermark sideways	£900
Tête-bêche pair (Horiz)	£3250
Cyl. 2. Block of Six	£6250

1953 *(May).* **2½d.** Type II Wmk Tudor Crown

S51 = SG 519b	Mint	Used
2½d. Carmine-red	1·25	1·25
a. Watermark inverted *(5.53)*	1·00	1·00

This issue appeared from booklets only. See Section SB, Nos. SB80/a.

1955 *(28 September).* **2½d.** Type I Wmk St Edward's Crown

S52 = SG 544	Mint	Used
2½d. Carmine-red	30	25
a. Imperf. between stamp and top margin	£1200	
b. Watermark sideways *(23.3.56)*	1·50	1·75
c. "b" for "D" in value (Cyl. 30 Dot, R. 19/11)	35·00	
d. White flaw below oval (Cyl. 44 Dot, R. 1/4)	35·00	
e. Frame retouch (sideways coil, Roll 7)	30·00	

Stamps with sideways watermark are from M coils with sideways delivery.

S52c   S52d

For illustration of No. S52e, see No. S50d

SA Dorothy Wilding issues *2½d. Carmine-red*

Cylinder Numbers (Blocks of Six)
Perforation Type A (E/I)

Cyl. No.	No dot	Dot
22	12·00	12·00
24	£500	£1000
25	10·00	10·00
27	10·00	10·00
30	10·00	10·00
32	10·00	10·00
33	10·00	10·00
34	†	75·00
37	10·00	10·00
38	12·00	12·00
39	10·00	10·00
40	12·00	12·00
42	10·00	10·00
43	10·00	10·00
44	10·00	10·00
45	£100	£100

Perforation Type E

Cyl. No.	No dot (AE/I)	Dot (E/I)
32	75·00	**
37	75·00	**

** Same price and appearance as perforation type A with extension holes in left margin.
In Cylinder 42, both panes, the marginal arrows at the top and bottom were omitted at first, but added later.

Minor Constant Sheet Flaws
Multipositive flaws as for No. S50
Cylinder flaw

| Cyl. 43 | 18/5 | Red spot on Queen's lip (Th. D3) |

Coil Leaders
Double-pane cylinder L1 was used for the vertical delivery coils and L3 for the sideways delivery coils.
Printed in continuous reels
(a) Vertical delivery. Watermark upright

Code No.	Number in roll	Face value	
F	960	£10	55·00
U	1920	£20	£150

(b) Sideways delivery. Watermark sideways

| M | 480 | £5 | 25·00 |

Imprimaturs from the NPM or BPMA
Imperforate, watermark Type W.**23**

Watermark upright	£900
Cyl. 30 Block of Six	£6250

1957 2½d. Type II. Wmk St Edward's Crown
S53 = SG 544b

	Mint	Used
2½d. Carmine-red	45	45
a. Tête-bêche (horiz. pair)	£3250	
d. Imperf. between stamp and top margin	£1200	
e. Watermark inverted *(9.55)*	55	70

Cylinder Numbers (Blocks of Six)
Perforation Type A (E/I)

Cyl. No.	No dot	Dot
46	10·00	10·00

Imprimaturs from the NPM or BPMA
Imperforate, watermark Type W.**23**

Watermark upright	£900
Watermark inverted	£900
Tête-bêche pair	£3250

1957 (19 November). **2½d.** With graphite lines, Type SA8. Wmk St. Edward's Crown. Type II
S54 = SG 565

	Mint	Used
2½d. Carmine-red	8·50	7·00
a. Coil join (horiz. pr.)	30·00	

Cylinder Numbers (Blocks of Six)
Single pane cylinder

Cyl. No.		Perf Type	No Dot
49		B (I/P)	70·00
49		C (E/P)	70·00

Coil Leader
Made up from sheets with sheet margin joins.
Sideways delivery

Code No.	Number in roll	Face value	
M	480	£5	£120

Imprimaturs from the NPM or BPMA
Imperforate, watermark Type W.**23**

Watermark upright	£900
Cyl. 49 Block of Six	£6250

Quantity Issued: 20,578,800

1959 (15 September)†. **2½d.** Wmk Crowns.
A. Type II Cream Paper
S55

	Mint	Used
2½d. Carmine-red	60	30
a. Tête-bêche (horiz. pair)	—	
b. Imperf. strip of 3		
c. Imperf. between stamp and bottom margin		
d. Watermark inverted *(11.58)*	4·50	3·00
e. State 1. Leaf and extra rose stem flaws (Cyl. 50 Dot, R. 9/4)	35·00	
ea. State 2. Extra rose stem. Leaf flaw retouched (Cyl 50 Dot, R. 9/4)	35·00	
f. White emblems (Cyl. 52 No dot, R. 12/4)	35·00	

B. Type I. Cream Paper *(4 October 1961)*
S56

	Mint	Used
2½d. Carmine-red	3·50	2·00
b. Watermark sideways *(10.11.60)*	1·25	70
ba. Imperf, strip of 6		
bb. Frame retouch (Sideways coil, Roll 7)	30·00	

C. Type I. Whiter Paper *(30 October 1963)*
S56C = SG 574e

	Mint	Used
2½d. Carmine-red	70	70
d. Watermark sideways *(3.8.62)*	40	60
da. Frame retouch (Sideways coil, Roll 7)	30·00	

D. Type II. Whiter Paper *(7 May 1962)*
S57 = SG 574

	Mint	Used
2½d. Carmine-red	10	20
a. Watermark inverted *(29.7.62)*	4·50	3·00
b. Imperf. between stamp and top margin		

2½d. Carmine-red — Dorothy Wilding issues — SA

D. Type II. Whiter Paper *(7 May 1962)*
S57 = SG 574

	Mint	Used
c. Watermark Crown to left (coils, 9.65 and booklets, 1.7.64)	70	1·25
d. Watermark Crown to right	70	1·25
e. State 2. Extra rose stem. Leaf flaw retouched (Cyl. 50 Dot, R. 9/4)	35·00	
f. Serif to "A" (Cyl. 55 No dot, R. 11/8)	35·00	

E. Type II. Chalk-surfaced Paper. Booklets only *(15 July 1963)*
S58 = SG 574k

	Mint	Used
2½d. Carmine-red	50	80
a. Watermark inverted *(15.7.63)*	75	1·25

Imperf. stamps, No. S55b comes from a booklet with watermark upright and No. S56ba is from an M coil with sideways watermark. *Sideways watermark*. Nos. S56b, S56d and S57c came from M coils with sideways delivery and Nos. S57c/d are from 2s. Holiday Booklets No. NR2.

For illustration of Nos. S56bb and S56da, see No. S50d. No. S56da is known in a second state showing a vertical line adjoining the right-hand frame not filled in with colour.

S55e State 1. Triangular white flaw adjoining left leaf and extra stem to rose.

State 2. Later printings exist with the leaf flaw retouched (Nos S55ea, S57e, S61c, S62b, S63e).

State 3. Both flaws retouched (S65d).

S55f Later retouched

Normal

S57f

Cylinder Numbers (Blocks of Six)
Type II. (No. S55) Cream paper
Perforation Type A (E/I)

Cyl. No.	No dot	Dot
50	10·00	10·00
51	12·00	12·00
52	12·00	12·00
53	12·00	12·00
54	12·00	12·00

Perforation Type B (I/P no dot) and C (E/P dot)

Cyl. No.	No dot	Dot
50	45·00	25·00
51	45·00	25·00
52	45·00	25·00

Type I. (No. S56) Cream Paper.
Perforation Type A (E/I)

Cyl. No.	No dot	Dot
42	35·00	35·00

Perforation Type B (I/P no dot) and C (E/P dot) Cream paper

Cyl. No.	No dot	Dot
42	£1000	£1000

Type I. (No. S56c). Whiter Paper
Perforation Type A (E/I)

Cyl. No.	No dot	Dot
42	70·00	70·00

Type II. (No. S57). Whiter Paper
Perforation Type A (E/I)

Cyl. No.	No dot	Dot
50	10·00	10·00
51	12·00	12·00
52	10·00	10·00
53	10·00	10·00
54	10·00	10·00
55	10·00	10·00
56	10·00	10·00
57	10·00	10·00
58	10·00	10·00
59	10·00	10·00

Perforation Type B (I/P no dot) and C (E/P dot)

Cyl. No.	No dot	Dot
51	25	25
52	45	25

Marginal arrows. In Type II these exist hand-engraved at left as well as photo-etched. Also sheets are known with the arrows omitted at bottom. On cylinder 55 the faint outline of the "V" shaped arrow is below rows 8/9 in addition to the etched arrow below vertical rows 6/7.

Minor Constant Sheet Flaws

Cyl. 42	1/4	Red spot over left of crown (Th. A3)
	12/4	Red spot in leaf of shamrock (Th. G1)
Cyl. 42.	4/1	Red and white dots in oval (Th. B2)
	5/8	Red dot in thistle (Th. G2)
	11/9	White spot in "R" of "E R"
	14/5	Slight retouch in forehead above Queen's right eye (Th. C2)
	16/3	White dot between thistle and leaf (Th. G2)
	17/2	Small white flaw on tail of "R" of "E R"
	18/10	Red dot between Queen's lip and nose (Th. D3). Later partially removed
	20/10	White flaw by oval at left (Th. D1–2)
Cyl. 50.	6/10	Background retouched behind "P" of "POSTAGE" and "R" of "REVENUE"
Cyl. 51.	7/5	Retouch to left of hair (Th. C2)
	9/6	White dot at bottom left of "R" of "REVENUE"
Cyl. 55.	11/8	Spur on "A" of "POSTAGE" (Th. G4)

Coil Leaders
Double-pane cylinder L1 was used for the vertical delivery coils and cylinders L3 for sideways delivery Type I coils and L5 for Type II coils.

Printed in continuous reels

(a) Vertical delivery. Watermark upright

Code No.	Number in roll	Face value		
F	960	£10	Type I. Cream or whiter paper	50·00

(b) Sideways delivery. Watermark sideways

M	480	£5	Type I. Cream or whiter paper	25·00
M	480	£5	Type II. Whiter paper	£150

SA Dorothy Wilding issues 2½d. Carmine-red

Imprimaturs from the NPM or BPMA
Type II. Imperforate, watermark Type W.**24**. Cream or whiter paper

Watermark upright	£900
Watermark inverted	£900
Watermark sideways	£900
Tête-bêche pair (Vert)	£3250
Cyl. 50. Block of Six (Cream paper)	£6250
Cyl. 51. Block of Six (Whiter paper)	£6250
Cyl. L1 (coils) Block of Six	£6750

1959 (9 June). **2½d.** Type II. With graphite lines, Type **SA8**. Wmk Crowns.

S59 = SG 591	Mint	Used
2½d. Carmine-red	12·00	10·00
a. Watermark inverted (21.8.59)	65·00	50·00

Cylinder Numbers (Blocks of Six)
Single pane cylinder

Cyl. No.	Perf Type	No Dot
49	B (I/P)	85·00
49	C (E/P)	85·00

Imprimaturs from the NPM or BPMA
Imperforate, watermark Type W.**24**

Watermark upright	£900
Watermark inverted	£900
Tête-bêche pair (Horiz)	£3250
Cyl. 49 Block of Six	£6250

Quantity Issued: 10,012,800

1959 (18 November). **2½d.** Type II. Phosphor-graphite issue. Wmk Crowns

S60 = SG 606	Mint	Used
2½d. Carmine-red	22·00	18·00
a. One 6 mm band at left or right (stamp with vert. margin)	30·00	
b. One 8 mm band	£180	
ba. As b but 6 mm band		

No. S60 has two graphite lines (Type **SA8**), on the back and two phosphor bands on the front, applied letterpress., which react green under the lamp.

The phosphor-graphite value with St Edward's Crown watermark Type W.**23**, is listed under "Dollis Hill" Phosphor trials at the end of Section SA (No. ST6 (1)b).

Cylinder Numbers (Blocks of Six)
Single pane cylinder

Cyl. No.	Perf Type	No Dot
49	B (I/P)	£175
49	C (E/P)	£175

Imprimatur from the NPM or BPMA
Perf. 15×14, watermark Type W.**24**

Watermark upright	—

Quantity Issued: 689,280

1960 (22 June). **2½d.** Type II. Two phosphor bands reacting green. Wmk Crowns.

S61	Mint	Used
2½d. Carmine-red	1·75	1·40
a. Watermark inverted (9.60)	£175	£175
b. One broad band (wmk. upright)	45·00	
c. State 2. Extra rose stem. Leaf flaw retouched (Cyl. 50 Dot, R. 9/4)	40·00	

The bands were applied by photogravure. For illustration of No. S61c, see No. S55e.

Cylinder Numbers (Blocks of Six)
Perforation Type B (I/P no dot) and C (E/P dot)

Cyl. No.	No dot	Dot
50	35·00	35·00

Minor Constant Sheet Flaw

Cyl. 50 6/10	Background retouch behind "P" of "POSTAGE" and "R" of "REVENUE"

Imprimaturs from the NPM or BPMA
Imperforate, watermark Type W.**24**

Watermark upright	£900
Watermark inverted	£900
Tête-bêche pair	£3250

1961 (5 June). **2½d.** Phosphor bands reacting blue. Wmk Crowns.
A. Two 8 mm Bands (applied photogravure).
Type II. Cream Paper

S62	Mint	Used
2½d. Carmine-red	6·00	3·00
a. Watermark inverted (3.61)	£175	£175
b. State 2. Extra rose stem. Leaf flaw retouched (Cyl. 50 Dot, R. 9/4)	40·00	

B. One Band at left (applied letterpress.).
Type II. Cream Paper (4 October 1961)

S63	Mint	Used
2½d. Carmine-red	4·00	4.00
a. Band applied photo. (3.11.61)	15·00	15·00
b. Watermark inverted (photo.) (3.62)	50·00	45·00
c. Error. Two bands (photo.)*	£110	
ca. Error. Band (photo.) omitted in pair with one band at right	£200	
d. Error. Band (I/press.) omitted in pair with one band at right	£225	
e. State 2. Extra rose stem. Leaf flaw retouched (Cyl. 50 Dot, R.9/4)	40·00	

C. One Band at left (applied letterpress.).
Type I. Cream Paper (4 October 1961)

S64 = SG 614b	Mint	Used
2½d. Carmine-red	45·00	40·00
b. Error. Band omitted, in pair with one band at right	£200	
c. Error. Two bands (I/press.)*	£120	

D. One Band at left (applied photogravure.).
Type II. Whiter Paper (22 June 1962)

S64 = SG 614a	Mint	Used
2½d. Carmine-red	60	75
a. Band applied I/press.	£225	90·00
b. Watermark inverted (3.6.63)	50·00	45·00
c. Error. Two bands (Photo.)	—	
d. State 3. Rose stem and leaf flaws retouched (Cyl. 50 Dot, R, 9/4)	35·00	
e. Horiz. pair ex. pane. Band at right and one stamp missing phosphor	—	

2½d. Carmine-red, 3d. Deep lilac **Dorothy Wilding issues** **SA**

* Two Band Errors. These can be identified by the distance between the bands. On the normal two band S62, this is 12 mm but it is 16 mm on the two band errors, Nos. S63c, S64c, and S65c. These three varieties have the 4 mm left band applied in error over the vertical perforations at each side of the stamp.

E. Two 8 mm Bands (applied photogravure).
Type II. Whiter Paper *(20 September 1964)*

S66 = SG 614	Mint	Used
2½d. Carmine-red	40	30
a. Bands applied l/press.	£2000	
b. One 8 mm band (photo.)	15·00	

No. S66 was a reissue of No. S62 but from cylinder 57 and on whiter paper. The shade is slightly more carmine. It was first released in error in the S.E. London area in September 1964 and then put on sale in Birmingham in December 1964 as electronic sorting machines were not in use there at that time. To prepare for the alteration in postal rates on 17 May 1965 when the 2½d. ceased to be the printed paper rate, it was released in the phosphor areas on 3 May 1965 in place of the single band stamps. However, as there was no longer a postal need for this value it was not reprinted.

For description of Nos. S62b, S63e and S65d, see illustration No S55e.

Cylinder Numbers (Blocks of Six)
Two bands (No. S62). Type II Cream paper.
Perforation Type A (E/I)

Cyl. No.	No dot	Dot
50	60·00	60·00

One band at left. Type II. Cream paper
Perforation Type A (E/I). Applied letterpress. (No. S63)

Cyl. No.	No dot	Dot
50	50·00	50·00

Perforation Type B (I/P no dot) or C (E/P dot)
Applied photogravure. (No. S63a)

Cyl. No.	No dot	Dot
50	£100	£100
53	£100	£100

One band at left. Type I. Cream paper.
Perforation Type A (E/I)
Applied letterpress. (No. S64)

42	£350	£350

Type II. Whiter paper,
Perforation Type A (E/I)
One band. Applied photogravure. (No. S65)

Cyl. No.	No dot	Dot
51	15·00	15·00
52	15·00	15·00
54	12·00	12·00
56	15·00	15·00
57	20·00	20·00

One band. Applied letterpress. (No. S65a)

50	£1750	£1750

Two bands. Applied photogravure. (No. S66)

57	10·00	10·00

Minor Constant Sheet Flaws
As recorded for Nos. S55/7

Imprimaturs from the NPM or BPMA
One band at left. Type II. Imperforate, watermark Type W.**24**.
Cream or whiter paper

Watermark upright	£900
Watermark inverted	£900
Tête-bêche pair (Horiz)	£3250
Cyl. 50 Block of Six (Cream paper)	£6250

3d. Deep lilac, Type SA2 (1954–1967)
Variations in the Multipositives
There are similar variations in the tilt of the portrait in the multipositives used as occurred in the 2½d. value (see notes and illustration at the beginning of the 2½d. list).

The second multipositive, corresponding to Type B, was used for cylinders 25 to 33 and the third multipositive, corresponding to Type C, was employed for cylinders 36 and 37. A fourth multipositive, also Type C, was introduced for cylinders 41 onwards.

1954 *(18 January)*. **3d.** Wmk Tudor Crown

S67 = SG 520	Mint	Used
3d. Deep lilac	1·50	90
a. Imperf. between stamp and top margin	£1000	
ab. Imperf. Between stamp and bottom margin	£1000	
b. Coil join (horiz. pair)	4·00	
c. Coil join (vert. pair)	12·00	

See General Notes under Paper – this stamp exists on very thick paper for this issue. (*Price £75 mint*)

Cylinder Numbers (Blocks of Six)
Perforation Type A (E/I)

Cyl. No.	No dot	Dot
3	25·00	25·00

Perforation Type B (I/P no dot) and C (E/P dot)

Cyl. No.	No dot	Dot
3	15·00	15·00

Minor Constant Sheet Flaws
Multipositive flaws

No dot	1/3	White scratch to bottom right of "R" of large "E R" (Th. A–B6)
Dot	9/8	Dark patch to left of central cross of tiara (Th. B3)

Coil Leaders
Made up from sheets with sheet margin joins.
Watermark upright

Code No.	Number in roll	Face value	
C	960	£12 Vertical delivery	60·00
S	480	£6 Sideways delivery	60·00

Imprimaturs from the NPM or BPMA
Imperforate, watermark Type W.**22**

Watermark upright	£900
Cyl. 3 Block of Six	£6250

1956 *(17 July)*. **3d.** Wmk St Edward's Crown.

S68 = SG 545	Mint	Used
3d. Deep lilac	40	25
a. Tête-bêche (horiz. pair)	£3250	
b. Imperf. three sides (pair)	£2750	
c. Imperf. between stamp and bottom margin	£1000	
d. Watermark inverted *(1.10.57)*	1·25	1·25
e. Watermark sideways *(22.11.57)*	18·00	17·00
f. Coil join (horiz. pair)	7·00	
g. Coil join (vert. pair)	14·00	
h. White flaw over Queen's eye (Cyl. 2 Dot, R.13/7)	50·00	

Stamps with sideways watermark are from S coils with sideways delivery.

No. S68b comes from a partly perforated booklet pane of six. No complete panes showing this error have been recorded.

33

SA Dorothy Wilding issues 3d. Deep lilac

S68h

Cylinder Numbers (Blocks of Six)
Perforation Type A (E/I)

Cyl. No.	No dot	Dot
2	10·00	10·00
3	10·00	10·00
4	12·00	12·00
5	10·00	10·00
9	10·00	10·00
10	10·00	10·00
15	10·00	12·00
16	15·00	15·00
17	15·00	15·00

Perforation Type B (I/P no dot) and C (E/P dot)

Cyl. No.	No dot	Dot
2	50·00	50·00
3	50·00	50·00

Single-pane cylinder
Perforation: Type F (L) (I/E)

Single-pane cylinder	No Dot
5	£150

Marginal arrows:
"V" shaped, hand engraved at top and bottom
"W" shaped, photo-etched at both sides
Early printings from cylinder 2 had the "V" shaped arrow omitted from the bottom of the sheet on no dot and dot panes (Price for positional block showing arrow omitted £20 no dot £30 dot)

Minor Constant Sheet Flaws
Multipositive flaws on all cylinders

No dot	1/3	White scratch to bottom right of "R" of large "E R" (Th. A–B6)
Dot	9/8	Dark patch to left of central cross of tiara (Th. B3)

Cylinder flaw		
Cyl. 17	17/3	Coloured scratches through "E" of large "E R" (Th. A1)

Coil Leaders
(a) Made up from sheets with sheet margin joins.
Watermark upright

Code No.	Number in roll	Face value		
C	960	£12	Vertical delivery	50·00
S	480	£6	Sideways delivery	50·00

(b) Printed in continuous reels.
Double-pane cylinder M2 was used for the vertical delivery coils and cylinder M5 for the sideways delivery coil.
(a) Vertical delivery. Watermark upright

Code No.	Number in roll	Face value	
C	960	£12	60·00
U	1920	£24	60·00

(b) Sideways delivery. Watermark sideways

S	480	£6	40·00

Imprimaturs from the NPM or BPMA
Imperforate, watermark Type W.23

Watermark upright	£900
Watermark upright White flaw over Queen's eye R. 13/7	£1500
Watermark inverted	£900
Watermark sideways	£900
Tête-bêche pair (Horiz or Vert)	£3250
Cyl. 2. Block of Six	£6250
Cyl. M5 (coils) Watermark sideways Block of Six	£6750

1957 (19 November). **3d.** With graphite lines, Type **SA8**. Wmk St Edward's Crown

S69 = SG 566	Mint	Used
3d. Deep lilac	1·50	1·50
a. Coil join (horiz. pair)	2·50	

Cylinder Numbers (Blocks of Six)
Single pane cylinders

Cyl. No.	Perf. Type	No Dot
7	B (I/P)	15·00
7	C (E/P)	15·00
11	B (I/P)	15·00
11	C (E/P)	15·00

Coil Leader
Made up from sheets with sheet margin joins.
Watermark upright

Code No.	Number in roll	Face value		
S	480	£6	Sideways delivery	£120

Imprimaturs from the NPM or BPMA
Imperforate, watermark Type W.23

Watermark upright	£900
Cyl 7 Block of Six	£6250

Quantity Issued: 91,466,400

1958 (8 December)†. **3d.** Wmk Crowns.

A. Cream Paper

S70	Mint	Used
3d. Deep lilac	25	25
c. Imperf. between stamp and top margin	£500	
d. Watermark Crown to left (Coils, 24.10.58 and booklets, 26.5.61)	1·25	75
e. Watermark inverted (11.58)	50	55
f. Watermark Crown to right (Booklets, 26.5.61)	1·25	65
g. Spot on "T" of "POSTAGE" (Cyl. 37 No dot, R. 19/11)	35·00	
h. Phantom "R" (Cyl. 37 No dot, below R. 20/12)	55·00	
i. Do. Retouch	20·00	

3d. Deep lilac   **Dorothy Wilding issues**   **SA**

1958 *(8 December)*†. **3d.** Wmk Crowns.

A. Cream Paper

S70		Mint	Used
j.	Phantom "R" (Cyl. 41 No dot, below R.20/12)	£375	
k.	Do. First retouch	30·00	
l.	Do. Second or third retouch	30·00	

B. Whiter Paper *(30 April 1962)*

S71 = SG 575		Mint	Used
3d.	Deep lilac	20	15
a.	Watermark Crown to left (Coils, *(30.4.62)* and booklets, *(5.6.62)*	50	55
b.	Watermark Crown to right (Booklets, *5.6.62)*)	50	55
c.	Watermark inverted *(16.7.62)*	50	55
d.	Experimental T watermark* (marginal block of 6)	35·00	35·00
e.	Serif on "E" (Cyl. 68 Dot, R.16/5)	35·00	
f.	Flaw on "E" (R.14/11 on Cyls. 60 No dot and others)	35·00	
g.	White spur on thistle left of "P" (Cyl. 70 No dot, "R". 4/2)	35·00	

* In 1964 No. S71 was printed from Cylinder 70 no dot and dot on an experimental paper which is distinguished by an additional watermark letter "T" lying on its side, which occurs about four times in the sheet, usually in the side margins where it is easiest to see. It is difficult to see when it occurs on the stamps themselves. 48,000 sheets were issued.

Variations in the Multipositives. See the notes at the beginning of the 3d. list about the variations in the tilt of the portrait on the different multipositives used.

Tête-bêche. No. S70 exists *tête-bêche*, also separated by gutters. These are from booklet sheets which were not issued.(£70*per pair*)

S70g

S70h

S70i

S70j, S74c

S70k First retouch

S70l Second or third retouch

S71f

S71e, S77g

S71g

An incomplete masking of the stamp image beneath the marginal rule revealed an "R" on Cyls. 37 and 41 no dot. It is more noticeable on the latter because of the wider marginal rule. The retouch on Cyl. 37 is not easily identified. There is no trace of the "R" but the general appearance of that part of the marginal rule is uneven. However, the retouch can be confirmed in a positional block by the presence of the Spot on "T" variety on R.19/11, No. S70g.

The "R" on Cyl. 41 was retouched three times, the first being as illustrated here (No. S70k) and traces of the "R" can still be seen in the others.

Cylinder Numbers (Blocks of Six)

A. Cream Paper. (No. S70)
Perforation Type A(E/I)

Cyl. No.	No dot	Dot
15	12·00	12·00
16	90·00	90·00
22	10·00	10·00
25	10·00	10·00
26	10·00	10·00
28	10·00	10·00
29	10·00	10·00
30	10·00	10·00
31	10·00	10·00
33	20·00	20·00
36	10·00	10·00
37	10·00	10·00
41	10·00	10·00
46	10·00	10·00
47	50·00	50·00
49	10·00	10·00
51	10·00	10·00
52	10·00	10·00
53	80·00	80·00
54	10·00	10·00
55	10·00	10·00
58	35·00	35·00

SA Dorothy Wilding issues 3d. Deep lilac

Cyl. No.	No dot	Dot
60	10·00	10·00
61	10·00	10·00
62	10·00	10·00
64	10·00	10·00

Perforation Type B (I/P no dot) and C (E/P dot)

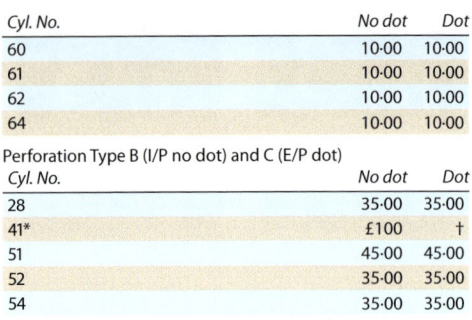

Cyl. No.	No dot	Dot
28	35·00	35·00
41*	£100	†
51	45·00	45·00
52	35·00	35·00
54	35·00	35·00

* This has been seen Perf. Type B (I/P no dot) and may be an example of No. S74 with phosphor bands omitted.

Perforation Type H

Cyl. No.	(E/I)	(P/I)
31	**	£100
36	**	£100
37	**	£125
41	**	£100

** Same price and appearance as perforation type A with extension holes in left margin.

B. Whiter Paper. (No. S71)
Perforation Type A (E/I)

Cyl. No.	No dot	Dot
51	10·00	—
52	15·00	15·00
54	15·00	15·00
58	10·00	10·00
60	15·00	10·00
61	10·00	10·00
62	10·00	10·00
63	10·00	10·00
64	10·00	10·00
66	10·00	10·00
67	10·00	10·00
68	10·00	10·00
69	10·00	10·00
70	10·00	10·00
70 with T wmk*	50·00	†
71	10·00	10·00
72	10·00	10·00
73	12·00	12·00
75	10·00	10·00
78	10·00	10·00
79	10·00	10·00
80	10·00	10·00
81	10·00	10·00
82	10·00	10·00

* See S71d, above.

Marginal arrows: These vary from cylinder to cylinder. The following combinations are known:
(a) All hand-engraved. "V" shaped at top and bottom; "W" shaped at both sides
(b) "V" shaped, hand-engraved at top and bottom; "W shaped, photo-etched at both sides
(c) All photo-etched. "W" shaped at top and bottom and at both sides

Minor Constant Sheet Flaws
Multipositive flaws (Cyls. 15, 16 and 22 only)

No dot	1/3	White scratch to bottom right of "R" of large "E R" (Th. A-B6)
Dot	9/8	Dark patch to left of central cross of tiara (Th. B3)

Cylinder flaws

Cyl. 46.	20/2	White flaw on leaves of oval at left (Th. E-F1)
Cyl. 52	17/9	White spur to circle around 3d. by "D" (Th. G6)
Cyl. 52.	18/2	Coloured line from Queen's hair to top of oval (Th. B2)
Cyl. 60.	4/11	Coloured flaw on thistle leaf (Th. G2)
Cyl. 63.	4/11	White flaw on leaf (Th. G2)
Cyl. 69	5/10	White flaw on wreath (Th. F6)
Cyl. 70.	10/4	White flaw above "PO" of "POSTAGE" (Th. G3)
	10/11	White flaw on daffodil stem giving appearance of thick stalk (Th. G-H2)
	19/8	Coloured scratch from tiara to oval (Th. C5)

Coil Leaders
Printed in continuous reels. Double-pane cylinder M2 was used for the vertical delivery coils and cylinders M5, M9, M10, M13 and M14 for the sideways delivery coils. Cylinders M5, M9 and M10 were used on cream paper and M13 and M14 on the whiter paper.

(a) Vertical delivery. Watermark upright.
Cream or whiter paper

Code No.	Number in roll	Face value	
C	960	£12	50·00
U	1920	£24	45·00
AC	480	£6	35·00
AD	960	£12	40·00

(b) Sideways delivery. Watermark sideways.
Cream or whiter paper

S	480	£6	20·00

Imprimaturs from the NPM or BPMA
Imperforate, watermark Type W.**24**. Cream or whiter paper

Watermark upright	£900
Watermark inverted	£900
Watermark sideways	£900
Tête-bêche pair (Horiz or Vert)	£3250
Cyl. 25 Block of Six (Cream paper)	£6250
Cyl. M5 (coils) Watermark sideways Block of Six	£6250

1958 (24 November). **3d.** With graphite lines, Type **SA8**. Wmk Crowns

S72 = SG 592		Mint	Used
3d. Deep lilac		90	65
a. Watermark inverted (4.8.59)		1·00	1·25
b. Two lines at left (5.61)		£550	£425
c. Three lines		£150	£120
d. One line		£2500	£2500
e. Coil join (horiz. pair)		12·00	

The misplaced graphite lines (varieties b/d) came from sheets from Cyls. 51 no dot and dot printed after the graphite line experiment had ended to use up residual stock of graphite-lined paper.

Examples of No. S72b have both graphite lines printed clear of the perforations. Stamps showing lines cutting the perforations are common and worth a fraction of the price of the genuine variety. This applies particularly to cylinder blocks.

Cylinder Numbers (Blocks of Six)
Single-pane cylinder

Cyl. No.	Perf. Type	No Dot
11	B (I/P)	25·00
11	C (E/P)	25·00

3d. Deep lilac — Dorothy Wilding issues — SA

Coil Leaders
Double-pane cylinder M2 was used.
Printed in continuous reels. Watermark upright.

Code No.	Number in roll	Face value		
C	960	£12	Vertical delivery	—

Made up from sheets with sheet margin joins. Watermark upright.

| S | 480 | £6 | Sideways delivery | £250 |

Imprimaturs from the NPM or BPMA
Imperforate, watermark Type W.**24**

Watermark upright	£900
Watermark inverted	£900
Tête-bêche pair (Horiz)	£3250
Cyl. 11 Block of Six	£6250

Quantity Issued: 57,222,960

1959 (18 November). **3d.** Phosphor-graphite issue. Wmk Crowns

S73 = SG 607	Mint	Used
3d. Deep lilac	12·00	9·00
a. One 6 mm band at left or right (stamp with vert. margin)	22·00	

No. S73 has two graphite lines, Type **SA8**, on the back and two phosphor bands on the front, applied by letterpress., which react green under the lamp.

Cylinder Numbers (Blocks of Six)
Single-pane cylinder

Cyl. No.	Perf Type	No Dot
11	B (I/P)	90·00
11	C (E/P)	90·00

Imprimatur from the NPM or BPMA
Perf. 15×14, watermark Type W.**24**

Watermark upright	—

Quantity Issued: 4,625,040

1960 (22 June). **3d.** Two phosphor bands reacting green. Wmk Crowns

S74	Mint	Used
3d. Deep lilac	1·75	1·75
a. Watermark inverted (14.8.60)	1·75	1·75
b. One 8 mm band (wmk. upright)	40·00	
c. Phantom "R" (Cyl. 41 No dot, below R. 20/12)	55·00	
ca. As c but one 8 mm band		
d. One 8 mm band (wmk. inverted)		
da. As d but 6 mm band		

The bands were applied by photogravure. No. S74b is from sheets and booklet panes.
For illustrations of No. S74c, see No S70j.

Cylinder Numbers (Blocks of Six)
Perforation Type B (I/P no dot) and C (E/P dot)

Cyl. No.	No dot	Dot
41	35·00	35·00

Imprimaturs from the NPM or BPMA
Imperforate, watermark Type W.**24**

Watermark upright	£900
Watermark inverted	£900
Tête-bêche pair (Horiz)	£3250
Cyl. 41. Block of Six	£6250

1961 (5 June)†. **3d.** Phosphor bands reacting blue. Wmk Crowns

A. Two Bands. Cream Paper

S75	Mint	Used
3d. Deep lilac	1·25	1·25
a. Watermark inverted (3.61)	1·25	1·25
b. Watermark Crown to left (14.7.61)	3·00	3·00
c. Watermark Crown to right	3·00	3·00
d. One 8 mm band (wmk. sideways)	28·00	

B. (24 October 1962) †

S76 = SG 615		
3d. Deep lilac	60	55
a. Watermark Crown to left (15.8.62)	1·75	1·75
b. Watermark Crown to right	1·75	1·75
c. Watermark inverted (25.9.62)	50	90
d. Error. One band on each stamp (horiz. pair)	£100	
e. Imperf three sides (pair)		

The 8 mm bands on both stamps of No. S76d prove that the bands were displaced for this issue in addition to No. S77 (see No. S77f).
No. S76e comes from booklet pane SB100, but only one pair is known.

C. (29 April 1965)

S77		
3d. Deep lilac (side band at left)	2·75	2·50
a. Side band at right	2·75	2·50
ab. Nos. S77/a (horiz. pair)	7·00	5·00
b. Watermark Crown to left, band at left (16.8.65)	30·00	18·00
c. Watermark Crown to left, band at right	60·00	35·00
d. Watermark Crown to right, band at left	35·00	22·00
e. Watermark Crown to right, band at right	65·00	40·00
f. Error. Pair, left-hand stamp with phosphor omitted, right-hand stamp with one 8 mm band	£100	
g. Serif on "E" (Cyl. 68 Dot, R. 16/5)	40·00	

The bands were all applied by photogravure on the stamps with upright and inverted watermark and by letterpress on those with watermark sideways.
* The one side band stamps were produced by an 8 mm band applied down alternate vertical rows of the sheet over the perforations so that alternate stamps have the band at left (No. S77) or right (No. S77a). In theory the width of the band on a single stamp should be 4 mm but this will vary if the bands have not been perfectly positioned. For illustration of No. S77g see No. S71e.

Cylinder Numbers (Blocks of Six)

Two bands (No. S75). Cream paper.
Perforation Type B (I/P no dot) and C (E/P dot)

Cyl. No.	No dot	Dot
52	90·00	90·00
60	£100	£100

Two bands. (No. S76) Whiter paper.
Perforation Type A (E/I)

Cyl. No.	No dot	Dot
60	20.00	20.00
61	25.00	25.00
62	10.00	10.00
64	15·00	10.00
67	10.00	10.00
71	15·00	15·00

SA   Dorothy Wilding issues   3d. Deep lilac

One side band. (No. S77)

Cyl. No.	No dot	Dot
67	50·00	50·00
68	50·00	50·00
71	50·00	50·00
72	50·00	50·00

Minor Constant Sheet Flaws

Cyl. 52	17/9	As for S70/71
Cyl. 52.	18/2	As for S70/71
Cyl. 60.	4/11	As for S70/71

Coil Leaders
Double-pane cylinder M2 was used. Watermark upright. Two bands.

Vertical delivery in continuous reels.
Cream or whiter paper

Code No.	Number in roll	Face value	
AC	480	£6	60·00
AD	960	£12	75·00
U	1920	£24	—

One side band (left or right).
Vertical delivery in continuous reels. Whiter paper

Code No.	Number in roll	Face value	
AC	480	£6	—
AD	960	£12	—
U	1920	£24	—

Imprimaturs from the NPM or BPMA
Two Bands. Imperforate, watermark Type W.**24**. Cream or whiter paper

Watermark upright	£900
Watermark inverted	£900
Watermark sideways	£900
Tête-bêche pair (Horiz or Vert)	£3250
Cyl. 52. Block of Six (Cream paper)	£6250
Cyl. 52. Block of Six (Whiter paper)	£6250
Cyl. M2 (coils) Block of Six	£6750

One Side Band. Imperforate, watermark Type W.**24**. Whiter paper

Watermark sideways	£900
Vertical *Tête-bêche* pair with sideways watermark	£3250

1965 (13 August). **3d.** Phosphor bands reacting violet. Wmk Crowns

A. One Side Band*
S78 = SG 615c

	Mint	Used
3d. Deep lilac (side band at left)	60	70
a. Side band at right	60	55
ab. Nos. S78/a (horiz. pair)	1·25	1·25
b. One 8 mm band (wmk. sideways)	10·00	
ba. Pair, left-hand stamp with phosphor omitted, right-hand stamp with one band (wmk. upright)	50·00	
bb. One 8 mm band (wmk. upright)	15·00	
c. Watermark Crown to left, band at left (10.65)	5·50	5·00
d. Watermark Crown to left, band at right	5·50	5·00
e. Watermark Crown to right, band at left	5·50	5·00
f. Watermark Crown to right, band at right	5·50	5·00
g. Watermark inverted (band at left) (2.67) †	80·00	80·00
h. Watermark inverted (band at right) †	8·00	7·00
ha. Nos. S78g/h (horiz. pair)	90·00	

B. One 4 mm Centre Band (8 December 1966)
S79 = SG 615e

	Mint	Used
3d. Deep Lilac	40	45
a. Watermark sideways (19.6.67)	1·00	1·00
b. Watermark inverted (8.67)	4·00	4·00

C. Two 9·5 mm Bands.
Se-tenant 2s. Booklets only (November 1967)

S80 = SG 615b

3d. Deep lilac (Watermark Crown to left)	1·75	1·75
a. Watermark Crown to right	1·75	1·75
b. One 9·5 mm band (wmk. sideways)	25·00	

The bands applied by photogravure, except for stamps with sideways watermark where they were applied by letterpress.

* The one side band stamps were produced by an 8 mm band applied down alternate vertical rows of the sheet over the perforations so that alternate stamps have the band at left (No. S78) or right (No. S78a). In theory the width of the band on a single stamp should be 4 mm but this will vary if the bands have not been perfectly positioned. In addition, one side band stamps with sideways watermark were produced by applying a 9·5 mm band over the perforations but these only came in the October 1967 2s. Booklet N30p(b)) *se-tenant* with the 1d. value. As it is not possible to distinguish these from the 8 mm bands (Nos. S78c/f) in singles, the complete panes only are listed under No. SB50 to SB53.

† **Inverted watermark.** Nos. S78g/h only come from the 10s. Booklet of February 1967 (X15p(a/b)). Each pane, No. SB103a comprises two stamps with band at left and four stamps with band at right.

Sideways watermark. Nos. S78c/f come from 2s. Booklets N22p(b), N23p(b), N24p/30p(a), N31p(c) and N32p(c). No. S79a comes from S coils with sideways delivery and Nos. S80/a come from 2s. Booklets N31p(a/b) and N32p(a/b).

Cylinder Numbers (Blocks of Six)
Perforation Type A (E/I)
One side band. (No. S78)

Cyl. No.	No dot	Dot
67	12·00	12·00
71	15·00	15·00
72	12·00	12·00
81	15·00	15·00
82	12·00	12·00

Perforation Type A(E/I)
One centre band. (No. S7)

Cyl. No.	No dot	Dot
78	10·00	10·00
79	10·00	10·00
81	10·00	10·00
82	10·00	10·00

Coil Leaders
Double-pane cylinder M2 was used for the vertical delivery coils and cylinders M13 and M14 for the sideways delivery coils.

(a) One side band. Vertical delivery printed in continuous reels with the watermark upright

Code No.	Number in roll	Face value	
AC	480	£6	—
AD	960	£12	—
U	1920	£24	55·00

(b) One centre band. Printed in continuous reels
(i) Vertical delivery. Watermark upright

Code No.	Number in roll	Face value
AC	480	£6	35·00
AD	960	£12	50·00

(ii) Sideways delivery. Watermark sideways

S	480	£6	35·00

4d. Ultramarine, Type SA3 (1953–1967)

1953 (2 November). **4d.** Type W.**22** Wmk Tudor Crown

S81 = SG 521	Mint	Used
4d. Ultramarine	3·25	1·30
a. Coil join (horiz. pair)	15·00	
b. Dotted "R" (Cyl. 1 No dot, R.10/8)	50·00	
c. Scar on neck (Cyl. 1 No dot R.16/9)	50·00	

S81c The scar was the object of a major retouch (See No. 582d)

S81b, S82c The blue dot is of varying size and was eventually touched out on the St Edward's Crown watermark.

Cylinder Numbers (Blocks of Six)
Perforation Type A (E/I)

Cyl. No.	No dot	Dot
1	25·00	25·00

Perforation Type B (I/P no dot) and C (E/P dot)

Cyl. No.	No dot	Dot
1	28·00	28·00

Minor Constant Sheet Flaws
| Cyl.1 | 1/4 | Retouch on cheek left of ear (Th. D4) |

Coil Leader
Made up from sheets with sheet margin joins. Sideways delivery with the watermark upright

Code No.	Number in roll	Face value	
H	480	£8	70·00

Imprimaturs from the NPM or BPMA
Imperforate, watermark Type W.**22**

Watermark upright	£900
Cyl. 1. Block of Six	£6250

1955 (14 November). **4d.** Wmk St Edward's Crown

S82 = SG 546	Mint	Used
4d. Ultramarine	1·30	45
a. Coil join (vert. pair)	12·00	
b. Coil join (horiz. pair)	10·00	
c. Dotted "R" (Cyl. 1 No dot, R.10/8)	45·00	
ca. Dotted "R" retouched	40·00	
d. Retouched neck (Cyl. 1 No dot, R.16/9)	40·00	

For illustration of No. S82c, see No. S81b.

S82d, S83c   Normal

This is the major retouch of S81c. The blue line joining the Queen's neck to the frame is also constant.

S82ca, S83e

Cylinder Numbers (Blocks of Six)
Perforation Type A (E/I)

Cyl. No.	No dot	Dot
1	20·00	20·00
3	45·00	45·00

Perforation Type B (I/P no dot) and C (E/P dot)

Cyl. No.	No dot	Dot
1	35·00	35·00

Minor Constant Sheet Flaws
| Cyl. 1 | 1/4 | As for S81 |
| | 16/9 | As for S81 |

Coil Leaders
Made up from sheets with sheet margin joins with the watermark always upright

Code No.	Number in roll	Face value	
A	960	£16 Vertical delivery	75·00
H	480	£8 Sideways delivery	75·00

Imprimatur from the NPM or BPMA
Imperforate, watermark Type W.**23**

Watermark upright	£900
Cyl. 1. Block of Six	£6250

1958 (29 October). **4d.** Wmk Crowns

A. Ultramarine. Cream Paper

S83	Mint	Used
4d. Ultramarine	1·60	90
a. Coil join (vert. pair)	15·00	
b. Coil join (horiz. pair)	15·00	
c. Retouched neck (Cyl 1 No dot, R.16/9)	40·00	
d. Imperf. between stamp and top margin	£650	
e. Dotted "R" retouched	30·00	

B. Ultramarine. Whiter Paper (18 October 1962)

S84 = SG 576	Mint	Used
4d. Ultramarine	45	35
a. Coil join (vert. pair)	9·00	
b. Coil join (horiz. pair)	9·00	

C. Deep Ultramarine†. Whiter Paper (28 April 1965)

S85 = SG 576a	Mint	Used
4d. Deep ultramarine	15	15
b. Double impression	—	
c. Imperf. between stamp and top margin	£350	
d. Wmk. Crown to left (Coils, (31.5.65) and booklets, (16.8.65))	70	55
e. Watermark inverted (21.6.65)	60	75
f. Watermark Crown to right (Booklets only, (16.8.65)	70	55

† This "shade" was brought about by making more deeply etched cylinders from a new multipositive, resulting in apparent depth of colour in parts of the design but there is no difference in the colour of the ink. The change was made deliberately and coincided with the change in the letter rate from 3d. to 4d. on 17 May 1965.
Examples of No. S85b were the result of slight paper movement during printing rather than the sheet actually being presented twice in the press.
For illustration of No. S83c, see No. S82d.

SA Dorothy Wilding issues 4d. Ultramarine,

Cylinder Numbers (Blocks of Six)
Perforation Type A(E/I)

(a) Ultramarine, Cream paper (No S83)

Cyl. No.	No dot	Dot
1	20·00	20·00
6	20·00	20·00
8	15·00	15·00

Whiter paper (No S84)

Cyl. No.	No dot	Dot
8	5·50	5·50

(b) Deep Ultramarine, Whiter paper (No S85)

Cyl. No.	No dot	Dot
12	15·00	10·00
13	10·00	10·00
16	10·00	10·00
18	10·00	10·00
20	15·00	15·00
23	12·00	12·00
25	12·00	12·00
26	10·00	10·00
27	10·00	10·00

Minor Constant Sheet Flaws

Cyl. 1	1/4	As for S81
	10/8	Darker shading to right of and below large R caused by retouching the dot variety
Cyl. 18	18/11	Two patches of retouching by frame at left (Th. C1)

Coil Leaders

(a) Ultramarine. Cream or whiter paper
Made up from sheets with sheet margin joins. Watermark upright

Code No.	Number in roll	Face value		
A	960	£16	Vertical delivery	—
H	480	£8	Sideways delivery	50·00

(b) Deep ultramarine
Printed in continuous reels. Cylinder P2 was used for the vertical delivery coil and was a double-pane cylinder but cylinder P1 was used for the sideways delivery coil and was a single-pane cylinder.

(i) Vertical delivery. Watermark upright

Code No.	Number in roll	Face value	
A	960	£16	50·00

(ii) Sideways delivery. Watermark sideways

H	480	£8	40·00

Imprimaturs from the NPM or BPMA
Imperforate, watermark Type W.**24**. Cream or white paper

Watermark upright	£900
Watermark upright Re-touched neck Variety. R.16/9	£1500
Cyl. 1 Block of Six. (Cream paper)	£6250
Cyl. 8 Block of Six. (White paper)	£6250

•⎯⎯

1959 (29 April). **4d.** With graphite lines, Type **SA8**. Wmk Crowns
S86 = SG 593

	Mint	Used
4d. Ultramarine	5·50	5·00
a. Two lines at left	£2400	

The misplaced graphite lines listed as No. S86a result in two lines at left (with the left line down the perforations) and traces of a third line down the opposite perforations.

Cylinder Numbers (Blocks of Six)
Perforation Type A(E/I)

Cyl. No.	No dot	Dot
6	65·00	65·00

Imprimaturs from the NPM or BPMA
Imperforate, watermark Type W.**24**

Watermark upright	£900
Cyl. 6. Block of Six	£6250

Quantity Issued: 6,891,600

•⎯⎯

1959 (18 November). **4d.** Phosphor-graphite issue. Wmk Crowns
S87 = SG 608

	Mint	Used
4d. Ultramarine	20·00	16·00
a. One 6 mm band at left or right (stamp with vert. margin)	30·00	

No. S87 has two graphite lines (Type **SA8**) on the back and two phosphor bands on the front, applied by letterpress, which react green under the lamp.

Cylinder Numbers (Blocks of Six)
Perforation Type A(E/I)

Cyl. No.	No dot	Dot
6	£160	£140

Imprimatur from the NPM or BPMA
Perf. 15 × 14, watermark Type W.**24**

Watermark upright	—

Quantity Issued: 490,560

•⎯⎯

1960 (22 June). **4d.** Two phosphor bands reacting green. Wmk Crowns
S88

	Mint	Used
4d. Ultramarine	9·00	8·00

The bands were applied by photogravure.

Cylinder Numbers (Blocks of Six)
Perforation Type B (I/P no dot) and C (E/P dot)

Cyl. No.	No dot	Dot
8	£100	£100

Imprimaturs from the NPM or BPMA
Imperforate, watermark Type W.**24**

Watermark upright	£900
Cyl. 8. Block of Six	£6250

•⎯⎯

1961 (5 June). **4d.** Two phosphor bands reacting blue. Wmk Crowns

A. Ultramarine. Cream Paper
S89 = SG 616

	Mint	Used
4d. Ultramarine	3·50	3·50
a. Error. One 8 mm band	£150	

B. Deep Ultramarine †. Whiter Paper (28 April 1965)
S90

	Mint	Used
4d. Deep ultramarine	70	60
b. Watermark inverted (21.6.65)	1·40	1·00
c. Watermark Crown to left (16.8.65)	2·00	2·00
d. Watermark Crown to right (16.8.65)	2·00	2·00
e. One broad band (wmk. sideways)	50·00	

The bands were applied by photogravure on the stamps with upright and inverted watermark and by letterpress on those with watermark sideways.
† The note below No. S85 concerning deep ultramarine applies here.

4d. Ultramarine, Dorothy Wilding issues — SA

Cylinder Numbers (Blocks of Six)
(a) Ultramarine. (No. S89)
Perforation Type B (I/P no dot) and C (E/P dot)

Cyl. No.	No dot	Dot
8	50·00	50·00

(b) Deep ultramarine. (No. S90)
Perforation Type A (E/I)

Cyl. No.	No dot	Dot
12	10·00	10·00
13	10·00	10·00
18	50·00	50·00
20	50·00	50·00

Minor Constant Sheet Flaw

Cyl. 18	18/11	Two patches of retouching by frame at left (Th. C1)

Imprimaturs from the NPM or BPMA
Imperforate, watermark Type W.**24**

Watermark upright	£900
Cyl. 8. Block of Six (Cream paper)	£6250

●────

1965 *(13 August)*. **4d.** Two 8 mm phosphor bands reacting violet. Wmk Crowns

S91		Mint	Used
4d.	Deep ultramarine	60	60
a.	Watermark inverted *(9.65)*	75	75
b.	Wmk. Crown to left (photo.) *(1.67)*	1·10	1·10
c.	Wmk. Crown to right (photo.) *(1.67)*	1·10	1·10
d.	One 8 mm band (photo.) (wmk. sideways)	40·00	
e.	Wmk. Crown to left (l/press.) *(10.65)*	15·00	
f.	Wmk. Crown to right (l/press.) *(10.65)*	15·00	

The bands were applied by photogravure, except for the sideways watermark stamps from 2s. Booklets N22p(b), N23p(b) and N24p/26p which had them applied by letterpress.

No. S91 is known with a very wide "phantom" band in addition to the normal two bands. This was probably due to a weak mixture of the phosphor ink, which leaked under the doctor blade. This occurred in the first and second vertical rows in a sheet.

Cylinder Numbers (Blocks of Six)
Perforation Type A (E/I)

Cyl. No.	No dot	Dot
18	10·00	10·00
20	20·00	20·00

Minor Constant Sheet Flaw

Cyl. 18	18/11	As for S90

●────

1967 *(Early)*. **4d.** Two 9·5 mm phosphor bands reacting violet. Wmk Crowns

S92 = SG 616a		Mint	Used
4d.	Deep ultramarine	25	25
a.	Watermark inverted *(2.67)*	75	75
b.	Wmk. Crown to left (Booklets, 4.67 and Coils, *(24.4.67)*)	1·10	1·10
c.	Wmk. Crown to right (Booklets, 4.67)	1·10	1·10
e.	One 9·5 mm band (wmk. sideways)	25·00	

The bands were applied by photogravure.

Cylinder Numbers (Blocks of Six)
Perforation Type A (E/I)

Cyl. No.	No dot	Dot
16	10·00	10·00
18	10·00	10·00
23	10·00	10·00
26	10·00	10·00
27	25·00	25·00

Minor Constant Sheet Flaw

Cyl. 18	18/11	As for S90

Coil Leader
Printed in continuous reels. Cylinder P1 was used and it was a single-pane cylinder.

Sideways delivery. Watermark sideways

Code No.	Number in roll	Face value	
H	480	£8	50·00

SA Dorothy Wilding issues 4½d. Chestnut,

4½d. Chestnut, Type SA3 (1959–1966)

1959 (9 February). **4½d.** Wmk Crowns
A. Cream Paper

S93	Mint	Used
4½d. Chestnut	55	55

B. Whiter Paper (29 May 1962)

S94 = SG 577	Mint	Used
4½d. Chestnut	10	25
a. Phantom frame (Cyl. 8 No dot below R.20/12)	£100	

S94a, S98c An incomplete marginal rule revealed a right-angled shaped frame-line on cylinder 8 no dot below R.20/12. Later retouched on No. S98.

Cylinder Numbers (Blocks of Six)
Perforation Type A(E/I)

Cream paper (No. S93)

Cyl. No.	No dot	Dot
2	12·00	12·00
6	15·00	15·00
7	10·00	10·00

Whiter paper. (No. S94)

| 7 | 10·00 | 10·00 |
| 8 | 10·00 | 10·00 |

Minor Constant Sheet Flaws
Multipositive flaw:

No dot	5/6	Pale top half of rose in bottom left corner (Th. F1–2)

Cylinder flaws

Cyl. 2	1/9	White spot on cheek level-with mouth (Th. D3)
	1/11	Break in bottom frame line at left corner
	5/5	Three dots to right of curve in "S" of "POSTAGE"
	10/8	White dot in laurel oval (Th. E6)
	16/2	Dotted line in bottom right corner (Th. H6)
	19/10	White dot on tail of "R" of "E R"
Cyl. 6	5/5	Nick in laurel oval at left (Th. D1)
	16/9	Extra jewel on dress above "O" of "POSTAGE"
Cyl. 7	18/6	White flaw in thistle flower (Th. G2)

Imprimaturs from the NPM or BPMA
Imperforate, watermark Type W.**24**. Cream or whiter paper

Watermark upright	£900
Cyl. 2 Block of Six (Cream paper)	£6250
Cyl. 7 Block of Six (White paper)	£6250

1959 (3 June). **4½d.** With Graphite Lines, Type **SA8**. Wmk Crowns

S95 = SG 594	Mint	Used
4½d. Chestnut	6·50	5·00

Cylinder Numbers (Blocks of Six)
Perforation Type A(E/I)

Cyl. No.	No dot	Dot
6	70·00	70·00

Minor Constant Sheet Flaw

| Cyl. 6 | 5/6 | As for S93 |

Imprimaturs from the NPM or BPMA
Imperforate, watermark Type W.**24**

Watermark upright	£900
Cyl. 6 Block of Six	£6250

Quantity Issued: 5,388,480

1959 (18 November). **4½d.** Phosphor-graphite issue. Wmk Crowns

S96 = SG 609	Mint	Used
4½d. Chestnut	30·00	20·00
a. One 6 mm band at left or right (stamp with vert. margin)	42·00	
b. One 8 mm band	£150	

This has two graphite lines (Type **SA8**), on the back and two phosphor bands on the front, applied by letterpress, which react green under the lamp. No. S96 is known with the phosphor bands additionally printed on the back of the stamp.

Cylinder Numbers (Blocks of Six)
Perforation Type A(E/I)

Cyl. No.	No dot	Dot
6	£250	£250

Minor Constant Sheet Flaw

| Cyl. 6 | 5/6 | As for S93 |

Imprimatur from the NPM or BPMA
Perf. 15 × 14, watermark Type W.**24**

| Watermark upright | — |

Quantity Issued: 696,000

1961 (13 September). **4½d.** Two phosphor bands reacting blue. Wmk Crowns

A. Cream Paper. Bands applied by Letterpress

S97	Mint	Used
4½d. Chestnut	3·50	2·50
a. One 6 mm band at left or right (stamp with vert. margin)	30·00	
b. One 8 mm band	30·00	
ba. As b but 6 mm band	40·00	
c. Bands applied photo. (3.4.62)	22·00	15·00

B. Whiter Paper. Bands applied by photogravure
(24 January 1963)

S98 = SG 616b	Mint	Used
4½d. Chestnut	55	30
a. Bands applied l/press. (6.65)	2·00	2·00
ab. One 6 mm band at left or right (stamp with vert. margin)	10·00	
b. One 8 mm band (l/press.)	30·00	
ba. As b but 6 mm band	30·00	
c. Phantom frame (Cyl. 8, below R.20/12)	£100	

For illustration of No. S98c, see No. S94a.

4½d. Chestnut, 5d. Brown,   **Dorothy Wilding issues**   **SA**

Cylinder Numbers (Blocks of Six)

A. Cream Paper
Applied I/press. (No. S97)
Perforation Type A (E/I)

Cyl. No.	No dot	Dot
7	50·00	50·00

Applied photo. (No. S97c)
Perforation Type B (I/P no dot) and C (E/P dot)

Cyl. No.	No dot	Dot
7	£150	£150

B. Whiter Paper
Applied photo. (No. S98)
Perforation Type A (E/I)

Cyl. No.	No dot	Dot
7	15·00	10·00
8	20·00	15·00

Applied I/press. (No. S98a)
Perforation Type A (E/I)

Cyl. No.	No dot	Dot
8	40·00	40·00

Minor Constant Sheet Flaws

Cyls. 7/8	5/6	Pale top half of rose in bottom left corner (Th. F1–2)
Cyl. 7	18/6	White flaw in thistle flower (Th. G2). Later retouched

Imprimaturs from the NPM or BPMA
Imperforate, watermark Type W.**24**. Cream or whiter paper

Watermark upright	£900
Cyl. 7 Block of Six (Cream paper)	£6250
Cyl. 7 Block of Six (White paper)	£6250

5d. Brown, Type SA4 (1953–1967)

1953 *(6 July)*. **5d.** Wmk Tudor Crown

S99 = SG 522		Mint	Used
	5d. Brown	1·00	3·50
a.	Spot by "E" of "POSTAGE" (No dot, R. 4/8)	50·00	
b.	Spot on daffodil (No dot, R. 10/12)	45·00	
c.	Neck retouch (Dot, R. 2/12)	45·00	
d.	Imperf between stamp Right sheet margin*	†	—

S99a/S103a   S99b/S103b   S99b/S103b retouched

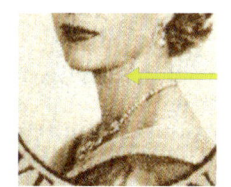

Normal   S99c/S103c

S99d recorded on a single used damaged example with an indistinct cancellation.

Cylinder Numbers (Blocks of Six)
Perforation Type A (E/I)

Cyl. No.	No dot	Dot
1	15·00	15·00

Imprimaturs from the NPM or BPMA
Imperforate, watermark Type W.**22**

Watermark upright	£900
Watermark upright with Spot on "E" of "POSTAGE" R. 4/8	£1500
Watermark upright with Spot on Daffodil R. 10/12	£1550
Cyl. 1 Block of Six	£6250

1955 *(21 September)*. 5d. Wmk St Edward's Crown

S100 = SG 547		Mint	Used
	5d. Brown	6·00	6·00
a.	Spot by "E" of "POSTAGE" (No dot, R. 4/8)	50·00	
b.	Spot on daffodil (No dot, R. 10/12)	45·00	
c.	Neck retouch (Dot, R. 2/12)	45·00	

For illustrations of Nos. S100a/c, see Nos. S99a/c.

Cylinder Numbers (Blocks of Six)
Perforation Type A (E/I)

Cyl. No.	No dot	Dot
1	60·00	60·00

SA Dorothy Wilding issues 5d. Brown, 6d. Purple

Imprimaturs from the NPM or BPMA
Imperforate, watermark Type W.**23**

Watermark upright	£900
Watermark upright with "Neck retouch" variety R./12	£1500
Cyl. **1.** Block of Six	£6250

●────

1958 (10 November). **5d.** Wmk Crowns

A. Cream Paper

S101	Mint	Used
5d. Brown	3·00	1·50
a. Spot by "E" of "POSTAGE" (Cyl. 1 No dot, R. 4/8)	45·00	
b. Spot on daffodil (Cyl 1. No dot, R. 10/12)	40·00	
c. Neck retouch (Cyl. 1 Dot, R. 2/12)	40·00	

B. Whiter Paper (1 May 1963)

S102 = SG 578	Mint	Used
5d. Brown	30	40
a. Spot by "E" of "POSTAGE" (No dot, R. 4/8)	45·00	
b. Spot on daffodil (No dot, R. 10/12)	40·00	
c. Neck retouch (Dot, R. 2/12)	40·00	

For illustrations of Nos. S101/2a, S101/2b and S101/2c, see Nos. S99a, S99b and S99c respectively.

Cylinder Numbers (Blocks of Six)

Cream Paper. (No. S101)
Perforation Type A(E/I)

Cyl. No.	No dot	Dot
1	25·00	25·00
2	30·00	30·00

Whiter Paper. (No. S102)
Perforation Type A(E/I)

Cyl. No.	No dot	Dot
1	10·00	10·00

Cylinder blocks with Perforation Type F(L)* (I/E no dot and P/E dot) are believed to be No. S103 but with phosphor omitted.

Imprimaturs from the NPM or BPMA
Imperforate, watermark Type W.**24**. Cream or whiter paper

Watermark upright	£900
Cyl. **2.** Block of Six (Cream paper)	£6250
Cyl. **1.** Block of Six (White paper)	£6250

●────

1967 (9 June). **5d.** Two 9·5 mm phosphor bands reacting violet. Wmk Crowns

S103 = SG 616c	Mint	Used
5d. Brown	55	35
a. Spot by "E" of "POSTAGE" (No dot, R. 4/8)	25·00	
b. Spot on daffodil (No dot, R. 10/12)	20·00	
c. Neck retouch (Dot, R. 2/12)	20·00	

The bands were applied by photogravure.
 For illustrations of Nos. S103a/c, see Nos S99a/c.

Cylinder Numbers (Blocks of Six)
Perforation Type A(E/I)

Cyl. No.	No dot	Dot
1	10·00	10·00

Perforation Type F (L)*

Cyl. No.	No dot (I/E)	Dot (P/E)
1	10·00	10·00

6d. Purple, Type SA4 (1954–1967)

1954 (18 January). **6d.** Wmk Tudor Crown

S104 = SG 523	Mint	Used
6d. Reddish purple	4·00	1·00
a. Imperforate three sides (pair)	£3750	
b. Imperf. between stamp and bottom margin	£1000	
c. Coil join (vert. pair)	30·00	

S104a, S105a, S107a

Cylinder Numbers (Blocks of Six)
Single-pane cylinders

Cyl. No.		Perf type	No Dot
1		B (I/P)	45·00
1		C (E/P)	45·00
1		F(L)(I/E)	45·00

Minor Constant Sheet Flaws
Multipositive flaws for cylinders 1, 2 and 3 used for S104 to S109

8/8	Small purple flaw joining "C" of "PENCE" to inner frame line
19/6	Small dark flaw on daffodil stem (Th. G2)
20/3	Coloured dot in top leaf of thistle (Th. A6)

Coil Leader
Made up from sheets with sheet margin joins.

Vertical delivery with the watermark upright

Code No.	Number in roll	Face value	
J	480	£12	£125

Imprimaturs from the NPM or BPMA
Imperforate, watermark Type W.**22**

Watermark upright	£900
Cyl. **1.** Block of Six	£6250

●────

1955 (20 December). **6d.** Wmk St Edward's Crown

A. Reddish Purple

S105 = SG 548	Mint	Used
6d. Reddish purple (shades*)	4·50	1·25
a. Imperforate three sides (pair)	£5250	
b. Imperf. between stamp and left margin		
c. Coil join (vert. pair)	40·00	
d. Pink tinted paper (stamp with selvedge) ††	75·00	

B. Deep Claret† (8 May 1958)

S106 = SG 548a	Mint	Used
6d. Deep claret (shades*)	4·50	1·40
a. Imperforate three sides (pair)	£5250	
b. Coil join (vert. pair)	40·00	
c. Pink tinted paper (stamp with selvedge) ††		

† This was a deliberate change of colour although shade variations exist. See footnote after No. S108.

6d. Purple Dorothy Wilding issues SA

†† These listings are for a deep tint of the paper showing on the selvedge. It is known from Cylinder 1, Perforation type C (E/P) and from Cylinder 3 Perforation type F(L) (I/E). Lighter shades of tinting are common and worth much less.
Also see General notes.

Cylinder Numbers (Blocks of Six)
Single-pane cylinders

Reddish purple (No. S105)
Perforation Type B (I/P)

Cyl. No.	No dot
1	45·00
2	45·00

Perforation Type C (E/P)

Cyl. No.	No dot
1	45·00
2	45·00

Deep claret (No. S106)
Perforation Type B (I/P)

Cyl. No.	No dot
2	45·00
3	45·00

Perforation Type C (E/P)

Cyl. No.	No dot
2	45·00
3	45·00

Perforation Type F (L) (I/E)

Cyl. No.	No dot
3	£100

Minor Constant Sheet Flaws
Multipositive flaws as shown for No. S104

Coil Leaders
Made up from sheets with sheet margin joins.

Vertical delivery with the watermark upright

Code No.	Number in roll	Face value	
J	480	£12 Reddish purple	£100
J	480	£12 Deep claret	—

Imprimaturs from the NPM or BPMA
A. Reddish Purple. Imperforate, watermark Type W.**23**

Watermark upright	£900
Cyl. 2 Block of Six	£6250

B. Deep Claret. Imperforate, watermark Type W.**23**

Watermark upright	£900
Cyl. 1 Block of Six	£6250

•———

1958 (23 December). **6d.** Wmk Crowns

A. Cream Paper

S107

	Mint	Used
6d. Deep claret (shades*)	1·25	70
a. Imperforate three sides (pair)	£4000	
b. Imperf. (pair)	£4500	
c. Coil join (vert. pair)	25·00	

B. White Paper (29 June 1962)
S108 = SG 579

6d. Deep claret (shades*)	30	25
a. Coil join (vert. pair)	12·00	
b. Spur to frame (Cyl. 10 No dot. R.17/2)	40·00	

* This colour is unstable and a range of shades exists which also vary according to the colour of the paper. One of the more marked variations is a purple-claret on the cream paper from cylinder 8.

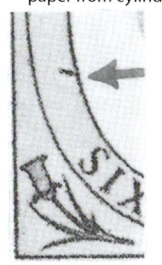

S108b

Cylinder Numbers (Blocks of Six)
A. Cream Paper (No. S107)
Single-pane cylinders
Perforation Type B (I/P)

Cyl. No.	No dot
2	15·00
3	15·00

Perforation Type C (E/P)

Cyl. No.	No dot
2	15·00
3	15·00

Double-pane cylinders
Perforation Type B (I/P no dot) and C (E/P dot)

Cyl. No.	No dot	Dot
5	—	—
7	15·00	15·00

Perforation Type A (E/I)

Cyl. No.	No dot	Dot
7	15·00	15·00
8	15·00	15·00

B. Whiter Paper. (No. S108)
Perforation Type A (E/I)

Cyl. No.	No dot	Dot
8	15·00	15·00
10	15·00	15·00
11	75·00	75·00

Perforation Type F (L)*

Cyl. No.	No dot (I/E)	Dot (P/E)
10	30·00	30·00

Perforation Type H

Cyl. No.	No dot (E/I)	Dot (P/I)
10	**	£1500

** Same price and appearance as perforated Type A with extension holes in left margin.
The marginal rule is damaged in most positions on cyl. 8

Minor Constant Sheet Flaws
Multipositive flaws on cylinders 2 and 3 as shown for No. S104
A second multipositive was used for cylinder 5 and a third for cylinders 7 onwards.

SA Dorothy Wilding issues 6d. Purple

Coil Leaders

Vertical delivery with the watermark upright
(a) Made up from sheets with sheet margin joins.

Code No.	Number in roll	Face value	
J	480	£12 Cream paper	85·00
J	480	£12 Whiter paper	85·00

(b) Printed in continuous reels. Single-pane cylinder Q1 was used. Vertical delivery. Watermark upright

J	480	£12 Whiter paper	75·00

Imprimaturs from the NPM or BPMA
Imperforate, watermark Type W.**24**. Cream or whiter paper

Watermark upright	£900
Cyl. 2 Block of Six (Cream paper)	£6250
Cyl. 8 Block of Six (Whiter paper)	£6250

1960 (27 June). **6d.** Two phosphor bands reacting green. Wmk Crowns

S109		Mint	Used
6d.	Deep claret (shades*)	2·75	2·25

* See footnote after No. S108
The bands were applied by photogravure.

Cylinder Numbers (Blocks of Six)
Single-pane cylinder
Perforation Type

Cyl. No.	Perf type	No dot
2	B (I/P)	35·00
2	C (E/P)	35·00

Minor Constant Sheet Flaws
Multipositive flaws as shown for No. S104

Imprimaturs from the NPM or BPMA
Imperforate, watermark Type W.**24**

Watermark upright	£900
Cyl. 2 Block of Six	£6250

1961 (5 June). **6d.** Two phosphor bands reacting blue. Wmk Crowns

A. Cream Paper. Bands applied by photogravure

S110		Mint	Used
6d.	Deep claret (shades*)	4·50	3·50
a.	Bands applied l/press.	£600	

B. White Paper. Bands applied by photogravure (3 October 1963)

S111			
6d.	Deep claret (shades*)	1·00	80
a.	Bands applied l/press.	£450	
ab.	Narrow band at left or right (stamp with vert. margin)	£500	

* See footnote after No. S108

Cylinder Numbers (Blocks of Six)
Cream paper (No. S110)
Perforation Type A (E/I)
Bands applied photo

Cyl. No.	No dot	Dot
7	40·00	40·00
8	60·00	60·00

Cream paper (No. S110a)
Perforation Type A (E/I)
Bands applied l/press.

Cyl. No.	No dot	Dot
8	†	

Whiter paper (No. S111)
Perforation Type A (E/I)
Bands applied photo.

Cyl. No.	No dot	Dot
8	25·00	25·00
10	10·00	10·00

Whiter paper (No. S111a)
Perforation Type A (E/I)
Bands applied l/press.

Cyl. No.	No dot	Dot
8	—	—

The marginal rule is damaged in most positions on cyl. 8

Imprimaturs from the NPM or BPMA
Imperforate, watermark Type W.**24** Cream paper

Watermark upright	£900
Cyl. 7. Block of Six	£6250

1965 (13 August). **6d.** Two 8 mm phosphor bands reacting violet. Wmk Crowns

S112		Mint	Used
6d.	Deep claret (shades*)	12·00	9·00
a.	One 6 mm band at left or right (stamp with vert. margin)	40·00	
b.	One 8 mm band	40·00	

* See footnote after No. S108
The bands were applied by letterpress.

Cylinder Numbers (Blocks of Six)
Perforation Type A (E/I)

Cyl. No.	No dot	Dot
8	£100	£100

1967 (Early). **6d.** Two 9·5 mm phosphor bands reacting violet. Wmk Crowns

S113 = SG 617		Mint	Used
6d.	Deep claret (shades*)	55	30

* See footnote after No. S108
The bands were applied by photogravure only.

Cylinder Numbers (Blocks of Six)
Perforation Type A (E/I)

Cyl. No.	No dot	Dot
10	20·00	25·00
11	10·00	10·00

Perforation Type F (L)*

Cyl. No.	No dot (I/E)	Dot (P/E)
10	10·00	10·00

Coil Leader
Printed in continuous reels. It is believed that cylinder Q1 was used and that it was a single-pane cylinder.

Vertical delivery. Watermark upright

Code No.	Number in roll	Face value	
J	480	£12	75·00

7d. Bright green, Type SA4 (1954–1967)

1954 *(18 January)*. **7d.** Wmk Tudor Crown

S114 = SG 524	Mint	Used
7d. Bright green	9·50	5·50

Cylinder Numbers (Blocks of Six)
Perforation Type A (E/I)

Cyl. No.	No dot	Dot
2	85·00	85·00

Perforation Type B (I/P no dot) and C (E/P dot)

Cyl. No.	No dot	Dot
2	85·00	85·00

Imprimaturs from the NPM or BPMA
Imperforate, watermark Type W.**22**

Watermark upright	£900
Cyl. 2 Block of Six	£6250

1956 *(23 April)*. **7d.** Wmk St Edward's Crown

S115 = SG 549	Mint	Used
7d. Bright green	50·00	10·00

Cylinder Numbers (Blocks of Six)
Perforation Type A (E/I)

Cyl. No.	No dot	Dot
2	£350	£350

Imprimaturs from the NPM or BPMA
Imperforate, watermark Type W.**23**

Watermark upright	£900
Cyl. 2 Block of Six	£6250

1958 *(26 November)*. **7d.** Wmk Crowns

A. Cream Paper

S116	Mint	Used
7d. Bright green	2·50	70

B. Whiter Paper *(3 July 1962)*

S117 = SG 580		
7d. Bright green	50	45

Cylinder Numbers (Blocks of Six)

Cream Paper (No. S116)
Perforation Type A (E/I)

Cyl. No.	No dot	Dot
1	25·00	25·00
2	20·00	20·00

Perforation Type B (I/P no dot) and C (E/P dot)

Cyl. No.	No dot	Dot
2	25·00	25·00

Whiter Paper (No. S117)
Perforation Type A (E/I)

Cyl. No.	No dot	Dot
1	10·00	10·00
2	10·00	10·00

Perforation Type F (L)*

Cyl. No.	No dot (I/E)	Dot (P/E)
1*	£500	£500

* This is probably No. S118 but with phosphor omitted.

Imprimaturs from the NPM or BPMA
Imperforate, watermark Type W.**24**. Cream or whiter paper

Watermark upright	£900
Cyl. 2. Block of Six (Cream paper)	£6250
Cyl. 1 Block of Six (Whiter paper)	£6250

1967 *(15 February)*. **7d.** Two 9·5 mm phosphor bands reacting violet. Wmk Crowns

S118 = SG 617a	Mint	Used
7d. Bright green	70	50
a. Imperf. between stamp and top margin	£1200	

The bands were applied by photogravure.
No. S118a came from the top row of 12 examples of which six were defective.

Cylinder Numbers (Blocks of Six)
Perforation Type F (L)*

Cyl. No.	No dot (I/E)	Dot (P/E)
1	12·00	12·00

Perforation Type A (E/I)

Cyl. No.	No dot	Dot
2	10·00	10·00

Imprimaturs from the NPM or BPMA
Imperforate, watermark Type W.**24**

Watermark upright	£900
Cyl. 2 Block of Six	£6250

SA Dorothy Wilding issues *8d. Magenta*

8d. Magenta, Type SA5 (1953–1967)

1953 *(6 July).* **8d.** Wmk Tudor Crown

S119 = SG 525	Mint	Used
8d. Magenta	1·25	85

Cylinder Numbers (Blocks of Six)
Perforation Type A (E/I)

Cyl. No.	No dot	Dot
3	15·00	15·00

Perforation Type B (I/P no dot) and C (E/P dot)

Cyl. No.	No dot	Dot
3	45·00	45·00

Minor Constant Sheet Flaw

Cyl. 3	20/1	Coloured dot between rose at top left and "A" of "POSTAGE" (Th. B2)

Imprimaturs from the NPM or BPMA
Imperforate, watermark Type W.**22**

Watermark upright	£900
Cyl. 3 Block of Six	£6250

1955 *(21 December).* **8d.** Wmk St Edward's Crown

S120 = SG 550	Mint	Used
8d. Magenta	7·00	1·25

Cylinder Numbers (Blocks of Six)
Perforation Type A (E/I)

Cyl. No.	No dot	Dot
3	75·00	65·00

Minor Constant Sheet Flaw

Cyl. 3	20/1	Coloured dot between rose at top left and "A" of "POSTAGE" (Th. B2). Later retouched

Imprimaturs from the NPM or BPMA
Imperforate, watermark Type W.**23**

Watermark upright	£900
Cyl. 3 Block of Six	£6250

1960 *(24 February).* **8d.** Wmk Crowns

A. Cream Paper

S121	Mint	Used
8d. Magenta	4·00	1·00

B. Whiter Paper *(6 July 1962)*

S122 = SG 581	Mint	Used
8d. Magenta	60	40
a. Diadem flaw (Cyl. 4 No dot, R. 18/2)	30·00	
b. Extra pearl (Cyl. 4 Dot, R. 16/2)	35·00	

S122a, S123a Multipositive white flaw on diadem, lower left of "E" of "POSTAGE". Exists as a minor flaw on Cyl. 3

S122b, S123b

Cylinder Numbers (Blocks of Six)
Cream Paper (No. S121)
Perforation Type A (E/I)

Cyl. No.	No dot	Dot
3	35·00	35·00

Whiter Paper (No. S122)
Perforation Type A (E/I)

Cyl. No.	No dot	Dot
3	40·00	15·00
4	35·00	10·00

Perforation Type F (L)

Cyl. No.	No dot (I/E)	Dot (P/E)
4**	—	—

** This is probably No. S123 but with phosphor omitted.

Marginal arrows:
"V" shaped, hand-engraved at top and bottom of sheet (Cyls. 3 and 4)
"W" shaped, photo-etched at both sides (Cyl. 3) or photo-etched at left and hand-engraved at right (Cyl. 4)

Imprimaturs from the NPM or BPMA
Imperforate, watermark Type W.**24**. Cream or whiter paper

Watermark upright	£900
Cyl. 3 Block of Six (Cream paper)	£6250
Cyl. 3 Block of Six (Whiter paper)	£6250

1967 *(28 June).* **8d.** Two 9·5 mm phosphor bands reacting violet. Wmk Crowns

S123 = SG 617b	Mint	Used
8d. Magenta	70	55
a. Diadem flaw (Cyl. 4 No dot, R. 18/2)	30·00	
b. Extra pearl (Cyl. 4 Dot, R. 16/2)	35·00	
c. Petal joined to frame (Cyl. 4 Dot, R. 13/11)	35·00	

The bands were applied by photogravure.
For illustrations of Nos. S123a/b, see Nos. S122a/b.

S123c

Cylinder Numbers (Blocks of Six)
Perforation Type A (E/I)

Cyl. No.	No dot	Dot
4	35·00*	10·00

Perforation Type F (L) *

Cyl. No.	No dot (I/E)	Dot (P/E)
4	35·00*	10·00

Marginal arrows:
"V" shaped, hand-engraved at top and bottom of sheet
"W" shaped, photo-etched at left and hand-engraved at right

Imprimaturs from the NPM or BPMA
Imperforate, watermark Type W.**24**

Watermark upright	£900
Watermark upright with extra pearl variety R.16/2	£1500
Cyl. 4. Block of Six	£6250

9d. Bronze-green Dorothy Wilding issues **SA**

9d. Bronze-green, Type SA5 (1954–1966)

1954 (8 February). **9d.** Wmk Tudor Crown

S124 = SG 526	Mint	Used
9d. Bronze-green	23·00	4·75
a. Frame break at upper right (Cyl. 1 No dot, R. 8/6)	45·00	
b. Imperf. between stamp and top margin*	—	

* No. S124b was caused by a paper fold.

S124a, S125a, S126a

Frame broken at upper right and shading below it missing. Later retouched on Crowns watermark. A very similar variety occurs on Cyl. 2, R. 11/11; see Nos. S126c. etc

Cylinder Numbers (Blocks of Six)
Perforation Type A (E/I)

Cyl. No.	No dot	Dot
1	£175	£175

Perforation Type B (I/P no dot) and C (E/P dot)

Cyl. No.	No dot	Dot
1	£175	£175

Imprimaturs from the NPM or BPMA
Imperforate, watermark Type W.**22**

Watermark upright	£900
Watermark upright with Frame break variety R.8/6	£1500
Cyl. **1.** Block of Six	£6250

1955 (15 December). **9d.** Wmk St Edward's Crown

S125 = SG 551	Mint	Used
9d. Bronze-green	20·00	2·75
a. Frame break at upper right (Cyl. 1 No dot, R. 8/6)	50·00	
b. Imperf between stamp and top margin*	—	

* No 125b was caused by a paper fold
For illustration of No. S125a, see No. S124a.

Cylinder Numbers (Blocks of Six)
Perforation Type A (E/I)

Cyl. No.	No dot	Dot
1	£150	£150

Perforation Type B (I/P no dot) and C (E/P dot)

Cyl. No.	No dot	Dot
1	£175	£175

Imprimaturs from the NPM or BPMA
Imperforate, watermark Type W.**23**

Watermark upright	£900
Cyl. **1.** Block of Six	£6250

1959 (24 March). **9d.** Wmk Crowns
A. Cream Paper

S126	Mint	Used
9d. Bronze-green	7·00	1·00
a. Frame break at upper right (Cyl. 1 No dot, R. 8/6)	40·00	
b. Broken daffodil (Cyl. 2 No dot, R. 7/2)	40·00	
c. Frame break at upper right (Cyl. 2 No dot, R. 11/11)	35·00	
d. Frame flaw (Cyl. 2 Dot, R. 12/5)	35·00	

B. Whiter Paper (4 June 1962)

S127 = SG 582	Mint	Used
9d. Bronze-green	60	40
a. Broken daffodil (Cyl. 2 No dot, R.7/2)	35·00	
b. Frame break at upper right (Cyl. 2 No dot, R. 11/11)	30·00	
c. Frame flaw (Cyl. 2 Dot, R. 12/5)	30·00	

For illustration of No. S126a, see No. S124a.

S126b, S127a, S128b Stem of daffodil is broken

S126c, S127b, S128c A very similar variety to the one on Cyl. 1, R. 8/6 but more pronounced

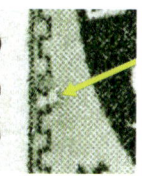

S126d, S127c, S128d Flaw on frame at lower left

Cylinder Numbers (Blocks of Six)

Cream paper (No. S126)
Perforation Type A (E/I)

Cyl. No.	No dot	Dot
1	40·00	40·00
2	30·00	30·00

Whiter paper (No. S127)
Perforation Type A (E/I)

Cyl. No.	No dot	Dot
2	10·00	10·00

Imprimaturs from the NPM or BPMA
Imperforate, watermark Type W.**24**. Cream or whiter paper

Watermark upright	£900
Watermark upright with Frame break variety R.11/11	£1500
Cyl. 1 Block of Six (Cream paper)	£6250
Cyl. 2 Block of Six (Whiter paper)	£6250

SA Dorothy Wilding issues 9d. Bronze-green, 10d. Prussian blue

1966 *(29 December).* **9d.** Two 9·5 mm phosphor bands reacting violet. Wmk Crowns

S128 = SG 617c

		Mint	Used
9d.	Bronze-green	70	65
a.	Imperf. between stamp and top margin	£2000	
b.	Broken daffodil (Cyl. 2 No dot, R. 7/2)	35·00	
c.	Frame break at upper right (Cyl. 2 No dot, R. 11/11)	30·00	
d.	Frame flaw (Cyl. 2 Dot, R. 12/5)	30·00	

The bands were applied by photogravure.
For illustrations of Nos. S128b/d, see Nos. S126b/d.

Cylinder Numbers (Blocks of Six)
Perforation Type A (E/I)

Cyl. No.	No dot	Dot
2	10·00	10·00

Imprimaturs from the NPM or BPMA
Imperforate, watermark Type W.**24**

Watermark upright	£900
Watermark upright with Frame break variety R.11/11	£1500
Cyl. 2 Block of Six (Cream paper)	£6250

●─────

10d. Prussian blue, Type SA5 (1954–1966)

1954 *(8 February).* **10d.** Wmk Tudor Crown

S129 = SG 527

	Mint	Used
10d. Prussian blue	18·00	4·75

Cylinder Numbers (Blocks of Six)
Perforation Type A (E/I)

Cyl. No.	No dot	Dot
1	£175	£175

Perforation Type B (I/P no dot) and C (E/P dot)

Cyl. No.	No dot	Dot
1	£175	£175

Minor Constant Sheet Flaws

Cyl. 1	3/3	White spur on right fork of "V" of "REVENUE"
	10/12	White flaw on thistle shows as a cut into the left-hand side of the flower (Th. A6)
	13/10	White flaw on rim of diadem below emblems (Th. B4)

Imprimaturs from the NPM or BPMA
Imperforate, watermark Type W.**22**

Watermark upright	£900
Cyl. 1 Block of Six	£6250

●─────

1955 *(22 September).* **10d.** Wmk St Edward's Crown

S130 = SG 552

	Mint	Used
10d. Prussian blue	20·00	2·75

Cylinder Numbers (Blocks of Six)
Perforation Type A (E/I)

Cyl. No.	No dot	Dot
1	£175	£175

Minor Constant Sheet Flaws

All Cyl. 1	As S129

Imprimaturs from the NPM or BPMA
Imperforate, watermark Type W.**23**

Watermark upright	£950
Cyl. 1 Block of Six	£6250

●─────

1958 *(18 November).* **10d.** Wmk Crowns

A. Cream Paper

S131

	Mint	Used
10d. Prussian blue	3·75	1·00

B. Whiter Paper *(13 November 1962)*

S132 = SG 583

	Mint	Used
10d. Prussian blue	1·00	75

Cylinder Numbers (Blocks of Six)

Cream paper (No. S131)
Perforation Type A (E/I)

Cyl. No.	No dot	Dot
1	30·00	30·00

Perforation Type B (I/P no dot) and C (E/P dot)

Cyl. No.	No dot	Dot
1	50·00	50·00

10d. Prussian blue, 11d. Brown-purple, **Dorothy Wilding issues** **SA**

Whiter Paper (No. S132)
Perforation Type A (E/I)

Cyl. No.	No dot	Dot
1	10·00	10·00

Perforation Type F (L)*

Cyl. No.	No dot (I/E)	Dot (P/E)
1**		£2250

** This is probably No. S133 but with the phosphor omitted.

Minor Constant Sheet Flaws

Cyl. 1	All Cyl. 1 as S129. All later retouched

Imprimaturs from the NPM or BPMA
Imperforate, watermark Type W.**24**. Cream or whiter paper

Watermark upright	£900
Cyl. 1 Block of Six (Cream paper)	£6250
Cyl. 1 Block of Six (Whiter paper)	£6250

●────

1966 *(30 December).* **10d.** Two 9·5 mm phosphor bands reacting violet. Wmk Crowns

S133 = SG 617d	Mint	Used
10d. Prussian blue	1·00	1·00
a. One 9·5 mm band	£250	

The bands were applied by photogravure.

Cylinder Numbers (Blocks of Six)
Perforation Type A (E/I)

Cyl. No.	No dot	Dot
1	10·00	10·00

Perforation Type F (L) *

Cyl. No.	No dot (I/E)	Dot (P/E)
1	10·00	10·00

Minor Constant Sheet Flaws

Cyl. 1	3/3	White spur on right fork of "V" of "REVENUE". Later retouched
	14/3	Retouch on Queen's nose (Th. D3)

Imprimaturs from the NPM or BPMA
Imperforate, watermark Type W.**24**

Watermark upright	£950
Cyl. 1. Block of Six	£6250

●────

11d. Brown-purple, Type SA5 (1954–1965)

1954 *(8 February).* **11d.** Wmk Tudor Crown

S134 = SG 528	Mint	Used
11d. Brown-purple	35·00	15·00

Cylinder Numbers (Blocks of Six)
Perforation Type B (I/P no dot) and C (E/P dot)

Cyl. No.	No dot	Dot
1	£275	£275

Minor Constant Sheet Flaw

Cyl. 1	19/3	White flaw in frame pattern at left by "O" of "POSTAGE" (Th. D1)

Imprimaturs from the NPM or BPMA
Imperforate, watermark Type W.**22**

Watermark upright	£950
Cyl. 1 Block of Six	£6250

●────

1955 *(28 October).* **11d.** Wmk St Edward's Crown

S135 = SG 553	Mint	Used
11d. Brown-purple	1·00	1·10

Cylinder Numbers (Blocks of Six)
Perforation Type A (E/I)

Cyl. No.	No dot	Dot
1	50·00	50·00

Perforation Type B (I/P no dot) and C (E/P dot)

Cyl. No.	No dot	Dot
1	20·00	20·00

Minor Constant Sheet Flaw

Cyl. 1	19/3	As for S134

Imprimaturs from the NPM or BPMA
Imperforate, watermark Type W.**23**

Watermark upright	£900
Cyl. 1 Block of Six	£6250

●────

SA Dorothy Wilding issues 1s. Bistre-brown

1s. Bistre-brown, Type SA6 (1953–1967)

1953 *(6 July).* **1s.** Wmk Tudor Crown

S136 = SG 529	Mint	Used
1s. Bistre-brown	80	50

Cylinder Numbers (Blocks of Six)
Perforation Type A (E/I)

Cyl. No.	No dot	Dot
1	20·00	20·00
2	75·00	75·00

Perforation Type B (I/P no dot) and C (E/P dot)

Cyl. No.	No dot	Dot
1	£100	£100

Minor Constant Sheet Flaws

Cyl. 1.	3/10	Coloured flaw between left-hand leaves of thistle (Th. B6)
	5/10	Coloured spur to top of lacing at right of value (Th. G5)
Cyl. 2.	3/10	As on Cyl. 1. (multipositive flaw)

Imprimaturs from the NPM or BPMA
Imperforate, watermark Type W.22

Watermark upright	£950
Cyl. 1. Block of Six	£6250

1955 *(3 November).* **1s.** Wmk St Edward's Crown

S137 = SG 554	Mint	Used
1s. Bistre-brown	22·00	65
a. Thistle flaw (Cyl. 3 Dot, R. 4/5)	65·00	

S137a, S138b, S139a

Cylinder Numbers (Blocks of Six)
Perforation Type A (E/I)

Cyl. No.	No dot	Dot
2	£150	£150
3	£150	£150

Perforation Type B (I/P no dot) and C (E/P dot)

Cyl. No.	No dot	Dot
4	£200	£200

Minor Constant Sheet Flaws

Cyl. 2.	3/10	Coloured flaw between left-hand leaves of thistle (Th. B6). Later retouched leaving a pale mark
Cyl. 3.	3/10	As on Cyl. 2, but flaw is retouched and appears much smaller (multipositive flaw)
Cyl. 4.	3/10	As for Cyl. 3.
	11/12	Coloured spur to foot of first "E" of "REVENUE"

Imprimaturs from the NPM or BPMA
Imperforate, watermark Type W.23

Watermark upright	£900
Cyl. 2 Block of Six	£6250

1958 *(30 October).* **1s.** Wmk Crowns
A. Cream Paper

S138	Mint	Used
1s. Bistre-brown	3·75	80
a. Double impression	£275	
b. Thistle flaw (Cyl. 3 Dot, R. 4/5)	40·00	

B. Whiter Paper *(22 July 1962)*

S139 = SG 584	Mint	Used
1s. Bistre-brown	75	30
a. Thistle flaw (Cyl. 3 Dot, R. 4/5)	40·00	

The note below No. S85 4d. deep ultramarine concerning paper movement applies to No. S138a.

S138a

For illustration of Nos. S138b and S139a, see No. S137a.

Cylinder Numbers (Blocks of Six)

Cream paper (No. S138)
Perforation Type A (E/I)

Cyl. No.	No dot	Dot
2	35·00	35·00
3	35·00	35·00
4	35·00	35·00

Whiter paper (No. S139)
Perforation Type A (E/I)

Cyl. No.	No dot	Dot
2	15·00	15·00
3	15·00	15·00
4	12·00	12·00

Minor Constant Sheet Flaws
Multipositive flaw

| Dot | 3/10 | Coloured flaw between left-hand leaves of thistle (Th. B6) now only exists retouched. Cyls. 2. and 3. show as a smudge and Cyl. 4. as a much smaller flaw |
| Cyl. 4. | 11/12 | Coloured spur to foot of first "E" of "REVENUE" |

Imprimaturs from the NPM or BPMA
Imperforate, watermark Type W.24. Cream or whiter paper

Watermark upright	£900
Watermark upright with Thistle flaw R.4/5	£1500
Cyl. 3. Block of Six (Cream paper)	£6250
Cyl. 3 Block of Six (Whiter paper)	£6250

1967 *(28 June).* **1s.** Two 9·5 mm phosphor bands reacting violet. Wmk Crowns

S140 = SG 617e	Mint	Used
1s. Bistre-brown	1·00	35

The bands were applied by photogravure.

Cylinder Numbers (Blocks of Six)
Perforation Type F (L)*

Cyl. No.	No dot (I/E)	Dot (P/E)
4	10·00	10·00

1s. Bistre-brown, 1s.3d. Green **Dorothy Wilding issues** **SA**

Minor Constant Sheet Flaws

Cyl. 4.	3/10	Coloured flaw between left-hand leaves of thistle (Th. B6) is now retouched leaving a much smaller flaw
	11/12	Coloured spur to foot of first "E" of "REVENUE"

Imprimaturs from the NPM or BPMA
Imperforate, watermark Type W.**24**

Watermark upright	£950
Cyl. 4. Block of Six	£6250

1s.3d. Green, Type SA7 (1953–1967)

1953 *(2 November).* **1s.3d.** Wmk Tudor Crown

S141 = SG 530		Mint	Used
1s.3d.	Green	4·50	3·25
	a. White flaw in Queen's hair (Dot, R. 2/9)	45·00	
	b. "P" flaw (Dot, R. 6/10)	45·00	

S141a, S142a, S143a, S144a, S145a, S146a, S147b   S141b, S142b, S143b, S144b, S145b, S146b, S147c

Cylinder Numbers (Blocks of Six)
Perforation Type A (E/I)

Cyl. No.	No dot	Dot
1	55·00	55·00

Perforation Type B (I/P no dot) and C (E/P dot)

Cyl. No.	No dot	Dot
1	70·00	70·00

Imprimaturs from the NPM or BPMA
Imperforate, watermark Type W.**22**

Watermark upright	£900
Cyl. 1 Block of Six	£6250

●———

1956 *(27 March).* **1s.3d.** Wmk St Edward's Crown

S142 = SG 555		Mint	Used
1s.3d.	Green	30·00	1·60
	a. White flaw in Queen's hair (Dot, R. 2/9)	70·00	
	b. "P" flaw (Dot, R. 6/10)	70·00	

For illustrations of Nos. S142a/b, see Nos. S141a/b.

Cylinder Numbers (Blocks of Six)
Perforation Type A (E/I)

Cyl. No.	No dot	Dot
1	£225	£225

Imprimaturs from the NPM or BPMA
Imperforate, watermark Type W.**23**

Watermark upright	£900
Watermark upright with White flaw in Queen's hair R.2/9	£1500
Watermark upright with "P" flaw variety R.6/10	£1500
Cyl. 1. Block of Six	£6250

●———

1959 *(17 June).* **1s.3d.** Wmk Crowns

A. Cream Paper

S143		Mint	Used
1s.3d.	Green	3·00	1·25
	a. White flaw in Queen's hair (Cyl. 1 Dot, R. 2/9)	40·00	
	b. "P" flaw (Cyl, 1, Dot, R. 6/10)	40·00	

53

SA Dorothy Wilding issues 1s.3d. Green

B. Whiter Paper *(29 August 1962)*

S144 = SG 585	Mint	Used
1s.3d. Green	75	30
a. White flaw in Queen's hair (Cyl. 1 Dot, R. 2/9)	35·00	
b. "P" flaw (Cyl. 1 Dot, R. 6/10)	35·00	

For illustrations of Nos. S143a/b and S144a/b, see Nos. S141a/b.

Cylinder Numbers (Blocks of Six)
Cream Paper No (S143)
Perforation Type A (E/I)

Cyl. No.	No dot	Dot
1	35·00	35·00

Whiter Paper No (S144)
Perforation Type A (E/I)

Cyl. No.	No dot	Dot
1	25·00	25·00
2	10·00	10·00

Imprimaturs from the NPM or BPMA
Imperforate, watermark Type W.**24**. Cream or whiter paper

Watermark upright	£900
Watermark upright with White flaw in Queen's hair R.7/9	£1500
Watermark upright with "P" flaw variety R.6/10	£1500
Cyl. 1 Block of Six (Cream paper)	£6250
Cyl. 1 ■ Block of Six (Whiter paper)	£6250

1960 *(22 June).* **1s.3d.** Two phosphor bands reacting green. Wmk Crowns

S145	Mint	Used
1s.3d. Green	7·00	4·50
a. White flaw in Queen's hair (Dot, R. 2/9)	45·00	
b. "P" flaw (Dot, R. 6/10)	45·00	

The bands were applied by photogravure.
For illustrations of Nos. S145a/b, see Nos. S141a/b.

Cylinder Numbers (Blocks of Six)
Perforation Type B (I/P no dot) and C (E/P dot)

Cyl. No.	No dot	Dot
1	75·00	75·00

Imprimatur from the NPM or BPMA
Imperforate, watermark Type W.**24**

Watermark upright	£900
Watermark upright with White flaw in Queen's hair R.7/9	£1500
Cyl. 1 ■ Block of Six	£6250

1961 *(5 June).* **1s.3d.** Two phosphor bands reacting blue. Wmk Crowns

A. Cream Paper

S146	Mint	Used
1s.3d. Green	22·00	10·00
a. White flaw in Queen's hair (Cyl. 1 Dot, R. 2/9)	55·00	
b. "P" flaw (Cyl. 1 Dot, R. 6/10)	55·00	

B. Whiter Paper *(21 January 1963)*

S147 = SG 618	Mint	Used
1s.3d. Green	1·90	2·50
a. One 8 mm band	10·00	
b. White flaw in Queen's hair (Cyl. 1 Dot, R. 2/9)	40·00	

B. Whiter Paper *(21 January 1963)*

c. "P" flaw (Cyl. 1 Dot, R. 6/10)	40·00	

The bands were applied by photogravure.
For illustrations of Nos. S146a/b and S147b/c, see Nos. S141a/b.

Cylinder Numbers (Blocks of Six)
Cream Paper (No. S146)
Perforation Type A (E/I)

Cyl. No.	No dot	Dot
1	£180	£160

Whiter Paper (No. S147)
Perforation Type A (E/I)

Cyl. No.	No dot	Dot
1	40·00	20·00
2	20·00	20·00

Imprimaturs from the NPM or BPMA
Imperforate, watermark Type W.**24**. Cream or whiter paper

Watermark upright	£900
Watermark upright with White flaw in Queen's hair R.7/9	£1500
Cyl. 1 ■ Block of Six (Cream paper)	£6250
Cyl. 1 Block of Six (Whiter paper)	£6250

1965 *(13 August).* **1s.3d.** Two 8 mm phosphor bands reacting violet. Wmk Crowns

S148	Mint	Used
1s.3d. Green	18·00	4·50
a. One 6 mm band at left or right (stamp with vert. margin)	40·00	
b. Bands applied photo. (1966)	7·50	3·50
c. Error. One 8 mm band (photo.)	40·00	
d. Error. One 8 mm band (l/press.)	45·00	
da. Error. As d but 6 mm band (l/press.)	50·00	

The bands were originally applied by letterpress.

Cylinder Numbers (Blocks of Six)
Perforation Type A (E/I)
Applied l/press (No. S148)

Cyl. No.	No dot	Dot
2	£175	£175

Perforation Type B (I/P no dot) and C (E/P dot)
Applied photo (No. S148b)

Cyl. No.	No dot	Dot
2	75·00	75·00

1967 *(Early).* **1s.3d.** Two 9·5 mm phosphor bands reacting violet. Wmk Crowns

S149	Mint	Used
1s.3d. Green	9·00	5·00

The bands were applied by photogravure.

Cylinder Numbers (Blocks of Six)
Perforation Type A (E/I)

Cyl. No.	No dot	Dot
2	£100	75·00

1s.6d. Grey-blue, Type SA6 (1953–1966)

1953 (2 November). **1s.6d.** Wmk Tudor Crown

S150 = SG 531	Mint	Used
1s.6d. Grey-blue	14·00	3·75
a. White flaw in Queen's hair below diadem (Dot, R.20/1)	55·00	
b. White flaw in Queen's hair opposite "N" of "REVENUE" (Dot, R.20/2)	55·00	

S150a, S151a, S152a, S153a, S154a

S150b, S151b, S152b Later retouched on Crowns watermark

Cylinder Numbers (Blocks of Six)
Perforation Type A (E/I)

Cyl. No.	No dot	Dot
1	£135	£150*

Perforation Type B (I/P no dot) and C (E/P dot)

Cyl. No.	No dot	Dot
1	£135	£150*

Imprimaturs from the NPM or BPMA
Imperforate, watermark Type W.**22**

Watermark upright	£900
Cyl. 1 Block of Six	£6250

1956 (27 March). **1s.6d.** Wmk St Edward's Crown

S151 = SG 556	Mint	Used
1s.6d. Grey-blue	23·00	1·60
a. White flaw in Queen's hair below diadem (Dot, R.20/1)	60·00	
b. White flaw in Queen's hair opposite "N" of "REVENUE" (Dot, R.20/2)	60·00	

For illustrations of Nos. S151a/b, see Nos. S150a/b.

Cylinder Numbers (Blocks of Six)
Perforation Type A (E/I)

Cyl. No.	No dot	Dot
1	£140	£175*

Perforation Type B (I/P no dot) and C (E/P dot)

Cyl. No.	No dot	Dot
1	£140	£175*

Imprimaturs from the NPM or BPMA
Imperforate, watermark Type W.**23**

Watermark upright	£900
Cyl. 1. Block of Six	£6250

1958 (16 December). **1s.6d.** Wmk Crowns

A. Cream Paper

S152	Mint	Used
b. White flaw in Queen's hair opposite "N" of "REVENUE" (Cyl. 1 Dot, R.20/2)	40·00	

B. Whiter Paper (14 November 1962)

S153 = SG 586	Mint	Used
1s.6d. Grey-blue	5·00	40
a. White flaw in Queen's hair below diadem (Cyl. 1 Dot, R.20/1)	35·00	

For illustrations of Nos. S152a/b and S153a, see Nos. S150a/b.

Cylinder Numbers (Blocks of Six)

Cream paper (No. S152)
Perforation Type A (E/I)

Cyl. No.	No dot	Dot
1	£100	£130
3	£110	£110

Perforation Type B (I/P no dot) and C (E/P dot)

Cyl. No.	No dot	Dot
1	£120	£150*
3	£120	£120

Whiter paper (No. S153)
Perforation Type A (E/I)

Cyl. No.	No dot	Dot
1	40·00	40·00

Imprimaturs from the NPM or BPMA
Imperforate, watermark Type W.**24**. Cream or whiter paper

Watermark upright	£950
Cyl. 1. Block of Six (Cream paper)	£6250
Cyl. 1 Block of Six (Whiter paper)	£6250

1966 (12 December). **1s.6d.** Two 9·5 mm phosphor bands reacting violet. Wmk Crowns

S154 = SG 618a	Mint	Used
1s.6d. Grey-blue	2·00	2·00
a. White flaw in Queen's hair below diadem (Cyl. 1 Dot, R.20/1)	35·00	

The bands were applied by photogravure.
For illustration of No. S154a, see No. S150a.

Cylinder Numbers (Blocks of Six)
Perforation Type A (E/I)

Cyl. No.	No dot	Dot
1	20·00	40·00*

Perforation Type F (L)*

Cyl. No.	No dot (I/E)	Dot (P/E)
8	25·00	25·00

Imprimaturs from the NPM or BPMA
Imperforate, watermark Type W.**24**

Watermark upright	£950
Cyl. 1. Block of Six	£6250

Presentation Packs

SPP1 (issued 1960)	18 values	£275

The issued pack contained one of each value. The 1½d. and 11d. were with St Edward's Crown watermark (Nos. S26 and S135) and the remainder were Crowns watermark all on cream paper, ½d. (No. S4), 1d (S16), 2d. (S40), 2½d. (S55), 3d. (S70), 4d. (S83), 4½d. (S93), 5d. (S101), 6d. (S107), 7d. (S116), 8d. (S121), 9d. (S126), 10d. (S131), 1s. (S138), 1s.3d. (S144), 1s.6d. (S152).
Two forms of the pack exist:
(a) Inscribed 10s 6d for sale in the U.K. and
(b) Inscribed $1·80 for sale in the U.S.A.

SPP2 (issued 1960)	16 values	£300

The issued pack contained two of each value of the Phosphor-Graphite experimental issue, ½d. (No. S8), 1d. (S19), 1½d. (S31), 2d. (S43), 2½d. (S60), 3d. (S73), 4d. (S87), 4½d. (S96). The ½d., 1d. and 1½d. were with St Edward's Crown watermark and the remainder with Crowns watermark. Although the details printed on the pack erroneously describe the stamps as all having Crowns watermark, the packs usually bear a sticker inscribed "CORRECTION. The ½d., 1d., & 1½d. stamps bear the St. Edward Crown Royal Cypher watermark."
Two forms of the pack exist:
(a) Inscribed 3s 8d for sale in the U.K. and
(b) Inscribed 50c for sale in the U.S.A.

"Dollis Hill" Phosphor Trials

This is a listing of unused trial stamps except for the used ½d. and 2½d. values on cover, the subject of notes 1 and 7 below. The majority of extant trial stamps are 2d. values. There is a significant proportion of 3d. values and a very few ½d. and 2½d. values. Substantially, the colours of the trial stamps are similar to issued stamps and the same colours are used in this list. However, it should be noted that the 2d. Red-brown trials are a much less deep shade than the stamps issued in 1953 and 1955 but are a deeper shade than the issued and trial stamps in the Light red-brown shade. Thus, the trials may be subject to lack of colour consistency (which would not be important to the phosphor experiments) if printed specially for the Post Office laboratory. All watermarked stamps are Watermark Crowns, Type W.**24** except ST6 (1) 2½d. trial which has Watermark St Edward's Crown, Type W.**23**. Prices are for unused trial stamps.

ST1 ½d. Orange-red

(1) Green phosphor, three 3 mm bands (note 1)
To date, no unused ½d. trial stamps have been found.

ST4 2d. Red-brown

(1)	No phosphor bands	
a.	No watermark	£300
b.	Watermark sideways right	£425
(2)	Green phosphor within the paper, no watermark, imperforate (note 2)	£1200
(3)	Green all-over phosphor (note 3)	
a.	No watermark	£300
b.	Watermark sideways left	£325
c.	Watermark sideways right	£300
(4)	Green phosphor bands, Watermark sideways left	
a.	Two side 1.5 mm bands	£425
b.	As a. and one, two or five additional 1·5 mm bands	£425
c.	As a. and a circular band	£1200

ST5 2d. Light red-brown

(1)	No phosphor bands, no watermark	£300
(2)	Green phosphor within the paper, no watermark	
a.	Imperforate	£1200
b	Perforated	£500
(3)	Green all-over phosphor (note 4)	
a.	No watermark, variable printing, gummed or not gummed	£300
b.	Watermark upright	80·00
c.	Watermark sideways left	£225
d.	Watermark sideways right	£275
e.	Watermark sideways right, phosphor front and back	£475
(4)	Yellow all-over phosphor no watermark (note 5)	£500
(5)	Green phosphor bands	
a.	No watermark, one wide central band	£300
b.	No watermark, two side bands	£425
c.	Watermark upright, 3 mm band at left	90·00
(6)	Green honeycomb, (mainly 5 rows of 5 dots) (note 6)	£500

There is considerable variation in the print and paper quality of these 2d. Light red-brown trial stamps ranging from mottled and powdery to high quality.

ST6 2½d. Carmine-red

(1)	Yellow phosphor, watermark St Edward's Crown upright	—
a.	One band at left	—
b.	Two 8mm bands and graphite lines on reverse*	£1800
(2)	Imperforate, Green all-over phosphor (note 7)	
(3)	Yellow phosphor bands	
a.	Watermark upright, two l/press 8 mm bands	—
b.	Watermark upright, l/press 6 mm band at left with selvedge and 8 mm band at right (see Section S Notes)	—

*See note after No. S60

ST7 3d. Deep lilac

(1)	No phosphor bands, watermark upright, with imperforate selvedge at left	—
(2)	Blue all-over phosphor	
a.	No watermark (note 8)	£350
b.	Watermark upright	95·00
c.	Watermark sideways right	£170
(3)	Blue phosphor bands, over the ink	
a.	Watermark upright, one 2 mm central band (note 9)	£170
b.	Watermark upright, one 2 mm band at left or right	£275
c.	Watermark upright, two 3 mm side bands	70·00
d.	Watermark sideways left, two 3 mm side bands	£200
da.	Watermark sideways Right	£200
e.	Watermark upright, one 4 mm central band (note 10)	£325
f.	Watermark sideways right, one 4 mm band at left	£375
(4)	Blue phosphor bands, under the ink	
a.	Watermark upright, one 1.5 mm band at left or right	£225

b.	Watermark upright, two 1.5 mm side bands	£225
c.	Watermark upright, one 2 mm central band	£225
d.	Watermark upright, one 4 mm central band	£300

The blue phosphor on these trials is a greenish-blue, which is more blue than the green phosphor on the trials but less blue than on the blue phosphor issued stamps.

Generally, some of the paper, particularly for the 2d. trial stamps, was susceptible to tearing. Torn paper was mended with repair tape prior to printing and this produced varieties such as printed on double paper, printed part on paper and tape and phosphor on stamp but not on tape.

Notes

The following is a brief list of trial usages.

1. On blank postcard with slogan postmark Norwich 29 February 1972
2. On blank cover with slogan postmark Norwich 14 February 1972
3. On blank postcard with slogan postmark Norwich 14 February 1972
4. On addressed covers to PO Research Station with slogan postmarks Harrow 15 December 1958, 16 December 1958 and 29 December 1958
5. On addressed cover to PO Research Station with postmark Gloucester 22 December 1971
6. On blank postcard with slogan postmark Norwich 24 February 1972
7. On blank postcard with slogan postmark Norwich 29 February 1972
8. On addressed cover to PO Research Station with slogan postmark Norwich 29 February 1972
9. On blank postcard with slogan postmark Norwich 29 February 1972
10. On blank postcard with slogan postmark Norwich 29 February 1972

Examples exist of other dates of trial usage on cover or postcard. Also, many of the trial stamps are known with postmarks but off cover. These used stamps show considerable variation in phosphor after-glow, possibly due to the stamps having been soaked to remove them from their original trial cover.

Section SB
Dorothy Wilding Issues
1953–1968. Booklet Panes in Photogravure

General Notes

Introduction. All panes were printed in photogravure by Harrison & Sons. As for counter sheets described in section SA, panes of six were printed in the reel in double-panes of 480 stamps, consisting of two panes (no dot and dot), each of 240 stamps arranged in 20 rows of 12. From 1957 most cylinders were engraved every 21 rows resulting in cylinder numbers appearing on either the top or bottom rows when guillotined into double panes of 20 rows. Panes of four for 2s. booklets with sideways watermark were printed in the reel as above, but being printed sideways, the double pane of 480 stamps comprised 24 rows of 20. Panes of four for 1s. and 2s. booklets with upright/inverted watermark were printed from single-pane cylinders on sheet-fed machines, all being 18 rows of 12 stamps; except for the 1963 Holiday Booklet (NRI) which was 20 rows of 12. See the detailed notes under Section S for information on printing, paper, gum and phosphor application.

Arrangement. The panes are listed in face value order of the stamps they include (for *se-tenant* panes under the lowest denomination). The main listing is followed by errors and varieties.

Perforation. Wilding booklet stamps exist in panes of two, four and six and details together with illustrations of the perforation types will be found in Appendix G, section 4. The type abbreviations found above the pane prices refer to the appearance of the binding margin, i.e. I = imperforate, AP = alternate perf., P = perforated, E = extension hole and AP(2E) = alternate perf with two extension holes only.

Booklet errors. Those listed as "Imperf. pane" show one row of perforations either at top or bottom of the booklet pane. Those listed as "part perf." pane have one row of three stamps imperforate on three sides. The *tête-bêche* errors derive from booklets but these are listed in Section SA.

Booklet cylinder numbers. These are listed for panes where the prefix letter and/or the number is visible. Some panes of four had the number engraved wide of the stamps so that they never showed on panes, but information on the cylinders used is given in most cases. Phosphor cylinder numbers have not been found on Wilding panes. The cylinder numbers being hand-engraved varied slightly as to their position in relation to the stamp so that some were invariably trimmed. A pane showing a complete cylinder number placed away from the stamp will only exist with trimmed perforations on the opposite side.

Where panes were printed from 21-row cylinders, resulting in the cylinder number appearing alongside either the top or the bottom row of the pane, these are differentiated in the listings, where a "T" after the number indicates that the cylinder number appears alongside the top row.

Booklet cylinder flaws. Cylinder flaws on booklet stamps are listed under the panes in which they occur. Prices are for the variety in a complete pane with its binding margin intact. In cases where a 21-row cylinder has been used both possible positions in the pane are given. Where a cylinder pane contains a variety, that variety is listed additionally as a pane and the cylinder listing bears an asterisk to identify that it contains a variety. Where a listed pane contains a variety, a description of it follows the listing.

When quoting the position on booklet panes no attention is paid to the labels. In a pane of six with the binding margin at the left, stamp 3 would be the third stamp in the row counting from left to right. Again "R. 1/3" refers to row one, third stamp from the left margin. Panes of four from 1s. and 2s. booklets contain panes with a top binding margin and "R. 2/2" refers to row two second stamp – viewing the pane with stamps upright.

Phosphor band widths and misplacement. See notes in Section S; the booklet stamps being similar to those printed in Post Office counter sheets. The 4 mm and 5·5 mm bands were printed on both top and bottom of the booklet sheets in letterpress on panes of four, but these can only be identified when the bands are slightly misplaced. Normally, panes of six showing 8 mm bands have a 6 mm band printed *over the first vertical row of perforations at the left*. Major shifts result in stamps from the first column having one 6 mm wide band and the other four stamps a misplaced band of 8 mm. This, in effect, changes the number of bands on a single stamp and these have always been popular with collectors. In order to be treated as a wide band variety, each band must be printed wholly on the stamp and not overlap any part of the adjacent stamp or the binding margin. Partial shifts of phosphor bands are common and command much reduced prices. A different kind of variety exists where 9·5 mm phosphor bands were printed one side band on 3d. stamps instead of two but this only occurred on a small printing of the 1d./3d. *se-tenant* panes in 2s. booklets listed as varieties of SB50 to SB53.

See Section SA for phosphor bands misplaced on singles derived from panes. Although complete panes with full perforations showing listable band shifts are included some remain unpriced due to their scarcity. It is possible that such panes were split up later especially if the perforations were no better than average. *Prices quoted in this Section are for good perfs all round.*

Phosphor application. Refer to the notes in Section S under "Phosphor Issues" for information on the types of phosphor employed.

Stamps overprinted "SPECIMEN". Panes exist with a handstamped overprint in two sizes. These derive from the National Postal Museum archive sales mentioned in the Introductory Notes. The handstamp can be found inverted or overlapping the perforations but these are not listed as varieties.

> **BOOKLET PANE PRICES.** The prices quoted are for panes with good perforations all round and with binding margin attached. Panes showing some degree of trimming will be worth less than the published prices in this Catalogue. It should be appreciated that some panes are scarce with full perforations and the prices shown in the Catalogue reflect this. Panes from the 2s. booklets are particularly difficult to find with full perforations on the three sides.

> **BOOKLET PANE VARIETIES.** Panes of six with listed varieties have been placed in the I perf column for typographic convenience. However, the variety will occur on a pane with I perf or Ie perf, depending on its location in the booklet sheet. It will not occur on a pane with the other perf selvedge.

Wilding Booklet Panes

Index to Booklet panes

SB No.	Face Value	Watermark	Size of Pane	Further description	Page
1	½d.	Tudor Crown	6		61
2	½d.	Tudor Crown	4		61
3	½d.	Tudor Crown	2		61
4	½d.	St Edward's Crown	6		61
5	½d.	St Edward's Crown	4		62
6	½d.	St Edward's Crown	2		62
7	½d.	Crowns	6	Cream paper	62
8	½d.	Crowns	6	Whiter paper	62
9	½d.	Crowns	4	Cream paper	63
10	½d.	Crowns, sideways	4	Cream paper	63
11	½d.	Crowns, sideways	4	Whiter paper	63
12	3×½d. +2½d.	Crowns	4	Chalky paper	63
13	2×½d. +2×2½d.	Crowns, sideways	4	Whiter paper	64
14	½d.	Crowns	6	Graphite lines	64
15	½d.	Crowns	6	Green phosphor	65
16	½d.	Crowns	6	Blue phosphor, cream paper	65
17	½d.	Crowns	6	Blue phosphor, whiter paper	65
18	½d.	Crowns, sideways	4	Blue phosphor, cream paper	65
19	½d.	Crowns, sideways	4	Blue phosphor, whiter paper	65
20	1d.	Tudor Crown	6		65
21	1d.	Tudor Crown	4		66
22	1d.	Tudor Crown	2		66
23	1d.	Tudor Crown	6	Including 3 labels: "MINIMUM INLAND PRINTED PAPER RATE 1½d."	66
24	1d.	Tudor Crown	6	Including 3 labels: "PLEASE POST EARLY IN THE DAY" – NORMAL SETTING	67
24A	1d.	Tudor Crown	6	Including 3 labels: "PLEASE POST EARLY IN THE DAY" – MODIFIED SETTING	67
25	1d.	Tudor Crown	6	Including 3 different labels	67
26	1d.	St Edward's Crown	6		68
27	1d.	St Edward's Crown	4		68
28	1d.	St Edward's Crown	2		68
29	1d.	St Edward's Crown	6	Including 3 different labels	68
30	1d.	Crowns	6	Cream paper	69
31	1d.	Crowns	6	Whiter paper	69
32	1d.	Crowns	4	Cream paper	70
33	1d.	Crowns, sideways	4	Cream paper	70
34	1d.	Crowns, sideways	4	Whiter paper	70
35/38	2 × 1d. +2 × 3d.	Crowns, sideways	4	Whiter paper	70
39	1d.	Crowns	6	Graphite lines	71
40	1d.	Crowns	6	Green phosphor	71
41	1d.	Crowns	6	Blue phosphor, cream paper	71
42	1d.	Crowns	6	Blue phosphor, whiter paper	71
43	1d.	Crowns, sideways	4	Blue phosphor, cream paper	72
44	1d.	Crowns, sideways	4	Blue phosphor, whiter paper	72
45/48	2 × 1d. +2 × 3d.	Crowns, sideways	4	Blue phosphor, whiter paper	72
49	1d.	Crowns	6	Violet phosphor, 8 mm.	72
50/53	2 × 1d. +2 × 3d.	Crowns, sideways	4	3d. with 1 side violet 8 mm band	73
54	1d.	Crowns	6	Violet phosphor, 9·5 mm.	73
55/56	2 × 1d.+2 × 3d.	Crowns	4	3d. with 2 violet 9·5mm bands	73
57/58	2 × 1d.+2 × 3d.	Crowns	4	3d. with 2 violet 9·5mm bands	74
59	1½d.	Tudor Crown	6		74
60	1½d.	Tudor Crown	4		74
61	1½d.	Tudor Crown	2		74
62	1½d.	St Edward's Crown	6		75
63	1½d.	St Edward's Crown	4		75
64	1½d.	St Edward's Crown	2		75
65	1½d.	Crowns	6	Cream paper	75
66	1½d.	Crowns	6	Whiter paper	75
67	1½d.	Crowns	4	Cream paper	76
68	1½d.	Crowns, sideways	4	Cream paper	76
69	1½d.	Crowns, sideways	4	Whiter paper	76

SB — Wilding Booklet Panes

SB No.	Face Value	Watermark	Size of Pane	Further description	Page
70	1½d.	Crowns	6	Graphite lines	76
71	1½d.	Crowns	6	Green phosphor	77
72	1½d.	Crowns	6	Blue phosphor, cream paper	77
73	1½d.	Crowns	6	Blue phosphor, whiter paper	77
74	1½d.	Crowns, sideways	4	Blue phosphor, cream paper	77
75	1½d.	Crowns, sideways	4	Blue phosphor, whiter paper	77
76	2d.	Tudor Crown	6		77
77	2d.	St Edward's Crown	6	Red-brown	78
78	2d.	St Edward's Crown	6	Light red-brown	78
79	2d.	Crowns	6	Cream paper	79
80	2½d.	Tudor Crown	6	Type II	79
81	2½d.	St Edward's Crown	6	Type II	80
82	2½d.	Crowns	6	Type II. Cream paper	81
83	2½d.	Crowns	6	Type II. Whiter paper	81
84	2½d.	Crowns	4	Type II. Chalky paper	81
85	2½d.	Crowns	6	Type II. Graphite lines	81
86	2½d.	Crowns	6	Type II. Green phosphor	82
87	2½d.	Crowns	6	Type II. Blue phosphor, 2 bands, cream paper	82
88	2½d.	Crowns	6	Type II. Blue phosphor, 1 band, cream paper	82
89	2½d.	Crowns	6	Type II. Blue phosphor, 1 band, whiter paper	82
90	3d.	St Edward's Crown	6		82
91	3d.	St Edward's Crown	4		83
92	3d.	Crowns	6	Cream paper	83
93	3d.	Crowns	6	Whiter paper	83
94	3d.	Crowns	4	Cream paper	84
95	3d.	Crowns, sideways	4	Cream paper	84
96	3d.	Crowns, sideways	4	Whiter paper	84
97	3d.	Crowns	6	Graphite lines	84
98	3d.	Crowns	6	Green phosphor	85
99	3d.	Crowns	6	Blue phosphor, cream paper	85
100	3d.	Crowns	6	Blue phosphor, whiter paper	85
101	3d.	Crowns, sideways	4	Blue phosphor, cream paper	85
102	3d.	Crowns, sideways	4	Blue phosphor, whiter paper	85
103	3d.	Crowns	6	Violet phosphor, 1 side band	86
104	3d.	Crowns	6	Violet phosphor, 1 centre band	86
105	4d.	Crowns	6	Deep ultramarine	86
106	4d.	Crowns, sideways	4	Deep ultramarine	87
107	4d.	Crowns	6	Deep ultramarine. Blue phosphor	87
108	4d.	Crowns, sideways	4	Deep ultramarine. Blue phosphor	88
109	4d.	Crowns	6	Violet phosphor, 8 mm.	88
110	4d.	Crowns, sideways	4	Violet phosphor, 8 mm.	88
111	4d.	Crowns	6	Violet phosphor, 9·5 mm.	88
112	4d.	Crowns, sideways	4	Violet phosphor, 9·5 mm.	89

½d. **Wilding Booklet Panes** **SB**

½d. Panes of six, *Wmk* Tudor Crown

From 2s.6d. Booklets F14/38 and F42/43 and 5s. Booklets H6/19 and H21.

	Perf. Type	
A. Watermark upright	I	Ie
SB1 Pane of 6×½d. (containing No. S1×6) *(3.54)*	4·00	4·50

	Perf. Type	
B. Watermark inverted	I	Ie
SB1a Pane of 6×½d. (containing No. S1a×6) *(3.54)*	4·00	4·50

Booklet Cylinder Numbers
Panes of six (20-row cylinders)

Cylinder No.	No Dot	Dot
E1	60·00	60·00
E2	35·00	35·00
E4	45·00*	45·00

* The no dot pane of cylinder E4 originally had a dot inserted in error. This can be distinguished from the true dot cylinder in which the "4" is broader and further from the "E", and the dot is more circular than the erroneous dot. The erroneous dot was not noticed until the Crowns watermark which exists in three states: I with the erroneous dot; II with dot removed leaving a smudge; and III with smudge removed. These are shown in the following illustration:

True dot   I   II   III

½d. Panes of four, *Wmk* Tudor Crown

From 1s. Booklet K1/a for use in "E" slot machines.

	Perf. Type P
A. Watermark upright	
SB2 Pane of 4×½d. (containing No. S1×4) *(22.7.54)*	8·00
B. Watermark inverted	
SB2a Pane of 4×½d. (containing No. S1a×4) *(22.7.54)*	10·00

Booklet Cylinder Number
Cylinder No. E3 was used, but it does not appear in the finished booklets.

½d. Panes of two, *Wmk* Tudor Crown

From 1s. Booklet E1 for use in experimental "D" slot machines.

	Perf. Type	
Watermark upright	E	E(½v)
SB3 Pane of 2× ½d. (containing No. S1×2) *(2.9.53)*	5·00	10·00

Made up from vertical columns 1 and 2 from sheets.

Booklet Cylinder Numbers
Panes of two (from sheets). *Perf. Type* E

Cylinder No.	No Dot	Dot
1	80·00	£100
3	65·00	65·00

Imprimaturs from the NBM or BPMA
Booklet Pane of six. Imperforate, watermark Type W.**22**

Two Panes as No. SB1 arranged *tête-bêche* with cylinder E2	£14500

Booklet panes of four. Imperforate, watermark Type W.**22**

Two panes as No. SB2 arranged vertically *tête-bêche* with a 12 mm vertical gutter margin between	£10000
Two panes as No. SB2 arranged vertically *tête-bêche* with a 12 mm horizontal gutter margin between with cylinder E3	£10500

½d. Panes of six, *Wmk* St Edward's Crown

From 2s.6d. Booklets F34/61, 3s. Booklets M1/10 and 5s. Booklets H17/37.

	Perf. Type	
A. Watermark upright	I	Ie
SB4 Pane of 6×½d. (containing No. S2×6) *(9.55)*	2·50	3·00
b. Part perf. pane*	£4500	
c. White flaw in Queen's hair (R. 1/3 or 2/3)	40·00	
B. Watermark inverted		
SB4a Pane of 6×½d. (containing No. S2b×6) *(9.55)*	4·00	5·00
ab. Part perf pane	£4500	

* Booklet error see General Notes.

SB4c, SB7e, SB14b
(Cyl. E4 dot)

Booklet Cylinder Numbers
Panes of six (20/21-row cylinders)

Cylinder No.	No Dot	Dot
E4	45·00*	35·00
E4 T	50·00*	40·00

* See notes after booklet panes of No. SB1.

The ½d. double-pane cylinders E1, E2 and E4 contained 20 rows and the cylinder number always occurred opposite row 18 so that it always appears next to the bottom row of the pane.

Cylinder E4 was later modified by adding another row of 24. In this and later 21-row cylinders, which are printed continuously on the web, the perforated web is cut at every 20th row to make sheets of 480. Consequently on successive sheets the cylinder number appears one row lower and thus a pane can have it adjoining the top or bottom row. Where the cylinder number adjoins the top row of the pane it is designated by the letter "T".

SB Wilding Booklet Panes ½d.

½d. Panes of four, *Wmk* St Edward's Crown
From 1s. Booklets K2/b for use in "E" slot machines and 2s. Booklet N1

	Perf. Type	
A. Watermark upright	AP	P
SB5 Pane of 4×½d. (containing No. S2×4) *(5.7.56)*	8·00	10·00
B. Watermark inverted		
SB5a Pane of 4×½d. (containing No. S2b×4) *(5.7.56)*	8·00	10·00

Booklet Cylinder Number
Cylinder No. E3 was used, but it does not appear in the finished booklets.

½d. Panes of two, *Wmk* St Edward's Crown
From 1s. Booklet E2 for use in experimental "D" slot machines.

	Perf. Type	
Watermark upright	E	E(½v)
SB6 Pane of 2×½d. (containing No. S2×2) *(11.57)*	25·00	40·00

Made up from vertical columns 1 and 2 from sheets.

Booklet Cylinder Numbers
Panes of two (from sheets). Perf. Type E

Cylinder No.	No Dot	Dot
3	£120	£180

Imprimaturs from the NPM or BPMA
Booklet pane of six. Imperforate, watermark Type W.**23**
Two panes as No. SB4 arranged *tête-bêche* with cylinder E4.	£14500

Booklet panes of four. Imperforate, watermark Type W.**23**
Two panes as No. SB5 arranged vertically *tête-bêche* with a 12 mm horizontal gutter margin between	£10000
Two panes as No. SB5 arranged *tête-bêche* with a 12 mm horizontal gutter margin between with cylinder E3	£10500

½d. Panes of six, cream or whiter paper. *Wmk* Crowns
From 3s. Booklets M9(a)/74, 5s. Booklets H35(a) and H37/74 and 10s. Booklets X1/2

Cream Paper	Perf. Type	
A. Watermark upright	I	Ie
SB7 Pane of 6×½d. (containing No. S4×6) *(11.58)*	5·50	7·00
b. Part perf. pane*	£4000	
c. Dot on left fraction bar (R. 1/1 or R. 2/1)	45·00	
d. Extended right fraction bar (R. 1/1 or R. 2/1)	45·00	
e. White flaw in Queen s hair (R. 1/3 or R. 2/3)	45·00	
B. Watermark inverted		
SB7a Pane of 6×½d. (containing No. S4c×6) *(11.58)*	5·50	6·50

Whiter Paper		
A. Watermark upright		
SB8 Pane of 6×½d. (containing No. S5×6) *(29.7.62)*	9·00	15·00
b. Dot on left fraction bar (R. 2/1)	55·00	
c. Extended right fraction bar (R. 1/1 or R. 2/1)	55·00	
B. Watermark inverted		
SB8a Pane of 6×½d. (containing No. S5c×6) *(29.7.62)*	9·00	15·00

* Booklet error. See General Notes.
For illustration of No. SB7e see No. SB4c.

SB7b

SB7c, SB8b, SB16c, SB17c
(Cyl. E12 no dot)

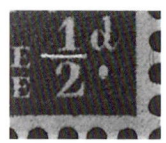

SB7d, SB8c, SB16b, SB17b
(Cyl. E12 no dot)

Booklet Cylinder Numbers
Panes of six (21-row cylinders)

Cream paper

Cylinder No.	No Dot	Dot
E4 With erroneous dot	65·00*	65·00
E4 No dot with smudge	80·00*	†
E4 Smudge removed	70·00*	†
E4 T With erroneous dot	65·00*	65·00
E4 T No dot with smudge	70·00*	†
E4 T Smudge removed	65·00*	†
E11	55·00	65·00
E11T	60·00	60·00
E12	65·00	65·00
E12T	70·00	70·00

* For explanation see notes below No. SB1.

Whiter paper

E11	90·00	90·00
E11T	90·00	90·00
E12	90·00	90·00
E12T	90·00	90·00

Specimen overprints from the NPM
Booklet pane of six. Perf. 15×14, watermark Type W.**24** inverted
Each stamp handstamped "SPECIMEN" (15×2½ mm.)	£1250

½d. Wilding Booklet Panes **SB**

½d. Panes of four, cream paper. *Wmk* Crowns
From 1s. Booklets K3/a for use in "E" slot machines and 2s. Booklets N2/3.

	Perf. Type
A. Watermark upright	AP
SB9 Pane of 4×½d. (containing No. S4×4) *(13.8.59)*	6·00
B. Watermark inverted	
SB9a Pane of 4×½d. (containing No. S4c×4) *(13.8.59)*	6·00

Booklet Cylinder Number
Cylinder No. E3 was used, but it does not appear in the finished booklets.

Specimen overprints from the NPM
Booklet pane of four. Perf. 15×14, watermark Type W.**24** inverted
Each stamp handstamped "Specimen" (13×2 mm.) £1250

½d. Panes of four, cream or whiter paper *Wmk* Crowns sideways
From 2s. Booklets N4/20

Cream Paper

	Perf. Type			
A. Watermark Crown to left	I	I(½v)	AP	AP(2E)
SB10 Pane of 4×½d. (containing No. S4d×4) *(26.5.61)*	25·00	60·00	15·00	40·00
B. Watermark Crown to right				
SB10a Pane of 4×½d. (containing No. S4e×4) *(26.5.61)*	25·00	60·00	15·00	†

Whiter Paper

A. Watermark Crown to left				
SB11 Pane of 4×½d. (containing No. S5a×4) *(5.6.62)*	30·00	55·00	12·00	45·00
B. Watermark Crown to right				
SB11a Pane of 4×½d. (containing No. S5b×4) *(5.6.62)*	30·00	55·00	12·00	†

Booklet Cylinder Number

Pane of four	Perf Type I
Cylinder No.	No Dot
E.13 (wmk Crown to left)	£120

Due to the width of the selvedge, the "3" was normally trimmed off.

Specimen overprints from the NPM
Booklet pane of four. Perf. 15×14, watermark Type W.**24**
Wmk Crown to left, perf type AP(2E)
Each stamp handstamped "Specimen" (13×2 mm.) £1000

Imprimaturs from the NPM or BPMA
Booklet panes of six. Imperforate, watermark Type W.**24**

Two Panes as Nos. SB7 or SB8 arranged *tête-bêche* (Cream or whiter paper)	£14000
Two Panes as Nos. SB7 or SB8 arranged *tête-bêche* with cylinder E4. (Cream paper)	£14500
Two Panes as Nos. SB7 or SB8 arranged *tête-bêche* with cylinder E12. (Whiter *paper*)	£14500

Booklet panes of four. Imperforate, watermark Type W.**24**

Two as No. SB9 panes arranged vertically *tête-bêche* with a 12mm horizontal gutter margin between	£10000
Two as No. SB9 panes arranged vertically *tête-bêche* with a 12mm horizontal gutter margin between with cylinder E3 (Cream paper)	£10500

SB12

SB13

½d. and 2½d. *Se-tenant* panes of four, *Wmk* Crowns
from Holiday Booklets,

Chalk-surfaced paper. 3×½d. with 2½d. from 2s. Booklet NR1/1a

	Perf. Type		
A. Watermark upright	I	I(½v)	AP
SB12 Pane of ½d./2½d. (containing No. S6×3, S58) *(15.7.63)*	15.00	25·00	9·00
b. Screen damage on 2½d. (R. 2/2)	†	†	55·00
B. Watermark inverted			
SB12a Pane of ½d./2½d. (containing No. S6a×3, S58a) *(15.7.63)*	15·00	25·00	9·00
ab. Daffodil flaw on ½d. (R. 2/1)	†	†	60·00
ac. Daffodil trumpet flaw on ½d (R. 1/2)	†	†	60·00

SB12b

SB12ab Bottom left stamp of pane (2½d. to right)

SB12ac Upper right stamp of pane

63

SB Wilding Booklet Panes ½d.

Whiter paper. Wmk Crowns sideways
Pair of ½d. with pair of 2½d. from 2s. Booklet NR2

		Perf. Type	
A. Watermark Crown to left	I	I(½v)	AP
SB13 Pane of 2× ½d./2½d. (containing Nos. S5a×2, S57c×2) (1.7.64)	12·00	20·00	2·25
b. Comma flaw (R. 1/2)	35·00	†	†
c. Spot to right of d (R. 1/1)	35·00	†	†
d. Rose flaw (R. 1/2)	†	†	30·00
e. "P" for "D" (R. 2/1)	†	†	35·00
f. Wreath flaw (R. 2/1)	†	†	30·00
g. White spot above "2" (R. 2/2)	†	†	30·00
B. Watermark Crown to right			
SB13a Pane of 2× ½d./2 ½d. (containing Nos. S5b×2, S57d×2) (1.7.64)	12·00	20·00	2·25
ab. Rose stem flaw (R. 1/2)	†	†	35·00
ac. Frame flaw (R. 1/2)	†	†	40·00
ad. White spot by daffodil (R. 1/1)	†	†	40·00

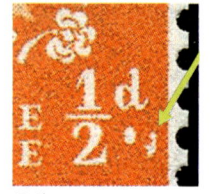

SB13b Upper right stamp of pane

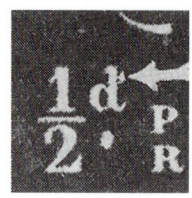

SB13c Upper left stamp of pane

SB13d Upper right stamp of pane

SB13e Lower left stamp of pane

SB13f Lower left stamp of pane

SB13g Lower right stamp of pane

SB13ab Upper right stamp of pane

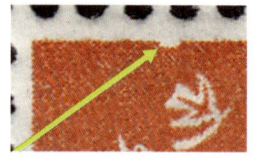

SB13ac Upper right stamp of pane

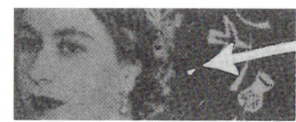

SB13ad Upper left stamp of pane

Booklet Cylinder Numbers
Panes of four *Perf. Type* I.
Cylinder Nos. 3 (½d.) and 2 (2½d.) were used, but they do not appear in the finished booklets NR1/1a but the following exists from the Holiday Booklet NR2 on whiter paper, *Perf. Type* I, watermark crowns to right.

Cylinder Nos.	No Dot
E14 (½d.), J15 (2½d.)	35·00

Due to the width of the selvedge "E" and "J" were normally trimmed off.

Imprimaturs from the NPM or BPMA
Se-tenant booklet panes of four.
Imperforate, watermark Type W.**24**

Two panes as No. SB12 arranged vertically *tête-bêche* with binding margin at top and bottom	£12250
Two panes as No. SB12 arranged vertically *tête-bêche* with binding margin at top and bottom with cylinders 3 + 2	£13000
Two panes as No. SB13 arranged sideways *tête-bêche* with binding margin at top and *bottom*	£12250
Two panes as No. SB13 arranged sideways *tête-bêche* with binding margin at top and *bottom* with cylinders J15 + E14	£13000

½d. Panes of six, graphite lines as Type SA8, shown above No. S3. *Wmk* Crowns

From 3s. Booklets M13g/15g, M19g/21g and 5s. Booklets H39g, H43g and H46g

	Perf. Type	
A. Watermark upright	I	Ie
SB14 Pane of 6×½d. (containing No. S7×6) (4.8.59)	65·00	75·00
b. White flaw in Queen's hair (R. 1/3 or 2/3)	£120	
B. Watermark inverted		
SB14a Pane of 6× ½d. (containing No. S7a×6) (4.8.59)	25·00	30·00

For illustration of No. SB14b, see No. SB4c.

Booklet Cylinder Numbers
Panes of six (21-row cylinder)

Cylinder No.	No Dot	Dot
E4	£180	£180
E4 T	£180	£180

Imprimaturs from the NPM or BPMA
Booklet panes of six. Imperforate, watermark Type W.**24** with graphite lines as **SA8**.

Two panes as No. SB14 arranged *tête-bêche*	£14000
Two panes as No. SB14 arranged *tête-bêche* with cylinder E4.	£14500

½d., 1d. **Wilding Booklet Panes** **SB**

½d. Panes of six, two phosphor bands reacting green applied by photogravure. *Wmk* Crowns

From 3s. Booklets M25p, M28p/29p and M37p(a) and 5s. Booklet H46p

	Perf. Type	
A. Watermark upright	*I*	*Ie*
SB15 Pane of 6×½d. (containing No. S9×6) *(14.8.60)*	35·00	45·00
B. Watermark inverted		
SB15a Pane of 6×½d. (containing No. S9a×6) *(14.8.60)*	95·00	£110

Booklet Cylinder Number
Panes of six (21-row cylinder)

Cylinder No.	No Dot	Dot
E11	£180	£180
E11 T	£180	£180

Specimen overprints from the NPM
Booklet pane of six, perf. 15×14, watermark type W.**24** upright.

Each stamp handstamped "Specimen" (13×2 mm). £1250

½d. Panes of six, two phosphor bands reacting blue applied by photogravure. Cream or whiter paper

From 3s. Booklets M33p, M36p, M37p(b), M38p/39p, M43p/47p, M49p/53p, M55p/61p, M64p/74p, and 5s. Booklets H49p, H51p/52p and H54p/74p

Cream Paper	Perf. Type	
A. Watermark upright	*I*	*Ie*
SB16 Pane of 6×½d. (containing No. S10×6) *(3.61)*	7·00	9·00
b. Extended right fraction bar (R. 1/1 or 2/1)	55·00	
c. Dot on left fraction bar (R. 1/1 or 2/1)	55·00	
d. One band on each stamp	£450	
B. Watermark inverted		
SB16a Pane of 6×½d. (containing No. S10a×6) *(3.61)*	10·00	12·00

Whiter Paper		
A. Watermark upright		
SB17 Pane of 6×½d. (containing No. S11×6) *(3.6.63)*	30·00	40·00
b. Extended right fraction bar (R. 1/1 or 2/1)	80·00	
c. Dot on left fraction bar (R. 1/1 or 2/1)	80·00	
B. Watermark inverted		
SB17a Pane of 6×½d. (containing No. S11c×6) *(3.6.63)*	30·00	40·00

For illustrations of Nos. SB16b/c and SB17b/c, see Nos. SB7c/d.

Booklet Cylinder Numbers
Panes of six (21-row cylinder)

Cream paper		
Cylinder No.	No Dot	Dot
E12	90·00	90·00
E12 T	90·00	90·00
Whiter paper		
E12	£100	£100
E12 T	£100	£100

Specimen overprints from the NPM
Booklet pane of six. Perf. 15×14, watermark Type W.**24** upright.

Each stamp handstamped "Specimen" (15×2½ mm). £1250

½d. Panes of four, two phosphor bands reacting blue applied by letterpress. Cream or whiter paper *Wmk* Crowns Sideways

From 2s. Booklets N4p, N8p/10p, N12p/20p

Cream Paper	Perf. Type			
A. Watermark Crown to left	*I*	*I(½v)*	*AP*	*AP(2E)*
SB18 Pane of 4×½d. (containing No. S10b×4) *(14.7.61)*	75·00	£100	45·00	75·00
b. One 8 mm band on each stamp	£200	—	£120	—
B. Watermark Crown to right				
SB18a Pane of 4×½d. (containing No. S10c×4) *(14.7.61)*	75·00	£100	45·00	†
ab. One 8 mm band on each stamp	—	—	£120	†

Whiter Paper	Perf. Type			
A. Watermark Crown to left	*I*	*I(½v)*	*AP*	*AP(2E)*
SB19 Pane of 4×½d. (containing No. S11a×4) *(15.8.62)*	90·00	£130	65·00	85·00
B. Watermark Crown to right				
SB19a Pane of 4×½d. (containing No. S11b×4) *(15.8.62)*	90·00	£130	65·00	†

Booklet Cylinder Number
Pane of four Perf. Type I

Cylinder No.	
E13 (wmk Crown to left)	£180

Due to the width of the selvedge, the "3" was usually trimmed off.

Specimen overprints from the NPM
Booklet pane of four. Perf. 15×14, watermark Type W.**24** Crown to right, perf Type AP.

Each stamp handstamped "Specimen" (13×2 mm). £1000

Imprimaturs from the NPM or BPMA
Booklet panes of six. Imperforate, watermark Type W.**24**.

Two panes as No. SB15 arranged horizontally *tête-bêche*	£14000
Two panes as No. SB15 arranged horizontally *tête-bêche* with cylinder E11	£14500
Two panes as Nos. SB16 or SB17 arranged horizontally *tête-bêche* (Cream or whiter paper)	£14000
Two panes as Nos. SB16 or SB17 arranged horizontally *tête-bêche* with cylinder E12.T (Cream paper)	£14500
Two panes as No. SB18 arranged sideways *tête-bêche*	£10000
Two panes as No. SB18 arranged sideways *tête-bêche* with cylinder E.13	£10500

1d. Panes of six, *Wmk* Tudor Crown

From 5s. Booklets H7/19 and H21

	Perf. Type	
A. Watermark upright	*I*	*Ie*
SB20 Pane of 6×1d. (containing No. S13×6) *(3.54)*	35·00	40·00
b. Hair flaw (R. 1/1)	65·00	
B. Watermark inverted		
SB20a Pane of 6×1d. (containing No. S13a×6) *(3.54)*	75·00	85·00
ab. Extended leaf on shamrock (R. 2/1)	90·00	

SB Wilding Booklet Panes *1d.*

SB20b, SB26d
(Cyl. F4 no dot)

SB20ab, SB26ad, SB30ac, SB31ad, SB39ac, SB40ac, SB41ab, SB42ab, SB49ab, SB54ab

The "Extended leaf on shamrock" is a multipositive flaw on panes with all watermarks and phosphors (Cyls. F3, F4 and F10 from the dot pane)

Booklet Cylinder Numbers
Panes of six from 5s. Booklets

Cylinder No.	No Dot	Dot
F4	£120	60·00*

*Contains the dot in serif flaw (R. 1/3), see below.

1d. Panes of four, *Wmk* Tudor Crown
From 1s. Booklet K1/a for use in "E" slot machines.

A. Watermark upright

		Perf. Type P
SB21	Pane of 4×1d. (containing No. S13×4) *(22.7.54)*	12·00

B. Watermark inverted

SB21a	Pane of 4×1d. (containing No. S13a×4) *(22.7.54)*	45·00

Booklet Cylinder Number
Cylinder No. F8 was used, but it does not appear in the finished booklets.

Imprimaturs from the NPM or BPMA
Booklet pane of six. Imperforate, watermark Type W.**22**

Two panes as No. SB20 arranged *tête-bêche* with cylinder F4	£14500

Booklet panes of four. Imperforate, watermark Type W.**22**

Two panes as No. SB21 arranged vertically *tête-bêche* with a 12mm horizontal gutter margin between	£10000
Two panes as No. SB21 arranged vertically *tête-bêche* with a 12mm horizontal gutter margin between with cylinder F8	£10500

1d. Panes of two, *Wmk* Tudor Crown
From 1s. Booklet E1 for use in experimental "D" slot machines.

Watermark upright

		Perf. Type			
		I	I(½v)	E	E(½v)
SB22	Pane of 2×1d. (containing No. S13×2) *(2.9.53)*	6·00	10·00	5·00	12·00
	a. Shamrock flaw on cyl. 2 No dot pane (as on No. S13c)	†	†	45·00	†

Made up from columns 1 and 2 from sheets.

Booklet Cylinder Numbers
Panes of two (from sheets)

	Perf. Type	
	I	E
Cylinder No.	No Dot	Dot
1	60·00	70·00
	Perf. Type	
	E	
2	60·00*	£120

SB23

1d. *Se-tenant* with printed labels, *Wmk* Tudor Crown
"MINIMUM INLAND PRINTED PAPER RATE 1½d."
3×1d. Tudor Crown
From 2s.6d. Booklet F15

		Perf. Type	
		I	Ie
A. Watermark upright			
SB23	Pane of 3×1d. (containing S13×3) *(3.54)*	£500	£500
c.	Dot in serif (R. 1/3)	£600	
d.	Daffodil flaw (R. 1/1)	£550	
B. Watermark inverted			
SB23a	Pane of 3×1d. (containing S13a×3) *(3.54)*	£500	£500
ab.	Spacing error	—	

All issues of label panes were printed on 20-row cylinders to accommodate the format of the stamps and labels on alternate rows. On panes SB23 and SB24, the labels were printed in a separate operation by letterpress whereas on panes SB25 and SB29 the labels were printed in photogravure, similar to the stamps.

The "Minimum" label has a height of 15mm and is the same letterpress plate as that used for the George VI issue, QB19. Accordingly, the spacing error, whereby the distance between "RATE" and "1½d" on the third label measures 2mm, occurs on the cylinder panes, described as "Spacing error" and the overall height of that label measures 16mm.

Rarely, sheets of the stamps prior to printing the labels by letterpress were rotated top to bottom resulting in the inverted watermark pane diagonally opposite having the spacing error and the cylinder pane being the normal measurement, described as "Spacing corrected".

In some cases of sheet preparation for this March 1954 booklet edition, a scissor cut was made in the left selvedge (perf 1½v) and the bottom selvedge was torn off by hand resulting in torn bottom perforations.

SB23c, SB24ba, SB24c, SB25b, SB26b, SB29b, SB30e, SB31b, SB41b, SB42b, SB49b, SB54b

Dot in serif of "1". Right-hand stamp
This is a multipositive flaw which is found only in booklet panes, stamp 3 in either the first or second horizontal rows; all watermarks and phosphors on the dot cylinder panes F3, F4 and F10 also on the ordinary panes from cylinders F3, F5, F6, F9 and F10. On cylinder F3 dot the flaw exists as a retouched state leaving the dot as a blemish and later the mark was removed. The later state occurs only in the position R. 2/3 and is not listed separately. Note that the flaw is present on all panes of six (R. 1/3) with cylinder number in bottom position.

66

1d. Wilding Booklet Panes **SB**

Booklet Cylinder Numbers
Panes with printed labels from 2s.6d. Booklet F15

Cylinder No.	No Dot	Dot
F5	†	£1750
F6 Spacing error	£650	£650
F6 Spacing corrected	—	†
F6 Spacing error and perf 1½v	†	£800

AVC pane with labels only (see Appendix HA, general notes) £1500

SB24

Cylinder No.	No Dot	Dot
F6 perf 1½v (normal setting)	£400	†
F6 (modified setting)	£300	£300

On panes SB25 and SB29, the labels were printed by photogravure instead of letterpress.
AVC pane with labels only, normal setting (see Appendix HA, General Notes) £350

SB25, SB29

1d. *Se-tenant* with printed labels, *Wmk* Tudor Crown
"PLEASE POST EARLY IN THE DAY"
3×1d. Tudor Crown
From 2s.6d. Booklets F16/25

	Perf. Type	
Normal label setting	I	Ie
A. Watermark upright		
SB24 Pane of 3×1d. (containing S13×3) (4.54)	50·00	60·00
c. Dot in serif (R. 1/3)	70·00	
d. Daffodil flaw (R. 1/1)	£100	
B. Watermark inverted		
SB24a Pane of 3×1d. (containing S13a×3) (4.54)	50·00	60·00
Modified label setting	Perf. Type	
A. Watermark upright	I	Ie
SB24A Pane of 3×1d. (containing S13×3) (1.55)	£120	£140
b. Dot in serif (R. 1/3)	£150	
c. Daffodil flaw (R. 1/1)	£170	
B. Watermark inverted		
SB24Aa Pane 3×1d. (containing S13a×3) (1.55)	£120	£140

Normal Setting   Modified setting

In the normal label setting, the space between "IN" and "THE" measures 1½ mm, whereas in the modified setting the distance is 1mm and this is only found on the majority of the Jan. 1955 edition (Booklet F25).

In some cases of sheet preparation for the April 1954 edition, a scissor cut was made in the left selvedge (perf 1½v) and the bottom selvedge was torn off by hand resulting in bottom torn perforations.

Booklet Cylinder Numbers
Panes with printed labels from 2s.6d. Booklets F16/F25

Cylinder No.	No Dot	Dot
F6 setting)	95·00	75·00

1d. *Se-tenant* with printed labels, *Wmk* Tudor Crown
"PACK YOUR PARCELS SECURELY" (1st LABEL)
"ADDRESS YOUR LETTERS CORRECTLY" (2nd label)
"AND POST EARLY IN THE DAY" (3rd label)
3×1d. Tudor Crown
From 2s.6d. Booklets F26/36

	Perf. Type	
A. Watermark upright	I	Ie
SB25 Pane of 3×1d. (containing No. S13×3) (1.55)	55·00	65·00
b. Dot in serif (R. 1/3)	80·00	
c. Daffodil flaw (R. 1/1)	80·00	
B. Watermark inverted		
SB25a Pane of 3×1d. (containing No. S13a×3) (1.55)	50·00	55·00

On panes SB25 and SB29, the labels were printed by photogravure instead of letterpress.

SB23d, SB24d, SB24Ac, SB25c, SB29c
(Cyl. F6 no dot)

Booklet Cylinder Numbers
Panes with printed labels from 2s.6d. Booklets F26/36

Cylinder No.	No Dot	Dot
F6	£120	£120

Imprimaturs from the NPM or BPMA
Booklet panes with printed labels. Imperforate, watermark Type W.**22**

Single pane (wmk upright) as No. SB24 but labels blank	£3250
Single pane (wmk inverted) as No. SB24 but labels blank	£3250
Two panes as No. SB24 but labels blank arranged tête-bêche	£7000
Two panes as No. SB24 but labels blank arranged tête-bêche with cylinder F6	£7500
Single pane (wmk upright) as No. SB25	£3250

67

SB Wilding Booklet Panes 1d.

Single pane (wmk inverted) as No. SB25	£3250
Two panes as No. SB25 arranged *tête-bêche*	£7000
Two panes as No. SB25 arranged *tête-bêche* with cylinder F6	£7500

1d. Panes of six, *Wmk* St Edward's Crown
From 3s. Booklets M1/10 and 5s. Booklets H17/37

		Perf. Type	
A. Watermark upright		I	Ie
SB26	Pane of 6×1d. (containing No. S14×6) *(8.55)*	5·00	6·00
b.	Dot in serif (R. 1/3 or 2/3)	50·00	
c.	Dew drop (R. 1/1 or 2/1)	50·00	
d.	Hair flaw (R. 1/1)	60·00	
B. Watermark inverted			
SB26a	Pane of 6×1d. (containing No. S14b×6) *(8.55)*	5·00	6·00
ab.	Spot on "d" (R. 1/1 or 2/1)	50·00	
ac.	White flaw by rose (R. 1/2 or 2/2)	50·00	
ad.	Extended leaf on shamrock (R. 1/1 or 2/1)	35·00	
ae.	Rose flaw (R. 1/1 or 2/1)	50·00	

For illustrations of No. SB26b, see No. SB23c, for No. SB26d, see No. SB20b and for No. SB26ad, see No. SB20ab.

SB26c, SB30d, SB39b Later retouched on Crowns and phosphor (Cyl. F3 dot)

SB26ab, SB30ab, SB31ac SB39ab, SB40ab (Cyl. F3 dot)

SB26ac (Cyl. F3 dot)

SB26ae, SB30ad, SB39ad, SB40ad (Cyl. F3 no dot)

Booklet Cylinder Numbers
Panes of six

Cylinder No.	No Dot	Dot
F3	50·00	60·00*
F3T	55·00	55·00
F4	55·00	50·00*

Cylinder F3 contained 21 rows so that cylinder numbers adjoin either the top (T) or the bottom row. It was used in all 5s. Booklets H31/37. Cylinder F4 was a 20-row cylinder and used for the 5s. Booklets H17/30.

1d. Panes of four, *Wmk* St Edward's Crown
From 1s. Booklets K2/b for use in "E" slot machines and 2s. Booklet N1

		Perf. Type	
A. Watermark upright		AP	P
SB27	Pane of 4×1d. (containing No. S14×4) *(5.7.56)*	10·00	10·00
b.	Spur to shamrock (R. 2/1)	55·00	†
B. Watermark inverted			
SB27a	Pane of 4×1d. (containing No. S14b×4) *(5.7.56)*	10·00	10·00

SB27b, SB32b Later retouched on Crowns wmk.

Booklet Cylinder Numbers
Cylinder Nos. F8 and F11 were used, but they do not appear in the finished booklets.

Imprimaturs from the NPM or BPMA
Booklet panes of six. Imperforate, watermark Type W.**23**

Two panes as No. SB26 arranged *tête-bêche* with cylinder F4.	£14500
Single pane with "hair flaw" variety R.1/1	£6000

Booklet panes of four. Imperforate, watermark Type W.**23**

Two panes as No. SB27 arranged vertically *tête-bêche* with a 12mm horizontal gutter margin between	£10000
Two panes as No. SB27 arranged vertically *tête-bêche* with a 12mm horizontal gutter margin between with cylinder F8	£10500

1d. Panes of two, *Wmk* St Edward's Crown
From 1s. Booklet E2 for use in experimental "D" slot machines.

		Perf.Type	
Watermark upright		E	E(½v)
SB28	Pane of 2×1d. (containing No. S14×2) *(11.57)*	25·00	40·00

Made up from columns 1 and 2 from sheets.

Booklet Cylinder Numbers
Panes of two (from sheets). Perf. Type E

Cylinder No.	No Dot	Dot
1	£200	£200

1d. Se-tenant with printed labels, *Wmk* St Edward's Crown
"PACK YOUR PARCELS SECURELY" (1st label),
"ADDRESS YOUR LETTERS CORRECTLY" (2nd label)
"AND POST EARLY IN THE DAY" (3rd label)
From 2s.6d. Booklets F33/52

		Perf. Type	
A. Watermark upright		I	Ie
SB29	Pane of 3×1d. (containing No. S14×3) *(8.55)*	18·00	19·00
b.	Dot in serif (R. 1/3)	40·00	
c.	Daffodil flaw (R. 1/1)	50·00	
B. Watermark inverted			
SB29a	Pane of 3×1d. (containing No. S14b×3) *(8.55)*	18·00	19·00

68

1d. Wilding Booklet Panes

For illustration of No. SB29b see No. SB23c and for No. SB29c see No. SB25c.

Booklet Cylinder Numbers
Panes with printed labels from 2s.6d. Booklets F33/52

Cylinder No.	No Dot	Dot
F6	75·00	60·00
F9	£130	£130

Cylinder F6 was used for the 2s.6d. Booklets F33/40 and part of F41/52 and F9 for 2s.6d. Booklets F41/52.

Imprimaturs from the NPM or BPMA
Booklet panes with printed labels. Imperforate, watermark Type W.**23**

Two panes as No. SB29 arranged *tête-bêche*	£7000
Two panes as No. SB29 arranged *tête-bêche* with cylinder F6	£7500
Single pane (wmk upright) as No. SB29	£3250
Single pane (wmk upright) as No. SB29 with "Daffodil flaw" R.1/1	£3750

1d. Panes of six, cream or whiter paper. *Wmk* Crowns
From 3s. Booklets M9(b)/(e), M10/74, 4s.6d. Booklets L59/65, 5s. Booklets H35(b)/(e), H36(a) and H37/74 and 10s. Booklets X1/14

Cream Paper	Perf. Type I	le
A. Watermark upright		
SB30 Pane of 6×1d. (containing No. S16×6) *(11.58)*	7·00	9·00
b. Imperf. pane*	£6000	
c. Part perf. pane*	£4500	
d. Dew drop (R. 1/1 or 2/1)	45·00	
e. Dot in serif (R. 2/3)	40·00	
B. Watermark inverted		
SB30a Pane of 6×1d. (containing No. S16d×6) *(11.58)*	7·00	9·00
ab. Spot on "d" (R. 1/1 or 2/1)	45·00	
ac. Extended leaf on shamrock (R. 1/1 or 2/1)	35·00	
ad. Rose flaw (R. 1/1 or 2/1)	40·00	

Whiter Paper	Perf. Type I	le
A. Watermark upright		
SB31 Pane of 6×1d. (containing No. S17×6) *(29.7.62)*	10·00	12·00
b. Dot in serif (R. 2/3)	35·00	
B. Watermark inverted		
SB31a Pane of 6×1d. (containing No. S17c×6) *(29.7.62)*	10·00	12·00
ab. Part perf. pane*	£4500	
ac. Spot on "d" (R. 1/1 or 2/1)	60·00	
ad. Extended leaf on shamrock (R. 1/1 or 2/1)	45·00	
ae. Imperf pane*	£6000	

* Booklet Errors See General Notes.

SB30b

SB30c

For illustrations of No. SB30d see No. SB26c; for Nos. SB30ab and SB31ac see No. SB26ab; for Nos. SB30ac and SB31ad see No. SB20ab and for No. SB30ad see No. SB26ae.

On the cream paper the dot in serif flaw (Cyl. F3 dot) was removed by retouching but a smudged state exists.

For illustration of No. SB30e, see No SB23c. On white paper the flaw exists from Cyl. F10 dot.

Booklet Cylinder Numbers
Panes of six (21-row cylinders)

Cream paper

Cylinder No.	No Dot	Dot
F3	50·00	50·00*
F3 T	50·00	50·00
F10	50·00	50·00*
F10 T	75·00	50·00

Whiter paper

F3	80·00	80·00
F3 T	80·00	80·00
F10	80·00	80·00
F10 T	80·00	80·00

Specimen overprints from the NPM
Booklet pane of six. Perf. 15×14, watermark Type W.**24**

Each stamp handstamped "SPECIMEN" (13×2 mm.) wmk. upright	£1250
Each stamp handstamped "SPECIMEN" (15×2½ mm.) wmk. inverted	£1250

SB Wilding Booklet Panes 1d.

1d. Panes of four, cream paper. Wmk Crowns
From 1s. Booklets K3/a for use in "E" slot machines and 2s. Booklets N2/3.

A. Watermark upright	Perf. Type AP
SB32 Pane of 4×1d. (containing No. S16×4) *(13.8.59)*	8·00
b. Spur to shamrock (R. 2/1)	40·00

B. Watermark inverted

SB32a Pane of 4×1d. (containing No. S16d×4) *(13.8.59)*	8·00

For illustration of No. SB32b see No. SB27b.

Booklet Cylinder Number
Cylinder No. F11 was used, but it does not appear in the finished booklets.

Imprimaturs from the NPM or BPMA
Booklet pane of six. Imperforate, watermark Type W.**24**

Two panes as Nos. SB30 or SB31 arranged *tête-bêche* (cream of whiter paper)	£14000
Two panes as Nos. SB30 or SB31 arranged *tête-bêche* (cream of white paper) with cylinder F3 (Cream paper)	£14500

Booklet panes of four. Imperforate, watermark Type W.**24**

Two panes as No. SB32 arranged vertically *tête-bêche* with a 12mm horizontal gutter margin between	£10000
Two panes as No. SB32 arranged vertically *tête-bêche* with a 12mm horizontal gutter margin between cylinder F11	£10500

Specimen overprints from the NPM
Booklet pane of four. Perf. 15×14, watermark Type W.**24** upright

Each stamp handstamped "SPECIMEN" (13×2 mm.)	£1000

1d. Panes of four, cream or whiter paper. Wmk Crowns sideways
From 2s. Booklets N4/20

Cream paper

A. Watermark Crown to left	Perf. Type			
	I	I(½v)	AP	AP(2E)
SB33 Pane of 4×1d. (containing No. S16e×4) *(26.5.61)*	20·00	80·00	12·00	50·00

B. Watermark Crown to right

	I	I(½v)	AP	AP(2E)
SB33a Pane of 4×1d. (containing No. S16f×4) *(26.5.61)*	20·00	80·00	12·00	†

Whiter Paper
A. Watermark Crown to left

	I	I(½v)	AP	AP(2E)
SB34 Pane of 4×1d. (containing No. S17a×4) *(5.6.62)*	30·00	£100	12·00	60·00

B. Watermark Crown to right

	I	I(½v)	AP	AP(2E)
SB34a Pane of 4×1d. (containing No. S17b×4) *(5.6.62)*	30·00	£100	12·00	†

Booklet Cylinder Numbers
Pane of four, Perf Type I

Cyl. No F12 (wmk Crown to left)	£170

Due to the width of the selvedge, the "2" was normally trimmed off.

Specimen overprints from the NPM
Booklet pane of four. Perf. 15×14, watermark Type W.**24** Perf. Type AP

Each stamp handstamped "SPECIMEN" (13×2 mm.)	£1000

SB35, SB37, SB45, SB47, SB50, SB52, SB55, SB57
(1d. values at left)

SB36, SB38, SB46, SB48, SB51, SB53, SB56, SB58
(1d. values at right)

1d. and 3d. Se-tenant panes of four, Pair of 1d. with pair of 3d. Whiter paper. Wmk Crowns sideways.
From 2s. Booklets N21/27

Panes SB35 and SB37 Panes of four with 1d. at left
Panes SB36 and SB38 Panes of four with 1d. at right

A. Watermark Crown to left

	Perf. Type			
	I	I(½v)	AP	AP(2E)
SB35 Pane of 2×1d./3d. (containing Nos. S17a×2, S71a×2) *(16.8.65)*	15·00	†	12·00	†
SB36 Pane of 2×3d./1d. (containing Nos. S71a×2, S17a×2) *(16.8.65)*	15·00	80·00*	13·00	†

*The I (½v) pane has the thistle flaw on 1d. (R.2/2).

B. Watermark Crown to right

	I	I(½v)	AP	AP(2E)
SB37 Pane of 2×1d./3d. (containing Nos. S17b×2, S71b×2) *(16.8.65)*	15·00	90·00	12·00	£250
SB38 Pane of 2×3d./1d. (containing Nos. S71b×2, S17b×2) *(16.8.65)*	15·00	†	13·00	£250
a. "R" flaw on 1d. (R. 2/2)	†	†	60·00	†

70

1d. Wilding Booklet Panes SB

Perf AP(2E). It is known that this perforator format was not used for this issue, but was used for later phosphor issues. Accordingly, these rare panes are from booklets N30pc, N31pc and N32pc, where the *se-tenant* pane has phosphor omitted.

SB36a, SB46c, SB51, SB56
Large white flaw to right of left thistle. Occurs on bottom right stamp of l(½v) pane with 3d. at left

SB38a, SB48c, SB53c, SB58a, SB58ba Flaw on P which appears as R and occurs on bottom right stamp of pane with 3d. at left

Booklet Cylinder Numbers
Pane of four (24-row single-pane cylinder of 480 stamps, sideways).
From 1d./3d./ *se-tenant* pane Perf. Type I, wmk Crown to left

Cylinder No.	No Dot
F13 (1d.), K22 (3d.)	65·00

1d. Panes of six, graphite lines as Type SA8. Wmk Crowns
From 3s. Booklets M13g/15g, M19g/21g and 5s. Booklets H39g, H43g and H46g

	Perf. Type I	le
A. Watermark upright		
SB39 Pane of 6×1d. (containing No. S18×6) *(4.8.59)*	30·00	35·00
b. Dew drop (R. 1/1 or 2/1)	75·00	
B. Watermark inverted		
SB39a Pane of 6×1d. (containing No. S18a×6) *(4.8.59)*	20·00	22·00
ab. Spot on "d" (R. 1/1 or 2/1)	75·00	
ac. Extended leaf on shamrock (R. 1/1 or 2/1)	65·00	
ad. Rose flaw (R. 1/1 or 2/1)	75·00	

For illustrations of No. SB39b see No. SB26c; for Nos. SB39ab/ad see Nos. SB26ab, SB20ab and SB26ae.

Booklet Cylinder Numbers
Panes of six (21-row cylinder)

Cylinder No.	No Dot	Dot
F3	£180	£180
F3 T	£180	£180

Imprimaturs from the NPM or BPMA
Booklet panes of six. Imperforate, watermark Type W.**24** with graphite lines Type **SA8**.

Two panes as No. SB39 arranged *tête-bêche*	£14000
do. with cylinder F3	£14500

1d. Panes of six, 6×1d. with two phosphor bands reacting green applied by photogravure. Wmk Crowns
From 3s. Booklets M25p, M28p/29p and M37p(a) and 5s. Booklet H46p

	Perf. Type I	le
A. Watermark upright		
SB40 Pane of 6×1d. (containing No. S20×6) *(14.8.60)*	35·00	40·00
b. One 8mm. band on each stamp	£200	
B. Watermark inverted		
SB40a Pane of 6×1d. (containing No. S20a×6) *(14.8.60)*	45·00	50·00
ab. Spot on "d" (R. 1/1 or 2/1)	95·00	
ac. Extended leaf on shamrock (R. 1/1 or 2/1)	95·00	
ad. Rose flaw (R. 1/1 or 2/1)	95·00	
ae. One 8mm. band on each stamp	£200	
af. Stamps 1 and 4 with one 6mm. band, others with one 8mm band	£200	

For illustrations of Nos. SB40ab/ad see Nos. SB26ab, SB20ab and SB26ae.

Booklet Cylinder Numbers
Panes of six (21-row cylinder)

Cylinder No.	No Dot	Dot
F3	£170	£170
F3 T	£170	£170

Specimen overprints from the NPM
Booklet pane of six. Perf. 15×14, watermark Type W.**24** inverted Each stamp handstamped "SPECIMEN" (13×2 mm.) £1250

Imprimaturs from the NPM or BPMA
Booklet panes of six. Imperforate, watermark Type W.**24**.

Two panes as No. SB40 arranged horizontally *tête-bêche*	£14000
do. with cylinder F3.	£14500

1d. Panes of six, with two phosphor bands reacting blue applied in photogravure. Cream or whiter paper. Wmk Crowns
From 3s. Booklets M33p, M36p, M37p(b), M38p/9p, M43p/7p, M49p/53p, M55p/61p, M64p/74p, 4s.6d. Booklets L59p/60p(a), L61p(a), L62p(a) and 5s. Booklets H49p, H51p/2p, H54p/74p

Cream Paper

	Perf. Type I	le
A. Watermark upright		
SB41 Pane of 6×1d. (containing No. S21×6) *(3.61)*	7·00	9·00
b. Dot in serif (R. 2/3)	50·00	
B. Watermark inverted		
SB41a Pane of 6×1d. (containing No. S21a×6) *(3.61)*	8·00	10·00
ab. Extended leaf on shamrock (R. 1/1 or 2/1)	55·00	

Whiter Paper

	Perf. Type I	le
A. Watermark upright		
SB42 Pane of 6×1d. (containing No. S22×6) *(3.6.63)*	12·00	15·00
b. Dot in serif (R. 2/3)	60·00	
c. One 8mm band on each stamp	—	
B. Watermark inverted		
SB42a Pane of 6×1d. (containing No. S22c×6) *(3.6.63)*	15·00	18.00
ab. Extended leaf on shamrock (R. 1/1 or 2/1)	65·00	
ac. One 8mm band on each stamp	—	

For illustrations of Nos. SB41b and SB42b see No. SB23c; for Nos. SB41ab and SB42ab see No. SB20ab.

Booklet Cylinder Numbers
Panes of six (21-row cylinders).

Cream paper

Cylinder No.	No Dot	Dot
F10	£100	£100
F10 T	£100	£100

Whiter paper

	No Dot	Dot
F10	£120	£120
F10 T	£120	£120

Specimen overprints from the NPM
Booklet pane of six. Perf. 15×14, watermark Type W.**24** inverted Each stamp handstamped "SPECIMEN" (15×2½ mm.) £1250

71

SB Wilding Booklet Panes 1d.

1d. Panes of four with Two phosphor bands, reacting blue. applied by letterpress. Cream or whiter paper. *Wmk* Crowns sideways
From 2s. Booklets N4p, N8p/10p, N12p/20p

Cream Paper

		Perf. Type		
A. Watermark Crown to left	I	I(½v)	AP	AP(2E)
SB43 Pane of 4×1d. (containing No. S21b×4) *(14.7.61)*	25·00	90·00	18·00	45·00
b. One 8mm. band on each stamp	—	—	85·00	—
B. Watermark Crown to right				
SB43a Pane of 4×1d. (containing No. S21c×4) *(14.7.61)*	25·00	90·00	18·00	†
ab. One 8mm. band on each stamp	—	—	85·00	†

Whiter Paper

A. Watermark Crown to left				
SB44 Pane of 4×1d. (containing No. S22a×4) *(15.8.62)*	30·00	£100	22·00	35·00
b. One 8mm. band on each stamp	£200	—	£200	—
B. Watermark Crown to right				
SB44a Pane of 4×1d. (containing No. S22b×4) *(15.8.62)*	30·00	£100	22·00	†
ab. One 8mm band on each stamp	£200	—	£200	†

Booklet Cylinder Numbers

Pane of four, Perf. Type I cyl. No. F12 (wmk. Crown to left)	£200

Due to the width of the selvedge, the "2" was normally trimmed off.

Specimen overprints from the NPM

Booklet pane of four. Perf. 15×14, watermark Type W.**24** Crown to right, Perf Type AP. Each stamp handstamped "SPECIMEN" (13×2 mm.)	£1000

Imprimaturs from the NPM or BPMA

Booklet panes of six. Imperforate, watermark Type W.**24**. Two panes as Nos. SB41 or SB42 arranged horizontally *tête-bêche* (cream or whiter paper)	£14000
Two panes as Nos. SB41 or SB42 arranged horizontally *tête-bêche* (cream or whiter paper) with cylinder F10. (whiter paper)	£14500
Booklet panes of four. Imperforate, watermark Type W.**24**. Two panes as No. SB43 arranged sideways *tête-bêche*	£10000
Two panes as No. SB43 arranged sideways *tête-bêche* with cylinder F12 (Cream paper)	£10500

1d. and 3d. *Se-tenant* panes of four, pair of 1d. (two bands) with pair of 3d. (one side 8mm band left or right) applied by letterpress. Phosphor bands reacting blue. *Wmk* Crowns sideways.

Whiter paper
From 2s. Booklets N21p/22p(a) and N23p(a)

Panes SB45 and SB47   Panes of four with 1d. at left
Panes SB46 and SB48   Panes of four with 1d. at right

		Perf. Type	
A. Watermark Crown to left	I	I(½v)	AP
SB45 Pane of 2×1d./3d. (containing Nos. S22a×2, S77b×2) *(16.8.65)*	£140	†	£100
SB46 Pane of 2×3d./1d. (containing Nos. S77c×2, S22a×2) *(16.8.65)*	£140	£200	£100
a. One band on each stamp	—	—*	—
b. One band on 1d. and no bands on 3d.	—	—*	—

*The I(½v) pane has the thistle flaw on the 1d. (R.2/2)

B. Watermark Crown to right			
SB47 Pane of 2×1d./3d. (containing Nos. S22b×2, S77d×2) *(16.8.65)*	£140	£200	£100
a. One band on each stamp	†	†	
SB48 Pane of 2×3d./1d. (containing Nos. S77e×2, S22b×2) *(16.8.65)*	£140	†	£100
a. One band on each stamp			
b. One band on 1d. and no bands on 3d.	—	†	—
c. "R" flaw on 1d. (R. 2/2)	†	†	£150

For illustrations of Nos. SB46 and SB48c see Nos. SB36 and SB38a.

The following illustration shows how the *se-tenant* stamps with one phosphor band on 3d. are printed and the arrows indicate where the guillotine falls. The result gives 1d. stamps with two bands and 3d. stamps with one band, either at left or right.

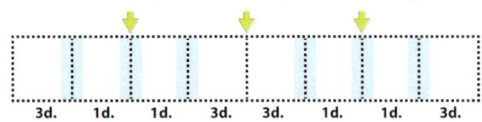

3d. 1d. 1d. 3d. 3d. 1d. 1d. 3d.

The stamps were printed sideways, as indicated by the position of the watermark.

Booklet Cylinder Numbers
Pane of four (24-row single pane cylinder of 480 stamps sideways).

From 1d./3d. *se-tenant* Perf. Type I, wmk Crown to left

Cylinder No.	No Dot
F13 (1d.), K22 (3d.)	£225

1d. Panes of six, with Two 8 mm phosphor bands reacting violet applied by photogravure. *Wmk* Crowns
From 4s.6d. Booklets L60p(b), L61p(b) and L62p(b)/65p(a) and 10s. Booklet X15p(a)

	Perf. Type	
A. Watermark upright	I	Ie
SB49 Pane of 6×1d. (containing No. S23b×6) *(9.65)*	10·00	12·00
b. Dot in serif (R. 2/3)	30·00	
B. Watermark inverted		
SB49a Pane of 6×1d. (containing No. S23c×6) *(9.65)*	10·00	12·00
ab. Extended leaf on shamrock (R. 1/1 or 2/1)	30·00	

1d. Wilding Booklet Panes SB

For illustrations of Nos. SB49b and SB49ab see Nos. SB23c and SB20ab.

Booklet Cylinder Numbers
Panes of six (21-row cylinder).

Cylinder No.	No Dot	Dot
F10	75·00	75·00
F10 T	75·00	75·00

●———

1d. and 3d Se-tenant panes of four, Pair of 1d. (two bands) with pair of 3d. (1 side 8 mm band left or right) applied by letterpress. Phosphor bands reacting violet. *Wmk* Crowns sideways

From 2s. Booklets N22pb, N23pb, N29p, N30pa, N31pc and N32pc

Panes SB50 and SB52   Panes of four with 1d. at left
Panes SB51 and SB53   Panes of four with 1d. at right

A. Watermark Crown to left

	Perf. Type			
	I	I(½v)	AP	AP(2E)
SB50 Pane of 2×1d./3d. (containing Nos. S23d×2, S78c×2) (10.65)	20·00	†	18·00	—
a. Phosphor printed both sides	†	†	—	†
d. 9·5mm band between 1d. and 3d.	£300	†	£200	†
SB51 Pane of 2×3d./1d. (containing Nos. S78d×2, S23d×2) (10.65)	20·00	75·00*	18·00	—
a. One 8mm band on each stamp	60·00	—*	50·00	†
b. One 8mm band on 1d. and no bands on 3d.	80·00	†	70·00	†
c. Phosphor printed both sides)	†	†	—	†
d. 9·5mm band between 1d. and 3d.	£300	†	£200	†

*The I(½ v) pane has the thistle flaw on the 1d. (R. 2/2)

B. Watermark Crown to right

SB52 Pane of 2×1d./3d. (containing Nos. S23e×2, S78e×2) (10.65)	20·00	75·00	18·00	20·00
SB53 Pane of 2×3d./1d. (containing Nos. S78f×2, S23e×2) (10.65)	20·00	†	18·00	20·00
a. One 8mm band on each stamp	80·00	†	70·00	80·00
b. One 8mm band on 1d. and no bands on 3d.	80·00	†	70·00	80·00
c. "R" flaw on 1d. (R. 2/2)	†	†	30·00	†
d. 9·5mm band between 1d. and 3d.	£300	†	£300	†

For illustrations of Nos. SB51 and SB53c see Nos. SB36 and SB38a.

SB50d/53d are replacement listings of previous SB55a, 56b, 57a and 58b as 9·5mm bands were experimental and the panes used in October 1967 booklet N30pb. As these bands are applied across the perforations and are liable to shift, it is not possible to distinguish the 3d. side band 9·5 mm bands from the 8mm bands of Nos. SB50, etc. in singles, and hence these are not listed as varieties under the 3d. value.

Booklet Cylinder Numbers
Pane of four (24-row single pane cylinder of 480 stamps sideways). From 1d./3d. *se-tenant* Perf. Type I, Wmk Crown to left.

Cylinder No.	No Dot
F13 (1d.), K22 (3d.) 8mm side band	75·00
F13 (1d), K22 (3d) 9·5mm side band	£400

●———

1d. Panes of six, with two 9·5mm phosphor bands reacting viole. *Wmk* Crowns

Two phosphor bands applied by photogravure
From 4s.6d. Booklets L65p(b)/71p and 10s. Booklets X16p/17p

	Perf Type	
	I	Ie
A. Watermark upright		
SB54 Pane of 6×1d. (containing No. S24×6) (2.67)	7·00	8·00
b. Dot in serif (R. 2/3)	35·00	
B. Watermark inverted		
SB54a Pane of 6×1d. (containing No. S24a×6) (2.67)	7·00	8·00
ab. Extended leaf on shamrock (R. 1/1 or 2/1)	35·00	

For illustrations of Nos. SB54b and SB54ab see Nos. SB23c and SB20ab.

Booklet Cylinder Numbers
Panes of six (21-row cylinder)

Cylinder No.	No Dot	Dot
F10	75·00	75·00
F10 T	75·00	75·00

●———

1d. and 3d. Se-tenant panes of four, with 9·5mm phosphor bands reacting violet. Pair of 1d. (two bands) with pair of 3d. (two bands) applied by letterpress. *Wmk* Crowns sideways

From 2s. Booklets N31p(a/b) and N32p(a/b)

Panes SB55 and SB57   Panes of four with 1d. at left
Panes SB56 and SB58   Panes of four with 1d. at right

A. Watermark Crown to left

	Perf. Type			
	I	I(½v)	AP	AP (2E)
SB55 Pane of 2×1d./3d. (containing Nos. S24b×2, S80×2) (11.67)	15·00	†	10·00	†
SB56 Pane of 2×3d./1d. (containing Nos. S80×2, S24b×2) (11.67)	15·00	65·00*	10·00	†
c. One 9·5mm band on each stamp	£100	£130*	85·00	†
d. One 9·5mm band on 1d. and no bands on 3d.	£100	—*	£100	†
e. One 9·5 mm band on 1d. and 5·5 mm band on 3d.	—	£300*	£150	†

*The I (½v) pane has the thistle flaw on 1d. (R.2/2)

73

SB Wilding Booklet Panes 1d., 1½d.

B. Watermark Crown to right

		Perf. Type		
	I	I(½v)	AP	AP (2E)
SB57 Pane of 2×1d./3d. (containing Nos. S24c×2, S80a×2) (11.67)	15·00	55·00	10·00	15·00
e. One 9·5 mm band on 1d. and 5·5 mm band on 3d.	†	†	£150	†
SB58 Pane of 2×3d./1d. (containing Nos. S80a×2, S24c×2) (11.67)	15·00	†	10·00	15·00
a. "R" flaw on 1d. (R. 2/2)	†	†	45·00	†
c. One 9·5mm band on each stamp	£100	†	85·00	—

For illustrations of Nos. SB56b/d and SB58a/ba, see Nos. SB36 and SB38a.

Booklet Cylinder Numbers
Pane of four (24-row single-pane cylinder of 480 stamps sideways). From 1d./3d. *se-tenant* Perf. Type I, wmk Crown to left

Cylinder No.	No Dot
F13 (1d.), K22 (3d.)	50·00

Imprimatur from the NPM or BPMA
Booklet pane of four. Imperforate, watermark Type W.**24**
Two panes as Nos. SB50 and SB53 arranged *tête-bêche* £12250

1½d. Panes of six, *Wmk* Tudor Crown
From 2s.6d. Booklets F1/36 and 5s. Booklets H1/17

	Perf. Type	
A. Watermark upright	I	Ie
SB59 Pane of 6×1½d. (containing No. S25×6) (5.53)	4·00	5·00
b. Extra jewel (R. 1/1)	55·00	
c. Extra bud on daffodil stem (R. 2/1)	55·00	
B. Watermark inverted		
SB59a Pane of 6×1½d. (containing No. S25c×6) (5.53)	4·00	5·00
ab. Imperf. pane*		

* Booklet error. This pane of six stamps is completely imperf. (see General Notes).

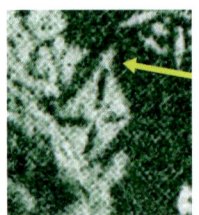

SB59b, SB62c
Multipositive flaw on Tudor and Edward Crown watermarks

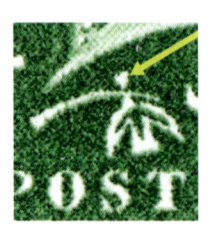

SB59c

Booklet Cylinder Numbers
Panes of six (20-row cylinders)

Cylinder No.	No Dot	Dot
G2	50·00	35·00
G3	50·00	35·00
G6	£140	£120

1½d. Panes of four, *Wmk* Tudor Crown
From 1s. Booklet K1/a for use in "E" slot machines.

	Perf. Type P
A. Watermark upright	
SB60 Pane of 4×1½d. (containing No. S25×4) (22.7.54)	12·00
b. Rose petal flaw (R. 1/1)	55·00
B. Watermark inverted	
SB60a Pane of 4×1½d. (containing No. S25c×4) (22.7.54)	15·00

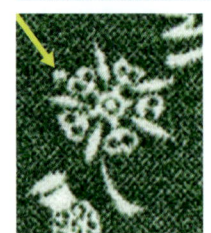

SB60b, SB63b, SB67b

Booklet Cylinder Number
Cylinder No. G5 was used, but it does not appear in the finished booklets.

1½d. Panes of two, *Wmk* Tudor Crown
From 1s. Booklet E1 for use in experimental "D" slot machines.

	Perf. Type			
Watermark upright	I	I(½v)	E	E(½v)
SB61 Pane of 2×1½d. (containing No. S25×2) (2.9.53)	12·00	85·00	9·00	25·00
a. Flaw on daffodil stem (as on No. S25f)	†	†	75·00	†

Made up from columns 1 and 2 from sheets.
No. SB61a was later retouched on cylinder 9 dot.

Booklet Cylinder Numbers
Panes of two (from sheets)

	No Dot	Dot
	Perf	Perf
Cylinder No.	Type I	Type E
2	£200	£200
4	†	—

	No Dot	Dot
	Perf	Perf
Cylinder No.	Type E	Type E
6	£200	£200
9	£130	85·00*
12	£130	85·00

Panes purporting to have come from cylinder 1 are believed to have been forged.

Imprimaturs from the NPM or BPMA
Booklet pane of six. Imperforate, watermark Type W.**22**
Two panes as No. SB59 arranged *tête-bêche* with cylinder G2**.** £14500
Booklet panes of four. Imperforate, watermark Type W.**22**
Two panes as No. SB60 arranged vertically *tête-bêche* with a 12mm horizontal gutter margin between £10000
Two panes as No. SB60 arranged vertically *tête-bêche* with a 12mm horizontal gutter margin between with cylinder G5 £10500

74

1½d. Wilding Booklet Panes SB

1½d. Panes of six, Wmk St Edward's Crown
From 2s.6d. Booklets F33(b) and F34/52, 3s. Booklets M1/11 and 5s. Booklets H17/31

	Perf. Type	
A. Watermark upright	I	Ie
SB62 Pane of 6×1½d. (containing No. S26×6) *(8.55)*	3·50	4·00
b. Rabbit's ears (R. 2/2)	45·00	
c. Extra jewel (R. 1/1 or 2/1)	50·00	
d. Large dot by daffodil (R. 1/1)	50·00	
e. Major retouch around emblems (R. 2/2)	65·00	
f. Flaw on rose at right (R. 1/2)	50·00	
B. Watermark inverted		
SB62a Pane of 6×1½d. (containing No. S26b×6) *(8.55)*	5·00	6·00
ab. Flaw on rose at top left (R. 1/2 or 2/2)	50·00	

For illustration of No. SB62c see No. SB59b

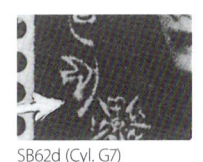

SB62b
Two white dots extending upwards from shamrock at left appearing as rabbit's ears (Cyl. G7 no dot)

SB62d (Cyl. G7)

SB62e
Major retouch affecting a pair with weak shading in the emblems. (Cyl. G7 dot)

Normal

SB62f (Cyl. G10 dot)

SB62ab
White flaw on rose at top left (Cyl. G10 dot)

Booklet Cylinder Numbers
Panes of six (G6 and G7 20-row cylinders, others 21-row cylinders)

Cylinder No.	No Dot	Dot
G6	70·00	40·00
G7	60·00	50·00
G9	£120	£120
G9 T	£140	£120
G10	£140	£100
G10 T	£140	£100

1½d. Panes of four, Wmk St Edward's Crown
From 1s. Booklet K2/b for use in "E" slot machines and 2s. Booklet N1

	Perf. Type	
A. Watermark upright	AP	P
SB63 Pane of 4×1½d. (containing No. S26×4) *(5.7.56)*	12·00	12·00
b. Rose petal flaw (R. 1/1)	40·00	55·00
B. Watermark inverted		
SB63a Pane of 4×1½d. (containing No. S26b×4) *(5.7.56)*	12·00	12·00

For illustration of No. SB63b see No. SB60b.

Booklet Cylinder Number
Cylinder No. G5 was used, but it does not appear in the finished booklets.

Imprimaturs from the NPM or BPMA
Booklet panes of six. Imperforate, watermark Type W.**23**

Pane of six (wmk upright) with hair flaw variety R.1/1	£6000
Two panes as No. SB62 arranged *tête-bêche* with cylinder F4.	£14500

Booklet panes of four. Imperforate, watermark Type W.**23**

Two panes as No. SB63 arranged vertically *tête-bêche* with a 12 mm horizontal gutter margin between	£10000
Two panes as No. SB63 arranged vertically *tête-bêche* with a 12 mm horizontal gutter margin between with cylinder F8	£10500

1½d. Panes of two, Wmk St Edward's Crown
From 1s. Booklet E2 for use in experimental "D" slot machines.

	Perf. Type	
Watermark upright	E	E(½v)
SB64 Pane of 2×1½d. (containing No. S26×2) *(11.57)*	30·00	40·00

Made up from columns 1 and 2 from sheets

Booklet Cylinder Numbers
Panes of two (from sheets)

Cylinder No.	No Dot	Dot
13	—	†
14	£200	£140

1½d. Panes of six, Cream or whiter paper. Wmk Crowns
From 3s. Booklets M9/74 and 10s. Booklets X1/9

Cream Paper	Perf. Type	
A. Watermark upright	I	Ie
SB65 Pane of 6×1½d. (containing No. S28×6) *(12.58)*	10·00	12·00
b. Dot on thistle (R. 1/3 or 2/3)	55·00	
B. Watermark inverted		
SB65a Pane of 6×1½d. (containing No. S28a×6) *(12.58)*	12·00	14·00

Whiter Paper		
A. Watermark upright		
SB66 Pane of 6×1½d. (containing No. S29×6) *(18.9.62)*	40·00	45·00
b. Dot on thistle (R. 1/3 or 2/3)	65·00	
c. Part perf pane*	£6500	
B. Watermark inverted		
SB66a Pane of 6×1½d. (containing No. S29d×6) *(18.9.62)*	50·00	55·00

* Booklet error. See general notes.

SB Wilding Booklet Panes 1½d.

SB65b, SB66b
Dot on thistle. Retouched on whiter paper (Cyl. G15 dot)

Booklet Cylinder Numbers
Panes of six (21-row cylinders)

Cream paper

Cylinder No.	No Dot	Dot
G10	£100	£100
G10 T	£100	£100
G11	90·00	90·00
G11 T	90·00	90·00
G15	60·00	60·00
G15 T	60·00	60·00

Whiter paper

Cylinder No.	No Dot	Dot
G15	90·00	90·00
G15 T	90·00	90·00
G16	£150	£150
G16 T	£150	£150

Specimen overprints from the NPM
Booklet pane of six. Perf. 15×14, watermark Type W.**24** upright

Each stamp handstamped "Specimen" (13×2 mm.)	£1250

1½d. Panes of four, Cream paper. *Wmk* Crowns
From 1s. Booklet K3/a for use in "E" slot machines and 2s. Booklets N2/3.

A. Watermark upright — *Perf Type AP*

SB67	Pane of 4×1½d. (containing No. S28×4) *(13.8.59)*	10·00
	b. Rose petal flaw (R. 1/1)	50·00

B. Watermark inverted

SB67a	Pane of 4×1½d. (containing No. S28a×4) *(13.8.59)*	12·00

For illustration of No. SB67b see No. SB60b.

Booklet Cylinder Number
Cylinder No. G5 was used, but it does not appear in the finished booklets.

Specimen overprints from the NPM
Booklet pane of four. Perf. 15×14, watermark Type W.**24** inverted

Each stamp handstamped "SPECIMEN" (13×2 mm.)	£1000

1½d. Panes of four, Cream or white paper. *Wmk* Crowns sideways
From 2s. Booklets N4/20

Cream Paper

		Perf. Type		
A. Watermark Crown to left	I	I(½v)	AP	AP(2E)
SB68 Pane of 4×1½d. (containing No. S28b×4) *(26.5.61)*	60·00	£120	50·00	75·00
B. Watermark Crown to right				
SB68a Pane of 4×1½d. (containing No. S28c×4) *(26.5.61)*	60·00	£120	50·00	†

Whiter Paper

A. Watermark Crown to left

SB69 Pane of 4×1½d. (containing No. S29b×4) *(5.6.62)*	40·00	85·00	35·00	75·00

B. Watermark Crown to right

SB69a Pane of 4×1½d. (containing No. S29c×4) *(5.6.62)*	40·00	85·00	35·00	†

Booklet Cylinder Number
Pane of four, Perf. Type, I (wmk Crown to left)

Cylinder No.	No Dot
G.17	£150

Due to the width of the selvedge the "7" was usually trimmed off.

Specimen overprints from the NPM
Booklet pane of four. Perf. 15×14, watermark Type W.**24** Crown to left, Perf. AP(2E)

Each stamp handstamped "SPECIMEN" (13×2 mm.)	£1000

Imprimaturs from the NPM or BPMA
Booklet panes of six. Imperforate, watermark Type W.**24**

Two panes as Nos. SB65 or SB66 arranged horizontally *tête-bêche* (cream or whiter paper)	£14000
Two panes as Nos. SB65 or SB66 arranged horizontally *tête-bêche* (Cream or Whiter paper) with cylinder G11 cream paper	£14500
Two panes as Nos. SB65 or SB66 arranged horizontally *tête-bêche* (cream or whiter paper) with cylinder G16 whiter paper	£14500

Booklet panes of four. Imperforate, watermark Type W.**24**

Panes as No. SB67 arranged vertically *tête-bêche* with 12mm gutter margin between on cream paper	£10000
Panes as No. SB67 arranged vertically *tête-bêche* with 12mm gutter margin between on cream paper with cylinder G5 cream paper	£10500

1½d. Panes of six, with graphite lines as Type **SA8**. *Wmk* Crowns
From 3s. Booklets M13g/15g and M19g/21g

	Perf Type	
A. Watermark upright	I	Ie
SB70 Pane of 6×1½d. (containing No. S30×6) *(4.8.59)*	£500	£500
B. Watermark inverted		
SB70a Pane of 6×1½d. (containing No. S30a×6) *(4.8.59)*	£250	£250

Booklet Cylinder Numbers
Panes of six (21-row cylinder)

Cylinder No.	No Dot	Dot
G11	£1000	£1000
G11 T	£1000	£1000

Imprimaturs from the NPM or BPMA
Booklet panes of six. Imperforate, watermark Type W.**24** with graphite lines.

Two panes as No. SB70 arranged *tête-bêche*	£14000
Two panes as No. SB70 arranged *tête-bêche* with cylinder G11	£14500

1½d., 2d. Wilding Booklet Panes SB

1½d. Panes of six, Two phosphor bands reacting green applied by photogravure. *Wmk* Crowns.
From 3s. Booklets M25p, M28p/29p and M37p(a)

	Perf Type	
	I	Ie
A. Watermark upright		
SB71 Pane of 6×1½d. (containing No. S32×6) *(14.8.60)*	55·00	65·00
B. Watermark inverted		
SB71a Pane of 6×1½d. (containing No. S32a×6) *(14.8.60)*	£120	£120

Booklet Cylinder Numbers
Panes of six (21-row cylinders)

Cylinder No.	No Dot	Dot
G11	£250	£250
G11 T	£250	£250

1½d. Panes of six, Two phosphor bands applied by photogravure reacting blue. Cream or whiter paper. *Wmk* Crowns
From 3s. Booklets M33p, M36p, M37p(b), M38p/9p, M43p/7p, M49p/53p, M55p/61p and M64p/74p

Cream Paper

	Perf. Type	
	I	Ie
A. Watermark upright		
SB72. Pane of 6×1½d. (containing No S33×6) *(4.61)*	70·00	80·00
b. One 8mm. band on each stamp	£400	
B. Watermark inverted		
SB72a Pane of 6×1½d. (containing No. S33a×6) *(4.61)*	£120	£130
ab. One 8mm. band on each stamp	£400	

Whiter Paper

	Perf. Type	
	I	Ie
A. Watermark upright		
SB73 Pane of 6×1½d. (containing No. S34×6) *(7.64)*	85·00	95·00
b. One 8mm. band on each stamp	£500	
B. Watermark inverted		
SB73a Pane of 6×1½d. (containing No. S34c×6) *(7.64)*	£200	£225
ab. One 8mm band on each stamp	£550	
ac. Phosphor displaced with stamps 1 and 4 showing 6mm. left and centre bands, others with one 8mm band in centre	—	

Booklet Cylinder Numbers
Pane of six (21-row cylinders)

Cream paper

Cylinder No.	No Dot	Dot
G15	£120	£120
G15 T	£120	£120

Whiter paper

Cylinder No.	No Dot	Dot
G16	£250	£250
G16 T	£250	£250

1½d. Panes of four, Two phosphor bands reacting blue, applied by letterpress. Cream or whiter paper. *Wmk* Crowns Sideways
From 2s. Booklets N4p, N8p/10p, N12p/20p

Cream Paper

	Perf. Type			
	I	I(½v)	AP	AP(2E)
A. Watermark Crown to left				
SB74 Pane of 4×1½d. (containing No. S33b×4) *(14.7.61)*	85·00	£150	60·00	£100
b. One 8mm band on each stamp	£150	—	£125	—
B. Watermark Crown to right				
SB74a Pane of 4×1½d. (containing No. S33c×4) *(14.7.61)*	85·00	£150	60·00	†
ab. One 8mm band on each stamp	£150	—	£125	†

Whiter Paper
A. Watermark Crown to left

	I	I(½v)	AP	AP(2E)
SB75 Pane of 4×1½d. (containing No. S34a×4) *(15.8.62)*	90·00	£170	70·00	£120

B. Watermark Crown to right

| SB75a Pane of 4×1½d. (containing No. S34b×4) *(15.8.62)* | 90·00 | £170 | 70·00 | † |

Booklet Cylinder Numbers
Pane of four Perf. Type I (wmk Crown to left)

Cylinder No.		No Dot
G.17		£275

Due to the width of the selvedge the "7" was usually trimmed off.

Imprimaturs from the NPM or BPMA
Booklet panes of six. Imperforate, watermark Type W.**24**

Two panes as No. SB71 arranged *tête-bêche*	£14000
Two panes as No. SB71 arranged *tête-bêche* with cylinder G11.	£14500
Two panes as No. SB72 arranged *tête-bêche*	£14000
Two panes as No. SB72 arranged *tête-bêche* with cylinder G15T	£14500

Booklet panes of four. Imperforate, watermark Type W.**24**

Two panes as No. SB75 arranged vertically *tête-bêche*	£10000
Two panes as No. SB75 arranged vertically *tête-bêche* with cylinder G.17	£10500

Specimen overprints from the NPM
Booklet pane of four. Perf. 15×14, watermark Type W.**24**, Crown to right, Perf. Type AP.

Each stamp handstamped "SPECIMEN" (13×2 mm.)	£1000

2d. Red-brown panes of six, *Wmk* Tudor Crown
From 5s. Booklets H8/19 and H21a

	Perf. Type	
	I	Ie
A. Watermark upright		
SB76 Pane of 6×2d. (containing No. S36×6) *(3.54)*	60·00	65·00
B. Watermark inverted		
SB76a Pane of 6×2d. (containing No. S36a×6) *(3.54)*	£200	£225

SB Wilding Booklet Panes 2d.

Booklet Cylinder Numbers
Panes of six (20-row cylinder)

Cylinder No.	No Dot	Dot
H1	£130	£110

* Includes retouched face variety (R. 2/1). Two states exist showing as a small retouch to left of ear and in state two the retouched area includes the forehead and cheek. Same price for either state included in the cylinder pane with upright watermark.

Imprimatur from the NPM or BPMA
Booklet pane of six. Imperforate, watermark Type W.**22** Two panes as No. SB76 arranged *tête-bêche* with cylinder H1**.**   £14500

2d. Red-brown panes of six, *Wmk* St Edward's Crown
From 5s. Booklets H17/25

	Perf. Type I	Perf. Type Ie
A. Watermark upright		
SB77 Pane of 6×2d. (containing No. S37×6) *(9.55)*	30·00	35·00
B. Watermark inverted		
SB77a Pane of 6×2d. (containing No. S37c×6) *(9.55)*	90·00	£100

Booklet Cylinder Numbers
Panes of six (20-row cylinder)

Cylinder No.	No Dot	Dot
H1	£130	£120

* Includes the second state of the retouched face variety (R. 2/1).

Imprimatur from the NPM or BPMA
Booklet pane of six. Imperforate, watermark Type W.**23** Two panes as No. SB77 arranged *tête-bêche* with cylinder H1**.**   £14500

2d. Light red-brown panes of six, *Wmk* St Edward's Crown
From 2s.6d. Booklets F53/61 and 5s. Booklets H26/31

	Perf. Type I	Perf. Type Ie
A. Watermark upright		
SB78 Pane of 6×2d. (containing No. S38×6) *(1.57)*	15·00	18·00
b. Imperf. pane*	£5000	
ba. Part perf. pane*	£5000	
c. Daffodil flaw (R. 1/3 or 2/3)	65·00	
ca. Daffodil flaw retouched	55·00	
d. Shamrock flaw (R. 1/3 or 2/3)	50·00	
e. Bud on thistle stem (R. 1/3 or 2/3)	55·00	
f. White flaw on thistle (R. 1/1 or 2/1)	55·00	
g. Daffodil stem flaw (R. 2/2)	60·00	
B. Watermark inverted		
SB78a Pane of 6×2d. (containing No. S38d×6) *(1.57)*	40·00	50·00
ab. Imperf. pane*	—	
ac. "D" for "P" (R. 1/2 or 2/2)	80·00	
ad. Spot after "2" (R. 1/2 or 2/2)	70·00	
ae. Dew drop (R. 1/2 or 2/2)	70·00	
af. Diadem flaw (R. 1/3 or 2/3)	70·00	
ag. White flaw at top of thistle (R. 1/2 or 2/2)	70·00	
ah. Accent on first "2" and spot on shamrock (R. 1/3 or 2/3)	£100	
aha. Retouched state. Spot on shamrock (R. 1/3 or 2/3)	85·00	

* Booklet Errors. See General Notes.

SB78ba

SB78c Later retouched (SB78ca) (Cyl. H6 no dot)

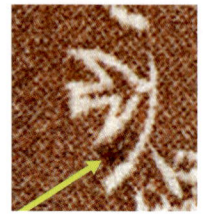

SB78ca

SB78d Later retouched (Cyl. H6 no dot)

SB78e, SB79b Later retouched (Cyl. H6 dot)

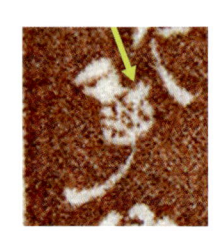

SB78f, SB79c (Cyl. H6 dot)

SB78g Later retouched (Cyl. pane H6 dot and on ordinary pane)

SB78ac, SB79ab (Cyl. H6 dot)

2d., 2½d. **Wilding Booklet Panes** **SB**

SB78ad, SB79ac (Cyl. H6 no dot)

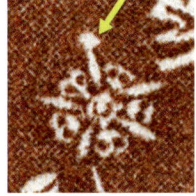

SB78ae Later retouched (Cyl. H6 no dot)

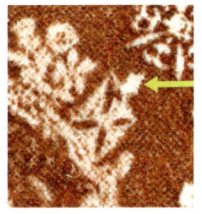

SB78af Later retouched (Cyl. H6 dot)

SB78ag Later retouched (Cyl. H6 no dot)

SB78ah

SB78aha The flaw on value was later retouched but the spot on shamrock remained. (Cyl. H6 no dot)

2d. Light red-brown panes of six, Cream paper.
Wmk Crowns

From 10s. Booklets X1/2

	Perf Type	
A. Watermark upright	I	Ie
SB79 Pane of 6×2d. (containing No. S40×6) *(10.4.61)*	£100	£110
b. Bud on thistle stem (R. 1/3 or 2/3)	£150	
c. White flaw on thistle (R. 1/1 or 2/1)	£150	
d. Daffodil flaw retouched	£130	
B. Watermark inverted		
SB79a Pane of 6×2d. (containing No. S40c×6) *(10.4.61)*	£900	£900
ab. "D" for "P" (R. 1/2 or 2/2)	£950	
ac. Spot after "2" (R. 1/1 or 2/2)	£950	

For illustration of Nos. SB79b/c, see Nos. SB78e/f and for Nos. SB79ab/ac see Nos. SB78ac/ad.

Booklet Cylinder Numbers
Panes of six (21-row cylinder). Cream paper

Cylinder No.	No Dot	Dot
H6	£600	£600
H6 T	£600	£600

> All stamps in the 2½d. panes show the frontal cross of the diadem with the top line extending the full width of the cross (Type II).

2½d. Panes of six, *Wmk* Tudor Crown

From 2s.6d. Booklets F1/36, F37a, F42b/43b, 3s.9d. Booklets G1/10 and 5s. Booklets H1/19

	Perf Type	
A. Watermark upright	I	Ie
SB80 Pane of 6×2½d. (containing No. S51×6) *(5.53)*	6·00	7·00
b. Jewels flaw (R. 2/2)	65·00	
B. Watermark inverted		
SB80a Pane of 6×2½d. (containing No. S51a×6) *(5.53)*	4·50	5·00
ab. "R" flaw (R. 1/1)	65·00	

SB80b (Cyl. J1 or J3 no dot)

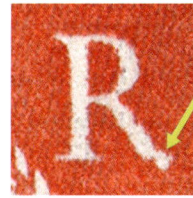

SB80ab, SB81ad (Cyl. J5 no dot)

Booklet Cylinder Numbers
Panes of six (20-row cylinders)

Cylinder No.	No Dot	Dot
J1	40·00	30·00
J3	40·00	30·00
J5	35·00	35·00

Booklet Cylinder Numbers
Panes of six (21-row cylinder)

Cylinder No.	No Dot	Dot
H6	£140	£100
H6 T	£150	£110

Early printings of the Cyl. H6 dot pane show a white dot below the daffodil stem flaw as SB78g but on R.1/2. This was later removed by retouch. *Cylinder No.* H6 no dot *with variety price* £180.

Imprimaturs from the NPM or BPMA
Booklet pane of six. Imperforate, watermark Type W.**23**

Pane with "bud on thistle" variety R.1/3 as No. SB78e	£6000
Pane with "white flaw on thistle" variety R.2/1 as No. SB78f	£6000
Two panes as No. SB78c arranged *tête-bêche* with cylinder H6. & "daffodil flaw" variety R.1/2	£15000

Imprimaturs from the NPM or BPMA
Booklet pane of six. Imperforate, watermark Type W.**22**

Two panes as No. SB80 arranged *tête-bêche* with cylinder J3 (dot)	£14500

SB Wilding Booklet Panes *2½d.*

2½d. Panes of six, *Wmk* St Edward's Crown

From 2s.6d. Booklets F34(d)/36(c) and F37/61, 3s.9d. Booklets G9(a)/(c) and G10(a)/21 and 5s. Booklets H17/36

		Perf Type	
A. Watermark upright		*I*	*Ie*
SB81	Pane of 6×2½d. (containing No. S53×6) (9.55)	3·50	4·00
b.	Imperf. pane*	£5000	
c.	Part perf pane*	£4250	
d.	Swan's head (R. 1/1 or 2/1)	£100	
e.	Wreath flaw (R. 1/3 or 2/3)	60·00	
f.	Damaged "P" (R. 1/3 or 2/3)	60·00	
g.	Dot by shamrock (R. 1/1 or 2/1)	60·00	
h.	Forehead retouch R. 1/2 or 2/2)	75·00	
i.	White flaw below thistle (R. 1/2 or 2/2)	60·00	
B. Watermark inverted			
SB81a	Pane of 6×2½d. (containing No. S53e×6) (9.55)	3·50	4·00
ab.	Imperf pane*	£5000	
ac.	Part perf. pane*	£4250	
ad.	"R" flaw (R. 1/1)	60·00	
ae.	Dotted "R" (R. 1/3 or 2/3)	60·00	
af.	Spur to "1" (R. 1/1 or 2/1)	50·00	

* Booklet Errors. See General Notes.
For illustration of No. SB81ad, see No. SB80ab.

SB81b

SB81c

SB81d, SB82d
Top of figure 2 is extended and curled, resembling a swan's head (Cyl. J8 no dot)

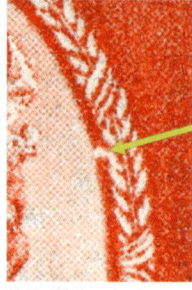

SB81e, SB82e
(Cyl. J9 no dot)

SB81f, SB82f
Red flaw almost obliterates the loop on "P". St Edward's and Crown wmks., (Cyl. J8 dot)

SB81g
Retouched later (Cyl. J9 dot)

SB81h, SB82g
(Cyl. J9 no dot)

SB81i, SB82h
(Cyl. J8 no dot)

SB81ae
Later retouched on Crowns wmk. (Cyl. J9 no dot)

SB81af, SB82ac, SB85ab
(Cyl. J9 dot)

Booklet Cylinder Numbers

Panes of six (J5 20-row cylinder, others 21-row cylinders)

Cylinder No.	No Dot	Dot
J5	45·00	35·00
J6	85·00	85·00
J6 T	85·00	55·00
J8	£100	55·00
J8 T	£100	55·00
J9	£120	£100
J9 T	£120	£100

Imprimaturs from the NPM or BPMA

Booklet panes of six. Imperforate, watermark Type W.**23**

Pane with "R flaw" variety R.1/1 as No. SB81ad	£6000
Two panes as No. SB81 arranged *tête-bêche* with cylinder J5	£14500

80

2½d. Wilding Booklet Panes SB

2½d. Panes of six, Cream or whiter paper. *Wmk* Crowns
From 5s. Booklets H36(b)/(c), (e) and H37/74 and 10s. Booklets X3/9

Cream Paper	Perf Type	
A. Watermark upright	*I*	*Ie*
SB82 Pane of 6×2½d. (containing No. S55×6) *(11.58)*	17·00	18·00
d. Swan's head (R. 1/1 or 2/1)	£100	
e. Wreath flaw (R. 1/3 or 2/3)	65·00	
f. Damaged "P" (R. 1/3 or 2/3)	65·00	
g. Forehead retouch (R. 1/2 or 2/2)	75·00	
h. White flaw below thistle (R. 1/2 or 2/2)	65·00	
B. Watermark inverted		
SB82a Pane of 6×2½d. (containing No. S55d×6) *(11.58)*	30·00	32·00
ac. Spur to "1" (R. 1/1 or R.2/1)	65·00	

Whiter Paper		
A. Watermark upright		
SB83 Pane of 6×2½d. (containing No. S57×6) *(29.7.62)*	35·00	38·00
b. Imperf. pane*	—	
c. Part perf. pane*	£4000	
B. Watermark inverted		
SB83a Pane of 6×2½d. (containing No. S57a×6) *(29.7.62)*	70·00	75·00

* Booklet Errors. See General Notes.
For illustrations of Nos. SB82d/f, see Nos. SB81d/f, for Nos. SB82g/h, see Nos. SB81h/i and for No. SB82ac see No. SB81af.

Booklet Cylinder Numbers
Panes of six (21-row cylinders)

Cream paper

Cylinder No.	No Dot	Dot
J6	£140	£140
J6 T	£140	£140
J8	£160	£160
J8 T	£160	£160
J9	£140	£140
J9 T	£140	£140
J13	£130	£130
J13 T	£130	£130

Whiter paper

Cylinder No.	No Dot	Dot
J13	£150	£150
J13 T	£150	£150
J14	£200	£200
J14 T	£200	£200

Specimen overprints from the NPM
Booklet pane of six. Perf. 15×14, watermark Type W.**24** inverted Each stamp handstamped "SPECIMEN" (15×2½ mm.) £1250

Imprimaturs from the NPM or BPMA
Booklet panes of six. Imperforate, watermark Type W.**24**

Two panes as No. SB82 arranged *tête-bêche*	£14000
Two panes as No. SB82 arranged *tête-bêche* with cylinder J6. T	£14500
Two panes as No. SB83 arranged *tête-bêche*	£14000
Two panes as No. SB83 arranged *tête-bêche* with cylinder J13 T	£14500

2½d. Panes of four, Chalk-surfaced paper. *Wmk* Crowns
From 2s. Booklet NR1/1a

	Perf. Type		
A. Watermark upright	*I*	*I(½v)*	*AP*
SB84 Pane of 4×2½d. (containing No. S58×4) *(15.7.63)*	5·00	15·00	2·00
B. Watermark inverted			
SB84a Pane of 4×2½d. (containing No. S58a×4) *(15.7.63)*	5·00	15·00	2·00

Booklet Cylinder Numbers
Panes of four (20-row single pane cylinder of 240 stamps).
Cylinder No. J1 was used, but it does not appear on the finished panes.

Imprimaturs from the NPM or BPMA
Booklet panes of four. Imperforate, watermark Type W.**24**

Two panes as No. SB84 arranged vertically *tête-bêche*	£10000
Two panes as No. SB84 arranged vertically *tête-bêche* with cylinder 1	£10500

2½d. Panes of six, with graphite lines as Type SA8. *Wmk* Crowns.
From 5s. Booklets H39g, H43g and H46g

	Perf Type	
A. Watermark upright	*I*	*Ie*
SB85 Pane of 6×2½d. (containing No. S59×6) *(21.8.59)*	£120	£120
b. Forehead retouch (R. 1/2 or 2/2)	£170	
B. Watermark inverted		
SB85a Pane of 6×2½d. (containing No. S59a×6) *(21.8.59)*	£400	£400
ab. Spur to "1" (R. 1/1 or 2/1)	£475	

For illustration of No. SB85b, see No. SB81h and for No. SB85ab, see No. SB81af.

Booklet Cylinder Numbers
Panes of six (21-row cylinders)

Cylinder No.	No Dot	Dot
J6	£750	£750
J6 T	£750	£750
J9	£750	£750
J9 T	£750	£750

Imprimaturs from the NPM or BPMA
Booklet panes of six. Imperforate, watermark Type W.**24** with graphite lines.

Two panes as No. SB85 arranged *tête-bêche*	£14000
Two panes as No. SB85 arranged *tête-bêche* with cylinder J9. T	£14500

SB Wilding Booklet Panes 2½d., 3d.

2½d. Panes of six, with two phosphor bands reacting green applied by photogravure. Wmk Crowns.
From 5s. Booklet H46p

	Perf Type	
A. Watermark upright	*I*	*Ie*
SB86 Pane of 6×2½d. (containing No. S61×6) *(9.60)*	£130	£140
b. One 8mm band on each stamp	£500	
B. Watermark inverted		
SB86a Pane of 6×2½d. (containing No. S61a×6) *(9.60)*	£1200	£1200

Booklet Cylinder Numbers
Panes of six (21-row cylinder)

Cylinder No.	No Dot	Dot
J13	£650	£650
J13 T	£650	£650

Specimen overprints from the NPM
Booklet pane of six. Perf. 15×14, watermark Type W.**24** upright
Each stamp handstamped "SPECIMEN" (13×2 mm.) £1250

2½d. Panes of six, with two phosphor bands reacting blue applied by photogravure. Cream paper. Wmk Crowns.
From 5s. Booklets H49p, H51p/52p and H54p

	Perf Type	
A. Watermark upright	*I*	*Ie*
SB87 Pane of 6×2½d. (containing No. S62×6) *(3.61)*	£120	£120
B. Watermark inverted		
SB87a Pane of 6×2½d. (containing No. S62a×6) *(3.61)*	£1200	£1200

Booklet Cylinder Numbers
Panes of six (21-row cylinders)

Cylinder No.	No Dot	Dot
J13	£600	£600
J13 T	£600	£600

2½d. Panes of six, with one phosphor band at left reacting blue applied by photogravure. Cream or whiter paper. Wmk Crowns.
From 5s. Booklets H55p/74p

Cream Paper	Perf Type	
A. Watermark upright	*I*	*Ie*
SB88 Pane of 6×2½d. (containing No. S63×6) *(3.62)*	£110	£120
B. Watermark inverted		
SB88a Pane of 6×2½d. (containing No. S63b×6) *(3.62)*	£300	£300

Whiter Paper		
A. Watermark upright		
SB89 Pane of 6×2½d. (containing No. S65×6) *(3.6.63)*	£120	£140
b. One 4 mm band at right but omitted on stamps 3 and 6	—	—
c. Two narrow bands over perforations	—	—
B. Watermark inverted		
SB89a Pane of 6×2½d. (containing No. S65b×6) *(3.6.63)*	£300	£300

No. SB89b was the source of No. S65e and No. SB89c was the source of No. S65c.

Booklet Cylinder Numbers
Pane of six (21-row cylinders)

One band. Cream paper		
Cylinder No.	No Dot	Dot
J13	£600	£600
J13 T	£600	£600

One band. Whiter paper		
Cylinder No.	No Dot	Dot
J13	£450	£450
J13 T	£450	£450
J14	£450	£450
J14 T	£450	£450

Specimen overprints from the NPM
Booklet pane of six. Perf. 15×14, watermark Type W.**24** upright
Each stamp handstamped "SPECIMEN" (15×2½ mm.) £1250

Imprimaturs from the NPM or BPMA
Booklet panes of six. Imperforate, watermark Type W.**24**

Two panes as No. SB86 arranged *tête-bêche*	£14000
Two panes as No. SB86 arranged *tête-bêche* with cylinder J13. T	£14500
Two panes as No. SB87 arranged *tête-bêche*	£14000
Two panes as No. SB87 arranged *tête-bêche* with cylinder J13.	£14500
Two panes as No. SB89 arranged *tête-bêche*	£14000
Two panes as No. SB89 arranged *tête-bêche* with cylinder J13.	£14500

3d. Panes of six, Wmk St Edward's Crown
From 3s. Booklets M1/10, 4s.6d. Booklets L1/7 and 5s. Booklets H32/36

	Perf Type	
A. Watermark upright	*I*	*Ie*
SB90 Pane of 6×3d. (containing No. S68×6) *(1.10.57)*	5·00	6·00
b. White dot on laurel leaf (R. 1/2 or 2/2)	55·00	
B. Watermark inverted		
SB90a Pane of 6×3d. (containing No. S68d×6) *(1.10.57)*	10·00	11·00

SB90b
(Cyl. K2 no dot)

Booklet Cylinder Numbers
Panes of six (K8 20-row cylinder, others 21-row cylinders)

Cylinder No.	No Dot	Dot
K1	80·00	80·00
K1 T	90·00	90·00
K2	70·00	70·00
K2 T	70·00	55·00
K7	60·00	50·00
K7 T	60·00	50·00
K8 T	60·00	45·00

K8 was engraved, incorrectly probably, by row 19 and only occurs at the top of the pane.

3d. Wilding Booklet Panes **SB**

3d. Panes of four, Wmk St Edward's Crown
From 2s. Booklet N1.

		Perf. Type AP
A. Watermark upright		
SB91	Pane of 4×3d. (containing No. S68×4) (22.4.59)	60·00
B. Watermark inverted		
SB91a	Pane of 4×3d. (containing No. S68d×4) (22.4.59)	75·00

Booklet Cylinder Numbers
Cylinder numbers did not appear in the finished booklets, but it is known that K9 was used.

Imprimaturs from the NPM or BPMA
Booklet pane of six. Imperforate, watermark Type W.**23**

Two panes as No. SB90 arranged *tête-bêche* with cylinder K1. T	£14500

Booklet panes of four. Imperforate, watermark Type W.**23**

Two panes as No. SB91 arranged vertically *tête-bêche* with a 12mm horizontal gutter margin between	£10000
2mm horizontal gutter margin between with cylinder K9	£10500

3d. Panes of six, Cream or whiter paper Wmk Crowns
From 3s. Booklets M9d/74, 4s.6d. Booklets L8/58, 5s. Booklets H36(d)/(e) and H37/74 and 10s. Booklets X1/14

Cream Paper	Perf Type	
A. Watermark upright	I	Ie
SB92 Pane of 6×3d. (containing No. S70×6) (11.58)	3·50	4·00
b. Imperf. pane*	£4250	
c. Part perf. pane*	£4000	
B. Watermark inverted		
SB92a Pane of 6×3d. (containing No. S70e×6) (11.58)	4·00	5·00
ab. Long tailed "R" (R. 1/1)	55·00	
ac. Background retouch (R. 1/1)	55·00	
ad. Part perf. pane*	£4000	

Whiter Paper		
A. Watermark upright		
SB93 Pane of 6×3d. (containing No. S71×6) (16.7.62)	6·00	7·00
b. Imperf pane*	£4250	
B. Watermark inverted		
SB93a Pane of 6×3d. (containing No. S71c×6) (16.7.62)	3·75	4·50
ab. Long tailed "R" (R. 1/1)	60·00	
ac. Background retouch (R. 1/1)	60·00	

* Booklet Errors. See General Notes.

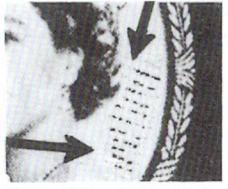

SB92ac, SB93ac, SB97ac, SB99ac, SB100ac Retouched area of fine dots behind Queen's head (Cyl. K15 no dot)

SB92b

SB92c

SB92ab, SB93ab, SB97ab, SB99ab, SB100ab (Cyl. K15 no dot)   Normal

Booklet Cylinder Numbers
Panes of six (K13, K15, K16 and K21 20-row cylinders, others 21-row cylinders)

Cream paper

Cylinder No.	No Dot	Dot
K7	£100	£100
K7 T	£100	£100
K13	35·00	35·00
K15	45·00	45·00
K17	60·00	50·00
K17 T	60·00	50·00
K18	70·00	70·00
K18 T	70·00	70·00
K20	60·00	60·00
K20 T	60·00	60·00

Whiter paper

Cylinder No.	No Dot	Dot
K15	60·00	60·00
K16	£225	£225

83

SB Wilding Booklet Panes 3d.

Cylinder No.	No Dot	Dot
K18	70·00	70·00
K18 T	70·00	70·00
K20	70·00	70·00
K20 T	70·00	70·00
K21	£1000	£1000

Specimen overprints from the NPM
Booklet panes of six. Perf. 15×14, watermark Type W.**24** upright
Each stamp handstamped "SPECIMEN" (13×2 mm.) £1250
Each stamp handstamped "SPECIMEN" (15×2½ mm.) £1250

3d. Panes of four, Cream paper. *Wmk* Crowns
From 2s. Booklets N2/3.

	Perf Type
	AP
A. Watermark upright	
SB94 Pane of 4×3d. (containing No. S70×4) (2.11.60)	25·00
B. Watermark inverted	
SB94a Pane of 4×3d. (containing No. S70e×4) (2.11.60)	25·00
ab. Break in bottom ribbon (R. 1/2)	85·00

SB94ab

Booklet Cylinder Numbers
Cylinder No. K12 was used, but it does not appear in the finished booklets.

Specimen overprints from the NPM
Booklet pane of four. Perf. 15×14, watermark Type W.**24** inverted
Each stamp handstamped "SPECIMEN" (13×2 mm.) £1000

3d. Panes of four, Cream or whiter paper. *Wmk* Crowns sideways
From 2s. Booklets N4/20 and NX1

Cream Paper

		Perf. Type		
	I	*I*(½v)	AP	AP(2E)
A. Watermark Crown to left				
SB95 Pane of 4×3d. (containing No. S70d×4) (26.5.61)	20·00	75·00	5·00	35·00
B. Watermark Crown to right				
SB95a Pane of 4×3d. (containing No. S70f×4) (26.5.61)	20·00	75·00	5·00	†

Whiter Paper
A. Watermark Crown to left
SB96 Pane of 4×3d. (containing No. S71a×4) (5.6.62)	18·00	75·00	9·00	35·00
B. Watermark Crown to right				
SB96a Pane of 4×3d. (containing No. S71b×4) (5.6.62)	18·00	75·00	9·00	†

Booklet Cylinder Number
Pane of four, Perf. Type I Cyl. No. K19 (Wmk Crown to left) £200

Due to the width of the selvedge, the "19" was normally trimmed off.

Specimen overprints from the NPM
Booklet pane of four. Perf. 15×14, watermark Type W.**24** Crown to left, Perf. AP(2E)
Each stamp handstamped "SPECIMEN" (13×2 mm.) £1000

Imprimaturs from the NPM or BPMA
Booklet panes of six. Imperforate, watermark Type W.**24**
Two panes as No. SB92 arranged *tête-bêche* £14000
Two panes as No. SB92 arranged *tête-bêche* with cylinder K7. £14500
Booklet panes of four. Imperforate, watermark Type W.**24**
Two panes as No. SB94 arranged *tête-bêche* vertically with 12mm gutter between £10000
Two panes as No. SB94 arranged *tête-bêche* vertically with 12mm gutter between with cylinder K12. £10500

3d. Panes of six, Graphite lines as Type **SA8**, *Wmk* Crowns
From 3s. Booklets M13g/15g, M19g/21g, 4s.6d. Booklets L11g, L15g/16g, L18g/19g and 5s. Booklets H39g, H43g and H46g

	Perf Type	
	I	*Ie*
A. Watermark upright		
SB97 Pane of 6×3d. (containing No. S72×6) (4.8.59)	6·00	7·50
B. Watermark inverted		
SB97a Pane of 6×3d. (containing No. S72a×6) (4.8.59)	7·00	8·50
ab. Long tailed "R" (R. 1/1)	75·00	
ac. Background retouch (R. 1/1)	75·00	

For illustrations of Nos. SB97ab/ac, see Nos. SB92ab/ac.

Booklet Cylinder Numbers
Panes of 6 (K7 21-row cylinder, others 20-row cylinders)

Cylinder No.	No Dot	Dot
K7	85·00	85·00
K7 T	85·00	85·00
K13	£100	£100
K15	£100	£100

3d. Wilding Booklet Panes

Imprimaturs from the NPM or BPMA
Booklet pane of six. Imperforate, watermark Type W.**24**

Two panes as No. SB97 arranged tête-bêche	£14000
Two panes as No. SB97 arranged tête-bêche with cylinder K7	£14500

3d. Panes of six, two phosphor bands reacting green applied by photogravure. *Wmk* Crowns.
From 3s. Booklets M25p, M28p/9p and M37p(a), 4s.6d. Booklets L21p, L24p, and L27p(a) and 5s. Booklet H46p

	Perf Type I	Perf Type Ie
A. Watermark upright		
SB98 Pane of 6×3d. (containing No. S74×6) *(14.8.60)*	20·00	22·00
b. One 8mm. band on each stamp	£350	
B. Watermark inverted		
SB98a Pane of 6×3d. (containing No. S74a×6) *(14.8.60)*	20·00	22·00
ab. Stamps 1 and 4 with one 6mm band, others with one 8mm band	£400	

See No. S74b,d for the one 8mm band variety and No. S74da for the one 6mm band variety.

Booklet Cylinder Numbers
Panes of six (21-row cylinders)

Cylinder No.	No Dot	Dot
K17	£120	£120
K17 T	£120	£120

Specimen overprints from the NPM
Booklet pane of six, Perf. 15×14, Wmk Type W.**24** upright
Each stamp handstamped "SPECIMEN" (13×2 mm.) £1250

3d. Panes of six, with two phosphor bands reacting blue applied by photogravure. Cream or whiter paper. *Wmk* Crowns.
From 3s. Booklets M33p, M36p, M37p(b), M38p/9p, M43p/7p, M49p/53p, M55p/61p, M64p/74p, 4s.6d. Booklets L25p, L27p(b), L28p, L30p/42p, L44p/57p and 5s. Booklets H49p, H51p/2p and H54p/74p

Cream Paper

	Perf Type I	Perf Type Ie
A. Watermark upright		
SB99 Pane of 6×3d. (containing No. S75×6) *(3.61)*	8·00	9·00
B. Watermark inverted		
SB99a Pane of 6×3d. (containing No. S75a×6) *(3.61)*	8·00	9·00
ab. Long tailed "R" (R. 1/1)	75·00	
ac. Background retouch (R. 1/1)	75·00	

Whiter Paper

	Perf Type I	Perf Type Ie
A. Watermark upright		
SB100 Pane of 6×3d. (containing No. S76×6) *(25.9.62)*	9·00	10·00
B. Watermark inverted		
SB100a Pane of 6×3d. (containing No. S76c×6) *(25.9.62)*	9·00	10·00
ab. Long tailed "R" (R. 1/1)	75·00	
ac. Background retouch (R. 1/1)	75·00	

For illustrations of Nos. SB99ab/ac and SB100ab/ac, see Nos. SB92ab/ac.

Booklet Cylinder Numbers
Panes of six (K15 20-row cylinder, others 21-row cylinders). Two bands.

Cream paper

Cylinder No.	No Dot	Dot
K15	85·00	85·00*
K18	£120	£120
K18 T	£120	£120

Whiter paper

Cylinder No.	No Dot	Dot
K15	£100	£100*
K18	£100	£100
K18 T	£100	£100
K20	£120	£120
K20 T	£120	£120

* K15 Dot panes have the extension hole at the centre of the selvedge as a result of the triple comb perforator starting from the bottom row of each booklet sheet.

Specimen overprints from the NPM
Booklet pane of six. Perf. 15×14, watermark Type W.**24** upright
Each stamp handstamped "SPECIMEN" (15×2½ mm.) £1250

3d. Panes of four, with two phosphor bands reacting blue applied by letterpress. Cream or whiter paper. *Wmk* Crowns.
From 2s. Booklets N4p, N8p/10p, N12p/20p

Cream Paper

A. Watermark Crown to left	Perf. Type I	I(½v)	AP	AP(2E)
SB101 Pane of 4×3d. (containing No. S75b×4) *(14.7.61)*	45·00	£125	30·00	75·00
b. One 8 mm band on each stamp			£200	—
B. Watermark Crown to right				
SB101a Pane of 4×3d. (containing No. S75c×4) *(14.7.61)*	45·00	£125	30·00	†
ab. One 8 mm band on each stamp			£200	†

Whiter Paper

A. Watermark Crown to left	Perf. Type I	I(½v)	AP	AP(2E)
SB102 Pane of 4×3d. (containing No. S76a×4) *(15.8.62)*	60·00	£150	40·00	£100
B. Watermark Crown to right				
SB102a Pane of 4×3d. (containing No. S76b×4) *(15.8.62)*	60·00	£150	40·00	†

Booklet Cylinder Numbers.
Pane of four, Perf. Type I Cyl. No. K19 (Wmk Crown to left) £200

Due to the width of the selvedge, the "19" was normally trimmed off.

Specimen overprints from the NPM
Booklet pane of four. Perf. 15×14, watermark Type W.**24**. Crown to right, Perf. Type AP
Each stamp handstamped "SPECIMEN" (13×2 mm.) £1000

SB Wilding Booklet Panes *3d., 4d.*

SB103

3d. Panes of six, with 4mm phosphor band reacting violet at side. 2×3d. (band at left) and 4×3d. (band at right). Phosphor bands applied by photogravure. Wmk Crowns.

From 10s. Booklet X15p(a/b)

	Perf Type	
A. Watermark upright	I	Ie
SB103 Pane of 6×3d. (containing Nos. S78×2, S78a×4) *(2.67)*	35·00	40·00
B. Watermark inverted		
SB103a Pane of 6×3d. (containing Nos. S78g×2, S78h×4) *(2.67)*	£120	£130

Booklet Cylinder Numbers
Panes of six (21-row cylinder)

Cylinder No.	No Dot	Dot
K18	£225	£225
K18 T	£225	£225

3d. Panes of six, with one 4mm centre phosphor band reacting violet. The centre phosphor bands were applied by photogravure using a mixed screen. *Wmk* Crowns.

From 10s. Booklets X16p/17p

	Perf Type	
A. Watermark upright	I	Ie
SB104 Pane of 6×3d. (containing No. S79×6) *(8.67)*	7·00	8·00
B. Watermark inverted		
SB104a Pane of 6×3d. (containing No. S79b×6) *(8.67)*	10·00	12·00

Booklet Cylinder Numbers
Panes of six (21-row cylinder)

Cylinder No.	No Dot	Dot
K18	£120	£120
K18 T	£120	£120

Imprimaturs from the NPM or BPMA
Booklet panes of six. Imperforate, watermark Type W.**24**

Two panes as No. SB98 arranged *tête-bêche*	£14000
Pane as No. SB98 with cylinder K17. T	£6000
Two panes as No. SB99 arranged *tête-bêche*	£14000
Two panes as No. SB99 arranged *tête-bêche* with cylinder K18	£14500
Two panes as No. SB100 arranged *tête-bêche*	£14000
Pane as No. SB100 with cylinder K20 T	£6000

Booklet panes of four. Imperforate, watermark Type W.**24**

Two panes as No. SB101 arranged *tête-bêche*	£10000
Two panes as No. SB101 arranged *tête-bêche* with cylinder K19	£10500
Two panes as No. SB102 arranged *tête-bêche*	£10000
Two panes as No. SB102 arranged *tête-bêche* with cylinder K19	£10500

4d. Deep ultramarine panes of six, *Wmk* Crowns
From 4s.6d. Booklets L59/65, 6s. Booklets Q1/23 and 10s. Booklets X10/14

	Perf Type	
A. Watermark upright	I	Ie
SB105 Pane of 6×4d. (containing No. S85×6) *(21.6.65)*	6·00	7·50
b. Imperf. pane*	£5000	
c. Part perf. pane*	£4500	
d. Line through diadem (R. 1/1 or 2/1)	70·00	
e. Dot below top frame (R. 1/1 or 2/1)	65·00	
f. "Y" flaw (R. 1/2 or 2/2)	50·00	
B. Watermark inverted		
SB105a Pane of 6×4d. (containing No. S85e×6) *(21.6.65)*	12·00	14·00
ab. Ink marks to right of "4"	£100	
ac. Ink marks to right of "4" retouched	65·00	

* Booklet Errors. See General Notes.

SB105b

SB105c, SB111b (illustrated), SB111ab

86

4d. **Wilding Booklet Panes** **SB**

SB105d
Later retouched (Cyl. N1 no dot)

SB105e, SB107c, SB109b, SB111b (Cyl. N1 dot)

SB105ab before retouch

SB105f, SB107d, SB109c, SB111c
Multipositive flaw from No Dot panes showing N1, N2 (T), N3 also without cylinder no.

SB105ac, SB107ab, SB109ab, SB111ac (Cyl. N1 no dot)

Booklet Cylinder Numbers (Deep ultramarine)
Panes of six (21-row cylinders N1/2 or 20-row cylinder N3)

Cylinder No.	No Dot	Dot
N1	60·00*	60·00
N1 T	65·00	65·00
N2		65·00
N2 T	65·00*	65·00
N3	65·00*	65·00

Specimen overprints from the NPM
Booklet pane of six. Perf. 15×14, watermark Type W.**24** inverted
Each stamp handstamped "SPECIMEN" (13×2 mm)   £1250

4d. Deep ultramarine panes of four, *Wmk* Crowns sideways
From 2s. Booklets N21/27

	Perf. Type			
	I	I(½v)	AP	AP(2E)
A. Watermark Crown to left				
SB106 Pane of 4×4d. (containing No. S85d×4) *(16.8.65)*	15·00	95·00	7·00	£150
B. Watermark Crown to right				
SB106a Pane of 4×4d. (containing No. S85f×4) *(16.8.65)*	10·00	95·00	6·00	†

Perf. AP(2E). It is known that this perforator format was not used on this issue, but was used on later phosphor issues. Accordingly, these rare panes are from booklets N31pd and N32pd where the 4d. pane has phosphor omitted.

Booklet Cylinder Numbers
Pane of four (24-row single pane cylinder of 480 stamps sideways).

	Perf. Type I
Cylinder No.	No Dot
N4 (Wmk. Crown to left)	£150
N4 (Wmk. Crown to right)	£150

On single-pane cylinders with sideways printing the number is engraved in the left margin by row 22. As some of the 4d. value was printed with the watermark either upright or inverted to the direction of print, this issue and the phosphor issues applied by photogravure occur with the cylinder number on panes with sideways watermark either to the left or to the right.

4d. Deep ultramarine panes of six, with two phosphor bands reacting blue. Applied by photogravure. *Wmk* Crowns.
From 4s.6d. Booklets L59p, L60pa/62pa. Booklets Q1p/3p, Q4pa/8pa.

	Perf Type	
	I	Ie
A. Watermark upright		
SB107 Pane of 6×4d. (containing No. S90×6) *(21.6.65)*	12·00	14·00
c. Dot below top frame (R. 1/1 or 2/1)	65·00	
d. "Y" flaw (R. 1/2 or 2/2)	50·00	
B. Watermark inverted		
SB107a Pane of 6×4d. (containing No. S90b×6) *(21.6.65)*	18·00	20·00
ab. Retouch over "4" (R. 1/1 or 2/1)	60·00	

For illustrations of Nos. SB107c/d and SB107ab, see Nos. SB105e/f and SB105ab.

Booklet Cylinder Numbers
Panes of six (21-row cylinder)

Cylinder No.	No Dot	Dot
N1	85·00*	85·00
N1 T	85·00	85·00

SB Wilding Booklet Panes 4d.

4d. Deep ultramarine panes of four, with two phosphor bands reacting blue. Applied by letterpress. *Wmk* Crown sideways

From 2s. Booklets N21p, N22pa and N23pa

	Perf. Type		
A. Watermark Crown to left	I	I(½v)	AP
SB108 Pane of 4×4d. (containing No. S90c×4) *(16.8.65)*	25·00	85·00	15·00
b. One 8 mm band on each stamp			
B. Watermark Crown to right			
SB108a Pane of 4×4d. (containing No. S90d×4) *(16.8.65)*	25·00	85·00	15·00
ab. One 8 mm band on each stamp			

Booklet Cylinder Numbers
Pane of four (24-row single pane cylinder of 480 stamps sideways).

	Perf. Type I
Cylinder No.	No Dot
N4 (Wmk. Crown to right)	£175

4d. Deep ultramarine panes of six, Two 8 mm phosphor bands reacting violet applied by photogravure. Wmk Crowns.

From 4s.6d. Booklets L60pb, L62pb, L63p, L65pa and 6s. Booklets Q4pb/8pb. Q9p/20p and 10s. Booklet X15pa

	Perf Type	
A. Watermark upright	I	Ie
SB109 Pane of 6×4d. (containing No. S91×6) *(9.65)*	5·50	6·50
b. Dot below top frame (R. 1/1 or 2/1)	55·00	
c. "Y" flaw (R. 1/2 or 2/2)	40·00	
B. Watermark inverted		
SB109a Pane of 6×4d. (containing No. S91a×6) *(9.65)*	5·50	6·50
ab. Retouch over "4" (R. 1/1 or 2/1)	65·00	

For illustrations of Nos. SB109b/c and SB109ab, see Nos. SB105e/f and SB105ab.

Booklet Cylinder Numbers
Panes of six (21-row cylinders N1 and N2 or 20-row cylinder N3)

Cylinder No.	No Dot	Dot
N1	70·00	70·00
N1 T	70·00	70·00
N2	80·00	80·00
N2 T	80·00	80·00
N3	80·00*	80·00

4d. Deep ultramarine panes of four, with two 8 mm phosphor bands reacting violet. Applied by photogravure or letterpress. *Wmk* Crowns sideways

From 2s. Booklets N22pb, N23pb/28p, N29p, N30pa, N31pb and N32

	Perf. Type			
A. Watermark Crown to left	I	I(½v)	AP	AP(2E)
SB110 Pane of 4×4d. (containing No. S91b×4) *(1.67)*	10·00	85·00	5·00	10·00
b. One 8 mm band on each stamp	—	—	—	—
c. Bands l/press. *(10.65)*	70·00	—	60·00	†
d. Phosphor printed both sides	†	†	—	†
B. Watermark Crown to right				
SB110a Pane of 4×4d. (containing No. S91c×4) *(1.67)*	10·00	85·00	5·00	15·00
ab. One 8 mm band on each stamp	—	—	—	—
ac. Bands l/press. *(10.65)*	70·00	—	60·00	†
ad. Phosphor printed both sides	†	†	—	†

Letterpress bands from booklets N22pb/26p, Photogravure bands from all later editions.

Booklet Cylinder Numbers
Pane of four (24-row single pane cylinder of 480 stamps sideways).

Photogravure bands	Perf. Type I
Cylinder No.	No Dot
N4 (Wmk. Crown to left)	£125
N4 (Wmk. Crown to right)	95·00

Letterpress bands	
Cylinder No.	No Dot
N4 (Wmk. Crown to left)	†
N4 (Wmk. Crown to right)	—

See note below SB106 cylinder numbers.

4d. Deep ultramarine panes of six, with two 9·5mm. phosphor bands reacting violet. Applied by photogravure. *Wmk* Crowns.

From 4s.6d. Booklets L65pb/71p, 6s. Booklets Q21p/27p and 10s. Booklet X15p(b), X16p/17p

	Perf Type	
A. Watermark upright	I	Ie
SB111 Pane of 6×4d. (containing No. S92×6) *(2.67)*	3·50	4·00
b. Part perf. pane*	£4750	
c. Dot below frame (R. 1/1 or 2/1)	60·00	
d. "Y" flaw (R. 1/2 or 2/2)	40·00	
B. Watermark inverted		
SB111a Pane of 6×4d. (containing No. S92a×6) *(2.67)*	3·50	4·00
ab. Part perf. pane*	£4750	
ac. Retouch over "4" (R. 1/1 or 2/1)	60·00	

* Booklet error. See General Notes.
For illustrations of Nos. SB111c/d and SB111ac, see Nos. SB105e/f and SB105ab.

4d. **Wilding Booklet Panes** **SB**

Booklet Cylinder Numbers
Panes of six (21-row cylinders)

Cylinder No.	No Dot	Dot
N1	60·00	60·00
N1 T	60·00	60·00
N2	55·00	55·00
N2 T	55·00	55·00
N2 (Wmk inverted)	£1000	£1000
N2 T (Wmk inverted)	£1000	£1000

Cylinder panes showing watermark inverted come from Booklet X17p. Due to the paper being re-reeled before printing.

Specimen overprints from the NPM
Booklet pane of six. Perf. 15×14, watermark Type W.**24** inverted

Each stamp handstamped "SPECIMEN" (13×2 mm.)	£1250

4d. Deep ultramarine panes of four, two 9·5 mm phosphor bands reacting violet. Applied by photogravure. *Wmk* Crown sideways

From 2s. Booklets N31pa, N31pc, N32pa and N32pc

		Perf. Type		
	I	I(½v)	AP	AP(2E)
A. Watermark Crown to left				
SB112 Pane of 4×4d. (containing No. S92b×4) *(4.67)*	10·00	65·00	2·50	15·00
b. One 9·5 mm band on each stamp	£100		90·00	—
c. Bands l/press	†	†	£500	†
B. Watermark Crown to right				
SB112a Pane of 4×4d. (containing No. S92c×4) *(4.67)*	10·00	65·00	2·50	35·00
ab. One 9·5 mm band on each stamp	£100		90·00	—
ac. Bands l/press	†	†	£500	†

The rare letterpress phosphor panes were experimental and, with the similar 1d./3d. panes (SB50/53d) probably derive from October 1967 booklet N30pb.

Booklet Cylinder Numbers
Pane of four (24-row single-pane cylinder of 480 stamps sideways).

	Perf. Type I
Cylinder No.	No Dot
N4 (Wmk. Crown to left)	—
N4 (Wmk. Crown to right)	£130

See note below SB106 cylinder numbers.

Section SC
Post Office Booklets of Stamps Containing Wilding Issues in Non-pictorial Covers (1953–1968)

General Notes

The booklets are listed in value and date order except for the 2 shilling booklets for Holiday Resorts (1963/64) and Christmas Cards (1965) which follow the ordinary 2s. booklets. All booklets had stitched panes

Booklet sheet arrangement. Booklets are made up from specially printed sheets which are differently arranged from Post Office counter sheets in order to facilitate manufacture, with the binding margin on the left, so that all booklets open at the right. The arrangement of the sheet varies according to the size and format of the booklet pane required. For example, in the case of booklet panes of six, the printers sheet of 480 stamps, consisting of two panes (no dot and dot) each of 240 stamps arranged in 20 rows of 12 stamps, has additional gutters provided between the 6th and 7th vertical rows in both panes, and the stamps in the 4th, 5th and 6th, and 10th, 11th and 12th vertical rows in both panes are inverted in relation to the others (i.e. tête-bêche). Two horizontal rows of the sheet (producing eight booklets) would be arranged thus:

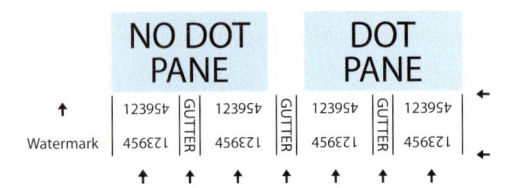

	NO DOT PANE				DOT PANE				
↑	123956	GUTTER	123956	GUTTER	123956	GUTTER	123956		←
Watermark	456EZL		123956		456EZL		123956		←
	↑	↑	↑	↑	↑	↑	↑	↑	

The sheets of stamps, interleaving sheets and covers are stitched vertically, once at the two outer edges of the double pane and twice in each of the gutters as shown by the vertical rules in the diagram. Finally, the booklets are guillotined both horizontally and vertically as indicated by the arrows. This stitching and quilotining of the mass of booklets is done after the sheet has been divided into the no dot and dot panes, resulting in 40 complete booklets at a time.

Inverted watermarks. From the diagram it is easy to see how 50% of Wilding booklet stamps have inverted watermarks.

Watermark positions. Although 50% of booklet panes of six have the watermark inverted, in describing the contents of the booklets reference is made to the catalogue numbers in section SA of the stamps with upright watermark throughout the list. This is to avoid continual reference to the catalogue numbers of the inverted watermarks. Also this applies to some booklets with panes of four and similarly, for panes of four with sideways watermark, reference is made only to the stamp with watermark sideways to the left (*as seen from the front of the stamp*).

Whiter paper. During the changeover period cream and whiter paper stamps could occur in the same booklet and we make no attempt to distinguish these.

Tête-bêche errors. These occur in booklets due to faulty manufacture, usually the result of a corner of the sheet being folded over.

Errors of make-up. Errors exist and we list those that are well known, but caution should be exercised as it is possible to break up booklets and remake them to agree with known errors.

Booklet covers. All covers are printed in black except where otherwise stated.

Booklet pane cylinder numbers. These occur in the left-hand margin of both panes of booklet sheets (i.e no dot and dot) similar to Post Office counter sheets. They are illustrated in Section S except that they always have prefix letters, e.g. E4, F5, G3, but the letters are liable to be partly or completely trimmed off.

All booklet panes of six printed from 20-row cylinders have the cylinder number adjoining the bottom row of stamps but in the case of 21-row cylinders, the perforated web is cut at every 20th row to make sheets of 480. Consequently, on successive sheets the cylinder number appears one row lower and thus a pane can have it adjoining the top or bottom row.

Booklet panes of four with sideways watermark invariably show the cylinder numbers trimmed, while panes of two (from counter sheets) show cylinder numbers.

Booklet panes of four with upright watermark and Machin panes of four and fifteen have the cylinder numbers trimmed off completely.

Dates. The month and year dates are those found printed on the booklets, either on the outer back cover or on the white interleaves. No dates are given on the 1s. booklets, the 2s. booklets Nos. N1/3, the 5s. Philympia booklet No. HP34 and the £1 booklet No. ZP1. The dates of issue of every booklet in a new cover design or composition are given in brackets where known.

Quantities. The quantities given are of the numbers manufactured, but some of the figures are shared by two or more booklets and this is indicated in the listing.

Pattern books. These were dummy books, including the postal rates interleaf dated December 1952, with SPACE AVAILABLE FOR COMMERCIAL ADVERTISING printed on the reverse of the front cover, reverse of the second interleaf and on both sides of the back cover. The panes of stamps were represented by perforated and gummed labels. In the 2s.6d. booklet the third pane had the three labels in the upper row inscribed 1d. and SPACE AVAILABLE FOR COMMERCIAL ADVERTISING printed across the lower row. The panes in the 2s.6d. book were unwatermarked but those in the 5s. booklet had a large Crown multiple watermark.

The books exist with a red handstamp panel at the top of the front cover stating "This is the pattern (Book A) (Book B)..." inserted in manuscript for the 2s.6d. and 5s. books respectively and they exist without the handstamp, presumably being unused examples. On the handstamped 5s. booklets the stamp contents were changed in manuscript to the new contents for issues from January 1953.

These pattern books were produced prior to the re-introduction of commercial advertising and were distributed to potential advertising contractors so that they could tender for the appointment as the Post Office advertising contractor for stamp books. This resulted in the appointment of J. Weiner Ltd., who were at the time the advertising contractor for Post Office telephone directories.

Paste-up books. The contractor was responsible for selling the advertising space and for the provision of copy to the printer. The commercial printed material was submitted to the Post Office Supplies Department in galley form for approval. These proofs were then used to prepare paste-up examples of each edition, so that the make-up could be checked. If the contractor failed to attract sufficient advertising for an edition, numerous official notices (apart from postal rate information) could be used to fill up interleaves and covers.

Paste-up books were prepared using a previous advertiser voucher copy by marking the front cover with the new edition date, pasting in proofs of new commercial advertisements and annotating pages with any other changes. Four copies of each paste-up were prepared, three of which were sent to the Post Office Supplies Department, who forwarded one to the printer, Harrison and Sons Ltd. It appears that an additional copy, marked "Duplicate" was prepared by J. Weiner Ltd., making two copies for their records.

Many paste-up books are similar, with new or repeat commercial advertisements. Of particular interest are new series or booklets showing changes in postal rates or changes in the number of interleaves, where previous editions needed to be changed on the front cover or split and stapled with additional copy. This occurred on the changes from the 2s.6d. to the 3s. series (1957/8), the 3s.9d. to the 4s.6d. series (1957) and the 4s.6d. to the 6s. series (1965). Of further interest are paste-up books showing dates that were never issued due to a lack of sales, resulting in cancellation or a change in postal rates or impending decimalisation in February 1971. These more interesting editions are identified in the listings and priced separately. The listing commences with February 1956 as earlier editions are not known. If they exist, earlier editions will be included in future listings

Advertiser voucher copy books. With the re-introduction of commercial advertising in September 1953 the Post Office advertising contractor began to supply a voucher copy of each edition to the firms whose advertisements appeared in them.

In 1953, the 2s.6d. September, October and November issued books, together with the 5s. September book, were supplied as voucher copies with the stamps torn out. From November 1953, nearly all editions, including the £1 (sewn and without black binding) were made up as voucher copies without the stamp panes. All 1s. and 2s. Holiday and Christmas books had no commercial advertising and a few other editions have not been found as voucher copies.

Of particular interest are the 2s.6d. booklets containing the *se-tenant* pane of three 1d. stamps and three labels. From January 1954 to January 1955 voucher copies of these booklets come with these se-tenant labels shown, but not the stamps. In the January 1954 edition the labels were printed on unwatermarked, ungummed paper, imperforate, but in subsequent editions they are perforated on gummed paper with the Harrison "house" watermark. The panes for the March and April 1954 to January 1955 editions are listed with the issued panes, SB23 and SB24.

Also, the January 1954 edition comes in three types, with the se-tenant pane on medium cream paper or thin buff paper and as a normal voucher copy without the pane. These dummy se-tenant panes are all specific to the voucher copies and do not have proof status.

The scarcer advertisers' voucher copy editions are listed and priced separately and the other editions are listed and priced at the end of each series, in each case being abbreviated to AVC.

Catalogue numbers. In order to avoid confusion we have used the same booklet numbers as in the *Concise Catalogue*. Many of these booklets bear the same prefix letters as other stamps listed in the Great Britain Specialised Catalogues so that when quoting numbers in this Appendix it should be made clear that booklets are being referred to.

Varieties shown thus (a) are those listed in the Great Britain Specialised Catalogues only.

Illustrations. The illustrations of the covers are ¾ size except where otherwise stated.

> **BOOKLET PRICES.** Prices in this Appendix are for booklets containing panes with "average" perforations (i.e. full perforations on two edges of the pane only). Booklets containing panes with complete perforations are worth more.

Non-pictorial types of booklet covers

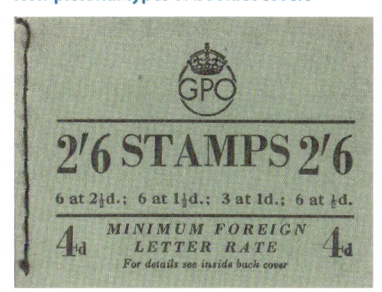

Type A Circular GPO Cypher

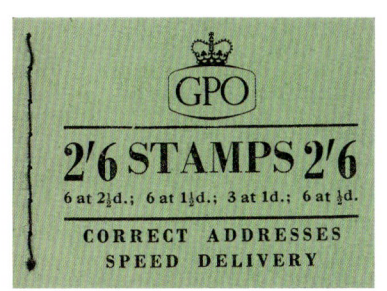

Type B Oval Type GPO Cypher

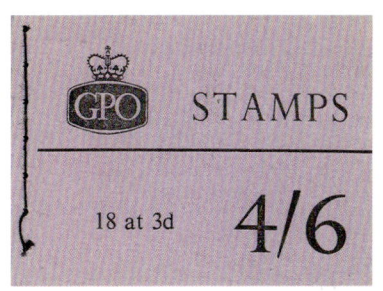

Type C Oval Type GPO Cypher 15 mm wide

Type D Larger Oval GPO Cypher 17 mm wide

SC Dorothy Wilding Booklets — 1s. Booklets, 2s. Booklets

1s. Booklets for use in slot machines

Booklet Series D
Contents: 4×1½d., 4×1d., 4×½d. in panes of two

I. White Unprinted Cover. Not interleaved. For use in experimental machines

Watermark Tudor Crown (Nos. S1, S13, S25)

E1	No date (issued 2.9.53)	56,650	5·00

Watermark St Edward's Crown (Nos. S2, S14, S26)

E2	No date (issued 11.57)	7,180	40·00
E2a	Ditto Stitched back to front		£100

These booklets were made up from columns 1 and 2 from sheets and so do not have inverted watermarks. D booklet machines were withdrawn in November 1960.

A booklet is known with watermark Tudor Crown on the ½d. panes and watermark St Edward's Crown on the 1d. and 1½d. panes (see also mixed watermarks for 2s.6d. and 5s. books). This is due to the ½d. stamp, S2, with watermark St Edward's Crown not being issued until December 1955, whereas the 1d. and 1½d. stamps were available earlier, resulting in later production of some E1 booklets with mixed watermarks between October and December 1955.

Booklet Series E
Contents: 4×1½d., 4×1d., 4×½d. in panes of four

II. White Printed Cover as Type B. Not interleaved. For use in F1 machines.

Watermark Tudor Crown (Nos. S1, S13, S25)

K1	No date (Back cover MINIMUM FOREIGN LETTER RATE FOUR PENCE) (issued 22.7.54)	180,360	8·00
K1a	No date (Back cover MONEY BY POST) (issued 11.54)	572,900	5·00

Watermark St Edward's Crown (Nos. S2, S14, S26)

K2	No date (Back cover £5 only). (issued 5.7.56)	373,000	5·00
K2a	No date (Back cover £10 only. Inland letter rate 2½d.) (issued 6.57)	532,000	5·00
K2b	No date (Back cover £10 only. Inland letter rate 3d.) (issued 8.58)	541,000	5·00

Watermark Crowns (Nos. S4, S16, S28)

K3	No date (Back cover £10 only. Overseas letter rate 6d.) (issued 13.8.59)	623,500	5·00
K3a	No date (Back cover £10 only. Overseas letter rate 4d.) (issued 10.60)	250,000	6·00

1s. booklets continued to be available until 1964. The machines were then converted to issue the thicker 2s. booklets.

2s. Booklets for use in slot machines

Contents: 4×3d., 4×1½d., 4×1d., 4×½d. in panes of four

I. Salmon Cover as Type B. Fully interleaved
Watermark St. Edward's Crown (Nos. S2, S14, S26, S68)

N1	No date (issued 22.4.59)	452,470	9·00

II. Salmon Cover as Type C. Fully interleaved
Watermark Crowns (upright) (Nos. S4, S16, S28, S70)

N2	No date (issued 2.11.60)	300,500	10·50

III. Lemon Cover as Type C. Fully interleaved
Watermark Crowns (upright) (Nos. S4, S16, S28, S70)

N3	No date (issued 9.2.61)	1,330,750	10·50

IV. Lemon Cover as Type C. Fully interleaved
Watermark Crowns (sideways) (Nos. S4d or S5a, S16e or S17a, S28a or S29a, S70d or S71a) or blue phosphor (Nos. S10b or S11a, S21b or S22a, S33b or S34a, S75b or S76a)

N4	Apr 1961 (issued 26.5.61)	1,381,440	32·00
	p. With blue phosphor bands (issued 14.7.61)	171,400	55·00
	pa. Error. 3d. pane missing phosphor		£200
N5	Sept 1961	889,000	50·00
N6	Jan 1962	911,600	45·00
N7	Apr 1962	958,600	55·00
N8	July 1962	935,600	50·00
	p. With blue phosphor bands	51,600	90·00
N9	Nov 1962	975,000	70·00
	p. With blue phosphor bands	56,000	90·00
N10	Jan 1963	1,105,400	55·00
	p. With blue phosphor bands	58,390	£180
N11	Mar 1963	1,090,800	55·00
N12	June 1963	1,014,800	55·00
	p. With blue phosphor bands	57,800	75·00
N13	Aug 1963	989,000	55·00
	p. With blue phosphor bands	56,400	£100
N14	Oct 1963	1,018,800	55·00
	p. With blue phosphor bands	11,200	£140
N15	Feb 1964	1,122,400	55·00
	p. With blue phosphor bands	76,600	95·00
N16	June 1964	386,570	55·00
	p. With blue phosphor bands	63,400	£120
N17	Aug 1964	122,300	80·00
	p. With blue phosphor bands	58,800	£120
N18	Oct 1964	1,179,800	55·00
	p. With blue phosphor bands	94,200	70·00
N19	Dec 1964	109,170	65·00
	p. With blue phosphor bands	34,000	70·00
N20	Apr 1965	1,435,400	55·00
	p. With blue phosphor bands	40,800	65·00

2s. booklets in this composition were withdrawn from sale on 31 August 1965

Paste-up books N4 to N20   each £100
AVC books N1 to N20   each 8·00

Contents changed: 4×4d. in pane of four, 2×1d. and 2×3d. in pane of four arranged *se-tenant* horizontally

V. Orange-Yellow Cover as Type C. Printed in black. Fully interleaved

Watermark Crowns (sideways) (Nos. S17a, S71a, S85d) and blue or violet phosphor with one band on 3d. (Nos. S22a, S23d, or S24d; S77b or S78c; S90c, S91b or S92b)

N21	July 1965 (issued 16.8.65)	2,671,800	3·50
	p. With blue phosphor bands (issued 16.8.65)	109,600	75·00

N22	Oct 1965	1,852,800	3·75
	pa. With blue phosphor bands	223,200	75·00
	pb. With violet 8 mm. phosphor bands)		12·00
N23	Jan 1966	1,633,200	6·25
	pa. With blue phosphor bands.	350,600	75·00
	pb. With violet 8 mm. phosphor bands)		16·00
N24	Apr 1966	2,125,200	6·25
	p. With violet 8 mm. phosphor bands	240,000	8·00
	pa. Error. 4d. pane missing phosphor		£100
N25	July 1966	1,981,800	7·50
	p. With violet 8 mm. phosphor bands	97,400	£150
N26	Oct 1966	1,787,400	6·00
	p. With violet 8 mm. phosphor bands	471,400	10·00
N27	Jan 1967	644,200	8·00
	p. With violet 8 mm. phosphor bands	2,100,400	5·00
N28p	Apr 1967 (a) With violet 8 mm. phosphor bands	2,330,200	6·00
	pa. Error. 4d. pane missing phosphor		75·00
N29p	July 1967. With violet 8 mm. phosphor bands	3,209,800	4·00
N30p	Oct 1967 (issued 15.9.67)		
	pa. With violet 8 mm. phosphor bands.	3,924,600	4·00
	pb. With violet 9·5 mm. phosphor bands on se-tenant pane		£250
	pc. Error. Se-tenant. pane missing phosphor		50·00

For illustration showing how the *se-tenant* stamps with one phosphor band on the 3d. are printed, see listing of No. SB45/8.

Watermark Crowns (sideways), 3d. with two violet phosphor bands (Nos. S23b or S24b; S78c or S80; S91b or S92b)

N31p	Jan 1968 (issued early 11.67)		
	pa. Violet 9·5 mm. bands.	1,864,800	4·00
	pb. 8 mm. bands on 4d. pane		£100
	pc. 8 mm. bands on se-tenant pane		£100
	pd. Error. 4d. pane missing phosphor		25·00
	pe. Error. Se-tenant pane missing phosphor		25·00
N32p	Mar 1968 (issued mid 1.68)		
	pa. Violet 9·5 mm. bands.	3,078,800	4·50
	pb. 8 mm. bands on 4d. pane		£100
	pc. 8 mm. bands on se-tenant pane		£100
	pd. Error. 4d. pane missing phosphor		25·00
	pe. Error. Se-tenant pane missing phosphor		25·00
Paste-up books N21 to N32			each £100
AVC books N21 to N32			each 8·00

Nos. N31pc and N32pc have one band on 3d.
2s. booklets were withdrawn on 11 February 1971 prior to decimalisation on 15 February.

2s. Booklets for Holiday Resorts

Contents: 8×2½d. in panes of four and 3×½d. and 1×2½d. in pane of four arranged *se-tenant*

Lemon Cover as Type C. Printed in red. Fully interleaved Watermark Crowns. Chalk-surfaced paper (Nos. S6, S58)

A. Black stitching
NR1 No date (issued 15.7.63)		415,000	4·00

B. White stitching
NR1a No date (issued 3.9.63)		50,000	4·00

Contents changed: 8×½d. and 8×2½d. in panes of four arranged *se-tenant* vertically.

Lemon Cover as Type C. Printed in red. Fully interleaved Watermark Crowns (sideways) (No. S5a/b, S57b/c)

NR2	1964 (issued 1.7.64)	827,800	1·50

These replaced the normal 2s. booklets in the resort towns to which they were issued.

2s. Booklet for Christmas Cards

Contents: 8×3d. in two panes of four
Orange-yellow Cover as Type C. Printed in red. Fully interleaved

Watermark Crowns (sideways) (No. S71a)

NX1	1965 (issued 6.12.65)	1,208,000	1·00

The above was withdrawn on 3.1.66 but reissued on 16.5.66 as a holiday resort booklet.

2s.6d. Booklets

Contents: 6×2½d., 6×1½d., 3×1d. (pane completed by three perforated labels), 6×½d. in panes of six
Pattern Book A. Dec 1952 (see Notes)
(a) with red handstamp on cover	£750
(b) without handstamp on cover	£750

LABELS. The wording printed on the labels differs as follows:

"PPR"	"MINIMUM INLAND PRINTED PAPER RATE 1½d." Two types exist: (a) 17 mm. high. Printed in photogravure (b) 15 mm. high. Printed by letterpress
"SHORTHAND"	"SHORTHAND IN 1 WEEK" (covering all three labels)
"POST EARLY"	"PLEASE POST EARLY IN THE DAY"
"PAP"	"PACK YOUR PARCELS SECURELY" (1st label), "ADDRESS YOUR LETTERS CORRECTLY" (2nd label) "AND POST EARLY IN THE DAY" (3rd label)

I. Composite Booklets containing Stamps of King George VI and Queen Elizabeth II

A. Green Cover as Type A. Not interleaved
K.G. VI ½d. (No. Q3), 1d. (No. Q6) and Q.E. II 1½d. (No. S25), 2½d. (No. S51)

F 1	May 1953	PPR 17 mm.	2,272,000	25·00
	a. Date error May 195 for May 1953			£150
	b. Date error May 19 for May 1953			£200
F 2	June 1953	PPR 17 mm.	2,751,000	30·00

SC Dorothy Wilding Booklets 2s.6d. Booklets

F 3	July 1953	PPR 17 mm.	2,199,000	35·00
F 4	Aug 1953	PPR 17 mm.	2,464,000	32·00

B. Green Cover as Type A. With the addition of two interleaves, one at each end K.G. VI ½d. (No. Q3), 1d. (No. Q6) and Q.E. II 1½d. (No. S25), 2½d. (No. S51)

F 5	Sept 1953	PPR 17 mm.	2,386,000	£250
F 6	Sept 1953	PPR 15 mm.		£130
	a. Date error missing "B" in "SEPTEMBER"			£160

C. Green Cover as Type B. Contents as Nos. F 5/6 K.G. VI ½d. (No. Q3), 1d. (No. Q6) and Q.E. II 1½d. (No. S25), 2½d. (No. S51)

F 7	Oct 1953	PPR 17 mm.	2,532,000	50·00
F 8	Oct 1953	PPR 15 mm.		£150
F 9	Nov 1953	PPR 17 mm.	4,308,000*	60·00
	AVC book			50·00
F10	Nov 1953	PPR 15 mm.		£250
F11	Dec 1953	PPR 17 mm.	2,918,000	55·00
	AVC book			50·00
F12	Jan 1954	SHORTHAND	2,199,000	75·00
	AVC book (with printed label pane)			£1500
	AVC book (without label pane)			80·00
F13	Feb 1954	SHORTHAND	2,202,000	85·00
	AVC book (with printed label pane)			£1500

* The quantity given for F9 includes F10.

D. Green Cover as Type B. Contents as Nos. F 5/6 but Q.E. II ½d. in place of K.G. VI ½d. K.G. VI 1d. (No. Q6) and Q.E. II ½d. (No. S1), 1½d. (No. S25), 2½d. (No. S51)

F14	Mar 1954	PPR 17 mm.	139,000	£650
F14a	Mar 1954	SHORTHAND		—

II. Booklets containing only Queen Elizabeth II Stamps

Green Cover as Type B. Watermark Tudor Crown (Nos. S1, S13, S25, S51)

A. Two interleaves pages, one at each end

F15	Mar 1954	PPR 15 mm.	2,085,000	£325
F16	Apr 1954	POST EARLY	3,176,000	65·00
F17	May 1954	POST EARLY	2,435,000	65·00
F18	June 1954	POST EARLY	2,419,000	65·00
F19	July 1954	POST EARLY	2,876,000	65·00
F20	Aug 1954	POST EARLY	2,871,000	65·00
F21	Sept 1954	POST EARLY	2,799,000	65·00
F22	Oct 1954	POST EARLY	2,803,000	50·00
F23	Nov 1954	POST EARLY	3,739,000	50·00
F24	Dec 1954	POST EARLY	2,813,000	50·00
AVC book F15 (with printed label pane)				£1500
AVC books F16 to F24 (with printed label pane)				each £350

B. Fully interleaved

F25	Jan 1955	POST EARLY		
	(a) (original setting)		2,551,000	80·00
	(b) (modified setting)			75·00
F26	Jan 1955	PAP	160,000	£200
F27	Feb 1955	PAP	2,694,000	50·00
F28	Mar 1955	PAP	2,530,000	50·00
F29	Apr 1955	PAP	2,522,000	50·00
F30	May 1955	PAP	2,530,000	65·00
F31	June 1955	PAP	2,522,000	50·00
F32	July 1955	PAP	2,431,000	50·00
AVC book F25(a) (with printed label pane)				£450

In the modified setting the distance between IN THE is 1 mm. and this is only found on the majority of the Jan. 1955 edition (Booklet F25). The normal spacing is 1½ mm.

> **MIXED WATERMARKS.** Nos. F33/8 and F42/3 exist with mixed Tudor Crown and St Edward's Crown watermarks. The mixed watermarks are indicated by the code letters "T" (Tudor) and "E" (Edward) starting with the first pane of the booklet, i.e. 2½d., 1½d., 1d., ½d. We only quote one price for each booklet and this is the minimum price. Some combinations are scarcer and worth more.

Tudor Crown, St Edward's Crown and mixed watermarks.
All have PAP labels.

F33	Aug 1955 PAP (TTTT)		
	(a) Combination TTET	2,563,000	50·00
	(b) Combination TEET		
F34	Sept 1955 (TTTT)		
	(a) Combination TTET		
	(b) Combination TEET		
	(c) Combination TEEE	2,275,000	60·00
	(d) Combination ETET		
	(e) Combination EEET		
	(f) Combination EEEE		
F35	Oct 1955 (TTTT)		
	(a) Combination TEET		
	(b) Combination EEET	2,289,000	35·00
	(c) Combination TEEE		
	(d) Combination EEEE		
F36	Nov 1955 (TTTT)		
	(a) Combination TEEE		
	(b) Combination EEET	4,125,000	35·00
	(c) Combination EEEE		

AVC books F27 to F36 each 30·00

Watermark St Edward's Crown (Nos. S2, S14, S26, S53). All have PAP labels

F37	Dec 1955		
	(a) Combination TEET	2,789,000	35·00
	(b) Combination EEET		
F38	Jan 1956		
	(a) Combination EEET	2,001,000	35·00
F39	Feb 1956	2,031,000	35·00
F40	Mar 1956	2,289,000	35·00
F41	Apr 1956	2,283,000	45·00
F42	May 1956		
	(a) Combination EEET	2,275,000	35·00
	(b) Combination TEEE		
F43	June 1956		
	(a) Combination EEET	2,293,000	35·00
	(b) Combination TEEE		
F44	July 1956	2,279,400	35·00
F45	Aug 1956	2,264,400	25·00
F46	Sept 1956	2,533,000	45·00
F47	Oct 1956	2,536,000	35·00
F48	Nov 1956	4,165,800	35·00
F49	Dec 1956	2,724,600	35·00
F50	Jan 1957	2,212,800	35·00
F51	Feb 1957	2,772,790	35·00
F52	Mar 1957	2,497,800	35·00

Paste-up books F39 to F52 each £150

2s.6d.. Booklets, 3s. Booklets **Dorothy Wilding Booklets** **SC**

Contents changed: 6×2½d., 6×2d., 6×½d. in panes of six

III.
Watermark St Edward's Crown (Nos. S2, S38, S53)

F53	Apr 1957	2,451,800	35·00
F54	May 1957	2,062,400	35·00
F55	June 1957	1,843,000	30·00
F56	July 1957	2,305,000	30·00
F57	Aug 1957	2,265,000	30·00
F58	Sept 1957	2,482,200	30·00
F59	Oct 1957	2,505,600	30·00
F60	Nov 1957	3,085,600	25·00
F61	Dec 1957	281,000	45·00

Paste-up books F53 to F61   each £150
AVC books F37 to F61   each 15·00

The 2s.6d. booklets were withdrawn from sale on 27 July 1958.

3s. Booklets

Contents: 6×3d., 6×1½d., 6×1d., 6×½d. in panes of six

I. Red Cover as Type B. Fully interleaved
Watermark St Edward's Crown (Nos. S2, S14, S26, S68)

M1	Jan 1958	1,815,000	28·00
M2	Feb 1958	2,224,000	38·00
M3	Mar 1958	2,271,000	30·00
M4	Apr 1958	2,654,000	28·00
M5	May 1958	2,146,000	28·00
M6	June 1958	2,222,000	28·00
M7	July 1958	885,000	30·00
M8	Aug 1958	896,000	32·00
M9	Nov 1958		
	(a) Combination EEEC		
	(b) Combination EECE		
	(c) Combination EECC	1,367,000	32·00
	(d) Combination CECE		
	(e) Combination CCCE		

> **MIXED WATERMARKS** See notes above No. F33. The mixed watermarks here are indicated by the code letters "E" (Edward) and "C" (Crowns), starting with the first pane of the booklet, i.e. 3d., 1½d., 1d., ½d.

Watermark Crowns (Nos. S4, S16, S28, S70), or graphite lines (Nos. S7, S18, S30, S72)

M10	Dec 1958		
	(a) Combination ECEC		
	(b) Combination CEEE		
	(c) Combination CECE	886,000	35·00
	(d) Combination CEEC		
	(e) Combination CECC		
M11	Jan 1959		
	(a) Combination CECC	} 1,145,000	35·00
M12	Feb 1959	1,125,000	35·00
M13	Aug 1959	1,038,000	40·00
	g. With graphite lines (issued 4.8.59)	47,000	£250
M14	Sept 1959	1,542,000	40·00
	g. With graphite lines	74,000	£325

Paste-up books M1 to M4 (using 2s.6d. AVC to make up)   each £200
M5 to M14   each £150
AVC books M1 to M14   each 20·00

II. Brick-red Cover as Type C. Fully interleaved.
Watermark Crowns (Nos. S4, S16, S28, S70), graphite lines (Nos. S7, S18, S30, S72) or green phosphor (Nos. S9, S20, S32, S74)

M15	Oct 1959	1,016,000	35·00
	g. With graphite lines	74,000	£350
M16	Nov 1959	2,287,000	35·00
M17	Dec 1959	1,027,000	35·00
M18	Jan 1960	752,000	35·00
M19	Feb 1960	750,000	50·00
	g. With graphite lines	37,600	£325
M20	Mar 1960	966,000	50·00
	g. With graphite lines	39,600	£375
M21	Apr 1960	941,000	45·00
	g. With graphite lines	38,200	£325
M22	May 1960	911,000	60·00
M23	June 1960	982,000	60·00
M24	July 1960	989,200	50·00
M25	Aug 1960	897,000	45·00
	p. With green phosphor bands (issued 14.8.60)	39,800	75·00
M26	Sept 1960	1,326,600	50·00
M27	Oct 1960	1,343,400	50·00
M28	Nov 1960	2,068,200	38·00
	p. With green phosphor bands	11,900	75·00
	pa. Error. 1½d. pane missing phosphor		£250

Paste-up books M15 to M28   each £150
AVC books M15 to M28   each 10·00

III. Brick-red Cover as Type D. Fully interleaved.
Watermark Crowns (Nos. S4 or S5, S16 or S17, S28 or S29, S70 or S71), green or blue phosphor (Nos. S9 or S10, S20 or S21, S32 or S33, S74 or S75)

M29	Dec 1960	905,200	48·00
	p. With green phosphor bands	31,800	75·00
M30	Jan 1961	731,800	60·00
M31	Feb 1961	727,000	60·00
	a. Date error 196 for 1961		£150
M32	Mar 1961	754,000	60·00
M33	Apr 1961	760,800	60·00
	p. With blue phosphor bands	142,600	75·00
M34	May 1961	738,000	60·00
M35	June 1961	768,000	60·00
M36	July 1961	783,400	55·00
	p. With blue phosphor bands	7,800	75·00
M37	Aug 1961	747,400	60·00
	pa. With green phosphor bands	} 54,400	75·00
	pb. With blue phosphor bands		85·00
	pc. Error. 3d. pane missing phosphor		£250
M38	Sept 1961	513,600	60·00
	p. With blue phosphor bands	19,200	85·00
M39	Oct 1961	494,600	60·00
	p. With blue phosphor bands	18,800	£100
M40	Nov 1961	467,600	60·00
M41	Dec 1961	356,800	60·00
M42	Jan 1962	447,000	60·00
M43	Feb 1962	654,200	60·00
	p. With blue phosphor bands	11,800	£100
M44	Mar 1962	655,200	50·00
	p. With blue phosphor bands	19,400	£100
M45	Apr 1962	569,600	60·00
	p. With blue phosphor bands	19,600	£100

SC — Dorothy Wilding Booklets — 3s. Booklets, 3s.9d. Booklets

M46	May 1962	475,000	60·00
	p. With blue phosphor bands	27,000	£100
M47	June 1962	468,400	60·00
	p. With blue phosphor bands	27,200	£100
M48	July 1962	729,400	60·00
M49	Aug 1962	691,200	60·00
	p. With blue phosphor bands	28,800	90·00
M50	Sept 1962	687,400	55·00
	p. With blue phosphor bands	11,800	£100
M51	Oct 1962	864,600	70·00
	p. With blue phosphor bands	35,200	£100
M52	Nov 1962	1,125,600	70·00
	p. With blue phosphor bands	51,800	£100
M53	Dec 1962	1,035,000	70·00
	p. With blue phosphor bands	19,200	£100
M54	Jan 1963	499,400	70·00
M55	Feb 1963	462,400	70·00
	p. With blue phosphor bands	39,400	£100
M56	Mar 1963	512,800	70·00
	p. With blue phosphor bands	39,200	£100
M57	Apr 1963	512,800	70·00
	p. With blue phosphor bands	39,600	£100
M58	May 1963	520,800	70·00
	p. With blue phosphor bands	19,400	£500
M59	June 1963	532,400	75·00
	p. With blue phosphor bands	19,800	70·00
M60	July 1963	712,000	60·00
	p. With blue phosphor bands	17,800	£100
M61	Aug 1963	698,600	70·00
	p. With blue phosphor bands	19,800	£100
M62	Sept 1963	503,000	70·00
	a. Date error 196 for 1963		£150
M63	Oct 1963	660,400	80·00
M64	Nov 1963	670,000	70·00
	p. With blue phosphor bands	39,400	£100
M65	Dec 1963	711,400	85·00
	p. With blue phosphor bands	19,350	£200
M66	Jan 1964	619,600	80·00
	p. With blue phosphor bands	67,000	75·00
M67	Mar 1964	666,600	80·00
	p. With blue phosphor bands	30,400	£100
M68	May 1964	636,600	80·00
	p. With blue phosphor bands	46,600	£120
M69	July 1964	865,800	60·00
	p. With blue phosphor bands	27,400	£100
M70	Sept 1964	915,600	60·00
	p. With blue phosphor bands	39,800	£100
M71	Nov 1964	2,157,600	45·00
	a. Date error 196 for 1964		£150
	p. With blue phosphor bands	99,200	55·00
M72	Jan 1965	1,009,800	45·00
	p. With blue phosphor bands	50,000	70·00
M73	Mar 1965	944,600	35·00
	p. With blue phosphor bands	38,200	65·00
M74	May 1965	765,600	60·00
	p. With blue phosphor bands	58,200	£100

Paste-up books M29 to M74	each £150
July 1965 (not issued)	£250
AVC books M29 to M38	each 10·00
M39 to M42	each 50·00
M44 and M45	each 50·00
M46 to M74	each 10·00

3s. booklets were withdrawn from sale on 31 August 1965.

3s.9d. Booklets

Contents: 18×2½d. in panes of six

Red Cover as Type B.
A. Two interleaves, one at each end
Watermark Tudor Crown (No. S51)

G1	Nov 1953	1,446,000	40·00
G2	Jan 1954	1,572,000	60·00
G3	Mar 1954	1,474,000	40·00
G4	Dec 1954	1,477,000	40·00
G5	Feb 1955	925,000	40·00
G6	Apr 1955	1,112,000	40·00
G7	June 1955	675,000	40·00
G8	Aug 1955	636,000	40·00

AVC books G1 to G4   each 30·00

Tudor Crown, St Edward's Crown and mixed watermarks
(see notes above No. F33)

G9	Oct 1955 (TTT)		
	(a) Combination TET		
	(b) Combination EET	1,661,000	40·00
	(c) Combination EEE		
G10	Dec 1955 (TTT)		
	(a) Combination TET	616,000	40·00
	(b) Combination EEE		

B. Fully interleaved. Watermark St Edward's Crown (No. S53)

G12	Feb 1956	638,000	30·00
G13	Apr 1956	642,000	30·00
G14	June 1956	634,000	30·00
G15	Aug 1956	747,200	30·00
G16	Oct 1956	1,762,800	30·00
G17	Dec 1956	1,065,800	30·00
G18	Feb 1957	1,376,000	30·00
G19	Apr 1957	1,139,600	30·00
G20	June 1957	1,115,200	17·00
G21	Aug 1957	39,600	40·00

Paste-up book G12 (stapled to make up)	£200
G13 to G21	each £150
AVC books G5 to G21	each 15·00

3s.9d. booklets were withdrawn from sale on 30 September 1957.

4s.6d. Booklets

Contents: 18×3d. in panes of six

**I. Purple Cover as Type B. Fully interleaved.
Watermark St. Edward's Crown** (No. S68)

L1	Oct 1957	2,249,000	30·00
L2	Dec 1957	4,539,000	30·00
L3	Feb 1958	1,789,000	35·00
L4	Apr 1958	2,691,000	30·00
L5	June 1958	1,096,000	32·00
L6	Oct 1958	1,796,000	30·00
L7	Dec 1958	1,808,000	30·00

Watermark Crowns (No. S70)

L8	Dec 1958	(incl. above)	£130

Paste-up books L1 or L2 (using 3s.9d. AVC books to make up)	each £200
Paste-up books L3 to L8	each £150
Aug 1958 (not issued)	£250
AVC books L1 to L8	each 20·00

**II. Purple Cover as Type C. Fully interleaved.
Watermark Crowns** (No. S70) or graphite lines (No. S72)

L9	Feb 1959	(with L14) 2,260,000	35·00
L10	June 1959	(with L16) 2,195,000	40·00
L11	Aug 1959	1,710,000	30·00
	g. With graphite lines	97,600	45·00
L12	Oct 1959	1,852,000	45·00
L13	Dec 1959	(with L17) 1,409,000	35·00

**III. Violet Cover as Type C. Fully interleaved.
Watermark Crowns** (No. S70), graphite lines (No. S72) or green phosphor (No. S74)

L14	Feb 1959	(incl. in L9)	£100
L15	Apr 1959	2,137,000	35·00
	g. With graphite lines	99,200	30·00
L16	June 1959	(incl. in L10)	60·00
	g. With graphite lines	99,400	30·00
L17	Dec 1959	(incl. in L13)	60·00
L18	Feb 1960	1,801,000	35·00
	g. With graphite lines	79,600	60·00
L19	Apr 1960	1,730,000	35·00
	g. With graphite lines	78,800	35·00
L20	June 1960	1,832,000	40·00
L21	Aug 1960	1,771,600	40·00
	p. With green phosphor bands	39,800	60·00
L22	Oct 1960	2,723,600	55·00

Paste-up books L9 to L22	each £150
AVC books L9 to L14 and L16 to L22	each 10·00

IV. Violet Cover as Type D. Fully interleaved.
Watermark Crowns (No. S70 or S71), green or blue phosphor (Nos. S74, S75 or S76)

L23	Dec 1960	1,772,000	75·00
L24	Feb 1961	1,982,200	75·00
	p. With green phosphor bands	27,200	50·00
L25	Apr 1961	3,428,400	50·00
	p. With blue phosphor bands	297,400	45·00
L26	June 1961	1,825,600	75·00
L27	Aug 1961	2,679,800	70·00
	pa. With green phosphor bands	63,120	90·00
	pb. With blue phosphor bands		80·00
L28	Oct 1961	3,061,000	70·00
	p. With blue phosphor bands	31,400	60·00
L29	Dec 1961	1,942,800	70·00
L30	Feb 1962	2,405,200	65·00
	p. With blue phosphor bands	43,600	40·00
L31	Apr 1962	1,985,000	75·00
	p. With blue phosphor bands	75,400	80·00
L32	June 1962	2,190,600	80·00
	p. With blue phosphor bands	74,000	90·00
L33	Aug 1962	2,533,800	60·00
	p. With blue phosphor bands	83,600	90·00
L34	Oct 1962	3,525,400	60·00
	p. With blue phosphor bands	83,200	£275
L35	Dec 1962	1,822,000	70·00
	p. With blue phosphor bands	82,200	80·00
L36	Feb 1963	2,352,600	70·00
	p. With blue phosphor bands	117,000	80·00
L37	Apr 1963	2,390,200	70·00
	p. With blue phosphor bands	119,000	55·00
L38	June 1963	2,873,600	70·00
	p. With blue phosphor bands	178,600	55·00
L39	Aug 1963	2,474,200	80·00
	p. With blue phosphor bands	111,000	65·00
L40	Oct 1963	1,829,200	75·00
	p. With blue phosphor bands	99,400	£100
L41	Nov 1963	1,821,000	80·00
	p. With blue phosphor bands	99,600	65·00
L42	Dec 1963	2,431,400	75·00
	p. With blue phosphor bands	46,400	£300
L43	Jan 1964	1,043,800	£125
L44	Feb 1964	1,069,000	80·00
	p. With blue phosphor bands	87,000	55·00
L45	Mar 1964	1,014,200	£125
	p. With blue phosphor bands	82,800	£180
L46	Apr 1964	1,006,600	£125
	p. With blue phosphor bands	62,400	65·00
L47	May 1964	1,028,800	80·00
	p. With blue phosphor bands	105,200	£100
L48	June 1964	1,067,400	80·00
	p. With blue phosphor bands	70,400	£100
L49	July 1964	1,673,600	80·00
	p. With blue phosphor bands	56,200	65·00
L50	Aug 1964	1,622,600	80·00
	a. Date error 196 for 1964		£150
	p. With blue phosphor bands	78,200	55·00
L51	Sept 1964	1,561,200	80·00
	p. With blue phosphor bands	98,000	65·00
L52	Oct 1964	1,781,800	80·00
	p. With blue phosphor bands	197,800	£100
L53	Nov 1964	1,686,000	80·00
	p. With blue phosphor bands	138,000	65·00
L54	Dec 1964	1,684,000	80·00
	p. With blue phosphor bands	119,200	65·00
L55	Jan 1965	1,519,200	70·00
	p. With blue phosphor bands	95,000	60·00
L56	Feb 1965	1,504,600	60·00
	p. With blue phosphor bands	94,200	80·00
L57	Mar 1965	1,479,600	35·00
	p. With blue phosphor bands	18,800	£500
L58	Apr 1965	1,438,400	55·00

Paste-up books L23 to L58	each £150
AVC books L23 to L27	each 10·00
AVC books L28 to L31	each 50·00
AVC books L32 to L58	each 10·00

An edition dated MAY 1965 was prepared, but not issued, due to the increase in letter rate from 3d. to 4d. on 17 May.

Paste-up May 1965	£400
AVC May 1965	£400

SC Dorothy Wilding Booklets   4s.6d.. Booklets, 5s. Booklets

Contents changed: 12×4d., 6×1d. in panes of six

Slate-blue Cover as Type D.
Watermark Crowns (Nos. S17, S85), blue or violet phosphor (Nos. S22, S23 or S24; S90, S91 or S92)

L59	July 1965 (issued 26.7.65)	2,191,600	30·00
	p. With blue phosphor bands (issued 26.7.65)	75,400	32·00
	pa. Error. 4d. pane missing phosphor		£150
L60	Sept 1965	1,839,600	30·00
	pa. With blue phosphor bands.	} 200,800	32·00
	pb. With violet 8 mm. phosphor bands		32·00
L61	Nov 1965	2,005,000	30·00
	pa. With blue phosphor bands	} 165,800	35·00
	pb. With violet 8 mm. phosphor bands		35·00
L62	Jan 1966	1,671,000	35·00
	pa. With blue phosphor bands	} 334,600	32·00
	pb. With violet 8 mm. phosphor bands		32·00
L63	Mar 1966	1,201,600	30·00
	p. With violet 8 mm. phosphor bands	153,200	30·00
L64	Jan 1967	98,800	40·00
	p. With violet 8 mm. phosphor bands	396,600	30·00
L65	Mar 1967	97,200	70·00
	pa. With violet 8 mm. phosphor bands	} 255,400	25·00
	pb. With violet 9·5 mm. phosphor bands		25·00

Watermark Crowns, violet 9·5 mm. phosphor (Nos. S24, S92)

L66p	May 1967	697,200	15·00
	pa. Error. 4d. pane missing phosphor		£100
L67p	July 1967	569,000	25·00
L68p	Sept 1967	750,800	20·00
L69p	Nov 1967	1,802,600	15·00
L70p	Jan 1968	729,400	15·00
L71p	Mar 1968	729,400	10·00
	pa. Error. 4d. pane missing phosphor		£100

Paste-up books L59 (using 5s. AVC to make up)		£200
L60 to L71		each £150
AVC books L59 to L71		each £10·00

5s. Booklets
Contents: 12×2½d., 6×2d., 6×1½d., 6×1d., 6×½d. in panes of six
Pattern Book B Dec 1952 (see Notes)

(a) with red handstamp on cover	£600
(b) without handstamp on cover	£600

I. Composite Booklets containing Stamps of King George VI and Queen Elizabeth II

A. Buff Cover as Type A. Not interleaved K.G. VI ½d. (No. Q3), 1d. (No. Q6), 2d. (No. Q12) and Q.E. II 1½d. (No. S25), 2½d. (No. S51)

H1	May 1953	1,309,000	40·00
	a. Date error May 195 for May 1953		£300
	b. Date error May 195 for May 1953		£300
H2	July 1953	1,716,000	50·00

B. Buff Cover as Type A. With the addition of two interleaves, one at each end. K.G. VI ½d. (No. Q3), 1d. (No. Q6), 2d. (No. Q12) and Q.E. II 1½d. (No. S25), 2½d. (No. S51)

H3	Sept 1953	1,070,000	65·00

C. Buff Cover as Type B. Contents as No. H3. K.G. VI ½d. (No. Q3), 1d. (No. Q6), 2d. (No. Q12) and Q.E. II 1½d. (No. S25), 2½d. (No. S51)

H4	Nov 1953	2,126,000	50·00
H5	Jan 1954	692,000	65·00

D. Buff Cover as Type B. Contents as Nos. H4/5 but Q.E. II ½d. in place of K.G. VI ½d. K.G. VI 1d. (No. Q6), 2d. (No. Q12) and Q.E. II ½d. (No. S1), 1½d. (No. S25), 2½d. (No. S51)

H6	Mar 1954	16,000	£1000

E. Buff Cover as Type B. Contents as No. H6 but Q.E. II 1d. in place of K.G. VI 1d. K.G. VI 2d. (No. Q12) and Q.E. II ½d. (No. S1), 1d. (No. S13), 1½d. (No. S25), 2½d. (No. S51)

H7	Mar 1954	160,000	£275
	a. Error. Extra 1½d. pane		£600

II. Booklets containing only Queen Elizabeth II Stamps

A. Buff Cover as Type B.
Watermark Tudor Crown (Nos. S1, S13, S25, S36, S51)

A. Two interleaves, one at each end

H8	Mar 1954	1,092,000	£225
H9	May 1954	1,884,000	£120
H10	July 1954	1,351,000	£130
H11	Sept 1954	1,357,000	95·00
H12	Nov 1954	2,309,000	£120

AVC books H4 to H12	each 40·00

B. Fully interleaved

H13	Jan 1955	1,349,000	95·00
H14	Mar 1955	1,450,000	75·00
H15	May 1955	1,461,000	80·00
H16	July 1955	1,460,000	£120

MIXED WATERMARKS. Nos. H17/19 and H21 exist with mixed Tudor Crown and St Edward's Crown watermarks. The mixed watermarks are indicated by the code letters "T" (Tudor) and "E" (Edward) starting with the first pane of the booklet, i.e. 2½d. (2), 2d., 1½d., 1d., ½d.

5s. Booklets   Dorothy Wilding Booklets   SC

Watermark Tudor Crown, St. Edward's Crown and mixed watermarks.

H17	Sept 1955		
	(a) Combination TTTETT		
	(b) Combination TTTEET		
	(c) Combination TTTETE		
	(d) Combination TTEETT		
	(e) Combination TTEEET		
	(f) Combination TTEEEE		
	(g) Combination TETETT		
	(h) Combination TETEET		
	(i) Combination TEEETT		
	(j) Combination TETETE		
	(k) Combination TEEETE		
	(l) Combination ETTETT		
	(m) Combination ETTEET	1,328,000	40·00
	(n) Combination ETEETT		
	(o) Combination ETEEET		
	(p) Combination EETETT		
	(q) Combination EETEET		
	(r) Combination EETETE		
	(s) Combination EETEEE		
	(t) Combination EEETTT		
	(u) Combination EEETET		
	(v) Combination EEETEE		
	(w) Combination EEEETT		
	(x) Combination EEEEET		
	(y) Combination EEEEEE		
H18	Nov 1955		
	(a) Combination TTEEEE		
	(b) Combination EETEEE		
	(c) Combination TEEEEE	2,147,000	42·00
	(d) Combination EEEETE		
	(e) Combination EEEEET		
	(f) Combination ETEEEE		48·00
H19	Jan 1956		
	(a) Combination TTTEET		
	(b) Combination EETETT	1,337,000	45·00
	(c) Combination EEEEET		

Watermark St Edward's Crown (Nos. S2, S14, S26, S37, S53)

H20	Mar 1956	1,403,000	55·00
H21	May 1956		
	(a) Combination EETETT	1,572,000	55·00
	(b) Combination EEEEET		48·00
H22	July 1956	1,465,190	45·00
H23	Sept 1956	1,589,000	48·00
H24	Nov 1956	2,430,600	48·00
	a. Date error missing "B" in "NOVEMBER"		£150
H25	Jan 1957	100,000	55·00
H25a	Date error missing "J" in "JANUARY"		£120

Introduction of 2d. light red-brown (No. S38) in place of No. S37

H26	Jan 1957	1,417,800	48·00
	a. Date error missing "J" in "JANUARY"		£120
H27	Mar 1957	1,435,400	65·00
H28	May 1957	1,375,200	50·00
H29	July 1957	1,453,600	40·00
H30	Sept 1957	2,104,600	40·00
H31	Nov 1957	1,708,400	40·00

Contents changed: 12×3d., 6×2½d., 6×1d., 6×½d. in panes of six III.

Watermark St Edward's Crown (Nos. S2, S14, S53, S68)

H32	Jan 1958	1,528,000	40·00
H33	Mar 1958	442,000	40·00
H34	May 1958	795,000	42·00
H35	July 1958 (11.58)		
	(a) Combination EEEEC		
	(b) Combination EEECE	1,313,000	28·00
	(c) Combination EEECC		
H36	Nov 1958		
	(a) Combination EEECE		
	(b) Combination EECEE		
	(c) Combination EECEE	1,235,000	28·00
	(d) Combination CCEEE		
	(e) Combination CCCEE		

Paste-up books H20 to H36	each £150
AVC books H13 to H17	each 40·00
AVC books H18 to H36	each 25·00

> **MIXED WATERMARKS** See notes above No. H17. The mixed watermarks here are indicated by the code letters "E" (Edward) and "C" (Crowns) starting with the first pane of the booklet, i.e. 3d. (2), 2½d., 1d., ½d..

Blue Cover as Type C. Fully interleaved.
Watermark Crowns (Nos. S4, S16, S55, S70), graphite lines (Nos. S7, S18, S59, S72) or green phosphor (Nos. S9, S20, S61, S74)

H37	Jan 1959		
	(a) Combination CCCCE		
	(b) Combination CCCEC	1,330,000	35·00
	(c) Combination CCCEE		
	(d) Combination CCECC		
H38	Mar 1959	895,000	45·00
H39	July 1959	1,122,000	42·00
	g. With graphite lines (issued 21.8.59)	46,200	£130
H40	Sept 1959	1,541,000	45·00
H41	Nov 1959	1,340,000	45·00
H42	Jan 1960	1,092,000	45·00
H43	Mar 1960	1,042,000	45·00
	g. With graphite lines	38,000	£170
H44	May 1960	1,023,000	50·00
H45	July 1960	1,104,000	55·00
H46	Sept 1960	1,158,800	80·00
	g. With graphite lines	65,999	£170
	p. With green phosphor bands	39,600	£120
	pa. Error. ½d. pane missing phosphor		£300
	pb. Error. 2½d. pane missing phosphor		£300
H47	Nov 1960	1,308,400	60·00

Paste-up books H37 to H47	each £150
AVC books H37 to H47	each £15·00

Blue Cover as Type D. Fully interleaved.
Watermark Crowns (Nos. S4, S16, S55, S70) or blue phosphor with two bands on 2½d. (Nos. S10, S21, S62, S75)

H48	Jan 1961	1,344,600	60·00
H49	Mar 1961	2,382,800	60·00
	p. With blue phosphor bands	97,400	£160
H50	May 1961	1,219,200	60·00
	a. Error. 2½d. pane with blue phosphor bands		£400

99

SC Dorothy Wilding Booklets — 5s. Booklets, 6s. Booklets

H51	July 1961	1,148,200	95·00
	p. With blue phosphor bands	7,200	£170
H52	Sept 1961	1,728,600	60·00
	p. With blue phosphor bands	15,200	£225
H53	Nov 1961	1,367,000	60·00
H54	Jan 1962	963,800	95·00
	p. With blue phosphor bands	38,600	£225

Watermark Crowns (Nos. S4 or S5, S16 or S17, S55 or S57, S70 or S71) or blue phosphor with one phosphor band on 2½d. (Nos. S10 or S11, S21 or S22, S63 or S65, S75 or S76).

H55	Mar 1962	1,006,200	85·00
	p. With blue phosphor bands	23,600	£180
H56	May 1962	1,120,800	60·00
	p. With blue phosphor bands	50,800	£200
H57	July 1962	1,309,600	95·00
	p. With blue phosphor bands	16,600	£180
H58	Sept 1962	1,523,800	90·00
	p. With blue phosphor bands	49,800	£250
H59	Nov 1962	1,543,200	90·00
	p. With blue phosphor bands	51,000	£250
H60	Jan 1963	1,024,600	60·00
	p. With blue phosphor bands	38,800	£600
H61	Mar 1963	1,116,800	60·00
	p. With blue phosphor bands	15,800	£250
H62	May 1963	1,102,200	80·00
	p. With blue phosphor bands	78,600	£250
H63	July 1963	1,456,400	95·00
	p. With blue phosphor bands	44,600	£170
H64	Sept 1963	1,402,200	60·00
	p. With blue phosphor bands	36,200	£250
H65	Nov 1963	1,400,000	60·00
	p. With blue phosphor bands	78,800	£250
H66	Jan 1964	831,600	60·00
	p. With blue phosphor bands	43,000	£150
H67	Mar 1964	760,200	60·00
	p. With blue phosphor bands	55,800	£120
	pa. Error. Green covers, as 10s. booklet		£400
H68	May 1964	760,200	95·00
	p. With blue phosphor bands	66,000	£225
H69	July 1964	1,647,200	95·00
	p. With blue phosphor bands	29,400	£200
H70	Sept 1964	1,574,200	60·00
	p. With blue phosphor bands	38,400	£200
H71	Nov 1964	1,152,400	85·00
	p. With blue phosphor bands	98,600	£120
	pa. Error. 1d. pane missing phosphor		£250
H72	Jan 1965	1,119,000	50·00
	p. With blue phosphor bands	55,200	£120
H73	Mar 1965	657,600	48·00
	p. With blue phosphor bands	19,000	£225
H74	May 1965	1,076,600	45·00
	p. With blue phosphor bands	56,800	£140

Paste-up books H48 to H74		each £150
AVC books H48 to H52		each 15·00
H53 to H56		each 50·00
H57 and H58		each 15·00
H59		50·00
H60 to H74		each 15·00

5s. booklets were withdrawn from sale on 31 August 1965.

6s. Booklets

Contents: 18×4d. in panes of six

Claret Cover as Type D. Fully interleaved.

Watermark Crowns (No. S85), blue or violet phosphor (Nos. S90, S91 or S92)

Q1	June 1965 (issued 21.6.65)	1,166,800	45·00
	p. With blue phosphor bands (issued 21.6.65)	101,800	45·00
Q2	July 1965	1,718,000	45·00
	p. With blue phosphor bands	136,200	80·00
Q3	Aug 1965	1,192,400	80·00
	p. With blue phosphor bands	87,600	60·00
Q4	Sept 1965	1,907,800	60·00
	pa. With blue phosphor bands		60·00
	pb. With violet 8 mm. phosphor bands	244,400	
			£100
Q5	Oct 1965	1,889,600	90·00
	pa. With blue phosphor bands		90·00
	pb. With violet 8 mm. phosphor bands	263,600	
			90·00
Q6	Nov 1965	1,788,800	90·00
	pa. With blue phosphor bands		90·00
	pb. With violet 8 mm. phosphor bands	98,200	
			90·00
Q7	Dec 1965	1,662,000	90·00
	pa. With blue phosphor bands.		£100
	pb. With violet 8 mm. phosphor bands	93,000	
			£100
Q8	Jan 1966	1,114,800	90·00
	pa. With blue phosphor bands.		90·00
	pb. With violet 8 mm. phosphor bands	349,200	
			90·00
Q9	Feb 1966	1,448,600	90·00
	p. With violet 8 mm. phosphor bands	116,800	90·00
Q10	Mar 1966	1,038,000	90·00
	p. With violet 8 mm. phosphor bands	122,400	£100
Q11	Apr 1966	1,124,200	90·00
	p. With violet 8 mm. phosphor bands	119,600	£200
Q12	May 1966	1,099,000	90·00
	p. With violet 8 mm. phosphor bands	121,000	£100
Q13	June 1966	1,070,400	90·00
	p. With violet 8 mm. phosphor bands	121,000	90·00
Q14	July 1966	667,600	90·00
	p. With violet 8 mm. phosphor bands	46,800	90·00
Q15	Aug 1966	1,503,200	90·00
	p. With violet 8 mm. phosphor bands	42,400	£250
Q16	Sept 1966	1,402,400	55·00
	p. With violet 8 mm. phosphor bands	227,200	55·00
Q17	Oct 1966	986,600	£100
	p. With violet 8 mm. phosphor bands	227,200	£175
Q18	Nov 1966	1,078,000	75·00
	p. With violet 8 mm. phosphor bands	271,200	45·00
Q19	Dec 1966	1,069,400	45·00

6s. Booklets, 10s. Booklets **Dorothy Wilding Booklets** **SC**

	p. With violet 8 mm. phosphor bands		270,500	80·00
Q20	Jan 1967		231,400	90·00
	p. With violet 8 mm. phosphor bands		622,400	90·00
Q21	Feb 1967		253,800	90·00
	p. With violet 9·5 mm. phosphor bands		566,200	50·00
Q22	Mar 1967		395,000	60·00
	p. With violet 9·5 mm. phosphor bands		580,800	50·00
	pa. Error. 4d. pane missing phosphor			£110
Q23	Apr 1967		395,400	45·00
	p. With violet 9·5 mm. phosphor bands		632,200	50·00

Watermark Crowns violet 9·5mm. phosphor (No. S92)

Q24p	May 1967	1,612,600	40·00
Q25p	June 1967	1,596,800	40·00
Q26p	July 1967	776,600	£100
Q27p	Aug 1967	750,600	75·00

Paste-up books Q1 to Q2 (using 4s.6d. AVC to make up)	each £200
Q4 (stapled to make up)	£200
Q3 and Q5 to Q27	each £150
AVC books Q1 to Q27	each 15·00

10s. Booklets

Contents: 30×3d., 6×2d., 6×1½d., 6×1d., 6×½d. in panes of six

I. Green Cover as Type D. Fully interleaved.
Watermark Crowns (Nos. S4, S16, S28, S40, S70)

X1	No date (issued 10.4.61)	902,000	£150
X2	Oct 1961	483,200	£300

Paste-up books X1 or X2	each £400
AVC books X1 or X2	each £200

Contents changed: 30×3d., 6×2½d., 6×1½d., 6×1d. in panes of six

Watermark Crowns (Nos. S17, S29, S57, S71)

X3	Apr 1962	524,680	£130
X4	Aug 1962	474,600	£180
X5	Mar 1963	493,200	£275
X6	July 1963	620,600	£180
X7	Dec 1963	606,600	£160
X8	July 1964	599,400	£130
X9	Dec 1964	415,200	£600

Paste-up book X3 or X4	each £300
X5 to X9	each £200
AVC books X3 or X4	each £200
X5 to X9	each 50·00

10s. booklets in this composition were withdrawn from sale on 31 August 1965.

Contents changed: 24×4d., 6×3d., 6×1d. in panes of six

II. Ochre Cover as Type D. Fully interleaved.

Watermark Crowns (Nos. S17, S71, S85)

X10	Aug 1965 (issued 23.8.65)	854,200	40·00
X11	Dec 1965	658,800	80·00
X12	Feb 1966	663,600	65·00
X13	Aug 1966	686,800	40·00
X14	Nov 1966	796,000	38·00

Watermark Crowns, violet phosphor with one side band on 3d. (Nos. S23, S78, S91 or S92)

X15p	Feb 1967		
	pa. With violet 8 and 4 mm. phosphor bands	301,800	10·00
	pb. With violet 9·5 mm. phosphor bands on 4d. panes		10·00
	pc. Error. 1d. pane missing phosphor		£150

Watermark Crowns, violet 9·5 mm. phosphor with one centre 4 mm. band on 3d. (Nos. S24, S79, S92)

X16 p	Aug 1967	1,488,800	7·00
	pa. Error. 1d. pane missing phosphor		£150
X17 p	Feb 1968	474,400	8·00
	pa. Error. 1d. pane missing phosphor		£150
	pb. Error. 4d. pane missing phosphor		£150

Paste-up books X10	each £200
AVC books X10 to X17	each 20·00

Section T
Dorothy Wilding Issues
1955–68. High Values. Recess-printed

General Notes

Plate preparation
The original master dies were engraved in three stages at Waterlows by HJ Bard. First the Queen's head was engraved, based on that on the 2½d. stamp. Following transfer by roller to a second die, the embrasure and word 'POSTAGE' were added, before being transferred to a third die, on to which the individual castles and values were engraved. Transfer roller impressions were taken from the finished dies for creation of the plates.

The finished dies were used by all three printers, although Waterlow and De La Rue prepared their own sets of transfer rollers for plate production. Bradbury Wilkinson initially employed the Waterlow and De La Rue transfer rollers, but subsequently prepared their own for the 2s.6d., 10s. and £1 values.

Waterlow experimented with a new method of plate production, by preparing a 'master' plate (46936) from which a mould (60555) was taken; two plates (46959 and 46992) being taken from that mould. The plates were not used and all were subsequently destroyed, but the nickel mould is held at The Postal Museum.

De La Rue also used ('alto') moulds for the production of some of their printing plates.

Bradbury Wilkinson produced their printing plates direct from transfer rollers.

Crowns Watermark. The Crowns are slightly smaller than in the low values.

Paper. The stamps are all on unsurfaced paper except the 2s.6d., No. T6 which is on chalk-surfaced paper.

Bradbury, Wilkinson printings are found with a degree of fluorescence when viewed under a short-wave u.v. lamp. This is due to the use of optical brightening agents in the rags used for paper making.

Stamps printed by Waterlow and De La Rue tend to curl from top to bottom while Bradbury, Wilkinson printings curl at the sides.

Perforation. All stamps in this Section are comb perforated 11×12 and the sheet perforation is always Type A.

Bradbury, Wilkinson Plate No.

Plate Numbers. All plates were made from the original Waterlow die. All stamps were printed from double plates producing left and right panes which were guillotined to make Post Office sheets of 40 (4×10). Plate numbers were used both by Waterlow and De La Rue but they appeared between the panes and were trimmed off. The Bradbury, Wilkinson plate numbers appear below stamps 3/4 in the bottom margin, the whole numbers on the left pane and the "A" numbers on the right pane. All three printers used rotary sheet-fed machines, although Waterlow's 2s.6d. plate 47316, still held at The Postal Museum is flat.

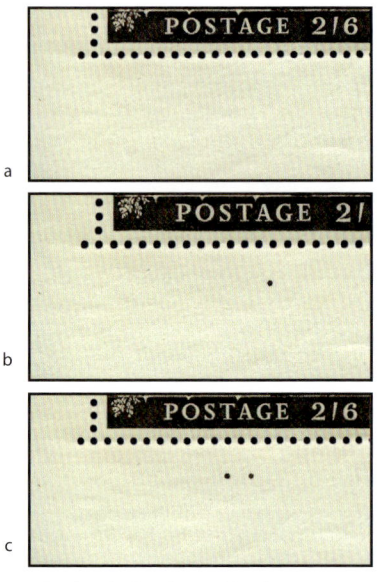

a. No dot   b. One dot   c. Two dots

De La Rue Plate Dots. De La Rue printed on paper with St Edward's Crown watermark and with Crowns watermark and as a control to distinguish the two papers during the changeover period, dots were inserted in the bottom margin below the first stamp in the bottom row.

In the case of the 2s.6d. the first printings on St Edward's Crown paper were without dot, but later a single dot appeared on this paper, whilst early printings of stamps on the Crowns paper had two dots. The stamps with one dot in the bottom margin were released on 17 April 1959.

In the 10s. the dots are 7mm from the design and 5mm apart and in the other values they are 6mm from the design and 2½ mm apart.

The number of sheets printed with double dots were:

2s.6d.	93,630	10s.	37,510
5s.	60,158	£1	18,660

Distinguishing the work of the three printers. Waterlow printed the stamps up to 31 December 1957 and then De La Rue held the contract until 31 December 1962, after which all printings were made by Bradbury, Wilkinson. The following characteristics will help to distinguish their work:

Paper

Waterlow	De La Rue	Bradbury, Wilkinson
(a) Wmk. W.**23** Creamy	(a) Wmk. W.**23** Light cream	(a) Wmk. W.**24** Whiter
(b) Wmk. W.**23** Light cream (From Feb., '57)	(b) Wmk. W.**24** Light cream	(b) Wmk. W.**24** Chalk-surfaced (2s.6d. only)
	(c) Wmk. W.**24** Whiter (From 1962)	(c) No wmk. White

High Values – General Notes **Dorothy Wilding issues**

Shades

	Waterlow	De La Rue
2s.6d.	Blackish brown	More chocolate
5s.	Rose-carmine	Lighter red, less carmine
10s.	Ultramarine	More blue
£1	Black	Less intense

The shade variations result in part from the differences in paper.

Gutters. The width of gutters between the stamps varies, particularly the horizontal, as follows:—

Waterlow	De La Rue
3·8 to 4·0 mm.	3·4 to 3·8 mm.

Later De La Rue plates were less distinguishable in this respect.

Perforation. The vertical perforation of the Bradbury, Wilkinson is 11.9 to 12 as against 11.8 for the De La Rue.

Impression. The individual lines of the De La Rue impression are cleaner and devoid of the whiskers of colour of Waterlow's, and the whole impression is lighter and softer. The Bradbury, Wilkinson stamps are generally more deeply engraved than the De La Rue, showing more of the diadem detail and heavier lines on the Queen's face.

Waterlow Sheet Markings

Perforation Markings. As a check for the alignment of the perforations the following marks occur between the stamps in the Waterlow printings only:

(a) 3 mm cross in the centre of the sheet.

(b) 2½ mm vertical lines in centre at top and bottom of sheet.

(c) 2½ mm horizontal lines in centre at each side of sheet.

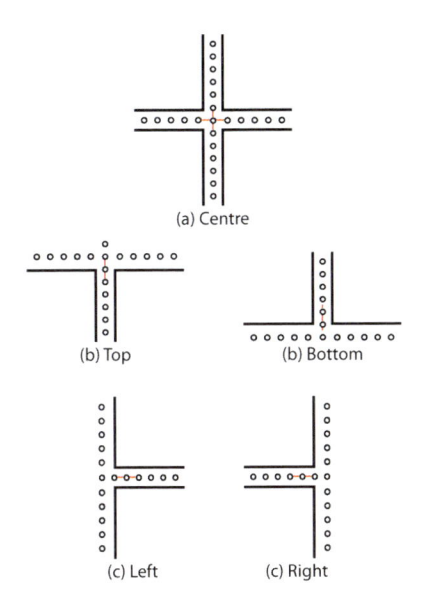

(a) Centre

(b) Top   (b) Bottom

(c) Left   (c) Right

Perforation Pin-holes. Coloured circles with a pin-hole through appear at left and right opposite row six at left and right, although one is usually trimmed off.

Three types of perforation pin-holes can be distinguished on the 2s.6d. stamp sheets.

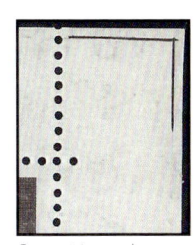

Pin-hole   Corner trim mark

Corner Trim Marks. These occur in the corners but naturally one or both sides may be trimmed off.

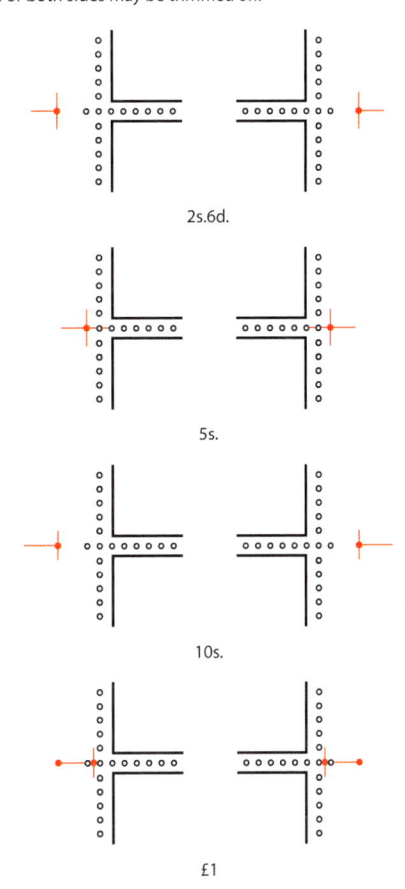

2s.6d.

5s.

10s.

£1

De La Rue Sheet Markings

Guide Marks. The only markings on De La Rue sheets are the guide marks which appear in the side margins between rows 5 and 6 which also serve to distinguish the left and right panes. Their position varies with each value and also in some cases in format between the different plates used from time to time. The circles or crosses also have pin-holes.

St Edward's Crown Watermark
2s.6d., 5s., 10s. Type 1. £1 Type 1a

Multiple Crowns Watermark
2s.6d. Types 1, 2, 2a, 2b, 2c, 4. 5s. Types 1, 2c, 2d, 3. 10s. Types 1, 2, 2d. £1 Types 1, 1b, 2, 4a.

Specialists recognise four basic types of guide marks which are described as seen from left panes. Reverse for right.

Type 1 Horizontal "T" shaped mark with spot at intersection.

a   As above but dot added to left extremity of horizontal arm.

T Dorothy Wilding issues *High Values – General Notes*

b As above but with "target" added between the two dots.

The "target" mark is small, circular with open centre which was pierced by the perforating machine.

Type 2 This is as type 1 but with the addition of a "target" between the horizontal "T" and stamp

a As type 2 but intersection dot to right of cross over point.
b As type 2 but intersection dot to left of cross over point.
c As type 2 but no dot.
d As type 2c but "target" joined to "T".

Type 3 This is as type 1 but "target" is added first followed by "T".

Type 4 "Target" centred on "T" and without dot at intersection.

a As type 4 but arms partly erased (south and east arms erased left pane; north and west arms for right pane).

Bradbury, Wilkinson Sheet Markings

Guide Holes. These appear in a coloured circle opposite row 6, at left on left-hand panes and at right on right-hand panes.

Lay Dots. On the 2s.6d. plates 1/1A to 7/7A small "lay" dots appear in the top sheet margin, above the first vertical row on the left-hand pane and on the right-hand pane above the fourth vertical row. Only one copy of the 5s. is known but examples may exist on the other values. These were guide marks to check any movement of the plate.

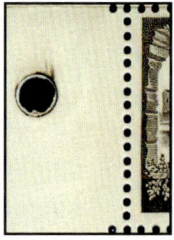

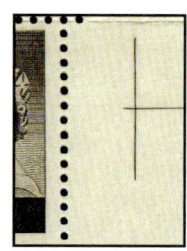

Guide hole   Guide cross

Guide Crosses. These occur in the region of rows 5 and 6 at right on left-hand panes and at left on right-hand panes. However, these do not appear on all plates, being omitted for instance on plates 8/8A, 9/9A of the 2s.6d. and 4/4A of the 5s.

Tinted sheet margins. Some sheets show a background wash or tint of the colour in which the stamps are printed. This is an indication of a new state of a plate or a plate that has been rechromed. The explanation for this is that in wiping off the excess ink from the surface of the plate a small amount may be left at the edge of the plate and this will continue until the plate is sufficiently smooth for the surface to be thoroughly wiped clean of ink. These marginal tints stop short of the edge of the sheet as the extremities of the plate do not come into contact with the inking roller.

All Bradbury Wilkinson plates were subsequently destroyed.

Dates of issue. Where a change of watermark or paper occurs the date given is generally that on which the stamps were first issued by the Supplies Department to Postmasters.

Post Office Training School stamps. All values of the Waterlow printings exist overprinted with thick vertical bars and stamps from the other printings with thin vertical bars. These were supplied to Post Office Training Schools, and their issue to the public was unauthorised.

"Cancelled" Overprint. Nos. T5, T17 and T24 come overprinted "CANCELLED" (size 40×5mm) as part of the test programme carried out by the Forensic Department of the Post Office.

The values overprinted "CANCELLED" (size 24×3 mm) from the De La Rue archive are listed below No. T2.

Withdrawal dates. It is known that the following went off sale at the Philatelic Bureau in the months shown:

Mar. 1968	£1 No. T24
Nov. 1968	2s.6d. No. T6
Nov. 1968	5s. No. T12
Jan. 1969	2s.6d. No. T5
Mar. 1970	10s. No. T18

The 2s.6d., 5s., 10s. and £1 no watermark, white paper (Nos. T7, T13, T19 and T25) were all withdrawn on 15 May 1970.

All 2s.6d., 5s. and 10s. stamps were invalidated as from 1 March 1972.

Type **T1.** Carrickfergus Castle

Type **T2.** Caernarvon Castle

Type **T3.** Edinburgh Castle

Type **T4.** Windsor Castle

(Des. Lynton Lamb. Portrait by Dorothy Wilding, Ltd.)

Eng Harold Bard (portrait) and Mr Ward (vignette)

2s.6d. Black-brown — Dorothy Wilding issues

2s.6d. Type T1 (1955–1968)

1955 *(23 September).* **2s.6d.** *Wmk* St Edward's Crown

(a) Waterlow Printings
T1 =SG 536

	Mint	Used
2s.6d. Black-brown	15·00	2·00
a. Re-entry (R.2/2)	70·00	

Quantity Issued: 47,919,460

(b) De La Rue Printings *(17 July 1958)*
T2 =SG 536a

2s.6d. Black-brown	30·00	2·50
a. Watermark inverted	†	£3000
b. With one plate dot in bottom margin (R.10/1) (released 17.4.59)	£150	

No T2a: Three used examples are recorded

T1a The doubling occurs down the left-hand margin

Quantity Issued: 21,350,400

Cancelled Overprints from the De La Rue Archives
Nos. T2, T9, T15 and T21 overprinted "CANCELLED" (24×3 mm)
Set of four £950.

The overprint was handstamped in violet and impressions vary slightly in position.

One sheet of each of the above values was provided by the Post Office Supplies Department to De La Rue as reference copies of their work and retained in the De La Rue Museum. They were placed on the market in 1990.

Plates. Plates numbered 46725, 46936, 47001, 47145 and 47316, each double-pane, are known to have been used by Waterlow. The first two plates were later destroyed but the remaining three are all held at The Postal Museum. Oddly, plate 47316 is flat (although stamps printed from it are known). All other printing plates are curved for the rotary press. The De La Rue plates were made using the original Waterlow dies. No plate numbers were found on the issued sheets, but it is now known that they were numbered 47320, 47321 and 47322. 47321 was issued as a "master" plate from which seven further printing plates were produced designated N1, N2 (the "one dot" printing), N3 (the "two dot" and "no dot" printings), N8, N9, N10 and N12.

Imprimaturs from the NPM or BPMA

No. T1 imperforate, watermark Type W.**23**	£2200
No. T2 imperforate, watermark Type W.**23**	£2200

1959 *(22 July).* **2s.6d.** *Wmk* Crowns

(a) De La Rue Printings

A. Light Cream Paper
T3

	Mint	Used
2s.6d. Black-brown	15·00	1·00
a. With two plate dots in bottom margin (R.10/1)	95·00	

B. Whiter Paper *(13 July 1962)*
T4 (=SG 595)

2s.6d. Black-brown	10·00	75
a. Watermark inverted	†	£3250
b. Imperf to top margin	—	—

No. T4a. Nine used examples are recorded.

Quantity Issued (both papers) 95, 999, 880

(b) Bradbury, Wilkinson Printings

A. Whiter Paper *(1 July 1963)*
T5 =SG 595a

2s.6d. Black-brown	35	40
a. Watermark inverted	£3250	£300
b. Weak entry (Pl. 5A, R. 5/4 or 6/4)	25·00	
c. Re-entry (Pl. 9A, R. 8/4)	30·00	
d. Re-entry (Pl. 9, R. 10/2)	25·00	

B. Chalk-surfaced Paper *(30 May 1968)*
T6 (=SG 595k)

2s.6d. Black-brown	50	1·50
a. Re-entry (Pl. 9A, R. 8/4)	30·00	
b. Re-entry (Pl. 9, R. 10/2)	25·00	

T5b
Lines of shading weak or omitted at base of collar, on dress, and at foot of background. Occurs on R.5/4 and 6/4 (the illustration is of R.6/4

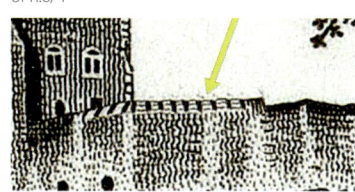

T5c, T6a
Re-entry shows in the form of brown dots over battlements. The re-entry on Nos. T5d and T6b occurs in the same place but is less marked

105

T Dorothy Wilding issues 2s.6d. Black-brown

Plate Numbers (Blocks of Four)
Bradbury, Wilkinson Printings

Whiter Paper. (No. T5)

Plate No.		Plate No	
1	30·00	1A	30·00
2	30·00	2A	30·00
3	30·00	3A	30·00
4	£700	4A	£700
5	15·00	5A	15·00
6	8·00	6A	8·00
7	8·00	7A	8·00
8	8·00	8A	8·00
9	8·00	9A	8·00

Chalk-surfaced Paper. (No. T6)

9	8·00	9A	8·00

A perforation variety exists on plates 5 and 6, of which 21,000 sheets were reported to come with double extension holes in the side margins. It is now known that this was an error, rather than a "trial", as previously thought.

Minor Constant Flaws
On Plate 9 there are a number of faint scratch marks in the top and bottom margins and these are particularly noticeable on the chalky paper. They occur in the top margin on R. 10/3 and in the bottom margin on R. 1/1, 1/2, 2/1, 3/3, 3/4, 7/2, 7/4 and 8/2.

Plates 8A, 10 and 10A all show evidence of progressive wear around the guide hole. On plates 10 and 10A this takes the form of a crack extending from the guide hole towards the stamps.

Plate 13A R. 1/2 shows a 2 cm. long scratch on the left-hand side of the bottom margin.

Plate Proofs
In the preparation of the printing plates, Bradbury, Wilkinson used a transfer roller and took black printings periodically in the course of production to check for flaws and alignment of the images. Two examples of imperforate black plate printings are recorded; three rows, comprising a block of 12 stamps and four rows comprising a block of 16, both in private hands.

Imprimaturs from the NPM or BPMA

No. T3 imperforate, watermark Type W.**24**	£2200
No. T3 with two plate dots R.10/1	£2750
No. T4 imperforate, watermark Type W.**24**	£2200
No. T5 imperforate, watermark Type W.**24**	£2200
No. T5 plate 1A block of four	£12000
No. T6 imperforate, watermark Type W.**24**	£2200
No. T6 plate 9A block of four	£12000

1968 (July 1). **2s.6d.** .White paper No Wmk.

Bradbury, Wilkinson Printings

T7 =SG 759	Mint	Used
2s.6d. Black-brown	30	45

Plate Numbers (Blocks of Four)

Plate No.		Plate No	
10	8·00	10A	8·00
11	8·00	11A	8·00
12	8·00	12A	8·00
13	8·00	13A	8·00

Imprimaturs from the NPM or BPMA

No. T7 imperforate, No watermark	£2200
No. T7 plate 10A block of four	£12000

5s. Type T2 (1955–1968)

1955 *(September 23).* **5s.** Wmk St Edward's Crown,

(a) Waterlow Printings

T8 (=SG 537)	Mint	Used
5s. Rose-carmine	40·00	4·00
a. Re-entry (R.8/1)	£110	

Quantity Issued: 16, 571, 120

(b) De La Rue Printings *(30 April 1958)*
T9 =SG 537a

	Mint	Used
5s. Rose-carmine	65·00	10·00

Quantity Issued: 7, 466, 880

T8a

Major re-entry showing doubling of vertical lines of background above the diadem, and in the diadem along the left edge of the frontal cross, both sides of the side cross and the diagonals

Plates. It is known that a double-pane plate numbered 46726 was used by Waterlow. De La Rue created further plates, all double-pane. Plate numbers did not occur on the issued sheets although it is now known that they were numbered 47317, 47323 and 47325. 47325 was used as a master plate to produce four printing plates; N1, N2, N3 and N4.

Imprimaturs from the NPM or BPMA

No. T8 imperforate, watermark Type W.**23**	£2200
No. T9 imperforate, watermark Type W.**23**	£2200

1959 *(June 15).* **5s.** Wmk Crowns, Type W.**24**

(a) De La Rue Printings
A. Light Cream Paper

T10	Mint	Used
5s. Scarlet-vermilion	65·00	3·00
a. Watermark inverted	£9000	£600
b. With two plate dots in bottom margin (R.10/1)	£150	

Some sheets of No. T10 are known perforated through the bottom margin and imperf in the top margin having been fed into the perforator the wrong way up (see Appendix G)

Two unused examples of T10a have been recorded and at least 25 used are known.

B. Whiter Paper *(7 May 1962)*
T11 =SG 596

	Mint	Used
5s. Scarlet-vermilion	45·00	2·00

Quantity issued (both papers): 30, 200, 320

(b) Bradbury, Wilkinson Printings
Whiter Paper *(3 September 1963)*
T12 =SG 596a

5s. (1) Red	2·50	70
(2) Brownish red (Plates 3, 4)	1·25	50
a. Watermark inverted	£400	£300
b. Printed on the gummed side	£1600	†

At least 30 examples of T12a are recorded.

Plate Numbers (Blocks of Four)
Bradbury, Wilkinson Printings. (No. T12)

Plate No.		Plate No	
1	65·00	1A	65·00
2	65·00	2A	65·00
3	10·00	3A	10·00
4	12·00	4A	12·00

Imprimaturs from the NPM or BPMA

No. T10 imperforate, watermark Type W.**24**	£2200
No. T10 with two plate dots R.10/1	£2750
No. T11 imperforate, watermark Type W.**24**	£2200
No. T12 imperforate, watermark Type W.**24**	£2200
No. T12 plate 2A block of four	£12000

1968 *(April 10).* **5s.** White paper. No Watermark.

Bradbury, Wilkinson Printings

T13 =SG 760	Mint	Used
5s. Brownish red	70	75

Plate Numbers (Blocks of Four)

Plate No.		Plate No	
4	9·00	4A	9·00
5	9·00	5A	9·00
6	11·00	6A	11·00

Imprimaturs from the NPM or BPMA

No. T13 imperforate, No watermark	£2200
No. T13 plate 5 block of four	£12000

T Dorothy Wilding issues *10s. Blue*

10s. Type T3 (1955–1968)

1955 *(September 1).* **10s.** Wmk St Edward's Crown, Type W.**23**

(a) Waterlow Printings	Mint	Used
T14 =SG 538		
10s. (1) Ultramarine	90·00	14·00
(2) Pale ultramarine	90·00	14·00
a. Weak value tablet (R.1/2)	£175	40·00

Quantity Issued: 7, 967, 800

(b) De La Rue Printings *(25 April 1958)*		
T15 =SG 538a		
10s. Dull ultramarine	£225	22·00
a. Weak frame (R.4/1)	£300	

A used example of No. T15 with inverted watermark has been reported.
Quantity Issued: 3, 680, 240

T14a
Weak print to right of lower panel gives ragged appearance

T15a, T17a

T15a, T16b and T17a occur due to spasmodic under-inking and differ slightly in frame position on each example. The variety has been reported on position R. 4/1, but can occur elsewhere.

Minor Sheet Flaws
In rows 8, 9 and 10 there are blue marks on the extremity of the white letters and figures of "POSTAGE" and value which are more marked on the bottom two rows. These may not be fully constant but could be helpful for purposes of identification.

Plates. It is known that Waterlow used a double-pane plate numbered 46728. De La Rue plates are now known to have been numbered 47318, 47324 and 47326. 47326 was used as a master plate to produce two printing plates; N1 and N2.

Imprimaturs from the NPM or BPMA

No. T14 imperforate, watermark Type W.**23**	£2200
No. T15 imperforate, watermark Type W.**23**	£2200

T15a, T17a

108

10s. Blue, £1 Black **Dorothy Wilding issues** **T**

1959 *(July 21).* **10s.** *Wmk* Crowns, Type W.**24**

(a) De La Rue Printings
A. Light Cream Paper
T16

		Mint	Used
10s.	Blue	70·00	8·00
	a. With two plate dots in bottom margin (R.10/1)	£250	

B. Whiter Paper *(30 April 1962)*
T17 =SG 597

		Mint	Used
10s.	Blue	55·00	5·00
	a. Weak frame (R.4/1)	£110	

Quantity Issued (both papers): 12, 704, 720

(b) Bradbury, Wilkinson Printings
Whiter Paper *(16 October 1963)*
T18 =SG 597a

		Mint	Used
10s.	Bright ultramarine	4·50	4·50
	a. Watermark inverted	†	£3250

No. T18a. Four used examples have been recorded.

Plate Numbers (Blocks of Four)
Bradbury, Wilkinson Printings. (No. T18)

Plate No.		Plate No	
1	£100	1A	£100
2	30·00	2A	30·00

Imprimaturs from the NPM or BPMA

No. T16 imperforate, watermark Type W.**24**	£2200
No. T16 with two plate dots R.10/1	£2750
No. T17 imperforate, watermark Type W.**24**	£2200
No. T18 imperforate, watermark Type W.**24**	£2200
No. T18 plate 1 block of four	£1200

1968 *(April 10).* **10s.** No Watermark. White paper

Bradbury, Wilkinson Printings
T19 =SG 761

		Mint	Used
10s.	Bright ultramarine	7·75	4·00

Plate Numbers (Blocks of Four)

Plate No.		Plate No	
2	30·00	2A	30·00

Imprimaturs from the NPM or BPMA

No. T19 imperforate, No watermark	£2200
No. T19 plate 2 block of four	£12000

£1   Type T4 (1955–1967)

1955 *(September 1).* **£1** *Wmk* St Edward's Crown, Type W.23

(a) Waterlow Printings
T20 =SG 539

	Mint	Used
£1 Black	£140	35·00
a. Re-entry (R.7/1)	£500	

Quantity Issued: 2, 769, 780

(b) De La Rue Printings *(28 April 1958)*
T21 =SG 539a

	Mint	Used
£1 Black	£350	65·00

Quantity Issued: 1, 521, 960

T20a

Minor Re-entries
Waterlow Printings
1/2 Slight doubling (Th. B1 and D–F1)
4/4 Slight doubling (Th. B1)
5/2 Slight doubling (Th. B1 and D–E1)
6/1 Slight doubling (Th. A–C13)
Other minute signs of doubling of left frame line occur on R. 7/2 and of right frame line on R. 1/1, 2/1, 3/3, 4/1, 4/2 and 9/2.

Plates. It is known that the double-pane plate used by Waterlow was numbered 46727. A further two plates were created by De La Rue, which are now known to be numbered 47319 and 47327. 47327 was used as a master plate to produce two printing plates; N1 and N2.

Imprimaturs from the NPM or BPMA

No. T20 imperforate, watermark Type W.**23**	£2200
No. T21 imperforate, watermark Type W.**23**	£2200

1959 *(June 30).* **£1** *Wmk* Crowns, Type W.**24**

(a) De La Rue Printings
A. Light Cream Paper
T22

	Mint	Used
£1 Black	£130	15·00
a. With two plate dots in bottom margin (R.10/1)	£325	
b. Watermark inverted	†	£3000

Two used examples of No. T22b have been recorded.

B. Whiter Paper *(30 April 1962)*
T23 =SG 598

	Mint	Used
£1 Black	£120	12·00
a. Watermark inverted	—	£3000

Two unused and four used examples of No T23a have been recorded.

109

T Dorothy Wilding issues £1 Black

Quantity Issued: 6, 281, 120

(b) Bradbury, Wilkinson Printings
Whiter Paper *(14 November 1963)*
T24 =SG 598a

£1 Black	13·00	8·00
a. Watermark inverted	£15000	£3750
b. Chalk-surfaced paper	£5250	†

Two unused and three used examples of No. T24a have been recorded.

10,000 sheets of the £1 were printed on chalk-surfaced paper (as 2s.6d., No. T6) but they were never issued. Nevertheless, at least 30 examples exist in private hands.

Die proofs of the £1 value on gummed, unwatermarked paper were taken from the original die by Bradbury, Wilkinson, probably in 1963. Two examples are known in private hands, both from the Goaman archive.

Plate Numbers (Blocks of Four)
Bradbury, Wilkinson Printings. (No. T24)

Plate No.		Plate No	
1	70·00	1A	70·00

Imprimaturs from the NPM or BPMA

No. T22 imperforate, watermark Type W.**24**	£2200
No. T22 with two plate dots R.10/1	£2750
No. T23 imperforate, watermark Type W.**24**	£2200
No. T23 plate 1 block of four	£8500
No. T24 imperforate, watermark Type W.**24**	£2200

1967 *(December 4).* **£1** White Paper. No Watermark.

Bradbury, Wilkinson Printings
T25 =SG 762

	Mint	Used
£1 Black	7·50	4·50

Plate Numbers (Blocks of Four)

Plate No.		Plate No	
1	30·00	1A	30·00

Imprimaturs from the NPM or BPMA

No. T25 perf. 11×12, No watermark	—
No. T25 plate 1 block of four	—

Presentation Pack

TPP1 (issued 1960) Four values	from £1400

The issued pack contained one of each value in the De La Rue printing with Crowns watermark on the light cream paper (Nos. T3, T10, T16 and T22).

Three forms of the pack exist:
(a) Inscribed "$6·50" for sale in the USA £2000
(b) Without price for sale in the UK —
(c) With "£1.18s." for sale at 1960 Festival Hall, International Stamp Exhibition £1400

Section U
Machin £.s.d. Issues
1967–1970. Sheet and Coil Stamps in Photogravure

General Notes

The Genesis of the Machin Design.

When Tony Benn became Postmaster General in 1964 one of the first subjects for discussion with the Stamp Advisory Committee (SAC) of the time was a new portrait of The Queen for definitive stamps. Designers did not like the current three-quarter profile Wilding photograph and a true profile was preferred. But it was not until November 1965 that five artists were formally invited to submit a new version. They were: Reginald Brill, Stuart Devlin, David Gentleman, Arnold Machin and John Ward.

Gentleman and Machin had already begun work but all had to submit a portrait "rendering" of the Queen and some sample stamp designs by 15 January 1966. Machin based his initial ideas on work he had previously done for his portrait of the Queen for the forthcoming decimal coinage. This had been based on photographs taken by Lord Snowdon and these photographs were supplied again to all invited artists. The images and models created by artists other than Machin are all in the collections of The Postal Museum, but none of them had any part to play in the later story.

Machin supplied six portraits (*Fig 1*) and created a total of nearly 70 sketches, far more than anyone else. Several of these sketches hark back very strongly to the Penny Black. Others have elaborate frames and many give the appearance of a cameo, reflecting his previous work for Wedgwood. Nearly all showed the Queen wearing a tiara as in the Snowdon photographs and on Machin's effigy for coins (*Fig 2*).

Figure 2. Machin's main rendering of The Queen's portrait made in January 1966

Creating the "Coinage" Head.
Before he created his first clay model Machin worked on photographs of the mould which he had previously created for the plaster cast of the effigy for decimal coins. On coins the Queen faced right but on stamps she needed to face left. So, in these reverse photographs the effigy of the Queen now faced in the correct direction for stamps.

Figure 1. One of a series of preliminary sketches created by Machin in January 1966, featuring elaborate frames and a Wedgwood-style cameo

The Stamp Advisory Committee asked Machin to develop his ideas and, as he was a sculptor, he did this in the form of a plaster cast.

Figure 3. Revised plaster cast of Machin's "Coinage" head made in March 1966 with The Queen wearing a tiara

First, he eliminated the coinage lettering and then drew over the portrait, adding highlights, and colouring the

111

background. At this point, images retained the round contours of the coin. This then became the basis for a clay model. Plaster was poured over the clay to create a mould and from this the first plaster cast was made. This cast was created very quickly in February 1966. After some comments from the Committee a new gentler portrait emerged and this is called Machin's "Coinage Head" (*Fig 3*).

A number of photographs were taken of this new plaster cast to be used in several frame designs prepared by Harrison & Sons Ltd., the printers. These frames included the words POSTAGE and REVENUE and symbols of the various countries making up the United Kingdom. When the head of The Queen was inserted it was cut at the neck in order to fit into the frames (*Fig 4*). A very large variety of essays, about 40 in all, were printed in different colours, many bicoloured, in April and May 1966 but postal officials were not impressed, describing the head as "unrecognisable".

Figure 4. Two of the many essays created in April/May 1966 featuring the "Coinage" head surrounded by country symbols

Simplified "Tiara" Head. Over the next few months Machin worked to simplify his image and to improve the design as a whole. First, he removed all symbols of the various countries. Then, in response to criticism of the lettering used by the printers, he produced plaster casts of the wording considered necessary – POSTAGE REVENUE – together with the 6d value. These he then combined on glass artwork with a version of the head from his Coinage plaster cast, with an added, slender neckline (*Fig 5*). The wording "Postage" and "Revenue" was then regarded as superfluous and also eliminated. This new, simple design, still with the tiara, (the "Tiara" head) was then essayed on 19 October by Harrisons with clear background colours of mauve, turquoise, leaf green (*Fig 6*), indigo blue and cyclamen. It is likely that the colours would have been chosen by Machin in collaboration with the printers.

Figure 5. Glass artwork based on the simplified "Coinage" head

Figure 6. One of the essays created by Harrison and Sons in October 1966 featuring the "Coinage" head, cropped and simplified with only the denomination

Hedgecoe photographs. Although Machin was working on a sculptured profile of the Queen throughout 1966, the Stamp Advisory Committee wanted a photographic alternative in case he was not successful. The Queen agreed to a request by Tony Benn for a photographic sitting and the Advisory Committee proposed John Hedgecoe as the photographer. At the time, Hedgecoe was head of the Photographic Department of the Royal College of Art. The sitting took place on 22 June and Hedgecoe supplied the Post Office with more than 60 prints in July or August. They showed the Queen wearing a different tiara, but also the diadem seen in the Wilding photographs of 1952, and as shown on the Penny Black (*Fig 7*). All showed a true profile facing left, some in very dark shadow or silhouette. The Queen returned these from Balmoral, having annotated the prints herself. On some she had written "good", others "yes" but a few "No".

Figure 7. One of the series of photographs taken by John Hedgecoe in August 1966 with The Queen wearing the diadem

These photographs, where the Queen is wearing the diadem, and simple essays prepared from them by Harrisons, were shown to the Stamp Advisory Committee at the same time as the essays featuring Machin's simplified "Tiara Head". The Committee liked the simplified essays but asked Machin to replace the tiara with the diadem, as on the Hedgecoe photographs.

The "Diadem" Head. When Machin was given the Hedgecoe photographs a remarkable transformation took place in his sculpture. During October 1966 he created a new clay model complete with diadem and necklace and prepared a new plaster cast sculpture instantly recognisable today. It had the Queen's neck cut away sharply at the shoulder but photographs were sent to the printers at the end of the month. From these, essays were ready by 31 October in colours similar to those of the simplified tiara version, but with no value (*Fig 8*). They were described as "a big improvement" but Machin wanted to "retouch" the sculpture to eliminate the sharp cut at the shoulder.

General Notes **Machin £.s.d. Issues**

Figures 1 – 8 are copyright Royal Mail Group, courtesy of The Postal Museum.

Figure 8. Essay created in October 1966, made from the first plaster cast of the "Diadem" head without corsage

The "Dressed Head". In fact, he created a totally new sculpture, adding a corsage. This new cast is described as the "Dressed Head" in official documents. Under different lighting conditions many photographs were taken of two versions of this plaster cast. They can be distinguished by minor variations in the necklace and lines of the hair. One (with a single line in the hair) was used for essays with a gradated, pastel background, the other (with two lines in the hair) for darker, solid backgrounds. A retouched version of the latter came to be used alone in later years.

A multitude of essays were printed from three different head types: the Diadem Head couped at the neck; a modified version of this, larger with more shoulder; and the full Dressed Head. Essays were in pastel and solid colours and sometimes they were bicoloured. A few were even in metallic inks. From these a selection of 30 was made for presentation to the Queen in January 1967. Included were examples of the Dressed head with and without value, and the larger head without corsage.

The Queen Approves. After showing the essays to the Queen the Postmaster General, now Edward Short, reported that "the Queen was very pleased with the definitive design; that she preferred the design with corsage" and that she "expressly requested" the olive brown with sepia colour for the 4d denomination (the basic inland letter rate). This was deliberately intended to imitate the original Penny Black. Later, the Queen commented further that she was "glad to give her approval to these stamps which she considers admirable."

The first three values, 4d., deep sepia, 1s. and 1s.9d., of the sterling Machin definitives appeared on 5 June 1967. The remaining values were issued in stages during the following 13 months and the low value series was completed on 1 July 1968, although subsequent changes of stamp colours and variations in the number of phosphor bands on some values introduced further additions to the basic series. This was the first definitive issue to be printed on paper without watermark, thus eliminating some of the factors which complicated the listing for previous issues.

Printers. All the low value £.s.d. Machin issues were printed in photogravure by Harrison & Sons. They were printed on continuous reels of paper on the web generally in double-pane width, i.e. 480 stamps consisting of two panes (no dot and dot) each of 240 stamps arranged in 20 rows of 12 stamps, the panes being guillotined before issue. The 10d., 1s.6d., 1s.9d. and part of the 1s. printings were made from single cylinders printing sheets of 240 stamps (i.e. no dot panes only). The bulk of the £.s.d Machin series were printed on Timson presses. The 4d. (both colours) from cylinders 14, 15, 16 and 17 and the 5d. from cylinders 11 and 13 were printed variously on the Halley or Thrissell presses as were the 1s.6d. and 1s.9d. values. The 1s. multi-value coils were printed on the five-colour Thrissell press. The single-value panes for the £1 'Stamps for Cooks' booklet were sheet fed printed on the L & M No. 4 press.

Single-colour booklet panes of six were printed on the Timson press while booklet panes of four and *se-tenant* panes (both panes of four and six) were printed on the Halley press.

The phosphor bands were applied at the same operation. The bi-coloured 1s.6d. and 1s.9d. were printed by the three-colour (including the phosphor cylinder) Halley machine and the remainder by the two-colour Timson machine. The multi-value coils and *se-tenant* panes from the £1 Stamps for Cooks booklet were printed by the five-colour Thrissell machine.

Master negatives and multipositives. The process of engraving a new Machin definitive photogravure cylinder started with a master negative from photographs (sometimes referred to as masterpositives) of one of the two casts of the Queen's head in profile. Further master negatives were taken and there is evidence that these were retouched as needed. For each value another master negative was then prepared of the value alone. The next step was the transfer of the head and value images on the master negatives by means of a step-and-repeat camera on to a photographic plate known as a multipositive. This was normally rather larger than the pane size of 240 or double-pane size of 480.

The multipositive was exposed on to a light-sensitive, gelatine-coated sheet (the carbon tissue) which was then transferred to the print cylinder by the normal chemical etching process. The relative positioning of the head and value negatives was not always uniformly precise and could result in tiny variations in distance between head and value digits described under Machin heads in these notes.

After an application of a thin layer of chrome, the cylinder was ready for use. (This process differed from the subsequent decimal photogravure issues, for which separate multipositives of the head and value were produced and individually exposed on to the carbon tissue).

Paper. Unwatermarked chalk-surfaced paper was used for all values. Exceptionally, examples of all four panes from the £1 Stamps for Cooks booklet and the 3d. and 10d. from sheets exist on uncoated paper. It may be distinguished from the normal chalk-surfaced paper by the fibres which clearly show on the surface, resulting in the printing impression being rougher, and by the screening dots which are not so evident.

Paper Thickness and Fluorescence. Variation in the thickness of paper sometimes occurs in the making and is undetected where the finished reel conforms to the prescribed weight. Within the reel there may be sections where the paper is unusually thick or thin. A particular example is the 2s. booklet of March 1970 which is known with panes UB15 and UB18 on very thick paper. This has an effect on the thickness of the booklet and could cause jamming in the vending machine. Such varieties are not listed. Certain coil issues were on translucent paper, the design showing clearly on the back of the stamps.

On some printings the fluorescent reaction varies. This is best seen on marginal examples, but the difference is not sufficient or consistent to warrant separate listing and, indeed, the brighter paper can be made to appear dull by exposure to sunlight. Stamps cannot be made to appear brighter, however, and none of the pre-decimal paper is as bright under u.v. as the fluorescent coated paper which was introduced in 1971.

Gum. Polyvinyl alchohol (PVA) was introduced by Harrison & Sons in place of gum arabic in 1968. It is almost invisible except that a small amount of pale yellowish colouring matter was introduced to make it possible to see that the stamps had been gummed. Although this can be distinguished from gum arabic in unused stamps there is, of course, no means of detecting it in used examples. Where the two forms of gum exist on the same value they are listed separately.

It should be further noted that gum arabic is normally shiny in appearance, and that, normally, PVA has a matt appearance. However, depending upon the qualities of the paper ingredients and the resultant absorption of the gum, occasionally, PVA has a slightly shiny appearance, and in cases of severe under-gumming gum arabic may appear matt. In such cases it is sometimes impossible to be absolutely sure which gum has been used except by testing the stamps with a very expensive infra-red spectrometer. Chemical tests unfortunately destroy the stamps. Therefore, whilst very shiny gum is gum arabic it does not follow that all matt gum is PVA. A few late printings of stamps originally issued on PVA were made on gum arabic paper, either in error or to use up stocks.

Paper treated with gum arabic is passed over a fracture bar before printing to reduce its tendency to curl. This results in a crazy paving appearance, often visible under magnification, not present on PVA.

Machin £.s.d. Issues — General Notes

The term PVA is used because it is generally accepted, but the official abbreviation is PVAl to distinguish it from PVAc, polyvinyl acetate, another adhesive which has not so far been used for stamps, although it does occur on postal stationery. De La Rue use the term PVOH, polyvinyl hydroxyl, to describe the same adhesive.

Machin Heads. Basically two master negatives were used for preparing the multipositive for each value comprising (a) head with background and (b) value. The portrait negative used for the initial releases had a three-dimensional effect only in the 10d. and 1s. values where a light background was used. On the other values, for which a different portrait master negative was used, the darker background merged with the outline and much of the relief effect was lost.

Beginning with coils and booklets in March 1968 a modified portrait negative was used giving greater contrast at those points where it had been lost. Thus there are three clearly different portraits; the original Head A with a flatter base to the bust, Head B with a curved shadow beneath the bust and Head C the three-dimensional version from the light background stamps.

These differences are listed and, for ease of reference, appear in tabulated form, together with details of the phosphor screens, at the beginning of the catalogue list.

As a result of the combination of two master negatives described above, the position of the value in relation to the frame varies from one multipositive to another. The 2d. Types I and II show an extreme case of this, where the change was made deliberately. Taking the 4d. for example the distance to the left frame varies from 0·9 mm on the early sheet cylinders to 1·2 mm on the multi-value coils, while the spacing to the bottom is normally 0·9 mm but decreases to 0·6 mm in the £1 Stamps for Cooks booklet.

Phosphor bands. See the General Notes for Section S for a detailed description of these. The Machin definitives were normally issued with violet phosphor bands only. Most values have appeared with the phosphor omitted in error and these are listed separately.

The 1s.6d. (No. U29) was issued as an experiment in 1969 with violet phosphor incorporated into the coating.

Phosphor screens. The phosphor bands were applied in photogravure, some of the cylinders having a 150-line screen and others a 250-line screen. The absence of a screen on parts of a printing is due to the cylinder becoming clogged.

The phosphor screen used for the single centre band on the 3d., 4d. sepia and 4d. vermilion booklet panes of six is unique in having a mixed screen. Continuous 21-row cylinders are normally produced from two pieces of carbon tissue, thus giving two joins. On this particular phosphor cylinder, the pieces of carbon tissue had different screens. Thus four types of booklet panes can be found (1) 150 screen; (2) screen join 150/250; (3) 250 screens; (4) screen join 250/150. It is calculated that out of 100 panes the proportions are 67 150 screen, 14 250 screen and 19 screen joins.

It is not easy to distinguish the different screens but we include them in the following check-list of the Machin Head Types.

Perforation. Harrisons used the same 15×14 comb perforation as for the previous Wilding definitives. A number of different perforators were used for both sheets and booklets and these are described and illustrated in Appendix G. The cylinder numbers are listed and priced according to the type of perforator used. The 1s. multi-value coils, for the first time, used a new rotary perforator - the Swedish 'Lawnmower'.

Booklet panes. In Section UB we list separately the booklet panes and the varieties on them and priced according to perforator types. See General Notes to that Section.

Coils. See general notes for Section S for detailed notes on these. Vertical delivery coils were printed from double-pane cylinders, except for the 3d. and 6d. These, together with all sideways delivery coils were printed from single-pane cylinders.

Coil leaders are listed with their codes and are priced as a leader with a single stamp attached or, for the multi-value coil, the five stamps attached. Additional stamps would be priced as normal. No distinction is made for the roll number.

Shades. There are numerous shades in these issues and we have restricted our listing to the most marked ones and related them to the cylinders which produced them where possible.

Dates of issue. The dates given are those announced by the Post Office, except in the case of dates for changes of gum or in the number of phosphor bands when we have quoted either the dates of release by the Philatelic Bureau or the earliest dates known. As in Section S the dates given in bold type in the headings are those on which stamps first appeared in sheet form. Where a date is followed by a dagger it means that the stamp appeared earlier in coils or booklets as indicated in footnotes.

First Day Covers. They are listed after the Presentation Pack but we only quote for official covers, prepared and issued by the Post Office, cancelled by FIRST DAY OF ISSUE circular postmarks.

Presentation Packs. See General Notes under Section W.

"Unprinted stamps". Widely trimmed sheet margins may produce the effect of unprinted stamps as illustrated above. The blank paper has the phosphor bands printed as on the normal stamps. In the Machin and Regional issues they come from either the left or right margins; in the special issues they are known from the top of the sheet.

Invalidation. All £.s.d. Machin definitives were withdrawn from sale on 25 November 1971, and were, with the exception of the £1 value, invalidated as from 1 March 1972. They ceased to be valid in Guernsey and Jersey from 1 October 1969 when these islands each established their own independent postal administrations and introduced their own stamps.

Sheet Markings. Reference should be made to the descriptions of Sheet Markings given in the General Notes for Section S, as most of these apply to this Section and the information given there is not repeated here. In the case of the 1s.6d. and 1s.9d. bicoloured Machin definitives reference should be made to the descriptions of Sheet Markings given in Section W as many of them also apply to these two values. Additional information to that provided in Sections S and W is given here.

Cylinder Numbers. In the Machin definitives ½d. to 1s. values they appear in the left-hand margin opposite Row 18 No. 1 in the style as illustrated in Section S. In the case of the 1s.6d. and 1s.9d. values the cylinder numbers appear boxed in the left-hand margin opposite Row 19 No. 1 in the style as illustrated in Section W.

Phosphor Cylinder Numbers. As with the 1970 General Anniversaries, special issue in Section W, phosphor cylinder numbers were introduced during 1970, "Ph 1" appearing on the Machin issues. It only occurs on the dot panes and appears in the right-hand margin and therefore not on the cylinder block. Moreover it is not synchronised with the ink cylinders and so can appear anywhere in the margin, and the "1" is often trimmed off. Its existence is recorded under the Sheet Markings.

Varieties in Cylinder Blocks. Where a cylinder block contains a listed variety the price is adjusted accordingly and bears an asterisk.

Marginal Arrows. In the Machin definitives these are "W" shaped (photo-etched) at top, bottom and sides, unless otherwise stated.

General Notes **Machin £.s.d. Issues** **U**

Perforation Guide Holes. A number of different styles of guide hole box have been used for the Machin definitives and these are fully illustrated as for Sections S and W.

In addition to guide hole boxes of one type or another opposite rows 14/15 (used for perforation Type A), the earlier cylinders of nearly all the values from ½d. to 1s. also show a single traffic light type box above and below the eighth vertical row in the no dot panes. This latter type would only be used in conjunction with perforation Type F(L)* and it is illustrated here to explain its presence on the sheets. When Type F(L)* is used the circular central part of the box is either partly or completely removed.

Colour trials. In preparation for the decimal currency Machin stamps, colour trials were prepared by Harrisons, using three values from the pre-decimal series. It is believed that as many as 40 different colours may have been tested in the trials which were conducted to determine which would be the most suitable for sorting mail under different lighting conditions.

It is probable that a small hand press would have been used to print the trials which were on ordinary coated paper with PVA gum and did not have phosphor bands. Due to the size of the press it is believed that a maximum of four stamps were printed in each colour, a;though in some cases as few as two examples have been recorded.

The 8d. value was used to trial stamps with solid backgrounds, the 1s. for light and gradated backgrounds and the 1s.6d. for bi-coloured stamps. Those which are known to exist are listed under the relevant values. All have been hinged and most have a letter and/or number annotated in pencil on the gummed side.

A full account of these colour trials conducted at Cambridge University in 1969, together with a listing of the identification letters and numbers, is recorded in the *GB Journal*, Volume 48 (2010), in three articles at pages 63, 92 and 123, published by the Great Britain Philatelic Society.

THREE TYPES OF MACHIN HEAD

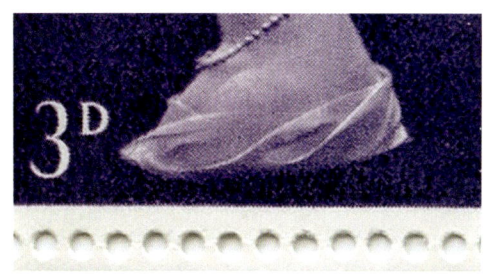

Head A Flatter base to the bust

Head B Curved shadow beneath the bust

Head C Three-dimensional effect with light background

115

U Machin £.s.d. Issues *Checklist*

CHECKLIST OF MACHIN HEADS AND PHOSPHOR SCREENS
For fuller explanations see General Notes.

Abbreviations
Phosphor bands: 1C = one centre; 1L = one left side; 1R = one right side
Booklet panes: s/t = stamps *se-tenant*; s/t labels = stamps *se-tenant* with labels
Coils: MV = multi-value; S = sideways delivery; V = vertical delivery

Face Value	Cat. No.	Description	Phosphor Bands	Gum	Head	Screen	Sheet Cylinders	Sources Booklet Panes	Coils
½d.	U 1		2	PVA	A	150	2, 3	—	—
1d.	U 2		2	PVA	A	150	2	—	—
	U 2		2	PVA	B	150	4, 6	6	V
	U 2		2	PVA	B	250	—	s/t, 6 s/t 15 s/t	—
	U 3		1C	PVA	B	250	—	6 s/t	—
	U 4		1C	GA	B	250	—	—	MV
2d.	U 5	Type I	2	PVA	A	150	1	—	—
	U 6	Type II	2	PVA	B	150	5, 6	—	V
	U 6	Type II	2	PVA	B	250	—	—	V, S
	U 7	Type II	1C	GA	B	250	—	—	MV
3d.	U 8		1C	GA	A	150	1	—	V
	U 8		1C	GA	A	250	—	—	S
	U 8		1C	GA	B	250	—	—	MV
	U 9		1C	PVA	A	150	1, 3, 4	—	—
	U 9		1C	PVA	A	250	—	—	S
	U 9		1C	PVA	B	150	—	6	—
	U 9		1C	PVA	B	Join	—	6	—
	U 9		1C	PVA	B	250	—	6	—
	U10		2	PVA	A	150	3, 4	—	V
	U10		2	PVA	B	150	—	—	V
	U10		2	PVA	B	250	—	4 s/t	—
4d.	U11	Sepia	2	GA	A	150	4, 8	6	V
	U11	Sepia	2	GA	A	250	—	—	S
	U11	Sepia	2	GA	B	250	14	—	—
	U12	Sepia	2	PVA	A	150	4, 10, 12, 13	6	—
	U12	Sepia	2	PVA	B	250	14, 15	4	—
	U13	Sepia	1C	PVA	A	150	4, 12, 13	6	V
	U13	Sepia	1C	PVA	A	Join	—	6	—
	U13	Sepia	1C	PVA	A	250	—	6	S
	U13	Sepia	1C	PVA	B	250	14, 15	4, 4 s/t labels 6 s/t	—
4d.	U14	Vermilion	1C	PVA	A	150	4, 10, 13	6	V
	U14	Vermilion	1C	PVA	A	Join	—	6	—
	U14	Vermilion	1C	PVA	A	250	—	6	S
	U14	Vermilion	1C	PVA	B	150	—	6	—
	U14	Vermilion	1C	PVA	B	Join	—	6	—
	U14	Vermilion	1C	PVA	B	250	15, 16, 17	4, 4 s/t labels 6, 15	S
	U15	Vermilion	1C	GA	B	250	—	—	MV
	U15	Vermilion Feb/Mar	1C	GA	A	150	—	6	—
	U15	Vermilion '69 6s. &	1C	GA	A	Join	—	6	—
	U15	Vermilion May '69 10s	1C	GA	A	250	—	6	—
	U16	Vermilion	1L	PVA	B	250	—	6 s/t, 15 s/t	—
	U16A	Vermilion	1R	PVA	B	250	—	15 s/t	—
5d.	U17		2	PVA	A	150	1	—	—
	U17		2	PVA	B	150	7, 10, 15	6	V
	U17		2	PVA	B	250	11, 13	15, 15 s/t	S
6d.	U18		2	PVA	A	150	2, 3, 4, 5	—	—
	U18		2	PVA	B	150	—	—	V
	U18		2	PVA	B	250	—	—	V
7d.	U19		2	PVA	B	150	3, 4	—	—
8d.	U20	Vermilion	2	PVA	A	150	2	—	—

116

Checklist **Machin £.s.d. Issues**

Face Value	Cat. No.	Description	Phosphor Bands	Gum	Head	Screen	Sheet Cylinders	Sources Booklet Panes	Coils
	U21	Turquoise-blue	2	PVA	B	150	3	—	—
9d.	U22		2	GA	A	150	2	—	—
	U23		2	PVA	A	150	2	—	—
10d.	U24		2	PVA	C	150	1	—	—
	U24		2	PVA	C	250	1	—	—
1s.	U25		2	GA	C	150	3, 11	—	—
	U26		2	PVA	C	150	11	—	—
	U26		2	PVA	C	250	11	—	—
1s.6d.	U27		2	GA	A	150	2A–2B, 3A–2B	—	—
	U27	(3) Phosphor omitted	—	GA	A	—	5A–2B	—	—
	U28		2	PVA	A	150	3A–2B, 5A–2B	—	—
	U28		2	PVA	A	250	3A–1B	—	—
	U29	"All-over" phos.	—	PVA	A	—	5A–2B	—	—
1s.9d.	U30		2	GA	A	150	1A–1B	—	—
	U31		2	PVA	A	250	1A–1B	—	—

INDEX TO COIL STAMPS

Face Value	Phosphor Bands	Gum	Head	Further description	Delivery		See stamp No.
1d.	2	PVA	B		V		U2
2d.	2	PVA	B	Type II	V	S	U6
3d.	1C	GA	A		V	S	U8
3d.	1C	PVA	A			S	U9
3d.	2	PVA	A		V		U10
3d.	2	PVA	B		V		U10
4d.	2	GA	A	Deep olive-brown	V	S	U11
4d.	1C	PVA	A	Deep olive-brown	V	S	U13
4d.	1C	PVA	A	Bright vermilion	V	S	U14
4d.	1C	PVA	B	Bright vermilion		S	U14
5d.	2	PVA	B		V	S	U17
6d.	2	PVA	B		V		U18
2×2d.	1C	GA	B	Multi-value coil. 4d. Bright vermilion		S	U32
+3d.	1C	GA	B	Multi-value coil. 4d. Bright vermilion		S	U32
+1d.	1C	GA	B	Multi-value coil. 4d. Bright vermilion		S	U32
+4d.	1C	GA	B	Multi-value coil. 4d. Bright vermilion		S	U32

UA Machin £.s.d. issues ½d., 1d.

PAPER AND WATERMARK
All the following issues are printed on chalk-surfaced paper, except for the uncoated errors, and are without watermark.

Type **U1** Value at left

Type **U2** Value at right

Queen Elizabeth II
(Des. after plaster cast by Arnold Machin)

½d. Type U1 (1968)

1968 (5 February). **½d.** Two 9·5 mm phosphor bands. PVA gum. Head A

U1 = SG 723	Mint	Used
½d. Orange-brown	10	10
a. Phosphor omitted	30·00	
b. Dot in "1" of "½" (Cyl. 3 No dot, R. 20/2)	10·00	

U1b

Cylinder Numbers (Blocks of Six)
Perforation Type A

Cylinder No.	No dot	Dot
2	2·00	2·00
3	10·00*	5·00

* Includes variety U1b.

Minor Constant Sheet Flaws

Cyl. 2.	5/12	Small retouch at base of Queen's hair (Th. E4–5)
	9/5	Dark horizontal strip of shading behind Queen's neck (Th. F5–6)
Cyl. 3	12/9	Dark patch below Queen's chin (Th. E2–3)

A number of stamps from cylinder 2 dot display irregularities of the background in the form of dark patches and lines. This is most prominent on R. 9/5 recorded above; others occur on R. 2/2, 7/6, 8/6, 9/11, 10/1, 13/2–5, 14/5, 17/4–5 and 18/1.

Sheet Markings

Guide holes: In double "SON" box opposite rows 14/15, at left (no dot) or right (dot). In addition a single traffic light type box appears above and below the eighth vertical row in the no dot pane only. (These would only be used in conjunction with perforation Type F(L)*).

Others: As given in General Notes

Sold Out: 10.2.70.

1d. Type U1 (1968–1970)

1968 (5 February). **1d.** Yellowish olive

A. Two 9·5 mm phosphor bands. PVA Gum.

U2 = SG 724	Mint	Used
1d. (1) Light olive (A) Head A	50	15
(2) Yellowish olive (B) Head B	10	10
(3) Greenish olive	10	10
a. Imperf. (coil strip)*	£3750	
b. Uncoated paper (1970)**	£150	
c. Phosphor omitted	4·00	
d. Phosphor omitted on front but printed on the gummed side	£300	
e. Error. One 9·5 mm phosphor band	8·00	
g. Neck retouches (Cyl. 4 No dot, R. 20/3)	15·00	
h. Flaw by Queen's chin (Vertical coil)	15·00	
i. Thick "1 D" (Vertical coil)	20·00	
j. Flaw by Queen's chin (Vertical coil)	15·00	
k. Imperforate at bottom (Vertical coil)	†	—
s. Optd. "Specimen" (14 mm.)	£250	

B. One 4 mm Centre Phosphor band. PVA Gum.
Se-tenant Booklet pane only (*16 September 1968*)

U3 = SG 725		
1d. Yellowish olive (Head B)	45	45

C. One 4 mm Centre Phosphor band. Gum Arabic.
Multi-value coil only (*27 August 1969*)

U4 = SG 725Eg		
1d. Yellowish olive (Head B)	1·00	
a. Dark vert. line (Roll 7 etc)	3·00	

* No. U2a occurs in a vertical strip of four, top stamp perforated on three sides, bottom stamp imperf. three sides and the two middle stamps completely imperf.
** Uncoated paper. No. U2b comes from the *se-tenant* pane of 15 in the £1 Stamps for Cooks Booklet (see No. UB2ab); see also General Notes.
No. U2d came from the *se-tenant* pane No. UB2ad of which six examples are believed to exist.
No. U3 only comes from the 10s. Booklet of September 1968 (XP6). It also occurs with the phosphor omitted but since a single stamp would be difficult to distinguish from No. U2c it is only listed when in a complete se-tenant booklet pane (see No. UB3a).
No. U4 only comes from the multi-value coil strip which is listed as No. U32.
A single used example is known of No. U2k.

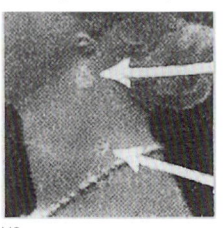

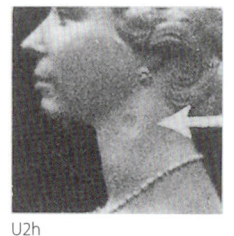

U2g U2h

Normal U2i

118

Cylinder Numbers (Blocks of Six)
Two bands. Perforation Type A

Cylinder No.	No dot	Dot
2 (Shade 1) (Head A)	7·00	7·00
4 (Shades 2, 3) (Head B)	2·00	2·00
6 (Shade 3) (Head B)	2·00	2·00

Minor Constant Sheet Flaws

Cyl. 2.	5/11	Small flaw at back of Queen's collar (Th. F5)
Cyl. 4	6/9	White flaw at top of Queen's hair (Th. B3)
Cyl. 6.	11/7	Horizontal line of coloured dots across Queen's shoulder (Th. F3–5)
	12/10	Vertical lines of coloured dots through Queen's forehead and cheek (Th. B2, C2–3 and D2)

Coils Leaders
Two bands. Vertical delivery printed in continuous reels from double-pane cylinders B1 or B2. Head B.

Code No.	Number in roll	Face value	
E	480	£2	35·00
X	960	£4	10·00
Z	1920	£8	12·00

One centre band. Multi-value coil, see No. U32.

Sheet Markings
Guide holes: Cyl. 4, in single "SN" box opposite rows 14/15, at left (no dot) or right (dot)
Cyls. 2 and 6, in double "SON" box opposite rows 14/15, at left (no dot) or right (dot)

Marginal arrows:
Cyls. 2 and 6, "W" shaped, photo-etched at top, bottom and sides
Cyl. 4, "W" shaped, hand-engraved at top, bottom and sides

Marginal rule:
Cyl. 2, at bottom of sheet, 2 mm wide
Cyls. 4 and 6, at bottom of sheet, 2 ½ mm wide

Others: As given in General Notes

2d. Type U1 (1968–1969)

Two Types

Type I. Value spaced away from left side of stamp (Cyls. 1 no dot and dot)

Type II. Value closer to left side from new multipositive (Cyls. 5 no dot and dot onwards). The portrait appears in the centre, thus conforming to the other values.

1968 (5 February). **2d.** Type I. Two 9·5 mm phosphor bands. PVA gum. Head A

U5 = SG 726	Mint	Used
2d. Lake-brown	10	10
a. Phosphor omitted	40·00	

Cylinder Numbers (Blocks of Six)
Perforation Type A

Cylinder No.	No dot	Dot
1	1·75	1·75

Minor Constant Sheet Flaws

Cyl. 1	3/11	Small white spot in band of diadem (Th. C5)
	8/8	Dark spot by emblems at rear of diadem (Th. B5)
	12/9	Retouching in Queen's hair just by ear (Th. C–D4)

Sheet Markings
Guide holes: In double "SON" box opposite rows 14/15, at left (no dot) or right (dot)

Others: As given in General Notes

1969 (February)†. **2d.** Change to Type II. Head B

A. Two 9·5 mm phosphor bands. PVA Gum

U6 = SG 727	Mint	Used
2d. Lake-brown	10	10
a. Phosphor omitted	2·00	
b. Error. One 9·5 mm phosphor band	60·00	

B. One 4 mm Centre Phosphor band. Gum Arabic.
Multi-value coil only (27 August 1969)

U7 = SG 728		
2d. Lake-brown	35	40

† No. U6 was issued on 4 April 1968 in sideways delivery coils, and on 19 March 1969 in vertical delivery coils.
No. U7 only comes from the multi-value coil strip which is listed as No. U32.

Cylinder Numbers (Blocks of Six)
Two bands. Perforation Type A

Cylinder No.	No dot	Dot
5	4·00	4·00
6	4·00	4·00
(6) Ph1	—	25·00

The phosphor cylinder number Ph1 is found on later printings of cyl. 6 dot, in the right margin.

Minor Constant Sheet Flaws

Cyl. 5.	6/8	Dark area above "2" (Th. F1)
	8/1	Small flaw on Queen's shoulder (Th. F3)
	10/1	Coloured line through Queen's nose and upper lip (Th. C–D2)
	10/3	Dark spot below Queen's chin (Th. E2)
	19/5	Retouch to background to left of diadem (Th. A2–3). There are two states of this
Cyl. 6.	18/4	Small retouch at top of Queen's neck and vertical scratch extending to her dress (Th. E3–G3). Several states exist

Coil Leaders
Two bands. Printed in continuous reels from single-pane cylinder D2 (vertical) or single-pane D1 (sideways)

Code No.	Number in roll	Face value		
T	480	£4	Sideways delivery	60·00
V	960	£8	Vertical delivery	90·00

One centre band. Multi-value coil, see No. U32.

Sheet Markings
Guide holes: In double "SON" box opposite rows 14/15, at left (no dot) or right (dot). In addition a single traffic light type box appears above and below the eighth vertical row in the no dot pane only (These would only be used in conjunction with perforation Type F(L)*).

Others: As given in General Notes

3d. Type U1 (1967–1969)

1967 (8 August). **3d.** One 4 mm centre phosphor band

A. Gum Arabic

U8 = SG 729	Mint	Used
3d. (1) Violet (A) Head A	10	10
(2) Bluish violet (sideways coils)	2·00	25
(1) Violet (multi-value coils) (B) Head B	40	20
a. Imperf (vertical pair)	£950	
b. Phosphor omitted	4·00	
c. Spot on nose (Sideways coil, Roll 10)	15·00	
d. Gash on diadem (Multi-value coil, Roll 1)	15·00	

B. PVA Gum (12 March 1968)

U9 = SG 729Ev		
3d. (1) Violet (A) Head A	1·00	
(2) Bluish violet (sideways coils)	30·00	
(1) Violet (booklets) (B) Head B	4·00	
a. Phosphor omitted	4·00	
b. Spot on nose (Sideways coil, Roll 10)	50·00	

No. U8 is known pre-released on 7 August at Bournemouth, Hyde (Cheshire), in South London and at Torquay.

U8c, U9b From sideways delivery coils

U8d Occurs in sideways delivery multi-value GS and GL coils on every fifth 3d. stamp

Cylinder Numbers (Blocks of Six)

Gum Arabic

Perforation Type A

Cylinder No.	No dot	Dot
1	25·00	28·00

Perforation Type F(L)*

| 1 | 2·50 | 2·50 |

PVA Gum

Perforation Type A

Cylinder No.	No dot	Dot
1	2·50	2·50
3	2·50	2·50
4	8·00	8·00

Perforation Type F(L)*

| 1 | † | — |

There are two states of cyl. 1 no dot: (a) "1" is hatched, the bottom part lacks colour and the serifs are short (gum arabic printings); (b) "1" is solid and the serifs are long (gum arabic perf. type F(L)* and PVA).

Cylinder blocks from the no dot pane of Cylinder 3 show a phantom "3", slightly smaller and just below and to the right of the normal cylinder number. This occurred on part of the printing.

Minor Constant Sheet Flaws

Cyl. 1	1/9	Vertical scratch on Queen's neck (Th. E3–4)
	3/9	Pale patch in background around "D" of value
	7/1	Small white flaw inside cross of diadem (Th. B5)
Cyl. 1.	1/4	Small retouch on Queen's neck below ear (Th. D4). PVA only
	1/7	White scratch in Queen's hair below diadem at right (Th. C5). PVA only
	4/11	Small retouch on Queen's neck (Th. E3).
	12/4	Retouch at front of Queen's collar (Th. G3)
	19/6	Small retouch by Queen's mouth (Th. D3)
Cyl. 3.	8/3	Scratch on Queen's temple (Th. C3)
	12/7	Retouch on Queen's neck below necklace (Th. F4)
	16/4	Flaw on Queen's shoulder (Th. F4). Later retouched

Coil Leaders

Printed in continuous reels from double-pane cylinder M1 (vertical) or single pane M2 (sideways). Head A

Gum Arabic.

Code No.	Number in roll	Face value		
S	480	£6	Sideways delivery	50·00
AC	480	£6	Vertical delivery	30·00
AD	960	£12	do.	30·00
U	1920	£24	do.	25·00

PVA Gum

| S* | 480 | £6 | Sideways delivery | £250 |

* Stamps from this coil can be distinguished from all other PVA centre-band stamps in singles. The coil stamps have Machin Head Type A and 250-line phosphor screen. The sheet stamps have Head Type A and 150-line screen, whilst the booklet stamps have Head Type B.

One centre band. Multi-value coil, see No. U32

Sheet Markings

Guide holes: Perf. Type A, in double "SON" box opposite rows 14/15, at left (no dot) or right (dot). In addition a single traffic light type box appears above and below the eighth vertical row in the no dot pane from cyl. 1 (latter only used in conjunction with perforation Type F (L)*).

Perf. Type F (L)*, boxed above and below the eighth vertical row in the no dot pane only. The usual "SON" boxes opposite rows 14/15 remain.

Others: As given in General Notes

1969 (20 August)†. **3d.** Change to Two 9·5 mm phosphor bands. PVA Gum

U10 = SG 730	Mint	Used
3d. Violet (A) Head A	10	15
(B) Head B (Booklets and coils)	25	15
a. Uncoated paper* (A) Head A	£6000	
b. Error. One 9·5 mm phosphor band	4·00	

* Uncoated paper see General Notes.
† Issued on 6.4.68 in 2s. Booklets dated May 1968, on 26 September 1968 in vertical delivery coils.

Cylinder Numbers (Blocks of Six)
Perforation Type A

Cylinder No.	No dot	Dot
3 (Head A)	3·75	3·75
4 (Head A)	6·50	6·50

The note about the phantom "3" mentioned under No. U9 also applies here and the whole of the printing was affected.

3d., 4d. Machin £.s.d. issues UA

Minor Constant Sheet Flaws

Cyl. 3.	8/3	Scratch on Queen's temple (Th. C3)
	12/7	Retouch on Queen's neck below necklace (Th. F4)

Coil Leaders
Vertical delivery printed in continuous reels from double pane cylinders M1 (Head A) or M4 (Head B)

Code No.	Number in roll	Face value	
AD (Head A)	960	£12	20·00
AD (Head B)	960	£12	25·00

Sheet Markings
Guide holes: In double "SON" box opposite rows 14/15, at left (no dot) or right (dot)
Others: As given in General Notes

4d. Deep sepia, Type U1 (1967–1968)

1967 (5 June). **4d.** Two 9·5 mm phosphor bands

A. Gum Arabic
U11 = SG 731/Ea

		Mint	Used
4d.	(1) Deep sepia (A) Head A	10	10
	(2) Deep olive-brown	1·00	1·00
	(2) Deep olive-brown (B) Head B	£1400	
a.	Phosphor omitted. Shade (1)	4·00	
ab.	Phosphor omitted. Shade (2)	6·00	
b.	Error. One 9·5 mm phosphor band	50·00	

B. PVA Gum (22 January 1968)
U12 = SG 731Eav

4d.	(2) Deep olive-brown (A) Head A	1·00	
	(3) Deep olive-sepia	1·00	30
	(2) Deep olive-brown (B) Head B	1·00	30
	(3) Deep olive-sepia	1·00	30
a.	Error. One 9·5 mm phosphor band	8·00	
b.	Phosphor omitted	4·00	
c.	White patch in hair (Cyl. 13 No dot, R. 20/12)	20·00	
d.	Nick in hair (Cyl. 15 Dot, R. 16/5)	20·00	

A wide range of shades exist on these issues from olive-brown to sepia-black. At the time, the Post Office stated this was the result of variations in depth of inking on the cylinder and that there was no change in the composition of the ink.

No. U11 (1) in shades of washed out grey are colour changelings which we understand are caused by the concentrated solvents used in modern dry-cleaning methods.

No. U11 (1) is known pre-released on 25 May at Gravesend.

U12c, U13b, U14e White patch over eye and hair
U12d, U13c, U14f Reported as being later retouched

Cylinder Numbers (Blocks of Six)
Gum Arabic
Perforation Type F(L)

Cylinder No.	No dot	Dot
(a) Shade (1) Deep sepia		
4 (Head A)	5·50	5·50
8 (Head A)	6·75	6·75
(b) Shade (2) Deep olive-brown		
4 (Head A)	12·00	12·00
8 (Head A)	12·00	12·00
Perforation Type A		
14 (Head B)	—	—

PVA Gum
Perforation Type F(L)*

Cylinder No.	No dot	Dot
(a) Shade (2) Deep olive-brown		
4 (Head A)	24·00	20·00
Perforation Type A		
4 (Head A)	12·00	12·00
10 (Head A)	4·00	4·00
12 (Head A)	12·00	12·00
13 (Head A)	20·00	20·00
14 (Head B)	3·00	3·00
15 (Head B)	70·00	70·00
(b) Shade (3) Deep olive-sepia		
Perforation Type A		
4 (Head A)	12·00	12·00
10 (Head A)	4·00	4·00
13 (Head A)	20·00	20·00
14 (Head B)	3·00	3·00
15 (Head B)	70·00	70·00

Stamps from cylinder 12 show traces of screening dots within the white area of the face value. Cylinder 15 has the number close to the stamp resulting in the dot often being removed by the perforations. The dot pane has a tiny dot on the horizontal rule below R. 20/1 whilst in the no dot pane the marginal rule below R. 20/1 is damaged and there is a line in the margin below R. 20/2.

Minor Constant Sheet Flaws

Cyl. 4.	1/1	Nick in neck (Th. F5)
	2/9	Dark flaw in Queen's hair (Th. C4)
	20/8	Scar on Queen's forehead (Th. C2–3)
Cyl. 8	18/12	Diagonal line through back of Queen's hair (Th. C5)
Cyl. 8.	9/9	White spot in band of diadem (Th. B3–4)
	15/3	Diagonal coloured line on Queen's shoulder and dress (Th. F–G4)
	15/5	Prominent retouch on Queen's neck just below jawline (Th. E3–4)
Cyl. 10	18/12	As Cyl. 8
Cyl. 10.	3/4	Coloured flaw on Queen's shoulder (Th. F3)
	3/6	Two coloured flaws on Queen's shoulder (Th. F3)
	10/8	Pale patch in background to left of Queen's throat (Th. E2)
	11/7	Dark flaw at back of Queen's neck, just above necklace (Th. E4)
	12/5	Dark flaw on Queen's shoulder, just below necklace (Th. F3)
	15/3	As Cyl. 8
	15/5	As Cyl. 8
	19/2	Dark coloured vertical line in lower right-hand stamp margin (Th. G7)
Cyl. 12	18/12	As Cyl. 8.
Cyl. 12.	15/3	As Cyl. 8
	15/5	As Cyl. 8

UA Machin £.s.d. issues 4d.

Cyl. 13	9/12	Large area of retouching behind Queen's head (Th. C5–6 and D5–6)
	18/12	As Cyl. 8
Cyl. 13.	15/3	As Cyl. 8
	15/5	As Cyl. 8 but more prominent
Cyl. 14	6/11	Vertical white scratch on Queen's neck (Th. E–F4)
	18/7	White flaw at back of Queen's dress (Th. F5)

Coil Leaders
Printed in continuous reels from double-pane cylinders P2, P3 or P4 (vertical) or single-pane P1 (sideways).

Head A
Gum Arabic. Shade (1) Deep sepia

Code No.	Number in roll	Face value		
H	480	£8	Sideways delivery	80.00
A	960	£16	Vertical delivery	£160

Sheet Markings
Guide holes: Perf. Type A, in double "SON" box opposite rows 14/15, at left (no dot) or right (dot). In addition a single traffic light type box appears above and below the eighth vertical row in the no dot pane only (latter only used in conjunction with perforation Type F(L)*).

Perf. Type F(L)*, boxed above and below the eighth vertical row in the no dot pane only. The usual "SON" boxes opposite rows 14/15 remain.

Others: As given in General Notes

1968 (16 September). **4d.** Change to one 4 mm centre phosphor band. PVA Gum

U13 = SG 732		Mint	Used
4d. (2) Deep olive-brown (A) Head A		10	10
(2) Deep olive-brown (B) Head B		10	10
(3) Deep olive-sepia		10	10
b. White patch in hair (Cyl. 13 No dot, R. 20/12)		20·00	
c. Nick in hair (Cyl. 15 Dot, R. 16/5)		20·00	

For illustrations of Nos. U13b/c see Nos. U12c/d.

No. U13 also occurs with the phosphor omitted but since a single stamp would be indistinguishable from No. U12b it is only listed when in a complete *se-tenant* booklet pane (see No. UB3a).

Cylinder Numbers (Blocks of Six)
Perforation Type A

(a) Shade (2) Deep olive-brown

Cylinder No.	No dot	Dot
4 (Head A)	2·50	2·50
12 (Head A)	2·50	2·50
13 (Head A)	70·00	70·00
14 (Head B)	3·00	3·00
15 (Head B)	3·00	3·00

(b) Shade (3) Deep olive-sepia

	No dot	Dot
14 (Head B)	3·00	3·00
15 (Head B)	3·00	3·00

The notes, concerning cylinders 12 and 15, under No. U12 also apply here.

Minor Constant Sheet Flaws

Cyl. 4.	1/1	Nick in neck (Th. F5)
	2/9	Coloured flaw in Queen's hair (Th. C4)
	19/1	Flaw on lower rim of Queen's diadem shows as missing pearls (Th. C5)
	20/8	Scar on Queen's forehead (Th. C2–3)

Cyl. 12	18/12	Diagonal line through back of Queen's hair (Th. C5)
Cyl. 12.	15/3	Diagonal coloured line on Queen's shoulder and dress (Th. F–G4)
	15/5	Prominent retouch on Queen's neck just below jawline (Th. E3–4)
Cyl. 13	9/12	Large area of retouching behind Queen's head (Th. C5–6 and D5–6)
	18/12	As Cyl. 12
Cyl. 13.	15/3	As Cyl. 12
	15/5	As Cyl. 12, but more prominent
Cyl. 15.	5/12	Two small white dots on Queen's shoulder (Th. F–G4). Later retouched
	17/12	White scratch in background above value, extending to Queen's shoulder. Later retouched but flaw still shows on Queen's shoulder

Coil Leaders
Printed in continuous reels from double-pane cylinder P3 (vertical) or single-pane P1 (sideways). Head A

Code No.	Number in roll	Face value		
H	480	£8	Sideways delivery	70·00
A	960	£16	Vertical delivery	80·00

Sheet Markings
Guide holes: As for perf. Type A under Nos. U11/12
Others: As given in General Notes

4d. bright vermilion, Type U1 (1969)

1969 (6 January). **4d.** Colour changed. One 4 mm Centre Phosphor band

A. PVA Gum

U14 = SG 733	Mint	Used
4d. Bright vermilion (A) Head A	10	10
(B) Head B	10	10
a. Tête-bêche (horiz. pair)	£5000	
b. Uncoated paper ('70)**	20·00	
c. Phosphor omitted	4·00	
d. Red nick in "D" (Cyl. 4 Dot, R. 15/1)	20·00	
e. White patch in hair (Cyl. 13 Dot, R. 20/12)	20·00	
f. Nick in hair (Cyl. 15 Dot, R. 16/5)	20·00	
g. Imperf. between stamp and top margin	£180	
h. Error. Two bands*	75·00	
s. Opt. "Specimen" (14 mm.)	45·00	

B. Gum Arabic. (20 February 1969)

U15 = SG 733Eg		
4d. Bright vermilion (A) Head A (booklets)	25·00	
(B) Head B (multi-value coil)	1·00	
a. Phosphor omitted (Head A)	£1750	
b. Diagonal scratch in background (Multi-value coil)	15·00	

** Uncoated paper. No. U14b comes from the £1 Stamps for Cooks Booklet (see Nos. UB16ab and UB17ab); see also General Notes.

Nos. U14 and U16/A from the £1 Stamps for Cooks Booklet (ZP1) show slight differences compared with stamps from normal sheets and all other booklets. The main stem of the "4" is thicker and it is only 0·6 mm from its foot to the base of the design compared with 0·9 mm on stamps from sheets and all

122

other booklets. Also, the cross-bar of the "4", normally opposite the point of the Queen's gown, is lower on the £1 booklet stamps. See under Machin Heads in General Notes.

Misplaced Phosphor Bands, *No. U14h comes from Method pane UB17af which has the central phosphor bands printed over the vertical perforations at each side.

No. U15A comes from the February and part of March 1969 6s. Barn Owl and Jay Booklets (QP46/7) and also part of May 1969 10s. Mary Kingsley Booklets (XP8).

No. U15B comes from the multi-value coil strip, issued 27 August 1969, which is listed as No. U32.

For illustrations of Nos. U14e/f, see Nos. U12c/d.

U14d
Believed later retouched

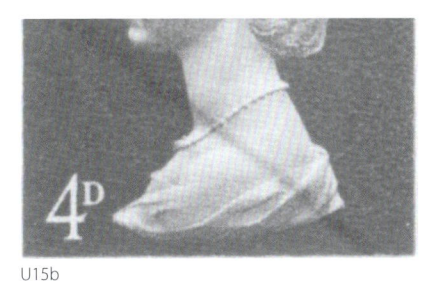

U15b

Cylinder Numbers (Blocks of Six)
PVA Gum. Perforation Type A

Cylinder No.	No dot	Dot
4 (Head A)	2·00	2·00
10 (Head A)	2·00	2·00
13 (Head A)	2·00	2·00
15 (Head B)	2·50	2·50
16 (Head B)	5·50	5·50
17 (Head B)	2·50	2·50

The note about the cylinder number being close to the stamp on Cylinder 15 mentioned under No. U12 also applies here.

Minor Constant Sheet Flaws

Cyl. 4.	1/1	Nick in neck (Th. F5)
	19/1	Flaw on lower rim of Queen's diadem shows as missing pearls (Th. C5)
	20/8	Scar on Queen's forehead (Th. C2–3)
Cyl. 10	18/12	Diagonal line through back of Queen's hair (Th. C5).
Cyl. 10.	15/3	Diagonal coloured line on Queen's shoulder and dress (Th. F–G4)
	15/5	Prominent retouch on Queen's neck just below jawline (Th. E3–4)
Cyl. 13	9/12	Large area of retouching behind Queen's head (Th. C5–6 and D5–6)
	18/12	As Cyl. 10
Cyl. 13.	15/3	As Cyl. 10
	15/5	As Cyl. 10, but more prominent
Cyl. 15.	17/12	Scratch on Queen's shoulder at left (Th. F3)
Cyl. 17	4/7	Small coloured spot in band of diadem (Th. B4)
	7/3	Small retouch on Queen's shoulder (Th. F3)
	18/4	Small flaw in band of diadem (Th. B4)
Cyl. 17.	19/10	White scratch at back of Queen's shoulder (Th. F5)

Coil Leaders
PVA Gum. Printed in continuous reels from double-pane cylinder P3 (vertical) or single-pane P1 (Head A) and P5 (Head B) (sideways)

Code No.	Number in roll	Face value		
H	480	£8	Sideways delivery	
			Head A	£160
			Head B	£140
A	960	£16	Vertical delivery	
			Head A	£160

One centre band, gum arabic. Multi-value coil, see No. U32

Sheet Markings
Guide holes: As for perf. Type A under Nos. U11/12
Others: As given in General Notes

1969 (6 January) **4d.** bright vermilion

A. One Side Phosphor band at left*. PVA Gum. Head B
From 10s. Booklets XP7/12 and £1 Booklet ZP1

U16 = SG 734	Mint	Used
4d. Bright vermilion	65	75
b. Uncoated paper ('70)**	£425	
c. Error. One 9·5 mm phosphor band	£250	
d. Phosphor omitted on front but printed at left on the gummed side	£425	
s. Optd. "Specimen" (14 mm.)	£275	

B. One Side Phosphor band at right*. PVA Gum. Head B
From £1 Booklet ZP1 only (1 December 1969)

U16A = SG 734Eb		
4d. Bright vermilion	2.00	2·75
b. Uncoated paper ('70)**	£425	
c. Phosphor omitted on front but printed at right on the gummed side	£425	
s. Optd. "Specimen" (14 mm.)	£275	

* The one side band stamps were produced by applying a 9·5 mm band over the vertical perforations between the 4d. and its adjoining stamp in the booklet panes. In theory the width of the band on a single stamp should be 4¾ (or 4·75) mm but this will vary if the band has not been perfectly positioned.

** Uncoated paper. Nos. U16b and U16Ab came from the se-tenant pane of 15 in the £1 Stamps for Cooks Booklet (see No. UB2ab.); see also General Notes.

No. U16 also occurs with the phosphor omitted but since a single stamp would be indistinguishable from No. U14c it is only listed when in a complete se-tenant booklet pane (see No. UB4a.).

No. U16d and No. U16Ac came from the se-tenant pane No. UB2ad of which three examples of each are believed to exist.

See note after No. U15 describing the differences between 4d. stamps in the £1 Booklet (ZP1) and those in sheets and all other booklets.

UA Machin £.s.d. issues 5d.,

5d., Type U1 (1968–1970)

1968 (1 July). **5d.** Two 9·5 mm phosphor bands. PVA Gum.

U17 = SG 735		Mint	Used
5d.	(1) Royal blue (A) Head A	10	10
	(2) Deep blue (B) Head B	1.00	1.00
a.	Imperforate (pair)	£350	
ab.	Imperf. between stamp and top margin	£500	
b.	Uncoated paper ('70)**	40·00	
c.	Two bands and phosphor coating (Cyl. 15)	£350	
d.	Phosphor omitted. Shade (1)	6·00	
da.	Phosphor omitted. Shade (2)	6·00	
db.	Right-hand band omitted		
e.	Phosphor omitted on front but printed on the gummed side	£425	
f.	Error. One 9·5 mm phosphor band	60·00	
g.	Neck retouch (Cyls. 7, 10, 11, No dot, R. 18/1 and Cyl. 15 R. 19/1)	15·00	
h.	Scratch severing neck (Cyl. 13 No dot, R. 19/4)	25·00	
s.	Optd. "Specimen" (14 mm.)	60·00	

No. U17a comes from the original state of cylinder 15 which is identifiable by the screening dots in the gutters (see note after cylinder number list). This must not be confused with imperforate stamps from cylinder 10, a large quantity of which was stolen from the printers early in 1970.

** Uncoated paper. No. U17b comes from the £1 Stamps for Cooks Booklet (see Nos. UB2ab and UB20ab and b); see also General Notes.

No. U17c is thought to result from the issue, in error, of stamps on phosphor-coated paper, intended for experiments only. Examples were purchased from various sources in 1972.

No. U17e came from the *se-tenant* pane No. UB2ad of which three examples are believed to exist.

No. U17 from the £1 Stamps for Cooks Booklet (ZP1) and cylinders 7, 10 and 11 (no dot and dot panes) show slight differences compared with stamps from cylinder 1 (no dot and dot) and all other booklet panes. The "5D" is slightly thicker and is positioned fractionally lower than on stamps from cylinder 1 and all other booklet panes. See under Machin Heads in the General Notes.

No. U17 is known postmarked at Trafalgar Square (London) on 29 June and at Dorking and Guildford on 30 June 1968.

Tête-bêche Pairs. Examples of No. U17 in *tête-bêche* pairs were not issued.

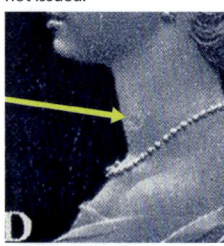

U17g

This variety is due to damage on the multipositive. Cyl. 1 is normal and the most marked retouch is on cyl. 11. Cyl. 15 was formed by moving up one row of the multipositive (which is 28 rows by 31 columns) and the variety occurs on R. 19/1. All on no dot panes.

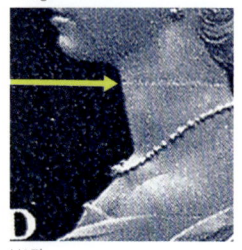

U17h

Cylinder Numbers (Blocks of Six)
Perforation Type A

Cylinder No.	No dot	Dot
1 (Shade 1) (Head A)	2·50	2·50
7 (Shade 2) (Head B)	15·00*	2·00
10 (Shade 2) (Head B)	15·00*	2·00
11 (Shade 2) (Head B)	20·00*	8·50
13 (Shade 2) (Head B)	£1200	£1200
15 (Shade 2) (Head B)	18·00	3·50
(15) Ph1	—	30·00

The phosphor cylinder number Ph1 is found on later printings of cyl. 15 dot, in the right margin.

Cylinder. 13 was produced from a different multipositive to cylinders 7, 10, 11 and 15 and thus does not display the retouch.

Cylinder. 15 dot has a smudge so that it looks like "151". Original printings of cylinder 15 (no dot and dot) had screening dots extending through the gutters of the stamps and into the margins of the sheet. Later the cylinder was cleaned and re-chromed.

Minor Constant Sheet Flaws

Cyl. 1	7/1	Coloured spot in band of diadem (Th. C5)
	7/5	Short white flaw in Queen's hair (Th. C4)
	12/2	White flaw in band of diadem (Th. B4)
Cyl. 1.	1/11	Pale patch in background below top bar of "5" (Th. G1)
	20/4	White spot in band of diadem (Th. C5)
Cyl. 7	18/2	Scratch on Queen's shoulder (Th. F4)
Cyl. 7.	1/10	White flaw on Queen's forehead (Th. C3)
	14/12	Small retouch on Queen's shoulder (Th. G4)
Cyl. 10	15/8	Coloured flaw below Queen's earring (Th. D4)
	18/2	Scratch on Queen's shoulder (Th. F4)
	20/5	Two diagonal scratches on Queen's neck (Th. E3–4, F4 and G4)
	20/6	Retouch on Queen's neck (Th. E4)
Cyl. 13	5/6	White flaw in Queen's hair (Th. C3)
	12/4	White ring flaw on Queen's forehead (Th. C2)
	13/3	Flaw on Queen's shoulder (Th. G3)
	14/5	Necklace flaw (Th. E4)
	18/2	Coloured flaw on Queen's neck (Th. F5)
Cyl. 15	16/8	Coloured flaw below Queen's earring (Th. D4)
	19/2	Scratch on Queen's shoulder (Th. F4)
Cyl. 15.	1/10	Scratch on Queen's nose (Th. C2)

Coil Leaders

Printed in continuous reels from double-pane cylinders S1, S3 or S4 (vertical) or single-pane S2 (sideways). Head B

Code No.	Number in roll	Face value		
AF	480	£10	Sideways delivery	85·00
AE	960	£20	Vertical delivery	£100

Sheet Markings

Guide holes: In double "SON" box (or "SO" box cyl. 10) opposite rows 14/15, at left (no dot) or right (dot). In addition a single traffic light type box appears above and below the eighth vertical row in the no dot pane only. (These would only be used in conjunction with perforation Type F(L)*).

Others: As given in General Notes.

6d., Machin £.s.d. issues **UA**

6d., Type U1 (1968)

1968 *(5 February).* **6d.** Two 9·5 mm phosphor bands. PVA Gum

		Mint	Used
U18 = SG 736			
6d.	(1) Bright reddish purple (shades) (A) Head A	10	10
	(2) Bright magenta	9·00	9·00
	(3) Claret	1·25	1·25
	(1) Bright reddish purple (B) Head B (coils)	15·00	10·00
	(3) Claret	80·00	35·00
a.	Phosphor omitted. Shade (1) Head A	35·00	
ab.	Phosphor omitted. Shade (3) Head A	45·00	
b.	Hair flaws (Cyl. 2 No dot, R. 18/1)	15·00	
c.	Background retouch (Cyl. 2 Dot, R. 11/1)	15·00	
d.	Diadem flaw (Cyl. 3 No dot, R. 2/3)	15·00	
e.	Two spots in front of neck (Vert. coil, Roll 12)((1) Head B)	20·00	
f.	Retouch above "6 D" (Vert. coil) ((1) Head B)	20·00	

U18b Two coloured lines crossing base of diadem, one extending in curves through the hair

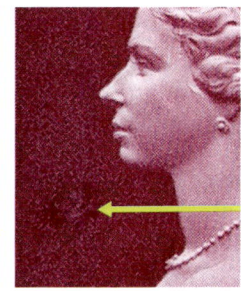

U18c Large circular retouch above value

U18d Coloured flaw in band of diadem

U18e Two spots in front of neck

U18f

Cylinder Numbers (Blocks of Six)
Perforation Type A

(a) Shade (1) Bright reddish purple

Cylinder No.	No dot	Dot
2	18·00*	5·50
3	3·50	3·50
4	£150	£150
5	4·00	4·00
(5) Ph1	—	£150

(b) Shade (2) Bright magenta

3	70·00	70·00

(c) Shade (3) Claret

5	10·00	10·00

The phosphor cylinder number Ph1 is found on later printings of cyl. 5 dot, in the right margin.

Minor Constant Sheet Flaws

Cyl. 2.	2/4	White flaw in band of diadem (Th. B4)
	4/4	Coloured line in band of diadem (Th. B3–4)
	4/11	Small retouch on Queen's collar (Th. G4)
	10/11	Vertical flaws in Queen's hair and in band of diadem (Th. B–C4)
Cyl. 3	13/5	Two small white flaws on Queen's neck above necklace (Th. F3)
	19/9	Small coloured dot in band of diadem (Th. B3)
Cyl. 3.	5/3	Line of white dashes on Queen's collar (Th. G3–4)
	11/5	Small retouch on Queen's collar (Th. G4)
Cyl. 4	11/10	Small background retouch left of Queen's forehead (Th. B2)
Cyl. 5	18/1	White tail below D

Coil Leaders
Vertical delivery printed in continuous reels from single-pane cylinder Q2. Head B

Code No.	Number in roll	Face value	
J (Shade 1)	480	£12	£250
(Shade 3)			£400

Sheet Markings
Guide holes: In double "SON" box opposite rows 14/15, at left (no dot) or right (dot). In addition a single traffic light type box appears above and below the eighth vertical row in the no dot pane only (These would only be used in conjunction with perforation Type F(L)*.)

Others: As given in General Notes

UA Machin £.s.d. issues 7d., 8d., 9d.

7d. Type U2 (1968)

1968 *(1 July).* **7d.** Two 9·5 mm phosphor bands. PVA Gum. Head B

U19 = SG 737	Mint	Used
7d. Bright emerald	25	25
a. Phosphor omitted	£100	

No. U19 is known postmarked at Dorking and at Guildford on 30 June 1968.

Cylinder Numbers (Blocks of Six)
Perforation Type A

Cylinder No.	No dot	Dot
3	4·50	4·50
4	15·00	12·00
(4) Ph1	—	55·00

The phosphor cylinder number Ph1 is found on all sheets from cyl. 4 dot, in the right margin.

Minor Constant Sheet Flaws

Cyl. 3	8/6	Flaw in background by Queen's collar (Th. F5)
	12/6	Dark flaw on jewel in band of diadem (Th. C5)

Sheet Markings
Guide holes: in single hand engraved box opposite rows 14/15, at left (no dot) or right (dot).
Marginal arrows: "W" shaped, hand engraved at top, bottom and sides on cyl. 3, photo-etched on cyl. 4
Others: As given in General Notes

Imprimaturs from the NPM or BPMA

No. U19 imperforate	£900
No. U19 cylinder 3 (no dot) block of six	£6250

8d. Bright vermilion, Type U2 (1968)

1968 *(1 July).* **8d.** Two 9·5 mm phosphor bands. PVA gum. Head A

U20 = SG 738	Mint	Used
8d. Bright vermilion	10	15
a. Phosphor omitted	£450	

No. U20 is known postmarked at Dorking and at Guildford on 30 June 1968.

Cylinder Numbers (Blocks of Six)
Perforation Type A

Cylinder No.	No dot	Dot
2	2·50	2·50

Sheet Markings
Guide holes: In double "SON" box opposite rows 14/15, at left (no dot) or right (dot). In addition a single traffic light type box appears above and below the eighth vertical row in the no dot pane only. (These would only be used in conjunction with perforation Type F(L)*.)
Others: As given in General Notes

Imprimaturs from the NPM or BPMA

No. U20 imperforate	£900
No. U20 cylinder 2 (no dot) block of six	£6250

8d. Light turquoise-blue, Type U2 (1969)

1969 *(6 January).* **8d.** Colour changed. Two 9·5 mm phosphor bands. PVA Gum. Head B

U21 = SG 739	Mint	Used
8d. Light turquoise-blue	25	25
a. Phosphor omitted	80·00	
b. Left band omitted		
c. Missing pearls (Cyl. 3 No dot, R. 19/2)	15·00	

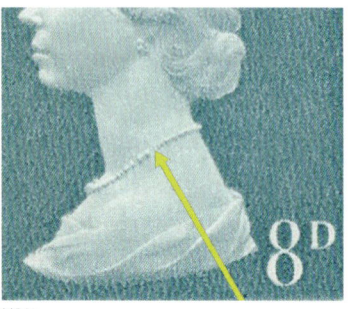

U21c

Cylinder Numbers (Blocks of Six)
Perforation Type A

Cylinder No.	No dot	Dot
3	20·00*	7·00

Minor Constant Sheet Flaw

Cyl. 3.	19/2	White flaw by Queen's mouth (Th. D2)

Sheet Markings
Guide holes: In single "SN" box opposite rows 14/15, at left (no dot) or right (dot). In addition a single traffic light type box appears above and below the eighth vertical row in the no dot pane only. (These would only be used in conjunction with perforation Type F(L)*.)
Others: As given in General Notes.

Colour trials
On coated paper with PVA gum. Perf 15×14 in blue, greenish blue, dull greenish blue, ultramarine, deep bright magenta, deep bright mauve, plum, purple, deep bluish violet, bright emerald or deep green.   *From* £1800 *(each)*

Imprimaturs from the NPM or BPMA

No. U21 imperforate	£900
No. U21 cylinder 3 (dot) block of six	£6250

9d. Type U2 (1967–1968)

1967 *(8 August).* **9d.** Two 9·5 mm phosphor bands. Head A

A. Gum Arabic

U22 = SG 740	Mint	Used
9d. Myrtle-green	25	25
a. Phosphor omitted	60·00	
b. Dots below necklace (Cyl. 2 Dot, R. 9/6)	20·00	

B. PVA Gum (29 November 1968)

U23 = SG 740Ev		
9d. Myrtle-green	1·00	
a. Phosphor omitted	85·00	

No. U22 is known pre-released on 7 August at Bournemouth and Torquay.

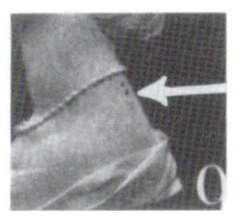

9d., 10d., 1s.   **Machin £.s.d. issues**   **UA**

U22b

Cylinder Numbers (Blocks of Six)
Gum Arabic

Perforation Type F(L)*

Cylinder No.	No dot	Dot
2	6·00	6·00

Perforation Type A

2	70·00	70·00

PVA Gum
Perforation Type A

2	5·50	5·50
(2) Ph1	—	£850

Cylinder 2 has the number close to the stamp resulting in the dot often being removed by the perforations. The no dot cylinder can be distinguished by a horizontal line below R. 20/2, although this may be trimmed off if the margin is narrow.

The phosphor cylinder number Ph1 is found on a later printing from cyl. 2 dot, in the right margin.

Minor Constant Sheet Flaws

Cyl. 2	2/7	Coloured line in gutter above stamp (Th. above A4–6)
	3/12	Retouch on Queen's shoulder (Th. F4)
	6/2	Pale area on Queen's shoulder (Th. F4). Retouched on PVA
	6/7	Dark patches on Queen's neck (Th. E–F3). Less noticeable on PVA
	7/3	Dark spot over "D" of value (Th. F6)
Cyl. 2.	6/10	Coloured line across Queen's shoulder and dress (Th. F–G4)
	8/11	Retouch on Queen's forehead (Th. B–C2)
	10/4	Coloured spot at rear of diadem (Th. C5)
	14/8	Two white flaws on Queen's neck by hair (Th. D–E4). Retouched on PVA
	14/11	Retouch on Queen's neck by necklace (Th. E4)
	15/11	Retouch on Queen's dress at front (Th. G3)
	19/10	Retouch on Queen's shoulder (Th. F4)

Sheet Markings
Guide holes: Perforation Type A, in double "SON" box opposite rows 14/15, at left (no dot) or right (dot). In addition a single traffic light type box appears above and below the eighth vertical row in the no dot pane only (latter only used in conjunction with perforation Type F(L)*).
Perforation Type F(L)*, boxed above and below the eighth vertical row in the no dot pane only. The usual "SON" boxes opposite rows 14/15 remain.
Others: As given in General Notes

Imprimaturs from the NPM or BPMA

No. U22 imperforate	£900
No. U22 imperforate with "dots below necklace" R.9/6	£1250
No. U22 cylinder 2 (dot) block of six	£6250

10d. Type U1 (1968)

1968 (1 July). **10d.** Two 9·5 mm phosphor bands. PVA gum. Head C

U24 = SG 741	Mint	Used
10d. Drab	25	25
a. Uncoated paper ('69)*	85·00	
b. Phosphor omitted	85·00	
c. Neck flaw (Cyl 1, R. 2/12)	20·00	

* Uncoated paper-see General Notes.
No. U24 is known postmarked at Dorking and at Guildford on 30 June 1968.

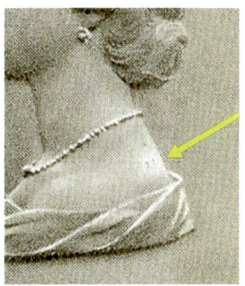

U24c Flaw comprises dark spots surrounded by white "halo" caused by lack of screening dots

Cylinder Number (Block of Six)
Single-pane cylinder
Perforation Type F(L)

Cylinder No.	No dot
1	6·00

Minor Constant Sheet Flaw

Cyl. 1	20/5	Coloured flaw in Queen's hair (Th. B3)

Sheet Markings
Guide holes: Through marginal arrow above vertical rows 6/7 and below vertical row 10
Others: As given in General Notes

Imprimaturs from the NPM or BPMA

No. U24 imperforate	£900
No. U24 cylinder 1 (no dot) block of six	£6250

1s. Type U1 (1967–1968)

1967 (5 June). **1s.** Two 9·5 mm phosphor bands. Head C

A. Gum Arabic

U25 = SG 742/Ea	Mint	Used
1s. (1) Light bluish violet	20	20
(2) Pale bluish violet	1·00	1·00
a. Phosphor omitted	£120	
b. Background retouches (Cyl. 3 No dot, R. 20/5)	20·00	

B. PVA Gum (26 April 1968)

U26 = SG 742v		
1s. Pale bluish violet	1·00	
a. Phosphor omitted	12·00	

No. U25(1) is known pre-released on 25 May at Gravesend.

127

UA   Machin £.s.d. issues   1s., 1s.6d.

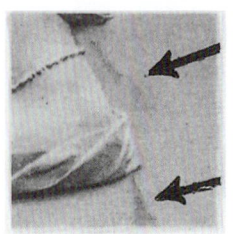

U25b Retouching extends from behind the Queen's neck to the base of the design where it is most noticeable. There are also minor retouches on the Queen's shoulder and on her dress.

Cylinder Numbers (Blocks of Six)

Gum Arabic
Double-pane cylinder
Perforation Type F(L)
Shade (1) Light bluish violet

Cylinder No.	No dot	Dot
3	5·50	5·50

Single-pane cylinder
Perforation Type F(L)
Shade (2) Pale bluish violet

11	11·00	—

PVA Gum
Single-pane cylinder
Perforation Type F(L)
Shade (2) Pale bluish violet

11	5·50	—

Minor Constant Sheet Flaws

Cyl. 3	1/10	Retouch in background above diadem (Th. A5)
	2/2	Light diagonal line extending from lowest point of Queen's hair to bottom right-hand corner (E5 through to G6)
	2/3	White spot in background left of Queen's shoulder (Th. G2)
	9/12	White spot in background to right of Queen's necklace (Th. E5)
	11/11	Coloured spot in band of diadem (Th. B4)
	17/2	As 11/11 but Th. B3
	18/12	Coloured spot in hyphen of value
	19/10	Coloured scratch through Queen's neck and background below portrait
	20/4	Horizontal scratch through Queen's neck and into background at right
Cyl. 3.	1/8	White spot in background at top of stamp (Th. A4)
	7/8	Coloured flaw in Queen's hair to right of earring (Th. D4)
	8/4	Coloured flaw in Queen's hair (Th. B3)
	9/7	Retouch to background to right of Queen's ear (Th. D5)
	19/8	Coloured spot in background above diadem emblems (Th. B5)
Cyl. 11	7/8	Coloured spot by band of diadem, also small spot in background at rear of diadem (Th. B4 and C5)
	7/9	Diagonal coloured line in background behind Queen's neck (Th. F5)
	15/4	Disturbed area in background at rear of diadem (Th. C–D5)
	16/9	Diagonal coloured scratches extending the depth of the stamp behind the Queen's portrait
	18/7	Diagonal coloured scratch about 10 mm long at left of Queen's portrait
	19/2	White flaw in Queen's hair to right of ear (Th. D4)

Sheet Markings

Guide holes: Perforation Type F(L)*, boxed above and below the eighth vertical row in the no dot pane only. In addition double "S O N" box appears opposite rows 14/15, at left (no dot) or right (dot). (These would only be used in conjunction with perforation Type A.)
    Perforation Type F(L), through marginal arrow above vertical rows 6/7 and below vertical row 10

Others: As given in General Notes

Colour trials. On coated paper with PVA gum. Perf 15×14. In olive-grey, light emerald, light violet-blue, pale magenta, mauve, pale chestnut, pale olive-green, turquoise-blue or slate-blue.   *From £1800 (each)*

Imprimaturs from the NPM or BPMA

No. U25 imperforate	£900
No. U25 cylinder 3 (no dot) block of six	£6250

●━━━

1s.6d.   Type U1 (1967–1969)

1967 *(8 August).* **1s.6d.** Two 9·5 mm phosphor bands. Head A

A. Gum Arabic

U27 = SG 743

1s.6d.		Mint	Used
(1)	Greenish blue and deep blue	25	25
(2)	Prussian blue and indigo (phosphor omitted)	15·00	
a.	Greenish blue omitted	£160	
b.	Phosphor omitted. Shade (1)	15·00	
c.	Retouch on dress (Cyl. 2A, R. 7/12)	20·00	
d.	Neck retouch (Cyl. 2A, R. 19/4)	20·00	
e.	Neck retouch (Cyl. 2A, R. 20/3)	20·00	

B. PVA Gum *(28 August 1968)*
U28 = SG 743Ev

1s.6d.			
(1)	Greenish blue and deep blue	1·00	
(2)	Prussian blue and indigo	7·00	7·00
a.	Greenish blue omitted	£100	
b.	Imperf. top margin. Shade (2)	£100	
c.	Phosphor omitted. Shade (1)	22·00	
ca.	Phosphor omitted. Shade (2)	18.00	
d.	Error. One 9·5 mm phosphor band	25·00	
e.	Greenish blue omitted and one 9·5 mm phosphor band	£225	

No. U27 is known pre-released on 7 August at Bournemouth and Torquay.

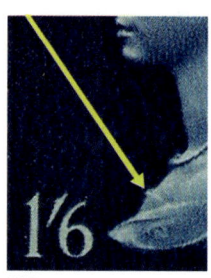

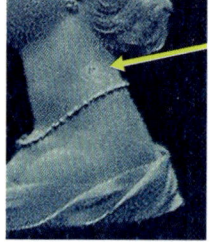

U27c   U27d

128

1s.6d., 1s.9d.   **Machin £.s.d. issues**   **UA**

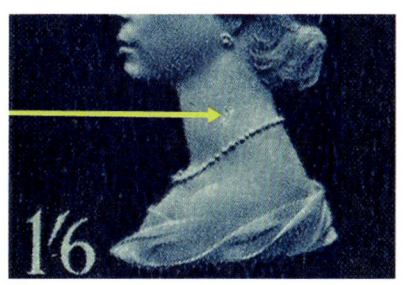

U27e

Cylinder Numbers (Blocks of Four)

Gum Arabic
Single-pane cylinders.
Perforation Type A

Cylinder No.	No dot
2A (deep blue) – 2B (greenish blue)	7·50
3A (deep blue) – 2B (greenish blue)	15·00
5A (indigo) – 2B (Prussian blue) (phosphor omitted)	£180
PVA Gum	
3A (deep blue) – 2B (greenish blue)	7·50
3A (indigo) – 1B (Prussian blue)	20·00
5A (indigo) – 2B (Prussian blue)	18·00

Minor Constant Sheet Flaws

Cyls. 2A–2B	3/12	Coloured spot in band of diadem (Th. B4)
	7/8	Coloured spots on Queen's collar (Th. G3)
	14/1	Coloured spot on Queen's shoulder (Th. F4–5)
	17/3	Coloured spot on Queen's temple (Th. C3)
	18/4	Coloured spot on Queen's shoulder (Th. F5)
	20/2	Pale patch on Queen's neck (Th. E3–4)
	20/7	Retouch on Queen's neck (Th. E4)
Cyls. 3A–2B	3/12	As for cyls. 2A–2B
Cyls. 5A–2B	19/1	Retouch on Queen's shoulder (Th. F5)

Sheet Markings

Cylinder numbers: Boxed, opposite R. 19/1

Guide holes: In single traffic light type box opposite rows 14/15, at both sides

Colour register marks: Opposite rows 3/4 and 17/18, at both sides

Autotron marks (solid): Deep blue and greenish blue opposite rows 7/8, left margin

Colour designations: G1 (greenish blue) opposite rows 7/8 and G2 (deep blue) opposite rows 5/6 both reading up in right margin

Traffic lights (boxed): Deep blue and greenish blue opposite row 19, right margin

Others: As given in General Notes

Colour trials
On coated paper with PVA gum. Perf 15×14 in rose-pink and deep blue-green, lilac and deep bright blue, pale bright blue and deep ultramarine, bright mauve and bright ultramarine, light violet and bluish violet, olive-yellow and brown-olive, pale magenta and deep carmine and pale dull green and deep bright purple. *From* £1800 (*each*)

Imprimaturs from the NPM or BPMA

No. U27 imperforate	£900
No. U27 imperforate with "retouch on dress" R. 7/12	£1250
No. U27 imperforate with "neck retouch" R. 20/3	£1250
No. U27 cylinder 2A, 2B block of six	£5000

1969 (10 December). **1s.6d**. Change to Phosphorised paper. PVA Gum. Head A

U29 = SG 743c	Mint	Used
1s.6d. Prussian blue and indigo	30	35
a. Prussian blue omitted	£450	

No. U29 was an experimental issue and the small printing represented approximately three months normal issue. After the supply was exhausted No. U28 again became the normal issue.

Cylinder Numbers (Block of Four)
Single-pane cylinders.
Perforation Type A

Cylinder No.	No dot
5A (indigo) – 2B (Prussian blue)	12·00

Minor Constant Sheet Flaws

Cyls. 5A–2B	12/5	Two white spots on Queen's dress (Th. G3)
	19/1	Retouch on Queen's shoulder (Th. F5)

Sheet Markings
All the same as for Nos. U27/8

Imprimaturs from the NPM or BPMA

No. U29 imperforate	£900
No. U29 cylinder 5A, 2B block of six	£6250

1s.9d. Type U1 (1967–1970)

1967 (5 June). **1s.**9d. Two 9·5 mm phosphor bands. Head A

A. Gum Arabic

U30 = SG 744	Mint	Used
1s.9d. (1) Dull orange and black	25	25
(2) Bright orange and black	1·00	1·00
a. Phosphor omitted	65·00	

B. PVA Gum (16 November 1970)
U31 = SG 744Ev

1s.9d. Bright orange and black	2·50

No. U30 is known pre-released on 25 May at Gravesend. The bright orange shade occurs on whiter paper and may be due to this.

Cylinder Numbers (Blocks of Four)

Gum Arabic
Single-pane cylinders
Perforation Type A

Cylinder No.	No dot
1A (black) – 1B (dull orange)	14·00
1A (black) – 1B (bright orange)	20·00
PVA Gum	
1A (black) – 1B (dull orange)	†
1A (black) – 1B (bright orange)	20·00

Minor Constant Sheet Flaws

Cyls. 1A–1B	4/6	White spot in Queen's ear (Th. D4)
	5/7	Coloured spots on Queen's upper lip (Th. D2)
	5/10	White patch in Queen's hair (Th. B4)
	8/1	Coloured flaw on Queen's neck (Th. E4)
	13/1	Retouch on Queen's shoulder (Th. F3–4)
	20/1	Pale patch in Queen's hair (Th. C4)

Sheet Markings

Cylinder numbers: Boxed, opposite R. 19/1

Guide holes: In single traffic light type box opposite rows 14/15, at both sides

129

UA Machin £.s.d. issues 1s.9d. Multi-value coil

Colour register marks: Opposite rows 3/4 and 17/18, at both sides
Autotron marks (solid): Black and orange opposite rows 7/8, left margin
Colour designations: G1 (orange) opposite rows 7/8 and G2 (black) opposite rows 5/6 both reading up in right margin
Traffic lights (boxed): Black and orange opposite row 19, right margin
Others: As given in General Notes

Imprimaturs from the NPM or BPMA

No. U30 imperforate	£900
No. U30 cylinder 1A, 1B block of six	£6250

Multi-value coil strip (1969)

1969 (27 August). **Strip of five (2d. + 2d. + 3d. + 1d. + 4d. *Se-tenant*)** each with one 4 mm Centre phosphor band. Gum Arabic. Head B

U32 = SG 725m	Mint	Used
1d. Light olive (No. U4), 2d. lake-brown (No. U7×2), 3d. violet (No. U8) and 4d. bright vermilion (No. U15)	2·50	

No. U32 was issued in strips from stamp vending machines taking a shilling or a decimal five pence piece. Complete coils only were available from the Philatelic Bureau in Edinburgh.
For listed varieties, see Nos. U4a, U8d and U15b.

A new type of perforation was adopted for these coils. The paper was drawn, gum upwards, over a cylinder containing short points pushing up pimples from the undersurface which were then shaved off.

It is understood that gum arabic was used for these coils, as also for the next decimal multi-value coil, because it is more brittle than PVA and facilitates the clean removal of the perforations.

First Day Covers

On official covers prepared and issued by the Post Office and stamps franked with circular "FIRST DAY OF ISSUE" postmarks.

UFC1	(5.6.67)	4d., 1s, 1s. 9d.	2·00
UFC2	(8.8.67)	3d., 9d., 1s. 6d.	2·00
UFC3	(5.2.68)	½d., 1d., 2d., 6d.	2·25
UFC4	(1.7.68)	5d., 7d., 8d., 10d.	3·00
UFC5	(1.12.69)	"Stamps for Cooks" pane stamps, four covers	20·00*

There was no First day cover service for the 4d. red and 8d. turquoise-blue values.

* The price is for covers with complete panes with recipe attached. The Milk Marketing Board issued a special handstamp cancellation reading "Visit the Stamps for Cooks Exhibition, Milk Marketing Board, Thames Ditton, Surrey".

Multi-value Coil Strip (1969)

Coil Leaders

Sideways delivery printed in continuous reels from cylinders B3-D3-M3-P6 (1d., 2d., 3d., 4d.), B4-D3-M3-P6 or B5-D3-M3-P6

Code No.	Number in roll	Face value	
GS	1500 (300 strips)	£15	18·00
GL	3000 (600 strips)	£30	20·00

Presentation Pack

UPP1	(Issued 5 March 1969) 14 values	7·00
	a. With German text	90·00

The issued Pack contained one each of the low value definitive stamps (½d. to 1s.9d.). The 4d. and 8d. were in the changed colours (Nos. U14 and U21 respectively).
UPP1 also exists with a Japanese insert card.

Section UB

Machin £.s.d. Issues
1967–1970. Booklet Panes in Photogravure

General Notes

Introduction. All panes were printed in photogravure by Harrison & Sons. See the detailed notes under Section U for information on printing, paper and gum. Reference to the note, "Booklet Cylinder Flaws", at the beginning of Section SB describes the panes which were printed from 21-row cylinders. These panes are found with varieties and the cylinder number in either the top or bottom row of the pane. In this Section the Panes of Six of the 1d., 3d., 4d. (both colours) and 5d. were printed from 21-row cylinders.

Booklet errors. Those listed as "Part perf. pane" have one row of three stamps imperforate on three sides.

Booklet Cylinder Number

Booklet cylinder numbers. These are listed for the panes of six only and the other panes had cylinder numbers engraved so that they did not occur in the finished booklet. The cylinders employed are recorded for reference. The cylinder numbers being hand-engraved varied as to their position in relation to the stamp so that some were invariably trimmed. A pane which shows a complete cylinder number placed away from the stamp will only exist with badly trimmed perforations on the opposite side.

Booklet cylinder flaws. Cylinder flaws on booklet stamps are listed under the panes in which they occur as in Section SB. The flaws are priced in panes since this is the preferred method of collecting wherever possible. In consequence when checking varieties on single stamps it will be necessary to look at the lists of the sheet and coil stamps as well as the booklet panes.

When quoting the position on booklet panes no attention is paid to the labels. Therefore a flaw on the first stamp in the pane No. UB13 (4d. (2) and pair of labels) will be described as being on "R. 1/1". Since this Catalogue is primarily concerned with stamps we do not list flaws which sometimes occur in the wording of the labels from booklet panes.

Booklet pane prices. The prices quoted are for panes in mint condition, good perforations all round and complete with binding margin. Prices for complete booklets in Appendix HA are for booklets with average perforations.

UB Machin £.s.d. Issues   Booklet Panes Checklist

CHECKLIST OF MACHIN £.s.d. BOOKLET PANES

UB No.	Face Value	Phos. Bands	Gum	Head	Size of Pane	Further description	Page
1	1d.	2	PVA	B	6	Yellowish olive	133
2	6×1d.	2	PVA	B	15	"Baked Stuffed Haddock" recipe	133
	3×4d.	1L					
	3×4d.	1R					
	3×5d.	2					
3	4×1d.	1C	PVA	B	6	4d. in sepia	134
	2×4d.	1C					
4	4×1d.	2	PVA	B	6	4d. in bright vermilion	134
	2×4d.	1L					
5	2×1d.	2	PVA	B	4	1d. at left	135
	2×3d.	2					
5a	2×1d.	2	PVA	B	4	1d. at right	135
	2×3d.	2					
6	3d.	1C	PVA	B	6	Violet	135
7	4d.	2	GA	A	6	Deep sepia	135
8	4d.	2	GA	A	6	Deep olive-brown	135
9	4d.	2	PVA	A	6	Deep olive-brown	135
10	4d.	2	PVA	B	4	Deep olive-brown	136
11	4d.	1C	PVA	A	6	Deep olive-brown	136
12	4d.	1C	PVA	B	4	Deep olive-sepia	136
13	4d.	1C	PVA	B	4	Deep olive-sepia, including 2 labels	137
14 (A)	4d.	1C	PVA	A	6	Bright vermilion	137
14 (B)	4d.	1C	PVA	B	6	Bright vermilion	137
14 (A)b	4d.	1C	GA	A	6	Bright vermilion	137
15	4d.	1C	PVA	B	4	Bright vermilion	137
16	4d.	1C	PVA	B	15	"Stuffed Cucumber" and "Method" recipe	138
17	4d.	1C	PVA	B	15	"Method" for Braised Shoulder of Lamb recipe	138
18	4d.	1C	PVA	B	4	Bright vermilion, including 2 labels	139
19	5d.	2	PVA	B	6	Deep Blue	139
20	5d.	2	PVA	B	15	"Method" for Cream of Potato Soup recipe	140

1d. Machin £.s.d. issues Booklet Panes — UB

1d. Panes of six 6×1d. (two bands). Head B. Shade (2)
Yellowish olive
From 4s.6d. Booklets LP45/LP59 and 10s. Booklets XP4/XP5

		Perf. Type I	Ie
UB1	Pane of 6×1d. (containing No. U2×6) (25.3.68)	2·00	2·50
a.	Part perf. pane*		
b.	Imperf. pane*	£5750	
c.	Phosphor omitted	35·00	

* Booklet error see General Notes.

Booklet Cylinder Numbers
Panes of Six (21-row cylinders)

Cylinder No.	Perforation Type I No Dot	Dot
F1	£175	£175
F1T	£175	£175
F3	10·00	10·00
F3T	10·00	10·00

In the above and all other 21-row cylinders, which are printed continuously on the web, the perforated web is cut at every 20th row to make sheets of 480. Consequently on successive sheets the cylinder number appears one row lower and thus a pane can have it adjoining the top or bottom row. Where the cylinder number adjoins the top row of the pane it is designated by the letter "T".
Examples of Cyl. No. pane F1 (lower position) are known with forged cylinder number.

"Stamps for Cooks" se-tenant pane of 15 with recipe label
Pane of 15 comprising 6×1d. (two bands) with 3×4d. (one side band at left), 3×4d. (one side band at right), 3×5d. and se-tenant recipe label. Head B. "Baked Stuffed Haddock" recipe from £1 "Stamps for Cooks" Booklet ZP1/ZP1a

A. Stapled

UB2	Pane of 3×4d./1d./5d./1d./4d. (containing Nos. U2×6, U16×3, U16A×3, U17×3) (1.12.69)	35·00
b.	Phosphor omitted	£500
c.	One 9·5 mm. phosphor band on each stamp, except first vertical row which has phosphor omitted	£750
d.	Mole on cheek (R. 1/2)	55·00
e.	White spot in necklace	55·00
s.	Optd. "Specimen" (14 mm)	£3500

B. Stitched

UB2a	Pane of 3×4d./1d./5d./1d./4d. (containing Nos. U2×6, U16×3, U16A×3, U17×3)	8·50
ab.	Uncoated paper*	£3000
ac.	Phosphor omitted	£225
ad.	Phosphor omitted from front, but shown on gummed side	—
ae.	Mole on cheek (R. 1/2)	15·00
af.	White spot in necklace	15·00
ag.	One 9·5 mm. phosphor band on each stamp except for first vertical row which has phosphor omitted	£750
ah.	As ag but phosphor omitted from first two vertical rows and one 9·5 mm. band at left on rows containing 5d., 1d., 4d.	£2250
aj.	One 9·5 mm. band at right on first row at left and phosphor omitted from vertical rows 1d., 5d., 1d., 4d.	

* Uncoated paper. See General Notes for Section U.

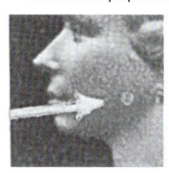

UB2d, UB2ae (1d.)

Nos. UB2e and UB2af are repairs of the multipositive 'Broken necklace' variety (UB16b, etc).

Booklet Cylinder Numbers
In the £1 Booklet (ZP1) the cylinder numbers were always trimmed off, however, the cylinders known to have been used were F7 (1d.), N8 (4d.) and R5 (5d.).

Imprimatur from the NPM or BPMA

No. UB2 imperforate, cyl. F7, N8, R5, se-tenant pane of 15	£15000

UB2

UB Machin £.s.d. issues Booklet Panes *1d.*

UB3

UB4

1d. and 4d. Sepia *se-tenant* booklet panes of six
  4×1d. (centre band) with vertical pair 4d. sepia (centre band). Head B

From 10s. Booklet XP6

	Perf. Type		
	I	I(½v)	P
UB3 Pane of 2×1d./1d./4d. (containing Nos. U3×4, U12×2) (16.9.68)	4·00	14·00	5·00
a. Phosphor omitted	35·00	65·00	45·00
b. Phosphor omitted on first column (2×1d.)			
c. Phosphor omitted on third column (2×4d.)			
d. Phosphor omitted on first column (2×1d.) and third column (2×4d.)			

Booklet Cylinder Numbers
Se-tenant pane of six (20-row cylinder)
One centre band

	Perforation Type I	
	I	P
Cylinder No.	No Dot	Dot
F4 (1d.), N5 (4d.) sepia	45·00	50·00

The phosphor cylinder appears to have suffered considerable damage during printing and other variants of misaligned and incomplete phosphor bands exist. In some cases a damaged band was replaced with a thinner 2·5mm band.

1d. and 4d. Bright vermilion *se-tenant* pane of six.
  4×1d. (two bands) with vertical pair 4d. bright vermilion (one left side band). Head B

From 10s. Booklets XP7/XP12

	Perforation Type P
UB4 Pane of 2×1d./1d./4d. (containing Nos. U2×4, U16×2) (6.1.69)	3·50
a. Phosphor omitted	£225

Booklet Cylinder Numbers
Se-tenant pane of six (20-row cylinder)
Two bands

	Perforation Type P
Cylinder No.	No Dot
F4 (1d.), N5 (4d. vermilion)	25·00

Imprimaturs from the NPM or BPMA
Booklet panes of six, imperforate.

Two panes as No. UB3 arranged *tête-bêche* with cylinder F4, N5	£10500
Two panes as No. UB4 arranged *tête-bêche* with cylinder F4, N5	£10500

1d., 3d., 4d.   Machin £.s.d. issues Booklet Panes   **UB**

3d. panes of six 6×3d. (centre band). PVA gum. Head B
From 10s. Booklets XP4/XP5

	Perf. Type	
	I	Ie
UB6 Pane of 6×3d.(containing No. U9×6) (25.3.68)	25·00	30·00
a. Phosphor omitted		

Booklet Cylinder Numbers
Panes of Six (21-row cylinder)

	Perforation Type I	
Cylinder No.	No Dot	Dot
K2	£325	£325
K2 T	£325	£325

4d. Deep olive-brown panes of six 6×4d. (two bands). Gum Arabic. Head A

(a) Shade (1) Deep sepia
From 6s. Booklets QP28/QP32

	Perf. Type	
	I	Ie
UB7 Pane of 6×4d. (containing No. U11×6) (21.9.67)	10·00	12·00
a. Phosphor omitted	28·00	

(b) Shade (2) Deep olive-brown
From 6s. Booklets QP33/QP36

UB8 Pane of 6×4d. (containing No. U11×6) (1.68)	12·00	14·00
a. Part perf. pane*	£4000	
b. Phosphor omitted	40·00	

* Booklet error–see General Notes.

6×4d. (two bands). PVA gum. Head A
From 4s.6d. Booklets LP45/LP46, 6s. Booklets QP37/QP40 and 10s. Booklets XP4/XP5

UB9 Pane of 6×4d. (containing No. U12×6) (25.3.68)	6·50	7·00
a. One 9·5 mm. phosphor band on each stamp	£190	
b. Phosphor omitted	28·00	
c. Patch on cheek (R. 1/2 or 2/2)	25·00	

UB9c, UB11b From 10s. Booklet

Booklet Cylinder Numbers
Panes of Six (21-row cylinders)

Gum Arabic
(a) Shade (1) Deep sepia

Cylinder No.	No Dot	Dot
N1	30·00	30·00
N1 T	30·00	30·00

(b) Shade (2) Deep olive-brown

Cylinder No.	No Dot	Dot
N1	30·00	30·00
N1 T	30·00	30·00

UB5

UB5a

1d. and 3d. *se-tenant* **pane of four** Pair 1d. (two bands) with pair 3d. (two bands). Head B
From 2s. Booklets NP27/NP29

Pane UB5 Pane of four with 1d. at left
Pane UB5a Pane of four with 1d. at right

	Perf. Type		
	I	I(½v)	AP
UB5 Pane of 2×1d./3d. (containing Nos. U2×2, U10×2) (6.4.68)	7·00	†	3·00
b. One 9·5 mm. phosphor band on each stamp	22·00	†	15·00
c. Phosphor omitted	£100	†	90·00
UB5a Pane of 2×3d./1d. (containing Nos. U2×2, U10×2) (6.4.68)	7·00	18·00	3·00
ab. One 9·5 mm. phosphor band on each stamp	22·00	50·00	15·00
ac. Phosphor omitted	£100	£150	90·00

Booklet Cylinder Numbers
Se-tenant panes of four
In the 2s. Booklets (NP27/NP29) the cylinder numbers were always trimmed off, but cylinders F2 and K1 were used.

135

UB Machin £.s.d. issues Booklet Panes 4d.

PVA Gum

Cylinder No.	No Dot	Dot
N1	10·00	10·00
N1 T	10·00	10·00
N2	10·00	10·00
N2 T	10·00	10·00

●────

4d. Deep olive-brown panes of four 4×4d. (two bands). PVA gum. Head B

From 2s. Booklets NP27/NP31

		Perf. Type	
	I	I(½v)	AP
UB10 Pane of 4×4d. (containing No. U12×4) (6.4.68)	4·50	15·00	4·50
a. One 9·5 mm. phosphor band on each stamp	25·00	38·00	22·00
b. Phosphor omitted	25·00	70·00	20·00
c. Dot on "D" (R. 1/2)	30·00	†	†
ca. Retouched state	25·00	†	†

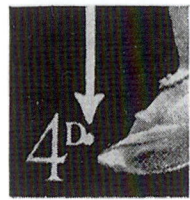

UB10c

Booklet Cylinder Numbers

In the 2s. Booklets (NP27/NP31) the cylinder numbers were always trimmed off, however, the cylinder known to have been used was N3.

●────

4d. Deep olive-brown pane of six 6×4d. (centre band). PVA gum. Head A

From 4s.6d. Booklets LP47/LP48, 6s. Booklets QP41/QP45 and 10s. Booklet XP6

		Perf. Type	
		I	Ie
UB11 Pane of 6×4d. (containing No. U13×6) (16.9.68)		2·50	3·00
a. Part perf. pane*		£4250	
b. Patch on cheek (R. 1/2 or 2/2)		20·00	

No. UB11 also occurs with the phosphor omitted but since a single pane would be indistinguishable from No. UB9b it is only listed there.
* Booklet error–see General Notes.

Booklet Cylinder Numbers
Panes of Six (21-row cylinders)

Cylinder No.	No Dot	Dot
N1	10·00	10·00
N1 T	10·00	10·00
N2	10·00	10·00
N2 T	10·00	10·00

●────

4d. Deep olive-sepia panes of four 4×4d. (centre band). PVA gum. Head B

From 2s. Booklets NP31a/NP33

		Perf. Types		
	I	I(½v)	AP	P
UB12 Pane of 4×4d. (containing No. U13×4) (16.9.68)	24·00	35·00	2·50	2·50
a. Phosphor omitted	*	*	*	50·00
b. Dot on "D" retouched	35·00	†	†	†

* Phosphor omitted errors exist from these booklets in Perf. Types I and AP, but the panes are identical with No. UB10b.

Booklet Cylinder Numbers

In the 2s. Booklets (NP31/3) the cylinder number was always trimmed off, however, the cylinder known to have been used was N3.

●────

136

4d. Machin £.s.d. issues Booklet Panes **UB**

UB13, UB18

4d. Deep olive-sepia *se-tenant* with printed labels
2×4d. (centre band). with two labels. PVA gum. Head B
"SEE OTHER PAGES" (left label) and "4,315 FOR YOU AT AGE 55" (right label) from 2s. booklets NP30/NP33

		Perf. Types			
		I	I(½v)	AP	P
UB13	Pane of 2×label/4d. (containing No. U13×2) (16.9.68)	3·50	12·00	1·00	2·75
a.	Phosphor omitted	75·00		60·00	
b.	Damaged pearls in crown (R. 1/2)	20·00		20·00	

UB13b, UB18b

Booklet Cylinder Numbers
In the 2s. Booklets (NP30/NP33) the cylinder number was always trimmed off, however, the cylinder known to have been used was N6.

4d. Bright vermilion panes of Six 6×4d. (centre band). PVA gum.
From 4s.6d. Booklets LP49/LP59, 6s. Booklets QP46/QP55 and 10s. Booklets XP7/XP12

		Perf. Type	
		I	Ie
UB14	Pane of 6×4d. (containing No. U14×6) (6.1.69) (A) Head A	1·75	2·00
	(B) Head B	2·50	2·75
a.	Phosphor omitted	75·00	
b.	Gum arabic (Head A)	£150	£170
ba.	Gum arabic (Head A). Phosphor omitted	—	

Booklet Cylinder Numbers
Panes of Six (21-row cylinders)

Pane No.	Cylinder No.	No Dot	Dot
UB14 (A)	N1 (Head A)	10·00	10·00
UB14 (A)	N1 T (Head A)	10·00	10·00
UB14 (A) b	N1 (gum arabic)	£400	£400
UB14 (A) b	N1 T (gum arabic)	£400	£400
UB14 (A)	N2 (Head A)	10·00	10·00
UB14 (A)	N2 T (Head A)	10·00	10·00
UB14 (B)	N7 (Head B)	15·00	15·00
UB14 (B)	N7 T (Head B)	15·00	15·00

4d. Bright vermilion panes of four 4×4d. (centre band). PVA gum. Head B
From 2s. Booklets NP34/NP45

		Perf.Types		
		I	I(½v)	P
UB15	Pane of 4×4d. (containing No. U14×4) (3.3.69)	3·50	16·00	90
a.	Phosphor omitted	60·00	£150	55·00
b.	Dot on "D" retouched	20·00	†	†
c.	Two narrow phosphor bands over perforations	†	†	£175

Booklet Cylinder Numbers
In the 2s. Booklets (NP34/NP45) the cylinder number was always trimmed off, however, the cylinder known to have been used was N3.

137

UB Machin £.s.d. issues Booklet Panes 4d.

UB16

4d. Bright vermilion panes of 15 *se-tenant* with recipe label. 15×4d. (centre band). PVA gum. Head B
"Stuffed Cucumber" recipe and "Method" from £1 "Stamps for Cooks" Booklet ZP1/ZP1a

A. Stapled
UB16	Pane of 15×4d. (containing No. U14×15) (1.12.69)	18·00
b.	Broken necklace (R. 1/1)	25·00
c.	Tail on "4" (R. 1/4)	25·00
s.	Opt. "Specimen" (14 mm)	£750

B. Stitched
UB16a	Pane of 15×4d. (containing No. U14×15)	3·00
ab.	Uncoated paper ('70)*	£250
ac.	Phosphor omitted	£120
aca.	Phosphor omitted from first column	£180
ad.	Broken necklace (R. 1/1)	15·00
ae.	Tail on "4" (R. 1/4)	15·00

UB17

"Method" only for Braised Shoulder of Lamb from £1 "Stamps for Cooks" Booklet ZP1/ZP1a

A. Stapled
UB17	Pane of 15×4d. (containing No. U14×15) (1.12.69)	18·00
b.	Broken necklace (R. 1/1)	25·00
c.	Spot over eye (R. 2/2)	25·00
s.	Opt. "Specimen" (14 mm)	£750

B. Stitched
UB17a	Pane of 15×4d. (containing No. U14×15)	3·00
ab.	Uncoated paper ('70)*	£250
ac.	Phosphor omitted	£120
ad.	Broken necklace (R. 1/1)	15·00
ae.	Spot over eye (R. 2/2)	15·00
af.	Two narrow bands on each stamp	£950

* Uncoated paper–see General Notes for Section U.
  The note below No. U15, describing No. U14h, also applies to pane UB17af.

4d., 5d.   Machin £.s.d. issues Booklet Panes   **UB**

UB16b, UB16ad, UB17b, UB17ad
This is a multipositive flaw which was repaired and appears as a white spot on pane UB2 (UB2e and UB2af)

UB16c, UB16ae

UB17c, UB17ae Later retouched on UB17 and exists retouched only on UB16

Booklet Cylinder Numbers
In the £1 Booklet (ZP1) the cylinder number was always trimmed off, however, the cylinder known to have been used was N9.

4d. Bright vermilion *se-tenant* pane with printed labels. 2×4d. (centre band). PVA gum. Head B
"SEE OTHER PAGES" (left label) and "4,315 FOR YOU AT AGE 55" (right label) from 2s. Booklets NP34/45

		Perf. Types		
		I	I(½v)	P
UB18	Pane of 2 x label/4d. (containing No. U14×2) (3.3.69)	3·25	20·00	1·00
a.	Phosphor omitted	90·00	£160	70·00
b.	Damaged pearls in crown (R. 1/2)			

Booklet Cylinder Numbers
In the 2s. Booklets (NP34/45) the cylinder number was always trimmed off, however, the cylinder known to have been used was N6.

For illustration of No. UB18b, see No. UB13b.

5d. Pane of six 6×5d. (two bands). PVA gum. Head B
From 5s. Booklets HP26/HP38 and 10s. Booklets XP6/XP12

		Perf. Type	
		I	Ie
UB19	Pane of 6×5d. (containing No. U17×6) (16.9.68)	1·75	2·00
a.	Imperf. pane*	£3500	
b.	Part perf. pane*	£2500	
c.	Phosphor omitted	40·00	
ca.	Third and fourth phosphor bands from left omitted	£120	
d.	White flaw on diadem (R. 1/2 or 2/2)	15·00	
e.	Scratch through hair (R. 1/1 or 2/1)	15·00	

* Booklet errors–see General Notes.

No. UB19ca is known with cylinder number R3 T. Single variety is No. U17db.

UB19d   UB19e

Booklet Cylinder Numbers
Panes of Six (21-row cylinders)

Pane No.	Cylinder No.	No Dot	Dot
UB19	R2	4·75	8·00
UB19	R2 T	4·75	8·00
UB19	R3	4·75	8·00
UB19	R3 T	4·75	8·00

UB Machin £.s.d. issues Booklet Panes 5d.

UB20

5d. Panes of 15 *se-tenant* with recipe label. 15×5d. (two bands). PVA gum. Head B

"Method" only for Cream of Potato Soup from £1 "Stamps for Cooks" Booklet ZP1/ZP1a

A. Stapled

UB20	Pane of 15×5d. (containing No. U17×15) (1.12.69)	25·00
b.	Uncoated paper ('70)*	£500
c.	White flaw below collar (R. 1/2)	35·00
d.	Flaw on shoulder (R. 1/2)	35·00
s.	Opt. "Specimen" (14 mm)	£900

B. Stitched

UB20a	Pane of 15×5d. (containing No. U17×15)	4·00
ab.	Uncoated paper ('70)*	£500
ac.	Phosphor and recipe omitted	£800
ad.	One 9·5 mm. band on each stamp	£800
ae.	Phosphor omitted	£200
af.	White flaw below collar (R. 1/2)	15·00
ag.	Flaw on shoulder (R. 1/2)	15·00

* Uncoated paper—see General Notes for Section U.

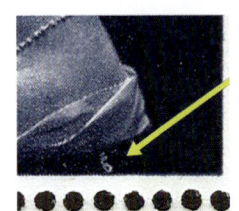

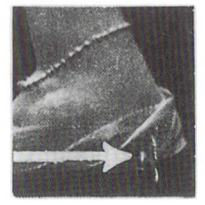

UB20c, UB20af

UB20d, UB20ag

Both varieties occur on the same stamp on the primary sheet and seem to be two states of the same retouch, other states exist.

Booklet Cylinder Numbers

In the £1 Booklet (ZP1) the cylinder number was always trimmed off, however, the cylinder known to have been used was R6 for UB20.

Section UC
Post Office Booklets of Stamps containing Machin £.s.d. Issues with Violet Phosphor Bands.

General Notes

The booklets are listed in value and date order. All booklets, except No. ZP1 which was stapled, had stitched panes. Most of the £1 booklets were stitched and these are listed under No. ZP1a.

Booklet sheet arrangement. See General Notes in Section SC.

Dates. The month and year dates are those found printed on the outer back cover. No dates are given on the 5s. Philympia booklet No. HP34 and the £1 booklet No. ZP1. The dates of issue of every booklet in a new cover design or composition are given in brackets where known.

Quantities. The quantities given are of the numbers manufactured, but some of the figures are shared by two or more booklets and this is indicated in the listing.

Advertiser voucher copy books. See General Notes in Section SC.

Publicity proofs for pictorial covers. From March 1968, the Post Office adopted a policy of pictorial covers for all booklets other than the 2s. slot machine editions. In order to publicise this policy, a distribution of 15 designs was made to the press and visitors to the Post Office stand at Stampex held at Central Hall, Westminster, in March 1968. The distribution comprised four 4s.6d. designs, six 6s. designs and five 10s. designs on coloured card relevant to each booklet value and on white glazed art paper, which assisted press reproduction. Generally, these publicity proofs were booklet size, but four art paper proofs were on paper 10cm square.

During the course of production of booklets with pictorial covers from 1968 to 1970, the printers, Harrison and Sons Ltd., produced a variety of booklet cover proofs in advance of booklet issues which show the evolution of the covers. Many of these proofs were provided to the Post Office advertising contractor, J. Weiner Ltd., but were not distributed generally to the press or the public as occurred in March 1968.

Following the loss of the Post Office contract by J. Weiner Ltd., in 1971 and the cessation of commercial advertising in booklets in 1975, this proof material became surplus to requirements and has been dispersed through the philatelic trade. As the material is widely available and collected by booklet specialists, a complete listing of the publicity proofs and related material is provided after the listing of 10s. booklets.

£1 "Stamps for Cooks" pattern books. On 31 March 1969, a meeting was held at Postal Headquarters to plan a "bigger" stamp book and Post Office design director, Stuart Rose, was instructed to prepare dummy pattern books for J. Weiner Ltd., the Post Office advertising contractor to use for marketing to prospective advertisers. The pattern books were prepared by Post Office studios on the theme of "Cookery".

They comprised hand-painted front and back card covers, two illustrative stamp panes, two illustrative interleaves and five or six plain interleaves, all to indicate the contents of the proposed book. The front showed cooking ingredients in a ladle and is inscribed "Stamps for Cooks" and "20s." and the back showed a prepared meal. Stamp panes had simulated stamps and text. The pattern books were stapled. At least seven books were produced, all slightly different, some remaining complete and some subsequently exploded for display.

The Milk Marketing Board accepted the proposal using recipes extracted from their *Dairy Book of Home Cookery*. The "Stamps for Cooks" £1 Book was experimental and was the first in the series later to become termed "prestige" books.

Catalogue numbers. In order to avoid confusion we have used the same booklet numbers as in the *Concise Catalogue*. Many of these booklets bear the same prefix letters as other stamps listed in the Great Britain Specialised Catalogues so that when quoting numbers in this Section it should be made clear that booklets are being referred to.

Varieties shown thus (a) are those listed in the Great Britain Specialised Catalogues only.

Illustrations. The illustrations of the covers are ¾ size except where otherwise stated.

> NOTE: All booklets in this Section are fully interleaved

Machin £.s.d. Issues — 2s. Booklets, 4s.6d. Booklets

2s. Booklets

Contents: 4×4d. in pane of four and 2×1d. and 2×3d. in pane of four arranged *se-tenant* horizontally

Orange-yellow Cover as Type C. PVA gum (Nos. U2, U10, U12)

NP27	May 1968 (issued 6.4.68)	3,112,400	1·25
NP28	July 1968	1,971,685	1·00
NP29	Aug 1968		3·75
	a. Inside front cover error "FOR YOU AT YOU"		50·00
	b. Error. Extra 4d. pane		£250

2s. booklets containing 3d. stamps were withdrawn on 14 September 1968.

Contents changed: 6×4d. in pane of four and in pane of two plus two printed labels *se-tenant* vertically

Grey Cover as Type C. One centre phosphor band on *se-tenant* pane. PVA gum (Nos. U12, U13)

NP30	Sept 1968 (issued 16.9.68)	2,497,400	75
	a. As NP29a		25·00
	b. Error. Extra 4d. pane		£250
	c. Error. Extra *se-tenant* pane		£250
NP31	Jan 1969	2,247,600	£250

Change to one centre phosphor band on 4×4d. pane. PVA gum (No. U13)

NP31a	Sept 1968 (issued 16.9.68) (incl. in NP30)		£600
NP32	Nov 1968	2,397,400	80
	a. As NP29a		25·00
	b. Error. Extra 4d. pane		£250
	c. Error. Extra *se-tenant* pane		£250
NP33	Jan 1969 (incl. in NP31)		75
	a. As NP29a		25·00

Change to 4d. bright vermilion with one centre phosphor band. PVA gum (No. U14)

NP34	Mar 1969 (issued 3.3.69)	1,952,000	1·10
	a. As NP29a		25·00
	b. Imprint error LOODON for LONDON		£150
NP35	May 1969	2,092,000	1·25
NP36	July 1969	436,000	1·75
	a. As NP29a		50·00
	b. Date error JU for JULY		40·00
NP37	Sept 1969	1,612,000	1·50
	a. Date error 196 for 1969		40·00
NP38	Nov 1969	1,470,400	1·25
	a. Imprint error HARRISOU for HARRISON		25·00
NP39	Jan 1970	1,172,000	2·00
NP40	Mar 1970	1,168,600	2·00
NP41	May 1970	1,390,800	2·00
NP42	July 1970	1,023,800	2·00
NP43	Aug 1970	1,037,800	2·00
NP44	Oct 1970	2,544,600	2·00
NP45	Dec 1970	2,273,400	2·00

Paste-up books NP27 to NP45 *each* £100
AVC books NP27 to NP45 *each* 5·00

4s.6d. Booklets

Contents: 12×4d., 6×1d. in panes of six

I. Slate-blue Cover as Type D. PVA gum (Nos. U2, U12)

LP45	May 1968 (issued 1.5.68)	742,600	4·00

Paste-up books £150
AVC books *each* 8·00

Type E. With GPO Cypher

Type F. With Post Office Crown Symbol

(Des. Stuart Rose)

(In Types E/F the design subject is changed from time to time and this is indicated in brackets after the date)

II. Blue Cover as Type E showing Ships. PVA gum (Nos. U2, U12)

LP46	July 1968 (*Cutty Sark*)	427,600	70

Change to one centre phosphor band on 4d. PVA gum (Nos. U2, U13)

LP47	Sept 1968 (*Golden Hind*) (issued 16.9.68)	1,052,800	70
LP48	Nov 1968 (*Discovery*)	1,009,000	70

Change to 4d. bright vermilion with one centre band. PVA gum (Nos. U2, U14)

LP49	Jan 1969 (*Queen Elizabeth 2*) (issued 6.1.69)	775,200	90
LP50	Mar 1969 (*Sirius*)	1,105,800	2·00
LP51	May 1969 (*Sirius*)	993,200	1·25
LP52	July 1969 (*Dreadnought*)	932,000	1·25
LP53	Sept 1969 (*Dreadnought*)	1,318,600	5·00
LP54	Nov 1969 (*Mauretania*)	1,469,400	1·50
LP55	Jan 1970 (*Mauretania*)	1,046,500	5·00
LP56	Mar 1970 (*Victory*)	872,400	1·50
LP57	May 1970 (*Victory*)	515,800	5·00

III. Blue Cover as Type F showing Ships. PVA gum (Nos. U2, U14)

LP58	Aug 1970 (*The Sovereign of the Seas*)	412,600	4·50
LP59	Oct 1970 (*The Sovereign of the Seas*)	746,600	5·00

Paste-up books LP46 to LP59 *each* £150
Paste-up book Dec 1970 (not issued) £250

AVC books LP46 to LP59 *each* 10·00

5s. Booklets

Type E. With GPO Cypher

Type F. With Post Office Crown Symbol
(Des. Stuart Rose)

Contents: 12×5d. in panes of six

I. Cinnamon Cover as Type E showing English Homes.
PVA gum (No. U17)

HP26	Dec 1968 (Ightham Mote) (issued 27.11.68)	978,000	2·00
HP27	Feb 1969 (Little Moreton Hall)	1,510,200	2·00
HP28	Apr 1969 (Long Melford Hall)	1,963,200	2·00
HP29	June 1969 (Long Melford Hall)	1,821,000	2·00
HP30	Aug 1969 (Long Melford Hall)	1,660,800	5·00

II. Cinnamon Cover as Type F showing English Homes.
PVA gum (No. U17)

HP31	Oct 1969 (Mompesson House)	2,251,200	2·25
HP32	Dec 1969 (Mompesson House)	960,200	2·50
HP33	Feb 1970 (Cumberland Terrace)	910,800	2·25

Type P
(Des. Peter Gauld)

Issued to publicise the Philympia International Philatelic Exhibition, London, September 1970

III. Cinnamon Cover as Type P. Stitched in red. PVA gum (No. U17)

HP34	(no date) (issued 3.3.70)	1,019,800	2·25

IV. Cinnamon Cover as Type F showing English Homes.
PVA gum (No. U17)

HP35	June 1970 (The Vineyard, Saffron Walden)	1,814,400	2·50
HP36	Aug 1970 (The Vineyard, Saffron Walden)	2,076,800	3·25
HP37	Oct 1970 (Mereworth Castle)	3,301,400	3·25
HP38	Dec 1970 (Mereworth Castle)	5,517,680	3·25

Paste-up books HP26 or HP27 (using 4s.6d. AVC to make up) £200
HP28 to HP38 *each* £150
AVC books HP26 to HP38 10·00

6s. Booklets

Contents: 18×4d. in panes of six

Claret Cover as Type D. Gum arabic (No. U11 (1))

QP28	Sept 1967 (issued 21.9.67)	1,345,000	50·00
QP29	Oct 1967	1,487,400	60·00
QP30	Nov 1967	1,522,200	50·00
QP31	Dec 1967	1,531,000	50·00
QP32	Jan 1968	1,251,400	48·00

Change to 4d. deep olive-brown. Gum arabic (No. U11 (2))

QP33	Feb 1968	1,314,400	48·00
QP34	Mar 1968	1,090,600	48·00
QP35	Apr 1968	1,127,800	35·00
QP36	May 1968	1,398,000	18·00

Change to PVA gum (No. U12 (2))

QP37	May 1968 (incl. in QP36)	£450

Paste-up books QP28 to QP31 *each* £150
QP32 (stapled to make up) £200
QP33 to QP37 *each* £150
AVC books QP28 to QP37 *each* 8·00

Type E. With GPO Cypher

Type F. With Post Office Crown Symbol
(Des. Stuart Rose)

UC Machin £.s.d. Issues — 6s. Booklets

II. Orange-red Cover as Type E showing Birds.
PVA gum (No. U12 (2))

QP38	June 1968 (Kingfisher) (issued 4.6.68)	1,212,000	2·00
QP39	July 1968 (Kingfisher)	1,195,000	10·00
QP40	Aug 1968 (Peregrine Falcon)	1,223,800	2·00

Change to one centre phosphor band. PVA gum (No. U13)

QP41	Sept 1968 (Peregrine Falcon) (issued 16.9.68)	1,010,200	1·40
QP42	Oct 1968 (Pied Woodpecker)	1,277,800	2·00
QP43	Nov 1968 (Pied Woodpecker)	1,006,200	1·50
QP44	Dec 1968 (Great Crested Grebe)	975,600	1·50
QP45	Jan 1969 (Barn Owl)	1,017,000	2·75

MIXED GUMS. Nos. QP46/QP47 exist with gum arabic and PVA panes in the same booklet. The mixed gums are indicated by the code letters "G" (Gum arabic) and "P" (PVA), starting with the first pane of the booklet.

Change to 4d. bright vermilion with one centre phosphor band. PVA gum (No. U14)

QP46	Feb 1969 (Barn Owl) (issued 20.2.69) (PPP)		3·50
	(a) Combination GGP		£170
	(b) Combination GPG		£170
	(c) Combination GPP		80·00
	(d) Combination PGG	1,035,200	£125
	(e) Combination PGP		80·00
	(f) Combination PPG		80·00
	(g) Combination GGG		£225
QP47	Mar 1969 (Jay) (PPP)		2·50
	(a) Combination GGP		£170
	(b) Combination PGP		80·00
	(c) Combination PPG	424,400	80·00
	(d) Combination GPP		80·00
	(e) Combination GPG		£170
	(f) Combination GGG		£225
QP48	May 1969 (Jay)	533,800	3·25
QP49	July 1969 (Puffin)	498,400	2·50
QP50	Sept 1969 (Puffin)	506,200	5·00

III. Orange-red Cover as Type F showing Birds.
PVA gum (No. U14)

QP51	Nov 1969 (Cormorant)	472,600	3·25
QP52	Jan 1970 (Cormorant)	487,800	3·75
QP53	Apr 1970 (Wren)	512,800	3·00
QP54	Aug 1970 (Golden Eagle)	570,600	3·00
QP55	Oct 1970 (Golden Eagle)	754,800	3·00

Paste-up books QP38 to QP55 *each* £150
Mar 1970 (not issued) £250
AVC books QP38 to QP43 *each* 10·00
QP44 25·00
QP45 to QP55 *each* 10·00

10s. Booklets

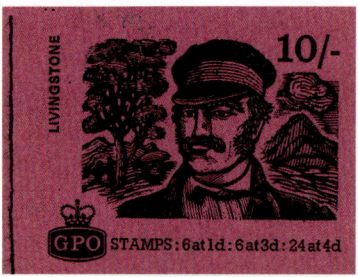

Type E I

Type E II

Pictorial Cover with GPO Cypher

(Des. Stuart Rose)

Two types of Cypher:
Type I. GPO in clear letters. 10s. Booklets XP4/XP5
Type II. GPO in black letters. 10s. Booklets XP6/XP10

Contents: 24×4d., 6×3d., 6×1d. in panes of six

Bright Purple Cover as Type E I showing Explorers.
PVA gum (Nos. U2, U9, U12)

XP4	May 1968 (Livingstone) (issued 25.3.68)	713,200	4·50
XP5	Aug 1968 (Livingstone)	39,497	4·50

Contents changed: 12×5d., 14×4d., 4×1d., in panes of six and one horizontally *se-tenant* pane of 2×4d., and 4×1d.

Yellow-green Cover as Type E II showing Explorers
PVA gum (Nos. U3, U13, U17)

XP6	Sept 1968 (Scott) (issued 16.9.68)	1,513,400	3·00

Content changed: 4d. bright vermilion but *se-tenant* pane comprises 1d. with two phosphor bands and 4d. with one left side phosphor band. PVA gum (Nos. U2, U14, U16, U17). For booklets with mixed gum, see note above No. QP46

XP 7	Feb 1969 (Mary Kingsley) (issued 6.1.69)	2,338,200	2·50
XP 8	May 1969 (Mary Kingsley) (PPPPP)		3·25
	(a) Combination PPPGP	1,165,200	70·00
	(b) Combination PPGPP		£200
XP 9	Aug 1969 (Shackleton)	1,765,600	3·50
XP10	Nov 1969 (Shackleton)	1,176,000	5·00

Type F

(Des. Stuart Rose)

Pictorial Cover with Post Office
Corporation Crown Symbol

Yellow-green Cover as Type F showing Explorers
PVA gum (Nos. U2, U14, U16, U17)

| XP11 | Feb 1970 (Frobisher) (issued 2.2.70) | 490,200 | 5·00 |
| XP12 | Nov 1970 (Captain Cook) | 737,400 | 6·00 |

Paste-up books XP4 to XP12 *each* £200
May 1970 (not issued) £300
AVC books XP4 to XP12 *each* 12·00

UC Machin £.s.d. Issues *Proofs*

Publicity proof covers and related material
All proofs are booklet cover size unless otherwise stated.

1. Cover proofs for issued booklets

4s.6d. Proofs

Blue card
(a) As Type E

Cutty Sark, Golden Hind, Discovery, Queen Elizabeth 2	each 30·00

(b) As Type E but with Type F value setting

Queen Elizabeth 2, Sirius, Dreadnought, Mauretania, Victory	each 40·00

White glazed art paper
(a) As Type E

(i) *Cutty Sark* (10 cm square)	50·00
(ii) *Golden Hind, Discovery, Queen Elizabeth 2*	each 30·00

5s. Proofs

Cinnamon card
(a) As Type E

Ightham Mote, Little Moreton Hall	each 50·00

White glazed art paper
(a) As Type E

Ightham Mote, Little Moreton Hall	each 50·00

6s. Proofs

Orange-red card
(a) As type E

Kingfisher, Peregrine Falcon, Pied Woodpecker, Great Crested Grebe, Barn Owl, Jay	each 30·00

(b) As Type E but with Type F value setting

Kingfisher, Peregrine Falcon, Pied Woodpecker, Great Crested Grebe, Jay, Puffin	each 60·00

White glazed art paper
(a) As Type E

(i) Kingfisher, Peregrine Falcon, Barn Owl (10 cm square)	each 50·00
(ii) Pied Woodpecker, Great Crested Grebe, Jay	each 30·00

10s. Proofs

Bright purple card
(a) As Type EI but with Type EII GPO Cypher

Livingstone, Scott, Shackleton, Cook	each 40·00

(b) As Type EII but with Type EI stamp contents

Livingstone, Scott, Kingsley, Frobisher, Cook	each 60·00

White glazed art paper
(a) As Type EI but with Type EII GPO Cypher

Livingstone, Scott, Shackleton, Cook	each 40·00

White card
(c) As Type EII

Scott, Shackleton, Kingsley, Frobisher, Cook	each 60·00

2. Cover proofs for booklets not issued

4s.6d. Proof
White glazed art paper, as Type F

Swallow	£120

5s. Proof
White glazed art paper, as Type F

The Red House	£700

10s. Proofs

Bright purple card, as Type EI but with Type EII GPO Cypher Drake	£100
White glazed art paper, as Type EI but with Type EII GPO Cypher Drake	£100
White card, as Type EII Drake	£120

3. Composite proof
White glazed art paper, as Type F (18 cm by 21cm)

10s. Cook and Drake, 6s. Curlew and Golden Eagle	£800

4. Poster Proof (PL(S) 331)
White glazed art paper (21 cm by 28 cm) illustrating six covers

4s.6d. *Queen Elizabeth 2 and Sirius*, as Type E but with Type F value setting	
6s. Barn Owl and Jay, as Type E but with Type F value setting	
10s. Kingsley, as Type EII	
5s. Little Moreton Hall, as Type E	£600

5. Preliminary Proofs and Essays

5s. Proof on cream paper, The Red House, as Type F (marked "5A")	£500
10s. Proof on Bright purple card, Livingstone, as Type EI, 120% booklet size	£500
10s. Essay on white paper, Kingsley with volcano and palm tree, no contents line, 120% booklet size	£500
10s. Essay on cream paper, palm tree and Drake ship (inverted), no contents line, 120% booklet size	£500
10s. Essay on cream paper, Frobisher, no contents line, 133% booklet size	£500
10s. Essay on cream paper, Cook, no contents line, 114% booklet size	£500

6. Zinc Metal Printing Blocks ("Zincos")

4s.6d. Golden Hind, Discovery, Queen Elizabeth II	each £400
5s. The Red House	£500
6s. Great Crested Grebe, Jay	each £400
10s. Scott, Shackleton, Cook, Drake	each £400

7. London Philympia booklet stitching trial
Trial booklet with front cover Type **P**, cover from December 1969, interleaves from January 1970, bound with coloured thread.
Thread coloured black, blue, green, yellow, pink, red *each* £200

£1 Booklet (Stamps for Cooks)

Type X

Contents: 18×5d., 36×4d., 6×1d., in panes of 15 including one horizontally *se-tenant* pane of 3×5d., 6×4d., and 6×1d. There are 12 recipes on interleaving pages and on *se-tenant* labels attached to each pane.

Pattern book (April 1969) (see Notes)
Full colour cover showing cooking ingredients on ladle and "Stamps for cooks" "20s." £2750

Full Colour Cover as Type X size 6×2⁷/₈ in. showing Baked Stuffed Haddock.

Pane of 15x5d. has two phosphor bands, panes of 15x4d. have one centre phosphor band but *se-tenant* pane has two phosphor bands on 1d. and 5d. and one side band on 4d. (three stamps with band at left and three stamps with band at right).

ZP1	(no date) (issued 1.12.69) (stapled)	10,848	£325
	s. Each stamp overprinted "Specimen" 14×2 mm		£5750
ZP1a	As last but booklet is sewn with thread	374,902	6·50
	as. Each stamp cancelled with Philatelic Bureau postmark of 8 June 1971		£2200
	at. Stamps overprinted double-line "SPECIMEN" 72×13 mm		£7500

Examples of this booklet are known with one or two colours omitted from the cover.

Upon issue in 1969, examples of ZP1s were provided to the advertising contractor for presentation as specimens to commercial advertising agencies for future editions of £1 books. During 1971, when a future edition was planned, examples of Nos. ZP1as and ZP1at were similarly provided to the advertising contractor.

AVC book (as ZP1a without black binding and no stamp panes) £100

Section UD
Machin £.s.d. Issues
1969. High Values. Recess-printed

General Notes

Introduction.
High Values.
The first proposals for designs for high values continued the idea of pictorial stamps as in the previous Castles series. Emphasis was laid on a regional motif illustrating some aspect of the architecture or beauty spots of England, Scotland, Northern Ireland and Wales. Printing would remain in intaglio, so the design(s) would need to be engraved as before. Machin produced sketches of an engraved print of Glencoe with an engraved "Dressed" head beside it. The printers, Bradbury Wilkinson, commissioned designs by Michael Goaman, one featuring HMS *Victory*, and another light coming through trees in a forest, together with engraved Machin heads in different sizes. All were ready by July 1967. None met with approval.

Edward Short, the Postmaster General, then asked for essays based on the photogravure stamp but at the same size as the first high values of George VI.

Working photographs created for the photogravure process did not provide enough contrast for the engraver. So, new starker versions, with greater highlights in the modelling, were taken of the plaster cast, which had now been blackened to assist this. Photography took place at Bradbury Wilkinson's factory. The engraving of the head was by two of their master craftsmen, R. G. Godbehear assisted by A. Dow. A second craftsman, J. G. Heymes, was responsible for engraving the background and lettering. Colour trials were produced based largely on those for the current Castles high values and four were approved on 25 January 1968. However, problems arose with the production of the plates and the issue date had to be postponed until 5 March 1969.

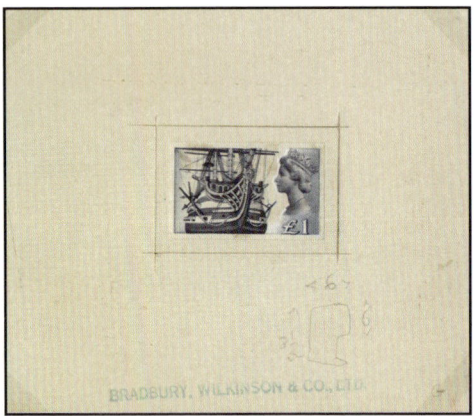

Proposed design by Michael Goaman featuring HMS *Victory*.

Printers. The Machin high values were recess-printed by Bradbury Wilkinson & Co. Ltd. on rotary sheet-fed machines.
Paper. Unwatermarked lightly coated paper was used for all values. Several types of coated paper appear to have been used and generally there is only a slight response to the chalky test. Variations in the thickness of the paper also exist. Shades are known but it is probable that they are due to the variations in the coating and thickness of the paper rather than to the use of different inks.

Gum. Only PVA gum was used for the Machin high values.

Sheet details. The printer's sheets comprised 160 stamps in four panes of 40 each arranged in five rows of eight stamps (see diagram above right), the sheet being guillotined into four before issue.

Perforation. All values are comb perforated 12. The printer's sheet was perforated as a complete sheet with perforation Type A*; therefore, the characteristics of each individual pane are different as is clearly shown in the diagram above. Perforator Type A* is described in Appendix G.

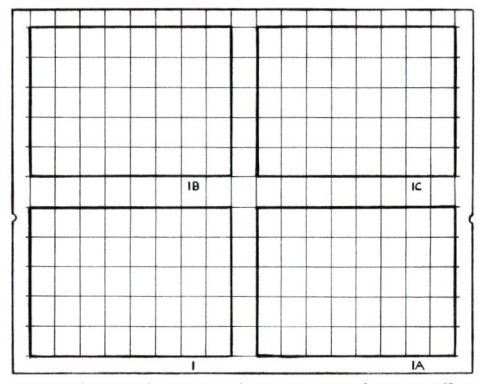

Diagram showing the printer's sheet comprising four Post Office panes, the method of perforation, and the positions of the plate numbers and perforation guide holes

Plate Numbers. See the General Notes for Section T for an illustration of these. Each printer's sheet produces four plate numbers comprising a "whole number" and "A", "B" and "C" numbered panes and these appear below stamp 7 in the bottom row of each pane, as shown in the diagram above. The arrangement of the panes is the same for all plates of all the values.

Guide hole and plugged impression

2s.6d. Brown, 5s. Red, 10s. Blue   Machin £.s.d.High Value Issues   **UD**

Perforation Guide Holes. The Machin high values have a single guide hole opposite the first row of stamps, in the left-hand margin of the "whole" number panes and in the right-hand margin of the "A" plates as shown in the diagram of the printer's sheet. Additionally for plate 2 of the 2s.6d., and 5s., and plate 1 of the 10s., there are "blind" perforation guide holes slightly below the punched holes.

The punched holes are usually heavily rimmed with colour and may be either partly or completely trimmed off. The appearance of the "blind" holes ranges from a thin outline to being completely coloured in.

U3. Queen Elizabeth II
(Des. after plaster cast by Arnold Machin)
(Eng. Robert Godbehear (head) and Alan Dow and JG Heymes (backgorund and lettering)

1969 Type U3

1969 *(5 March).* **2s.6d. Brown**

UD1 = SG 787	Mint	Used
2s.6d. Brown	20	20

Plate Numbers (Blocks of Four)

Plate No.	
	5·00
2	5·00
2 A	5·00
2 B	5·00
2 C	5·00
3	5·00
3 A	5·00*
3 B	5·00
3 C	5·00
6	8·00
6 A	8·00
6 B	8·00
6 C	40·00

* This contains the recorded minor constant flaw.

Minor Constant Flaw

| Pl. 3A | 5/8 | Dot to right of Queen's eye (Th. D–E4) |

Quantities Printed. Pl. 2/2C 7,840,000; Pl. 3/3C 27,200,000; Pl. 6/6C 9,360,000

1969 *(5 March).* **5s. Crimson-lake**

UD2 = SG 788	Mint	Used
5s. Crimson-lake	85	25

Plate Numbers (Blocks of Four)

Plate No.	
2	12·00
2 A	12·00
2 B	12·00
2 C	12·00
3	10·00
3 A	10·00
3 B	10·00
3 C	10·00

Quantities Printed. Pl. 2/2C 8,480,000; Pl. 3/3C 15,200,000

1969 *(5 March).* **10s. Deep ultramarine**

UD3 = SG 789	Mint	Used
10s. Deep ultramarine	3·00	3·75

Plate Numbers (Blocks of Four)

Plate No.	
1	30·00
1 A	30·00
1 B	30·00
1 C	30·00

Quantities Printed. Pl. 1/1C 8,880,000

149

UD Machin £.s.d. High Value Issues £1 Black

1969 (5 March). **£1 Bluish black**

UD4 = SG 790	Mint	Used
£1 Bluish black	1·75	75

The indigo shade, previously listed, is believed to have occurred by migration of colour during storage of a sheet within a blue-coloured enclosure and was not the result of faulty ink mix during printing.

Plate Numbers (Blocks of Four)

Plate No.

3	20·00
3 A	20·00
3 B	20·00
(3 C*)	†
4	30·00
4 A	30·00
4 B	30·00
4 C	30·00

* This plate number block is not known as there was a fault on the plate and only the left half of this pane was issued.

New plates were made for the decimal £1 in 1970, but in single pane settings of 100 (10×10) in place of the plates of four panes each of 40 (8×5). Plate blocks of four from Plate 3 of the decimal issue (No. UD11 in Vol. 4 of this catalogue) can easily be distinguished from Plate 3 blocks of the pre-decimal issue as they show part of the "TOTAL SHEET VALUE" inscription in the margin opposite R. 9/10.

However, specialists may also recognise single stamps by studying the background shading under a strong magnifying glass, particularly in the top left and bottom right corners. The pre-decimal issue has thicker horizontal lines of shading whilst the decimal issue has thicker vertical lines, each caused by the direction in which the transfer roller was rocked, both plates being produced by the conventional process of rocking in impressions from the die. (Illustrations taken from top left corner)

On 6 December 1972 the £1 value was reissued with the value shown in a new style.

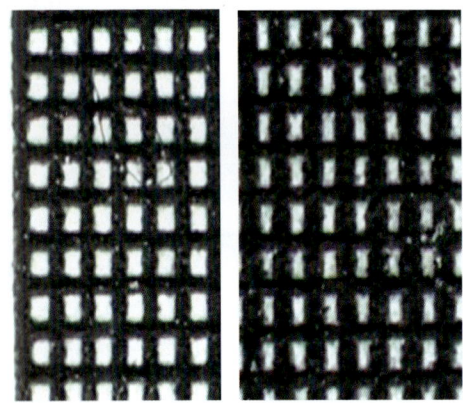

UD4 Pre-decimal issue Thicker horizontal lines   UD11 Decimal issue Thicker vertical lines

Quantities Printed. Pl. 3/3C 3,760,000; Pl. 4/4C 2,800,000

Proofs

Imperforate in the £1 design Type U3 each mounted on a Bradbury, Wilkinson card and marked "Approved by the Queen" signed and dated "14 Jan/Feb. 1968" in blue. The stamps are printed in the approved colours of Nos. UD1 to UD4
Card inscribed in red "A1" with £1 in brown as No. UD1
Card inscribed in red "A2" with £1 in crimson-lake as No. UD2
Card inscribed in red "A3" with £1 in deep ultramarine as No. UD3
Card inscribed in red "A4" with £1 in issued colour as No. UD4

As above but 2s.6d., 5s., 10s., and £1 imperforate proofs in the issued colours mounted on Bradbury, Wilkinson card
Card with four values imperforate inscribed "AS SUBMITTED 20.3.68"

The above were originally in the Bradbury, Wilkinson archive later acquired by De La Rue and sold by them in 2000.

Imprimaturs from the NPM or BPMA

Nos. UD1/UD4 imperforate (set of four)	£7000
No. UD1 plate 2B block of four	£8250
No. UD2 plate 2B block of four	£8250
No. UD3 plate 1 block of four	£8250
No. UD4 plate 3 block of four	£8250

Presentation Pack

UPP2	(issued 5 March 1969) Four values	16·00
	a. With German text	55·00

The issued Pack contained one each of Nos. UC1/UC4. UPP2 also exists with a Japanese insert card.

First Day Cover

UFC6	(5.3.69) 2s.6d., 5s., 10s., £1	6·50

150

Section W
Special Issues
(1953–1970)

General Notes

Special issues. Until 1966 it had been the policy of the Post Office to restrict commemorative issues to celebrating particular events, such as anniversaries or exhibitions, conferences and festivals. The introduction of the Landscape series in May 1966 heralded a new departure as this was followed by pictorial sets showing British Birds, Paintings, Bridges, Cathedrals, etc. and Technological Achievements. These cannot be described as being commemorative stamps, yet it is obviously convenient and logical for them to be listed here and so we have headed this section Special Issues.

Se-tenant **combinations.** *Se-tenant* means joined together. Some sets include stamps of different design arranged *se-tenant* as blocks or strips and, in mint condition, these are usually collected unsevered as issued. Where such combinations exist, the individual stamps are priced normally as mint and used singles but please note that Stanley Gibbbons generally only supply such issues in complete *se-tenant* units.

Printers. All the £.s.d. special issues were printed in photogravure by Harrison & Sons with the exception of the 1964 2s.6d. Shakespeare and 1966 2s.6d. Westminster Abbey which were recess-printed by Bradbury, Wilkinson & Co. and the 1969 Post Office Technology and 1970 Commonwealth Games issues which were printed by De La Rue & Co. by lithography.

Generally, the double-sized stamps were printed on continuous reels of paper on the web in double-pane width, i.e. 240 stamps consisting of two panes (no dot and dot) each of 120 stamps arranged in 20 rows of six stamps, the panes being guillotined before issue. However, the higher values were often printed in single panes, either on reel- or sheet-fed machines. After the listing of each issue we give the sheet arrangement and state whether printed in the reel or in sheets.

Queen's portrait. The portrait from the photograph by Dorothy Wilding Ltd. was used from the 1953 Coronation to the 1966 Westminster Abbey issues. This was replaced on the 1966 Landscapes to 1967 Christmas by the profile coinage design by Mrs. Mary Gillick, adapted by David Gentleman. The third, and final, change was made on the 1968 Bridges issue with the introduction of design from a plaster cast by Arnold Machin. The Machin head can be distinguished from the Gentleman adaptation of the Gillick profile by two, instead of one, laurel leaves on top of the Queen's head.

Paper. The same type of paper as for the definitive issues was used up to the 1960 General Letter Office issue and thereafter chalk-surfaced paper was used.

Screen. The 200-line screen as used for the Wilding definitives was employed up to the 1960 Europa issue but thereafter Harrisons used a finer 250-line screen.

Watermarks. These are illustrated in Section SA and were used as follows:

Tudor Crown 1953 Coronation issue
St Edward's Crown 1957 World Scout Jubilee and Inter-Parliamentary Union and 1958 Commonwealth Games
Crowns All later issues until 1967 Wild Flowers and British Discovery and Invention
No watermark 1967 Paintings and Sir Francis Chichester and all issues from 1967 Christmas onwards

The watermark normally appears sideways on upright designs. On certain stamps, the 2½d. and 3d. 1962 Productivity Year and the 1963 Freedom from Hunger and Paris Postal Conference issues, the watermark is normally inverted. These stamps were printed on the web and for technical reasons the paper had to be re-reeled and, to save time and expense, it was decided to print on the paper wound in the reverse direction to normal, thus resulting in the watermark being inverted. A large proportion of the printing for the 1967 Wild Flowers 9d. was similarly treated. Other inverted watermark varieties on commemorative issues are normally from sheet-printed issues where the paper has been accidentally fed the wrong way and these are often quite scarce.

Gum. The distinction between gum arabic and PVA gum is explained in the General Notes relating to Section UA. It is sufficient to state here that gum arabic was used for all commemorative stamps up to the 1967 Christmas issue and thereafter Harrisons and De La Rue only used PVA gum.

Perforation. Harrisons used the same 15×14 comb perforation as for the Wilding definitives but some of the upright designs are perforated 14×15. The 1964 2s.6d. Shakespeare and 1966 2s.6d. Westminster Abbey were comb perforated 11×12 by Bradbury, Wilkinson and the 1969 Post Office Technology and 1970 Commonwealth Games issues were comb perforated 13½×14 by De La Rue.

Cylinder and plate blocks are listed according to the perforator type as described in Appendix G together with abbreviations for the side and horizontal margins of the listed block. These are usually from the bottom left corner, therefore the first letter refers to the left margin and the second to the bottom margin. For details see Section S.

Phosphor bands. See the General Notes for Section S for a detailed description of these. In the special issues they were applied as follows:

Blue: From 1962 NPY to 1965 Salvation Army and 1965 ITU
    Generally 8 mm. but occasionally 9·5 mm. bands.
Violet 8 mm. bands: Other 1965 issues to 1966 Christmas.
Violet 9·5 mm. bands: 1967 EFTA to 1970 Christmas.

From 1962 until the 1967 Wild Flowers set the special issues appeared both with and without phosphor bands. From the 1967 British Paintings set onwards it was intended that all special issues should appear only with phosphor bands. However, it is quite common practice for sheets to be issued with the phosphor accidentally omitted and these are listed as varieties.

Methods of Application. All three methods, photogravure, flexography and letterpress were utilised to apply the phosphor bands to £.s.d. special issues (for the characteristics of each method see Section S Notes).

In the light of considerable research it now appears that from 1962 until 1969 the bands were applied either by flexography or photogravure, the only exceptions being the two special issues printed by De La Rue which had the bands applied by letterpress. These two issues used a slightly different substance known as SA, sulphanilic acid being the activator.

It is known that the first phosphor issue, 1962 National Productivity Year set, had the bands printed on the web by flexography and the following reel-fed issues used the same process or photogravure. Flexography was used for the few sheet-fed issues. Since 1970 Harrisons have only used photogravure to apply the bands, and phosphor cylinder numbers were introduced.

Some difficulty can arise in distinguishing between phosphor bands applied by photogravure and those printed

Special issues — General Notes

by flexography. The latter often do not run to the bottom of the sheet or show a break in the bottom margin. They also show, in some instances, a vertical split in the centre of the band.

In some instances the cylinders or stereos used to apply the bands were made-up with a narrow band at one side or both sides of the sheet. These narrow bands vary in size, as do the normal bands, but most are 6 mm. wide. Where such varieties occur they are included, listing being for a single stamp with vertical margin attached. Note that the 6 mm. band listings refer to the width of the band *as printed*, not the width of the part of the band that falls on the stamp.

Phosphor cylinder numbers. Starting with the 1970 Anniversaries issue cylinder numbers were introduced on the phosphor cylinders as an additional check on tracing errors in applying the bands.

Cylinder varieties and minor constant flaws. We have only listed or recorded those we have actually seen and know to be constant in the position given. Others have been reported and may be added in future editions as examples become available for inspection. To pinpoint the position of the flaws we give the reference according to the S.G. Thirkell Position Finder where this is appropriate. Please note that for designs which lack outer frame lines the position finder should be placed over the outside of the perforation. For further information see the General Notes to Section S under "Varieties" and "Varieties in Cylinder Blocks".

Flaws on Phosphor Issues. In the recorded lists of flaws on stamps which come both ordinary and phosphor, "O" means that the flaw occurs only on the ordinary stamp, "P" phosphor only and "OP" on ordinary and phosphor.

Multicoloured stamps. Colour descriptions are taken from the traffic lights to identify the colours of the cylinder numbers and also missing colour errors. Where colours are superimposed one over another, the colours that result will be different from those described. So far as possible we have followed the normal practice giving the colours starting first with the most prominent one in the centre of the stamp and then moving outwards, usually ending with the colours of the inscriptions, background and Queen's head.

Presentation Packs. Special Packs comprising slip-in cards with printed commemorative inscriptions and descriptive notes on the back and with protective covering, were introduced in 1964 with the Shakespeare issue. These are listed and priced.

Issues of 1968-1969 (British Paintings to the Prince of Wales Investiture) were also issued in packs with text in German for sale through the Post Office's German agency and these are also listed.

Subsequently, the packs sold in Germany, Japan and the Netherlands were identical to the normal English version with the addition of a separate printed card in German, Japanese or Dutch. These are noted where they exist.

Spelling and other errors on insert cards exist, but these are outside the scope of this catalogue.

Reprinted insert cards. In 1988 permission was granted to a British stamp dealer by the Post Office to reproduce, from an original, 1,000 sets of the Dutch insert cards for the 1969 Ships to the 1970 Literary Anniversaries issues.

"Specimen" and "Cancelled" stamps. The former practice of distributing these ceased during the reign of King George VI but occasionally such overprints were applied to Elizabethan Special Issues for advance publicity or exhibition purposes and these are listed.

Various issues of 1964, 1965 and 1966 are known overprinted "CANCELLED", usually without gum. These were for use in trials carried out by the Forensic Department of the Post Office, and should not have reached the general public.

Issues of 1969/1970 are known with "CANCELLED" applied with a violet rubber handstamp (26×3½ mm), generally across a corner of the stamps. This practice was introduced in an attempt to defeat the postal use of the stamps prior to their first day of issue and which could be obtained from advance publicity material distributed to shops supplied by the Post Office Agency in West Germany. When it was realised that the use of the rubber handstamp created material of a collectable nature the practice was discontinued but the following are known to exist, Nos. W159/W197. The Machin 1969 high values, Nos. U33/U36 were similarly obliterated. Later stamps were cancelled by a red pen line across the corner. Such publicity material is outside the scope of this catalogue.

Encapsulated Stamp Sets. Starting with the 1969 Post Office Technology set, publicity notices were prepared for a number of commemorative issues. These comprised complete sets of stamps mounted on card with details of issue date, description, designer and printer and encapsulated in perspex.

Scientific analysis of the stamps in these cards has concluded that they are printed on unsurfaced paper, unlike the issued stamps which are all on chalk-surfaced paper.

As the stamps cannot be removed from the perspex casing they are not individually listed, but those cards which we have seen are noted.

Withdrawal dates. The earlier commemorative issues were left on sale until exhaustion and definite withdrawal dates are not always known, but starting with 1963 Red Cross issue the Post Office announced a standard practice to keep commemorative stamps on sale at the Philatelic Bureau for 12 months from date of issue unless sold out before. All £.s.d. special stamps were invalidated as from 1 March 1972.

Quantities. Up to the end of the 1962 issues (NPY) it is believed that stamps were sold to exhaustion except where a definite withdrawal date was announced, and so the printing figures are quoted as being the quantities sold. Starting with the 1963 Freedom from Hunger issue the quantities are stated as being the number sold, issued or printed. These are defined as follows:

Sold: Actual quantities sold after accounting for undistributed stocks and unsold stocks returned to stores for destruction.

Issued: Quantities issued from Post Office Stores Department to post offices, including the Philatelic Bureau. These figures are given for the 1965 issues (Churchill to ITU) and for which we do not have actual sales figures. Some may have been withdrawn and destroyed.

Printed: Quantities actually supplied by the printers. These often differ from advance announcements of quantities ordered, owing to spoilage, etc.

Research at the Postal Museum has revealed that quantities noted in the printers' reports frequently differ from those previously announced by the Post Office and published in the philatelic press. There are also cylinder combinations recorded that have not been reported or listed in this catalogue. This research has not been incorporated into this edition as it is not clear whether they were ever put on sale.

We also quote figures for sales of Presentation Packs and these were only made available after the total quantities sold, etc., had been announced. The quantities for packs are not additional as they have already been included in the figures for the numbers sold, issued or printed.

We have noticed slight variations in the figures given for quantities sold, etc., stated in other publications and would point out that the figures we have given are those furnished to us by the Post Office. However, the differences are insignificant. See note above Type No. W 178.

Sheet markings. Reference should be made to the descriptions of sheet markings given in the General Notes for Section S, as most of these apply to this section and the information given there is not repeated here. In the commemorative issues the markings are most interesting as they begin with the same basic markings as for the definitives for the first monocoloured issues but as more colours were introduced other markings began to appear. They are described here in the order of their appearance.

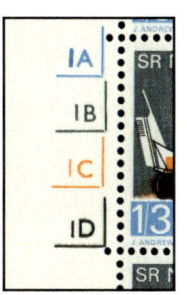

General Notes **Special issues**

Normal at side
Harrison

At foot

De La Rue

Cylinder Numbers. These are described in Section S but we show above how they occur on stamps printed in more than one colour. In the listing of cylinder number blocks for stamps printed in more than one colour we give the colour of each cylinder number in order, reading downwards. The information is sometimes helpful in connection with varieties and flaws where more than one cylinder has been used for the same colour in combination with others.

Plate Numbers. The Plate Numbers used by Bradbury Wilkinson for the 2s.6d. Shakespeare and the 2s.6d. Westminster Abbey are as shown in our notes on the sheet markings for Section T. It should be stated that some of the sheet-fed commemorative stamps were printed by Harrisons on a Linotype and Machinery No. 4 press which uses curved plates and on these the cylinder numbers are, strictly speaking, plate numbers. However, as they appear just like the cylinder numbers they are referred to as such.

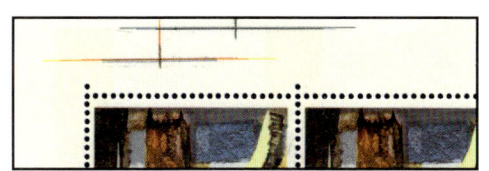

Colour Register Marks. These are coloured crosses of very fine lines, one for each colour superimposed as illustrated. They appear on all sheets of stamps printed in more than one colour, starting with the 1960 Europa issue.

Photo-etched Solid

Stippled

Autotron Marks. Coloured bars which may be photo-etched solid or stippled (dotted) lines. They serve as an electronic control on colour registration and were first used on the 1961 CEPT issue.

Colour Designations. These consist of colour names usually preceded by a figure and the letter "G" which stands for "Gear". They are usually trimmed off but sometimes appear on extra wide right-hand margins on double-pane and single-pane reel-fed printings. They are to indicate which side the cylinder should be fitted and aligned with the colour gear in the press. They are not always shown in the colour indicated. They began to be used on the 1961 CEPT issue, but do not appear on correctly trimmed sheets of £.s.d. stamps after the 1969 Notable Anniversaries issue.

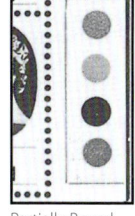

Boxed
Harrison

Partially Boxed

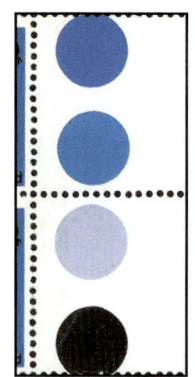

De La Rue

"Traffic Lights". This term is used to denote coloured check dots which were first introduced on the 1962 NPY issue. They are intended as a means of checking sheets for missing colours before delivery to the Post Office. They may be fully boxed or partially boxed as shown but we have not distinguished between these. We quote the colours in the order of their appearance reading downwards. Sometimes they are in the same order as the cylinder numbers in which case we state this to save space. Rather larger dots were used by De La Rue.

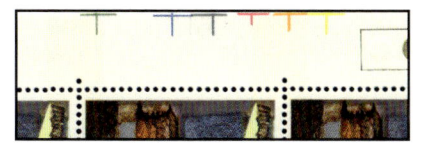

Coloured Crosses. These are most usually found on sheet-fed printings and they serve as trimming lines and as an additional check on colour registration. They are often trimmed off. They first appeared on the 1s.3d. 1964 Botanical stamp.

153

W Special issues *General Notes*

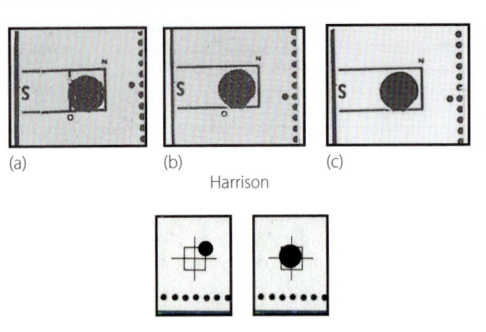

(a) (b) (c)
Harrison

De La Rue

Perforation Guide Holes. At first the styles as shown in the General Notes for Section S were used but the types illustrated above were introduced as follows:
- (a) Double "SON" box for the 6d. 1965 Parliament
- (b) Single "SON" box for the 4d. 1966 Landscapes
- (c) Single "SN" box for the 4d. 1966 World Football Cup

The letters stand for "Selvedge", "Off-side" and "Near-side" and they appear in the reverse order on the other side of the sheet. The "S" or "S O" and part of the box are liable to be trimmed off. We also show the styles used by De La Rue for the 1969 Post Office Technology set and 1970 Commonwealth Games issue respectively.

TOTAL SHEET VALUE £ 6. 0. 0.

Total Sheet Values. As an aid to counter clerks in stocktaking and in selling stamps by the sheet, the "TOTAL SHEET VALUE" and amount was printed in the margin. This practice was introduced with the 1969 Anniversaries issue and this was presumably found to be necessary with the introduction of stamps of unusual size and sheet make-up.

Embossed heads. Starting with the 1968 British Paintings set the Queen's head was sometimes embossed over the gold printing.

This gives rise to missing embossing varieties which are listed, although we do not list misplaced embossing. Provision is also made for an embossed dot in the traffic lights.

Design Index

This index gives an easy reference to the inscriptions and designs of the Special Stamps 1953 to 1970. Where a complete set shares an inscription or type of design, then only the catalogue number of the first stamp is given. Paintings, inventions, etc., are indexed under the name of the artist or inventor, where this is shown on the stamp.

Aberfeldy Bridge W131
Alcock, John W154
Antrim W86
Arbroath Declaration, 650th Anniversary W182
Architecture: Cathedrals W159
    Rural W178
Atlantic Flight, 50th Anniversary W154
Automatic Sorting W174

Battle of Britain, 25th Anniversary W67
Battle of Hastings, 900th Anniversary W101
Black Headed Gull W92
Blackbird W95
Blue Tit W93
Bridges W130
Brown, Arthur W154
Burns, Robert W81

Cairngorms W88
Canterbury Cathedral W162
CEPT W14, W21
Christmas 1966, Children's Paintings (3d., 1s.6d.) W109
    1967, Paintings (3d., 4d., 1s.6d.) W127
    1968, Children's Toys (4d., 9d., 1s.6d.) W142
    1969, Traditional Religious Themes (4d., 5d., 1s.6d.) W175
    1970, Lisle Psalter (4d., 5d., 1s.6d.) W198
Churchill, Winston W56
Commonwealth Arts Festival W65
Commonwealth Cable W40
Commonwealth Games (1958) W9
Commonwealth Games (1970) W192
Commonwealth Parliamentary Conference W24
"Concorde" W151
Constable, John W141
Cook's First Voyage of Discovery, 200th Anniversary W137
Coronation W1
Cotswold Limestone W179
Cutty Sark W148

de Montfort's Parliament, 700th Anniversary W59
Dickens, Charles, Death Centenary W187
Durham Cathedral W159

East Indiaman W147
EFTA W111
Elizabethan Galleon W146
"Elizabeth I" W138
England Winners World Cup Football Championships, 1966 .... W96
Europa, CEPT, 1st Anniversary W14
Europa, CEPT, 10th Anniversary W155

Fife Harling W178
First England–Australia Flight, 50th Anniversary W158
Flowers W113
Forth Road Bridge W54
Freedom from Hunger W29

Gandhi, Mahatma, Birth Centenary W170
General Letter Office, Tercentenary W12
Gipsy Moth W122
Great Britain W149

Harlech Castle W87
Hovercraft W99

International Botanical Congress W50
International Co-operative Alliance W184
International Geographical Congress W46
International Labour Organisation, 50th Anniversary W156
International Lifeboat Conference W34
International Telecommunications Union, Centenary W79

Jet Engine W125
Jubilee Jamboree (1957) W5

Landscapes W85
Lawrence, Thomas W119, W139
Le Nain, Louis W129
Lister, Joseph W63
Liverpool Metropolitan Cathedral W164
Lowry, L. S. W121

M4 Viaduct W133
Mauretania W150
Mayflower, 350th Anniversary of Voyage W185
Menai Bridge W132
Motor Cars W98
Murillo W128

National Giro W171
National Nature Week W32
National Productivity Year W26
Nightingale, Florence, 150th Birth Anniversary W183
North Atlantic Treaty Organisation (NATO),
    20th Anniversary W157
Nuclear Power W100

Paris Postal Conference, Centenary W31
Parliament, 700th Anniversary W59
Parliamentary Conference W8
Penicillin W124
Philympia 1970 .... W195
Piper, John W140
Post Office Savings Bank, Centenary W16
Post Office Tower W75
Prince of Wales, Investiture W165

Queen Elizabeth 2 .... W145

Radar W123
Radio Telescope W97
Red Cross Centenary Congress W37
Robin W94
Royal Air Force, 50th Anniversary W136
Royal Astronomical Society, 150th Anniversary W186

St Giles' Edinburgh W161
St Paul's Cathedral W163
Salvation Army Centenary W61
Seville School W127
Shakespeare Festival W41
Stubbs, George W120
Sussex W85

Tarr Steps W130
Telecommunications W172
Television W126
Trades Union Congress, Centenary W134

Ulster Thatch W181
United Nations, 20th Anniversary W77

Votes for Women, 50th Anniversary W135

Welsh Stucco W180
Westminster Abbey, 900th Anniversary W83
World Cup Football Championships, 1966 .... W89
Wordsworth, William, 200th Birth Anniversary W191

York Minster W160

W 1953 Coronation of Queen Elizabeth II

> **Important Note:**
> To eliminate confusion, the *Type* numbers (the bold, black numbers which appear beneath each illustration) have been altered for this edition to match the *Catalogue* numbers (the bold, blue numbers in the listings)..

Type **W1**

(Des. E. G. Fuller)

Type **W2**

(Des. Michael Goaman)

Type **W3**

(Des. Edmund Dulac)

Type **W4**

(Des. M. C. Farrar-Bell)
(Portrait by Dorothy Wilding Ltd (except 1s.3d.))

a. Mis-shapen emblems (Cyl. 1 Dot, R. 1/6)	35·00
b. Thistle flaw (Cyl. 1 Dot, R. 16/5)	40·00
First Day Cover (W1/W4)	75·00

Nos. W1/W4 are known used from an Army Post Office in Egypt and Lambeth, London S.W. on 2 June 1953. The latter example was an error as the UK offices were closed on 2 June.

Reprints, in black, of these four stamps were included in the Penrose Annual for 1954. These reprints were printed in photogravure by Harrisons, on ungummed paper, but were perforated. They were inscribed on the reverse "Reproduction only no postal or philatelic value".

For a £1 value as Type W3 see Nos. **MS**2147 and 2380 in the *Great Britain Concise Catalogue*.

W1a    W1b

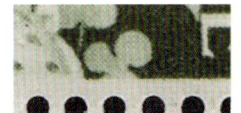

Normal    W3a

W2a    W4a

W4b

1953 *(3 June).* **Coronation of Queen Elizabeth II** Types W.**1**/**4**.
Watermark Tudor Crown, Type W.**22**

W1 =SG 532		Mint	Used
	2½d. carmine-red	20	20
	a. Missing pearl (Cyl. 3 Dot, R. 1/4)	40·00	
	b. Pearls retouched	35·00	
W2 =SG 533			
	4d. ultramarine	80	40
	a. Daffodil leaf flaw (Cyl. 1 No dot, R. 19/1)	20·00	
W3 =SG 534			
	1s.3d. deep yellow-green	3·00	1·00
	a. Clover leaf flaw (Cyl. 2 No dot, R. 20/1)	20·00	
W4 =SG 535			
	1s.6d. deep grey-blue	6·50	2·00

World Scout Jubilee Jamboree 1957

Cylinder Numbers (Blocks of Six)
Perforation Type A (E/I)

	Cylinder No.	No dot	Dot
2½d.	1	5·50	5·50
	2	3·50	3·50
	3	3·50	3·50
	4	3·50	3·50
4d.	1	25·00*	5·00
1s.3d.	2	40·00	12·00
1s.6d.	1	45·00	45·00

Minor Constant Flaws

2½d. Cyl. 1 no dot
19/2 Spur to top of "A" of "POSTAGE"

2½d. Cyl. 3 dot
13/2 Bulge on left-hand fraction bar

2½d. Cyl. 4 no dot
1/3 White flaw in diadem (Th. A7)
1/4 White spur on left-hand crown (Th. B2)
7/1 Red spot behind hair level with earring (Th. D8–9)
14/2 Red spot on face level with earring (Th. D7)
17/1 White spot on branch below left-hand crown (Th. C5)

4d. Cyl. 1 dot
1/4 Retouched stem of daffodil (Th. F2–3)

1s.3d. Cyl. 2 dot
2/6 Retouch behind upper part of "E" of "E R" and white flaw at top of sceptre (Th. B4)

1s.6d. Cyl. 1 no dot
18/2 Malformed foot to "R" of "REVENUE"

1s.6d. Cyl. 1 dot
19/1 White flaw on wreath below R of REVENUE (Th. B9)

Sheet Details

Sheet size: 120 (6×20). Double-pane reel-fed

Sheet markings:

Cylinder numbers: Opposite R. 18/1

Guide holes: Boxed opposite rows 14/15, at left (no dot) or right (dot)

Marginal arrows:
"V" shaped, hand-engraved at top and bottom of sheet
"W" shaped, photo-etched at both sides

Marginal rule: At bottom of sheet

Imprimaturs from the NPM or BPMA
Nos. W1/W4 imperforate, watermark Type W.**22**

Watermark upright (set of 4)	£4000

Quantities Sold:

2½d.	415,034,000
4d.	19,816,000
1s.3d.	8,012,000
1s.6d.	5,987,200

Type **W5**. Scout Badge and "Rolling Hitch"
(Des. Mary Adshead)

Type **W6**. "Scouts coming to Britain"
(Des. Pat Keely)

Type **W7**. Globe within a Compass
(Des. W. H. Brown)

1957 (1 August). **World Scout Jubilee Jamboree** Types **W5**/**W7**. Watermark St Edward's Crown, Type W.**23**

Commemorating the 50th Anniversary of the founding of the Boy Scout Movement. The Jubilee Jamboree was held at Sutton Coldfield.

W5 =SG 557		Mint	Used
2½d. carmine-red		20	20
a. Broken rope strand (Cyl. 4 Dot, R. 1/1)		40·00	
b Neck retouch (Cyl. 5 No dot, R. 11/5)		40·00	
W6 =SG 558			
4d. ultramarine		50	50
a. Solid pearl at right (Cyl. 1 No dot, R. 14/5)		40·00	
W7 =SG 559			
1s.3d. green		3·00	2·00
a. Major retouch (Cyl. 1 Dot, R. 2/4)		30·00	
First Day Cover (W5/W7)			25·00

W5a    W5b

1957 World Scout Jubilee Jamboree

W6a W7a

Sheet Details:
Sheet size: 120 (6×20). Double-pane reel-fed

Sheet markings:
Cylinder numbers: Opposite R. 18/1
Guide holes: Opposite rows 14/15, at left (no dot) or right (dot)
Marginal arrows:
"V" shaped, hand-engraved at top and bottom of sheet
"W" shaped, hand-engraved on both sides
Marginal rule: At bottom of sheet

Imprimaturs from the NPM or BPMA
Nos. W5/W7 imperforate, watermark Type W.23

Watermark upright (set of 3)	£3000
2½d. cylinder 5 block of six	£7000
2½d. "Neck retouch" R. 11/5	£1500
4d. cylinder 1. block of six	£7000
1s.3d. cylinder 1. block of six	£7000
1s.3d. "Major retouch" R. 2/4	£1500

Quantities Sold: Sheets and coils:
2½d. 137,235,286
4d. 9,318,477
1s.3d. 3,820,478

Cylinder Numbers (Blocks of Six)
Perforation Type A (E/1)

	Cylinder No.	No dot	Dot
2½d.	4	3·50	3·50
	5	3·50	3·50
4d.	1	15·00	15·00
1s.3d.	1	25·00	25·00

Perforation Type B (I/P)

| 4d. | 1 | | 4·00 | 4·00 |

Perforation Type C (E/P)

| 4d. | 1 | | † | 4·00 |

Coils Leaders:

Value	Size	Printed	Sold	Price
2½d.	4800	487	23	£750
	480	100	49	£600
4d.	4800	480	21	£900
	480	100	37	£700
1s.3d.	4800	482	20	£900
	240	100	33	£700

Total number of coil stamps sold or used on covers:
2½d. 133,920
4d. 118,560
1s.3d. 103,920

Only 60,632 covers were serviced and 14 large rolls of each value were used for this purpose.

Withdrawn: 11.9.57

Minor Constant Flaws
2½d. Cyl. 4 dot
- 11/2 Red spot over Queen's left eyebrow, later retouched (Th. C9)
- 14/1 Red spot in rope between "L E" (Th. G5)
- 16/5 White spot in rope at junction with fifth line at left (Th. C1)
- 17/3 Red spot in large "2" just left of curve
- 19/2 White dot after small "2"
- 20/4 White stop after "M"

2½d. Cyl. 5 dot
- 13/4 Red spot in top of "A"

1s.3d. Cyl. 1 dot
- 18/2 Green spot in compass point above badge (Th. E2)

Coils
Special rolls were prepared of this issue for servicing first day covers mechanically. They were produced from different cylinders and printed on continuous reels of paper. The cylinders bore 126 impressions in 21 rows of six. The cylinders were numbered J1 for the 2½d. and 4d. and J2 for the 1s.3d. The reels were cut so as to provide single rolls of 4800 stamps, numbered 1 to 6. Some very minor flaws have been noted on these coil stamps.

The rolls were put on sale at the London Chief Office but as the quantities were too large for stamp collectors, some were rewound into smaller rolls of 480 for the 2½d. and 4d. and 240 for the 1s.3d. and put on sale there on 2 September.

46th Inter-Parliamentary Union Conference 1957 W

Type **W8**

(Des. M. C. Farrar-Bell and adapted by Frank Langfield with added lettering)

1957 *(12 September).* **46th Inter-Parliamentary Union Conference** Type **W8.** Watermark St Edward's Crown, Type W.**23**

To mark the 46th Conference held at Church House, Westminster. The Union was founded in 1889.

W8 =SG 560	Mint	Used
4d. ultramarine	40	40
a. Broken wreath (R. 2/6)	35·00	
b. Broken frame (R. 12/5)	35·00	
c. Partial double frame line (R. 17/3, 17/6 and 18/6)	35·00	
First Day Cover (W8)		£150

W8a

W8b

W8c

Cylinder Numbers (Blocks of Six)
Perforation Type B (I/P)

	Cylinder No.	No dot	Dot
4d.	2	5·00	

Perforation Type C (E/P)

4d.	2	5·00	

Minor Constant Flaws

4d. Cyl. 2 no dot

- 1/5 Blue blob in frame over last "N" of "CONFERENCE" (Th. E6)
- 1/6 Outline of left-hand jewel of diadem incomplete (Th. A–B3)
- 2/1 Line joining shamrock leaf to bottom frame (Th. G–H1)
- 3/2 Blue scratch on right frame near bottom (Th. H6)
- 8/7 Small break in frame opposite last "E" in "CONFERENCE"
- 14/6 Fine scratch from ear right across neck (Th. E4)
- 15/8 Blue blob in bottom right corner (Th. H6)
- 18/1 Blue spot below "A" of "POSTAGE"

Sheet Details

Sheet size: 240 (12×20). Single-pane reel-fed

Sheet markings:

Cylinder number: Opposite R. 18/1

Guide holes: Six. Opposite rows 1 and 7/8 at both sides and also boxed opposite rows 14/15 at both sides

Marginal arrows:

"V" shaped, hand-engraved at top and bottom of sheet
"W" shaped, etched in photogravure at both sides

Marginal rule: At bottom of sheet

Imprimaturs from the NPM or BPMA

No. W8 imperforate, watermark Type W.**23**

Watermark upright	£1000
do. with "Broken wreath" R. 2/6	£1500
do. with "Partial double frame line" R.17/3	£1500
cylinder 2 block of six	£7000

Quantity Sold: 10,472,160

Withdrawn: 13.10.57

1958 Sixth British Empire and Commonwealth Games

Type **W9.** Welsh Dragon

(Des. Reynolds Stone)

Type **W10.** Flag and Games Emblem

(Des. W. H. Brown)

Type **W11.** Welsh Dragon

(Des. Pat Keely)

A

1958 (18 July). **Sixth British Empire and Commonwealth Games** Types **W9/W11**. Watermark St Edward's Crown, Type W.**23**

The 1958 Empire and Commonwealth Games were held at Cardiff.

W9 =SG 567		Mint	Used
3d.	deep lilac	10	10
a.	Short scale (Cyl. 2 Dot, R. 1/1)	40·00	
b.	Shoulder flaw (Cyl. 2 Dot, R. 12/2)	40·00	
c.	Shoulder flaw retouched	40·00	
d.	Body flaw. State 1 (Cyl. 2 Dot, R. 20/3)	40·00	
da.	Body flaw. State 2	40·00	
e.	Body flaw. State 3	40·00	
f.	Retouched face (Cyl. 7 Dot, R. 10/6)	40·00	
g.	"H" flaw (Cyl. 7 Dot, R. 11/2)	45·00	
h.	"H" flaw retouched	40·00	
s.	"SPECIMEN", Type A	65·00	
W10 =SG 568			
6d.	reddish purple	30	30
s.	"SPECIMEN", Type A	65·00	
W11 =SG 569			
1s.3d.	green	1·00	1·00
s.	"SPECIMEN" Type A	65·00	
First Day Cover (W9/W11)			75·00

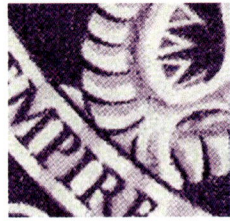

Normal 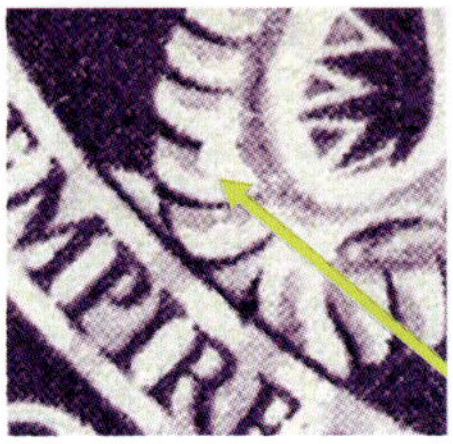   W9a

Part of the shading is missing on the scale near "M" of "EMPIRE".

W9b    W9c

White flaw on shading of dragon's body above shoulder. Later retouched with an irregular pattern of dots.

W9 State 1    W9d State 2

W9e State 3

Flaw on body above second "E" of "EMPIRE". This is a progressive flaw. Initially normal, the first stage showed the faintest outline of the flaw. State II shows the flaw solid and state III with a dark outline and pale centre.

W9f

The retouches across the Queen's cheek and below the chin are quite marked on Cyl. 7 dot, R. 10/6 but there are other minor retouches in this position in stamp No. 6 in rows 2 to 13.

Sixth British Empire and Commonwealth Games **1958**

W

W9g   W9h

White flaw crossing line behind dragon's left foreleg shows as a letter "H". After retouching there is a light vertical line across the flaw.

Imprimaturs from the NPM or BPMA
Nos. W9/W11 imperforate, watermark Type W.**23**

Watermark upright (set of 3)	£3000
3d. cylinder 2. block of six	£7000
6d. cylinder 6 block of six	£7000
1s.3d. cylinder 3 block of six	£7000

Quantities Sold:

3d.	320,400,000
6d.	28,595,880
1s.3d.	9,870,000

Cylinder Numbers (Blocks of Six)
Perforation Type A (E/I)

	Cylinder No.	No dot	Dot
3d.	2	1·50	1·50
	7	3·00	3·00
6d.	6	4·00	4·00
1s.3d.	3	8·50	8·50

Minor Constant Flaws

3d. Cyl. 2 no dot
- 13/1 Dark diagonal line across last two fins of dragon's tail; later the upper line was touched out (Th. F–G9)
- 19/3 Dots to left of right stroke of "H" in "BRITISH" (Th. D2)

3d. Cyl. 7 no dot
- 8/4 White spot on "M" in "EMPIRE"; later retouched (Th. E2)

3d. Cyl. 7 dot
- 3/4 White flaw on fin of dragon's tail above "E" of "COMMONWEALTH" (Th. F8)
- 4/5 Break in left frame by top of 3 (Th. E1)
- 20/3 White flaw on dragon's ankle above "N" of "COMMONWEALTH" (Th. F7)

6d. Cyl. 6 no dot
- 18/6 Dot between "O" and "N" of "COMMONWEALTH" (Th. A6)

6d. Cyl. 6 dot
- 10/1 "BRI" thicker than normal and retouch under left corner of flag (Th. G3)
- 11/1 "IRE" thicker than normal
- 16/1 "IR" thicker than normal
- 20/3 Dent in bottom frame below Queen (Th. H10–11)

1s.3d. Cyl. 3 no dot
- 12/3 Retouched background above "R". of "EMPIRE" (Th. G5)

1s.3d. Cyl. 3 dot
- 16–19/5 Vertical scratch of varying length in left-hand margin, petering out in rows 18/19

Sheet Details
 Sheet size: 120 (6×20). Double-pane reel-fed

Sheet markings:

Cylinder numbers: Opposite R. 18/1

Guide holes: Boxed opposite rows 14/15, at left (no dot) or right (dot)

Marginal arrows:
"V" shaped, hand-engraved at top and bottom of sheet
"W" shaped, photo-etched at both sides
In the early printings of the 6d. the arrow was omitted in the right margin on the no dot pane, and in the left margin on the dot pane. Later they were inserted by hand-engraving and appear quite rough

Marginal rule: At bottom of sheet

W 1960 Tercentenary of Establishment of General Letter Office.

W24

Crowns Watermark
The Multiple Crowns watermark, Type W.**24**, was used for all the following special issues up to the 1967 Wild Flowers issue.

Type **W12**.
Postboy of 1660
(Des. Reynolds Stone)

Type **W13**.
Posthorn of 1660
(Des. Faith Jaques)

1960 (7 July). **Tercentenary of Establishment of General Letter Office.** Types **W12/W13**. The watermark is sideways on the 1s.3d.

The Charles II Act of 1660 establishing the GPO legally settled the Post Office and was the first of a long series of laws for the regulation of postal matters.

W12 =SG 619		Mint	Used
3d.	deep lilac	20	20
a.	Broken mane (Cyl. 1 No dot, R. 17/2)	70·00	
b.	Face scratch (Cyl. 1 Dot, R. 17/3)	40·00	
W13 =SG 620			
1s.3d.	green	1·60	1·75
First Day Cover (W12/W13)			50·00

W12a

W12b
Scratch extends from eye to hair

Cylinder Numbers (Blocks of Six)
Perforation Type A (E/1)

	Cylinder No.	No dot	Dot
3d.	1	4·50	4·50

Perforation Type B (P/I)

1s.3d.	1	25·00	

Perforation Type C (P/E)

1s.3d.	1	25·00	

For Types B and C the 1s.3d is with sheet orientated showing head to right.

Minor Constant Flaws
3d. Cyl. 1 no dot

1/2	White dot in bottom of large "C" (Th. B1)
10/5	White notch in bottom frame below "r" of "Letter" (Th. H7)
13/1	"r" of "Letter" weak (Th. G7)
15/6	White patch on left foreleg of horse (Th. E5)

3d. Cyl. 1 dot

11/6	White dot in hair near top of ear (Th. D12)
20/5	White nick in back of boy (Th. D4)

1s.3d. Cyl. 1 no dot

1/18	White bulge inside "0" of "1960" (Th. E7)
2/20	White bulge on stem of acorn under horn (Th. L3)
5/19	White spot in centre of leaf on right of portrait (Th. G6)
6/5	White dot at junction of two acorns under Queen's shoulder (Th. G5)

Sheet Details
Sheet sizes:
   3d. 120 (6×20). Double-pane reel-fed;
   1s.3d. 120 (20×6). Single-pane reel-fed

Sheet markings:
Cylinder numbers:
   3d. opposite R. 18/1;
   1s.3d. opposite R. 4/1

Guide holes:
   3d. opposite rows 14/15, at left (no dot) or right (dot)
   1s.3d. Six. Above and below vertical rows 1, 7/8 and boxed above and below 14/15

Marginal arrows (hand-engraved):
   3d. "V" shaped at top and bottom of sheet; "W" shaped on both sides
   1s.3d. "V" shaped on both sides: "W" shaped at top and bottom of sheet.

Marginal rule: 3d. at bottom of sheet and 1s.3d. at right-hand side

Imprimaturs from the NPM or BPMA
Nos. W12/W13 imperforate, watermark Type W.**24**

Watermark upright (3d.) or sideways (1s.3d.) (set of 2)	£2000
3d. "Face scratch" flaw R. 17/3	£1500
3d. cylinder 1. block of six	£7000
1s.3d. cylinder 1 block of six	£7000

Quantities Sold:
   3d.   143,390,520
   1s.3d.   6,090,840

Withdrawn: 31.12.60

162

First Anniversary of European Postal and Telecommunications Conference 1960

Chalk-surfaced paper
All the following special issues are on chalk-surfaced paper, unless otherwise stated.

Type **W14**. Conference Emblem

Type **W15**. Conference Emblem

(Des. Reynolds Stone, emblem by P. Rahikainen)

1960 *(19 September).* **First Anniversary of European Postal and Telecommunications Conference** Types **W14/W15**

Celebrating the first Anniversary of the Conference of European Postal and Telecommunications Administrations.

W14 = S.G.621		Mint	Used
6d.	bronze-green and purple	1·00	20
	a. Broken diadem (R. 1/2)	35.00	
	b. Blurred "E" (R. 13/5)	35.00	

W15 =SG 622			
1s.6d.	brown and blue	6·00	2·25
	a. Broken diadem (R. 1/2)	40·00	
	b. Major retouch (R. 9/2)	40·00	
	c. Blurred "E" (R. 13/5)	25·00	
First Day Cover (W14/W15)			50·00

Printing Screen. Nos. W14/W15 were the last photogravure commemoratives from Harrisons to utilise the 200-line screen. On the 1s.6d. a 200-line screen was used for the portrait and the new 250-line version for the background.

Miniature Sheets

On the occasion of the Eurostamp–1962 London Stamp Exhibition, organised with the help of the Council of Europe, a miniature sheet, size 114×124 mm, was produced comprising three each of Nos. W14/W15 *se-tenant* in a block of six (2×3) printed in grey-blue, imperforate and surrounded by a brown frame and inscriptions in black on white unwatermarked gummed paper. The stamps were printed by Harrison & Sons in photogravure and the rest of the sheet was printed by Wm. Clowes & Sons by letterpress. The sheet had no franking value.

A similar sheet exists, size 110×125 mm, but with the stamps printed in black and surrounded by a green frame and inscription giving details of the issue in red. The stamps were printed in photogravure and the rest of the sheet in letterpress by Harrison & Sons. The sheet had no franking value.

W14/W15a

W14b, W15c

W15b

Cylinder Numbers (Blocks of Four)

Cylinder Nos.	Perforation Type B (E/P)	
	No dot	Dot
6d. 1 (purple)–1A (green)	6·00	
1s.6d. 2 (blue) –1A (brown)	30·00	

	Perforation Type C (I/P)	
	No dot	Dot
6d. 1 (purple) – 1A (green)	6·00	
1s.6d. 2 (blue) – 1A (brown)	30·00	

The same cylinder 1A was used for both values.

Minor Constant Flaws

6d. Cyls. 1–1A no dot

- 1/4 Pale purple spots in bottom of oval and below bottom frame (Th. G9–10 and H10)
- 6/2 Two short lines in scroll above "T" of "TELECOMMUNICATIONS" (Th. E2)
- 9/3 Small coloured line in scroll above "E" of "EUROPEAN" (Th. B1)
- 12/2 Dot in "M" of "ADMINISTRATION"
- 19/1 Vertical scratch left of scroll containing "EUROPEAN" (Th. B–D1)
- 20/5 Two scratches in scroll left of "C" of "CONFERENCE" (Th. A12)

1s.6d. Cyls. 2–1A no dot

- 10/4 Retouch to spine of "P" of "EUROPA"
- 12/2 Dot in "M" of "ADMINISTRATION"
- 17/4 Dotted retouch above "CO" (Th. F4)
- 18/5 Retouch in background above first "M" of "TELECOMMUNICATIONS"

Sheet Details

Sheet size: 120 (6×20). Single-pane reel-fed

Sheet markings:

Cylinder numbers: Bottom margin below R. 20/5

Guide holes: Opposite rows 1 and 7/8, at both sides and boxed opposite rows 14/15, at both sides

Marginal arrows (hand-engraved):

"V" shaped at top and bottom

"W" shaped at both sides

Marginal rule: At bottom of sheet

Colour register marks: Opposite rows 2 and 19 at both sides

Imprimaturs from the NPM or BPMA

Nos. W14/W15 imperforate, watermark Type W.**24**

Watermark upright (set of 2)	£2000
6d. "Broken diadem" R. 1/2	£1500
6d. "Blurred E" R. 13/5	£1500
6d. cylinder 1, 1A block of four	£5000
1s.6d. "Major retouch" R. 9/2	£1500
1s.6d. cylinder 2, 1A block of four	£5000

W 1961 *Post Office Savings Bank Centenary*

Quantities Printed:

6d.	16,990,320
1s.6d.	7,682,520

Withdrawn: 31.12.60, but placed on sale again during Stampex exhibition in March 1961

Type **W16**. Thrift Plant
(Timson printing)
(Des. Peter Gauld)

Type **W17**. Growth of Savings
(Timson printing)
(Des. Michael Goaman)

Type **W18**. Thrift Plant
(Des. Michael Goaman)

1961 *(28 August)*. **Post Office Savings Bank Centenary**
Types **W16/W20** The watermark is sideways on the 2½d.

To mark the centenary of the establishment of the PO Savings Bank.

Timson

Thrissell

Timson

Thrissell

A. TIMSON Machine
2½d. Cyls. 1E–1F no dot. Deeply shaded portrait (dull black)
3d. Cyls. 3D–3E no dot. Sharp portrait with good contrast and bright highlights

W16 =SG 623A		Mint	Used
2½d.	dull black and red	10	10
a.	Dull black (Queen's Head) omitted	—	
b.	Forehead retouch (R. 4/19)	40·00	

W17 =SG 624A			
3d.	orange-brown and violet	10	10
a.	orange-brown omitted	£600	
b.	Perf. through right sheet margin	35·00	38·00
ba.	Do. and orange-brown omitted	£1250	
c.	Extension hole in top or bottom sheet margin	35·00	
ca.	No extension hole in left margin	35·00	
d.	Nick in "S" (R. 9/3)	35·00	
e.	Nick retouched	30·00	

W18 =SG 625A			
1s.6d.	red and blue	1·00	1.20
a.	Phantom oval in light blue (R. 19/3)	35·00	

First Day Cover (W16/W18)		45·00

* No. W16a dull black omitted. The listing is for certificated examples without the grey ghosting present on some stamps.

B. THRISSELL Machine
2½d. Cyls. 1D–1B no dot or dot. Lighter portrait (grey-black)
3d. Cyls. 3C–3B no dot or dot. Dull portrait, lacking in contrast

W19 =SG 623B		Mint	Used
2½d.	grey-black and red	1·50	1·50

W20 =SG 624B			
3d.	orange-brown and violet	30	30
a.	Orange-brown omitted	£1750	
b.	Notch in flower (No dot, R. 7/1)	35·00	
c.	Notch in leaf (No dot, R. 14/4)	35·00	

A very small quantity of all values was pre-released at the Chorley, Lancs., PO on 21 August, 1961.

W16b

W17d
Nick in "S"

W17e
Nick filled in but centre of "S" is narrower

Post Office Savings Bank Centenary 1961 W

3d. Cyls. 3C–3B no dot
- 1/4 Additional serif at top of "K" of "BANK"
- 3/3 Notch in upper right leaf on lowest right-hand branch of tree (Th. E7)
- 4/2 Retouch on neck below earring (Th. E10)
- 4/6 Dot in "B" of "BANK"
- 7/3 Retouch above necklace (Th. E10)

Sheet Details

Sheet sizes:

	Timson	Thrissell
2½d.	120 (20×6) Single-pane reel-fed	Double-pane reel-fed
3d.	120 (6×20) Single-pane reel-fed	Double-pane reel-fed
1s.6d.	120 (6×20) Single-pane reel-fed	

Sheet markings:
Cylinder numbers:

2½d.	Bottom margin below R. 6/19	Bottom margin below R. 6/19
3d.	Bottom margin below R. 20/5	Bottom margin below R. 20/2 and R. 20/5
1s.6d.	As 3d.	

Guide holes:

2½d.	Above and below vertical rows 1, 7/8 and (boxed) 14/15	Below vertical rows 14/15 (no dot) or above (dot), boxed
3d.	Opposite rows 1, 7/8 and (boxed) 14/15, both sides	Opposite rows 14/15, at left (no dot) or right (dot), boxed
1s.6d.	As 3d.	

Marginal arrows (hand-engraved):

2½d.	"V" shaped on both sides; "W" shaped at top and bottom	As Timson
3d.	"V" shaped, all round	"V" shaped, at top and bottom; "W" shaped at both sides
1s.6d.	"V" shaped, at top and bottom; "W" shaped, at both sides	

Marginal rules:

2½d.	At right-hand side	As Timson
3d.	At bottom	As Timson
1s.6d.	At bottom	

Colour register marks:

2½d.	Above and below vertical rows 2/3 and 17/18	Below vertical rows 2/3 and 17/18 (no dot) or above (dot)
3d.	Opposite rows 3/4 and 17/18 at both sides	Opposite rows 3/4 and 17/18 at left (no dot) or right (dot)
1s.6d.	Opposite rows 2/3 and 18/19 at left (no dot) or right (dot)	

W18a

W20b   W17Ac

Cylinder Numbers (Blocks of Four)

A. Timson printings: Single-pane cylinders only (no dot). Nos. W16/18

	Perforation types		
Cylinder No.	B	C	F(L)
2½d. 1E (black)–1F (red)*	1·50 (P/I)	1·50 (P/E)	†
3d. 3D (violet)–3E (brown)	1·50 (E/P)	1·50 (I/P)	70·00 (P/E)
1s.6d. 2E (blue)–2C (red)	6·00 (E/P)	6·00 (I/P)	†

* The black number is superimposed over the red.

B. Thrissell printings: Double-pane cylinders. Nos. W19/W20

	Perforation Type A	
Cylinder Nos.	No dot	Dot
2½d. 1D (black)–1B (red)	7·50 (I/E)	7·50 (I/E)
3d. 3C (violet)–3B (brown)	5·50 (E/1)	2·00 (E/I)

In the 2½d. dot pane the dot was omitted in error after 1B.

In the 3d. no dot pane "3E" was wrongly inserted and the "C" was engraved over the "E".

Two blocks of four are needed to show both cylinders in the 3d. no dot Thrissell printing as the numbers are below R. 20/2 and R. 20/5 on the bottom margin.

For Types B and C the 2½d. is with sheet orientated showing head to right.

Minor Constant Flaws

2½d. Cyls. 1E–1F no dot
- 1/13 Two white dots on right curve below last "S" of "SAVINGS"
- 1/16 Two black dots right of Queen's left eye (Th. D4)
- 1/17 State I. Dark red patch left of top thrift flower (Th. H3)
State II. Later printings show whitish patch
- 2/3 White horizontal line from Queen's hair to "OF" of "OFFICE" (Th. C3)
- 5/3 White spot on top of right arm of V of SAVINGS

3d. Cyls. 3D–3E no dot
- 8/1 Diagonal retouch across Queen's cheek from right of her left eye to nose (Th. D9–10)
- 11/5 Brown spot on squirrel's neck (Th. D5)
- 17/1 Retouch on Queen's chin (Th. E9)
- 17/2 Retouch on neck (Th. E10)
- 19/2 Retouch above necklace (Th. E–F10)
- 20/1 Vertical violet line on branch in bottom right corner (Th. FG13)

165

W 1961 European Postal and Telecommunications (CEPT) Conference

Colour designations (usually trimmed off):
- **2½d.** None
- **3d.** BROWN opposite row 11 and BLUE opposite row 12, right margin, dot pane
- **1s.6d.** RED opposite row 15 and BLUE opposite row 16, right margin

In the case of marginal copies the differences in sheet markings, in conjunction with the different types of perforators used, provide helpful clues for identifying the printing machine used.
Autotron markings were engraved on the Thrissell cylinders during the printing run.

Imprimaturs from the NPM or BPMA
Nos. W16/W18 imperforate, watermark Type W.**24**

Watermark upright (3d., 1s.6d.) or sideways (2½d.) (set of 3)	£3000
2½d. "forehead retouch" R. 4/19	£1500
2½d. cylinder 1E, 1F block of four	£5000
3d. cylinder 3D, 3F block of four	£5000
1s.6d. cylinder 2E, 2C block of four	£5000

Quantities Sold:
2½d.	24,720,000
3d.	114,360,000
1s.6d.	7,560,000

Type **W21.** CEPT Emblem

Type **W22.** Doves and Emblem

Type **W23.** Doves and Emblem

(All values des. Michael Goaman, doves by T. Kurpeschoek)

1961 (18 September). **European Postal and Telecommunications (CEPT) Conference** Types W21/W23

Representatives of 19 countries met at Torquay on 11 September for the Second Anniversary Conference of the European Postal and Telecommunications Administrations. These were the first stamps of Great Britain to be printed in three colours

W21 =SG 626	Mint	Used
2d. orange, pink and brown	10	10
a. Orange omitted	£15000	
b. White ear (Dot, R. 11/2)	35·00	

W22 =SG 627		
4d. buff, mauve and ultramarine	10	10

W23 =SG 628	Mint	Used
10d. turquoise, pale green and Prussian blue	20	20
a. Pale green omitted	£24000	
b. Turquoise omitted	£7250	

First Day Cover (W21/W63)		4·00

Only the lower half of 4d. no dot sheets were issued to Post Offices.

W21b

Perforation Type A (E/I)

Cylinder Numbers (Blocks of Four)

		Perforation Type A (E/I)	
Cylinder Nos.		No dot	Dot
2d. 1A (brown)–1B (orange)1C (pink)		1·50	1·50
4d. 2E (ultramarine)–2B (buff)–2C (mauve)		1·50	1·50
10d. 3G (Prussian blue)–3D (green)–3A (turquoise)		2·50	2·50

The panes were transposed, the dot being on the left and the no dot on the right. The 2d. was originally issued without dots on either pane, but dots were subsequently added to the left-hand pane.

Minor Constant Flaws
2d. Cyls. 1A–1B–1C no dot
- 6/4 Pale spot on neck below necklace (Th. F10)
- 17/4 Dot in lower right pink horn (Th. F12)
- 18/1 Diagonal dark brown patch across Queen's cheek. Later retouched (Th. E10)

2d. Cyls. 1A–1B–1C dot (pane originally issued without dots)
- 6/4 Small white dot to left of "P"
- 18/6 Hairline from right-hand frame to sheet margin (Th. E13–14)

4d. Cyls. 2E–2B–2C dot
- 5/3 Flaw at top right of "E"
- 12/6 Dark patch above diadem (Th. A8)
- 15/3 Flaw down Queen's forehead and nose (Th. C–D6)
- 17/6 Pale patch on cheek (Th. D7)

10d. Cyls. 3G–3D–3A no dot
- 4/6 White patch above Queen's right eye (Th. C10)
- 6/1 Pale patch to right of Queen's neck (Th. E12-13, F12-13)
- 10/3 White patch on Queen's forehead (Th. C10). Started during the run gradually becoming more prominent
- 15/5 Small white patch at top centre of Queen's forehead (Th. C10)

10d. Cyls. 3G–3D–3A dot
- 4/3 Break in loop of posthorn around "P" (Th. C7)
- 4/6 Notch in frame at top right (Th. A13)
- 14/2 Dark patch to right of lower right posthorn (Th. C8)

Sheet Details
Sheet size: 120 (6×20). Double-pane reel-fed

Sheet markings:

Cylinder numbers: Bottom margin below R. 20/5

Guide holes: Opposite rows 14/15, at left (dot) or right (no dot), boxed

Seventh Commonwealth Parliamentary Conference. **1961**   **W**

Marginal arrow (hand-engraved):
"V" shaped at top and bottom
"W" shaped at both sides

Marginal rule: At bottom of sheet

Colour register marks:
- **2d.** Opposite rows 2/3 and 17/18 at left (dot) or right (no dot)
- **4d.** Opposite rows 2/3 and 18/19 at left (dot) or right (no dot)
- **10d.** None

Autotron marks (solid):
- **2d.** Respectively brown, pink and orange opposite rows 18/20, at left (dot) or right (no dot)
- **4d.** Respectively ultramarine and mauve opposite rows 18/19, at left (dot) or right (no dot)
- **10d.** Respectively Prussian blue, green and turquoise opposite rows 18/20, at left (dot) or right (no dot)

Colour designations:
- **2d.** BROWN in right margin reading upwards opposite rows 14/13 (no dot)
- **4d.** YELLOW, MAUVE, BLUE respectively in right margin opposite rows 11/12, 12/13 and 13 (no dot)
- **10d.** None

Imprimaturs from the NPM or BPMA
Nos. W21/W23 imperforate, watermark Type W.**24**

Watermark upright (set of 3)	£3000
2d. cylinder 1A, 1B, 1C (no dot) block of four	£5000
4d. cylinder 2E, 2B, 2C (dot) block of four	£5000
10d. cylinder 3G, 3D, 3A (no dot) block of four	£5000

Quantities Sold:
2d.	47,530,920
4d.	7,614,480
10d.	5,427,780

Type **W24.** Hammer Beam Roof, Westminster Hall

Type **W25.** Palace of Westminster

(Des. Faith Jaques)

1961 *(25 September).* **Seventh Commonwealth Parliamentary Conference. Types W24/W25.**
The watermark is sideways on the 1s.3d.

The Empire Parliamentary Association was formed at the Coronation of King George V and in 1948 its name was changed to its present form.

W24 =SG 629	Mint	Used
6d. purple and gold	10	10
a. Gold omitted	£2200	

W25 =SG 630		
1s.3d. green and blue	1·20	1·20
a. Blue (Queen's head) omitted	£40000	

b. Green omitted

First Day Cover (W24/W25)	25·00

Cylinder Numbers (Blocks of Four)

	Perforation Types	
Cyl. Nos. (No dot)	Type B	Type C
6d. 1B (gold)–1D (purple)	1·50 (E/P)	1·50 (I/P)
1s.3d. 2A (green)–2B (blue)	7·50 (P/I)	7·50 (P/E)

For Types B and C the 1s.3d. is with sheet orientated showing head to right.

Minor Constant Flaws
6d. Cyls. 1B–1D no dot
- 3/4 Dot in middle bar of second "E" in "CONFERENCE"
- 5/5 Enlarged white patch in Queen's hair (Th. C7)
- 6/3 Two small retouches in neck above necklace (Th. F7–8)
- 10/3 Patch of retouching below crossed maces (Th. G5–6)

1s.3d. Cyls. 2A–2B no dot
- 5/4 White patch on Queen's forehead (Th. D4)
- 6/2 Small white vertical line on Queen's forehead (Th. C–D4)

Sheet Details
Sheet sizes:
- **6d.** 120 (6×20); Single-pane reel-feed
- **1s.3d.** 120 (20×6). Single-pane reel-fed

Sheet markings:

Cylinder numbers: Bottom margin below R. 20/5 (6d.) or 6/19 (1s.3d.)

Guide holes:
- **6d.** opposite rows 1 and 7/8, at both sides and boxed opposite rows 14/15, at both sides
- **1s.3d.** above and below vertical rows 1 and 7/8 and boxed above and below vertical rows 14/15

Marginal arrows (hand-engraved):
- **6d.** "V" shaped at top and bottom
  "W" shaped at both sides
- **1s.3d.** "V" shaped at both sides
  "W" shaped at top and bottom

Marginal rule: 6d. at bottom of sheet; 1s.3d. at right side

Colour register marks:
- **6d.** Opposite both sides of rows 2/3 and 18/19
- **1s.3d.** Above and below vertical rows 2/3 and 18/19

Imprimaturs from the NPM or BPMA
Nos. W24/W25 imperforate, watermark Type W.**24**

Watermark upright (6d.) or sideways (1s.3d.) (set of 2)	£2000
6d. cylinder 1B, 1D block of four	£5000
1s.3d. cylinder 2A, 2B block of four	£5000

Quantities Sold:
6d.	16,680,000
1s.3d.	5,760,000

W 1962 National Productivity Year.

Type **W26.** "Units of Productivity"

Type **W27.** "National Productivity"

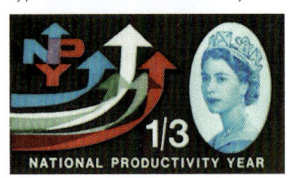

Type **W28.** "Unified Productivity"

(Des. David Gentleman)

The National Productivity Year issue was the first commemorative series to appear with phosphor bands and presents a number of other interesting facets:

The watermark on the 2½d. and 3d. is inverted for the reason explained in the General Notes to this section.

There were several printings of the low values which are characterised by their distinct shades and confirmed by different states of some of the flaws and varieties. It is believed that the second printing of the 2½d. comes from sheets numbered between about 439,000 and 450,000. Only the third printing was used for the phosphor stamps. There was considerable variation in the carmine-red during the printing and carmine-rose shades are quite common.

2½d. During the first printing both green cylinders were seriously damaged, hence the major repairs in the later printings.

3d. There were several printings of this value which fall into two shade groups. The violet cylinder 2A provided a number of minor flaws and was quickly replaced. It is believed that stamps from this cylinder were supplied only to Canterbury and Chelmsford.

1962 *(14 November)*. **National Productivity Year.**
The watermark is inverted on the 2½d. and 3d.
Types **W26/W28**

The stamps emphasised the need for greater productivity as an essential element in the continuing prosperity of Great Britain.

A. Ordinary

W26 =SG 631		Mint	Used
2½d.	(1) Myrtle-green and carmine-red	10	10
	(2) Deep green and bright carmine-red	25	15
	(3) Blackish olive and carmine-red	25	15
a.	Emblem and arrows retouch (No dot, R. 3/3) (2)	25·00	
b.	Ditto (3)	25·00	
c.	Arrow head retouch (No dot, R. 4/4) (2)	25·00	
d.	Ditto (3)	25·00	
e.	Retouches, arrows 2 and 6 (No dot, R. 4/5) (2)	25·00	
f.	Ditto (3)	25·00	
g.	White nose (Dot, R. 2/6) (1)	25·00	
h.	Neck retouch (Dot, R. 15/4) (1)	25·00	
i.	Ditto (2)	25·00	
j.	Ditto (3)	25·00	
k.	Smudged red centre cube (Dot R. 18/3) (2)	25·00	
l.	Ditto (3)	25·00	
m.	Arrow head retouch (Dot, R. 19/6) (2)	25·00	
n.	Ditto (3)	25·00	

W27 =SG 632			
3d.	(1) Light blue and violet	25	25
	(2) Light blue and deep bluish purple	30	30
a.	Light blue (Queen's head) omitted	£5750	
b.	Lake in Scotland (Cyls. 2A–2B Dot, R. 1/3	£150	
c.	Kent omitted (Cyls. 2C–2B No dot, R. 18/2)	70·00	
d.	Lake in Yorkshire (Cyls. 2C–2B Dot, R. 19/1)	35·00	
e.	Forehead line (Cyls. 2D–2B No dot, R. 17/6)	25·00	
f.	Ditto, removed	25·00	
g.	Ditto, retouched	25·00	

W28 =SG 633			
1s.3d. carmine, light blue and deep green		80	80
a. Light blue (Queen's head) omitted		£15000	

First Day Cover (W26/W28)	45·00

B. Phosphor

(2½d. has one band at left; others have three bands, all applied flexo.)

WP26 =SG 631p			
2½d. blackish olive and carmine-red		60	50
a.	Emblem and arrows retouch (No dot, R. 3/3)	25·00	
b.	Arrows head retouch (No dot, R. 4/4)	25·00	
c.	Retouches, arrows 2 and 6 (No dot, R. 4/5)	25·00	
d.	Neck retouch (Dot, R. 15/4)	25·00	
e.	Smudged red centre cube (Dot, R. 18/3)	25·00	
f.	Arrow head retouch (Dot, R. 19/6)	25·00	

WP27 =SG 632p			
3d. light blue and violet		1·50	80
a.	Left-hand band omitted		
b.	Narrow band at left or right (stamp with vert. margin)	5·00	
c.	Forehead line (Cyls. 2D-2B, No dot, R. 17/6)	25·00	
d.	Forehead line removed	25·00	

WP28 =SG 633p			
1s.3d. carmine, light blue and deep green		35·00	22·00
a. Narrow band at left or right (stamp with vert. margin)		50·00	

First Day Cover (W26/W28)	£125

About 60 2½d., 350 3d. and 20 1s.3d. were pre-released at a Lewisham post office, London, on 16 and 17 October, 1962.

National Productivity Year. 1962

2½d. Arrows numbered for easy identification of varieties and flaws

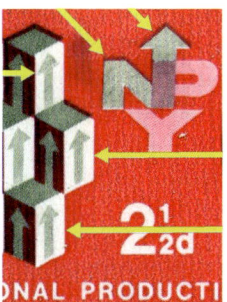

W26a/W26b, WP26a
"N" and arrowhead of emblem strongly shaded with diagonal cuts and dashes, also arrows 4, 10 and 14

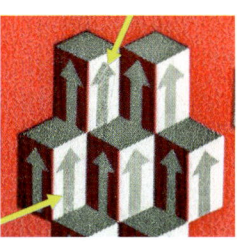

W26e/W26f, WP26c
In W26c/W26d, WP26b the arrowhead alone is retouched with diagonal lines and in W26m/W26n, WP 26f with irregular dots. Less marked retouches occur in the same area on dot cyl., R.19/2 and 19/4

W26g

W26h/W26j, WP26d

W27b

W27c

W27d

W27e, WP27c

W27f, WP27d

W27g

The original variety was a horizontal line from Queen's left eye to hair which was later removed, leaving a white gap and this was finally partly filled in by retouching

Cylinder Numbers (Blocks of Four)

(a) Ordinary

	Cylinder Nos.	Perforation Type A (E/I) No dot	Dot
2½d.	1D (red)–1B (green) (shade 1)	1·50	1·50
	1D–1B (shade 2)	2·50	15·00
	1D–1B–(shade 3)	2·50	15·00
3d.	2A (violet)–2B (blue)	40·00	40·00
	2C–2B	2·50	2·50
	2D–2B	3·50	3·50
1s.3d.	3C (carmine)–3B (blue)–3E (green)	5·00	

		No dot Type B (E/P)	Type C (I/P)
1s.3d.	3C (carmine)–3B (blue)–3E (green)	18·00	18·00

(b) Phosphor

		Perforation Type A (E/I) No dot	Dot
2½d.	1D (red)–1B (green) (shade 3)	4·25	8·00*
3d.	2D (violet)–2B (blue)	4·25	4·25
1s.3d.	3C (carmine)–3B (blue)–3E (green)	£150	†

Minor Constant Flaws

2½d. Cyls. 1D–1B no dot

1/2 Two small green dots right of arrow 2 (Th. B–C4) all shades, OP

3/2 Scratch through top of bottom right cube (Th. F–E4) all shades, OP

3/4 Minor retouches to face around mouth (Th. D–E10) shades 2/3, OP

5/1 White scratch below Queen's nose and through mouth (Th. D–E10) all shades, OP

17/5 Small retouch to cheek to right of mouth (Th. D10–11) all shades, OP

3d. Cyls. 2C–2B no dot

1/4 Retouch in Scotland (Th. C3), O

6/5 Dark patch above "R" of "PRODUCTIVITY" (Th. G6), O

13/5 Line of retouching above blue sea of Ireland (Th. C2), O

169

1962 National Productivity Year.

3d. Cyls. 2C–2B dot

7/1	Purple line across Solway Firth (Th. D3), O
15/6	Row of dots from Queen's left eye to hair (Th. C11), O

3d. Cyls. 2D–2B no dot

13/5	Lines of retouching in blue sea above Ireland (Th. C2), OP

3d. Cyls. 2D–2B dot

1/3	Retouch in Yorkshire (Th. D4), OP

1s.3d. Cyls. 3C–3B–3E no dot

3/4	White flaw at back of Queen's hair (Th. D12), OP
6/2	Retouch on tail of large blue arrow (Th. D2), OP
13/4	White flaw left of earring (Th. E11), OP

Sheet Details

Sheet size: 120 (6×20)

- **2½d., 3d.** Double-pane reel-fed on a Timson machine
- **1s.3d.** Single-pane reel-fed on a new Thrissell machine capable of using five colours

Sheet markings:

Cylinder numbers: Bottom row below R. 20/5

Guide holes:
- **2½d., 3d.** Opposite rows 14/15 (boxed), at left (no dot) or right (dot)
- **1s.3d.** Opposite rows 1 and 7/8, at both sides and boxed opposite rows 14/15, at both sides

Marginal arrows (photo-etched):
"W" shaped at top, bottom and sides

Marginal rule: At bottom of sheet

Colour register marks:
- **2½d., 3d.** Opposite rows 2/3 and 18/19, at left (no dot) or right (dot)
- **1s.3d.** Opposite rows 2/3 and 18/19, at both sides

Autotron marks (stippled):
- **2½d., 3d.** Bottom margin in various positions
- **1s.3d.** Respectively red, green, blue, green, red below vertical rows 4/6

Colour designations (usually trimmed off):
- **2½d.** G GREY (not green) opposite rows 8/9 and G RED opposite row 13, right margin on the dot cylinder
- **3d.** G BLUE opposite rows 8/9 and G MAUVE (Cyl. 2C) opposite row 13 or G PURPLE (Cyl. 2D) opposite rows 6/7, right margin on the dot cylinder
- **1s.3d.** G BLUE opposite row 9 and G GREEN opposite rows 12/3, left margin

Traffic lights (boxed):
- **2½d.** Green, red opposite R. 20/6 dot pane
- **3d.** Blue, violet opposite R. 20/6 dot pane
- **1s.3d.** Blue, red, green boxed opposite R. 20/6

Imprimaturs from the NPM or BPMA

A. Ordinary
Nos. W26/W28 imperforate, watermark Type W.**24**

Watermark upright (set of 3)	£3000
2½d. "Emblems + arrow retouch" R. 3/5	£1500
2½d. cylinder 1D, 1B (no dot) block of four	£5000
3d. "Forehead line" flaw R. 17/6	£1500
3d. cylinder 2D, 2B (no dot) block of four	£5000
1s.3d. cylinder 3B, 3C, 3E block of four	£5000

B. Phosphor
Nos. WP26/WP28 imperforate, watermark Type W.**24**

Watermark upright (set of 3)	£3000
2½d. "Arrows + emblems retouch" R. 3/3	£1500
2½d. "Arrow head retouch" R. 4/4	£1500
2½d. cylinder 1D, 1B (no dot) block of four	£5000
3d. "Forehead line" flaw R. 17/6	£1500
3d. cylinder 2D, 2B (no dot) block of four	£5000
1s.3d. cylinder 3C, 3B, 3E block of four	£5000

Quantities Sold:

	Ordinary	Phosphor
2½d.	99,240,000	7,320,090
3d.	182,580,000	13,320,000
1s.3d.	8,832,000	1,320,000

Of the 2½d. ordinary it is estimated that about 62 million came from the first printing. 3 million from the second printing and 34 million from the third printing

Freedom from Hunger. 1963

Type W29. Campaign Emblem and Family

Type W30. Children of Three Races

(Des. Michael Goaman)

1963 *(21 March).* **Freedom from Hunger.** Types **W29/W30**
The watermark is inverted.

The stamps were part of a world-wide co-operative effort to focus attention on the problem of hunger and malnutrition.

A. Ordinary

W29 =SG 634	Mint	Used
2½d. crimson and pink	10	10
a. Line through "MPA" (Cyls. 1D–1H Dot, R. 7/2)	35·00	
b. Broken "R" in "FREEDOM" (Cyls. 1D–1H No dot, R. 16/2)	35·00	

W30 =SG 635		
1s.3d. bistre-brown and yellow	1·00	1·00
First Day Cover (W29/W30)		25·00

B. Phosphor (applied flexo.)

WP29 =SG 634p		
2½d. One band	3·00	1·20
a. Line through "MPA" (Cyls. 1D–1H Dot, R. 7/2)	35·00	
b. Broken "R" in "FREEDOM" (Cyls. 1D–1H No dot, R. 16/2)	35·00	

WP30 =SG 635p		
1s.3d. Three bands	30·00	23·00
a. Vert. pair, one stamp with phosphor omitted, the other with short bands		
b. Narrow band at left or right (stamp with vert. margin.)	50·00	
c. Two bands only		

First Day Cover (WP29/WP30)	40·00

The 2½d. value was pre-released at Chipping Norton on 20 March 1963.

W29a, WP29a
An unsuccessful attempt was made to touch this out

W29b, WP29b

Cylinder Numbers (Blocks of Four)

	Perforation Type A (E/I)	
(a) Ordinary Cylinder Nos.	No dot	Dot
2½d. 1D (pink)–IG (crimson)	60·00	60·00
1D–1H	2·50	2·50
1s.3d. 2E (yellow)2G (brown)	8·00	8·00
(b) Phosphor		
2½d. 1D (pink)–1H (crimson)	15·00	15·00
1s.3d. 2E (yellow)–2G (brown)	£150	£150

Only the lower halves of sheets from the 2½d. 1D–1G cylinders were released.

In the 1s.3d. the cylinder numbers are reversed, the dot pane being on the left and the no dot pane on the right of the printer's double-pane sheet.

The 1s.3d. exists showing a single extension hole for alternate horizontal rows in the left margin. Cylinder blocks from the right-hand side of the sheets are identical to those from perforator Type A.

Minor Constant Flaws

2½d. Cyls. 1D–1H no dot
9/6 Dot in upper part of second "A" of "CAMPAIGN", OP
15/2 Retouch from base of portrait to "M" of "CAMPAIGN" (Th. E11 and F12–13), OP

2½d. Cyls. 1D–1H dot
8/1 and 7/1 Hairline extends from under "GN" on 8/1 to "CAMPAIGN" on 7/1, OP
19/1 Retouch on left cheek and jawbone (Th. D10), OP

1s.3d. Cyls. 2E–2G no dot
1/2 Small white line in extreme right wheatsheaf (Th. C6), OP

Sheet Details

Sheet size: 120 (6×20). Double-pane reel-fed

Sheet markings:

Cylinder numbers: Bottom row below R. 20/5

Guide holes:
2½d. Opposite rows 14/15 (boxed), at left (no dot) or right (dot)
1s.3d. Opposite rows 14/15 (boxed), at left (dot) or right (no dot)

Marginal arrows (photo-etched):
"W" shaped at top, bottom and sides

Marginal rule: At bottom of sheet

Colour register marks:
2½d. Opposite rows 2/3 and 18/19, at left (no dot) or right (dot)
1s.3d. Opposite rows 2/3 and 18/19, at left (dot) or right (no dot)

Autotron marks (stippled):
2½d. Below vertical rows 2/3, no dot pane
1s.3d. Below vertical rows 2/3, dot pane

Colour designation:
1s.3d. G2 in brown opposite row 7 at right, no dot, on wide cut margins

Traffic lights (boxed):
2½d. Red, pink opposite R. 20/6, dot pane
1s.3d. Brown, yellow opposite R. 20/6, no dot pane

Imprimaturs from the NPM or BPMA

A. Ordinary
Nos. W29/30 imperforate, watermark Type W.**24**

Watermark upright (set of 2)	£2000
2½d. "Line through MPA" R. 7/2	£1500
2½d. cylinder 1D, 1H (dot) block of four	£5000
1s.3d. cylinder 2E, 2G, (no dot) block of four	£5000

B. Phosphor
Nos. WP29/30 imperforate, watermark Type W.**24**

W 1963 *Paris Postal Conference Centenary.*

Watermark upright (set of 2)	£2000
2½d. "Line through MPA" R.7/2	£1500
2½d. cylinder 1D, 1H (dot) block of four	£5000
1s.3d. cylinder 2E, 2G, (no dot) block of four	£5000

Quantities Sold:	Ordinary	Phosphor
2½d.	97,050,000	2,784,920
1s.3d.	9,009,000	624,960

Withdrawn: 1.5.64

Type **W31**.
"1863 Paris Postal Conference Centenary"

(Des. Reynolds Stone)

1963 *(7 May).* **Paris Postal Conference Centenary.**
Type **W31** The watermark is inverted

A postal conference was held in Paris to commemorate the centenary of the first international meeting of postal authorities held in 1863.

A. Ordinary
W31 =SG 636

		Mint	Used
6d.	green and mauve	20	20
a.	Green omitted	£5500	
b.	White spot in frame line (No dot, R. 19/3)		35·00

First Day Cover (W31)		7·50

B. Phosphor (applied flexo.)
WP31 =SG 636p

		Mint	Used
6d.	Three bands	3·00	2·75
a.	Pair, with and without phosphor	70·00	
b.	Horiz. pair; one stamp without phosphor, the other with two bands	85·00	
c.	Narrow band at left or right (stamp with vert. margin)	8·00	
d.	White spot in frame line (No dot, R. 19/3)		35·00

First Day Cover (WP31)		30·00

W31b, WP31d

Cylinder Numbers (Blocks of Four)

	Perforation Type A (E/I)	
Cylinder Nos.	No dot	Dot
6d. 2A (mauve)–1B (green)		
Ordinary	2·50	2·50
6d. 2A–1B Phosphor	15·00	15·00

The panes were reversed, the dot being on the left and the no dot on the right.

Minor Constant Flaws
6d. Cyls. 2A–1B no dot
- 1/1   Flaw in oval frame at 11 o'clock (Th. B9) and lack of definition in top right rose (Th. B13), OP
- 14/6 First "N" of "CONFERENCE" appears white, OP
- 19/5 Dot under "R" of "CENTENARY", OP
- 20/5 White spot on ivy stem below first "E" of "CONFERENCE" and coloured dot in right frame near top (Th. A13), OP

6d. Cyls. 2A–1B dot
- 14/2 White spot in "R" of "CONFERENCE", OP

Sheet Details
Sheet size: 120 (6×20). Double-pane reel-fed
Sheet markings:
Cylinder numbers: Below R. 20/5
Guide holes: Opposite row 15 (boxed), at left (dot) or right (no dot)
Marginal arrows (photo-etched):
"W" shaped at top, bottom and sides
Marginal rule: At bottom of sheet
Colour register marks: Opposite rows 2/3 and 18/19, at left (dot) or right (no dot)
Autotron marks (stippled): Bottom margin, dot pane
Traffic lights (boxed): Green, mauve opposite R. 20/6, no dot pane

Imprimaturs from the NPM or BPMA

A. Ordinary
No. W31 imperforate, watermark Type W.**24**

Watermark upright	£1000
6d. "White spot in frame line" R. 19/3	£1500
6d. cylinder 2A, 1B (no dot) block of four	£5000

B. Phosphor
No. WP31 imperforate, watermark Type W.**24**

Watermark upright	£1000
6d. cylinder 2A, 1B (dot) block of four	£5000

Quantities Sold: Ordinary 18,536,400; phosphor 1,430,800

Withdrawn: 1.6.64

National Nature Week. 1963

Type **W32.** Posy of Flowers

(Des. Stanley Scott)

Type **W33.** Woodland Life

(Des. Michael Goaman)

1963 *(16 May).* **National Nature Week.** Types **W32/W33**

The Council for Nature organised a Nature Week from 18–25 May in order to draw attention to the natural history movement and the importance of wildlife conservation.
The 4½d. value was the first stamp of Great Britain to be printed in five colours.

A. Ordinary

W32	=SG 637	Mint	Used
3d.	yellow, green, brown and black	10	10
a.	Caterpillar flaw (Dot, R. 3/2)	75·00	
ab.	Retouched	60·00	
W33	**=SG 638**		
4½d.	black, blue, yellow, magenta and brown-red	15	15
a.	Nose retouch (Cyl. 2E, R. 14/4)	25·00	

First Day Cover (W32/W33)			12·00

B. Phosphor

WP32	**=SG 637p**		
3d.	Three bands, applied photo.	30	30
a.	Narrow band at left or right (stamp with vert. margin)	2·00	
b.	Caterpillar flaw (Dot, R. 3/2)	75·00	
ba.	Retouched	60·00	
WP33	**=SG 638p**		
4½d.	Three bands, applied flexo.	1·40	1·40
a.	Narrow band at left or right (stamp with vert. margin)	4·00	
b.	Nose retouch (Cyl. 2E. No dot, R. 14/4)	25·00	
c.	Error. Two bands		

First Day Cover (WP32/WP33)	35·00

No. W32 is known pre-released on 15 May 1963 at Highbury, London.

W32a, WP32b
Several states exist, later retouched

W33a, WP33b

Cylinder Numbers (Blocks of Six)

		Perforation Type A (E/I)	
(a) Ordinary	Cylinder Nos.	No dot	Dot
3d.	1A (black)–3B (brown)–1C (green)–1D (yellow)	2·00	2·00

		Rows 12/13	Rows 18/19
4½d.	1A (brown-red)–1B (yellow)–1C (magenta)–1D (blue)–2E (black)	2·50	8·00
	1A–1B–1C–1D–3E	4·00	15·00

		No dot	Dot
(b) Phosphor			
3d.	1A (black)–3B (brown)–1C (green)–1D (yellow)	3·50	3·50

		Rows 12/13	Rows 18/19
4½d.	1A (brown-red)–1B (yellow)–1C (magenta)–1D (blue)–2E (black)	12·00	25·00
	1A–1B–1C–1D–3E	15·00	25·00

In the 3d. the panes were reversed, the dot being on the left and the no dot on the right.
In the 4½d. there are two sets of cylinder numbers in the left-hand margin (perf. type E) opposite rows 12/13 and 18/19. In position 18/19 the "1D" is in grey-blue superimposed over an additional "1C" in magenta. Also in position 12/13 the black "2" is superimposed over a black "1". The cylinder numbers are engraved more boldly in position 12/13 and are boxed, the others being without boxes.

Minor Constant Flaws

3d. Cyls 1A–3B–1C–1D no dot

2/1 Retouch to Queen's left jaw (Th. D–E11), OP
2/5 Dot between top of "A" and "T" of "NATURE", OP
2/6 White line through top of 3 of value, OP
4/4 Green flaw at bottom right foot of "I" of "NATIONAL", OP
5/4 First "N" of "NATIONAL" blurred at top left, OP
6/5 Diagonal green line crosses petals of left-hand daisy (Th. B–C3), OP
7/1 Retouch on Queen's left cheek (Th. D11), OP
9/1 Green dot near centre of "N" of "NATURE", OP
9/2 White flaw at top of left-hand buttercup (Th. B2), OP
10/1 Patch of white to left of Queen's right eye (Th. C10), OP
10/4 Green dot at top right of "2", OP
12/6 White patch just above "NA" of "NATIONAL", OP
13/6 Green spot above "EK" of "WEEK", OP
14/1 White spot above "3" of value (Th. E8), OP
16/6 Dark spot to right of Queen's mouth (Th. E11–12), OP
18/3 Retouch above second "A" of "NATIONAL", later retouched, appearing as a whitish blob (Th. F5), OP

W 1963 Ninth International Lifeboat Conference.

18/5	White flaw under top left buttercup, at right (Th. C2), OP
19/3	Brown flaw to bottom right of "T" of "NATURE", later retouched, OP
19/5	Large green blob above second "A" of "NATIONAL", later touched out, OP
20/4	White dot between top of "3" of value and leaf (Th. E7–8), OP

3d. Cyls. 1A–3B–1C–1D dot

2/3	White dot just left of top of "3" of value, OP
6/6	Retouch under jaw extending to bottom of ear (Th. E10–11), OP
8/1	Brown dot under right leg of last "A" of "NATIONAL", OP
8/3	Retouch by "L" of "NATIONAL" (Th. G6), OP
9/6	Brown dot under right leg of second "N" of "NATIONAL", OP
14/1	Retouch above first "E" of "WEEK", OP
14/4	Retouch left of 3 of value (Th. F–78), OP
15/4	White flaw at bottom of oblique stroke in first "N" of "NATIONAL", OP
15/5	Greyish smear over dot of value, OP
16/5	Retouch from mouth to ear (Th. D11), OP
18/4	Green dot above upper lip (Th. D10), OP
19/6	Small white retouch between "63" of "1963" and dark hairline between "3" of value and leaf (Th. F8), OP

4½d. Cyls. 1A–1B–1C–1D–2E no dot and 1A–1B–1C–1D–3E no dot

3/3	Dark spot under fawn (Th. G10), OP
7/1	Yellow patch above fawn's right ear (Th. E11), OP
14/1	Brown spot in second upper leaf from butterfly (Th. B3), OP
19/3	Retouch in background behind woodpecker (Th. E9), OP

Sheet Details

Sheet size: 120 (6×20). 3d. double pane reel-fed; 4½d. single pane reel-fed

Sheet markings:

Cylinder numbers:

  3d. Below row 20/5
  4½d. Opposite rows 18/19 and boxed numbers opposite rows 12/13

Guide holes:

  3d. Opposite rows 14/15 (boxed), at left (dot) or right (no dot)
  4½d. Opposite rows 14/15 (boxed), at both sides

Marginal arrows (photo-etched):
"W" shaped at top, bottom and sides

Marginal rule: At bottom of sheet

Colour register marks:

  3d. Opposite rows 2/3 and 17/19, at left (dot) or right (no dot)
  4½d. Opposite rows 3/4 and 17/18, at left (no dot) or right (dot)

Autotron marks (stippled):

  3d. Between panes vertically, opposite rows 6/9 (seen either in right or left margin)
  4½d. Below vertical rows 1/3 and 4/6 but omitted from rows 1/3 in the first printing

Colour designations (usually trimmed off):

  3d. G BROWN (rows 4/5), G GREEN (rows 6/7), G YELLOW (row; 8/9), G ORANGE (row 13), left margin dot pane reading downwards
  4½d. G1 BROWN G2 YELLOW G3 RED G4 BLUE G5 BLACK in left margin reading downwards opposite rows 5/9

Traffic lights (boxed):

  3d. Yellow, black, green, brown opposite R. 20/6, no dot pane
  4½d. Black, blue, magenta, yellow, brown-red opposite rows 19/20 at right

Imprimaturs from the NPM or BPMA

A. Ordinary
Nos. W32/W33 imperforate, watermark Type W.**24**

Watermark upright (set of 2)	£2000
3d. cylinder 1A, 3B, 1C, 1D (no dot) block of six	£7000
4½d. cylinder 1A, 1B, 1C, 1D, 2E (no dot) block of six	£7000

B. Phosphor
Nos. WP32/WP33 imperforate, watermark Type W.**24**

Watermark upright (set of 2)	£2000
3d. cylinder 1A, 3B, 1C, 1D (dot) block of six	£7000
4½d. cylinder 1A, 1B, 1C, 1D, 2E (no dot) block of six	£7000

Quantities Sold:

	Ordinary	Phosphor
3d.	148,560,000	8,640,000
4½d.	12,480,000	1,140,000

Withdrawn: 1.6.64

Type **W34**. Rescue at Sea

Type **W35**. 19th-century Lifeboat

Type **W36**. Lifeboatmen

(Des. David Gentleman)

1963 *(31 May)*. **Ninth International Lifeboat Conference.** Types **W34/W36**

The International Lifeboat Conferences are held every four years. In 1963 the Conference was held at Edinburgh from 3 to 5 June.

A. Ordinary

W34 =SG 639		Mint	Used
2½d.	blue, black and red	10	10
a.	Missing neckline (No dot, col. 1)	20·00	
b.	Shaded diadem (Dot, R. 20/6)	30·00	
c.	White flaw in hair (no dot, R. 9/6)	30·00	

W35 =SG 640			
4d.	red, yellow, brown, black and blue	20	20
a.	Spot on boom (R. 6/6)	30·00	
b.	Spot under "I" (R. 13/3)	30·00	

174

Ninth International Lifeboat Conference. 1963

W36 =SG 641						
1s.6d. sepia, yellow and grey-blue		1·50	1·50			
First Day Cover (W34/W36)			20·00			

B. Phosphor (applied flexo.)

WP34 =SG 639p			
2½d. One band		50	60
a. Missing neckline (No dot, col. 1)		20·00	
b. Shaded diadem (Dot, R. 20/6)		30·00	
c. White flaw in hair (No dot, R. 9/6)		30·00	
WP35 =SG 640p			
4d. Three bands		50	60
a. Narrow band at left or right (stamp with vert. margin)		2·00	
b. Spot on boom (R. 6/6)		30·00	
c. Spot under "I" (R. 13/3)		30·00	
WP36 =SG 641p			
1s.6d. Three bands		48·00	28·00
a. Narrow band at left or right (stamp with vert. margin)		60·00	
First Day Cover (WP34/WP36)			55·00

In the 1s.6d. the grey-blue is lighter on the phosphor stamps, presumably in order to give better phosphor reaction.
All values are known pre-released on 30 May.

W34a, WP34a
Occurs on all stamps in first vertical row in varying degrees

W34b, WP34b
Occurred during the course of printing

W34c, WP34c

W35a, WP35b

W35b, WP35c

Cylinder Numbers (Blocks of Six)

(a) Ordinary

	Perforation Type A (E/I)			
	No dot		Dot	
Cylinder Nos.	Row 12	Row 19	Row 12	Row 19
2½d. 3A (red)–3B (black)–1C (blue)	1·80	2·00	1·80	2·00

4d. 1A (blue)–1B (black)–1C (red)–1D (brown)–1E (yellow)	2·50	2·50	†	†
		Row 18		
1s.6d. 3A (blue)–1B (sepia)–1C (yellow)	15·00	15·00		

(b) Phosphor

	Row 12	Row 19		
2½d. 3A (red)–3B (black)–1C (blue)	4·50	4·50	4·50	4·50
4d. 1A (blue)–1B (black)–1C (red)–1D (brown)–1E (yellow)	4·50	4·50	†	†
		Row 18		
1s.6d. 3A (blue)–1B (sepia)–1C (yellow)	£300	£300	†	†

In the 2½d. the cylinder numbers in row 12 are shown as A (red) B (black) 1C (blue) in left margin (perf. type E) of left pane and the same in the right margin of right pane but without dot after C.
In the 1s.6d. the 1C is shown twice opposite row 18.

Minor Constant Flaws

2½d. Cyls. 3A–3B–1C no dot
  7/5 Scratch down Queen's face from hair to chin (Th. C–D11), OP
  8/5 Scratch continues from hair to shoulder (Th. C–D11), OP
  9/1 White scratch on dress above "ENC" (Th. F12), OP
  11/1 Scratch from hair to ear (Th. C–D12), OP
  14/3 Black dot below lower lip (Th. D10), OP

2½d. Cyls. 3A–3B–1C dot
  3/4 Retouch left of Queen's ear (Th. C11), OP
  9/6 Retouch on Queen's forehead (Th. C10), OP
  19/6 Pale grey patch over back of shoulder, normal in State 1 (Th. F12–13), OP

4d. Cyls. 1A–1B–1C–1D–1E no dot
  1/6 Retouch on Queen's nose (Th. B–C10), OP
  3/5 Vertical line of retouching on Queen's face down to shoulder (Th. C–E11), OP
  4/2 Vertical black line through shoulder to just above "EN" (Th. E–F12), OP
  13/1 Pale blue streak across top frame line at apex of sail (Th. A5), OP
  13/2 Yellow scratch across main sail from mast to rigging (Th. D6), OP
  18/2 Black dot over Queen's left eye (Th. C10), OP
  20/2 Blue dot on Queen's neck (Th. E11), OP
  20/3 Vertical red line down first "N" of "CONFERENCE", OP

1s.6d. Cyls. 3A–1B–1C no dot
  6/5 Length of retouching on Queen's collar (Th. E11–12), OP
  15/6 Retouch over Queen's right eye (Th. B10), OP

Sheet Details

Sheet size: 120 (6×20). 2½d. double-pane reel-fed; others single-pane reel-fed

Sheet markings:

Cylinder numbers:
  2½d. Boxed opposite R. 12/1 (no dot pane) or R. 12/6 (dot pane) Also opposite R. 19/1 on both panes without box
  4d. Boxed opposite R. 12/1 and without box in left margin opposite rows 17/20

1963 Red Cross Centenary Congress.

1s.6d. Boxed opposite rows 11/12, left margin and unboxed opposite R. 18/1

Guide holes:
- **2½d.** Opposite rows 14/15 (boxed), at left (no dot) or right (dot)
- **4d., 1s.6d.** Opposite rows 14/15 (boxed), at both sides

Marginal arrows (photo-etched):
"W" shaped, at top, bottom and sides

Marginal rule: At bottom of sheet

Colour register marks:
- **2½d.** Opposite rows 3/4 and 18/19. at left (no dot) or right (dot)
- **4d.** Opposite rows 2/3 and 17/18, at both sides
- **1s.6d.** Opposite rows 2/4 and 18/19, at both sides

Autotron marks (stippled):
- **2½d.** Blue, black, red below vertical rows 4/6 on dot pane
- **4d.** Yellow. brown, black, red, blue below vertical rows 4/6
- **1s.6d.** Yellow, sepia, blue below vertical rows 4/6

Colour designations (usually trimmed off):
- **2½d.** G RED G BLACK G BLUE opposite rows 6, 7 and 9 respectively reading upwards at left (no dot) or right (dot)
- **4d.** G YELLOW G BROWN G BLACK G RED G BLUE in right margin reading upwards opposite rows 14/10
- **1s.6d.** G BLUE G BROWN G YELLOW in left margin reading downwards opposite rows 6/9

Traffic lights (boxed):
- **2½d.** Blue, black, red opposite R. 20/6, dot pane
- **4d.** Yellow, brown, black, red, blue opposite R. 20/6
- **1s.6d.** Yellow, sepia, blue opposite R. 20/6

Imprimaturs from the NPM or BPMA

A. Ordinary
Nos. W34/W36 imperforate, watermark Type W.**24**

Watermark upright (set of 3)	£3000
2½d. cylinder 3A, 3B, 1C (dot) block of six	£7000
4d. "spot on boom" R. 6/6 block of six	£1500
4d. cylinder 1A, 1B, 1C, 1D, 1E block of six	£7000
1s.6d. cylinder 3A, 1B, 1C block of six	£7000

B. Phosphor
Nos. WP34/WP36 imperforate, watermark Type W.**24**

Watermark upright (set of 3)	£3000
2½d. cylinder 3A, 3B, 1C (dot) block of six	£7000
4d. "spot on boom" R. 6/6	£1500
4d. "spot under I" R. 13/3	£1500
4d. cylinder 1A, 1B, 1C, 1D, 1E block of six	£7000
1s.6d. cylinder 3A, 1B, 1C block of six	£7000

Quantities Sold:

	Ordinary	Phosphor
2½d.	81,405,000	4,239,000
4d.	7,475,040	840,000
1s.6d.	7,484,780	886,000

Withdrawn: 1.6.64

Type **W37.** Red Cross

Type **W38.** Red Cross

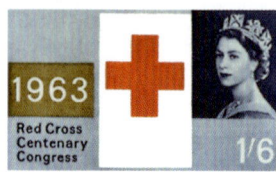

Type **W39.** Red Cross

(Des. H. Bartram)

1963 (15 August). **Red Cross Centenary Congress.** Types W37/W39

The congress which opened in Geneva on 2 September marked the Centenary of the establishment of the Red Cross organisation.

A. Ordinary

W37 =SG 642		Mint	Used
3d. red and deep lilac		25	25
a. Red omitted		£16000	
b. Repaired cross (Cyls. 2A–2B, No. dot, R. 5/6)		30·00	
W38 =SG 643			
1s.3d. red, blue and grey		1·25	1·25
W39 =SG 644			
1s.6d. red, blue and bistre		1·25	1·25
a. Retouch in "C" of "Cross" (R. 14/4)		30·00	
b. Retouch over "1" of "1/6" (R. 16/6)		30·00	
First Day Cover (W37/W39)			20·00

B. Phosphor (applied flexo.)

WP37 =SG 642p			
3d. Three bands		1·10	1·00
a. Red omitted		—	
b. Two bands only			
c. Narrow band at left or right (stamp with vert. margin)		2·00	
WP38 =SG 643p			
1s.3d. Three bands		35·00	30·00
a. Narrow band at left or right (stamp with vert. margin)		48·00	
WP39 =SG 644p			
1s.6d. Three bands		35·00	27·00
a. Narrow band at left or right (stamp with vert. margin)		55·00	
b. Retouch in "C" of "Cross" (R. 14/4)		60·00	
c. Retouch over "1" of "1/6" (R. 16/6)		60·00	
First Day Cover (WP37/WP39)			60·00

Red Cross Centenary Congress. 1963

W37b

W39a, WP39b

W39b, WP39c

Cylinder Numbers (Blocks of Four)

(a) Ordinary

		Perforation Types		
	Cylinder Nos.	A (E/I) No dot	A (E/I) Dot	E (AE/I) Dot
3d.	2A (lilac)–2B (red)	2·00	2·00	5·00
	3A–2B	2·00	2·00	†
	3A–3B	3·00	3·00	†
1s.3d.	1A (grey)–3B–(blue)–1C (red)	9·00	†	†
1s.6d.	1A–(blue)– 1B (red)–1C (bistre)	9·00	†	†

(b) Phosphor

3d.	3A (lilac)–2B (red)	6·50	6·50	†
	3A–3B	6·50	6·50	†
1s.3d.	1A–(grey)–3B (blue)–1C (red)	£180	†	†
1s.6d.	1A–(blue)–1B (red)–1C (bistre)	£180	†	†

Perforation Type A (E/I) shows an alternate extension hole in the left margin.

Minor Constant Flaws

3d. Cyl. 3A no dot in combination with red cyls. 2B or 3B no dot
- 2/3 Lilac coloured spot above "t" of "Centenary". Retouched with cyl. 3B (Th. F10–11), OP

3d. Cyl. 2B no dot in combination with lilac cyls. 2A or 3A no dot
- 4/1 Red retouch in top left centre of cross (Th. D4), OP
- 7/3 Pale centre to cross (with cyl. 3A only), OP

3d. Cyl. 3A dot in combination with red cyls. 2B or 3B dot
- 4/3 Coloured spur on "C" of "Congress" (Th. G9), OP
- 15/2 Scratch above "3D". Retouched with cyl. 3B (Th. B8–C9), OP
- 17/5 Retouching in and around "D" of "3D" (Th. D9), OP

3d. Cyl. 2B dot in combination with lilac cyls. 2A or 3A dot
- 16/1 Red retouches in left arm and top left centre of cross (Th. D3–4), OP
- 19/1 Red retouch in lower arm of cross (Th. E4), OP

1s.3d. Cyls. 1A–3B–1C no dot
- 11/4 Diagonal scratch from Queen's nose to jaw (Th. D7), OP
- 12/1 White spot to left of Queen's earring (Th. D8), OP

- 12/5 Dark patch to right of Queen's left eye (Th. C7), OP
- 15/3 Line through words "Red Cross", OP
- 18/4 Large retouch on Queen's neck (Th. E7), OP

1s.6d. Cyls. 1A–1B–1C no dot
- 15/3 Large retouch in right arm of cross (Th. C–D8), OP

Sheet Details

Sheet size: 120 (6×20). 3d. double-pane reel-fed; others single-pane reel-fed

Sheet markings:

Cylinder numbers: Opposite R. 19/1, boxed

Guide holes:
- **3d.** Opposite rows 14/15 (boxed), at left (no dot) or right (dot)
- **1s.3d.**, and **1s.6d.** Opposite rows 14/15 (boxed), at both sides

Marginal arrows (photo-etched):
"W" shaped, at top, bottom and sides

Marginal rule: At bottom of sheet

Colour register marks:
- **3d.** Opposite rows 2/3 and 18/19, at left (no dot) or right (dot)
- **1s.3d., 1s.6d.** Opposite rows 17/19, at both sides

Autotron marks (stippled):
- **3d.** Lilac, red below vertical rows 2/3 on no dot panes
- **1s.3d.** Grey, blue, red below vertical rows 1/3
- **1s.6d.** Blue, red, bistre below vertical rows 1/3 and 4/6

Colour designations (usually trimmed off):
- **3d.** G RED in right margin opposite rows 5/6 (Cyls. 3A3B dot)
- **1s.3d.** G1 GREY G2 BLUE G3 YELLOW in right margin reading downwards opposite rows 9/4
- **1s.6d.** None

Traffic lights (boxed):
- **3d.** Lilac, red opposite R. 19/6
- **1s.3d.** Grey, blue, red opposite R. 19/6
- **1s.6d.** Blue, red, bistre opposite R. 19/6

Imprimaturs from the NPM or BPMA

A. Ordinary

Nos. W37/W39 imperforate, watermark Type W.**24**

Watermark upright (set of 3)	£3000
3d. cylinder 3A, 2B (no dot) block of four	£5000
1s.3d. cylinder 1A, 3B, 1C block of four	£5000
1s.6d. "retouch over 1 of 1/6" R. 16/4	£1500
1s.6d. cylinder 1A, 1B, 1C block of four	£5000

B. Phosphor

Nos. WP37/WP39 imperforate, watermark Type W.**24**

Watermark upright (set of 3)	£3000
3d. cylinder 3A, 3B (no dot) block of four	£5000
1s.3d. cylinder 1A, 3B, 1C block of four	£5000
1s.6d. "retouch over 1 of 1/6" R. 16/4	£1500
1s.6d. cylinder 1A, 1B, 1C block of four	£5000

Quantities Sold:

	Ordinary	Phosphor
3d.	157,277,800	10,349,280
1s.3d.	7,278,120	929,040
1s.6d.	6,995,160	1,038,840

Withdrawn: 1.9.64

W 1963 Opening of COMPAC.

Type **W40**. Commonwealth Cable

B
(Des. Peter Gauld)

1963 *(3 December).* **Opening of COMPAC.** Type **W40**

The Commonwealth Trans-Pacific Cable (COMPAC) was the first telephone cable to be laid across the Pacific Ocean. It links Canada with Australia and New Zealand by way of Hawaii and Fiji.

A. Ordinary

W40 =SG 645	Mint	Used
1s.6d. blue and black	1·25	1·25
a. Black omitted	£7000	
s. "CANCELLED", Type B, in red	35·00	
First Day Cover (W40)		12·00

B. Phosphor (applied flexo.)

WP40 =SG 645p		
1s.6d. Three bands	7·25	7·00
a. Left band omitted	45·00	
b. Narrow band at left or right (stamp with vert. margin)	25·00	
First Day Cover (WP40)		35·00

The stamp handstamped "CANCELLED" was applied to *Philatelic Bulletin* No. 3 (November 1963) so that it only exists unused, no gum.

No. WP40 has a "blue" phosphor overprint but it is known with bands giving a short greenish after-glow after irradiation to ultraviolet light. It is probable that this was due to contaminated phosphor rather than the use of "green" phosphor.

Cylinder Numbers (Blocks of Four)

	Perforation Type F (P/E). No dot	
Cylinder. Nos.	Ordinary	Phosphor
1s.6d. 1A (blue)–1B (black)	9·00	40·00

Minor Constant Flaws
1s.6d. Cyls. 1A–1B no dot
   17/6 Bulge at top of figure "1" of value (Th. F10), OP
   19/1 Extra white dot on Queen's right eye (Th. C10), OP

Sheet Details
Sheet size: 120 (6×20). Single pane reel-fed

Sheet markings:

Cylinder numbers: Opposite R. 19/1, boxed

Guide holes: at top above R. 1/2 and at bottom below R. 20/4, cutting marginal arrow

Marginal arrows (photo-etched): "W" shaped, at top, bottom and sides

Marginal rule: At bottom of sheet

Colour register marks: Opposite rows 1/2 and 17/8, at both sides

Autotron marks (stippled): Below vertical rows 2/3

Colour designations: G1 BLUE (row 9), G2 BLACK (row 12), left margin

Traffic lights: Black, blue (boxed), opposite R. 19/6

Imprimaturs from the NPM or BPMA

A. Ordinary
No. W40 imperforate, watermark Type W.**24**
Watermark upright	£1000
1s.6d. cylinder 1A, 1B block of four	£5000

B. Phosphor
No. WP40 imperforate, watermark Type W.**24**
Watermark upright	£1000
1s.6d. cylinder 1A, 1B block of four	£5000

Quantities Sold: Ordinary 8,015,880; phosphor 824,280

Withdrawn: 1.9.64

Shakespeare Festival. **1964**

Type **W41.** Puck and Bottom
(A Midsummer Night's Dream)

Type **W42.** Feste *(Twelfth Night)*

Type **W43.** Balcony Scene
(Romeo and Juliet)

Type **W44.** Eve of Agincourt *(Henry V)*

(All the above des. David Gentleman)

Type **W45.**
Hamlet contemplating Yorick's Skull *(Hamlet)*

Des. Christopher and Robin Ironside.
Recess printed, Bradbury Wilkinson. Eng. Alan Dow.

1964 *(23 April).* **Shakespeare Festival.** Types **W41/W45.**
The 2s.6d. is perf. 11×12, comb.

Issued on the occasion of the 400th Anniversary of the Birth of William Shakespeare. An additional feature of this issue was the introduction of Presentation Packs by the then, General Post Office. The packs include one set of stamps and details of the designs, the designer and the stamp printer. They were issued for this and almost all later commemorative issues.

A. Ordinary

W41 =SG 646		Mint	Used
3d.	(1) Yellow-bistre, black and deep violet-blue	10	10
	(2) Bistre-brown, black and deep violet-blue	10	10
a.	Black dots across Puck's head (Dot, R. 7/6)	30·00	
b.	"Cancelled", Type B	£175	

W42 =SG 647			
6d.	(1) Yellow, orange, black and yellow-olive	20	20
	(2) Yellow, orange, black and olive-green	20	20
a.	Broken "H" (R. 12/3)	30·00	
b.	Missing floorboards (R. 20/1 and 20/2)	30·00	
c.	Olive spots by Queen's mouth (R. 9/6)	30·00	
d.	"Cancelled", Type B	£175	

W43 =SG 648			
1s.3d.	(1) Cerise, blue-green, black and sepia	18·00	
	(2) Cerise, turquoise, black and sepia	40	40
a.	Watermark inverted	£1500	
b.	Large pearl (Dot, R. 13/2)	10·00	
c.	"Cancelled", Type B (Shade (1))	£175	

W44 =SG 649			
1s.6d.	(1) Violet, turquoise, black and blue	60	60
	(2) Pale violet, turquoise, black and blue	1·10	1·10
a.	Watermark inverted	£1300	
b.	"Cancelled", Type B	£200	

W45 =SG 650			
2s.6d.	(1) Deep slate-purple	1.20	1.20
	(2) Blackish brown	2·00	2·00
	(3) Jet-black	£600	£250
a.	Watermark inverted	£1000	
b.	"Cancelled", Type B (jet-black shade)	£475	

First Day Cover (W41/W45)	5·00
Presentation Pack (W41/W45)	12·00

B. Phosphor (Three bands) (3d. applied photo.; others flexo.)

WP41 =SG 646p			
3d.	(1) Yellow-bistre, black and deep violet-blue	25	25
	(2) Bistre-brown, black and deep violet-blue	25	25
a.	Narrow band at left or right (stamp with vert. margin)	2·00	
b.	Black dots across Puck's head (Dot, R. 7/6)	30·00	

WP42 =SG 647p			
6d.	Yellow, orange, black and yellow-olive	75	75
a.	Narrow band at left or right (stamp with vert. margin)	2·75	
b.	Broken "H" (R. 12/3)	30·00	
c.	Missing floorboards (R. 20/1 and 20/2)	30·00	
d.	Olive spots by Queen's mouth (R. 9/6)	30·00	

WP43 =SG 648p			
1s.3d.	Cerise, turquoise, black and sepia	2·00	2·00
a.	Watermark inverted	£400	
b.	Narrow band at left or right (stamp with vert. margin)	5·00	
c.	Large pearl (Dot, R. 13/2)	30·00	

WP44 =SG 649p			
1s.6d.	Violet, turquoise, black and blue	2·50	2·50
a.	Narrow band at left or right (stamp with vert. margin)	6·00	

First Day Cover (WP41/WP44)	9·00

W 1964 Shakespeare Festival.

Shades. The listed shades of the 6d. to 2s.6d. result from different printings. The 3d. and 6d. shades are quite distinct, the blue-green shade of the 1s.3d. comes from the scarce first printing from cylinder 1B, and although the pale violet in the 1s.6d. may only be due to under-inking, it came from part of the second printing. There were three printings of the 2s.6d. which produced a number of shades, but they fall into the groups listed. The rare jet-black shade exists, possibly from proof sheets issued in error. Most examples have a "CANCELLED" overprint No. W45b.

The 3d. is known with yellow-bistre missing on the top two-thirds of the figures of Puck and Bottom. This occurred on the top row only of a sheet.

W41a, WP41b

W42a, WP42b
Also grey patch on Shakespeare's right cheek. Both later retouched

W42c, WP42d

W42b, WP42c
Other less prominent states of missing floorboards also occur on R. 19/1, 19/2, 19/6 and 20/6

W43b, WP43c

Cylinder Numbers (Blocks of Four)

(a) Ordinary

Cylinder Nos.	Perforation Type A (E/I) No dot	Dot
3d. 1A (violet-blue)–1B (black)–1C (bistre)	1·50	1·50
6d. 1A (olive-green)–1B (orange)–1C (yellow)–1D (black)	30·00	†

	Perforation Type A(T) (E/P) No dot	Dot
1s.3d. 3A (sepia)–1B (blue-green)–1C (cerise)–1D–(black)	90·00	90·00
3A–2B (turquoise)–1C–1D	2·50	2·50
1s.6d. 1A (blue)–1B (violet)–1C (black)–1D (turquoise)	4·00	4·00

b) Phosphor

	Perforation Type A (E/I) No dot	Dot
3d. 1A (violet-blue)–1B (black)–1C (bistre)	1·50	1·50
6d. 1A (olive-green)–1B (orange)–1C (yellow)–1D (black)	30·00	†

	Perforation Type A(T) (E/P) No dot	Dot
1s.3d. 3A (sepia)–2B (turquoise)–1C (cerise)–1D (black)	15·00	15·00
1s.6d. 1A (blue)–1B (violet)–1C (black)–1D (turquoise)	20·00	20·00

The 3d. no dot cylinders exist with a false dot after the 1B but this was later removed. In the dot cylinders of the 1s.6d. the dots appear to the left of 1C and 1D.

Plate Numbers (Blocks of Four)
Perforation Type A (E/I)

2s.6d. Plate 1		15·00
Plate 1A		15·00

Minor Constant Flaws

3d. Cyls. 1A–1B–1C no dot

9/5	White scratch on boards above "AL" (Th. F/9), OP
19/1	White line in floorboard division above "S" of "FESTIVAL" (Th. G8), OP
20/1	White patch on Queen's collar, later retouched (Th. E12), OP

3d. Cyls. 1A–1B–1C dot

2/5	White patch on floorboards above F (Th. G7), OP
7/5	Retouches on Queen's left cheek, later partly retouched (Th. D11), OP
11/5	Retouch below Queen's left eye (Th. C11), OP
16/2	White spur to bottom arc of "3", OP
20/1	Dark flaw in stage above "VA", later retouched (Th. G9), OP

1s.3d. Cyls. 3A–2B–1C–1D no dot

18/2	Outline of Shakespeare's nose cut short, later corrected (Th. C3), OP

1s.6d. Cyls. 1A–1B–1C–1D no dot

1/6	White flaw on stage above "EAR" (Th. F4-G5), OP
18/1	Black flaw at base of tent over last "A" of "SHAKESPEARE" (Th. F5), OP
20/2	Vertical scratches on Queen's face (Th. BD11), OP

1s.6d. Cyls. 1A–1B–1C–1D dot

13/3	Flaw on stage above "EA" (Th. G4), OP

Sheet Details

Sheet sizes:
- **3d.** 120 (6×20). Double-pane reel-fed
- **6d.** 120 (6×20). Single-pane reel-fed
- **1s.3d., 1s.6d.** 120 (6×20). Double-panes sheet-fed
- **2s.6d.** 40 (4×10). Double-pane sheet-fed

The 1s.3d. and 1s.6d. were printed by the Linotype and Machinery No. 4 machine, a rotary sheet-fed double-pane machine.

Sheet markings:

Cylinder numbers: Opposite R. 19/1, boxed

Plate numbers
- **2s.6d.:** Bottom margin below vertical rows 5/6

Guide holes:
- **3d.** Opposite rows 14/15 (boxed), at left (no dot) or right (dot)
- **6d.** Opposite row 13 (boxed), at both sides
- **1s.3d.** Opposite rows 15/16 (boxes only, no holes), at left (no dot) or right (dot)
- **1s.6d.** Opposite rows 14/15 (boxes only, no holes), at left (no dot) or right (dot)
- **2s.6d.** Opposite row 6 (unboxed), at left (Plate 1) or right (Plate 1A)

False boxes appear in both margins opposite rows 14/15 in the 6d. value and these are deleted by a diagonal black line.

Marginal arrows (photo-etched):
"W" shaped, at top, bottom and sides (none on 2s.6d.)

Marginal rule: At bottom of sheet (except 2s.6d.)

20th International Geographical Congress. 1964

Colour register marks:
- **3d**. Opposite rows 2 and 17/18, at left (no dot) or right (dot)
- **6d**. Opposite rows 1/3 and 17/18, at both sides (usually trimmed off)
- **Others:** none

Autotron marks:
- **3d**. In central gutter alongside rows 14/16
- **6d**. Below vertical rows 1/3: black (stippled), olive (solid), orange (stippled), yellow (solid)
- **Others:** none

Colour designations (usually trimmed off):
- **3d**. G BLUE (rows 13/12), G BLACK (rows 9/8), G YELLOW (rows 5/4) reading upwards, right margin dot pane
- **Others:** none

Traffic lights (boxed): All R. 19/6
- **3d**. Violet-blue, black, bistre
- **6d**. Black, yellow, orange, olive
- **1s.3d**. Black, cerise, turquoise, sepia
- **1s.6d**. Turquoise, black, violet, blue

Essays
Set of four gummed perforated esays mounted on Harrison & Sons presentation cards with the face value in black instead of white. £10000

Imprimaturs from the NPM or BPMA

A. Ordinary
Nos. W41/W45 imperforate, watermark Type W.**24**

Watermark upright (set of 5)	£5500
3d. cylinder 1A, 1B, 1C (no dot) block of four	£5000
3d. (esparto paper) cylinder 1A, 1B, 1C (no dot) block of four	£5000
6d. cylinder 1A, 1B, 1C, 1D* block of four	£5500
1s.3d. cylinder 3A, 2B, 1C, 1D (no dot) block of four	£5000
1s.6d. cylinder 1A, 1B, 1C, 1D (dot) block of four	£5000
2s.6d. Plate 1A block of four	£6000

B. Phosphor
Nos. WP41/WP44 imperforate, watermark Type W.**24**

Watermark upright (set of 4)	£4000
3d. cylinder 1A, 1B, 1C (no dot) block of four	£5000
6d. cylinder 1A, 1B, 1C, 1D* block of four	£5500
1s.3d. cylinder 3A, 2B, 1C, 1D (dot) block of four	£5000
1s.6d. cylinder 1A, 1B, 1C, 1D (dot) block of four	£5000

Quantities Sold:

	Ordinary	Phosphor
3d.	133,670,000	10,427,880
6d.	19,238,200	1,318,560
1s.3d.	7,067,200	727,800
1s.6d.	6,910,120	657,120
2s.6d.	3,664,920	—
Pack	108,541	—

Withdrawn: 31.3.65 (3d. ordinary sold out earlier)

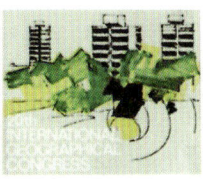

Type **W46.** Flats near Richmond Park ("Urban Development")

Type **W49.** Shipbuilding Yards, Belfast ("Industrial Activity")

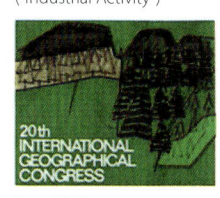

Type **W48.**
Beddgelert Forest Park, Snowdonia ("Forestry")

Type **W46.**
Nuclear Reactor, Dounreay ("Technological Development")

(Des. Dennis Bailey)

1964 (1 July). 20th International Geographical Congress. Types W46/W49

The first International Geographical Congress was held in 1871; since then one has normally been held at four-yearly intervals. London was chosen in 1964 and the Congress lasted from 20 to 28 July.

A. Ordinary

W46 =SG 651

	Mint	Used
2½d. black, olive-yellow, olive-grey and turquoise-blue	10	10
a. Short line under 2½d. (various)	14·00	
b. Line repaired (No dot, R. 18/5)	30·00	
c. Retouched lawn (No dot, R. 11/1 and 11/6)	30·00	

W47 =SG 652

4d. orange-brown, red-brown, rose, black and violet	30	30
a. Violet (face value) omitted	£275	
b. Red-brown (dock walls) omitted		
c. Violet and red-brown (dock walls) omitted	£500	
d. Watermark inverted	£850	
e. Scarred neck (R. 20/3)	30·00	

181

1964 20th International Geographical Congress

W48 =SG 653

8d.	yellow-brown, emerald, green and black	80	80
a.	Green (lawn) omitted	£24000	
b.	Watermark inverted	£2200	

W49 =SG 654

1s.6d.	yellow-brown, pale pink, black and brown	1·40	1·40
a.	Watermark inverted	55·00	
b.	Neck flaw (R. 8/4)	30·00	

First Day Cover (W46/W49)	10·00
Presentation Pack	£100

B. Phosphor (2½d. applied photo.; others flexo.)

WP46 =SG 651p

2½d.	One band	40	50
a.	Short line under 2½d. (various)	14·00	
b.	Line repaired (No dot, R. 18/5)	30·00	
c.	Retouched lawn (No dot, R. 11/1 and 11/6)	30·00	

WP47 =SG 652p

4d.	Three bands	1·20	1·20
a.	Narrow band at left or right (stamp with vert. margin)	5·00	
b.	Scarred neck (R. 20/3)	30·00	

WP48 =SG 653p

8d.	Three bands	2·50	3·50
a.	Narrow band at left or right (stamp with vert. margin)	8·00	

WP49 =SG 654p

1s.6d.	Three bands	28·00	22·00
a.	Narrow band at left or right (stamp with vert. margin)	35·00	
b.	Neck flaw (R. 8/4)	30·00	

First Day Cover (WP46/WP49)	35·00

A pair of No. WP47 exists with phosphor bands printed diagonally on the gum but omitted from the printed side. This was due to a paper fault which affected the corner of the sheet.

A used example of the 4d. (No. W47), is known with the red-brown omitted.

It was announced that quantities of Nos. W47/W49 were subsequently overprinted with phosphor bands 'because supplies ran out'.

W46a, WP46a

The short lower line occurs on no dot R.5/5, 9/5 (most marked) and 10/2 and on dot R.3/4, 4/5 and 7/5 (short at left). In no. W46b and WP46b the line has been repaired but there remains a short gap unfilled

W46b

W46c, WP46c
The illustration shows the retouch on R.11/1. On 11/6 it starts further over the line and is less extensive.

W47e, WP47b

W49b, WP49b
Later retouched

Cylinder Numbers (Blocks of Four)

(a) Ordinary

		Perforation Types		
		A (E/I)	A (E/I)	F (P/E)
	Cylinder Nos.	No dot	Dot	No dot
2½d.	3D (black)–1C (yellow)–1B (grey)–1A (blue)	1·00	1·00	†
4d.	1E (orange-brown)–1D (red-brown)–1C (rose)–1B (black)–1A (violet)	†	†	2·00
8d.	1D (brown)–1C (green)–1B (emerald)–1A (black)	7·50	†	4·50
1s.6d.	1D (yellow-brown)–1C (pink)–1B (black)–1A (brown)	9·00	†	†

(b) Phosphor

2½d.	3D (black)–1C (yellow)–1B (grey)–1A (blue)	2·50	2·50	†
4d.	1E (orange-brown)–1D (red-brown)–1C (rose)–1B (black)–1A (violet)	†	†	6·50
8d.	1D (brown)–1C (green)–1B (emerald)–1A (black)	†	†	12·00
1s.6d.	1D (yellow-brown)–1C (pink)–1B (black)–1A (brown)	£140	†	£125

Minor Constant Flaws

2½d. Cyls. 3D–1C–1B–1A no dot

- 2/4 Black line from Queen's left eye to base of back of diadem, later retouched and showing as faint white line (Th. C12–13), O
- 4/1 Blue spot on Queen's collar, later retouched (Th. E12), OP
- 12/3 Green spot at foot of hills above second "N" of "INTERNATIONAL" (Th. F5), OP
- 15/2 Blue dot left of oval and above left end of upper value bar, later retouched (Th. E10), OP
- 19/3 Green blob above "2" of "20th" (Th. E1), OP
- 20/3 White dot in portrait oval above right corner of central cross of crown (Th. A12), OP
- 20/5 White flaw in hair below central cross of crown (Th. B11), OP

2½d. Cyls. 3D–1C–1B–1A dot

- 7/5 Small retouch to right of Queen's nostril (Th. C11), OP
- 9/3 Retouch by Queen's left eye, later retouched on phosphor only (Th. B–C12), OP
- 12/3 White flaw in "h" of "20th", OP
- 12/5 Blue dot by grey panel opposite value (Th. G10), OP
- 13/5 Blue scratch on Queen's left cheek (Th. C11), OP
- 15/2 Two diagonal white lines above central cross of crown (Th. A12), OP
- 15/4 Blue patch in hills above black arrow (Th. D8) and slight retouch to right of "L" of "GEOGRAPHICAL", OP
- 15/5 White flaw in hair above Queen's left eye (Th. B12), OP
- 17/4 Retouch on Queen's neck above collar (Th. E12), OP

20th International Geographical Congress. **1964**

4d. Cyls. 1E–1D–1C–1B–1A no dot
- 1/1 Horizontal black line joining centre of "2" to left frame line, OP
- 1/2 Black spur on frame line below last "S" in "CONGRESS", OP
- 1/5 White dot in panel to right of rear cross of crown (Th. B13), OP
- 1/6 Small flaw under right arm of "N" of "CONGRESS" (Th. H2), OP
- 3/5 White flaw on left of crown (Th. A11), OP
- 3/6 White spike projecting from back of neck (Th. D12), OP
- 6/1 Several small black dots on collar (Th. E11–12), OP
- 7/1 Horizontal line between Queen's lips and ear (Th. C11–12), OP
- 7/2 Similar retouch but lower down (Th. D11–12), OP
- 8/1 Violet dot to right of "d" in value (Th. G12), OP
- 14/2 Horizontal grey line through "NATION", OP
- 16/5 Broken "R" in "GEOGRAPHICAL", OP
- 18/1 Break in vertical lines above "AT" of "INTERNATIONAL" and small black dot to left of break (Th. E3), OP
- 20/2 Black dot above Queen's nostril (Th. D11), and break in vertical frame line to left of value, OP
- 20/5 Corner break in frame line left of value (Th. H9), OP
  Numerous other minor frame breaks are known

8d. Cyls. 1D–1C–1B–1A no dot
- 1/1 Extensive retouching to back of Queen's collar (Th. E12–13), OP
- 4/2 Dark patch in front of Queen's neck (Th. D–E11), OP
- 4/6 Nick in final "A" of "GEOGRAPHICAL", OP
- 6/6 Retouch at back of Queen's collar (Th. E13), OP
- 7/6 Shading on Queen's forehead, later retouched appearing as white patch (Th. B11–12), OP
- 16/4–6 Green line runs through emerald field below brown area, OP
- 17/5 Horizontal white line across Queen's face (Th. C11–12), OP
- 18/5 Two horizontal white lines across face and chin (Th. C–D11–12), OP

1s.6d. Cyls. 1D–1C–1B–1A no dot
- 1/1 Dark flaw in front of Queen's collar (Th. E11), OP
- 2/2 White scratch across necklace (Th. D12), OP
- 13/3 White dot in panel below rear cross in crown (Th. B13), OP
- 20/6 Dark spot below Queen's nose (Th. C12), OP

Sheet Details

Sheet sizes: 20 (6×20).
    2½d. double-pane reel-fed; others single-pane sheet-fed

Sheet markings:

Cylinder numbers: Opposite rows 19/20 at left, boxed

Guide holes:
    2½d. Opposite rows 14/15 (boxed), at left (no dot) or right (dot)
    Others: Usually trimmed off

Marginal arrows (photo-etched):
"W" shaped, at top, bottom and sides

Marginal rule: At bottom of sheet

Colour register marks:
    2½d. Opposite rows 2/3 and 18/19, at left (no dot) or right (dot)
    Others: Above and below vertical rows 1 and 5/6

Autotron marks (stippled):
    2½d. Black, blue, yellow, grey opposite rows 6/8, at right (no dot) or left (dot)
    Others: Trimmed off

Colour designations (usually trimmed off):
    2½d. G1 GREY G2 DARK GREEN G3 YELLOW G4 BLACK reading upwards, right margin dot pane
    Others: Trimmed off

Traffic lights (boxed): All opposite rows 19/20 at right
    2½d. Black, yellow, blue, grey
    4d. Orange-brown, red-brown, rose, black, violet
    8d. Brown, green, black, emerald
    1s.6d. Order not known

Imprimaturs from the NPM or BPMA

A. Ordinary
Nos. W46/W49 imperforate, watermark Type W.**24**

Watermark upright (set of 4)	£4000
2½d. "Retouch lawn" flaw R. 11/1	£1500
2½d. cylinder 3D, 1C, 1B, 1A (no dot) block of four	£5000
4d. "Scarred neck" flaw R. 20/3	£1500
4d. cylinder 1E, 1D, 1C, 1B, 1A block of four	£5000
8d. cylinder 1D, 1C, 1B, 1A block of four	£5000
1s.6d. cylinder 1D, 1C, 1B, 1A block of four	£5000

B. Phosphor
Nos. WP46/WP49 imperforate, watermark Type W.**24**

Watermark upright (set of 4)	£4000
2½d. "Retouch lawn" flaw R. 11/1	£1500
2½d. cylinder 3D, 1C, 1B, 1A (no dot) block of four	£5000
4d. "Scarred neck" flaw R. 20/3	£1500
4d. cylinder 1E, 1D, 1C, 1B, 1A block of four	£5000
8d. cylinder 1D, 1C, 1B, 1A block of four	£5000
1s.6d. cylinder 1D, 1C, 1B, 1A block of four	£5000

Quantities Sold:

	Ordinary	Phosphor
2½d.	109,768,120	3,377,520
4d.	15,241,680	577,800
8d.	8,226,800	465,720
1s.6d.	10,154,040	519,000
Pack	29,952	—

Withdrawn: 2.7.65 (2½d. ordinary sold out earlier)

W 1964 Tenth International Botanical Congress.

Type **W50**. Spring Gentian

Type **W51**. Dog Rose

Type **W52**. Honeysuckle

Type **W53**. Fringed Water Lily

(Des. Sylvia and Michael Goaman)

1964 *(5 August).* **Tenth International Botanical Congress.** Types **W50/W53**

Botanical Congresses are held every five years each alternate one taking place in Europe. The King of Sweden was Hon. President of the 1964 Congress, which took place in Edinburgh.

A. Ordinary

W50 =SG 655		Mint	Used
3d.	violet, blue and sage-green	25	25
a.	Blue omitted	£20000	
b.	Sage-green omitted	£24000	
c.	Broken petal (Cyls. 3A–1B–1C Dot, R. 1/2)	65·00	
s.	"Cancelled", Type B	45·00	

W51 =SG 656			
6d.	apple-green, rose, scarlet and green	30	30
b.	Rose hip flaw (No dot, R. 2/2)	30·00	
s.	"Cancelled", Type B	45·00	

W52 =SG 657			
9d.	lemon, green, lake and rose-red	80	80
a.	Green (leaves) omitted	£22000	
b.	Watermark inverted	75·00	
c.	Line through "INTER" (R. 1/1)	65·00	
s.	"Cancelled", Type B	45·00	

W53 =SG 658			
1s.3d	yellow, emerald, reddish violet and grey-green	1·20	1·20
a.	Yellow (flowers) omitted	£45000	
b.	Watermark inverted	£2500	
c.	Fruit flaw (R. 14/2)	30·00	
s.	"Cancelled", Type B	45·00	

First Day Cover (W50/W53)		10·00
Presentation Pack		£125

B. Phosphor (applied flexo.)

WP50 =SG 655p			
3d.	Three bands	40	40
a.	Right band omitted		
b.	Narrow band at left or right (stamp with vert. margin)	2·50	
c.	Broken petal (Cyls. 3A–1B–1C Dot, R. 1/2)	65·00	

WP51 =SG 656p			
6d.	Three bands	2·50	2·75
a.	Four bands	22·00	
b.	Narrow band at left or right (stamp with vert. margin)	5·00	
c.	Rose hip flaw (No dot, R. 2/2)	30·00	

WP52 =SG 657p			
9d.	Three bands	4·50	4·50
a.	Narrow band at left or right (stamp with vert. margin)	6·00	
b.	Line through "INTER" (R. 1/1)	65·00	

WP53 =SG 658p			
1s.3d	Three hands	25·00	20·00
a.	Narrow band at left or right (stamp with vert. margin)	35·00	
b.	Fruit flaw (R. 14/2)	45·00	

First Day Cover (WP50/WP53)		35·00

Nos. W50s/W53s have the "CANCELLED" handstamp as used on No. W40 applied in black spread over two values. It was used on sample first day covers distributed by the Post Office with the notice announcing the service.

All values were accidentally released before the official date of issue at several post offices and by the Philatelic Bureau. The earliest known date is 27 July.

The, possibly unique, example of No. W53a shows the yellow printed on the gummed side due to a paper fold.

Normal

W50c, WP50c
Petal is broken where the violet overlaps the blue

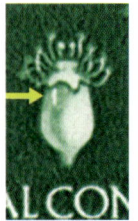

W51b, WP51c
White flaw in rose hip

W53b, WP53b
Grey-green overlaps centre of fruit

Tenth International Botanical Congress. **1964**

W52c, WP52b

Cylinder Numbers (Blocks of Four)

(a) Ordinary

	Perforation Types		
Cylinder Nos	A (E/I) No dot	A (E/I) Dot	F (P/E) No dot
3d. 2A (violet)–1B (blue)–1C (sage-green)	1·50	1·50	†
3A–1B–1C	1·50	1·50	†
6d. 1D (apple-green)–1C (rose)–1B (scarlet)–1A (green)	2·00	2·00	†
9d. 2D (lemon)–2C (green)–2B (lake)–2A (rose-red)	†	†	5·00
1s.3d. 1D (yellow)–1C (emerald)–1B (reddish violet)–1A (grey-green)	†	†	7·50

(b) Phosphor

3d. 3A (violet)–1B (blue)–1C (sage-green)	2·25	2·25	†
6d. 1D (apple-green)–1C (rose)–1B (scarlet)–1A (green)	15·00	12·50	†
9d. 2D (lemon)–2C (green)–2B (lake)–2A (rose-red)	†	†	22·00
1s.3d. 1D (yellow)–1C (emerald)–1B (reddish violet)–1A (grey-green)	†	†	£120

Minor Constant Flaws

3d. Cyls. 2A–1B–1C and 3A–1B–1C no dot
- 1/4 White dot between 3rd and 4th fruits below portrait (Th. E12), OP
- 2/4 Curved white line across right petal of left Gentian (Th. C3), OP
- 6/1 Small white vertical line on same petal as above (Th. C–D3), OP

3d. Cyl. 3A no dot
- 2/5 Retouch on upper lip, OP
- 7/5 Blue dash on small leaf pointing left below first flower (Th. F2), OP
- 10/5 White dot below first "S" of "CONGRESS", OP
- 12/5 Line of damage extends from Queen's upper lip to base of ear (Th. C10–12), OP
- 12/6 Line of damage extends from Queen's right cheek across nose to ear (Th. C10–12), OP
- 13/1 Clear line of white dots joins "SS" of "CONGRESS", OP
- 19/3 White flaw at edge of petal under "3" (Th. C1), OP
- 20/2 Retouch from Queen's left eye to ear (Th. B11–C12), OP

3d. Cyls. 2A–1B–1C and 3A–1B–1C dot
- 1/4 Small patch of white on Queen's forehead (Th. B10), OP
- 5/6 White dot in pod above "R" of "CONGRESS" (Th. F12), OP
- 15/5 Green dots in leaves above "OT" of "BOTANICAL" (Th. E–F7), OP
- 17/1 Retouch under necklace below earring (Th. D12), O but almost completely repaired on 3A phosphor
- 19/1 White dot on right petal of partly opened bud (Th. B8), OP
- 19/2 Retouch between Queen's left eyebrow and hair (Th. B11), OP

3d. Cyl. 2A dot
- 10/6 Coloured line across Queen's neck (Th. D11), O

3d. Cyl. 3A dot
- 6/4 Violet dot in Queen's forehead (Th. B10), OP
- 12/5 Flaw in Queen's left eye, OP
- 13/3 Thin white line from leaf to "R" of "INTER" (Th. G2), OP
- 13/6 Small white dash above "O" of "BOTANICAL" and violet spot above middle of collar (Th. D12), OP
- 19/6 Diagonal white line above "ES" of "CONGRESS", and retouch from centre of cheek to earring (Th. C11–12), OP
- 20/1 Light patch in background above 2nd "N" in "INTERNATIONAL", OP

6d. Cyls. 1D–1C–1B–1A no dot
- 2/6 Green flaws in "T" of "INTER", OP
- 5/4 Green spot between eyebrows (Th. B10), OP
- 6/4 Retouch above necklace (Th. D11) and green dot on lower petal of flower nearest to portrait (Th. C–D9), OP
- 10/1 White spot in hair below flowers of crown (Th. B12), OP
- 11/1 Retouch in Queen's collar (Th. D12), OP
- 17/2 Small retouch in front of Queen's ear (Th. C11), OP
- 18/2 Green indent in left side of seed pod (Th. F10), OP
- 20/1 Green spot in lowest leaf above "TE" of "INTER" (Th. F2), OP
- 20/4 Retouch on Queen's left cheek (Th. C11–12), OP

6d. Cyls. 1D–1C–1B–1A dot
- 2/6 Green flaws in "T" of "INTER" and line of yellow dots on middle leaf at left (Th. D1), OP
- 4/4 Three scarlet dots to right of Queen's left eye (Th. B11), OP
- 20/4 Retouch on Queen's left cheek (Th. C11–12), OP
- 20/5 Two green spots on seed pod (Th. F10), OP

9d. Cyls. 2D–2C–2B–2A no dot
- 4/4 "ON" of "INTERNATIONAL" joined by white line, OP
- 7/1 Red spot under jewel of necklace (Th. E11), OP
- 13/2 White dot between two left stamens of lower bloom (Th. F3), OP
- 14/2 Green dot above Queen's upper lip (Th. C11), OP
- 14/3 Red dot above Queen's right eye (Th. B10–11), OP

1s.3d. Cyls. 1D–1C–1B–1A no dot
- 5/1 White line through "NI" and above "C" of "BOTANICAL", OP
- 8/3 Grey-green flaw at base of "E" of "CONGRESS", OP
- 11/1 Retouch on Queen's jaw line and neck (Th. C11), OP
- 12/6 Horizontal dark line on left-hand bud (Th. B–C12), OP
- 13/2 Green spot on stem of largest bloom (Th. C5), OP
- 15/6 Pale patch in background adjoining Queen's lips (Th. C10), OP
- 18/3 Three dark horizontal dots above "L" of "INTERNATIONAL" (Th. G5–6), OP
- 19/1 Dark spot in leaf below left-hand flower (Th. D–E2), OP
- 20/1 Tops of "IN" of "INTER" joined, OP
- 20/6 White scratch through seed extending from above "C" of "BOTANICAL" to "R" of "CONGRESS" (Th. G8–12), OP

Sheet Details
Sheet size: 120 (6×20)
    3d., **6d.** double-pane reel-fed
    9d., **1s.3d.** single-pane sheet-fed

Sheet markings:

Cylinder numbers: Boxed, opposite R. 20/1 3d., 19–20/1 others

Guide holes:
    3d., **6d.** Opposite rows 14/15 (boxed), at left (no dot) or right (dot)
    9d., **1s.3d.** None

Marginal arrows (photo-etched):
"W" shaped, at top, bottom and sides

Marginal rule: At bottom of sheet

Colour register marks:
    3d., **6d.** None
    9d., **1s.3d.** Above and below vertical rows 1 and 6

W 1964 *Opening of Forth Road Bridge.*

Autotron marks:
- **3d.** Solid, violet, blue, sage-green opposite rows 4/5 and 15/16 at right (no dot) or left (dot)
- **6d.** Stippled, green, scarlet, rose, apple-green opposite rows 4/6 at right (no dot) or left (dot) and again apple-green, rose, scarlet opposite rows 14/15 at right (no dot) or left (dot)
- **9d., 1s.3d.** None

Coloured crosses (partly trimmed):
- **1s.3d.** Above and below vertical rows 1/2
- **Others:** None

Colour designations (usually trimmed off):
- **3d.** G1 GREEN G2 BLUE G3 MAUVE in right margin of dot panes

Traffic lights (boxed):
- **3d.** Violet, blue, sage-green opposite R. 20/6
- **6d.** Apple-green, rose, scarlet, green opposite R. 19–20/6
- **9d.** Lemon, green, lake, rose-red opposite R. 19–20/6
- **1s.3d.** Yellow, emerald, reddish violet, grey-green opposite R. 19–20/6

Essays
Perforated and gummed essays on Harrison & Sons presentation card. Various designs ex Goaman archive *from* £5000 each

Imprimaturs from the NPM or BPMA

A. Ordinary
Nos. W50/W53 imperforate, watermark Type W.**24**

Watermark upright (set of 4)	£4000
3d. cylinder 2A, 1B, 1C (no dot) block of four	£5000
6d. "rosehip" flaw R. 2/2	£1500
6d. cylinder 1D, 1C, 1B, 1A (no dot) block of four	£5000
9d. "line through INTER" flaw R. 1/1	£1500
9d. cylinder 2D, 2C, 2B, 2A block of four	£5000
1s.3d. "fruit flaw" R. 14/2	£1500
1s.3d. cylinder 1D, 1C, 1B, 1A block of four	£5000

B. Phosphor
Nos. WP50/WP53 imperforate, watermark Type W.**24**

Watermark upright (set of 4)	£4000
3d. cylinder 2A, 1B, 1C (no dot) block of four	£5000
6d. cylinder 1D, 1C, 1B, 1A (dot) block of four	£5000
9d. "line through INTER" flaw R. 1/1	£1500
9d. cylinder 2D, 2C, 2B, 2A block of four	£5000
1s.3d. cylinder 1D, 1C, 1B, 1A block of four	£5000

Quantities Sold:

	Ordinary	Phosphor
3d.	166,491,720	6,764,880
6d.	25,361,120	996,720
9d.	11,896,060	498,460
1s.3d.	15,664,600	650,920
Pack	16,140	—

Withdrawn: 2.7.65

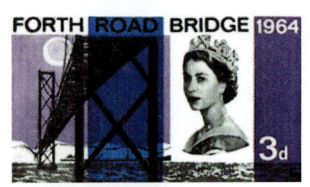

Type **W54.** Forth Road Bridge

Type **W55** Forth Road and Railway Bridges

(Des. Andrew Restall)

1964 *(4 September).* **Opening of Forth Road Bridge.** Types **W54/W55**

At that time the largest suspension bridge in Europe and the fourth largest in the world. Opened by Her Majesty The Queen.

A. Ordinary

W54 =SG 659		Mint	Used
3d. black, blue and reddish violet		10	10
a. Imperforate between stamp and top margin		£975
b. Dotted 3 (Cyl. 2A Dot, R. 15/1)		30·00

W55 =SG 660 | | |
---|---|---|---
6d. blackish lilac, light blue and carmine-red | | 20 | 20
a. Light blue omitted | | £6500 |
b. Watermark inverted | | 5·00 |

First Day Cover (W54/W55)	3·00

Presentation Pack (W54/W55)	£325

B. Phosphor (3d. applied photo., 6d. flexo.)

WP54 =SG 659p | | |
---|---|---|---
3d. Three bands | | 50 | 50
a. Narrow band at left or right (stamp with vert. margin) | | 5·00 |
b. Dotted 3 (Cyl. 2 A Dot, R. 15/1) | | 30·00 |

WP55 =SG 660p | | |
---|---|---|---
6d. Three bands | | 2·25 | 2·25
a. Watermark inverted | | £800 |
b. Narrow band at left or right (stamp with vert. margin) | | 7·00 |

First Day Cover (WP54/WP55)	10·00

W54b, WP54b

Opening of Forth Road Bridge. **1964** W

Cylinder Numbers (Blocks of Four)

(a) Ordinary

Cylinder Nos.	Perforation Type A (E/I) No dot	Dot
3d. 1C (blue)–1B (black)–2A (violet)	1·25	1·25
1C–1B–3A	15·00	15·00
1C–1B–4A	1·50	1·50
2C–1B–4A	2·00	2·00
6d. 1C (blue)–2B (blackish lilac)–2A (red)*	1·50	1·50

	Perforation Type A(T) (E/P) No dot	Dot
6d. 1C (blue)–2B (blackish lilac)–2A (red)*	4·75	4·75

(b) Phosphor

	Perforation Type A (E/I) No dot	Dot
3d. 1C (blue)–1B (black)–2A (violet)	3·00	3·00
1C–1B–4A	24·00	24·00

	Perforation Type A(T) (E/P) No dot	Dot
6d. 1C (blue)–2B (blackish lilac)–2A (red)*	24·00	24·00

* In the 6d. no dot pane the cylinder numbers are expressed in error thus: 1C2.B.2A

Minor Constant Flaws

3d. Cyl. 1C no dot in combination with cyls. 1B–2A or 1B–4A no dot
- 4/2 Blue spot to left and above "B" of "BRIDGE", OP
- 8/1 Blue spot below "B" of "BRIDGE", OP
- 13/6 Blue spot in sky S.W. of moon (Th. B1), O

3d. Cyl. 1C dot in combination with cyls. 1B–2A, 1B–3A or 1B–4A dot
- 18/6 Blue dash to left of 3d. (Th. F–G11); also blue spot to left of tanker (Th. G3), latter coincident with a similar violet spot on cyl. 2A

3d. Cyl. 1B no dot in combination with cyls. 1C–2A, 1C–3A, 1C–4A or 2C–4A no dot
- 1/3 Detail at rear of diadem is weak (Th. B–C10), OP
- 2/3 Scratch on necklace and collar (Th. E9), OP
- 4/4 Lack of detail at rear of diadem (Th. B–C10), OP
- 8/4 Black flaw on Queen's neck above large jewel (Th. E9), OP
- 9/2 White spot on Queen's nose (Th. D8), OP
- 9/4 Black scratch on Queen's forehead (Th. C8–9), OP
- 14/4 Black spot below Queen's left nostril (Th. D8), OP
- 16/4 Loss of detail at back of Queen's neck and collar. Almost normal with cyl. 3A (Th. E10–F10–11), OP
- 18/1 Black spots under "G" of "BRIDGE" (Th. A10), OP

3d. Cyl. 1B dot in combination with cyls. 1C–2A, 1C–3A, 1C–4A or 2C–4A dot
- 2/2 White flaw in sea appears as extra wave (Th. G8), OP
- 13/2 Weak top to "O" of "FORTH", OP
- 18/4 Small white flaw in hair above Queen's left eye (Th. B9), OP

3d. Cyls. 2A, 3A and 4A no dot (multipositive flaws)
- 17/4 White patch at left side of moon (Th. B2), OP. Less pronounced on cyl. 3A
- 19/4 Large retouch in sky left of bridge (Th. D1), OP. Most marked on cyl. 4A
- 20/1 White tower on hill above funnel (Th. F3), OP. Retouched on cyls. 3A and 4A
- 20/4 Large retouch in sky left of moon (Th. A–B1), OP. Most pronounced on cyls. 3A and 4A

3d. Cyls. 1C–1B–2A no dot
- 10/6 Violet retouches below "1" and "4" of "1964" (Th. B11 and B13), OP
- 18/5 White arc at top left of moon (Th. A–B2), OP

3d. Cyl. 4A no dot in combination with cyls. 1C–1B or 2C–1B no dot
- 12/6 Faint acute accent over "d" of "3d" (Th. F13), OP
- 14/4 Small nick in left edge of value panel (Th. D11), OP
- 16/2 Retouch in sky above funnel (Th. E–F3), OP

3d. Cyl. 4A dot in combination with cyls. 1C–1B or 2C–1B dot
- 14/2 Violet coloured flaw in sky at left of pylon (Th. E2), OP

3d. Cyls. 2C–1B–4A dot
- 17/3 Dark patch on skyline under bridge (Th. F5), O

6d. Cyls. 1C–2B–2A no dot
- 5/1 Small nick in top of "9" of "1964", OP
- 5/5 Red scratch over "D" of "BRIDGE", OP
- 7/1 Red scratch over "6" of "6d", OP
- 7/3 Two small breaks in bridge below portrait (Th. G8), OP
- 8/2 Black spot on Queen's collar (Th. E10), OP
- 15/6 Dark red patch below "4" of "1964" (Th. B13), OP
- 16/1 Black dot in front of "D" of "ROAD", OP
- 16/5 Mottled portrait, OP
- 17/6 Mottled portrait, OP
- 18/4 Black spot in water between left-hand towers of bridge (Th. F1), OP

6d. Cyls. 1C–2B–2A dot
- 1/4 White scratch on Queen's cheek (Th. D9), OP
- 15/5 Two small coloured flaws on Queen's forehead (Th. C9); also two small red spots below portrait by bridge (Th. G9), OP
- 17/2 Diagonal red stroke by value panel (Th. D11), OP
- 19/1 Queen's face is a mass of white dots (State 1) OP; later appears normal (State 2), O only. Other stamps in the sheet show a similar appearance but this is the most marked

Sheet Details
Sheet size: 120 (6×20). 3d. double-pane reel-fed; 6d. double-pane sheet-fed

Sheet markings:

Cylinder numbers: Opposite R. 19/1, boxed

Guide holes:
- **3d.** Opposite rows 14/15 (boxed), at left (no dot) or right (dot)
- **6d.** None

Marginal arrows (photo-etched): "W" shaped, at top, bottom and sides

Marginal rule: At bottom of sheet

Colour register marks:
- **3d.** Opposite rows 2/3 and 17/18, at left (no dot) or right (dot)
- **6d.** Opposite rows 1/2 and 17/18, at left (no dot) or right (dot)

Autotron marks (solid):
- **3d.** Black, blue, violet opposite rows 4/6 and violet, blue, black opposite rows 13/15 at right (no dot) or left (dot)
- **6d.** None

Colour designations (usually trimmed off):
- **3d.** G MAUVE G BLUE G BLACK in right margin reading upwards opposite rows 8/4 on dot panes only
- **6d.** None

Traffic lights (boxed):
- **3d.** Violet, blue, black opposite R. 19/6
- **6d.** Blue, red, blackish lilac opposite R. 19/6

W 1965 *Churchill Commemoration.*

Imprimaturs from the NPM or BPMA
A. Ordinary
Nos. W54/W55 imperforate, watermark Type W.**24**

Watermark upright (set of 2)	£2000
3d. cylinder 1C, 1B, 2A (no dot) block of four	£5000
6d. cylinder 1C, 2B, 2A (dot) block of four	£5000

B. Phosphor
Nos. WP54/WP55 imperforate, watermark Type W.**24**

Watermark upright (set of 2)	£2000
3d. cylinder 1C, 1B, 2A (dot) block of four	£5000
6d. cylinder 1C, 2B, 2A (dot) block of four	£5000

Quantities Sold:

	Ordinary	Phosphor
3d.	108,098,480	8,020,920
6d.	12,055,960	1,240,800
Pack	11,450	—

Withdrawn: 2.7.65

> **PHOSPHOR BANDS**
> From the Churchill issue onwards all phosphor bands were applied in photogravure, unless otherwise stated.

Type **W56.** Sir Winston Churchill

Type **W58.** Sir Winston Churchill

(Des. David Gentleman and Rosalind Dease, from photograph by Karsh)

1965 *(8 July).* **Churchill Commemoration.** Types W56/W58

Rembrandt

Timson

I. Rembrandt Machine
Cyls. 1A–1B dot and no dot. Lack of shading detail on Churchill's portrait. Queen's portrait appears dull and coarse. This was a sheet-fed rotary machine.

A. Ordinary
W56 =SG 661

		Mint	Used
4d.	black and olive-brown	15	10
a.	Watermark inverted	3·00	
b.	Vertical scratch (Dot, R. 20/3)	30·00	

B. Phosphor
WP56 =SG 661p

4d.	Three bands	20	20
a.	Left band omitted	25·00	
b.	Vertical scratch (Dot, R. 20/3)	30·00	

II. Timson Machine
Cyls. 5A–6B no dot. More detail on Churchill's portrait–furrow on forehead, his left eyebrow fully drawn and more shading on cheek. Queen's portrait lighter and sharper. This was a reel-fed, two-colour, 12-in. wide rotary machine. The differences in impression were due to the greater pressure applied by the cylinders.

Churchill Commemoration. 1965

Ordinary only
W57 =SG 661a

4d. black and pale olive-brown	50	50

III. Linotype and Machinery No. 4 Machine
Cyls. 1A–1B no dot. The Linotype and Machinery No. 4 machine was a sheet-fed rotary press machine. Besides being used for printing the 1s.3d. stamps it was also employed to overprint the phosphor bands on both values.

A. Ordinary
W58 =SG 662

1s.3d. black and grey	45	45
a. Watermark inverted	£140	
First Day Cover (W56 and W58)		4·75
Presentation Pack (W56 and W58)		40·00

B. Phosphor
WP58 =SG 662p

1s.3d. Three bands	1·00	1·00
a. Narrow band at left or right (stamp with vert. margin)		5·00
b. Error. Two broad bands		
First Day Cover (WP56 and WP58)		5·00

These are known postmarked 7 July.
Two examples of the 4d. value exist with the Queen's head omitted, one due to something adhering to the cylinder and the other due to a paper fold. The stamp also exists with Churchill's head omitted, also due to a paper fold.

W56b, WP56b

Cylinder Numbers (Blocks of Four)
(a) Ordinary

	Perforation Types		
	A(T) (E/P) No dot	A(T) (E/P) Dot	F (P/E) No dot
Cylinder Nos.			
4d. 1A (olive-brown)–1B (black) Rembrandt	1·25	1·25	†
4d. 5A (olive-brown)–6B (black) Timson	†	†	3·00
1s.3d. 1A (black)–1B (grey) Linotype and Machinery No. 4	†	†	2·50

(b) Phosphor

4d. 1A (olive-brown)–1B (black) Rembrandt	1·50	1·50	†
1s.3d. 1A (black)1B (grey) Linotype and Machinery No. 4	†	†	5·50

Minor Constant Flaws
4d. Cyls. 1A–1B no dot

1/1	Background retouch left of Churchill's right eye (Th. D2), scratch from Churchill's ear to Queen's chin (Th. D8–11), small background retouch to right of Churchill's left ear (Th. C9), OP
6/6	Queen's face mottled with white streaks (Th. B–D10–12), OP
14/1	Dark patch above Queen's left eye (Th. B11), OP

4d. Cyls. 1A–1B dot

1/6	Vertical line of white dots near hair above Churchill's right eye (Th. A–C3), OP
4/3	Disturbance under Churchill's left eye (Th. D6), OP
7/1	Queen's face mottled with white specks (Th. B–D10–12), OP
7/2	Queen's face mottled with white specks (Th. B–D10–12), OP
20/5	Brown diagonal line on bridge of Queen's nose (Th. C11), OP

The mottled face of the Queen varieties on no dot R. 6/6 and dot R. 7/1 and 7/2 are very marked and occur on ordinary and phosphor but only on some sheets. Many other stamps on this cylinder show signs of mottling

4d. Cyls. 5A–6B no dot (ordinary only)

4/2	Retouch in background between portraits (Th. B9)
6/4	Retouch at top of Churchill's nose (Th. D5)
10/4	Two spots in vertical white line level with Churchill's shoulder (Th. E10)
12/3	Small white flaw by Queen's right eye (Th. C10)
14/5	Background retouch just above Churchill's right shoulder (Th. E–F2) and brown flaw in margin below Churchill's chin (Th. H5)
15/5	Brown flaw left of Churchill's head (Th. A2)

1s.3d. Cyls. 1A–1B no dot

1/4	Line of white dots in Queen's hair (Th. C12), OP
7/1	Small white dot over Queen's left eyelid (Th. C11), OP
15/4	White flaw at base of Queen's neck (Th. D2), OP
19/4	Spur on top jewel of emblems in diadem (Th. A12), OP

Sheet Details
Sheet size: 120 (6×20)
    4d. Rembrandt double-pane sheet-fed
    Timson single pane reel-fed
    1s.3d. L. & M. No. 4 single-pane sheet-fed

Sheet markings:

Cylinder numbers: Opposite R. 19/1, boxed

Guide holes:
    4d. Timson above vertical row 2 (boxed) and below vertical rows 3/4 (unboxed and over arrow)
    Others: None

Marginal arrows (photo-etched):
"W" shaped, at top, bottom and sides; Rembrandt very small at bottom; others normal

Marginal rule: At bottom of sheet

Colour register marks:
    4d. Rembrandt, none
    4d. Timson, opposite rows 1/2 and 17/18, at both sides
    1s.3d. Above and below vertical rows 1/2 and 6

Autotron marks (solid):
    4d. Timson: Brown, black above R. 1/2 and 1/3
    Others: None

Colour designations: None

Traffic lights (boxed): All R. 19/6
    4d. Black, brown;
    1s.3d. Grey, black

W 1965 700th Anniversary of Simon De Montfort's Parliament.

Imprimaturs from the NPM or BPMA

A. Ordinary
Nos. W56, W58 imperforate, watermark Type W.**24**

Watermark upright (set of 2)	£2000
4d. cylinder 1A, 1B (no dot) block of four	£5000
1s.3d. cylinder 1A, 1B (no dot) block of four	£5000

B. Phosphor
Nos. WP56, WP58 imperforate, watermark Type W.**24**

Watermark upright (set of 2)	£2000
4d. cylinder 1A, 1B (no dot) block of four	£5000
1s.3d. cylinder 1A, 1B (no dot) block of four	£5000

Quantities Issued:		Ordinary	Phosphor
4d.	Rembrandt	103,217,520	10,322,760
4d.	Timson	32,040,000	—
1s.3d.		7,893,480	864,960
Pack		38,500	—

Withdrawn: 4d. phosphor sold out Dec. 1965, remainder withdrawn: 28.2.66

Type **W59**. Simon de Montfort's Seal
(Des. Stewart R. Black)

Type **W60**. Parliament Buildings (after engraving by Hollar, 1647)
(Des. Prof. Richard Guyatt)

1965 (19 July). **700th Anniversary of Simon De Montfort's Parliament.** Types **W59/W60**

Simon de Montfort summoned the first parliament representing many cities and shires and it met in various buildings at Westminster in January 1265.

A. Ordinary

W59 =SG 663		Mint	Used
6d.	olive-green	10	10
	a. Imperforate between stamp and top margin	£1250	

W60 =SG 664			
2s.6d.	black, grey and pale drab	50	50
	a. Watermark inverted	60·00	

| First Day Cover (W59/W60) | 6·00 |
| Presentation Pack (W59/W60) | 65·00 |

B. Phosphor

WP59 =SG 663p		Mint	Used
6d.	Three bands	50	50

| First Day Cover (WP59) | 15·00 |

Both values were accidentally released in several post offices in the London area on 8 July, the date of issue of the Churchill stamps. Covers are also known with both values, bearing the First Day cancellation of the Philatelic Bureau dated 8 July.

Cylinder Numbers (Blocks of Four)

		Perforation Type A (E/I)	
	Cylinder Nos.	No dot	Dot
6d.	2 (olive-green). Ordinary	1·25	1·25
6d.	2 Phosphor	2·75	2·75

The 2s.6d. sheets had no cylinder numbers. Perforation is Type A(T) (E/P)

Minor Constant Flaws
6d. Cyl. 2 no dot

1/1	Background scratch behind right cross of diadem (Th. C11–12), OP
5/3	Small background blemish above jewels in diadem (Th. B11), OP
9/4	Retouch at rear of horse's belly (Th. E4), OP
15/2	Dot below "e" of "Anniversary", OP
17/3	Cut in "m" of "Parliament", OP
17/5	Background retouch to right of diadem (Th. C11), OP

Salvation Army Centenary. **1965**   **W**

6d. Cyl. 2 dot
- 10/6 Spur to "m" of "Parliament", OP
- 14/5 White flaw on Queen's necklace (Th. E10), OP

2s.6d. No numbers
- 4/1 Vertical line running through river wall and building in centre of stamp (Th. E–F9)
- 4/6 Vertical line from left of steps at centre through Thames to frame line (Th. G–H7)
- 6/3 Blemish between 5th and 6th windows of building in front of Westminster Hall (Th. E10)
- 8/1 White scratches above "V" of "ANNIVERSARY"
- 10/1 Nick in "S" of "ANNIVERSARY"

Sheet Details
Sheet sizes:
- **6d**. 120 (6×20). Double-pane reel-fed
- **2s.6d**. 80 (8×10). Single-pane sheet-fed

Sheet markings:

Cylinder numbers: 6d. opposite R. 19/1, boxed; 2s.6d. none

Guide holes:
- **6d**. In double photo-etched box opposite rows 14/15, at left (no dot) or right (dot). In the left margin the boxes are lettered "SON", the "S" being in left box (usually trimmed off), the "O" below centre line and the "N" above right line. In the right margin the sequence is reversed. The letters are very small and denote respectively selvedge, off-side and near-side
- **2s.6d**. None

Marginal arrows (photo-etched): "W" shaped, at top, bottom and sides

Marginal rule: At bottom of sheet

Colour register marks, Autotron marks, Colour designations: None

Traffic lights (boxed):
- **6d**. None
- **2s.6d**. Grey, drab and black opposite R. 9/8, boxed

  This shows that the stamp was printed in three colours and accounts for misplacement of the Queen's head downwards in some badly registered sheets

Imprimaturs from the NPM or BPMA

A. Ordinary
Nos. W59/W60 imperforate, watermark Type W.**24**

Watermark upright (*set of* 2)	£2000
6d. cylinder 2 (dot) block of four	£5000

B. Phosphor
No. WP59 imperforate, watermark Type W.**24**

Watermark upright (set of 2)	£2000
6d. cylinder 2 (dot) block of four	£5000

Quantities Issued:

	Ordinary	Phosphor
6d.	12,973,800	1,537,920
2s.6d.	4,055,120	—
Pack	24,450	—

Withdrawn: 28.2.66

Type **W61**. Bandsmen and Banner

(Des. M. C. Farrar-Bell)

Type **W62**. Three Salvationists

(Des. G. Trenaman)

1965 *(9 August)*. **Salvation Army Centenary.** Types **W61/W62**

A religious movement, the Salvation Army was founded in 1865 by William Booth who became its General in 1880.

A. Ordinary

W61 =SG 665 — Mint — Used

	Mint	Used
3d. indigo, grey-blue, cerise, yellow and brown	10	10
a. Diadem flaw (R. 16/6)	30·00	
b. Retouch to V (R. 19/3)	30·00	

W62 =SG 666

	Mint	Used
1s.6d. red, blue, yellow and brown	60	60
a. Extra pearl (R. 17/1)	30·00	

First Day Cover (W61/W62)	10·00

B. Phosphor

WP61 =SG 665p

	Mint	Used
3d. One band	20	20
a. Diadem flaw (R. 16/6)	30·00	
b. Retouch to V (R. 19/3)	30·00	

WP62 =SG 666p

	Mint	Used
1s.6d. Three bands	90	90
a. Extra pearl (R. 17/1)	30·00	

First Day Cover (WP61/WP62)	22·00

W61a, WP61a    W61b, WP61b

W62a WP62a

W 1965 Salvation Army Centenary.

Cylinder Numbers (Blocks of Six)

(a) Ordinary

	Cylinder. Nos. (No dot)	Perforation Type A (E/I)
3d.	2A (blue)–2B (indigo)–1C (brown)–1D (cerise)–1E (yellow)	1·25
1s.6d.	1A (red)–1B (brown)–1C (blue)–1D (yellow)	5·00

(b) Phosphor

3d.	2A (blue)–2B (indigo)–1C (brown)–1D (cerise)–1E (yellow)	2·00
1s.6d.	1A (red)–1B (brown)–1C (blue)–1D (yellow)	8·00

Minor Constant Flaws

3d. Cyls. 2A–2B–1C–1D–1E no dot
- 1/6 Pale area below "D" of "3D" (Th. G13), OP
- 2/1 Dark spot on Queen's chin (Th. D11), OP
- 3/6 Vertical scratch below flag-bearer's collar (Th. D–E4), OP
- 8/1 Spur at foot of "T" of "SALVATION" at bottom of stamp, OP
- 11/2 Blue scratch in white vertical dividing line to left of Queen's lips (Th. D10); also blue spot to left of flag-bearer's lips (Th. D4), both OP
- 15/6 Grey flaw protruding from collar under Queen's chin (Th. E11), OP
- 16/1 Due to faulty registration on the multipositive, the cerise colour is positioned slightly to the right resulting in a white line at left of flag in sky, also cerise colour overlaps ear and face below ear (Th. B–C3 and C4), OP. Note This variety is not an ordinary colour shift and is therefore best collected in a positional block. A similar variety, although much less marked, is found on R. 14/1, also OP
- 17/4 White spot in lower part of "V" of "SALVATION" at bottom of stamp, OP

1s.6d. Cyls. 1A–1B–1C–1D no dot
- 1/1 Retouch on right arm of left-hand man (Th. D–12), OP
- 1/4 White flaw on Queen's hair behind ear (Th. D12), OP
- 15/6 Retouch on right leg of left-hand man (Th. G2), OP
- 19/3 Diagonal scratch across Queen's forehead and nose (Th. B–C10), OP
- 20/1 White flaw on Queen's neck by necklace (Th. E11), OP
- 20/3 Small red flaw at back of Queen's hair (Th. D12), OP
- 20/5 A wispy line of blue dots by left leg of right-hand man (Th. F7), OP

Sheet Details
Sheet size: 120 (6×20). Single-pane reel-fed

Sheet markings:

Cylinder numbers:
- **3d.** Opposite rows 18/19 at left, boxed
- **1s.6d.** Opposite row 19 at left, boxed

Guide holes: Opposite rows 14/15 (boxed), at both sides

Marginal arrows (photo-etched):
"W" shaped, at top, bottom and sides

Marginal rule: At bottom of sheet

Colour register marks:
Opposite rows 1/2 and 17/18, at both sides

Autotron marks (solid):
- **3d.** Blue, indigo, brown, cerise, yellow below vertical rows 1/3
- **1s.6d.** Red, brown, blue, yellow below vertical rows 1/3

Colour designations:
- **3d.** G1 YELLOW G2 RED G3 BROWN G4 BLUE BLACK G5 BLUE in right margin reading upwards opposite rows 9/3 ("G1 YELLOW" is very faint on some sheets)
- **1s.6d.** G1 YELLOW G2 BLUE G3 BROWN G4 RED in right margin reading upwards opposite rows 9/3.

Traffic lights (boxed):
- **3d.** Blue, indigo, brown, cerise, yellow opposite rows 18/19 at right
- **1s.6d.** Red, brown, blue, yellow opposite rows 18/19 at right

Imprimaturs from the NPM or BPMA

A. Ordinary
Nos. W61/W62 imperforate, watermark Type W.**24**

Watermark upright (set of 2)	£2000
3d. "Diadem flaw" R. 16/6	£1500
3d. cylinder 2A, 2B, 1C, 1D, 1E block of six	£7000
1s.6d. "Extra pearl" flaw R. 17/1	£1500
1s.6d. cylinder 1A, 1B, 1C, 1D block of six	£7000

B. Phosphor
Nos. WP61/WP62 imperforate, watermark Type W.**24**

Watermark upright (set of 2)	£2000
3d. "Diadem flaw" R. 16/6	£1500
3d. cylinder 2A, 2B, 1C, 1D, 1E block of six	£7000
1s.6d. "Extra pearl" flaw R. 17/1	£1500
1s.6d. cylinder 1A, 1B, 1C, 1D block of six	£7000

Quantities Issued:

	Ordinary	Phosphor
3d.	54,312,000	4,261,200
1s.6d.	5,244,120	652,320

Withdrawn: 28.2.66 (3d. ordinary sold out Dec. 1965)

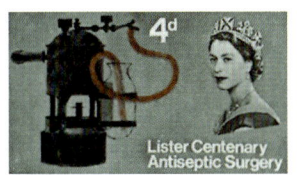

Centenary of Joseph Lister's Discovery of Antiseptic Surgery. **1965** **W**

Type **W63**. Lister's Carbolic Spray
(Des. Peter Gauld)

Type **W64**. Lister and Chemical Symbols
(Des. Frank Ariss)

W63c, WP63d

W63e
"e" of "Antiseptic" nearly filled by white flaw (later retouched leaving malformed "e"

W63d, WP63e
large grey retouch outlines face. Similar, but more minor flaws can be found on Row19/2, 20/1.

1965 (1 September). **Centenary of Joseph Lister's Discovery of Antiseptic Surgery.** Types W63/W64

A. Ordinary

W63 =SG 667

		Mint	Used
4d.	indigo, brown-red and grey-black	10	10
a.	Brown-red (tube) omitted	£600	
b.	Indigo omitted	£7000	
c.	Corner scratch (No dot, R. 17/1)	30·00	
d.	Face retouch (No dot, R. 18/1)	30·00	
e.	Filled "e" (Dot, R. 20/4)	30·00	

W64 =SG 668

1s.	black, purple and new blue	40	40
a.	Watermark inverted	£675	

First Day Cover (W63/W64)	5·00

B. Phosphor

WP63 =SG 667p

		Mint	Used
4d.	Three bands	25	25
a.	Brown-red (tube) omitted	£6750	
b.	Narrow band at left or right (stamp with vert. margin)	3·00	
c.	Error. Two broad bands	35·00	
ca.	Error. One thin and one broad band	40·00	
d.	Corner scratch (No dot, R. 17/1)	30·00	
e.	Face retouch (No dot, R. 18/1)	30·00	

WP64 =SG 668p

1s.	Three bands	1·00	1·00
a.	Watermark inverted	£550	
b.	Narrow band at left or right (stamp with vert. margin)	3·00	
c.	Error. Two broad bands	50·00	

First Day Cover (WP63/WP64)	9·00

Nos. W63/W64 exist postmarked 1 August 1965 at Skeabost Bridge (Skye) (probably a mis-print of 31 August), and can also be found cancelled 31 August elsewhere.

Nos. WP63c/WP63ca came from a sheet showing misplaced phosphor bands; No. WP63ca were from the left-hand vertical row only.

Cylinder Numbers (Blocks of Four)

	Perforation Types		
	A (E/I)	A (E/I)	F (P/E)
Cylinder Nos.	No dot	Dot	No dot
4d. 4A (black)–1B (blue)–1C (red). Ordinary	3·00	1·50	†
4A–1B–1C. Phosphor	4·00	1·50	†
1s. 1A (black)–1B (purple)–1C (blue). Ordinary	†	†	2·50
1A–1B–1C. Phosphor	†	†	5·50

Minor Constant Flaws

4d. Cyls. 4A–1B–1C no dot

4/1	Line of white dots under apparatus (Th. H3–4), OP
4/4	Two dark flaws to lower right of apparatus (Th. G5–6), OP
5/6	Prominent retouch in front of Queen's dress (Th. E–F10), OP
6/6	Grey flaw hanging from rear jewel of tiara (Th. B12), OP
10/3	Grey flaw on Queen's forehead (Th. B10), OP
11/4 to 12/4	Grey line under "g" of "Surgery" extending across gutter joining frames, OP
11/6	Diagonal grey line from top left corner to apparatus (Th. A1–B2), OP
16/5	Retouch on Queen's forehead (Th. B10), OP
17/2	White flaw in loop of d of value, OP
19/6	Grey spots on Queen's forehead (Th. B10–11), OP
19/6 and 20/6	Grey line extends down right-hand margin, OP
20/3	Vertical grey line from lower left corner of stamp to gutter (Th. H1), OP
20/6	Base of "4" joined to tube by dark line (Th. B7), OP

4d. Cyls. 4A–1B–1C dot

1/4	Blue spot between "p" and "t" of "antiseptic", OP
8/2	Retouch on Queen's collar (Th. E12), OP
10/2	Diagonal grey line above te of Lister and in front of Queen's collar (Th. F8–E10), OP
13/3	Retouch behind Queen's necklace (Th. D12), OP
18/1	Retouch on Queen's jaw close to ear (Th. D11), OP

193

W 1965 Commonwealth Arts Festival.

19/2	White scratch above "ur" of "Surgery", OP
20/1	Two dark spots at right of Queen's mouth (Th. D11), OP
20/6	Retouch in front of Queen's neck (Th. E10), OP

1s. Cyls. 1A–1B–1C no dot

1/5	Large black spot at rear of Queen's collar (Th. E13), OP
3/1	Retouch along Liste's right shoulder (Th. D3–C4), OP
3/2	Broken frame line behind Queen's portrait was retouched by dots (Th. C13), OP
6/1	Missing portions of jewels left of large cross on diadem heavily retouched (Th. A10), OP
8/1	White retouch on Queen's throat (Th. D11), OP
11/2	Extra pearl half way up necklace (Th. D11), OP
11/3	Small retouch on Queen's left cheek (Th. D11), OP
14/2	Retouch on Queen's collar (Th. E12), OP
15/6	Line from Queen's left eyebrow into hair (Th. B11), OP
16/4	Retouch on back of Queen's collar (Th. E13), OP
17/6	Blue spot normally found by Lister's right wrist is missing (Th. E6), OP
19/1	Dark spot under Queen's nose (Th. C10), OP
20/3	Retouch below Queen's necklace (Th. D12), OP

Sheet Details

Sheet size: 120 (6×20). 4d. double-pane reel-fed; 1s. single- pane sheet-fed

Sheet markings:

Cylinder numbers: Opposite R. 19/1, boxed

Guide holes: Opposite rows 14/15 (boxed), at left (no dot) or right (dot)

Marginal arrows (photo-etched):
"W" shaped, at top, bottom and sides

Marginal rule: At bottom of sheet

Colour register marks:
- **4d.** Opposite rows 2/3 and 16/17, at left (no dot)
- **1s.** Above and below vertical rows 1/2 and 5/6

Autotron marks (solid):
- **4d.** Black, indigo, brown-red opposite rows 3/5, at right (no dot) or left (dot)
- **1s.** None

Colour designations: None

Traffic lights (boxed):
- **4d.** Black, indigo, brown-red opposite R. 19/6
- **1s.** Black, purple, blue opposite R. 20/6

Imprimaturs from the NPM or BPMA

A. Ordinary
Nos. W63/W64 imperforate, watermark Type W.**24**

Watermark upright (set of 2)	£2000
4d. "filled e" variety R. 20/4	£1500
4d. cylinder 4A, 1B, 1C (dot) block of four	£5000
1s. cylinder 1A, 1B, 1C (dot) block of four	£5000

B. Phosphor
Nos. WP63/WP64 imperforate, watermark Type W.**24**

Watermark upright (set of 2)	£2000
4d. cylinder 4A, 1B, 1C (dot) block of four	£5000
1s. cylinder 1A, 1B, 1C (dot) block of four	£5000

Quantities Issued:	Ordinary	Phosphor
4d.	92,167,440	10,732,800
1s.	8,368,800	1,452,360

Withdrawn: 15.4.66

Type **W65.** Trinidad Carnival Dancers

Type **W66.** Canadian Folk-dancers

(Des. David Gentleman and Rosalind Dease)

1965 *(1 September).* **Commonwealth Arts Festival.**
Types **W65/W66**

The Festival was aimed at promoting the cultural traditions of Commonwealth countries and was held in London and other centres between 16 September and 2 October.

A. Ordinary

W65 =SG 669		Mint	Used
6d.	black and orange	10	10

W66 =SG 670			
1s.6d.	black and light reddish violet	40	40

First Day Cover (W65/W66)			7·00

B. Phosphor

WP65 =SG 669p			
6d.	Three bands	40	40
a.	Narrow band at left or right (stamp with vert. margin)	3·00	

WP66 =SG 670p			
1s.6d.	Three bands	1·25	1·25
a.	Narrow band at left or right (stamp with vert. margin)	3·50	
b.	Error. Two broad bands	30·00	
c.	Error. Two bands (9·5 and 6 mm.)	35·00	

First Day Cover (WP65/WP66)		14·00

Nos. W65/W66 are known postmarked 1 August 1965 at Skeabost Bridge (Skye) (probably a mis-print for 31 August).

No. WP66c come from the right-hand side of the sheet where the narrow band occurs on the stamp instead of the first vertical row of perforations.

Cylinder Numbers (Blocks of Four)

		Perforation Type F(L) (I/E)
Cylinder Nos.		No dot
6d.	1A (orange)–1B (black). (Ordinary)	1·25
	1A–1B. Phosphor	2·50
1s.6d.	1A (violet)1B (black). Ordinary	2·50
	1A–1B. Phosphor	6·50

Minor Constant Flaws

6d. Cyls. 1A–1B (no dot)

1/2	Damaged right arm of "v" of "Festival", OP
1/6	Black spot at back of Queen's neck under hair (Th. C12), OP
11/2	S shaped line of white dots on Queen's neck (Th. D–E11), OP

Commonwealth Arts Festival. **1965**

17/1 Pale area in background by right sleeve of central figure (Th. D3–4), OP

1s.6d. Cyls. 1A–1B no dot

2/3 White flaw under "n" of "Commonwealth", OP

3/4 Vertical scratch from Queen's ear to neck (Th. C–D12), OP

5/6 Vertical line from diadem to Queen's neck (Th. B–D11), OP

7/5 Pale area below "C" of "Commonwealth", OP

9/2 White triangle in Queen's hair (Th. B11), OP

13/6 White spot between emblems and rear cross of diadem (Th. B12), OP

15/1 Diagonal scratch to right of "C" of "Commonwealth" (Th. G–12), OP

20/6 Two dots to right of Queen's left eyebrow (Th. C11), OP

Sheet Details

Sheet size: 120 (6×20). Single-pane reel-fed

Sheet markings:

Cylinder numbers: Opposite R. 19/1, boxed

Guide holes: Above vertical rows 3/4 and below vertical row 5, unboxed

Marginal arrows (photo-etched):
"W" shaped, at top, bottom and sides

Marginal rule: At bottom of sheet

Colour register marks:

6d. Opposite rows 1/2 and 18/19, at both sides and opposite rows 10/11 (orange only), at left

1s.6d. Opposite rows 1/2, at both sides, rows 9/10 (violet only), at left and rows 18/19, at left and 17/18 at right

Autotron marks (solid):

6d. Orange, black above and below vertical rows 3/4

1s.6d. Violet, black above and below vertical rows 3/4

Colour designations:

6d. G ORANGE G BLACK reading upwards opposite rows 14/12, right margin

1s.6d. G MAUVE G BLACK reading upwards opposite rows 15/13, right margin

Traffic lights (boxed):

6d. Black, orange opposite R. 19/6

1s.6d. Black, violet opposite R. 19/6

Imprimaturs from the NPM or BPMA

A. Ordinary

Nos. W65/W66 imperforate, watermark Type W.**24**

Watermark upright (set of 2)	£2000
6d. cylinder 1A, 1B block of four	£5000
1s.6d. cylinder 1A, 1B block of four	£5000

B. Phosphor

Nos. WP65/WP66 imperforate, watermark Type W.**24**

Watermark upright (set of 2)	£2000
6d. cylinder 1A, 1B block of four	£5000
1s.6d. cylinder 1A, 1B block of four	£5000

Quantities Issued:	Ordinary	Phosphor
6d.	12,264,840	1,621,080
1s.6d.	5,003,000	788,880

Withdrawn: 15.4.66

Battle of Britain 1940

Type **W67.** Flight of Spitfires

Type **W68.** Pilot in Hurricane

Battle of Britain 1940

Type **W69.** Wing-tips of Spitfire and Messerschmitt ME-109

Battle of Britain 1940

Type **W70.** Spitfires attacking Heinkel HE-111 Bomber

Battle of Britain 1940

Type **W71.** Spitfire attacking Stuka Dive-bomber

Battle of Britain 1940

Type **W72.** Hurricanes over Wreck of Dornier DO-1722 Bomber

Battle of Britain 1940

Type **W73.** Anti-aircraft Artillery in Action

W 1965 25th Anniversary of Battle of Britain.

Type W74. Air-battle over St Paul's Cathedral

(Des. Andrew Restall (9d.), David Gentleman and Rosalind Dease (others))

1965 *(13 September).* **25th Anniversary of Battle of Britain.** Types W67/W74

The Battle of Britain was the first major campaign in world history to be fought entirely between opposing air forces.

The 4d. values were issued together se-tenant in blocks of six (3×2) within the sheet

A. Ordinary

		Mint	Used
W67 =SG 671			
4d.	yellow-olive and black	25	25
a.	Block of 6. Nos. W67/W72	2·50	2·50
W68 =SG 672			
4d.	yellow-olive, olive-grey and black	25	25
W69 =SG 673			
4d.	red, new blue, yellow-olive, olive-grey and black	25	25
b.	Damaged wing (Cyl. 3D Dot, R. 19/3)	30·00	
W70 =SG 674			
4d.	olive-grey, yellow-olive and black	25	25
W71 =SG 675			
4d.	olive-grey, yellow-olive and black	25	25
b.	Stuka retouch (Cyl. 1E No dot, R. 2/2)	30·00	
W72 =SG 676			
4d.	olive-grey, yellow-olive, new blue and black	25	25
b.	New blue omitted	†	£6500
c.	Damaged tailplane (Cyl. 3D Dot, R. 20/3)	30·00	
W73 =SG 677			
9d.	bluish violet, orange and slate-purple	1·75	1·75
a.	Watermark inverted	£100	
W74 =SG 678			
1s.3d.	light and deep grey, black and light and bright blue	1·75	1·75
a.	Watermark inverted	£190	
b.	Face value omitted	£1500	
First Day Cover (W67/W74)		10·00	
Presentation Pack (W67/W74)		40·00	

No. W72b is only known commercially used on cover from Truro.

No. W74b is caused by a 12mm downward shift of black which resulted in the value being omitted from the top row of one sheet.

B. Phosphor

WP67 =SG 671p			
4d.	Three bands	40	40
a.	Block of 6. Nos. WP67/WP72	3·75	3·75
b.	Narrow band at left (stamp with vert. margin)	2·50	
WP68 =SG 672p			
4d.	Three bands	40	40
WP69 =SG 673p			
4d.	Three bands	40	40
b.	Narrow band at right (stamp with vert. margin)	2·50	
c.	Damaged wing (Cyl. 3D Dot, R. 19/3)	30·00	
d.	Error. Two bands		
WP70 =SG 674p			
4d.	Three bands	40	40
b.	Narrow band at left (stamp with vert. margin)	2·50	
WP71 =SG 675p			
4d.	Three bands	40	40
b.	Stuka retouch (Cyl. 1E No dot, R. 2/2)	30·00	
WP72 =SG 676p			
4d.	Three bands	40	40
b.	Narrow band at right (stamp with vert. margin)	2·50	
c.	Damaged tailplane (Cyl. 3D Dot, R. 20/3)	30·00	
WP73 =SG 677p			
9d.	Three bands	2·00	2·00
a.	Narrow band at left or right (stamp with vert. margin)	5·00	
b.	Error. Two bands		
WP74 =SG 678p			
1s.3d.	Three bands	2·00	2·00
a.	Watermark inverted	5·00	
b.	Narrow band at left or right (stamp with vert. margin)	5·00	
First Day Cover (WP67/WP74)		30·00	

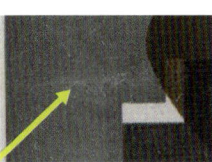

W69b, WP69c

W71b, WP71b
This variety only occurs in combination with cyls. 3A–1B–1C–3D. With cyls. 2A–1B–1C–3D it is normal

W72c, WP72c

25th Anniversary of Battle of Britain. 1965 W

Cylinder Numbers (Blocks of Twelve (3×4) (4d.), Four (9d.), Six (1s.3d.))

(a) Ordinary

	Perforation Types		
	A (E/1)	A (E/1)	F (P/E)
Cylinder Nos.	No dot	Dot	No dot
4d. 2A (black)–1B (blue)–1C (red)–3D (olive-grey)–1E (yellow-olive)	9·00	30·00	†
3A–1B–1C–3D–1E	9·00	35·00	†
9d. 1A (slate-purple)–1B (violet)–1C (orange)	†	†	8·50
1s.3d. 1A (black)–1B (light blue)–1C (light grey)–1D (deep grey)–1E (bright blue)	†	†	12·50

(b) Phosphor

4d. 3A (black)–1B (blue)–1C (red)–3D (olive-grey)–1E (yellow-olive)	11·00	35·00	
9d. 1A (slate-purple)–1B (violet)–1C (orange)	†	†	10·00
1s.3d. 1A (black)–1B (light blue)–1C (light grey)–1D (deep grey)–1E (bright blue)	†	†	14·00

Minor Constant Flaws

4d. Cyls. 1B–1C–3D–1E no dot in combination with black cyls. 2A or 3A no dot

- 1/3 Horizontal scratch retouch under right of cross (Th. F5–7), OP
- 1/6 Similar retouch under centre of cross (Th. F3–6), OP
- 15/2 Nick in centre line of fuselage at left (Th. D1), OP
- 20/1 Small dark area on left wing of bomber (Th. D2), OP

4d. Cyl. 3A no dot

- 1/4 Nick in lower curve of "B" in "BRITAIN", OP
- 7/2 Black spot in front of Queen's ear (Th. C12), OP
- 12/3 White scar across Queen's left cheek (Th. C12), OP
- 13/2 Fine vertical line on Queen's left cheek (Th. C12), OP
- 18/3 Extra white dot in Queen's hair behind earring (Th. C13), OP

4d. Cyls. 1B–1C–3D–1E dot in combination with black cyls. 2A or 3A dot

- 5/3 Dark horizontal line below right arm of cross (Th. F56), OP
- 8/1 Dark spot at left end of bomber's wing (Th. C1), OP
- 11/2 Line of white dots on pilot's right shoulder (Th. E8–F10), OP
- 16/1 Dark spot at right end of bomber's wing (Th. B9), OP
- 16/3 Notch in bomber's tail under "B" of "Battle" (Th. A4), OP

9d. Cyls. 1A–1B–1C no dot

- 11/2 Line across Queen's face under eyes (Th. C10–11), OP
- 12/3 Retouch in sky behind hat of man with flag (Th. C1), OP
- 20/5 White patch below where vapour trails cross (Th. C5–6), OP

1s.3d. Cyls. 1A–1B–1C–1D–1E no dot

- 4/4 Scratch below 1 of 1940 (Th. H5), OP
- 5/3 Horizontal bright blue line above building at right (Th. F8–10), OP
- 5/4 Dark line between "Br" of "Britain" (Th. G–H5), OP
- 9/5 Retouches in sky at lower right (Th. D–E9–10), OP
- 14/4 Blue dot in front of Queen's ear (Th. C12), OP
- 20/3 Line under value is shorter at right, OP

Sheet Details

Sheet size: 120 (6×20)

4d. In *se-tenant* blocks of six, double-pane reel-fed

9d., 1s.3d. Single-pane sheet-fed

Sheet markings:

Cylinder numbers:
- **4d., 1s.3d.** Opposite rows 18/19 at left, boxed
- **9d.** Opposite R. 19/1, boxed

Guide holes:
- **4d.** In double "SON" box opposite rows 14/15, at left (no dot) or right (dot)
- **Others:** None

Marginal arrows (photo-etched): "W" shaped, at top, bottom and sides

Marginal rule: At bottom of sheet

Colour register marks:
- **4d.** None
- **9d.** Above and below vertical rows 1/2 and 6
- **1s.3d.** Above and below vertical rows 1/2 and 5/6
  There is a large violet blob of colour under vertical rows 1/2 in the 9d. value

Autotron marks (solid):
- **4d.** Black, red, blue, olive-grey, yellow-olive opposite rows 3/7, at right (no dot) or left (dot)
- **Others:** None

Colour designations: None

Traffic lights (boxed):
- **4d.** Olive-grey, red, black, blue, yellow-olive opposite rows 18/19 at right
- **9d.** Violet, orange, slate-purple opposite R. 19/6
- **1s.3d.** Deep grey, light blue, light grey, black, bright blue opposite rows 18/19 at right

Imprimaturs from the NPM or BPMA

A. Ordinary
Nos. W67/W72 imperforate, watermark Type W.**24**
Watermark upright (*se-tenant* block of six)	£6000

Nos. W73/W74 imperforate, watermark Type W.**24**
Watermark upright (2 values)	£2000

B. Phosphor
Nos. WP67/WP72 imperforate, watermark Type W.**24**
Watermark upright (*se-tenant* block of six)	£6000

Nos. WP73/WP74 imperforate, watermark Type W.**24**
Watermark upright (2 values)	£2000

Quantities Issued:

	Ordinary	Phosphor
4d.	103,417,440	11,560,440
9d.	6,195,960	1,143,120
1s.3d.	6,469,440	1,239,840
Pack	28,524	—

Withdrawn: 31.5.66

W 1965 Opening of Post Office Tower.

W75b, WP75b

Type **W75**. Post Office Tower and Georgian Buildings
Type **W76**. Post Office Tower and Nash Terrace, Regent's Park 

(Des. Clive Abbott)

1965 (8 October). **Opening of Post Office Tower.**
Types **W75/W76**

At the time, the tallest building in London, the Post Office Tower is 620 feet high and helps to provide more long distance telephone circuits and more television channels. An additional feature of this issue was the inclusion of the names of both the designer and printers at the foot of the stamps and this became the practice for many later issues until 1969. Watermark sideways on 3d.

A. Ordinary

W75	=SG 679	Mint	Used
3d.	olive-yellow, new blue and bronze-green	10	10
a.	Olive-yellow (tower) omitted	£6000	£2250
b.	Extra window (Dot, R. 4/18)	30·00	
W76	**=SG 680**		
1s.3d.	bronze-green, yellow-green and blue	20	20
a.	Watermark inverted	£175	
First Day Cover (W75/W76)			2·50
Presentation Pack (W75/W76)			12·50

B. Phosphor

WP75	=SG 679p		
3d.	One band at left	15	15
a.	Band at right	15	15
ab.	Nos. WP75/WP75a (horiz. pair)	30	50
ac.	Error. Broad band *se-tenant* with missing phosphor (horiz. pair)	55·00	
b.	Extra window (Dot, R. 4/18)	30·00	
WP76	**=SG 680p**		
1s.3d.	Three bands	30	30
a.	Watermark inverted	£200	
b.	Error. Left-hand band omitted	30·00	
First Day Cover (WP75/WP76)			4·75
Presentation Pack* (WP75/WP76)			12·50

* See note under withdrawn at end of listing.
The above are known pre-released on 4 October at Aish, South Brent (Devon).
The one phosphor band on No. WP75 was produced by printing broad phosphor bands across alternate rows of vertical perforations. Individual examples show the band at right or left (same prices either way).

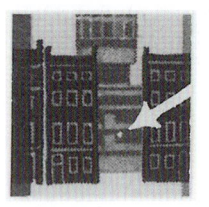

Cylinder Numbers (Blocks of Four)
(a) Ordinary

		Perforation Types		
		A (I/E)	A (I/E)	F (P/E)
	Cylinder Nos.	No dot	Dot	No dot
3d.	1A (blue)–1B (green)–1C (yellow)*	1·25	1·25	†
1s.3d.	1A (yellow-green)–1B (bronze-green)–1C (blue)	†	†	1·50

(b) Phosphor

| 3d. | 1A (blue)–1B (green)–1C (yellow)* | 1·25 | 1·25 | † |
| 1s.3d. | 1A (yellow-green)–1B (bronze-green)–1C (blue) | † | † | 1·75 |

* In the 3d. dot pane the dot after 1C is omitted in error.
For perforation Type A the 3d. is with sheet orientated showing head to left.

Minor Constant Flaws

3d. Cyls. 1A–1B–1C dot
- 1/20 White spot at base of tower (Th. L3), OP
- 2/19 Olive-yellow spot below second ground floor window of building at base of tower at right (Th. M4), OP
- 2/20 Blue spot below "SO" of "HARRISON", OP
- 5/2 White spot in "O" of "OFFICE", OP
- 5/8 Blue spot surrounded by pale area below "T" of "TOWER", OP
- 5/16 Pale spot in blue panel to left of "3d". (Th. J4), OP

1s.3d. Cyls. 1A–1B–1C no dot
- 1/5 Pale area around lower tip of "3" of "1/3", OP
- 3/1 Small retouch below "T" of "TOWER" (Th. C–D1), OP
- 4/1 Horizontal line of retouching below "1/3" (Th. D11–12), OP
- 6/2 Scratch in sky above roof of left-hand terrace (Th. E2), OP
- 10/3 Dark spot to left of Queen's nose (Th. C8), OP
- 10/4 Retouch to background at top right of "1" of "1/3", OP
- 15/4 White scratch through "E" and over "R" of "TOWER", OP

Sheet Details
Sheet sizes:
- 3d. 120 (20×6). Double-pane reel-fed
- 1s.3d. 120 (6×20). Single-pane sheet-fed

Sheet markings:
Cylinder numbers:
- 3d. Above vertical row 2, boxed
- 1s.3d. Opposite R. 19/1, boxed

Guide holes:
- 3d. In double "SON" box above vertical rows 6/7 (no dot) or below (dot)
- 1s.3d. None

Marginal arrows (photo-etched):
"W" shaped, at top, bottom and sides

Marginal rule:
- 3d. At left of sheet
- 1s.3d. At bottom of sheet

Colour register marks:
- 3d. None

20th Anniversary of the United Nations. **1965**

1s.3d. Above and below vertical rows 1/2 and 5/6

Autotron marks (solid):
3d. Yellow, green, blue below vertical rows 15/17 (no dot) or above (dot)
1s.3d. None

Colour designations: None

Traffic lights (boxed):
3d. Yellow, green, blue reading left to right below vertical row 2
1s.3d. Yellow-green, bronze-green, blue opposite R. 19/6

Imprimaturs from the NPM or BPMA

A. Ordinary
Nos. W75/W76 imperforate, watermark Type W.**24**

Watermark upright (1s.3d.) or sideways (3d.) (set of 2)	£2000
3d. "extra widow" variety R. 4/18	£1500
3d. cylinder 1A, 1B, 1C (dot*) block of four	£5000
1s.3d. cylinder 1A, 1B, 1C block of four	£5000

B. Phosphor
Nos. WP75/WP76 imperforate, watermark Type W.**24**

Watermark upright (1s.3d.) or sideways (3d.) (set of 2)	£2000
3d. "extra widow" variety R. 4/18	£1500
3d. cylinder 1A, 1B, 1C (dot*) block of four	£5000
1s.3d. cylinder 1A, 1B, 1C block of four	£5000

Quantities Issued:

	Ordinary	Phosphor
3d.	51,291,120	4,274,880
1s.3d.	5,722,320	1,107,480
Pack	25,060	(ordinary and phosphor)

Withdrawn: 30.6.66

When the Post Office Tower was opened on 19 May 1966 these stamps were issued from automatic machines giving a block of four of the 3d. and a pair of the 1s.3d. dispensed in envelopes, and packs were also issued from a machine. These continued to be available after the stamps had been withdrawn everywhere else and early in 1968 the ordinary stamps were replaced by phosphor stamps and packs. These were withdrawn on the introduction of decimal currency.

Type **W77**. UN Emblem

Type **W78**. ICY Emblem

(Des. Jeffery Matthews)

1965 *(25 October)*. **20th Anniversary of the United Nations.** Types **W77/W78**

Commemorating the 20th Anniversary of the formation of the United Nations in 1945. 1965 was also designated International Co-operation Year and the symbol of the clasped hands is shown on the 1s.6d. value.

A. Ordinary

W77 =SG 681

	Mint	Used
3d. black, yellow-orange and light blue	10	10
a. Broken circle (Dot, R. 11/4)	65·00	
b. Lake in Russia (Dot, R. 19/3)	65·00	
c. Flying saucer flaw retouched (Dot, R. 18/3)	25·00	
e. Imperf. between stamp and top margin*	£1800	

W78 =SG 682

1s.6d. black, bright purple and light blue	35	35
a. Watermark inverted		£2250

First Day Cover (W77/W78)		5·00

B. Phosphor

WP77 =SG 681p

3d. One centre band	25	25
a. Broken circle (Dot, R. 11/4)	65·00	
b. Lake in Russia (Dot, R. 19/3)	65·00	
c. Flying saucer flaw (Dot, R. 18/3)	30·00	
d. Retouched	25·00	

WP78 =SG 682p

1s.6d. Three bands	1·00	1·00
a. Error. Two bands	35·00	

First Day Cover (WP77/WP78)		9·00

* No. W77e was caused by a paper fold.

W77a, WP77a   W77b, WP77b

1965 20th Anniversary of the United Nations.

WP77c
Stroke over "S" of "ANNIVERSARY" and smudge

W77c, WP77d
Retouched. Smudge removed

Cylinder Numbers (Blocks of Four)
(a) Ordinary

Cylinder Nos.	Perforation Types		
	A (E/I) No dot	A (E/I) Dot	F (P/E) No dot
3d. 1A (black)–1B (blue)–1C (orange)*	1·25	1·25	
1s.6d. 1A (black)–1B (blue)–1C (purple)	†	†	2·75

(b) Phosphor

Cylinder Nos.	A (E/I) No dot	A (E/I) Dot	F (P/E) No dot
3d. 1A (black)–1B (blue)–1C (orange)*	1·50	1·50	†
1s.6d. 1A (black)–1B (blue)–1C (purple)	†	†	6·00

* On the 3d. dot pane the dot is before instead of after the "1C".

Minor Constant Flaws
3d. Cyls. 1A–1B–1C no dot

1/1	Diagonal scratch across Queen's face (Th. C11–12), OP
1/4	Round pale grey flaw by Queen's left eye (Th. C11–12), OP
2/2	Pale patch on Queen's neck (Th. E12), OP
8/5	Dotted white scratch on right side of "0" of large "20" (Th. D8–9), OP
9/2	Black flaw in lower loop of "3", OP
10/4	Small break in middle of "S" of "ANNIVERSARY", OP
13/1	Curved white scratch in bottom right-hand corner of blue panel (Th. H9–10), OP
14/4	Scratch on Queen's neck by necklace (Th. E12), OP
15/6	Black spot on Queen's forehead (Th. C11), OP
19/4	Horizontal white scratch over "VERSARY", OP
20/6	Black flaws between laurel leaves over middle of large 2 (Th. D3), OP

3d. Cyls. 1A–1B–1C dot

20/1	White scratch through "ARY" U, OP

1s.6d. Cyls. 1A–1B–1C no dot

2/1	White scratch behind Queen's neck (Th. D12–E12), OP
5/1	Small patch of white dots to right of Queen's head (Th. B13), OP
6/2	Pale patch to left of top of large "U" (Th. B1), OP
10/1	Pale patch in background to left of Queen's mouth (Th. D10), OP
11/2	Pink spot central below large "N" (Th. F7), OP
15/1	White scratch in base of large "U", (Th. E2), OP
20/1	Vertical white scratch in background behind Queen's head (Th. C–D13), OP
20/5	Retouch to background within upper thumb of symbol (Th. B5), OP

Sheet Details
Sheet size: 120 (6×20).3d. double-pane reel-fed; 1s.6d. single-pane sheet-fed

Sheet markings:
Cylinder numbers: Opposite R. 19/1, boxed

Guide holes:
  3d. In double "SON" box opposite rows 14/15, at left (no dot) or right (dot). An unusual feature of this stamp is that there is an additional single box printed in orange beneath the double box which is in black
  1s.6d. None

Marginal arrows (photo-etched):
"W" shaped, at top, bottom and sides

Marginal rule: At bottom of sheet

Colour register marks:
  3d. None
  1s.6d. Above and below vertical rows 1 and 6

Autotron marks (solid):
  3d. Black, blue, orange opposite rows 5/6 at right (no dot) or left (dot)
  1s.6d. None

Colour designations (usually trimmed off):
  3d. G1 BROWN G2 BLUE G3 BLACK in right margin reading upwards opposite rows 8/5 on dot panes
  1s.6d. None

Traffic lights (boxed):
  3d. Black, blue, orange opposite R. 19/6
  1s.6d. Black, blue, purple opposite R. 19/6

Imprimaturs from the NPM or BPMA

A. Ordinary
Nos. W77/W78 imperforate, watermark Type W.**24**

Watermark upright (set of 2)	£2000
3d. cylinder 1A, 1B, 1C (no dot) block of four	£5000
1s.6d. cylinder 1A, 1B, 1C block of four	£5000

B. Phosphor
Nos. WP77/WP78 imperforate, watermark Type W.**24**

Watermark upright (set of 2)	£2000
3d. "Flying saucer flaw" retouched R. 18/3	£1500
3d. cylinder 1A, 1B, 1C (dot) block of four	£5000
1s.6d. cylinder 1A, 1B, 1C block of four	£5000

Quantities Issued:

	Ordinary	Phosphor
3d.	50,598,720	4,488,240
1s.6d.	5,476,800	1,018,560

Withdrawn: 30.6.66

ITU Centenary. 1965

Type **W79**. Telecommunications Network

Type **W80**. Radio Waves and Switchboard

(Des. Andrew Restall)

1965 *(15 November)*. **ITU Centenary.** Types **W79/W80**

The aims of the Union created in 1865, then known as the International Telegraph Union, were to promote, maintain and extend international co-operation in telecommunications.

A. Ordinary

W79 =SG 683	Mint	Used
9d. red, ultramarine, deep slate-violet, black and pink	20	20
a. Watermark inverted	30·00	

W80 =SG 684		
1s.6d. red, greenish blue, indigo, black and light pink	40	40
a. Light pink omitted	£4000	£2500
b. Watermark inverted	—	
c. Red pin with arm (R. 1/4)	—	
d. Retouched arm	25·00	

First Day Cover (W79/W80)		8·00

B. Phosphor

WP79 =SG 683p		
9d. Three bands	75	75
a. Watermark inverted	£110	
b. Error. Two bands	70·00	
c. Narrow band at left (stamp with vert. margin)	3·00	

WP80 =SG 684p		
1s.6d. Three bands	2·00	2·00
a. Error. Two bands	30·00	
b. Narrow band at left (stamp with vert. margin)	8·00	
c. Red pin with arm (R. 1/4)	40·00	
d. Retouched arm	25·00	

First Day Cover (WP79/WP80)		13·00

Originally scheduled for issue on 17 May 1965, supplies from the Philatelic Bureau were sent in error to reach a dealer on that date and another dealer received his supply on 27 May. Ordinary and phosphor sets exist on cover postmarked Stretford on 18 May 1965.

WP80c, WP80c   W80d, WP80d

On the phosphor printing the red pin has a projecting arm at right; this was later retouched leaving faint traces of red on the pink background. The ordinary stamp has been reported with the variety (W80d), presumably from the phosphor printing but with phosphor omitted.

Cylinder Numbers (Blocks of Six)

		Perforation Type F (P/E)
(a) Ordinary		
Cylinder Nos. (No dot)		
9d. 1A (ultram.)–1B (red)–1C (violet)–1D (pink)–2E (black)		1·80
1s.6d. 2A (blue)–1B (indigo)–1C (pink)–1D (red)–2E (black)		3·50
(b) Phosphor		
9d. 1A (ultram.)–1B (red)–C (violet)–1D (pink)–2E (black)		6·50
1s.6d. 2A (blue)–1B (indigo)–1C (pink)–1D (red)–2E (black)		15·00

The same black cylinder was used for both values.

Minor Constant Flaws

9d. and **1s.6d.** Cyl. 2E
  2/4 Small white curl in hair behind Queen's ear (Th. C12), OP
  5/2 Small nick in diagonal stroke of first "N" of "UNION", OP

9d. Cyls. 1A–1B–1C–1D–2E
  6/5 Small break in diagonal blue network line at right (Th. B8), OP
  9/5 Diagonal white scratch in blue background above "ATIO" of "INTERNATIONAL" (Th. E3), OP
  10/5 Damaged lower half of 1 of 1865, shows as white nick and white scratch, OP
  17/6 Small nick in right-hand stroke of first "M" of "TELECOMMUNICATION", OP
  20/5 Wavy scratch in background over "OMMUNI" of "TELECOMMUNICATION" (Th. E79), OP

1s.6d. Cyls. 2A–1B–1C–1D–2E
  3/3 Retouches to background above first "C" of "TELECOMMUNICATION", P

Sheet Details
  Sheet size: 120 (6×20). Single-pane sheet-fed

Sheet markings:

Cylinder numbers: Opposite rows 18/19 at left, boxed

Guide holes: None

Marginal arrows (photo-etched):
"W" shaped, at top, bottom and sides

Marginal rule: At bottom of sheet

Colour register marks: Above and below vertical rows 1/2 and 5/6

Autotron marks: None

Colour designations: None

W 1966 Burns Commemoration

Traffic lights (boxed):
- **9d.** Ultramarine, red, violet, pink, black opposite rows 18/19 at right
- **1s.6d.** Blue indigo, pink, red, black opposite rows 18/19 at right

Imprimaturs from the NPM or BPMA

A. Ordinary
Nos. W79/W80 imperforate, watermark Type W.**24**

Watermark upright (set of 2)	£2000
9d. cylinder 1A, 1B, 1C, 1D, 2E block of six	£7000
1s.6d. "Retouched arm" variety R. 1/4	£1500
1s.6d. cylinder 2A, 1B, 1C, 1D, 2E block of six	£7000

B. Phosphor
Nos. WP79/WP80 imperforate, watermark Type W.**24**

Watermark upright (*set of 2*)	£2000
9d. cylinder 1A, 1B, 1C, 1D, 2E block of six	£7000
1s.6d. "Red pin with arm" flaw R. 1/4	£1500
1s.6d. cylinder 2A, 1B, 1C, 1D, 2E block of six	£7000

Quantities Issued:

	Ordinary	Phosphor
9d.	5,321,880	556,080
1s.6d.	5,287,920	589,800

Withdrawn:
30.6.66 (1s.6d. phosphor sold out December 1965)

Type **W81**.
Robert Burns (after Skirving chalk drawing)

Type **W82**.
Robert Burns (after Nasmyth portrait)

(Des. Gordon F. Huntly)

1966 (25 January). **Burns Commemoration**

Robert Burns (1759–1796), Scotland's celebrated national poet, was born in Alloway, near Ayr. Types **W81/W82**.

A. Ordinary
W81 =SG 685

		Mint	Used
4d.	black, deep violet-blue and new blue	10	10

W82 =SG 686

1s.3d.	black, slate-blue and yellow-orange	20	20
First Day Cover (W81/W82)			1·25
Presentation Pack (W81/W82)		40·00	

B. Phosphor
WP81 =SG 685p

4d.	Three bands	20	20
a.	Narrow band at left or right (stamp with vert. margin)	2·50	

WP82 =SG 686p

W78	1s.3d. Three bands	90	90
First Day Cover (WP81/WP82)			3·50

These are known postmarked 24 January 1966.

Cylinder Numbers (Blocks of Four)

(a) Ordinary

		Perforation Types		
		A (E/I) No dot	A (E/I) Dot	F (P/E) No dot
	Cylinder Nos.			
4d.	1A (violet-blue)–1B (black)–1C (new blue)	1·25	1·25	†
	1A–2B–1C	1·25	1·25	†
1s.3d.	2A (slate-blue)–1B (black)–1C (orange)	†	†	1·50

(b) Phosphor

4d.	1A (violet-blue)–1B (black)–1C (new blue)	1·50	1·50	†
1s.3d.	2A (slate-blue)–1B (black)–1C (orange)	†	†	4·50

Minor Constant Flaws
4d. Cyls. 1A–1B–1C dot and 1A–2B–1C dot
- 9/4 Small white flaw at front of diadem (Th. A10), OP
- 18/1 Coloured spot above Queen's upper lip (Th. C10), OP
- 19/3 White flaw on Queen's neck above centre of collar (Th. E11), OP

4d. Cyls. 1A–2B–1C dot only
- 15/1 White spot at back of Burns's hair by parting (Th. A5), OP

1s.3d. Cyls. 2A–1B–1C no dot

- 2/6 Pale background flaw in front of Queen's neck (Th. D9), OP
- 3/6 Grey spot on Burns's nose near his right eye (Th. C5), OP
- 4/6 Grey diagonal line through white line to panel at lower right (Th. E8–G9), OP
- 6/5 White patch to right of Queen's left eyebrow (Th. B11), OP
- 9/4 Large dark retouch in Burns's hair left of parting (Th. B4), OP
- 19/1 Flaw on Burns's right cheek (Th. D4), OP
- 19/5 Dark flaw on Burns's shirt touching left lapel (Th. F5), OP

Sheet Details
 Sheet size: 120 (6×20). 4d double-pane reel-fed: 1s.3d. single-pane sheet-fed

Sheet marking:

Cylinder numbers: R. 19/1, boxed

Guide holes:
 4d. In double "SON" box opposite rows 14/15, at left (no dot) or right (dot)
 1s.3d. None

Marginal arrows (photo-etched):
"W" shaped, at top, bottom and sides

Marginal rule: At bottom of sheet

Colour register marks:
 4d. None
 1s.3d. Above and below vertical rows 1 and 6

Coloured crosses:
 4d. None
 1s.3d. Above and below vertical row 2

Autotron marks (solid):
 4d. Violet-blue, black, new blue opposite rows 5/6, at right (no dot) or left (dot)
 1s.3d. None

Colour designations: None

Traffic lights (boxed):
 4d. New blue, black, violet-blue opposite R. 19/6
 1s.3d. Orange, black, slate-blue opposite R. 19/6

Imprimaturs from the NPM or BPMA

A. Ordinary
Nos. W81/W82 imperforate, watermark Type W.**24**

Watermark upright (set of 2)	£2000
4d. cylinder 1A, 2B, 1C (dot) block of four	£5000
1s.3d. cylinder 2A, 1B, 1C block of four	£5000

B. Phosphor
Nos. WP81/WP82 imperforate, watermark Type W.**24**

Watermark upright (set of 2)	£2000
4d. cylinder 1A, 1B, 1C (dot) block of four	£5000
1s.3d. cylinder 2A, 1B, 1C block of four	£5000

Quantities Sold.

	Ordinary	Phosphor
4d.	77,905,176	8,738,520
1s.3d.	5,685,096	1,226,160
Pack	38,968	—

Withdrawn: 29.7.66 but later put on sale again in error for a short time at the Philatelic Counter in London, the Philatelic Bureau in Edinburgh and at the Edinburgh Festival.

900th Anniversary of Westminster Abbey. 1966

Type **W83**. Westminster Abbey

(Des. Sheila Robinson)

Type **W84**. Fan Vaulting, Henry VII Chapel

(Des. and eng. Bradbury Wilkinson)

1966 (28 February). **900th Anniversary of Westminster Abbey.** Types **W83/W84**

Westminster Abbey, officially the Collegiate Church of St Peter, Westminster, is the nation's Coronation Church and a mausoleum for England's greatest men and women.

The 2s.6d. was engraved by Alan Dow (Queen's head) and Frederick Warner and was recess-printed on chalk-surfaced paper by Bradbury Wilkinson and comb perf. 11×12.

A. Ordinary

W83 =SG 687		Mint	Used
3d.	black, red-brown and new blue	10	10
a.	Diadem flaw (No dot, R.16/2)	30·00	
b.	Retouch on Queen's cheek (Dot, R. 15/6)	30·00	
W84 =SG 688			
2s.6d.	black	30	30
First Day Cover (W83/W84)			2·50
Presentation Pack (W83/W84)		40·00	

B. Phosphor

WP83 =SG 687p			
3d.	One band	10	10
a.	Diadem flaw (No dot, R. 16/2)	30·00	
b.	Retouch on Queen's cheek (Dot. R. 15/6)	30·00	
c.	Error. Two bands	10·00	
First Day Cover (WP83)			8·00

W83a, WP83a    W83b, WP83b

Cylinder and Plate Numbers (Blocks of Four)

		Perforation Type A (E/I)	
	Cylinder or Plate Nos.	No dot	Dot
3d.	2A (blue)–1B (black)–1C (brown). Ordinary	1·25	1·25
	2A–1B–1C. Phosphor	1·25	1·25
2s.6d.	Plate 1.	2·00	†
	Plate 1A	3·00	†

203

W 1966 Landscapes.

Minor Constant Flaws
3d. Cyls. 2A–1B–1C no dot
- 1/6 Vertical scratch to right of Queen's head and running through bottom frame of panel (Th. D–E12), OP
- 15/1 Small white dots touching "E" and second "A" of "ANNIVERSARY", OP

2s.6d. Plate 1
- 2/2 Broken horizontal line in top margin over "Y" of "ANNIVERSARY" (Th. A1)
- 6/1 Scratch in bottom margin below "Y" of "ABBEY" (Th. I13–14)
- 10/2 Second "0" of "900" joined to "t" of "th"

2s.6d. Plate 1A
- 5/3 Horizontal line in margin left of "Y" of "ANNIVERSARY" and vertical line in top margin at left (Th. A1 and A2)
- 7/4 Scratch through "Y" of "ANNIVERSARY"

Sheet Details
Sheet sizes:
- 3d. 120 (6×20). Double-pane reel-fed
- 2s.6d. 40 (4×10). Double-pane sheet-fed

Sheet markings:

Cylinder numbers: 3d. R. 19/1, boxed

Plate numbers: 2s.6d. Bottom margin below vertical rows 3/4

Guide holes:
- 3d. In double "SON" box opposite rows 14/15, at left (no dot) or right (dot)
- 2s.6d. In circle opposite row 6, at left (Pl. 1) or right (Pl. 1A)

Marginal arrows (photo-etched):
- 3d. "W" shaped, at top, bottom and sides
- 2s.6d. none

Marginal rule:
- 3d. at bottom of sheet
- 2s.6d. none.

Colour register marks: None

Coloured cross (black):
- 2s.6d. opposite row 6, at right (Pl. 1) or left (Pl. 1A)

Autotron marks (solid):
- 3d. Blue, black, red-brown opposite rows 6/7, at right (no dot) or left (dot);
- 2s.6d. none

Colour designations: None

Traffic lights (boxed):
- 3d. Blue, black, red-brown opposite R. 19/6

Imprimaturs from the NPM or BPMA

A. Ordinary
Nos. W83/W84 imperforate, watermark Type W.**24**

Watermark upright (set of 2)	£2500
3d. "Diadem flaw" R. 16/2	£1500
3d. cylinder 2A, 1B, 1C (no dot) block of four	£5000
2s.6d. Plate 1 block of four	£7000

B. Phosphor
No. WP83 imperforate, watermark Type W.24

Watermark upright	£1000
3d. "Diadem flaw" R. 16/2	£1500
3d. cylinder 2A, 1B, 1C (no dot) block of four	£5000

Quantities Sold:	Ordinary	Phosphor
3d.	48,703,426	5,247,720
2s.6d.	2,819,056	—
Pack	24,272	—

Withdrawn: 31.8.66 3d. (2s.6d. sold out in April 1966).
The 3d. was later put on sale again in error for a short time at the Philatelic Counter in London and at the Philatelic Bureau in Edinburgh.

Type **W85.** View near Hassocks, Sussex

Type **W86.** Antrim, Northern Ireland

Type **W87.** Harlech Castle, Wales

Type **W88.** Cairngorm Mountains, Scotland

(Des. Leonard Rosoman. Queen's portrait adapted by David Gentleman from coinage)

1966 (2 May). Landscapes. Types W85/W88

Britain's first special pictorial stamps featuring scenes in England, Northern Ireland, Wales and Scotland.

The Queen's profile design on this, and following special issues to 1967 Christmas, was taken from the coinage design by Mrs. Mary Gillick and adapted by David Gentleman.

A. Ordinary

W85 =SG 689		Mint	Used
4d. black, yellow-green and new blue		10	10
a. Dash before "ENGLAND" (No dot, R. 20/5)		30·00	
b. Green flaw on tree trunk (Dot, R. 3/4)		40·00	

W86 =SG 690			
6d. black, emerald and new blue		10	10
a. Watermark inverted		6·00	
b. "AN" for "AND" (R. 10/3)		65·00	
c. Retouched, with misaligned "D"		30·00	

W87 =SG 691			
1s.3d. black, greenish yellow and greenish blue		15	15
a. Broken "D" (R. 14/2)		35·00	

W88 =SG 692			
1s.6d. black, orange and Prussian blue		15	15
a. Watermark inverted		22·00	

First Day Cover (W85/W88)			3·50

Landscapes. 1966

B. Phosphor

WP85 =SG 689p

4d.	Three bands	10	10
a.	Narrow band at left or right (stamp with vert. margin)	3·00	
b.	Green flaw on tree trunk (Dot. R. 3/4)	35·00	

WP86 =SG 690p

6d.	Three bands	10	10
a.	Watermark inverted	£170	
b.	"AN" for "AND" (R. 10/3)	65·00	

WP87 =SG 691p

1s.3d.	Three bands	15	15
a.	Broken "D" (R. 14/2)	35·00	

WP88 =SG 692p

1s.6d.	Three bands	15	15

First Day Cover (WP85/WP88)	4·50

These are known postmarked 26 April in Winchester.

No. W85 exists with Queen's head and value omitted, due to a paper fold, with the stamp above showing value only omitted. A vertical pair of No. W86 exists with the Queen's head and value omitted from the upper stamp and partial omission on the lower stamp, both due to a paper fold (*Price* £10,000).

W86b and WP86b. 40,000 sheets, including all the phosphor stamps, were printed before this was discovered and the D was then added to the cylinder, forming W86c.

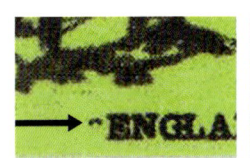

W85a (Later retouched)

W85b, WP85b

W86b, WP86b

W87a, WP87a

Cylinder Numbers (Blocks of Four)

	Perforation Type A (E/I)	
(a) Ordinary Cylinder Nos.	No dot	Dot
4d. 2A (blue)–1B (black)–1C (yellow-green)	1·25	1·25

	No dot	
	Type F (P/E)	Type F(L) (I/E)
6d. 1A (blue)–3B (black)–1C (green)	1·25	†
1s.3d. 2A (blue)–2B (black)–1C* (yellow)	1·50	†
1s.6d. 1A (blue)–1B (orange)–1C (black)	1·50	1·50

(b) Phosphor

	Perforation Types		
	A (E/I) No dot	A (E/I) Dot	F (P/E) No dot
4d. 2A (blue)–1B (black)–1C (yellow-green)	1·25	1·25	†
6d. 1A (blue)–3B (black)–1C (green)	†	†	1·25
1s.3d. 2A (blue)–2B (black)–1C* (yellow)	†	†	1·50
1s.6d. 1A (blue)–1B (orange)–1C (black)	†	†	1·50

* The figure 1 of this cylinder is inverted

Minor Constant Flaws

4d. Cyls. 2A–1B–1C no dot
- 11/2 Pale area behind Queen's collar above value (Th. E–F12–13), OP
- 14/5 Dark spot in green field at top left corner (Th. A1–2), OP

4d. Cyls. 2A–1B–1C dot
- 2/4 Retouching in sky between clouds (Th. A2), OP

6d. Cyls. 1A–1B–1C no dot
- 2/2 Horizontal blue line across Queen's neck, later retouched on ordinary (Th. D11), OP
- 5/4 Green spot between "N". and "I", OP
- 17/2 Curved green flaw on trees opposite Queen's chin (Th. D9), OP
- 18/1 Blue mark in field left of cottage (Th. F5), OP
- 19/2 Green line running across Queen's head (Th. B10–12), OP
- 20/6 Diagonal black flaw below second "R" of "HARRISON", OP

1s.3d. Cyls. 2A–2B–1C no dot
- 6/1 Pale diagonal white line above "ES" of "WALES", OP
- 9/2 Pale area between "1" and "3" of value (Th. F11–12), OP
- 19/1 Dot before "M" of "ROSOMAN" (Th. H2), OP

1s.6d. Cyls. 1A–1B–1C no dot
- 1/6 Blurred area at back of Queen's hair (Th. B–C12), OP
- 4/6 Several blemishes in background between mountains which appear as italic figures 20 (Th. A4–5), OP
- 8/1 Retouch above "d" of value (Th. F13), OP
- 13/4 Retouch behind Queen's neck (Th. D12), OP
- 18/3 White spot between "AN" of "SCOTLAND" and foot of "A" is enlarged, OP

Sheet Details

Sheet size: 120 (6×20). 4d. double-pane reel-fed; others single-pane sheet-fed

Sheet markings:

Cylinder numbers: R. 19/1, boxed

Guide holes:
- **4d.** In single "SON" box opposite rows 14/15, at left (no dot) or right (dot). The centre bar of the double box has been erased
- **Others:** None

Marginal arrows (photo-etched):
"W" shaped, at top, bottom and sides

Marginal rule: At bottom of sheet

Colour register marks:
- **4d.** None
- **Others:** Above and below vertical rows 1/2 and 5/6

Autotron marks (solid):
- **4d.** Blue, black, yellow-green opposite rows 5/6, at right (no dot) or left (dot)
- **Others:** None

W 1966 *World Football Cup Championship.*

Colour designations: None

Traffic lights (boxed):
- **4d.** Blue, black, yellow-green opposite R. 19/6
- **6d.** Blue, black, green opposite R. 19/6
- **1s.3d.** Blue, black, yellow opposite R. 19/6
- **1s.6d.** Black, blue, orange opposite R. 19/6

Imprimaturs from the NPM or BPMA

A. Ordinary
Nos. W85/W88 imperforate, watermark Type W.**24**

Watermark upright (*set of 4*)	£4000
4d. cylinder 2A, 1B, 1C (no dot) block of four	£5000
6d. cylinder 1A, 3B, 1C block of four	£5000
1s.3d. cylinder 2A, 2B, 1C block of four	£5000
1s.6d. cylinder 1A, 1B, 1C block of four	£5000

B. Phosphor
Nos. WP85/WP88 imperforate, watermark Type W.**24**

Watermark upright (*set of 4*)	£4000
4d. cylinder 2A, 1B, 1C (no dot) block of four	£5000
6d. cylinder 1A, 3B, 1C block of four	£5000
1s.3d. cylinder 2A, 2B, 1C block of four	£5000
1s.6d. cylinder 1A, 1B, 1C block of four	£5000

Quantities Sold:

	Ordinary	Phosphor
4d.	80,326,440	11,283,720
6d.	11,531,760	2,459,280
1s.3d.	5,286,000	1,242,720
1s.6d.	5,462,640	1,204,200

Withdrawn: 1.5.67 but 6d. phosphor was sold out in January

World Cup 1966

Type **W89.** Players with Ball   Type **W90.** Players with Ball

(Des. David Gentleman)   (Des. William Kempster)

Type **W91.** Goalkeeper saving Goal

(Des. David Caplan)

1966 *(1 June).* **World Football Cup Championship.**
Types **W89/W91.** Watermark sideways on 4d.

16 countries took part in the final stages of the World Football Championship for the Jules Rimet Cup in England during July, 1966. See also No. W96.

A. Ordinary

W89 =SG 693   Mint   Used

4d. red, reddish purple, bright blue, flesh and black		10	10
a. Patch on thigh (No dot, R. 3/20)		30·00	
b. Broken shadow (No dot, R. 5/17)		30·00	
c. Red patch below ball (no dot, R. 4/16)		30·00	

W90 =SG 694

6d. black, sepia, red, apple-green and blue	10	10
a. Black omitted	£200	
b. Apple-green omitted	£6000	
c. Red omitted	£10000	
d. Watermark inverted	5·00	

W91 =SG 695

1s.3d. black, blue, yellow, red and light yellow-olive	15	15
a. Blue omitted	£350	
b. Watermark inverted	£150	
c. Darned stocking (R. 19/2)	30·00	

First Day Cover (W89/W91)	9·00

Presentation Pack (W89/W91)	30·00

B. Phosphor

WP89 =SG 693p

4d. Two bands	10	10
a. Narrow band at left (stamp with vert. margin)	2·00	
b. Error. Extra phosphor band at right		
c. Error. One broad band	25·00	
d. Patch on thigh (No dot. R. 3/20)	30·00	
e. Red patch below ball (No dot, R. 4/16)	30·00	
f. Broken shadow (No dot, R. 5/17)	30·00	

… World Football Cup Championship. 1966

WP90 =SG 694p			
6d.	Three bands	10	10
a.	Black omitted	£2800	
WP91 =SG 695p			
1s.3d.	Three bands	15	15
a.	Watermark inverted	2.00	
b.	Darned stocking (R. 19/2)	30·00	
c.	Error. Two bands	16·00	
First Day Cover (WP89/WP91)			11·50

The 4d. ordinary has been seen postmarked 31 May in Hereford.

W89a, WP89d, W96a

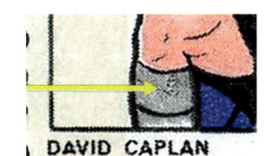

W89b, WP89f, W96c

W89c, WP89e, W96b

W91c, WP91b

Cylinder Numbers (Blocks of Six)

(a) Ordinary

	Perforation Type A (I/E)	
Cylinder Nos.	No dot	Dot
4d. 1A (black)–1B (blue)–1C (red)–1D (purple)–1E (flesh)**	1·25	1·25

	Perforation Types	
	F (P/E) No dot	F(L) (I/E) No dot
6d. 1A (blue)–1B (green)–1C (red)–1D (sepia)–1E (black)	1·25	†
2A–1B–1C–1D–1E	3·00	†
1s.3d. 1A (black)–1B (yellow)–1C (yellow-olive)–1D (blue)–1E (red)	32·00*	32·00*
1A–1B–1C–1D–2E	32·00*	32·00*

(b) Phosphor

	Perforation Types		
	A (I/E) No dot	A (I/E) Dot	F (P/E) No dot
4d. 1A (black)–1B (blue)–1C (red)–1D (purple)–1E (flesh)**	1·25	1·25	†
6d. 1A (blue)–1B (green)–1C (red)–1D (sepia)–1E (black)	†	†	1·25
1s.3d. 1A (black)–1B (yellow)–1C (yellow-olive)–1D (blue)–2E (red)	†	†	30·00*

** In the 4d. no dot pane the flesh cylinder is expressed in error with a dot thus: "1E.".
For perforation Type A the 4d. is with sheet orientated showing head to left.

Minor Constant Flaws

4d. Cyls. 1A–1B–1C–1D–1E no dot
- 3/1 Horizontal scratch through top of ball (Th. K1–2), OP
- 5/6 Blue patch below "u" of "Cup", OP
- 6/18 Blue spots over T of LTD, OP

4d. Cyls. 1A–1B–1C–1D–1E dot
- 4/20 Red line joins head and left arm of player at left (Th. F3), OP
- 5/10 Dark spot on ball (Th. K1), OP
- 5/17 Grey coloured spur to top of "l" of "World", OP

6d. Cyls. 1B–1C–1D–1E in combination with blue cyls. 1A or 2A no dot
- 5/4 Diagonal scratch on barrier next to grass below crowd (Th. G–57), OP

6d. Cyl. 1A no dot
- 17/4 Pale area around top of "1" of "1966", OP

1s.3d. Cyls. 1A–1B–1C–1D no dot in combination with red cyls. 1E or 2E
- 1/3 Patch on sock of central player (Th. G2), OP
- 9/2 Black spur on head of right-hand player (Th. B7), OP
- 14/5 Break in black frame line around players opposite "U" of "CUP", OP
- 18/1 Black spot to right of stroke of "1/3"; also black spot below second "R" of "HARRISON" OP
- 20/1 Black spot below second "A" of "CAPLAN", OP

1s.3d. Cyl. 2E no dot
- 1/6 Red scratch on face of central player, OP

Sheet Details
Sheet size:
- **4d.** 120 (20×6). Double-pane reel-fed
- **6d., 1s.3d.** 120 (6×20). Single-pane sheet-fed

Sheet markings:

Cylinder numbers:
- **4d.** Above vertical rows 2/3, boxed
- **6d., 1s.3d.** Opposite rows 18/19 at left, boxed

Guide holes:
- **4d.** In single photo-etched box above vertical rows 6/7 (no dot) or below (dot). On the no dot pane the box is now lettered "SN", the "S" being on the left in the box (usually trimmed off), and the "N" above the right line. On the dot pane the sequence is reversed.
- **6d., 1s.3d.** None

Marginal arrows (photo-etched):
"W" shaped, at top, bottom and sides, except that early printings of the 6d. from cylinder 1A both ordinary and phosphor were without any arrow markings in the margins. These were later inserted by hand.
Minimum price for marginal strip showing arrow omitted: £15 Ordinary or phosphor

Marginal rule:
- **4d.** At left of sheet
- **6d., 1s.3d.** At bottom of sheet

Colour register marks:
- **4d.** Above vertical rows 3/4 and 18/19 (no dot) or below (dot)
- **6d., 1s.3d.** Above and below vertical rows 1/2 and 6

Coloured crosses:
- **4d.** None
- **6d.** Above and below vertical row 3
- **1s.3d.** Above and below vertical rows 3/4

Autotron marks (solid):
- **4d.** Red, purple, flesh, blue, black below vertical rows 15/18 (no dot) or above (dot)
- **6d., 1s.3d.** None

W 1966 *British Birds.*

Colour designations:
- **4d**. 5 BLACK G4 BLUE MAROON G3 G2 RED G1 LIGHT RED below vertical rows 11/16 on dot panes only
- **6d., 1s.3d.** None

Traffic lights (boxed):
- **4d**. Black, blue, red, purple, flesh reading left to right below vertical rows 2/3
- **6d**. Blue, green, red, sepia, black opposite rows 18/19 at right
- **1s.3d**. Black, yellow, yellow-olive, blue, red opposite rows 18/19 at right

Imprimaturs from the NPM or BPMA

A. Ordinary
Nos. W89/W91 imperforate, watermark Type W.**24**

Watermark upright (6d., 1s.3d.) or sideways (4d.) (set of 3)	£3000
4d. cylinder 1A, 1B, 1C, 1D, 1E (dot) block of six	£7000
6d. cylinder 2A, 1B, 1C, 1D, 1E block of six	£7000
1s.3d. cylinder 1A, 1B, 1C, 1D, 2E block of six	£7500*

B. Phosphor
Nos. WP89/WP91 imperforate, watermark Type W.**24**

Watermark upright (6d., 1s.3d.) or sideways (4d.) (set of 3)	£3000
4d. "Broken shadow" flaw R. 5/17	£1500
4d. "Red patch below ball" flaw R. 4/16	£1500
4d. cylinder 1A, 1B, 1C, 1D, 1E (no dot*) block of six	£7000
6d. cylinder 1A, 1B, 1C, 1E block of six	£7000
1s.3d. cylinder 1A, 1B, 1C, 1D, 2E block of six	£7500*

Quantities Sold:

	Ordinary	Phosphor
4d.	129,764,160	16,397,880
6d.	17,086,680	3,357,480
1s.3d.	7,026,240	1,761,240
Pack	48,732	—

Withdrawn: 31.5.67

Type **W92**. Black-headed Gull

Type **W93**. Blue Tit

Type **W94**. Robin

Type **W95**. Blackbird

(Des. J. Norris Wood)

1966 (8 August). **British Birds.** Types **W92/W95**

These were the first British stamps to be printed in eight colours. On the blackbird design the black was printed over the bistre.

Issued together in *se-tenant* blocks of four within the sheet.

A. Ordinary

W92 =SG 696   Mint   Used

		Mint	Used
4d.	grey, black, red, emerald-green, bright blue, greenish yellow and bistre	10	10
a.	Block of 4. Nos. W92/W95	40	40
	Missing colours:		
c.	Black, bright blue, bistre and reddish brown	£5000	
d.	Greenish yellow	£950	
e.	Red	£1100	
f.	Emerald-green	£200	
g.	Bright blue	£700	
h.	Bistre	£200	
i.	Black (only)	—	
k.	HARRISO omitted (No dot R. 15/5)* Block of four	70·00	
l.	Watermark inverted	4·00	

W93 =SG 697

		Mint	Used
4d.	black, greenish yellow, grey, emerald-green, bright blue and bistre	10	10
b.	Black "4d" only ommitted	£2000	

208

British Birds. **1966**

Missing colours:		
c. Black, bright blue, bistre and reddish brown	£5000	
d. Greenish yellow	£950	
f. Emerald-green	£200	
g. Bright blue	£700	
h. Bistre	£200	
i. Watermark inverted	4·00	

W94 =SG 698

4d. red, greenish yellow, black, grey, bistre, reddish brown and emerald-green		10	10
Missing colours:			
c. Black, bright blue, bistre and reddish brown	£5000		
d. Greenish yellow	£950		
e. Red	£1100		
f. Emerald-green	£200		
g. Bistre	£200		
i. Black (only)	—		
j. Reddish brown	£125		
i. Watermark inverted	4·00		

W95 =SG 699

4d. black, reddish brown, greenish yellow, grey and bistre		10	10
b. Black "4d" only omitted	£2000		
Missing colours:			
c. Black, bright blue, bistre and reddish brown	£5000		
d. Greenish yellow	£950		
h. Bistre	£200		
j. Reddish brown	£125		
i. Watermark inverted	4·00		

First Day Cover (W92/W95)	8·00
Presentation Pack (W92/W95)	13·00

B. Phosphor

WP92 =SG 696p

4d. Three bands		10	10
a. Block of 4. Nos. WP92/WP95		40	40
Missing colours:			
b. Emerald-green	£200		
c. Bright blue	£5000		
d. Bistre	£2000		
e. Greenish yellow	£2000		
i. Watermark inverted	20·00		

WP93 =SG 697p

4d. Three bands		10	10
Missing colours:			
b. Emerald-green	£200		
c. Bright blue	£5000		
d. Bistre	£2000		
e. Greenish yellow	£2000		
i. Watermark inverted	20·00		

WP94 =SG 698p

4d. Three bands		10	10
Missing colours:			
b. Emerald-green	£200		
c. Bistre	£2000		
d. Reddish brown	£175		
e. Greenish yellow	£2000		
i. Watermark inverted	20·00		

WP95 =SG 699p

4d. Three bands		10	10
Missing colours:			
c. Bistre	£2000		
d. Reddish brown	£175		
e. Greenish yellow	£2000		
i. Watermark inverted	20·00		

First Day Cover (WP92/WP95)	8·00

Prices for missing colour errors and inverted watermarks in blocks of four:

	Ordinary	Phosphor
Black, bright blue, bistre and reddish brown	£20000	†
Greenish yellow	£3800	£8000
Red	£2200	†
Emerald-green	£600	£600
Bright blue	£1400	£10000
Bistre	£800	£8000
Reddish brown	£250	£350
Watermark inverted	16·00	80·00

* "HARRISON" is omitted except for fragments of the "N" and on the stamp below (W94) the imprint is very faint, particularly "AND SO". The price is for a block containing both varieties. The damage was quickly discovered and repaired during the early stages of the printing. Black omitted only is not known in a block.

These are known postmarked at various places with dates from 17 July 1966 due to supplies prematurely released by the Philatelic Bureau.

Cylinder Numbers (Blocks of Eight)

	Perforation Type F (P/E). No dot	
Cylinder Nos.	Ordinary	Phosphor
2A (black)–1B (grey)–1C (yellow)–1D (red)–1E (green)–2F (blue)–2G (bistre)–1H (Brown)	2·00	2·00
2A–1B–1C–1D–1E–2F–2G–2H	50·00	†

Minor Constant Flaws

4d. Cyls. 2A–1B–1C–1D–1E–2F–2G with 1H or 2H no dot
1/2 Small brown dot under main twig (Th. B3), OP
4/3 Small brown dot to right of Robin's tail (Th. B7), OP
5/1 Small black dot in gull's wing (Th. D5), OP
6/2 Red spot between blackbird's claws (Th. F6), OP
7/1 Small black dot in gull's wing (Th. D6), OP
7/4 Extension to main twig at right (Th. A6), OP
9/6 Horizontal bistre line above main twig at left (Th. A–B3–4), O

Sheet Details
Sheet size: 120 (6×20). In *se-tenant* blocks of four, single-pane sheet-fed

Sheet markings:
Cylinder numbers: Opposite rows 17/19 at left, boxed
Guide holes: None
Marginal arrows (photo-etched):
"W" shaped, at top, bottom and sides
Marginal rule: At bottom of sheet

W 1966 England's World Cup Football Victory.

Colour register marks: Above and below vertical rows 1/3 and 5/6
Coloured crosses: Above and below vertical rows 3/4
Autotron marks and Colour designations: None
Traffic lights (boxed): In same order as cylinder numbers opposite rows 18/19 at right

A number of sheets from the end of the printing run showed part of the design in the left-hand margin by row 20. This was caused by incomplete masking of the multipositive; touched out before printing, but then wearing through.

Imprimaturs from the NPM or BPMA

A. Ordinary
Nos. W92/W95 imperforate, watermark Type W.**24**

Watermark upright (*se-tenant* block of 4)	£4000
4d. cylinder 2A, 1B, 1C, 1D, 1E, 2F, 2G, 1H block of eight	£9000

B. Phosphor
Nos. WP92/WP95 imperforate, watermark Type W.**24**

Watermark upright (*se-tenant* block of 4)	£4000
4d. cylinder 2A, 1B, 1C, 1D, 1E, 2F, 2G, 1H block of eight	£9000

Quantities Sold:

	Ordinary :	phosphor
4d.	88,047,742	14,613,120
Pack	42,888	

Withdrawn: 7.8.57

World Cup 1966

Type **W96**. Cup Winners

(Des. David Gentleman)

1966 (18 August). **England's World Cup Football Victory.**
Watermark sideways. Type **W96**

England won the World Cup Football Championship by defeating West Germany 4–2 at Wembley on 30 July 1966.

W96	=SG 700	Mint	Used
4d.	red, reddish purple, bright blue, flesh and black	10	10
a.	Patch on thigh (No dot, R. 3/20)	30·00	
b.	Red patch below ball (No dot, R. 4/16)	30·00	
c.	Broken shadow (No dot, R. 5/17)	30·00	
First Day Cover (W96)		7·50	

The above was only put on sale at post offices in England, the Channel Islands and the Isle of Man, and the Philatelic Bureau in London and also, on August 22, in Edinburgh on the occasion of the opening of the Edinburgh Festival, as well as at Army post offices at home and abroad.

It was pre-released on 17 August at an Army Camp PO in Great Britain.

The Philatelic Bureau did not service First Day Covers for this stamp, but a First Day of Issue handstamp was provided inscribed "Harrow & Wembley" to replace the "Wembley, Middx" postmark of the initial issue.

An example of No. W89 with forged additional inscription on Edinburgh (22 August) first day cover is known.

For W96a, W96b and W96c. see illustrations after Nos. W89/W91.

Cylinder Numbers (Blocks of Six)

	Perforation Type A (I/E)
Cylinder Nos.	No dot Dot
4d 1A (black)–1B (blue)–1C (red)–1D (purple)–1E (flesh)*	1·25 1·25

* In the no dot pane the flesh cylinder is expressed in error thus: "1E". and on the dot pane the black cylinder is shown as ."1A".

Perforation Type A is with sheet orientated showing head to left.

Minor Constant Flaws

4d. Cyls. 1A–1B–1C–1D–1E no dot

1/15	Black dot in second "N" of "ENGLAND"
2/9	Black spur on left player's right boot (Th. J–K5)
3/1	Horizontal scratch through top of ball (Th. K1–2)
5/6	Blue patch below "u" of "Cup"
6/13	White patch on heel of left player's left boot (Th. J3)
6/18	Blue spots over "T" of "LTD"

4d. Cyls. 1A–1B–1C–1D–1E dot

4/11	Black dot between "W" and "I" of "WINNERS"
5/10	Dark spot on ball (Th. K1)
5/17	Grey coloured spur to top of l of World

British Technology. 1966

Sheet Details
Sheet size: 120 (20×6). Double-pane reel-fed

Sheet markings:

Cylinder numbers: Above vertical rows 2/3, boxed

Guide holes: In single "S N" box above vertical rows 6/7 (no dot) or below (dot)

Marginal arrows (photo-etched): "W" shaped, at top, bottom and sides

Marginal rule: At left of sheet

Colour register marks: Above vertical rows 3/4 and 18/19 (no dot) or below (dot)

Autotron marks (solid): Red, purple, flesh, blue, black below vertical rows 15/18 (no dot) or above (dot)

Colour designations: 5 BLACK G4 BLUE MAROON G3 G2 RED G1 LIGHT RED below vertical rows 11/16 on dot panes only

Traffic lights (boxed): Black, blue, red, purple, flesh reading left to right below vertical rows 2/3

Imprimatur from the NPM or BPMA
Ordinary paper
No. W96 imperforate, watermark Type W.**24**

Watermark sideways	£1000
4d. "Patch on thigh" variety R. 3/20	£1500
4d. "Red patch below ball" variety R. 4/16	£1500
4d. cylinder 1A, 1B, 1C, 1D, 1E (no dot*) block of six	£7000

Quantity Sold: 12,452,640
Sold out soon after issue

Type **W97.** Jodrell Bank Radio Telescope

Type **W98.** British Motor-cars
(Des. David and Ann Gillespie)

Type **W99.** SRN 6 Hovercraft

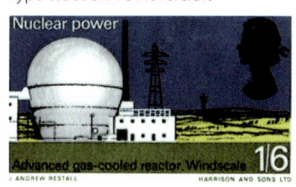

Type **W100.** Windscale Reactor
(Des. Andrew Restall)

1966 *(19 September).* **British Technology.** Types **W97/W100**

The designs represent British Technological achievements.

A. Ordinary

W97 =SG 701		Mint	Used
4d.	black and lemon	10	10
a.	Struts flaw (No dot, R. 4/6)	30·00	

W98 =SG 702			
6d.	red, deep blue and orange	10	10
a.	Red (Mini-cars) omitted	£20000	
b.	Blue (Jaguar and inscr.) omitted	£17000	
c.	Broken "D" (R. 19/6)	35·00	

W99 =SG 703			
1s.3d.	black, orange-red, slate and light greenish blue	15	15

W100 =SG 704			
1s.6d.	black, yellow-green, bronze-green, lilac and deep blue	15	15

First Day Cover (W97/W100)		2·50

Presentation Pack (W97/W100)	20·00	

B. Phosphor

WP97 =SG 701p			
4d.	Three bands	10	10
a.	Error. Pair, with and without phosphor	25·00	

b. Narrow band at left or right (stamp with vert. margin)		4·00	
c. Struts flaw (No dot, R. 4/6)		30·00	

WP98 =SG 702p

6d. Three bands		10	10
a. Narrow band at left or right (stamp with vert. margin)		4·00	
b. Broken "D" (R. 19/6)		35·00	

WP99 =SG 703p

1s.3d. Three bands		20	20

WP100 =SG 704p

1s.6d. Three bands		20	20
a. Narrow band at left or right (stamp with vert. margin)		4·00	
b. Error. Two broad bands		35·00	
First Day Cover (WP97/WP100)		2·50	

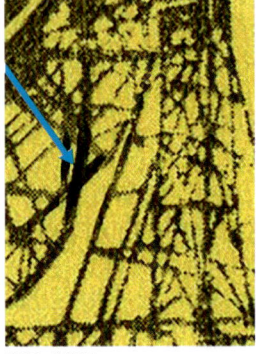

W97a, WP97c
Strong retouch consisting of three strong black strokes in the form of an arrow

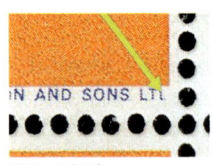

W98c, WP98b

Cylinder Numbers (Blocks of Six)

		Perforation Type \4A (E/I)	
(a) Ordinary			
Cylinder. Nos.		No dot	Dot
4d.	1A (lemon)–1B (black)	1·25	1·25
6d.	1A (orange)–1B (red)–1C (blue)	1·25	
1s.3d.	1A (blue)–1B (slate)–1C (orange)–1D (black)	1·50	
1s.6d.	1A (bronze-green)–1B (lilac)–1C (black)–1D (yellow-green)–1E (blue)	1·50	
(b) Phosphor			
4d.	1A (lemon)–1B (black)	1·50	1·25
6d.	1A (orange)–1B (red)–1C (blue)	1·25	
1s.3d.	1A (blue)–1B (slate)–1C (orange)–1D (black)	1·40	
1s.6d.	1A (bronze-green)–1B (lilac)–1C (black)–1D (yellow-green)–1E (blue)	1·50	

Minor Constant Flaws

4d. Cyls. 1A–1B no dot
- 1/1 Lines of retouching above Queen's head resemble a thumb-print (Th. A9–12); also small pale area in left of telescope bowl (Th. C3–4), both OP
- 1/2 Retouch to background right of value (Th. B3–4), OP
- 1/6 Retouch to background top left corner of stamp (Th. A1), OP
- 5/4 Retouch to background in front of Queen's neck (Th. E9), OP
- 10/6 Horizontal line of retouching to background behind Queen's head (Th. D12–13), OP
- 19/6 Horizontal white line above "ON AND SONS" of imprint, OP
- 20/5 Horizontal white line below portrait (Th. F10–12), OP
- 20/6 As 20/5 but stronger line, OP

4d. Cyls. 1A–1B dot
- 3/3 Retouch to background in front of Queen's neck (Th. E10), OP
- 5/5 White scratch in right of telescope bowl (Th. B6–7), OP
- 9/3 Small white patch in background below portrait (Th. F–G12), OP
- 9/5 Retouch to background at left of telescope bowl (Th. E–F1), OP
- 13/4 Small white patch in background bottom left of portrait (Th. FG9), OP
- 13/5 Pale patch in background to left of telescope bowl (Th. E–F2), OP
- 14/6 Yellow spot in right of telescope bowl (Th. D6), OP

6d. Cyls. 1A–1B–1C no dot
- 5/6 Retouch to background above Queen's head (Th. A10–11), OP
- 10/3 Vertical blue line in Queen's portrait (Th. AC10), OP
- 13/3 Pale area above value (Th. A2), OP
- 17/4 Spur of first "S" of "SONS", OP

1s.3d. Cyls. 1A–1B–1C–1D no dot
- 1/1 Retouch in background behind Queen's head (Th. CD13), OP
- 1/4 White spot below "e" of "Hovercraft", OP
- 1/6 Retouch in sea, bottom centre (Th. G7), OP
- 12/6 Horizontal orange coloured line extends from sea to sheet margin (Th. G13–15), OP

1s.6d. Cyls. 1A–1B–1C–1D–1E no dot
- 1/3 Retouch in sky in front of Queen's neck (Th. CD10), OP
- 1/5 Grey coloured flaw in sky top right of Queen's head (Th. A13), OP
- 2/2 Lower part of left stroke of "n" of "Advanced" is broken off, OP
- 16/3 Vertical blue line in gutter between design edge and perforation (Th. D–G13), OP
- 16/5 Wispy whitish line runs vertically above "v" of "Advanced" (Th. F–G2), OP
- 20/1 Small white flaw in large door of building (Th. F6), OP

Sheet Details

Sheet size: 120 (6×20). 4d. double pane reel-fed; others single pane reel-fed

Sheet markings:
Cylinder numbers:
    4d., 6d., 1s.3d. Opposite R. 19/1, boxed
    1s.6d. Opposite rows 18/19 at left, boxed

Guide holes:
    4d. In single "S N" box opposite rows 14/15, at left (no dot) or right (dot)
    Others. In single "S O N" box opposite rows 14/15, at both sides

Marginal arrows (photo-etched):
"W" shaped, at top, bottom and sides

Marginal rule: None

Colour register marks:
    4d. Opposite rows 1/2 and 20, at left (no dot) or right (dot)

British Technology. 1966

      6d., **1s.3d.** Opposite rows 2/3 and 17/18, at both sides
      1s.6d. Opposite rows 3/4 and 17/18, at both sides

Autotron marks (solid):
      4d. Black, lemon, opposite row 5, at right (no dot) or left (dot)
      6d. Blue, red, orange below vertical rows 1/3
      1s.3d. Black, orange, blue, slate below vertical rows 1/3. Additional black below vertical row 3
      1s.6d. Black, lilac, bronze-green, yellow-green, blue below vertical rows 1/3 and additionally black below vertical row 1. During printing the correct sequence, black, blue, bronze-green, lilac, yellow-green, was engraved below vertical rows 4/6

Colour designations:
      4d. G1 YELLOW G2 BLACK in right margin reading upwards opposite rows 8/5 on dot panes only
      6d. G2 RED G3 BLUE in right margin reading upwards opposite rows 7/6
      1s.3d. G1 GREY G2 BLUE G3 RED G4 BLACK in right margin reading upwards opposite rows 7/4
      1s.6d. G1 BLUE G2 YELLOW G3 GREEN G4 MAUVE G5 BLACK in right margin reading upwards opposite rows 9/5

Traffic lights (boxed):
      4d. Lemon, black opposite R. 19/6
      6d. Orange, red, blue opposite R. 19/6
      1s.3d. Blue, slate, orange, black opposite rows 18/19 at right
      1s.6d. Black, lilac, bronze-green, yellow-green, blue opposite rows 18/19 at right

Imprimaturs from the NPM or BPMA

A. Ordinary
Nos. W97/W100 imperforate, watermark Type W.**24**

Watermark upright (*set of 4*)	£4000
4d. "Struts flaw" R. 4/6	£1500
4d. cylinder 1A, 1B (no dot) block of four	£5000
6d. cylinder 1A, 1B, 1C block of four	£5000
1s.3d. cylinder 1A, 1B, 1C, 1D block of four	£5000
1s.6d. cylinder 1A, 1B, 1C, 1D, 1E block of four	£5000

B. Phosphor
Nos. WP97/WP100 imperforate, watermark Type W.**24**

Watermark upright (*set of 4*)	£4000
4d. cylinder 1A, 1B (no dot) block of four	£5000
6d. cylinder 1A, 1B, 1C block of four	£5000
1s.3d. cylinder 1A, 1B, 1C, 1D block of four	£5000
1s.6d. cylinder 1A, 1B, 1C, 1D, 1E block of four	£5000

Quantities Sold:

	Ordinary	Phosphor
4d.	79,112,278	12,737,520
6d.	11,087,516	2,388,720
1s.3d.	5,199,900	1,431,000
1s.6d.	5,284,069	1,414,320
Pack	35,437	—

Withdrawn: 18.9.67 (6d. phosphor sold out earlier)

Type **W101.**

Type **W102.**

Type **W103.**

Type **W104.**

Type **W105.**

Type **W106.**

Types W97/W102 show battle scenes and were issued together *se-tenant* in horizontal strips of six within the sheet

Type **W107.** Norman Ship

W 1966 900th Anniversary of Battle of Hastings

Type **W108**. Norman Horsemen attacking Harold's Troops

(Des. David Gentleman)
(Printed in photogravure with the Queen's head die-stamped in gold 6d., 1s.3d.)

1966 (14 October). **900th Anniversary of Battle of Hastings**
Types **W101/W108**. Watermark sideways on 1s.3d. (normal is top of crown pointing to left *when stamps are viewed from the back*)

The scenes depicted are all reproduced from the celebrated Bayeux Tapestry which records the Norman invasion of England.

A. Ordinary

W101 =SG 705		Mint	Used
4d. black, olive-green, bistre, deep blue, orange, magenta, green, blue and grey		10	10
a. Strip of 6. Nos. W101/W106		60	60
ab. Imperforate strip of six		£3500	
Missing colours:			
b. Olive-green		50·00	
c. Bistre		50·00	
d. Deep blue		60·00	
e. Orange		50·00	
f. Magenta		50·00	
g. Green		45·00	
h. Blue		35·00	
i. Grey		35·00	
j. Watermark inverted		7·00	

W102 =SG 706			
4d. black, olive-green, bistre, deep blue, orange, magenta, green, blue and grey		10	10
Missing colours:			
b. Olive-green		50·00	
c. Bistre		50·00	
d. Deep blue		60·00	
e. Orange		50·00	
f. Magenta		50·00	
g. Green		45·00	
h. Blue		35·00	
i. Grey		35·00	
j. Watermark inverted		7·00	

W103 =SG 707			
4d. black, olive-green, bistre, deep blue, orange, magenta, green, blue and grey		10	10
Missing colours:			
b. Olive-green		50·00	
c. Bistre		50·00	
d. Deep blue		60·00	
e. Orange		50·00	
f. Magenta		50·00	
g. Green		45·00	
h. Blue		35·00	
i. Grey		35·00	
j. Watermark inverted		7·00	

W104 =SG 708			
4d. black, olive-green, bistre, deep blue, magenta, green, blue and grey		10	10
Missing colours:			
b. Olive-green		50·00	
c. Bistre		50·00	
d. Deep blue		60·00	
f. Magenta		50·00	
g. Green		45·00	
h. Blue		35·00	
i. Grey		35·00	
j. Watermark inverted		7·00	

W105 =SG 709			
4d. black, olive-green, bistre, deep blue, orange, magenta, green, blue and grey		10	10
Missing colours:			
b. Olive-green		50·00	
c. Bistre		50·00	
d. Deep blue		60·00	
e. Orange		50·00	
f. Magenta		50·00	
g. Green		45·00	
h. Blue		35·00	
i. Grey		35·00	
j. Watermark inverted		7·00	

W106 =SG 710			
4d. black, olive-green, bistre, deep blue, orange, magenta, green, blue and grey		10	10
Missing colours:			
b. Olive-green		50·00	
c. Bistre		50·00	
d. Deep blue		60·00	
e. Orange		50·00	
f. Magenta		50·00	
g. Green		45·00	
h. Blue		35·00	
i. Grey		35·00	
j. Watermark inverted		7·00	

W107 =SG 711			
6d. black, olive-green, violet, blue, green and gold		10	10
a. Watermark inverted		42·00	

W108 =SG 712			
1s.3d. black, lilac, bronze-green, rosine, bistre-brown and gold		20	30
a. Lilac omitted		£5250	
b. Watermark sideways inverted (top of crown pointing to right)		50·00	
c. Club flaw (R. 7/2)		35·00	

First Day Cover (W101/W108)			2·00
Presentation Pack (W101/W108)			8·50

900th Anniversary of Battle of Hastings 1966

B. Phosphor

WP101 =SG 705p

4d. Three bands		10	10
a.	Strip of 6. Nos. WP101/WP106	60	60
	Missing colours:		
b.	Olive-green	50·00	
c.	Bistre	50·00	
d.	Deep blue	60·00	
e.	Orange	50·00	
f.	Magenta	50·00	
g.	Green	45·00	
h.	Blue	50·00	
i.	Grey	40·00	
j.	Magenta and green	—	
k.	Watermark inverted	3·00	

WP102 =SG 706p

4d. Three bands		10	10
	Missing colours:		
b.	Olive-green	50·00	
c.	Bistre	50·00	
d.	Deep blue	60·00	
e.	Orange	50·00	
f.	Magenta	50·00	
g.	Green	45·00	
h.	Blue	50·00	
i.	Grey	40·00	
j.	Magenta and green	—	
k.	Watermark inverted	3·00	

WP103 =SG 707p

4d. Three bands		10	10
	Missing colours:		
b.	Olive-green	50·00	
c.	Bistre	50·00	
d.	Deep blue	60·00	
e.	Orange	50·00	
f.	Magenta	50·00	
g.	Green	45·00	
h.	Blue	50·00	
i.	Grey	40·00	
j.	Magenta and green	—	
k.	Watermark inverted	3·00	

WP104 =SG 708p

4d Three bands		10	10
	Missing colours:		
b.	Olive-green	50·00	
c.	Bistre	50·00	
d.	Deep blue	60·00	
f.	Magenta	50·00	
g.	Green	45·00	
h.	Blue	50·00	
i.	Grey	40·00	
j.	Magenta and green	—	
k.	Watermark inverted	3·00	

WP105 =SG 709p

4d. Three bands		10	10
	Missing colours:		
b.	Olive-green	50·00	
c.	Bistre	50·00	
d.	Deep blue	60·00	
e.	Orange	50·00	
f.	Magenta	50·00	
g.	Green	45·00	
h.	Blue	50·00	
i.	Grey	40·00	
j.	Magenta and green	—	
k.	Watermark inverted	3·00	

WP106 =SG 710p

4d. Three bands		10	10
	Missing colours:		
b.	Olive-green	50·00	
c.	Bistre	50·00	
d.	Deep blue	60·00	
e.	Orange	50·00	
f.	Magenta	50·00	
g.	Green	45·00	
h.	Blue	50·00	
i.	Grey	40·00	
j.	Magenta and green	—	
k.	Watermark inverted	3·00	

WP107 =SG 711p

6d. Three bands		10	10
a.	Watermark inverted	75·00	

WP108 =SG 712p

1s.3d. Four bands		20	40
a.	Lilac omitted	£1250	
b.	Error. Three bands	8·00	
c.	Watermark sideways inverted (top of crown pointing to right)	35·00	
d.	Club flaw (R. 7/2)	35·00	

First Day Cover (WP101/WP108)	9·00

4d. Prices for missing colour errors and inverted watermarks in strips of six:

	Ordinary	Phosphor
Olive-green	£300	£300
Bistre	£300	£300
Deep blue	£360	£360
Orange (on five stamps)	£250	£250
Magenta	£300	£300
Green	£270	£270
Blue	£210	£300
Grey	£210	£240
Magenta and green	†	—
Watermark inverted	45·00	20·00

Nos. W101 and W105 with grey and blue omitted have been seen commercially used, posted from Middleton-in-Teesdale.

The 6d. and 1s.3d. were also issued with the die-stamped gold head omitted but as these can also be removed by chemical means we are not prepared to list them unless a way is found of distinguishing the genuine stamps from the fakes which will satisfy the Expert Committees. However, three examples of No. W108 in a right-hand top corner block of ten (2×5) are known with the Queen's head omitted as a result of a double paper fold prior to die-stamping. The perforation is normal. Of the other seven stamps, four have the Queen's head misplaced and three are normal.

W 1966 900th Anniversary of Battle of Hastings

W108c, WP108d
The fallen knight has what appears to be a large black club at his right hand

Cylinder Numbers (Blocks of 24 (4d.), Six (6d.), Eight (1s.3d.))

	Perforation Types	
Cylinder Nos	F (P/E) Ordinary	No dot Phosphor
4d. 1A (black)–1B (olive-green)–1C (bistre)–1D (deep blue)–1E (orange)–1F (magenta)–1G (green)–H (blue)–1J (grey)	6·00	5·00
2A–1B–1C–1D– 1E–1F–1G–1H–1J		5·00

	G (P/P)			
	Ordinary		Phosphor	
	No dot	Dot	No dot	Dot
6d. 1A (black)–1B (olive-green)–1C (violet)–1D (blue)–1E (green)	1·25	1·25	1·25	1·25

	A (T) (E/P) No dot	
	Ordinary	Phosphor
1s.3d. 1A (black)–1B (lilac)–1C (bronze-green)–1D (rosine)–1E (bistre-brown)	35·00*	35·00*

Minor Constant Flaws
4d. Cyls. 1B–1C–1D–1E–1F–1G–1H–1J no dot in combination with black cyls. 1A or 2A
  3/4 Spur on second "S" of "HASTINGS", OP
  4/1 Horizontal black line to left of Queen's forehead (Th. A10–11), OP (1A only)
  4/5 Black line under Queen's chin (Th. C11), OP (1A only)
  9/1 Right hind leg of dark horse is paler than normal (Th. F–G8), OP
  9/2 Second "S" of "SONS" pale and distorted, possibly hand drawn (OP) (1A only)
  19/4 White spot on horseman's leg (Th. F7), OP (1A only)
  20/3 "LTD" heavier than normal, OP (1A only)
  20/4 "HARRISON AND" heavier than normal, OP (1A only)

4d. Cyl. 2A no dot
  10/1 "H" of "HARRISON" is indistinct, O
  11/1 "Hastings 1066" weaker than normal, O

6d. Cyls. 1A–1B–1C–1D–1E no dot
  1/1 Blue patch on hull due to lack of black shading (Th. F9), OP
  4/1 Small dot after final "s" of "Hastings", OP
  6/1 Diagonal black line through figures in small boat (Th. C3–B5), OP
  8/4 Diagonal spur on first "t" of "Battle", OP

6d. Cyls. 1A–1B–1C–1D–1E dot
  1/1 Partial break in main left-hand rigging of main vessel (Th. D3), OP
  3/1 Extra gold enlarges Queen's throat at both sides (Th. C–D12), P
  8/5 Horizontal black line in upper part of first "6" of "1966", OP
  8/6 Horizontal black line through "HAR" of "HARRISON", OP

1s.3d. Cyls. 1A–1B–1C–1D–1E no dot
  6/2 Dot in "g" of "Hastings", OP
  7/1 Vertical line from "N" of "SONS"
  8/1 Diagonal hairline runs from bottom of red shield of second soldier through toes of right foot to bottom of stamp (Th. E–H12), O
  9/1 Line continues to right-hand arm of first soldier (Th. A12), O
  10/4 Bronze-green dot upper left of "1" of "1/3" (Th. F8), OP

Sheet Details
  Sheet sizes:
    4d. 120 (6×20). In *se-tenant* strips of six, single pane sheet-fed
    6d. 60 (6×10). Double pane sheet-fed
    1s.3d. 60 (6×10). Single pane sheet-fed

Sheet markings:
Cylinder numbers:
    4d. Opposite rows 17/19 at left, boxed
    6d. Opposite rows 8/9 at left, boxed
    1s.3d. Opposite rows 7/8 at left, boxed

Guide holes: None
Marginal arrows (photo-etched):
"W" shaped, at top, bottom and sides
Marginal rule: None
Colour register marks:
    4d. Above and below vertical rows 1 and 5/6
    6d. Above vertical rows 1 and 5/6 (no dot) or below them (dot)
    1s.3d. Opposite rows 1/2 and 9/10, at both sides
Coloured crosses:
    4d. Above and below vertical rows 3/4
    6d. Above vertical rows 3/4 (no dot) or below them (dot)
    1s.3d. Opposite rows 5/6, at both sides
Autotron marks and Colour designations: None
Traffic lights (boxed and in same order as cylinder numbers):
    4d. Opposite rows 17/19 at right
    6d. Opposite rows 8/9 at right
    1s.3d. Opposite rows 7/8 at right

Imprimaturs from the NPM or BPMA
A. Ordinary
Nos. W101/W106 imperforate, watermark Type W.**24**
Watermark upright (*se-tenant* strip of six) £6000
Nos. W107/W108 imperforate, watermark Type W.**24**
Watermark upright (6d.) or sideways (1s.3d.) (Each) £2000
6d. cylinder 1A, 1B, 1C, 1D, 1E (dot) block of six £7000

B. Phosphor
Nos. WP101/WP106 imperforate, watermark Type W.**24**
Watermark upright (*se-tenant* strip of six) £6000
No. WP107 imperforate, watermark Type W.**24**
Watermark upright (6d.) £2000
6d. cylinder 1A, 1B, 1C, 1D, 1E (no dot) block of six £7000
1s.3d. cylinder 1A, 1B, 1C, 1D, 1E block of eight £9000

Quantities Sold:

	Ordinary	Phosphor.
4d.	89,197,226	15,861,960
6d.	12,012,328	2,820,360
1s.3d.	5,721,426	1,646,280
Pack	51,332	

Withdrawn: 13.10.67 (6d. phosphor sold out in September)

Christmas. 1966

Type **W109**. King of the Orient
(Des. Miss Tasveer Shemza)

Type **W110**. Snowman
(Des. James Berry)

(Printed in photogravure with the Queen's head die-stamped in gold)

1966 *(1 December).* **Christmas.** Watermark sideways on 3d. Types **W109/W110**

These designs, executed by two six-year-old children, were chosen from nearly 5,000 entries in a Post Office competition for Britain's first adhesive Christmas stamps.

A. Ordinary

W109 =SG 713		Mint	Used
3d.	black, blue, green, yellow, red and gold	10	10
a.	Queen's head double	—	†
ab.	Queen's head double, one albino	£500	
b.	Green omitted		£4250
c.	Missing "T" (No dot, R. 6/2)	25·00	

W110 =SG 714			
1s.6d.	blue, red, pink, black and gold	10	10
a.	Pink (hat) omitted	£3800	
b.	Watermark inverted	30·00	

First Day Cover (W109/W110)		70
Presentation Pack (W109/W110)	10·00	

B. Phosphor

WP109 =SG 713p			
3d.	One band at left	10	10
a.	Band at right	10	10
ab.	Nos. WP109/WP109a (horiz. pair)	20	20
ac.	Error. Pair, with and without phosphor	20·00	
b.	Missing "T" (No dot. R. 6/2)	45·00	

WP110 =SG 714p			
1s.6d	Two bands	10	10
a.	Watermark inverted	90·00	

| First Day Cover (WP109/WP110) | | 70 |

The one phosphor band on No. WP109 was produced by printing broad phosphor bands across alternate vertical rows of perforations. Individual examples show the band at right or left (same prices either way).

W109c, WP109b

Both values were issued with the Queen's head embossed but with the gold omitted. However, as the colour can be removed by chemical means, we are not prepared to list them unless a way is found of distinguishing the genuine stamps from the fakes which will satisfy the Expert Committees.

It is understood that the gold heads (actually aluminium powder) were die-stamped on to the printed stamps one vertical column at a time. Sheets of both values are known with the Queen's heads and embossing omitted from the right-hand column and ten gold heads printed in the left margin. Examples with the head omitted from the right-hand stamp in a horizontal marginal pair from such sheets can be considered genuine. A marginal block of the 3d. is known with two gold head omissions, due to a paper-fold, with three partial gold heads on the gummed side. A paper-fold on the 1s.6d. resulted in the head being omitted from the bottom right-hand stamp and printed instead in the right margin, level with "1/6".

Either because the film from which the heads were applied was re-used or because it did not feed through the blocking press properly, examples of both values are known showing a row of only partial Queen's heads. In these cases the embossing is complete but the gold is only partially printed, with a colourless "silhouette" of the head encroaching into it; the result of the gold already having been die-stamped out of the film.

No. WP109 exists with a horizontal phosphor band across the top of the stamp. This was caused by phosphor spillage under the doctor blade and occurred on the top horizontal row of a sheet.

Cylinder Numbers (Blocks of Six)

		Perforation Types	
(a) Ordinary		A (I/E)	A (I/E)
	Cylinder Nos	No dot	Dot
3d.	1A (blue)–1B (black)–1C (green)–1D (yellow)–1E (red)	35·00	35·00
	1A–2B–1C–1D–1E	28·00	28·00
	1A–3B–1C–1D–1E	1·00	1·00
	1A–4B–1C–1D–1E	1·00	1·00
		A (I/E)	A (T) (P/E)
		No dot	No dot
1s.6d.	1A (blue)–1B (black)–2C (red)–1D (pink)	1·25	1·25

		Perforation Types	
(b) Phosphor		A (I/E)	A (I/E)
	Cylinder Nos	No dot	Dot
3d.	1A (blue)–3B (black)–1C (green)–1D (yellow)–1E (red)	1·00	1·00
	1A–4B–1C–1D–1E	1·00	1·00
		A (I/E)	A (T) (P/E)
		No dot	No dot
1s.6d.	1A (blue)–1B (black)–2C (red)–1D (pink)	15·00	1·25

Perforation Types A and A(T) are with sheets orientated showing head to left.

In the dot panes of the 3d. the dot is missing after B in the black colour.

W 1966 *Christmas.*

Minor Constant Flaws
3d. Cyls. 1A–1C–1D–1E no dot in combination with black cyls. 3B or 4B

2/1	During the course of printing a diagonal cut developed at base of Queen's neck and later the piece of gold foil separated and dropped downwards (Th. C–D5), OP
2/3	Blue dot in front of "H" of "HARRISON", OP
2/8	"A" of "AND" in imprint shorter than normal, OP
3/4	White patch at top left corner of panel is larger than normal (Th. A1), OP
3/8	Extra stop after "T." of "T. SHEMZA", OP
7/1	Damaged top to "A" of "AND", OP
8/8	Red dot under first leg of "H" of "HARRISON", OP

3d. Cyls. 1A–1C–1D–1E dot in combination with black cyls. 3B or 4B

1/5	Two red dots in the yellow above red circle in crown (Th. F–G3), OP (3B only)
2/1	As for no dot cyls.
4/6	Background retouch between points of crown at right (Th. F5), OP
4/7	First "S" of "SONS" incomplete, OP
5/5	Red spot in white area below Queen's portrait (Th. D5), OP (3B only)
8/1	Top of "S" of "HARRISON" incomplete, OP

1s.6d. Cyls. 1A–1B–2C–1D no dot

3/1	White spot normally found in red scarf is filled in (Th. E4), OP
6/7	Dark blue spot inside "6" of "1/6", OP
8/2	Small blue projection into right-hand margin (Th. L7), OP
9/1	Second "R" of "BERRY" is damaged, OP

Sheet Details
Sheet size: 80 (8×10)
    3d. double-pane reel-fed, with dot pane above no dot pane
    1s.6d. single-pane sheet-fed

Sheet markings:

Cylinder numbers:
    3d. Above vertical rows 2/3, boxed
    1s.6d. Opposite R. 8/1, boxed

Guide holes: **3d.** Boxed above vertical rows 6/7; **1s.6d.** none

Marginal arrows (photo-etched):
"W" shaped, at top, bottom and sides

Marginal rule: None

Colour register marks:
    3d. None;
    1s.6d. above and below vertical rows 1/2 and 7/8

Coloured crosses: **3d.** None; **1s.6d.** above and below vertical rows 4/5

Autotron marks (solid):
    3d. Green, yellow, red, black, blue opposite rows 8/10, left margin (dot); **1s.6d.** none

Colour designations: None

Traffic lights (boxed):
    3d. Black, blue, green, yellow, red below vertical rows 2/3
    1s.6d. Blue, red, pink, black opposite R. 8/10

Imprimaturs from the NPM or BPMA

A. Ordinary
Nos. W109/W110 imperforate, watermark Type W.**24**

Watermark upright (1s.6d.) or sideways (3d.) *(set of 2)*	£2000
3d. cylinder 1A, 3B, 1C, 1E (no dot) block of six	£7000
1s.6d. cylinder 1A, 1B, 2C, 1D (no dot) block of six	£7000

B. Phosphor
Nos. WP109/WP110 imperforate, watermark Type W.**24**

Watermark upright (1s.6d.) or sideways (3d.) *(set of 2)*	£2000
3d. cylinder 1A, 4B, 1C, 1D, 1E (dot) block of six	£7000
1s.6d. cylinder 1A, 1B, 2C, 1D (no dot) block of six	£7000

Quantities Sold:

	Ordinary	Phosphor
3d.	153,318,160	20,774,000
1s.6d.	8,756,960	2,109,280
Pack	33,672	—

Withdrawn: The 3d. phosphor was sold out in January, the 3d. ordinary and 1s.6d. phosphor were sold out in October, and the 1s.6d. ordinary was withdrawn on 30.11.67

European Free Trade Association. **1967** W

Type **W111**. Sea Freight

Type **W112**. Air Freight
(Des. Clive Abbott)

1967 *(20 February).* **European Free Trade Association.** Types **W111/W112**

Issued to commemorate the movement of trade between Austria, Denmark, Norway, Portugal, Sweden, Switzerland and the United Kingdom. Finland was an associate member.

A. Ordinary

W111 =SG 715	Mint	Used
9d. deep blue, red, lilac, green, brown, new blue, yellow and black	10	10
Missing colours:		
a. Black (Queen's head), brown, new blue and yellow	£1300	
b. Lilac	£140	
c. Green	£140	
d. Brown (rail trucks) omitted	95·00	
e. New blue	£140	
f. Yellow	£140	
g. Watermark inverted	£180	
h. Quay flaw (R. 8/3)	30·00	

W112 =SG 716		
1s.6d. violet, red, deep blue, brown, green, blue-grey, new blue, yellow and black	10	10
Missing colours:		
a. Red	—	
b. Deep blue	£550	
c. Brown	£140	
d. Blue-grey	£140	
e. New blue	£140	
f. Yellow	£140	
g. Green	£3750	
h. Broken ribbon (R. 11/3)	20·00	
i. Broken undercarriage leg (R. 13/6)	40·00	
j. Break in frame (R. 20/1)	30·00	

First Day Cover (W111/W112)	5·00
Presentation Pack (W111/W112)	20·00

B. Phosphor (9d. applied flexo.; 1s.6d. applied typo.)

WP111 =SG 715p		
9d. Three bands	10	10
Missing colours:		
a. Lilac	£225	
b. Green	£140	
c. Brown (rail trucks) omitted	95·00	
d. New blue	£140	
e. Yellow	£180	
f. Watermark inverted	£1200	
g. Quay flaw (R. 8/3)	30·00	

WP112 =SG 716p		
1s.6d. Three bands	10	10
Missing colours:		
b. Deep blue	£140	
c. Brown	95·00	
d. Blue-grey	£140	
e. New blue	£140	
f. Watermark inverted	50·00	
g. Broken ribbon (R. 11/3)	30·00	
h. Broken undercarriage leg (R. 13/6)	40·00	
j. Break in frame (R. 20/1)	20·00	
k. All over phosphor		

First Day Cover (WP111/WP112)	5·00

No. WP112k came from the first vertical column of a sheet. It was due to a weak mixture of the phosphor ink which leaked under the phosphor doctor blade.

W111h, WP111g
Black protuberance on quay between trucks

Normal

W112h, WP112g

W112i, WP112h
Broken undercarriage leg below wing

W112j, WP112j
Break in the frame of Portuguese flag

Cylinder Numbers (Blocks of Eight)

	Perforation Type	
	F (P/E)	No dot
Cylinder Nos	Ordinary	Phosphor
9d. 1A (deep blue)–1B (red)–1C (lilac)–1D (green)–1E (brown)–1F (new blue)–1G (yellow)–1H (black)	1·25	1·25
1s.6d. 2A (violet)–1B (red)–1C (deep blue)–1D (green)–1E (brown)–1F (new blue)–1G (yellow)–2H (blue-grey)–2J (black)	20·00	20·00

219

W 1967 *European Free Trade Association.*

Minor Constant Flaws
9d. Cyls. 1A–1B–1C–1D–1E–1F–1G–1H no dot

    6/5 Black colour on roof of bridge is smudged (Th. D8–9), OP
    11/5 Small blue dot in base of letter "E" (Th. B–C2), OP
    12/5 White spot in lilac superstructure (Th. E11), OP

1s.6d. Cyls. 2A–1B–1C–1D–1E–1F–1G–2H–2J no dot

    10/1 Small violet dot in top of letter "E" (Th. A2), OP
    19/1 White spur in "6" of "1/6", OP

Sheet Details
Sheet size: 120 (6×20). Single-pane sheet-fed

Sheet markings:
Cylinder numbers:
    9d. Opposite rows 17/19 at left, boxed
    1s.6d. Opposite rows 17/20 at left, boxed

Guide holes: None

Marginal arrows (photo-etched): "W" shaped, at top, bottom and side.

Marginal rule: At bottom of sheet

Colour register marks: Above and below vertical rows 1/2 and 5/6

Coloured crosses: Above and below vertical rows 4/5

Autotron marks and Colour designations: None

Traffic lights (boxed):
    9d. Opposite rows 17/19 at right, in same order as cylinder numbers
    1s.6d. Violet, red, deep blue, brown, green, blue-grey, new blue, yellow, black opposite rows 17/19 at right

Imprimaturs from the NPM or BPMA

A. Ordinary
Nos. W111/W112 imperforate, watermark Type W.**24**

Watermark upright (*set of* 2)	£2000
9d. cylinder 1A, 1B, 1C, 1D, 1E, 1F, 1G block of eight	£9000
1s.6d. "Broken undercarriage leg" flaw R. 13/6	£1500
1s.6d. cylinder 2A, 1B, 1C, 1D, 1E, 1F, 1G, 2H, 2J block of eight	£9000*

B. Phosphor
Nos. WP111/WP112 imperforate, watermark Type W.**24**

Watermark upright (*set of* 2)	£2000
9d. cylinder 1A, 1B, 1C, 1D, 1E, 1F, 1G block of eight	£9000
1s.6d. "Broken undercarriage leg" flaw R. 13/6	£1500
1s.6d. cylinder 2A, 1B, 1C, 1D, 1E, 1F, 1G, 2H, 2J block of eight	£9000*

Quantities Sold.	Ordinary	Phosphor
9d.	6,553,738	5,557,104
1s.6d.	6,363,483	4,237,944
Pack	42,906	—

Withdrawn: 19.2.68

Type **W113.** Hawthorn and Bramble

Type **W114.** Larger Bindweed and Viper's Bugloss

Type **W115.** Ox-eye Daisy, Coltsfoot and Buttercup

Type **W116.** Bluebell, Red Campion and Wood Anemone

The above were issued together *se-tenant* in blocks of four within the sheet

(Des. Rev. W. Keble Martin)

Type **W117.** Dog Violet

Type **W118.** Primroses

(Des. Mary Grierson)

British Wild Flowers. 1967

1967 (24 April). **British Wild Flowers.** Types **W113/W118**

A. Ordinary

W113 =SG 717		Mint	Used
4d.	grey, lemon, myrtle-green, red, agate and slate-purple	10	10
a.	Block of 4. Nos. W113/W116	40	40
b.	Grey double*		
c.	Red omitted	£4000	
d.	Watermark inverted	2·00	
e.	Slate-purple omitted	£5500	

W114 =SG 718			
4d.	grey, lemon, myrtle-green, red, agate and violet	10	10
b.	Grey double*		
d.	Watermark inverted	2·00	

W115 =SG 719			
4d.	grey, lemon, myrtle-green, red and agate	10	10
b.	Grey double*		
d.	Watermark inverted	2·00	

W116 =SG 720			
4d.	grey, lemon, myrtle-green, reddish purple, agate and violet	10	10
b.	Grey double*		
c.	Reddish purple omitted	£2000	
d.	Watermark inverted	2·00	
e.	Value omitted (see note)	£9500	

W117 =SG 721			
9d.	lavender-grey, green, reddish violet and orange-yellow	15	15
a.	Watermark inverted	1·30	
b.	Notch in leaf (R. 20/2)	20·00	

W118 =SG 722			
1s.9d.	lavender-grey, green, greenish yellow and orange	15	15

First Day Cover (W113/W118)			1·20
Presentation Pack (W113/W118)			20·00

B. Phosphor

WP113 =SG 717p			
4d.	Three bands	10	10
a.	Block of 4. Nos. WP113/WP116	40	40
b.	Agate omitted	£3500	
c.	Slate-purple omitted	£500	
d.	Watermark inverted	2·00	

WP114 =SG 718p			
4d.	Three bands	10	10
b.	Agate omitted	£3500	
c.	Violet omitted		
d.	Watermark inverted	2·00	

WP115 =SG 719p			
4d.	Three bands	10	10
b.	Agate omitted	£3500	
c.	Watermark inverted	2·00	

WP116 =SG 720p			
4d.	Three bands	10	10
b.	Agate omitted	£3500	
c.	Violet omitted		
d.	Watermark inverted	2·00	

WP117 =SG 721p			
9d.	Three bands	15	15
a.	Notch in leaf (R. 20/2)	20·00	

WP118 =SG 722p			
1s.9d.	Three bands	15	15

First Day Cover (WP113/WP118)	7·00
Presentation Pack (WP113/WP118)	20·00

Although officially titled "British Wild Flowers" the Post Office first day cover and presentation pack are both inscribed "British Flora".

4d. Prices for missing colour errors and inverted watermarks in blocks of four:

	Ordinary	Phosphor
Red	£4000	†
Reddish purple	£2000	†
Agate	†	£14000
Violet	†	
Slate purple	£5500	£500
Watermark inverted	8·00	8·00
Grey double		†

* The double impression of the grey printing affects the Queen's head, value and inscription.

The 1s.9d. is known postmarked 20 April in the Bristol area. No. W116e (Bluebell etc.) was caused by something obscuring the face value on R. 14/6 during the printing of one sheet.

W117b, WP117a

Cylinder Numbers (Blocks of Eight (4d.) or Six (others))

		Perforation Types	
		F (P/E) No dot	
Cylinder Nos.		Ordinary	Phosphor
4d.	3A (grey)–1B (lemon)–2C (myrtle-green)–1D (reddish purple)–1E (red)–1F (agate)–2G (violet)–1H (slate-purple)	1·50	1·50
	3A–1B–3C–1D–1E–1F–2G–1H	†	30·00
		A (E/I)	No dot
9d.	2A (lavender-grey)–3B (green)–3C (reddish violet)–2D (orange-yellow)	22·00*	22·00*
1s.9d.	2A (lavender-grey)–2B (green)–2C (greenish yellow)–2D (orange)	1·75	1·75

Minor Constant Flaws

4d. Cyls. 3A–1B–2C–1D–1E–1F–2G–1H no dot
  1/4 Green flaw in large leaf above flower (Th. A4), OP
  4/6 Yellow spot by Queen's chin (Th. C10), P
  8/6 Small spot by upper leaf of wood anemone (Th. A6), OP
  10/2 Small green spot in lower wood anemone (Th. D9), OP
  15/6 Style on left-hand flower of right-hand plant is incomplete (Th. A6), OP
  16/2 Green spot at left of bluebell leaf (Th. E1), P

9d. Cyls. 2A–3B–3C–2D no dot
  9/6 Diagonal hairline running down from small right-hand leaf (Th. F10), OP
  13/5 Green spot between left leaf and centre violet flower (Th. D3), OP

1967 British Wild Flowers.

| 14/1 | Fine vertical yellow line at right of right-hand leaf on top left-hand stamen (Th. BC3), OP |
| 20/6 | Green spot in lower left-hand leaf (Th. G1), OP |

1s.9d. Cyls. 2A–2B–2C–2D no dot

1/2	Diagonal yellow hairline in the white portion from Queen's neck to top of value (Th. CE11), OP
1/6	Retouch between top of stroke and "9" of value (Th. F12), OP
2/2	Retouch over "9" of value (Th. F13), OP
10/1	"M" of "MARY" is weak, OP
15/1	Line of green dots between two right-hand primroses (Th. E9), OP
19/4	Dotted green line projecting left from top left-hand leaf (Th. C–D1), OP
19/5	Horizontal green hairline on central primrose (Th. D4), OP
19/6	"N" of "HARRISON" is weak, OP
20/1	Break in outline of petals in topmost primrose (Th. B7), OP

Sheet Details

Sheet size: 120 (6×20)
   4d. In *se-tenant* blocks of four, single-pane sheet-fed
   9d., 1s.9d. Single-pane reel-fed

Sheet markings:

Cylinder numbers:
   4d. Opposite rows 17/19 at left, boxed
   9d., 1s.9d. Opposite rows 18/19 at left, boxed

Guide holes:
   4d. None
   9d., 1s.9d. Opposite row 15 (boxed), at both sides

Marginal arrows (photo-etched):
"W" shaped at top, bottom and sides

Marginal rule: At bottom of sheet

Colour register marks:
   4d. Above and below vertical rows 1/2 and 5/6
   9d., 1s.9d. Opposite rows 1/2 and 20, at both sides

Coloured crosses:
   4d. Above and below vertical rows 3/4
   9d., 1s.9d. None

Autotron marks (solid):
   4d. None
   9d. Lavender-grey, green, reddish violet, green over orange, below vertical rows 1/3
   1s.9d. Lavender-grey, orange, green, greenish yellow, below vertical rows 1/3

Colour designations:
   4d. None
   9d. G1 GREEN G2 MAUVE G3 ORANGE G4 GREY in right margin reading upwards opposite rows 9/3
   1s.9d. G1 YELLOW G2 GREEN G3 ORANGE G4 GREY in right margin reading upwards opposite rows 13/7

Traffic lights (boxed and in same order as cylinder numbers):
   4d. Opposite rows 17/19 at right
   9d., 1s.9d. Opposite rows 18/19 at right

Imprimaturs from the NPM or BPMA

A. Ordinary
Nos. W113/W116 imperforate, watermark Type W.**24**

Watermark upright (*se-tenant* block of four)	£4000
4d. cylinder 3A, 1B, 2C, 1D, 1E, 1F, 2G, 1H block of eight	£9000

Nos. W117/W118 imperforate, watermark Type W.**24**

Watermark upright (2 values only)	£2000
9d. cylinder 2A, 3B, 3C, 2D block of six	£7500*
1s.9d. cylinder 2A, 2B, 2C, 2D block of six	£7000

B. Phosphor
Nos. WP113/WP116 imperforate, watermark Type W.**24**

Watermark upright (*se-tenant* block of four)	£4000
4d. cylinder 3A, 1B, 2C, 1D, 1E, 1F, 2G, 1H block of four	£9000

Nos. WP117/WP118 imperforate, watermark Type W.**24**

Watermark upright (2 values only)	£2000
9d. cylinder 2A, 3B, 3C, 2D block of six	£7500*
1s.9d. cylinder 2A, 2B, 2C, 2D block of six	£7000

Quantities Sold.

	Ordinary	Phosphor
4d.	78,331,778	37,133,952
9d.	5,873,042	5,701,608
1s.9d.	3,259,521	4,929,648
Pack	53,446	(including ordinary and phosphor)

Withdrawn: 23.4.68

British Paintings. 1967

PHOSPHOR BANDS. All the following commemorative issues were normally issued with phosphor bands only; however, most also exist with phosphor omitted in error.

Type **W119**. Master Lambton (Sir Thomas Lawrence)

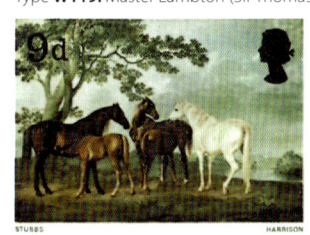

Type **W120**. Mares and Foals in a Landscape (George Stubbs)

Type **W121**. Children Coming Out of School (L. S. Lowry)

(Des. Stuart Rose)

1967 (10 July). **British Paintings.** No watermark. Two phosphor bands, applied by flexography. Types **W119/W121**

This is the first issue of British Paintings for which Harrisons made photographs from the originals.

W119 =SG 748	Mint	Used
4d. rose-red, lemon, brown, black, new blue and gold	10	10
a. Gold omitted (value and Queen's head)	£275	
b. New blue omitted	£15000	
c. Phosphor omitted	7·00	

W120 =SG 749		
9d. Venetian red, ochre, grey-black, new blue, greenish yellow and black	10	10
a. Black omitted (Queen's head and value)	£1000	
ab. Black (Queen's head only) omitted	£2100	
c. Phosphor omitted	£500	
d. Error. One broad band	15·00	

W121 =SG 750		
1s.6d. greenish yellow, grey, rose, new blue, grey-black and gold	10	10

a. Gold omitted (Queen's head)		
b. New blue omitted	£275	
c. Grey (clouds and shading) omitted	£150	
d. Phosphor omitted	£300	
e. Error. One broad band	8·00	
f. Extra window (No dot, R. 9/1)	28·00	

First Day Cover (W119/W121)	1·00
Presentation Pack (W119/W121)	20·00

No. W120ab with Queen's head only omitted, was due to a major colour shift. A similar shift caused the face value to be misplaced to the right of the Queen's head.

All values were put on sale in error on 30 June at the Lincoln head post office.

W121f

Cylinder Numbers (Blocks of Four (4d.) or Six (others))

	Perforation Type A(T) (I/E)	
Cylinder Nos.	No dot	Dot
4d. 3A (gold)–1B (lemon)–1C (rose-red)–1D (new blue)–1E (brown)–1F (black)	1·00	1·00
3A–1B–2C–1D–1E–1F	1·00	1·00
4A–1B–1C–1D–1E–1F	1·00	1·00
4A–1B–2C–1D–1E–1F	1·00	1·00
5A–1B–2C–1D–1E–1F	1·00	1·00

	Perforation Type A(T) (E/P)	
	No dot	Dot
9d. 2A (black)–1B (greenish yellow)–1C (Venetian red)–1D (ochre)–1E (new blue)–3F (grey-black)	1·25	1·25
1s.6d. 2A (grey-black)–1B (greenish yellow)–1C (rose)–1D (new blue)–1E (grey)–1F (gold)	1·25	1·25

Perforation Type A(T) on the 4d. is with sheet orientated showing head to right. In the 4A dot pane the dot is omitted for the gold cylinder and it appears before the C in the rose-red cylinder.

In the 9d. the greenish yellow 1B is very faint in the dot pane and is sometimes almost invisible. Also in the dot pane the dot appears before the 2A.

In the 1s.6d. dot pane the dot appears before the 1F.

Minor Constant Flaws

4d. Cyls. 1B–2C–1D–1E–1F in combination with gold cyls. 3A, 4A or 5A no dot

2/1 Two small dots on boy's left leg (Th. K6, L6)
3/1 Gold dot on boy's right collar (Th. F5)
5/4 Dark spot on right leg of boy's breeches (Th. 14)

4d. Cyls 1B–2C–1D–1E–1F in combination with gold cyls. 3A, 4A or 5A dot

1/11 Red spot in left gutter, sometimes lost in perforations (Th. J0)
2/11 Small red spot on boy's right collar (Th. E5)
3/4 Small spot in the V of boy's collar (Th. F5)
5/3 Dark spot on inside of boy's left elbow (Th. F7)

223

W 1967 *Sir Francis Chichester's World Voyage.*

9d. Cyls. 2A–1B–1C–1D–1E–3F no dot
- 3/1 Break in first "S" of "STUBBS"
- 4/3 Dark spot in foliage of lower centre branch (Th. C5)
- 7/1 Dark spot between right-hand foal's forelegs (Th. G7) and another in the grass just below (Th. H7)

9d. Cyls. 2A–1B–1C–1D–1E–3F dot
- 2/5 Slight nick in upright stroke of "d" of value
- 9/3 Small retouch in sky above white horse (Th. D10)
- 10/1 Break in first "R" of "HARRISON"
- 11/1 Dark dot below horse's hind hoof in bottom left corner (Th. H1)

1s.6d. Cyls. 2A–1B–1C–1D–1E–1F no dot
- 1/1 Circular patch in building below "1" of value (Th. C2)
- 1/5 Small dot by leg of foreground figure left of centre (Th. I6)
- 9/4 Small spot above roof of small house in side street (Th. E9)

1s.6d. Cyls. 2A–B1–C1–D–1E–1F dot
- 1/1 Break in "Y" of "LOWRY"
- 1/4 Lack of colour on second red door from right (Th. F–G11)
- 12/1 Line of small dots in top gutter

Sheet Details
Sheet size: 4d. 60 (12×5)
Others: (5×12). All double- pane sheet-fed

Sheet markings:
Cylinder numbers:
 4d. Opposite R. 4/1, boxed
 Others: Opposite rows 10/11 at left, boxed

Guide holes: None

Marginal arrows (photo-etched):
"W" shaped, at top and bottom (4d.) or at both sides (others)

Marginal rule: At bottom of sheet

Colour register marks, coloured crosses, autotron marks and Colour designations: None

Traffic lights (boxed and in same order as cylinder numbers):
 4d. Opposite R. 4/12
 Others: Opposite rows 10/11 at right

Imprimaturs from the NPM or BPMA
Nos. W119/W121 imperforate

No watermark (*set of 3*)	£3000
4d. cylinder 3A, 1B, 1C, 1D, 1E, 1F (dot) block of four	£5000
9d. cylinder 2A, 1B, 1C, 1D, 1E, 3F (dot) vertical strip of three	£4000
1s.6d. "Extra window" flaw R. 9/1	£1500
1s.6d. cylinder 2A, 1B, 1C, 1D, 1E, 1F (no dot) block of six	£7000

Quantities Sold:
4d.	102,443,229
9d.	9,568,991
1s.6d.	9,660,509
Pack	46,017

Withdrawn:
9.7.68 (4d. sold out October 1967, 9d. sold out January 1968)

Type W122. *Gipsy Moth IV*
(Des. Michael and Sylvia Goaman)

1967 *(24 July).* **Sir Francis Chichester's World Voyage.**
No watermark. Three phosphor bands, applied by flexography. Type **W122**

Sir Francis Chichester voyaged single-handed from England to Australia and back in Gipsy Moth IV and was knighted by the Queen on his return.

W122 =SG 751		Mint	Used
1s.9d.	black, brown-red, light emerald and blue	10	10
a.	Broken ribbon (R. 19/3)	28·00	
First Day Cover (W122)			40

Normal   W122a

Cylinder Numbers (Blocks of Six)

	Perforation Type A (E/I) No dot
Cylinder. Nos.	
1s.9d. 2A (black)–1B (light emerald)–1C (blue)–1D (brown-red)	1·25

Minor Constant Flaws
1s.9d. Cyls. 2A–1B–1C–1D no dot
- 1/6 Dark flaw in Queen's hair below ribbon (Th. B12–13)
- 2/1 Grey flaw at top of main sail (Th. A7) and flaw in rear sail (Th. C8–9)
- 6/5 Diagonal line running across main sail (Th. D6–7)
- 13/1 Line of small blue dots in rear sail (Th. D–E8)
- 14/4 White flaw in figure "1" of value (Th. G12)
- 16/2 Break in rigging near main-mast (Th. D5)
- 17/6 Line of blue dots on hull below main sail (Th. E4–5)
- 18/5 Scratch through rear sail to grey clouds (Th. E8–D11)
- 18/6 Same scratch extends to foresail (Th. C1–B5)
- 19/1 Small spur protrudes from top right of rear sail (Th. B–C9)
- 20/1 Curved dotted blue line between rear sail and Queen's portrait (Th. C9)
- 20/2 Diagonal blue line in top gutter (Th. O–13 in gutter)
- 20/3 Vertical white line at bottom left of main sail (Th. D–E5)
- 20/4 Blue flaw at top of main sail (Th. A7)
- 20/6 Dot between "ON" of "HARRISON"

Sheet Details
Sheet size: 120 (6×20). Single pane reel-fed

Sheet markings:
Cylinder numbers: Opposite rows 18/19 at left, boxed

Guide holes: Boxed, opposite row 14, at both sides. Boxes without holes also appear opposite row 15, at both sides

British Discovery and Invention. **1967**

Marginal arrows (photo-etched):
"W" shaped, at top, bottom and sides

Marginal rule: At bottom of sheet

Colour register marks: Opposite rows 1/2 and 20, at both sides

Autotron marks (solid): Black, blue, emerald, brown-red, below vertical rows 1/3

Coloured crosses and Colour designations: None

Traffic lights (boxed): Blue, brown-red, black, emerald, opposite rows 18/19 at right

Imprimatur from the NPM or BPMA
No. W122 imperforate

No watermark (single)	£1000
1s.9d. "Broken ribbon" variety R. 19/3	£1500
1s.9d. cylinder 2A, 1B, 1C, 1D block of six	£7000

Quantity Sold: 10,060,867

Withdrawn: 23.7.68

Type **W123.** Radar Screen

Type **W124.** Penicillin Mould
(Des. Clive Abbott)

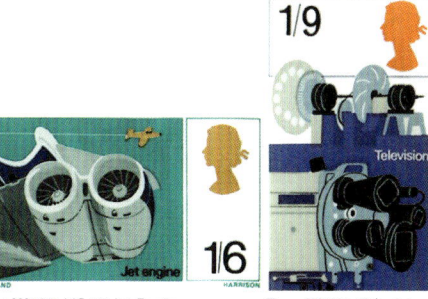

Type **W125.** VC-10 Jet Engines   Type **W126.** Television Equipment

(Des. Negus and Sharland team)

1967 *(19 September).* **British Discovery and Invention.** Three phosphor bands (4d.) or two phosphor bands (others). Types **W123/W126**

Watermark Multiple Crowns, sideways on 1s.9d. This was the last commemorative issue to bear a watermark.

		Mint	Used
W123 =SG 752			
4d.	greenish yellow, black and vermilion	10	10
a.	Phosphor omitted	5·00	
b.	Broken scale (R. 10/2)	45·00	
W124 =SG 753			
1s.	blue-green, light greenish blue, slate-purple and bluish violet	10	10
a.	Phosphor omitted	10·00	
b.	Watermark inverted	20·00	
W125 =SG 754			
1s.6d.	black, grey, royal blue, ochre and turquoise-blue	10	10
a.	Phosphor omitted	£600	
b.	Watermark inverted	£325	
c.	Cowling flaw (R. 1/2)	20·00	
W126 =SG 755			
1s.9d.	black, grey-blue, pale olive-grey, violet and orange	10	10
a.	Pale olive-grey omitted		£4500
b.	Orange (Queen's head) omitted	£30000	
c.	Phosphor omitted	£600	
d.	Error. One broad band	50·00	
First Day Cover (W123/W126)			70
Presentation Pack (W123/W126)		9·00	

225

W 1967 *British Discovery and Invention.*

All values are known on a special cover prepared by the Edinburgh GPO Philatelic Bureau but postmarked 8 August 1967.

W123b   W125c

Cylinder Numbers (Blocks of Six)

	Cyl. Nos. (No dot)	Perforation Types A (E/I)	F (P/E)
4d.	1A (vermilion)–1B (greenish yellow)–1C (black)	1·00	†
1s.	1A (bluish violet)–1B (blue-green)–1C (light greenish blue) 1D (slate-purple)	†	1·00
1s.6d.	1A (black)–1B (ochre)–1C (royal blue)–1D (grey)–1E (turquoise-blue)	†	1·25
		F (E/P)	
1s.9d.	1A (black)–1B (violet)–1C (pale olive-grey)–1D (grey-blue)–1E (orange)	†	1·25

Perforation Type F on the 1s.9d. is with sheet orientated showing head to right.

Minor Constant Flaws

4d. Cyls. 1A–1B–1C
- 2/2 Break in outer ring of radar screen at top centre (Th. A6)
- 8/5 Break in scale division of radar screen just to left of centre bottom mark (Th. G5)
- 14/5 Break in scale division of radar screen in centre left mark (Th. D3)

1s. Cyls. 1A–1B–1C–1D
- 19/3 Retouch to background at right of value (Th. F12–13)
- 19/6 Violet coloured flaw in bottom right of white outer ring (Th. G6)

1s.6d. Cyls. 1A–1B–1C–1D–1E
- 12/3 Small break in outer frame-line to right of 1/6 (Th. G13)
- 13/2 Pale area in background above first e of engine (Th. F8)
- 19/5 White scratch to background extends to next stamp (Th. G3–10)
- 19/6 White scratch to background extending from previous stamp (Th. G4–10)
- 20/3 The small grey coloured projection of the tailplane at right of the engines is malformed (Th. C8)

1s.9d. Cyls. 1A–1B–1C–1D–1E
- 1/18 Two of the holes of the disc at left are joined (Th. E1)
- 5/1 One of the slits in grey-blue disc below portrait is joined to hub by white flaw (Th. E5)

Sheet Details
Sheet sizes:
- **4d.** 120 (6×20). Single-pane reel-fed
- **1s., 1s.6d.** 120 (6×20). Single-pane sheet-fed
- **1s.9d.** 120 (20×6). Single-pane sheet-fed

Sheet markings:
Cylinder numbers:
- **4d., 1s.** Opposite R. 19/1, boxed
- **1s.6d.** Opposite rows 18/19 at left, boxed
- **1s.9d.** Opposite rows 5/6 at left, boxed

Guide holes:
- **4d.** Opposite rows 14/15 (boxed), at both sides; others, none

Marginal arrows (photo-etched): "W" shaped, at top, bottom and sides

Marginal rule: At bottom of sheet

Colour register marks:
- **4d.** Opposite rows 3/4 and 17/18, at both sides
- **1s., 1s.6d.** Above and below vertical rows 1 and 6
- **1s.9d.** Opposite rows 1 and 6 bottom margin, at both sides

Coloured crosses:
- **4d.** None
- **1s., 1s.6d.** Above and below vertical rows 2/3
- **1s.9d.** Opposite rows 4/5, at both sides

Autotron marks (solid):
- **4d.** Black, yellow, vermilion below vertical rows 1/3. An additional semi-solid mark in red appears below vertical row 1
- **Others:** none

Colour designations: None

Traffic lights (boxed):
- **4d., 1s.** In same order as cylinder numbers opposite R. 19/6
- **1s.6d.** In reverse order to cylinder numbers opposite rows 18/19 at right
- **1s.9d.** Violet, black, olive-grey, grey-blue, orange opposite rows 5/6 at right

Imprimaturs from the NPM or BPMA
Nos. W 123/W126 imperforate, watermark Type W.**24**

Watermark upright (4d., 1s., 1s.6d.) or sideways (1s.9d.) (*set of 4*)	£4000
4d. "Broken scale" flaw R. 10/2	£1500
4d. cylinder 1A, 1B, 1C block of six	£7000
1s. cylinder 1A, 1B, 1C, 1D block of six	£7000
1s.6d. cylinder 1A, 1B, 1C, 1D, 1E block of six	£7000
1s.9d. cylinder 1A, 1B, 1C, 1D, 1E block of six	£7000

Quantities Sold:
4d.	104,165,625
1s.	10,718,389
1s.6d.	10,380,413
1s.9d.	7,469,585
Pack	59,117

Withdrawn: 18.9.68

Christmas. 1967.

NO WATERMARK. All commemorative stamps from here onwards were printed on paper without watermark

Type **W127**. The Adoration of the Shepherds (School of Seville)

Type **W128**. Madonna and Child (Murillo)

Type **W129**. The Adoration of the Shepherds (Louis Le Nain)

(Des. Stuart Rose)

1967. Christmas. One phosphor band (3d.) or two phosphor bands (others), applied by flexography. Types **W127/W129**

The 4d. was issued on 18 October and the others were put on sale on 27 November.

W127 =SG 756		Mint	Used
3d.	olive-yellow, rose, blue, black and gold	10	10
a.	Gold omitted (value and Queen's head)	£110	
ab.	Gold (value only) omitted	£2750	
ac.	Gold (Queen's head only) omitted	£2750	
b.	Rose omitted	£3250	
c.	Imperforate between stamp and left margin	£850	
d.	Phosphor omitted	1·00	
da.	Phosphor omitted in pair with normal	1·25	
e.	Printed on the gummed side	£625	
f.	Olive-yellow omitted	—	—

W128 =SG 757			
4d.	bright purple, greenish yellow, new blue, black and gold	10	10
a.	Gold (value and Queen's head) omitted	80·00	
ab.	Gold (Queen's head only) omitted	£4500	
b.	Gold (value only) omitted	£2500	
c.	Greenish yellow (Child, robe and Madonna's face) omitted	£7500	
d.	Phosphor omitted	£125	
da.	Error. Right-hand band omitted		
e.	Error. One broad band	40·00	
f.	Brown flaw (Dot, R. 2/3)	28·00	
g.	Greenish yellow and gold omitted	£15000	

W129 =SG 758			
1s.6d.	bright purple, bistre, lemon, black, orange-red, ultramarine, gold	15	15
a.	Gold omitted (value and Queen's head)	£15000	
ab.	Gold (Queen's head only) omitted	£3000	
ac.	Gold (value only) omitted	£3000	
b.	Ultramarine omitted	£750	
c.	Lemon omitted	£20000	
d.	Phosphor omitted	12·00	
e.	Error. One broad band	45·00	

First Day Cover (2) (W127/W129)	3·00

The original printing of the 4d. was double-pane and printed on the Wood press (dot pane above no dot); cylinders 2A–1B–1C–1D–1E, 2A–2B–2C–2D–2E and 3A–2B–2C–2D–2E. The second printing was on the Thrissell press; cylinders 6A–3B–3C–3D–3E 8A–3B–3C–3D–3E.

There is a wide variation on shades of the 3d. and 4d. but they are not listed as there are a number of intermediate shades. For the 4d. value, stamps from one machine show a darker background and give the appearance of the greenish yellow being omitted, but this is not so and these should not be confused with the true missing greenish yellow, No. W128c.

The 3d. and 4d. are known with value omitted resulting from colour shifts. No. W128b comes from first vertical row of a sheet on which the gold cylinder was stopped so that it printed the head only.

No. W129ab comes from stamps in the first vertical row of a sheet. No. W127 ab was caused by a paper fold.

No. W128f. This marked variety on the 4d. consists of a large brown area in the lower right corner (Th. J–K 8–9) which can be clearly seen by the naked eye, but which would not show up in an enlarged illustration. It occurs on cylinders 2B–2C–2D–2E dot in conjunction with gold cylinders 2A or 3A.

Cylinder Numbers (Blocks of Six)

		Perforation Types A (P/E)	
Cylinder Nos.		No dot	Dot
3d.	1A (gold)–1B (olive-yellow)–1C (rose)–1D (blue)–1E (black)	1·00	
	2A–1B–1C–1D–1E	1·00	
		(I/E)	(I/E)
4d.	2A (gold)–1B (bright purple)–1C (new blue)–1D (greenish yellow)–1E (grey-black)	1·00	1·00
	2A–2B–2C–2D–2E	4·00	4·00
	3A–2B–2C–2D–2E	1·00	1·00
	6A–3B–3C–3D–3E	6·00	
	8A–3B–3C–3D–3E	6·00	
		A(T) (E/P) No dot	
1s.6d.	2A (gold)–1B (ultramarine)–1C (bright purple)–1D (orange-red)–1E (lemon)–1F (bistre)–2G (black)	1·25	

Perforation Type A on the 3d. and 4d. are with the sheet orientated showing the head to right.

The gold of the Queen's portrait and the value is normally further to the left on the 6A and 8A cylinders.

Minor Constant Flaws

3d. Cyls. 1B–1C–1D–1E in conjunction with gold cyls. 1A or 2A no dot
  1/7 Black horizontal line across triangle of red above Mary's head (Th. E2–3)

3d. Cyls. 1A–1B–1C–1D–1E no dot
  1/11 Break in upright wall of building shows against sky (Th. D6)

1967 Christmas

3d. Cyls. 2A–1B–1C–1D–1E no dot

3/10	Small black spot in Joseph's cloak (Th. D5)
4/9	Background retouch in left pillar (Th. D2)

4d. Cyls. 2B–2C–2D–2E in conjunction with gold cyls. 2A or 3A no dot

1/5	Prominent pale area in background at bottom right (Th. K–L 8–9)

4d. Cyls. 3A–2B–2C–2D–2E no dot

2/12	A cut at top of diagonal of "4" of value
7/5	Dark spot in Mother's right hand (Th. E5)

4d. Cyls. 2B–2C–2D–2E in conjunction with gold cyls. 2A or 3A dot

4/5	Line of pale dots over "4" of value (Th. J1)

4d. Cyls. 3A–2B–2C–2D–2E dot

2/12	Black dot over first "R" of "HARRISON"
3/6	Black dot on Child's forehead (Th. C6)
4/9	Spot on lower left margin of stamp (Th. K1)
7/2	Small spot just beyond little finger of Madonna's right hand (Th. E6)
7/12	Two small red dots over "H" of "HARRISON"

1s.6d. Cyls. 2A–1B–1C–1D–1E–1F–2G no dot

1/2	Background disturbance above "ll" of "shilling"
3/6	Curved green flaw left of cow's tail (Th. E1)
4/9	Background disturbance below "n" of "One"

Sheet Details

Sheet sizes:
- **3d.** 120 (12×10). Single pane sheet-fed
- **4d.** 120 (12×10). Double pane reel-fed for gold cyls. 2A and 3A and single pane reel-fed for gold cyls. 6A and 8A
- **1s.6d.** 60 (10×6). Single pane sheet-fed

Sheet markings:

Cylinder numbers:
- **3d.** Opposite R. 9/1, boxed
- **4d.** (Wood) Below vertical row 11, boxed
- **4d.** (Thrissell) Below vertical column 11 and open boxed
- **1s.6d.** Opposite rows 4/5 at right, boxed

Guide holes:
- **3d. 1s.6d** None
- **4d.** (Wood) Above and below vertical row 8
- **4d.** (Thrissell) Above and below vertical column 8 and open boxed

Marginal arrows (photo etched):
"W" shaped, at top, bottom and sides

Marginal rules: None

Colour register marks:
- **3d.** Above and below vertical rows 1/2 and 11/12
- **4d.** (Wood) Above and below vertical rows 1/3 (dot) and 8/10 (no dot)
- **4d.** (Thrissell) Above and below column 1 and column 12
- **1s.6d.** Opposite rows 1/2 and 6, at both sides

Coloured crosses:
- **3d.** Above and below vertical rows 3/4
- **4d.** None
- **1s.6d.** Next to cylinder numbers at left and traffic lights at right

Autotron marks (solid):
- **3d., 1s.6d.** None
- **4d.** (Wood) Greenish yellow, bright purple, new blue, grey-black, gold opposite rows 6/8, right margin (dot) with the 3A–2B–2C–2D–2E cylinders but the order of the colours is reversed with the 2A–1B–1C–1D–1E cylinders
- **4d.** (Thrissell) Opposite rows 7/8 right margin, yellow and red by row 7, blue and black by row 8 (there is no gold Autotron mark)

Colour designations:
- **3d., 1s.6d.** None
- **4d.** (Wood) G1 YELLOW above vertical row 12 on the dot pane and G2 GREY G3 GREEN G4 RED G5 GOLD above vertical rows 1/4 on the no dot pane, the whole inscription being upside down.
The G3 GREEN is printed in blue
- **4d.** (Thrissell) Above columns 1/6 and inverted. G1 YELLOW (Row 6) G2 RED G3 GREEN (printed in blue) G4 GREY and G5 GOLD (row 1/2)

Traffic lights (boxed):
- **3d.** In the same order as the cylinder numbers opposite R. 9/12
- **4d.** (both printings) Greenish yellow, bright purple, gold, new blue, grey-black above vertical rows 10/11
- **1s.6d.** Lemon, bright purple, orange-red, ultramarine, black, bistre, gold opposite rows 4/5 at right

Cut lines: 4d. (Thrissell) Opposite row 9, right margin. Below column 9.

Imprimaturs from the NPM or BPMA
Nos. W127/W129 imperforate

No watermark (set of 3)	£3000
3d. cylinder 1A, 1B, 1C, 1D, 1E (no dot) block of six	£7000
4d. cylinder 2A, 1B, 1C, 1D, 1E (dot) block of six	£7000
1s.6d. cylinder 2A, 1B, 1C, 1D, 1E, 1F, 2G vertical strip of three	£4000

The 3d. (missing phosphor) and 4d. (normal and missing gold) are known imperforate and were not issued. Care should be taken not to confuse these with NPM imprimaturs.

Quantities Sold:
- **3d.** 270,349,845
- **4d.** 287,827,440
- **1s.6d.** 17,913,209

Withdrawn: 3d. Sold out July 1968; 4d. 17.10.68; 1s.6d. 26.11.68

1967 (27 November). **Gift Pack 1967**

WGP1 Comprising Nos. WP111/WP118 and W119/W129	2·25

Quantity Sold: 105,577

British Bridges. 1968

PVA GUM. All commemorative issues from here onwards printed by Harrisons are on paper with PVA gum. For further particulars about this gum see notes at the beginning of Section UA on the Machin definitive issues.

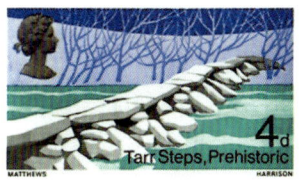

Type **W130**. Tarr Steps, Exmoor
(Des. Jeffery Matthews)

Type **W131**. Aberfeldy Bridge
(Des. Andrew Restall)

Type **W132**. Menai Bridge
(Des. Leonard Rosoman)

Type **W133**. M4 Viaduct
(Des. Jeffery Matthews)

1968 *(29 April)*. **British Bridges.** Two phosphor bands, applied by flexography (4d., 1s.9d.) or photogravure (others) Types **W130/W133**

W130 =SG 763	Mint	Used
4d. black, bluish violet, turquoise-blue and gold	10	10
a. Printed on the gummed side	35·00	
b. Phosphor omitted	10·00	
c. O retouch (R. 20/6)	30·00	
d. No curve to slab (R. 10/6)	30·00	

W131 =SG 764		
9d. red-brown, myrtle-green, ultramarine, olive-brown, black and gold	10	15
a. Gold (Queen's head) omitted	£225	
b. Ultramarine omitted	†	£7000
c. Phosphor omitted	15·00	
d. Phosphor bands diagonal	30·00	
e. Error. One broad band	22·00	
f. "HARRISON" redrawn (R. 18/3)	28·00	
g. "RESTALL" redrawn (R. 18/4)	28·00	

W132 =SG 765		
1s.6d. olive-brown, red-orange, bright green, turquoise-green and gold	15	20
a. Gold (Queen's head) omitted	£375	
b. Red-orange omitted	£375	
c. Phosphor omitted	50·00	
d. Broken corner stones (R. 15/1)	30·00	

W133 =SG 766		
1s.9d. olive-brown, greenish yellow, dull green, deep ultramarine and gold	15	25
a. Gold (Queen's head) omitted	£325	
b. Gold (Queen's head) and phospor omitted	£3500	
c. Phosphor omitted	10·00	
d. Error. One broad band	40·00	
e. Error. Left-hand band omitted		

First Day Cover (W130/W133)		90
Presentation Pack (W130/W133)		5·25

No. W131b is only known on first day covers posted from Canterbury, Kent or the Philatelic Bureau, Edinburgh.

Used examples of the 1s.6d. are known with both the gold and the phosphor omitted.

W130c

Normal

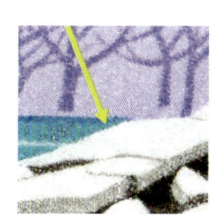

W130d
No curve at left to central slab

W132d

1968 British Bridges.

Normal

W131f W131g
Inscriptions redrawn by hand.

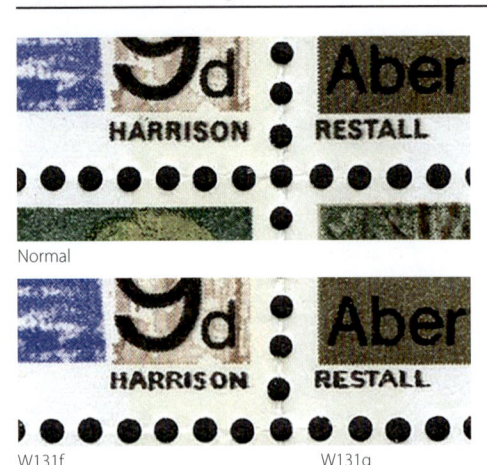

Cylinder Numbers (Blocks of Eight)

Cylinder Nos.	Perforation Type F (P/E) No dot
4d. 3A (black)–1B (turquoise-blue)–2C (bluish violet)–2D (gold)	1·00
9d. 1A (black)–1B (red-brown)–1C (ultramarine)–1D (olive- brown)–1E (myrtle-green)–1F (gold)	1·00
1s.6d. 2A (olive-brown)–1B (red-orange)–1C (bright green)–2D (turquoise-green)–3E (gold)	1·50
1s.9d. 2A (olive-brown)–1B (gold)–1C (dull green)–1D (deep ultramarine)–1E (greenish yellow)	1·50

Minor Constant Flaws
4d. Cyls. 3A–1B–2C–2D no dot
- 4/1 Diagonal dotted line across top of bridge near far end (Th. C10)
- 9/1 Lack of screening dots in left of pale green patch left of Tarr (Th G4–5)
- 11/1 Similar variety but more pronounced (Th. G4–5)
- 12/2 Broken tip to horizontal bar of "T" of "Tarr"
- 14/2 Scratch across lower stones near far end of bridge (Th. D10–C12)
- 17/2 Weakness behind and below "hi" of "Prehistoric" (Th. G11)
- 19/4 Damaged "H" in "HARRISON"

9d. Cyls. 1A–1B–1C–1D–1E–1F no dot
- 9/4 Break in olive-brown line at left of ultramarine area under main arch (Th. F6)
- 20/4 Small dark spot under "r" of "Bridge"

1s.6d. Cyls. 2A–1B–1C–2D–3E no dot
- 5/5 Two diagonal lines in sky at right (Th. B–C13)
- 5/6 Diagonal line in sky extending to base of Queen's neck (extension of one of the lines in 5/5) (Th. C1)
- 6/1 Small curved flaw in front of "H" of "HARRISON"
- 6/2 White flaw in first arch beyond the far tower (Th. E12)
- 14/5 Small white flaw at top right of near tower (Th. B8)
- 19/1 Green spot on near tower above right-hand arch (Th. D7–8)

1s.9d. Cyls. 2A–1B–1C–1D–1E no dot
- 2/5 Retouch in centre lane (Th. C–D8)
- 10/4 Disturbance at right of pale green area below Queen (Th. D3–4)
- 14/5 Vertical line appears as radio mast above building on skyline (Th. A6)
- 15/1 Retouch between buildings at bend in motorway (Th. C10)
- 17/4 Break at foot of s in value

Sheet Details
Sheet size: 120 (6×20). Single-pane sheet-fed

Sheet markings:

Cylinder numbers: Opposite rows 17/18 at left, boxed

Guide holes: None

Marginal arrows (photo-etched): "W" shaped, at top, bottom and sides

Marginal rule: At bottom of sheet

Colour register marks:
- 4d.,1s.9d. Above and below vertical rows 1/2 and 6
- 9d.,1s.6d. Above and below vertical rows 1 and 5/6

Coloured crosses:
- 4d., 1s.6d. Above and below vertical row 3
- 9d. Above and below vertical rows 3/4
- 1s.9d. Above and below vertical rows 2/3

Autotron marks and Colour designations: None

Traffic lights (boxed):
- 4d. Gold, bluish violet turquoise-blue, black above vertical row 5
- 9d. Black, red-brown, ultramarine, myrtle-green, gold, olive-brown above vertical rows 4/5
- 1s.6d. Gold, turquoise-green, bright green, red-orange, olive-brown above vertical row 5
- 1s.9d. Gold, dull green, olive-brown, deep ultramarine, greenish yellow above vertical row 5

Imprimaturs from the NPM or BPMA
Nos. W130/W133 imperforate

No watermark (set of 4)	£4000
4d. "O retouch" variety R. 20/6	£1500
4d. "No curve to slab" variety R. 10/6	£1500
4d. cylinder 3A, 1B, 2C, 2D block of eight	£9000
9d. "HARRISON" and "RESTALL" redrawn R. 18/3-4 (pair)	£3000
9d. cylinder 1A, 1B, 1C, 1D, 1E, 1F block of eight	£9000
1s.6d. "Broken corner stones" variety R. 15/1	£1500
1s.6d. cylinder 2A, 1B, 1C, 2D, 3E block of eight	£9000
1s.9d. cylinder 2A, 1B, 1C, 1D, 1E block of eight	£9000

Quantities Sold:

4d.	97,458,120
9d.	8,773,080
1s.6d.	9,451,400
1s.9d.	5,924,800
Pack	69,646

Withdrawn: 28.4.69

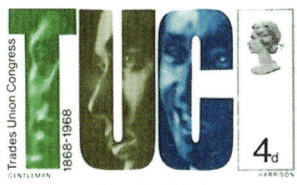

British Anniversaries. 1968

Type **W134**. "TUC" and Trade Unionists

Type **W135**.
Mrs. Emmeline Pankhurst (statue)

Type **W136**.
Sopwith Camel and Lightning Fighters

Type **W137**.
Captain Cook's *Endeavour* and Signature

(Des. David Gentleman (4d.), Clive Abbott (others))

1968 (29 May). **British Anniversaries.** Two phosphor bands, applied by flexography (1s., 1s.9d.) or photogravure (others). Types **W134/W137**

Four famous anniversaries, with the events described on the stamps.

W134 =SG 767		Mint	Used
4d.	emerald, olive, blue and black	10	10
a.	Phosphor omitted*	40·00	
b.	Retouch on large "C" (No dot, R. 3/2)	30·00	
W135 =SG 768			
9d.	reddish violet, grey and black	10	10
a.	Phosphor omitted	7·00	
b.	Error. One broad band	32·00	
W136 =SG 769			
1s.	olive-brown, blue, red, slate-blue and black	15	20
a.	Phosphor omitted	10·00	
W137 =SG 770			
1s.9d.	ochre, brownish ochre and blackish brown	20	25
a.	Phosphor omitted	£190	
b.	Broken bulwarks (R. 8/2)	30·00	
c.	Error. One broad band		
First Day Cover (W134/W137)		2·50	
Presentation Pack (W134/W137)		5·00	

* The phosphor bands are normally faint and difficult to see and care is needed in identifying the phosphor omitted on the 4d. value.

The 1s.9d. is known with phosphor removed by chemical means. These can be detected, but care is needed in identifying genuine examples.

This issue is known postmarked at Netheravon, Salisbury, Wiltshire on 28 May.

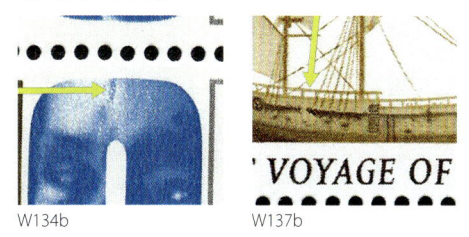

W134b   W137b

Cylinder Numbers (Blocks of Eight (4d., 1s.), Four (9d.), Six (1s.9d.))

		Perforation Types	
		A (E/I) No dot	A (E/I) Dot
Cylinder Nos.			
4d.	1A (black)–1B (blue)–1C (olive)–1D (emerald)	1·00	1·00
		F (P/E) No dot	
9d.	1A (black)–1B (reddish violet)–1C (grey)	1·00	
1s.	1A (black)–1B (olive-brown)–1C (blue)–1D (slate-blue)–1E (red)	1·25	
1s.9d.	2A (blackish brown)–1B (brownish ochre)–1C (ochre)	1·50	

Minor Constant Flaws

4d. Cyls. 1A–1B–1C–1D no dot
- 1/1 Small retouch in right cross bar of large "T"
- 2/2 Stop between "Union" and "Congress"
- 4/1 Retouch at top of large "C" (not as prominent as No. W134b)
- 10/6 Small retouch at top left of large "U"
- 11/3 Small flaw in "6" of "1968"
- 11/6 Vertical green line from right cross bar of large "T" (Th. B–E3)

4d. Cyls. 1A–1B–1C–1D dot
- 2/6 Small spot right of "4" of value
- 4/5 Green spots by "d" of "Trades" (Th. F–G1)
- 5/5 Dotted line across back of Queen's hair (Th. B–C12)
- 19/1 Retouch on cheek of face shown in large "T" (Th. D1–2)
- 20/5 Two tiny dots above "g" of "Congress"

9d. Cyls. 1A–1B–1C no dot
- 9/4 Spur at top right of Queen's head (Th. A13)
- 14/6 Dark flaw on collar (Th. D10/11) and small flaw on left sleeve (Th. F11)

1s. Cyls. 1A–1B–1C–1D–1E no dot
- 3/1 Dot over "O" of "ROYAL"
- 4/4 Extension of wing joining it to last "T" of "ABBOTT"

1s.9d. Cyls. 2A–1B–1C no dot
- 10/3 Small flaws in background above "Y" of "DISCOVERY" level with value (Th. F10–11)
- 11/2 Small cut in "Y" of "VOYAGE"
- 13/2 Flaw in lower part of "S" of "DISCOVERY"
- 16/2 Sliced "F" in "FIRST"
- 20/5 Tail of "9" of "1968" slightly shortened

W 1968 *British Paintings.*

Sheet Details
Sheet size: 120 (6×20).
4d. double pane reel-fed
Others: single pane sheet-fed

Sheet markings:
Cylinder numbers:
 4d., 1s. Opposite rows 17/18 at left, boxed
 9d. Opposite R. 19/1, boxed
 1s.9d. Opposite R. 18/1, boxed

Guide holes:
 4d. In double "S O N" box opposite rows 14/15, at left (no dot) or right (dot)
 Others: None

Marginal arrows (photo-etched):
"W" shaped, at top, bottom and sides

Marginal rule:
 4d. None
 Others: at bottom of sheet

Colour register marks:
 4d. Opposite rows 2/4 and 18/20 at left (no dot) or right (dot)
 Others: Above and below vertical rows 1 and 6

Coloured crosses:
 4d. None
 9d., 1s.9d. Above and below vertical row 3
 1s. Above and below vertical rows 2/3

Autotron marks (solid):
 4d. Black, blue, olive, emerald opposite rows 4/6, at right (no dot) or left (dot)
 Others: None

Colour designations: None

Traffic lights (boxed):
 4d. In same order as cylinder numbers opposite rows 1/2, at right
 9d. Black, grey, reddish violet above vertical row 5
 1s. Olive-brown, blue, slate-blue, red, black above vertical row 5
 1s.9d. Brownish ochre, blackish brown, ochre above vertical row 5

Imprimaturs from the NPM or BPMA
Nos. W134/W137 imperforate

No watermark (*set of 4*)	£4000
4d. "Retouch to large C" retouch	£1500
4d. cylinder 1A, 1B, 1C, 1D (no dot) block of eight	£9000
9d. cylinder 1A, 1B, 1C block of four	£5000
1s. cylinder 1A, 1B, 1C, 1D, 1E block of eight	£9000
1s.9d. cylinder 2A, 1B, 1C block of six	£7000

Quantities Sold:
4d.	97,757,920
9d.	9,135,240
1s.	9,872,160
1s.9d.	6,217,440
Pack	67,639

Withdrawn: 28.5.69

Type **W138.** Queen Elizabeth I (Unknown Artist)

Type **W139.** Pinkie (Sir Thomas Lawrence)

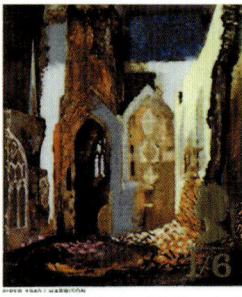

Type **W140.** Ruins of St Mary Le Port (John Piper)

Type **W141.** The Hay Wain (John Constable)

(Des. Stuart Rose)
(Printed in photogravure with the Queen's head embossed in gold)

1968 *(12 August).* **British Paintings.** Types **W138/W141.** Two phosphor bands applied by photogravure (1s.9d.) or flexography (others)

This is the second issue of British Paintings for which Harrisons made photographs from the originals.

W138 =SG 771	Mint	Used
4d. black, vermilion, greenish yellow, grey and gold	10	10
a. Gold omitted (value and Queen's head)	£300	
b. Gold (value and Queen's head) and phosphor omitted	£4000	
c. Vermilion omitted*	£700	
d. Phosphor omitted	1·50	
e. Embossing omitted	90·00	
f. Blister on hand (No dot, R. 2/8)	30·00	

W139 =SG 772		
1s. mauve, new blue, greenish yellow, black, magenta and gold	10	15
a. Gold omitted (value and Queen's head)	£7500	

232

British Paintings. **1968**

b. Gold (value and Queen's head), embossing and phosphor omitted	£650	
c. Embossing omitted		
d. Phosphor omitted	7·00	

W140 =SG 773

1s.6d. slate, orange, black, mauve, greenish yellow, ultramarine, and gold	15	20
a. Gold (value and Queen's head) omitted	£300	
b. Phosphor omitted	10·00	
c. Embossing omitted	£300	

W141 =SG 774

1s.9d. greenish yellow, black, new blue, red and gold	15	20
a. Gold (value and Queen's head), embossing and phosphor omitted	£900	
b. Red omitted	£10000	
c. Phosphor omitted	20·00	
d. Embossing omitted	£140	

First Day Cover (W138/W141)	1·00
Presentation Pack (W138/W141)	4·50
Presentation Pack (German) (W138/W141)	30·00

Pack also exists with a Japanese insert card.
* No. W138c shows the face and hands white, and there is more yellow and olive in the costume.

The 4d. also exists with the value only omitted resulting from a colour shift.

This issue is known pre-released on a first day cover postmarked 10 August from Vauxhall Bridge PO, SW1.

W138f

Cylinder Numbers (Blocks of Six)

	Perforation Type A(T) (I/E)	
Cylinder Nos.	No dot	Dot
4d. 2A (gold)–1B (embossing)–3C (black)–2D (grey–3E (vermilion)–2F (greenish yellow)	1·00	1·00
1s. 2A (gold)–1B (embossing)–2C (black)–2D (new blue)–2E (mauve)–2F (magenta)–2G (greenish yellow)	1·00	1·00
2A–2B–2C–2D–2E–2F–2G	1·00	1·00
1s.6d. 1A (gold)–1B (embossing)–1C (black)–1D (ultramarine)–1E (slate)–1F (mauve)–1G (orange)–1H (greenish yellow)	1·25	1·25
	Perforation Type A(T) (E/P)	
1s.9d. 2A (gold)–1B (embossing)–1C (black)–1D (new blue)–1E (red)–1F (greenish yellow)	1·25	1·25

Perforation Type A(T) on the 4d., 1s. and 1s.6d. are with sheet orientated showing head to right.

In each value the 1B cylinder number appears in colourless embossing; it is difficult to see but can often be discerned with the aid of a magnifying glass.

Minor Constant Flaws
4d. Cyls. 2A–1B–3C–2D–3E–2F no dot
  6/8 Thick "A" in "HARRISON"
4d. Cyls. 2A–1B–3C–2D–3E–2F dot
  4/2 Black flaw on dress above Queen's right hand (Th. J4–5)
1s. Cyls. 2A–1B–2C–2D–2E–2F–2G no dot
  2/4 Diagonal black line across Pinkie's shoulder (Th. D4)
  5/1 Black spur to "A" of "HARRISON"
  6/1 Thin diagonal black line across dress (Th. H3–5)
1s.6d. Cyls. 1A–1B–1C–1D–1E–1F–1G–1H no dot
  6/1 Dark coloured spot in top right corner of dark blue area (Th. A8–9)
1s.6d. Cyls. 1A–1B–1C–1D–1E–1F–1G–1H dot
  1/8 ? shaped black flaw in doorway (Th. J5)
  6/6 Extra patch at upper left corner of yellow wall (Th. E8)
1s.9d. Cyls. 2A–1B–1C–1D–1E–1F no dot
  9/2 Blue spot after "HARRISON"
  10/1 Green instead of brown bush in bottom left-hand corner

Sheet Details
  Sheet size: **1s.9d.** 60 (6×10)
  Others: 60 (10×6). All double pane sheet-fed

Sheet markings:
Cylinder numbers:
  4d. Opposite row 5, left margin, boxed
  1s., 1s.6d. Opposite rows 4/5, left margin, boxed
  1s.9d. Opposite rows 8/9, left margin, boxed

Guide holes: None
Marginal arrows (photo-etched):
"W" shaped, at top, bottom and sides
Marginal rule: None
Colour register marks:
  4d., 1s, 1s.6d. Above vertical rows 1/2 and 9/10 (no dot) or below (dot)
  1s.9d. Opposite rows 1/2 and 9/10, left margin (no dot) or right margin (dot)
Coloured crosses:
  4d., 1s. Above vertical rows 6/7 (no dot) or below (dot)
  1s.6d. Above vertical rows 7/8 (no dot) or below (dot)
  1s.9d. Opposite rows 7/8, left margin (no dot) or right margin (dot)
Autotron marks, Colour designations: None
Traffic lights (boxed):
  4d., 1s.,1s.6d. In same order as cylinder numbers, except that on the 1s.6d. the gold and embossing lights are transposed, reading left to right above vertical rows 8/9
  1s.9d. In same order as cylinder numbers, except that the gold and embossing lights are transposed, reading left to right above vertical row 5

Imprimaturs from the NPM or BPMA
Nos. W138/W141 imperforate

No watermark (set of 4)	£4000
4d. "Blister on hand" variety	£1500
4d. cylinder 2A, 1B, 3C, 2D, 3E, 2F (no dot) block of six	£7000
1s. cylinder 2A, 1B, 2C, 2D, 2E, 2F, 2G (no dot) block of four	£5000
1s.6d. cylinder 1A, 1B, 1C, 1D, 1E, 1F, 1G, 1H (dot) block of six	£7000
1s.9d. cylinder 2A, 1B, 1C, 1D, 1E, 1F (no dot) block of six	£7000

W 1968 Christmas

Quantities Sold:

4d.	185,034,000
1s.	17,953,440
1s.6d.	8,878,440
1s.9d.	5,739,000
English Pack	93,829
German Pack	7,880

Withdrawn: 11.8.69

1968 *(16 September).* **Gift Pack 1968**

WGP2	Comprising Nos. W130/W141		3·00
	a. German text		80·00

Quantities Sold: Ordinary 41,308; German 1,650

1968 *(16 September).* **Collectors Pack 1968**

WCP1	Comprising Nos. W123/W141	2·50

Quantity Sold: 26,284

Type **W142**. Boy and Girl with Rocking Horse

Type **W143**. Girl with Doll's House

Type **W144**. Boy with Train Set

(Des. Rosalind Dease)
(Printed in photogravure with the Queen's head embossed in gold)

1968 *(25 November).* **Christmas.** Types **W142/W144**. One centre phosphor band (4d.) or two phosphor bands (others), applied by flexography

The joy of giving is emphasised on this Christmas issue; all three designs show children playing with their Christmas toys.

W142 =SG 775

		Mint	Used
4d.	black, orange, vermilion, ultramarine, bistre and gold	10	10
a.	Gold omitted	£6000	
b.	Vermilion omitted*	£525	
c.	Ultramarine and phosphor omitted	£500	
d.	Embossing omitted	6·00	
e.	Phosphor omitted	5·00	
ea.	Phosphor and embossing omitted		
f.	Retouched dapples (Cyl. 1A. R. 12/4)	30·00	
g.	Bistre omitted	†	—
h.	Orange omitted	†	—

W143 =SG 776

		Mint	Used
9d.	yellow-olive, black, brown, yellow, magenta, orange, turquoise-green and gold	15	15
a.	Yellow omitted	£175	
b.	Turquoise-green (dress) omitted	£22000	
c.	Embossing and phosphor omitted	10·00	
d.	Embossing omitted	6·00	
f.	Phosphor omitted	10·00	

W144 =SG 777

		Mint	Used
1s.6d.	ultramarine, yellow-orange, bright purple, blue-green, black and gold	15	20
a.	Embossing omitted		
b.	Phosphor omitted	15·00	

First Day Cover (W142/W144)	1·00

Christmas. 1968

Presentation Pack (W142/W144)	9·00
Presentation Pack (German) (W142/W144)	30·00

* The effect of the missing vermilion is shown on the rocking horse, saddle and faces which appear orange instead of red. No. W142 is known pre-released on 24 November at Edinburgh.

A single used example of No. W142g has been seen with the bistre omitted from the mane of the rocking horse and the girl's hair. No. W142a also exists with a single complete omission and three partial gold heads on the gummed side due to a paper fold.

Two machines were used for printing the 4d. value:

Stamps from cylinders 1A–1B–2C–1D–1E in combination with 1F, 2F or 3F (gold) were printed entirely on the Rembrandt sheet-fed machine. They invariably have the Queen's head level with the top of the boy's head and the sheets are perforated through the left side margin (perforation type F).

Stamps from cylinders 2A–2B–3C–2D–2E in combination with 1F, 2F, 3F or 4F (gold) were printed on the reel-fed Thrissell machine in five colours (its maximum colour capacity) and subsequently sheet-fed on the Rembrandt machine for the gold Queen's head and the embossing. The position of the Queen's head is generally lower than on the stamps printed at one operation, but it varies in different parts of the sheet and is not, therefore, a sure indication for identifying single stamps. Another small difference is that the boy's grey pullover is noticeably "moth-eaten" in the Thrissell printings and is normal on the Rembrandt. The Thrissell printings are perforated through the top margin (perforation type A).

Marginal copies can usually be identified by the characteristics of the perforation (if any) in the sheet margin. Ideally, cylinder blocks of six are required to show examples of the two printing machines used.

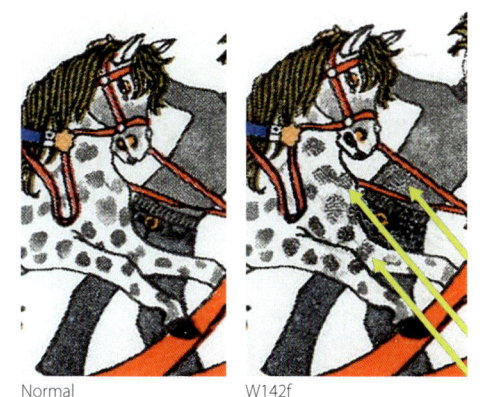

Normal   W142f

Grey dapples on the horse nearest to the boy and extending to the boy's belt and trousers, are heavily retouched

Cylinder Numbers (Blocks of Six)

A. Rembrandt only printings

Cylinder Nos. (No dot)	Perforation Types	
	A (E/I)	F (P/E)
4d. 1A (black)–1B (orange)–2C (vermilion)–1D (ultramarine)–1E (bistre)–1F (gold)	†	1·00
1A–1B–2C–1D–1E–2F	†	1·00
1A–1B–2C–1D–1E–3F	†	2·00
1A–1B–2C–1D–1E–4F	†	– (E/P)
9d. 1A (black)–1B (brown)–1C (yellow)–2D (magenta)–1E (orange) 1F (turquoise-green)–1G (yellow-olive)–1H (gold)	†	1·25
1s.6d. 1A (black)–1B (ultramarine)–1C (yellow-orange)–1D (bright purple)–1E (blue-green)–1F (gold)	†	1·25

B. Thrissell and Rembrandt printings

4d. 2A (black)–2B (orange)–3C (vermilion)–2D (ultramarine)–2E (bistre)–1F (gold)	1·00	†
2A–2B–3C–2D–2E–2F	2·00	†
2A–2B–3C–2D–2E–3F	5·00	†
2A–2B–3C–2D–2E–4F	5·00	†

Perforation Type F on the 9d. and 1s.6d. are with sheet orientated showing head to right. The 1s.6d. has cyl. nos. 1B–1E unboxed.

Minor Constant Flaws

4d. Cyls. 1A–1B–2C–1D–1E in combination with gold cyls. 1F, 2F, 3F, or 4F

- 3/6 Small black flaw in "m" of "Christmas"
- 12/5 Small nick on right edge of upright stroke of "4" of value

4d. Cyls. 2A–2B–3C–2D–2E in combination with gold cyls. 1F, 2F, 3F or 4F

- 16/4 Small black flaw above horse's left foreleg by boy's waist (Th. D9)
- 20/4 Break in outline at top centre of near rocker (Th. F4–5)

9d. Cyls. 1A–1B–1C–2D–1E–1F–1G–1H

- 4/3 Small black flaw between "a" and "s" of "Christmas"
- 6/18 Break in middle of final "s" of "Christmas"

1s.6d. Cyls. 1A–1B–1C–1D–1E–1F

- 2/18 Pale patch on boy's left shoulder (Th. F4)
- 3/8 Thick horizontal spur on left of lower central purple slotted plate (Th. D–E4)
- 5/2 Black flaws in background lower right of Queen's head (Th. C–D7)
- 5/3 Two black dots between "1" and stroke of "1/6"
- 6/20 Purple coloured flaws in background below boy's foot (Th. J7)

Sheet Details

	Rembrandt	Thrissell/Rembrandt
Sheet sizes:		
4d. 120 (6×20)	Single pane sheet-fed	Single pane reel-fed for five colours, and then single pane sheet fed for the gold and embossing
9d., 1s.6d. 120 (20×6)	Single pane sheet-fed	
Sheet markings:		
Cylinder numbers:		
4d.	Opposite rows 18/19, left margin, boxed	Opposite rows 18/19, left margin, boxed
9d., 1s.6d.	Opposite rows 4/5, left margin, boxed	
Guide holes:		
4d.	None	Opposite rows 14/15 (boxed), at both sides
9d., 1s.6d.	None	
Marginal arrows (photo-etched):		
4d.	"W" shaped, at top, bottom and sides	"W" shaped, at top, bottom and sides
9d, 1s.6d.	As 4d.	

W 1968 Christmas.

	Rembrandt	Thrissell/Rembrandt
Marginal rule:		
	None	None
Colour register marks:		
4d.	Above and below vertical rows 1/2 and 6	Opposite rows 2/3 and 19/20 at both sides
9d., 1s.6d.	Opposite rows 1/2 and 5/6 at both sides	
Coloured crosses:		
4d.	Above and below vertical row 3	Gold only below vertical row 3
9d., 1s.6d.	Opposite rows 3/4 at both sides	
Autotron marks (solid):		
4d.	None	Black, bistre, ultramarine, vermilion, orange below vertical rows 4/6
9d., 1s.6d.	None	
4d., 9d., 1s.6d	None	None
Colour designations:		
4d., 9d., 1s.6d.	None	None
Traffic lights (boxed):		
4d.	Orange, vermilion, ultramarine, bistre, black, gold, embossing opposite rows 18/19, right margin; also above vertical row 5 reading left to right	Orange, vermilion, ultramarine, bistre, black, gold, embossing opposite rows 18/19, right margin; also gold and embossing (unboxed) above vertical row 5 reading left to right
9d.	Gold, olive, green, orange, magenta, yellow, brown, black opposite rows 4/5, right margin; also embossing, gold, olive, green, orange, magenta, yellow, brown, black above vertical rows 17/19 reading left to right	
1s.6d.	Embossing, gold, green, purple, orange, ultramarine, black opposite rows 4/5, at right; also gold, green, purple, orange, ultramarine, black, above vertical rows 18/19 reading left to right	

Imprimaturs from the NPM or BPMA
Nos. W142/W144 imperforate

No watermark (*set of 3*)	£3000
4d. "Retouched dapples" R. 12/4	£1500
4d. cylinder 1A, 1B, 2C, 1D, 1E, 1F block of six	£7000
9d. cylinder 1A, 1B, 1C, 2D, 1E, 1F, 1G, 1H block of six	£7000
1s.6d. cylinder 1A, 1B, 1C, 1D, 1E, 1F block of six	£7000

Quantities Sold:

4d.	326,078,360
9d.	17,102,520
1s.6d.	21,344,760
English Pack	72,474
German Pack	7,298

Withdrawn: 24.11.69

Although the Traffic Light box in the right margin on the 9d. and the upper margin on the 1s.6d. were designed to accommodate an embossing light the space was not in fact used.

British Ships. 1969

Type **W145**. RMS *Queen Elizabeth 2*

Type **W146**. Elizabethan Galleon

Type **W147**. East Indiaman

Type **W148**. *Cutty Sark*

Type **W149**. *SS Great Britain*

Type **W150**. RMS *Mauretania*

(Des. David Gentleman)

1969 *(15 January)*. **British Ships.** Types **W145/W150**. Two phosphor bands at right (1s.), one horizontal phosphor band (5d.) or two phosphor bands (9d.), applied by flexography

Issued as a tribute to British shipbuilders and seamen, these stamps depict five famous ships of the past and the *Queen Elizabeth 2*, which sailed on her maiden voyage to New York on 2 May 1969.

The 9d. values were issued together *se-tenant* in strips of three throughout the sheet and the 1s. values were issued together *se-tenant* in pairs throughout the sheet.

		Mint	Used
W145	=SG 778		
	5d. black, grey, red and turquoise	10	10
	a. Black omitted (Queen's head, value, hull and inscr.)	£3500	
	b. Grey omitted (decks, etc.)	£225	
	c. Red (inscription) omitted	£225	
	d. Red and phosphor omitted	£190	
	e. Phosphor omitted	5·00	
W146	=SG 779		
	9d. red, blue, ochre, brown, black and grey	10	10
	a. Strip of 3. Nos. W146/W148	40	50
	ab. Red, blue and phosphor omitted	£3250	
	ac. Blue omitted	£3250	
	d. Phosphor omitted	12·00	
	da. Phosphor omitted. (strip of three)	40·00	
W147	=SG 780		
	9d. ochre, brown, black and grey	10	10
	b. Phosphor omitted	12·00	
W148	=SG 781		
	9d. ochre, brown, black and grey	10	10
	b. Phosphor omitted	12·00	
W149	=SG 782		
	1s. brown, black, grey, green and greenish yellow	15	15
	a. Pair, Nos. W149/W150	50	60
	b. Greenish yellow omitted	£4500	
	c. Phosphor omitted	28·00	
	ca. Phosphor omitted. (pair)	65·00	
W150	=SG 783		
	1s. red, black, brown, carmine and grey	15	15
	a. Carmine (hull overlay) omitted	£40000	
	b. Red (funnels) omitted	£30000	
	c. Carmine and red omitted	£30000	
	d. Phosphor omitted	30·00	

First Day Cover (W145/W150)		1·50
Presentation Pack (W145/W150)	3·00	
Presentation Pack (German) (W145/W150)	38·00	

Pack also exists with a Dutch or Japanese insert card

* In addition to the generally issued Presentation Pack (inscribed "RMS Queen Elizabeth 2... she sailed on her maiden voyage to New York on 17 January 1969") a further pack (inscribed "RMS Queen Elizabeth 2... she sails on her maiden voyage early in 1969") was issued for sale exclusively on board the *QE2* during her maiden voyage which had been postponed. (*Price* £15).

First Day covers are known postmarked 14 January, Buckley, Flintshire. The year date shown as 1968 instead of 1969 exists postmarked at Brighton, Sussex.

Cylinder Numbers (Blocks of Six (5d. and 1s.) or Twelve (9d.))

	Perforation Types	
Cyl. Nos. (No dot)	A(T) (E/P)	F (P/E)
5d. 1A (black)–1B (grey)–1C (red)–1D (turquoise)	1·25	†
9d. 1A (black)–2B (brown)–1C (ochre)–1D (grey)–1E (red)–1F (blue)	†	2·00
1s. 2A (black)–1B (grey)–1C (green)–1D (red)–1E (carmine)–1F (brown)–1G (yellow)	2·00	†

W 1969 First Flight of Concorde.

Minor Constant Flaws

5d. Cyls. 1A–1B–1C–1D
- 2/5 Disturbance in sea over "liz" of "Elizabeth"
- 3/2 Blue flaw on superstructure halfway between funnel and stern (Th. E6) (later removed)
- 4/5 Weak patch in hull directly below funnel (Th. F9)

9d. Cyls. 1A–2B–1C–1D–1E–1F
- 16/2 Rope between second and third masts is broken (Th. D5)

1s. Cyls. 2A–1B–1C–1D–1E–1F–1G
- 1/6 Small brown flaw lower right of stern mast (Th. D6)
- 2/8 Curved black flaw just above third funnel (Th. C10)
- 4/2 Weak patch in hull directly below foremast (Th. E17)
- 10/1 Wispy black flaw in front of Queen's chin (Th. B–C17)

Sheet Details

Sheet sizes: All single-pane sheet-fed
- **5d.** 72 (8×9)
- **9d.** 120 (6×20). In *se-tenant* strips of three
- **1s.** 80 (8×10). In *se-tenant* pairs

Sheet markings:

Cylinder numbers:
- **5d.** Opposite rows 7/8, left margin, boxed
- **9d.** Opposite rows 17/18, left margin, boxed
- **1s.** Below vertical row 7, boxed

Guide holes: None

Marginal arrows (photo-etched):
"W" shaped, at top and bottom (5d.); "W" shaped, at top, bottom and sides (others)

Marginal rule: None

Colour register marks:
- **5d.** Opposite rows 1/2 and 8/9 at both sides
- **9d.** Above and below vertical rows 1 and 6
- **1s.** Opposite rows 1/2 and 10 at both sides

Coloured crosses:
- **5d.** Opposite rows 5/6 at both sides
- **9d.** Above and below vertical rows 3/4
- **1s.** Opposite rows 5/7 at both sides

Autotron marks, Colour designations: None

Traffic lights (boxed):
- **5d.** In same order as cylinder numbers opposite rows 7/8, right margin; also above vertical row 7 reading left to right
- **9d.** In same order as cylinder numbers opposite rows 18/19, right margin; also above vertical rows 5/6 but in reverse order to cylinder numbers reading left to right
- **1s.** In reverse order to cylinder numbers opposite rows 8/9, right margin; also above vertical row 8 in reverse order to cylinder numbers reading left to right

Imprimaturs from the NPM or BPMA
Imperforate, no watermark

No W145 single	£1000
Nos. W146/W148 *se-tenant* strip of three	£3000
9d. cylinder 1A, 2B, 1C, 1D, 1E, 1F block of 12	£13000
Nos. W149/W150 *se-tenant* pair	£2000
1s. cylinder 2A, 1B, 1C, 1D, 1E, 1F, 1G block of six	£7000

Quantities Sold:

5d.	67,584,528
9d.	14,351,160
1s.	10,784,480
English Pack	116,526
German Pack	4.416

Withdrawn: 14.1.70

Type **W151.** Concorde in Flight
(Des. Michael and Sylvia Goaman)

Type **W152.** Plan and Elevation Views

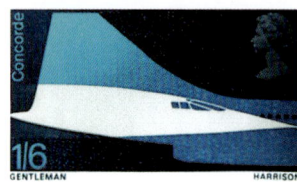

Type **W153.** Concorde's Nose and Tail
(Des. David Gentleman)

1969 *(3 March).* **First Flight of Concorde.** Types W151/W153. Two phosphor bands

Issued to commemorate the first flight of the "Concorde" supersonic airliner developed and produced jointly by Britain and France.

W151 =SG 784		Mint	Used
4d.	yellow-orange, violet, greenish blue, blue-green and pale green	10	10
a.	Violet omitted (value, etc.)	£750	
b.	Yellow-orange and phosphor omitted	£750	
c.	Yellow-orange omitted	£750	
d.	Phosphor omitted	1·00	
e.	Error. Left-hand band omitted	55·00	
f.	Oil slick flaw (R. 13/2)	30·00	

W152 =SG 785			
9d.	ultramarine, emerald, red and grey-blue	15	15
a.	Phosphor omitted	£100	
b.	Grey-blue (Face value and inscr. omitted)	—	
c.	One phosphor band		

W153 =SG 786			
1s.6d.	deep blue, silver-grey and light blue	15	15
a.	Silver-grey omitted*	£750	
b.	Phosphor omitted	10·00	

First Day Cover (W151/W153)	4·00
Presentation Pack (W151/W153)	7·50
Presentation Pack (German) (W151/W153)	75·00

Pack also exists with a Dutch or Japanese insert card
* No. W153a affects the Queen's head which appears in the light blue colour. This exists as a complete sheet with guide marks and sheet markings in grey-blue affecting the remaining five stamps of top row.
A cover with all three values is known postmarked 2 March, at Hindon, Salisbury.

First Flight of Concorde. **1969**

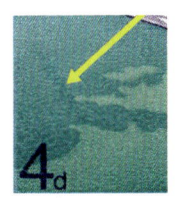

W151f
Dark flaw in Atlantic Ocean appears as an oil slick

Cylinder Numbers (Blocks of Six)

Cyl. Nos. (No dot)	Perforation Type F (P/E at left and I/E at right)
4d. 1A (violet)–1B (orange)–1C (greenish blue)–1D (pale green)–1E (blue-green)	1·25
9d. 2A (grey-blue)–1B (red)–1C (emerald)–1D (ultramarine)	1·50
1s.6d. 1A (deep blue)–1B (silver-grey)–3C (light blue)	1·50

In this issue cylinder blocks exist at the left or right of the sheets.

Minor Constant Flaws

4d. Cyls. 1A–1B–1C–1D–1E

| 1/2 | Disturbance in background below tail (Th. F–G11) |
| 2/2 | Disturbance in background below tail (Th. F–G12) |

9d. Cyls. 2A–1B–1C–1D

| 11/2 | Flaw on Queen's hair below ribbons (Th. B13) |

1s.6d. Cyls. 1A–1B–3C

| 18/2 | Small white patch below tip of Concorde's nose (Th. F13) |

Imprimaturs from the NPM or BPMA
Nos. W151/W153 imperforate

No watermark (*set of 3*)	£3000
4d. cylinder 1A, 1B, 1C, 1D, 1E block of six	£7000
9d. cylinder 2A, 1B, 1C, 1D block of six	£7000
1s.6d. cylinder 1A, 1B, 3C block of six	£7000

Quantities Sold:

4d.	91,551,720
9d.	9,488,520
1s.6d.	9,874,560
English Pack	100,608
German Pack	2,827

Withdrawn: 2.3.70

Sheet Details
Sheet size: 120 (6×20). Single-pane sheet-fed

Sheet markings:

Cylinder numbers:
- **4d.** Opposite rows 1/2 and 18/19, at both sides, boxed
- **9d.** Opposite rows 2/3 and 18/19, at both sides, boxed
- **1s.6d.** Opposite rows 2 and 19, at both sides, boxed

Guide holes: None

Marginal arrows (photo-etched):
"W" shaped, at top, bottom and sides

Marginal rule: At bottom of sheet

Colour register marks:
- **4d.** Above and below vertical rows 1/2 and 6
- **9d.** Above and below vertical rows 1 and 5/6
- **1s.6d.** Above and below vertical rows 1/2 and 6

Coloured crosses: Above and below vertical rows 2/3

Autotron marks, Colour designations: None

Traffic lights (boxed):
- **4d.** Blue-green, orange, violet, greenish blue, pale green reading left to right above vertical row 5
- **9d.** Ultramarine, emerald, red, grey-blue reading left to right above vertical row 5
- **1s.6d.** Deep blue, light blue, silver-grey reading left to right above vertical row 5

W 1969 Notable Anniversaries.

Type **W154**. Page from *Daily Mail* and Vickers Vimy Aircraft

(Des. Philip Sharland)

Type **W155**. Europa and CEPT Emblems

(Des. Michael and Sylvia Goaman)

Type **W156**. ILO Emblem

(Des. Philip Sharland)

Type **W157**. Flags of NATO Countries

(Des. Philip Sharland)

Type **W158**. Vickers Vimy Aircraft and Globe showing Flight

(Des. Michael and Sylvia Goaman)

1969 (2 April). **Notable Anniversaries.** Types **W154/W158**. Two phosphor bands, applied by photogravure (5d.) or flexography (others)

Five famous anniversaries, with the events described on the stamps.

W154 =SG 791		Mint	Used
5d.	black, pale sage-green, chestnut and new blue	10	10
a.	Phosphor omitted	£180	
b.	Missing windshield (R. 3/4)	30·00	

W155 =SG 792			
9d.	pale turquoise, deep blue, light emerald-green and black	10	15
a.	Uncoated paper*	£1800	
b.	Phosphor omitted	18·00	

W156 =SG 793			
1s.	bright purple, deep blue and lilac	15	20
a.	Phosphor omitted	10·00	

W157 =SG 794			
1s.6d.	red, royal blue, yellow-green, black, lemon and new blue	15	20
a.	Black omitted	£125	
b.	Yellow-green (from flags) omitted	85·00	
c.	Yellow-green and phosphor omitted	85·00	
d.	Phosphor omitted	9·00	
e.	Shadow variety (R. 18/6)	30·00	
f.	Lemon (from flags) omitted	†	£4500

W158 =SG 795			
1s.9d.	yellow-olive, greenish yellow and pale turquoise-green	25	30
a.	Uncoated paper*	£275	
b.	Phosphor omitted	6·00	

First Day Cover (W154/W158)	1·10
Presentation Pack (W154/W158)	4·50
Presentation Pack (German) (W154/W158)	50·00

Pack also exists with a Japanese insert

* **Uncoated paper.** See General Notes for Section UA also below Nos. W159/W164.

No. W154 is known postmarked 1 April.

No. W157f is only known used on a first day cover from Liverpool.

Normal 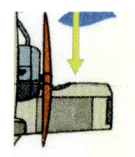   W154b

W157e
Deficient shading in shadow by fold

Cylinder Numbers (Blocks of Six (5d., 1s., 1s.9d.) or Eight (9d., 1s.6d.))

		Perforation Types	
	Cylinder Nos. (No dot)	A (E/I)	F (P/E)
5d.	1A (blue)–1B (chestnut)–1C (sage-green)–1D (black)	1·25	†
9d.	1A (blue)–1B (green)–1C (black)–1D (turquoise)	†	1·25
1s.	1A (blue)1B (purple)1C (lilac)	†	1·50
1s.6d.	1A (new blue)–1B (lemon)–1C (red)–1D (royal blue)–1E (black)–1F (green)	†	1·50
1s.9d.	2A (yellow-olive)–2B (green)–1C (yellow)	†	2·25

240

Notable Anniversaries. **1969**

Minor Constant Flaws
5d. Cyls. 1A–1B–1C–1D
- 3/4 Black horizontal line extending through the engine and fuselage (Th. E9–12)
- 4/6 Vertical black scratch top left of photograph of Alcock (Th. A–B3)
- 15/3 Retouch to base of engine (Th. E10)
- 15/5 White flaw on Brown's cap (Th. B6). Later retouched

9d. Cyls. 1A–1B–1C–1D
- 14/1 Retouch to background below "O" of "EUROPA" (Th. FG4)
- 15/3 Weak patch in background to left of CEPT symbol (Th. E11)
- 19/3 Retouch to background below "EU" of "EUROPA" (Th. F2)
- 20/2 Weak patch in background above "O" of "EUROPA" (Th. B–C4)

1s. Cyls. 1A–1B–1C
- 19/1 Dark patch in upper jaw of spanner (Th. F1)

1s.9d. Cyls. 2A–2B–1C
- 17/4 Horizontal scratch through value (Th. A1–3)
- 20/6 Pale patch in East Asia on globe (Th. B12)

Sheet Details
Sheet size: 120 (6 × 20).
- **5d.** single-pane reel-fed
- **Others:** single pane sheet-fed

Sheet markings:
Cylinder numbers:
- **5d.** Opposite rows 18/19, left margin, boxed
- **9d.** Opposite rows 17/18, left margin, boxed
- **1s.** Opposite row 18, left margin, boxed
- **1s.6d.** Opposite rows 17/18, left margin, boxed
- **1s.9d.** Opposite row 18, left margin, boxed

Guide holes:
- **5d.** Opposite rows 14/15 (boxed), at both sides
- **Others:** None

Marginal arrows (photo-etched):
"W" shaped, at top, bottom and sides

Marginal rule: None

Colour register marks:
- **5d.** Opposite rows 1/2 and 19/20 at both sides
- **Others:** Above and below vertical rows 1 and 6

Coloured crosses:
- **5d.** None
- **9d., 1s., 1s.9d.** Above and below vertical row 3
- **1s.6d.** Above and below vertical rows 3/4

Autotron marks (solid):
- **5d.** Black, sage-green, blue, chestnut below vertical rows 1/3
- **Others:** None

Colour designations:
- **5d.** G1 BROWN G2 BLUE G3 (blank) G4 BLACK in right margin reading upwards opposite rows 14/9
- **Others:** None

Sheet values: Opposite rows 4/7 and 14/17 reading upwards in left margin and downwards in right margin

Traffic lights (boxed):
- **5d.** Black, sage-green, blue, chestnut opposite rows 18/19, right margin; also in same order opposite rows 1/2, left margin
- **9d.** Black, green, blue, turquoise opposite rows 17/18, right margin; also in reverse order reading left to right above vertical row 5
- **1s.** In same order as cylinder numbers opposite row 18, right margin; also in reverse order reading left to right above vertical row 5
- **1s.6d.** In same order as cylinder numbers opposite rows 17/18, right margin; also in reverse order reading left to right above vertical row 5
- **1s.9d.** In same order as cylinder numbers opposite row 18, right margin; also in reverse order reading left to right above vertical row 5

Essay: Perforated and gummed essay on Harrison & Sons presentation card. Printed in black, green and red. Ex Goaman Archive £5000

Imprimaturs from the NPM or BPMA
Nos. W154/W158 imperforate

No watermark (*set of* 5)	£5000
5d. "Missing windshield" variety R. 3/4	£1500
5d. cylinder 1A, 1B, 1C, 1D block of six	£7000
9d. cylinder 1A, 1B, 1C, 1D block of eight	£9000
1s. cylinder 1A, 1B, 1C block of eight	£7000
1s.6d. "Shadow variety" R. 18/6	£1500
1s.6d. cylinder 1A, 1B, 1C, 1D, 1E, 1F block of eight	£9000
1s.9d. cylinder 2A, 2B, 1C block of six	£7000

Quantities Sold:

5d.	82,285,680
9d.	9,823,200
1s.	10,302,360
1s.6d.	10,512,480
1s.9d.	6,155,760
English Pack	90,282
German Pack	4,539

Withdrawn: 1.4.70

W 1969 British Architecture (Cathedrals).

Type **W159**. Durham Cathedral

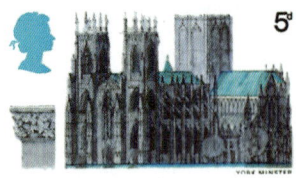

Type **W160**. York Minster

Type **W161**. St Giles', Edinburgh

Type **W162**. Canterbury Cathedral

Type **W163**. St Paul's Cathedral

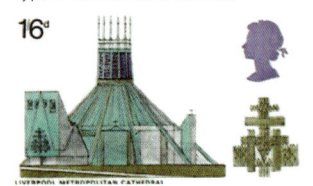

Type **W164**. Liverpool Metropolitan Cathedral

(Des. Peter Gauld)

1969 (28 May). **British Architecture (Cathedrals).** Types W161/W164. Two phosphor bands, applied by flexography (5d.) or photogravure (others)

The designs show six famous British Cathedrals dating from medieval times to the present, the Liverpool Metropolitan Cathedral being completed in 1967.

The 5d. values were issued together se-tenant in blocks of four throughout the sheet

W159 =SG 796		Mint	Used
5d.	grey-black, orange, pale bluish violet and black	10	10
a.	Block of 4. Nos. W159/W162	40	50
ac.	Uncoated paper* (block of four)	£1000	
b.	Pale bluish violet omitted	£12500	
c.	Uncoated paper*	£250	
d.	Missing "d"	£500	

W160 =SG 797			
5d.	grey-black, pale bluish violet, new blue and black	10	10
b.	Pale bluish violet omitted	£12500	
c.	Uncoated paper*	£250	

W161 =SG 798			
5d.	grey-black, purple, green and black	10	10
b.	Green omitted**	£100	
c.	Uncoated paper*	£250	
d.	Missing d	£500	

W162 =SG 799			
5d.	grey-black, green, new blue and black	10	10
c.	Uncoated paper*	£250	

W163 =SG 800			
9d.	grey-black, ochre, pale drab, violet and black	15	20
a.	Black (value) omitted.	£250	
b.	Black (value) and phosphor omitted	£325	
c.	Phosphor omitted	45·00	

W164 =SG 801			
1s.6d.	grey-black, pale turquoise-blue, pale reddish violet, pale yellow-olive and black	20	25
a.	Black (value) omitted	£2750	
b.	Black (value) double	£500	
c.	Phosphor omitted	20·00	
ca.	Error. Phosphor omitted and one stamp with diagonal phosphor band (pair)	60·00	
d.	One phosphor band		

First Day Cover (W159/W164)	1·00
Presentation Pack (W159/W164)	5·50
Presentation Pack (German) (W159/W164)	35·00

Pack also exists with a Dutch or Japanese insert card

* **Uncoated paper.** This does not respond to the silver test, and may be further distinguished from the normal chalk-surfaced paper by the fibres which clearly show on the surface, resulting in the printing impression being rougher, and by the screening dots which are not so evident.
For this issue hand-stamped "Cancelled" see Special Issues–Notes, "Specimen".

5d. Prices for missing colour errors in blocks of four:

Pale bluish violet	£25000
Green	£100

** The missing green on the roof top is known on R. 2/5, R. 8/5 and R. 10/5 but all from different sheets and it only occurred in part of the printing, being "probably caused by a batter on the impression cylinder". Examples are known with the green partly omitted.
Nos. W159d and W161d missing "d" affects stamps R. 1/1 and R. 2/1 in a block; the stamps at right were normal.

British Architecture (Cathedrals). 1969 W

Cylinder Numbers (Blocks of Eight (5d.) or Six (9d., 1s.6d.))

	Perforation Types		
Cylinder. Nos.	A (E/I) No dot	A (E/I) Dot	F (P/E) No dot
5d. 1A (black)–1B (purple)–1C (blue)–1D (orange)–2E (green)–2F (grey-black)–1G (violet)*	1·50	1·50	†
1A–1B–2C–1D–2E–2F–1G*	1·50	1·50	†
9d. 1A (black)–1B (grey-black)–2C (violet)–1D (drab)–1E (ochre)**	†	†	1·75
1s.6d. 1A (black)–1B (violet)–1C (turquoise-blue)–1D (yellow-olive)–1E (grey-black)	†	†	2·00

* In the 5d. dot panes the violet cylinder is expressed in error thus: "1.G" and the black cylinder "1.A".
** In the 9d. the violet 2C often appears battered, the 2 sometimes being hardly discernible.

Minor Constant Flaws
5d. Cyls. 1A–1B–1D–2E–2F no dot in combination with blue cyls. 1C or 2C no dot

1–2/4	Thin diagonal green line joins portrait to inset design (Th. C-E2)

5d. Cyls. 1A–1B–1D–2E–2F dot in combination with blue cyls. 1C or 2C dot

14/3	Green coloured scratch extends from bottom of third stamp in row 1 to top of third stamp in row 4. (Most noticeable in the sky of R. 3/3)
4/1	Damaged first "S" of "ST GILES"
10/3	Grey-black coloured spur at right of angel (Th. F13)

9d. Cyls. 1A–1B–2C–1D–1E

8/5	Dark spot in window on first floor just to right of centre of St Paul's (Th. F7)
9/1	Dot left of ground floor window next to entrance columns (Th. G3)

1s.6d. Cyls. 1A–1B–1C–1D–1E

1/1	Retouch on Queen's head (Th. A11)
15/1	Spur at left of third spike of central tower (Th. A5); also dot before "C" of "CATHEDRAL"

Sheet Details
Sheet sizes:
    5d. 72 (6×12). In *se-tenant* blocks of four, double-pane reel-fed, with dot pane above no dot pane
    9d., 1s.6d. 120 (6×20). Single-pane sheet-fed

Sheet markings:

Cylinder numbers:
    5d. Opposite rows 10/11, left margin, boxed
    9d., 1s.6d. Opposite rows 18/19, left margin, boxed

Guide holes:
    5d. Opposite rows 6/7 (boxed), at both sides
    Others: None

Marginal arrows (photo-etched):
"W" shaped, at top, bottom and sides

Marginal rule: None

Colour register marks:
    5d. Opposite rows 10/12, left margin, although usually trimmed off
    9d., 1s.6d. Above and below vertical rows 1 and 6

Coloured crosses:
    5d. None
    9d., 1s.6d. Above and below vertical rows 3/4

Autotron marks:
    5d. Normally trimmed off
    9d., 1s.6d. None

Colour designations: None

Sheet values:
    5d. Opposite rows 2/5 and 8/11 reading upwards in left margin and downwards in right margin
    9d., 1s.6d. Opposite rows 5/6 and 15/16 reading upwards in left margin and downwards in right margin

Traffic lights (boxed):
    5d. In same order as cylinder numbers opposite rows 10/11, right margin; also in same order reading left to right above vertical rows 4/5
    9d. In reverse order to cylinder numbers opposite rows 18/19, right margin; also above vertical row 5 but in same order as cylinder numbers reading left to right
    1s.6d. Black, yellow-olive, turquoise-blue, violet, grey-black opposite rows 18/19, right margin; also grey-black, yellow-olive, turquoise-blue, violet and black reading left to right above vertical row 5

Imprimaturs from the NPM or BPMA
Imperforate, no watermark

Nos. W159/W162 *se-tenant* block of four	£4000
5d. cylinder 1A, 1B, 1C, 1D, 2E, 2F, 1G block of eight	£9000
No. W163 single	£1000
9d. cylinder 1A, 1B, 2C, 1D, 1E block of six	£7000
No. W164 single	£1000
1s.6d. cylinder 1A, 1B, 1C, 1D, 1E block of six	£7000

Quantities Sold:

5d.	65,344,176
9d.	11,065,920
1s.6d.	11,414,280
English Pack	119,828
German Pack	7,200

Withdrawn: 27.5.70

W 1969 *Investiture of HRH The Prince of Wales.*

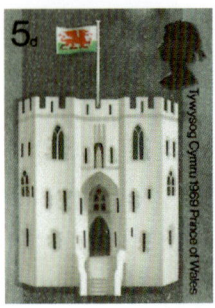

Type **W165**. The King's Gate, Caernarvon Castle

Type **W166**. The Eagle Tower, Caernarvon Castle

Type **W167**. Queen Eleanor's Gate, Caernarvon Castle

Types **W165/W167** were issued together *se-tenant* in horizontal strips of three within the sheet

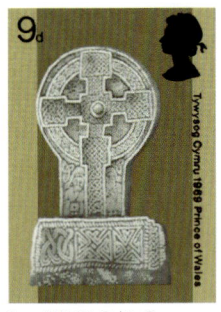

Type **W168**. Celtic Cross, Margam Abbey

Type **W169**. HRH The Prince of Wales (after photograph by G. Argent)

(Des. David Gentleman)

1969 *(1 July).* **Investiture of HRH The Prince of Wales.**
Types **W165/W169** . Two phosphor bands, applied by flexography, the phosphor being printed between two groups of colour units.

The ceremony of Investiture dates back to 1284 when King Edward I presented his son to the people of Caernarvon as the first Prince of Wales.

W165 =SG 802		Mint	Used
5d.	deep olive-grey, light olive-grey, deep grey, light grey, red, pale turquoise-green, black and silver	10	10
a.	Strip of 3. Nos. W165/W167	30	50
b.	Black (value and inscr.) omitted	£700	
c.	Red omitted*	£1250	
d.	Deep grey omitted**	£500	
e.	Pale turquoise-green omitted	£1250	
f.	Light grey omitted (see footnote)	£9500	
g.	Phosphor omitted	5·00	
ga.	Phosphor omitted (strip of three)	15·00	

W166 =SG 803			
5d.	deep olive-grey, light olive-grey, deep grey, light grey, red, pale turquoise-green, black and silver	10	10
b.	Black (value and inscr.) omitted	£700	
c.	Red omitted*	£1250	
d.	Deep grey omitted**	£500	
e.	Pale turquoise-green omitted	£1250	
f.	Light grey omitted (see footnote)	£9500	—
g.	Phosphor omitted	5·00	

W167 =SG 804			
5d.	deep olive-grey, light olive-grey, deep grey, light grey, red, pale turquoise-green, black and silver	10	10
b.	Black (value and inscr.) omitted	£700	
c.	Red omitted*	£1250	
d.	Deep grey omitted**	£500	
e.	Pale turquoise-green omitted	£1250	
f.	Light grey omitted (see footnote)	£9500	
g.	Phosphor omitted	5·00	

W168 =SG 805			
9d.	deep grey, light grey, black and gold	15	20
a.	Phosphor omitted	25·00	
b.	Error. One broad band	50·00	

W169 =SG 806			
1s.	blackish yellow-olive and gold	15	20
a.	Phosphor omitted	18·00	
b.	Error. One broad band	42·00	
c.	Error. Diagonal broad band	50·00	

First Day Cover (W165/W169)	1·00
Presentation Pack (W165/W169)	3·00
Presentation Pack (German) (W165/W169)	35·00

Pack also exists with a Dutch or Japanese insert card.

5d. Prices for missing colour errors in strips of three:

Black	£2100
Pale turquoise-green	£3750
Red	£3750
Light grey	£28500
Deep grey	£1500

The light grey (marks on walls, window frames, etc) omitted is unique in a mint strip of three and one. No. W166f commercially used on cover.

* The 5d. is also known with the red misplaced downwards and where this occurs the red printing does not take very well on the silver background and in some cases is so faint that it could be mistaken for a missing red. However, the red can be seen under a magnifying glass and caution should therefore be exercised when purchasing examples of W165c/W167c.

** The deep grey affects the dark portions of the windows and doorways.

In addition to the generally issued Presentation Pack a further pack in different colours and with all texts printed in both English and Welsh was made available exclusively through Education Authorities for free distribution to all schoolchildren in Wales and Monmouthshire. (*Price* £20).

First Day Covers are known postmarked in error "1 JUL 1968" at London NW1.

Investiture of HRH The Prince of Wales. 1969 W

Cylinder Numbers (Blocks of Nine (5d.) or Four (9d., 1s.))

Cylinder Nos.	Perforation Type F (E left margin) No dot			
5d. 1A (black)–1B (red)–1C (silver)–1D (green)–1E (deep olive- grey)–1F (light olive-grey)–1G (deep grey)–1H (light grey)	2·00			
	A (P/E) No dot	A (P/E) Dot	A(T) (I/E) No dot	A(T) (I/E) Dot
9d. 1A (black)–1B (gold)–1C (deep grey)–1D (light grey)	1·50	1·50	†	†
1s. 1A (gold)–2B (blackish yellow-olive)	1·50	1·50	†	†

The above are with sheets orientated showing head to right.

Minor Constant Flaws

9d. Cyls. 1A–1B–1C–1D dot
5/9 "yw" of "Tywysog" are joined together

1s. Cyls. 1A–2B no dot
1/10 Retouch to right of Prince's lower lip (Th. J-K6)
3/4 Small retouch below Prince's left eye (Th. G6)

1s. Cyls. 1A–2B dot
3/9 R Dark patch below Prince's left eye (Th. G6)

Sheet Details

Sheet sizes:
- **5d**. 72 (12×6). In *se-tenant* strips of three, single pane sheet-fed
- **9d., 1s.** 60 (10×6). Double pane sheet-fed, with no dot pane above dot pane

Sheet markings:

Cylinder numbers:
- **5d**. Opposite rows 4/5, left margin, boxed
- **9d., 1s.** Opposite row 6, left margin, boxed

Guide holes: None

Marginal arrows (photo-etched):
- **5d**. None
- **9d., 1s.** "W" shaped, at top, bottom and sides

Marginal rule: None

Colour register marks:
- **5d**. Opposite rows 1 and 6, at both sides
- **9d**. Above (no dot) or below (dot) vertical rows 1/2 and 10
- **1s.** Above (no dot) or below (dot) vertical rows 1/2 and 9/10

Coloured crosses:
- **5d**. Opposite rows 3/4, at both sides
- **9d., 1s.** Above (no dot) or below (dot) vertical row 4

Autotron marks, Colour designations: None

Sheet values:
- **5d**. Above and below vertical rows 2/5 and 8/11 reading left to right in top margin and right to left (upside-down) in bottom margin
- **9d., 1s.** Opposite rows 1/3 and 4/6 reading upwards in left margin and downwards in right margin

Traffic lights (boxed):
- **5d**. In same order as cylinder numbers opposite rows 4/5, right margin; also in same order reading left to right above vertical rows 10/11
- **9d**. In same order as cylinder numbers opposite row 6, right margin; also in same order reading left to right above vertical row 9
- **1s.** In reverse order to cylinder numbers opposite row 6, right margin; also in reverse order reading left to right above vertical row 9

Imprimaturs from the NPM or BPMA
Imperforate, no watermark

Nos. W165/W167 *se-tenant* strip of three	£3000
5d. cylinder 1A, 1B, 1C, 1D, 1E, 1F, 1G, 1H block of nine	£10000
Nos. W168 and W169	(Each) £1000

Quantities Sold:

5d.	99,467,496
9d.	13,384,380
1s.	12,972,720
English Pack	256,709
German Pack	9,360
Welsh Schoolchildren's Pack	146,958

Withdrawn: 30.6.70

W 1969 *Gandhi Centenary Year.*

Type **W170**. Mahatma Gandhi

(Des. Biman Mullick)

1969 *(13 August)*. **Gandhi Centenary Year.** Two phosphor bands, applied by flexography. Type **W170**

This was the first United Kingdom postage stamp to commemorate an overseas leader and the first to be designed by an overseas artist.

W170 =SG 807

1s.6d.	black, green, red-orange and grey	25	30
a.	Printed on the gummed side	£1750	
b.	Phosphor omitted	4·00	
c.	Tooth flaw (R. 20/3)	40·00	
ca.	Tooth flaw retouched	35·00	
First Day Cover (W170)			3·25

The above is known pre-released on 12 August at Penyfai (Bridgend), Glamorgan and also postmarked Paisley, Renfrewshire 13 July 1969, the latter being due to the use of an incorrect date-stamp on a first day cover.

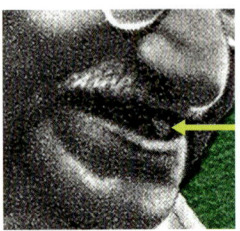

W170c   W170ca Retouched
White patch in Gandhi's mouth appears as tooth. Later retouched to near normal.

Cylinder Numbers (Blocks of Six)

	Perforation Type
Cylinder. Nos. (No dot)	F (P/E)
1s.6d. 2A (black)–1B (grey)–2C (green)–1D (orange)	2·75

Minor Constant Flaws
1s.6d. Cyls. 2A–1B–2C–1D

1/6	Second white spot in Gandhi's right eye (Th. D6). Later retouched; also small nick in left arm of "Y" of "Year"
3/4	Dark patch on arm of spectacles (Th. C4)
3/5	Retouch on Gandhi's nose (Th. E6)
5/3	Dark spot in front of Gandhi's right ear (Th. D3)
8/2	Dark spot on Gandhi's temple (Th. C4). Later retouched
12/4	White patch on Gandhi's right lapel (Th. G2)
16/1	Retouched "G" of "Gandhi"

Sheet Details
    Sheet size: 120 (6 × 20). Single-pane sheet-fed

Sheet markings:
Cylinder numbers: Opposite rows 18/19, left margin, boxed
Guide holes: None

Marginal arrows (photo-etched):
"W" shaped, at top, bottom and sides
Marginal rule: None
Colour register marks: Above and below vertical rows 1 and 6
Coloured crosses: Above and below vertical row 3
Autotron marks and Colour designations: None
Sheet values: Opposite rows 4/7 and 14/17 reading upwards in left margin and downwards in right margin
Traffic lights (boxed): Black, grey, green, orange opposite rows 19/20, right margin; also in reverse order reading left to right above vertical row 5

Imprimatur from the NPM or BPMA
No. W170 imperforate

No watermark (single)	£1000
do. with "Tooth flaw" R. 20/3	£1500
do. cylinder 2A, 1B, 2C, 1D block of six	£7000

Quantity Sold: 10,804,920

Withdrawn: 12.8.70

1969 *(15 September)*. **Collectors Pack**

WCP2	Comprising Nos. W142/W170	25·00

This pack also exists with a German or Japanese insert card.
Quantity Sold: 63,890

Type **W171**. National Giro "G" Symbol

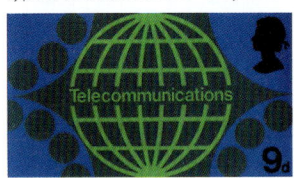

Type **W172**. Telecommunications – International Subscriber Dialling

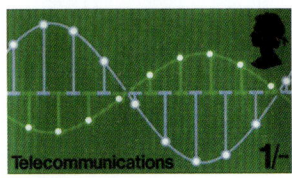

Type **W173**. Telecommunications – Pulse Code Modulation

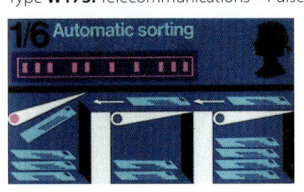

Type **W174**. Postal Mechanisation – Automatic Sorting

(Des. David Gentleman)

(Lithography by De La Rue)

Post Office Technology Commemoration. 1969

1969 (1 October). **Post Office Technology Commemoration.**
Comb perforation 13½×14. Two phosphor bands applied by letterpress. Types **W171/W174**

Issued on the day the Post Office became a public corporation, these stamps depict some of its technological achievements. This issue in itself was a technical departure for the Post Office being the first British stamps to be printed by lithography.

	Mint	Used
W171 =SG 808		
5d. new blue, greenish blue, pale lavender and black	10	10
a. Phosphor omitted	5·00	
b. Error. One broad band	20·00	
W172 =SG 809		
9d. emerald, violet-blue and black	10	10
a. Error. One broad band	20·00	
W173 =SG 810		
1s. emerald, lavender and black	15	15
a. Phosphor omitted	£325	
b. Error. One broad band	20·00	
W174 =SG 811		
1s.6d. bright purple, light turquoise-blue, grey-blue and black	20	20
a. Error. One broad band	22·00	
First Day Cover (W171/W174)		75
Presentation Pack (W171/W174)	5·00	

Pack also exists with a Dutch, German or Japanese insert card
No. W171a can be found with or without a dry impression of the letterpress plate.
The 1s. is known postmarked at Gloucester on 29 September and the 1s.6d. at Gutcher Yell (Shetland Isles) on 26 September.
For examples with "Cancelled" handstamp, see Special Issues–Notes, "Specimens".

Plate Numbers (Blocks of Four)

Plate Nos. (all Dot)	Perforation Type F (L) (I/E)
5d. 2A (new blue)–2B (greenish blue)–2C (lavender)–2D (black)	1·25
2A–3B–2C–2D	1·00
2A–3B–2C–3D	1·00
3A–4B–3C–4D	1·50
9d. 2A (emerald)–2B (violet-blue)–2C (black)	1·00
1s. 1A (emerald)–1B (lavender)–1C (black)	2·00
1A–1B–2C	1·50
1A–1B–3C	1·50
1s.6d. 1A (purple)–1B (light turquoise-blue)–1C (grey-blue)–1D (black)	1·75

Although all the plate numbers are followed by a dot they were in fact only printed in single panes.

Minor Constant Flaws
Numerous minor flaws caused by specks of dust settling on the printing plate and preventing the ink from reaching the area appear as white inkless rings and are known as litho ring flaws. Minor flecks of colour are similarly caused. As such flaws only affect part of a printing and cannot be regarded as constant we do not record them.

Sheet Details Sheet size: 120 (10×12). Single-pane sheet-fed

Sheet markings:

Plate numbers: Opposite rows 1/2, left margin, unboxed

Guide holes: Above and below vertical row 6 in crossed box. Reserve guide-hole boxes appear above and below vertical row 4 but these were not used

Marginal arrows (solid):
"W" shaped, at top, bottom and sides

Marginal rule: None

Colour register marks:
5d., 9d., 1s. Below vertical rows 1 and 10 and opposite rows 1 and 12, at both sides
1s.6d. Above and below vertical rows 1 and 10 and opposite rows 1 and 12, at both sides

Coloured crosses, Autotron marks, Colour designations: None

Sheet values: Above and below vertical rows 2/4 and 7/9 reading left to right in top margin and right to left (upside-down) in bottom margin

Traffic lights (unboxed):
5d. Opposite rows 8/10, right margin
9d., 1s. Opposite rows 9/10, right margin
1s.6d. Opposite rows 9/11, right margin

Encapsulated stamp card:
On pale green card, 3¾ × 5¾ encapsulated in perspex

Imprimaturs from the NPM or BPMA
Nos. W171/W174 imperforate

No watermark (set of 4)	£4000
5d. cylinder 2A, 3B, 2C, 2D block of four	£5000
9d. cylinder 2A, 2B, 2C block of four	£5000
1s. cylinder 1A, 1B, 3C block of four	£5000
1s.6d. cylinder 1A, 1B, 1C, 1D block of four	£5000

Quantities Sold:

5d.	72,405,720
9d.	8,472,000
1s.	10,296,120
1s.6d.	10,757,040
Pack	104,230

Withdrawn: 30.9.70

W 1969 Christmas.

Type **W175**. Herald Angel

Type **W176**. The Three Shepherds

Type **W177**. The Three Kings

(Des. Fritz Wegner)

(Printed in photogravure with the Queen's head (and stars 4d., 5d. and scroll-work 1s.6d. embossed in gold)

1969 (26 November). **Christmas.** One 7 to 8 mm. centre phosphor band (4d.) or two phosphor bands (others), applied by photogravure (W175b) or flexography (others) Types **W175/W177**

Traditional religious themes are featured on these stamps by Austrian-born designer Fritz Wegner.

W175	=SG 812	Mint	Used
4d.	vermilion, new blue, orange, bright purple, light green, bluish violet, blackish brown and gold	10	10
a.	Gold (Queen's head etc.) omitted	£12000	
b.	Centre band 3·5 mm	30	20

W176	=SG 813		
5d.	magenta, light blue, royal blue, olive-brown, green, greenish yellow, red and gold	10	10
a.	Light blue (sheep, etc.) omitted	£110	
b.	Red omitted*	£2200	
c.	Gold (Queen's head etc.) omitted	£1200	
d.	Green omitted	£375	
e.	Olive-brown, red, gold and phosphor omitted	£15000	
f.	Embossing omitted	25·00	
g.	Phosphor omitted	5·00	
h.	Imperf through left margin	£100	

W177	=SG 814		
1s.6d.	greenish yellow, bright purple, bluish violet, deep slate, orange, green, new blue and gold	15	15
a.	Gold (Queen's head etc.) omitted	£150	
b.	Deep slate (value) omitted	£525	
c.	Greenish yellow omitted	£475	
e.	New blue omitted	£140	
f.	Embossing omitted	12·00	
g.	Embossing and phosphor omitted	12·00	

h.	Phosphor omitted		6·00
i.	Broken arch (R. 1/6)		30·00
First Day Cover (W159/W164)			1·00
Presentation Pack (W159/W164)			5·00

* The effect of the missing red is shown on the hat, leggings and purse which appear as dull orange.

The 4d. is known postmarked at Dudley, Worcs. on 25 November.

No. W175 has one centre 8 mm band. This was ineffective in the automatic facing machines and after about three-quarters of the stamps had been printed the remainder were printed with a 3·5 mm. band (No. W175b). The wide band is sometimes difficult to see. Stamps have also been seen with a very wide phantom band measuring about 20 mm. which only reacts very faintly under the lamp and with a clear 3·5 mm. band over it.

No. W176e was caused by a paper fold.

No. W176h is believed to come from a single sheet which was fed into the perforator upside down.

No. W177d bluish violet omitted has been deleted as examples showed only a partial omission.

W 177i
Break in the arch above the crown of King at right

Cylinder Numbers (Blocks of Six (4d.) or Eight (5d., 1s.6d.))

	Perforation Types A (E/I)			
	7–8 mm. band		3·5 mm. band	
Cylinder. Nos.	No dot	Dot	No dot	Dot
4d. 1A (brown)–1B (vermilion)–2C (orange)–1D (purple)–1E (new blue)–1F (green)–1G (violet)–1H (gold)	1·25	1·25	†	†
1A–1B–2C–1D–1E–2F–1G–1H	3·00	3·00	3·00	3·00
	F (P/E) No dot		F (L) (I/E) No dot	
5d. 1A (royal blue)–1B (yellow)–1C (magenta)–1D (green)–2E (brown)–1F (light blue)–1G (red)–1H (gold)	1·75		£300	
1s.6d. 3A (slate)–1C (gold)–1D (blue)–1E (yellow)–1F (green)–1G (violet)–1H (purple)–1J (orange)	2·50		†	

On the 4d. cylinder numbers 1A and 1H often appear as 1A1 and 1H1 on the dot and no dot panes respectively; the 1B and 1E have what appear to be small letters "IN" in place of the dot, whilst the 2C is an alteration from 1C, all on the dot panes.

Minor Constant Flaws

4d. Cyls. 1A –1B–2C–1D–1E–2F–1G–1H dot

5/3 White flaw in hem of Angel's gown (later corrected) (Th. E1)

11/1 A break in the pattern of the pillar on the right (Th. E13)

11/4 White flaw in the pattern of the arch over the Queen's head (Th. A11)

British Rural Architecture. 1970

Sheet Details
Sheet sizes:
- **4d.** 72 (6×12). Double-pane reel-fed (one pane above the other) for four colours and phosphor, and then single-pane sheet-fed for remaining four colours and embossing
- **5d., 1s.6d.** 120 (6×20). Single-pane sheet-fed

Sheet markings:

Cylinder numbers:
- **4d.** Opposite rows 10/12, left margin, boxed
- **5d., 1s.6d.** Opposite rows 17/19, left margin, boxed

Guide holes:
- **4d.** Opposite rows 6/7 (boxed), at both sides
- **5d., 1s.6d.** None

Marginal arrows (photo-etched):
"W" shaped, at top, bottom and sides

Marginal rule: None

Colour register marks:
- **4d.** None
- **5d., 1s.6d.** Above and below vertical rows 1/2 and 5/6

Coloured crosses:
- **4d.** Usually trimmed off
- **5d., 1s.6d.** Above and below vertical rows 3/4

Autotron marks, Colour designations: None

Sheet values:
- **4d.** Opposite rows 3/4 and 9/10 reading upwards in left margin and downwards in right margin
- **5d.** Opposite rows 4/7 and 14/17 reading upwards in left margin and downwards in right margin
- **1s.6d.** Opposite rows 5/6 and 15/16 reading upwards in left margin and downwards in right margin

Traffic lights (boxed):
- **4d.** Vermilion, orange, purple, new blue, green, brown, violet, gold and embossing opposite rows 9/11, right margin; also in same order reading left to right above vertical rows 4/5
- **5d.** Embossing and then as cylinder numbers but in reverse order opposite rows 17/19, right margin; also in same order as cylinder numbers followed by embossing above vertical rows 4/5
- **1s.6d.** Embossing, gold, blue, yellow, slate, green, violet, purple and orange opposite rows 17/19, right margin; also in reverse order reading left to right above vertical rows 4/5

Encapsulated Stamp Card:
Imprimaturs from the NPM or BPMA
Nos. W175/W177 imperforate

No watermark (*set of 3*)	£3000
4d. (8 mm centre band) cylinder 1A, 1B, 2C, 1D, 1E, 1F, 1G, 1H block of six	£7000
do. (3.5 centre band) block of six	£7000
5d. cylinder 1A, 1B, 1C, 1D, 2E, 1F, 1G, 1H block of six	£7000
1s.6d. "BROKEN ARCH" flaw R. 1/6	£1500
1s.6d. cylinder 3A, 1C, 1D, 1E, 1F, 1G, 1H, 1J block of eight	£9000

Quantities Sold: 4d. 271,244,808; 5d. 139,845,600; 1s.6d. 19,136,520; Pack 121,454

Withdrawn: 25.11.70

Type **W178.** Fife Harling

Type **W179.** Cotswold Limestone

(Des. David Gentleman)

Type **W180.** Welsh Stucco

Type **W181.** Ulster Thatch

(Des. Sheila Robinson)

1970 (11 February). **British Rural Architecture.** Two phosphor bands. Types **W178/W181**

The designs feature typical cottage architecture in Scotland, England, Wales and Northern Ireland respectively.

W178 =SG 815	Mint	Used
5d. grey, grey-black, black, lemon, greenish blue, orange-brown, ultramarine and green	10	10
a. Lemon omitted	£160	
b. Lemon omitted from chimney at left (R. 12/2)	35·00	
c. Grey (Queen's head and cottage shading) omitted	—	
d. Greenish blue (door) omitted	†	£4800
e. Grey-black (inscription and face value) omitted	£20000	
ea. Grey-black (face value only) omitted	£17000	
eb. Green (cobblestones) omitted	—	
f. Phosphor omitted	2·00	
g. Nick in hair (R. 15/6)	30·00	

W 1970 British Rural Architecture.

W179 =SG 816

9d.	orange-brown, olive-yellow, bright green, black, grey-black and grey	15	15
a.	Phosphor omitted	30·00	

W180 = S.G. 817

1s.	deep blue, reddish lilac, drab and new blue	15	15
a.	New blue omitted	£130	
b.	Phosphor omitted	15·00	
c.	Error. One broad band		

W181 =SG 818

1s.6d.	greenish yellow, black, turquoise-blue and lilac	20	25
a.	Turquoise-blue omitted	£17500	
b.	Phosphor omitted	5·00	
c.	Broken panes in middle window (No dot, R. 3/2)	30·00	
d.	Error. One broad band	40·00	

First Day Cover (W178/W181)	85

Presentation Pack (W178/W181)	3·00

Pack also exists with a Dutch, German or Japanese insert card.

Examples showing "Fife harling" (No. W178) omitted were due to a partial omission of the grey-black (*Price mint £475*). The listed example of No.W178d is used and tied on piece, with the greenish blue colour omitted. No. W178e is a total omission and should only be purchased with certificate.

Misdated First Day covers are known postmarked 11 January (Doncaster) or 1969 (Farnham).

No. W178b. The lemon is omitted from the chimney at left once in every sheet (later added to cylinder and appearing normal).

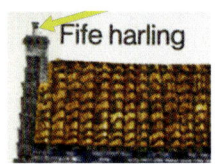

W178b

W178g   W181c

Cylinder Numbers (Blocks of Eight (5d.), Six (9d.), Four (1s., 1s.6d.))

	Perforation Types	
	F (P/E)	A (T) (E/P)
Cylinder Nos.	No dot No dot	Dot
5d. 1A (black)–1B (grey-black)1C (brown)–1D (ultramarine)–1E (greenish blue)–1F (green)–1G (grey)–1H (lemon)	1·50	† †
9d. 1A (grey-black)–1B (yellow)–1C (brown)–1D (black)–IE (green)–1F (grey)	1·50	† †

1s.	1A (deep blue)–2B (lilac)–1C (new blue)–1D (drab)	†	1·25 1·25
1s.6d.	1A (black)–1B (yellow)–1C (turquoise-blue)–1D (lilac)	†	1·50 1·50

Minor Constant Flaws

5d. Cyls. 1A–1B–1C–1D–1E–1F–1G–1H no dot
 4/2 Right leg of "h" of "harling" is broken
 9/6 Pale patch on wall above left-hand first-floor window of building at right (Th. D8)
 20/6 Pale patch on wall by top of upright at the bottom of the banisters and similar patch with grey spot in it just above (Th. F1); coloured spur to centre chimney (Th. A7); and orange-brown flaw below "F" of "Fife" (Th. A2)

9d. Cyls. 1A–1B–1C–1D–1E–1F no dot
 19/1 Dark flaw on gate at left (Th. G2)

1s.6d. Cyls. 1A–1B–1C–1D no dot
 2/3 Pale flaw on left stroke of "U" of "ULSTER" and two yellow dots in front of Queen's neck

1s.6d. Cyls. 1A–1B–1C–1D dot
 5/5 White flaw to right of sixth brick from bottom (Th. G7)

Sheet Details

Sheet sizes:
 5d., 9d. 120 (6×20). Single pane sheet-fed
 1s., 1s.6d. 60 (6×10). Double pane sheet-fed (etched sideways on the cylinder)

Sheet markings:

Cylinder numbers:
 5d. Opposite rows 17/19, left margin, boxed
 9d. Opposite rows 18/19, left margin, boxed
 1s., 1s.6d. Opposite rows 9/10, left margin, boxed

Guide holes: None

Marginal arrows (photo-etched):
"W" shaped, at top, bottom and sides

Marginal rule: None

Colour register marks:
 5d., 9d. Above and below vertical rows 1/2 and 6
 1s. Opposite rows 1/2 and 6, at left (no dot) or right (dot)
 1s.6d. Opposite rows 1 and 6, at left (no dot) or right (dot)

Coloured crosses:
 5d., 9d. Above and below vertical rows 3/4
 1s. Opposite row 7, at left (no dot) or right (dot)
 1s.6d. Opposite rows 6/7, at left (no dot) or right (dot)

Autotron marks, Colour designations: None

Sheet values:
 5d., 9d. Opposite rows 4/7 and 14/17 reading upwards in left margin and downwards in right margin 1s. Opposite row 2/4 and 7/9 reading upwards in left margin and downwards in right margin
 1s.6d. As 1s. but reading downwards in left margin and upwards in right margin

Traffic lights (boxed):
 5d. In same order as cylinder numbers opposite rows 18/19, right margin; also in reverse order reading left to right above vertical rows 4/6
 9d. In reverse order to cylinder numbers opposite rows 18/19; also in same order as cylinder numbers above vertical row 5
 1s. In same order as cylinder numbers opposite rows 6/7, right margin; also in same order reading left to right above vertical row 5

1s.6d. In same order as cylinder numbers opposite rows 7/8 at both sides; also in reverse order above vertical row 5

Imprimaturs from the NPM or BPMA
Nos. W178/W181 imperforate

No watermark (*set of* 4)	£4000
5d. "NICK IN HAIR" variety R. 15/6	£1500
5d. cylinder 1A, 1B, 1C, 1D, 1E, 1F, 1G, 1H block of eight	£9000
9d. cylinder 1A, 1B, 1C, 1D, 1E, 1F block of six	£7000
1s. cylinder 1A, 2B, 1C, 1D block of four	£5000
1s.6d. cylinder 1A, 1B, 1C, 1D block of four	£5000

Quantities Sold:

5d.	81,581,880
9d.	11,723,160
1s.	10,258,320
1s.6d.	8,969,280
Pack	116,983

Withdrawn: 10.2.71

Sales quantities. The figures quoted for quantities actually sold of the 1970 issues are according to the best estimates available from the Post Office, as exact records of unsold returns could not be made in the circumstances following the postal strike, and the change to decimal issues. In particular the estimates for the Philympia and Christmas issues cannot be guaranteed.

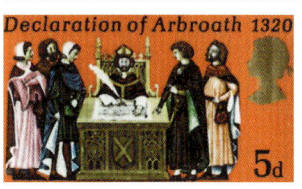

Type **W182**. Signing the Declaration of Arbroath

Type **W183**. Florence Nightingale attending Patients

(Des. Fritz Wegner)

Type **W184**. Signing the International Co-operative Alliance

(Des. Marjorie Saynor)

Type **W185**. Pilgrims and *Mayflower*

(Des. Fritz Wegner)

Type **W186**. Sir William Herschel, Francis Baily, Sir John Herschel and Telescope

(Des. Marjorie Saynor)

(Printed in photogravure with the Queen's head embossed in gold)

W 1970 General Anniversaries.

1970 *(1 April).* **General Anniversaries.** Two phosphor bands. Types **W182/W186**

Five famous anniversaries, with the events described on the stamps.

An additional feature of this issue was the introduction of cylinder numbers for the cylinders printing the phosphor bands. They are not easy to see but are printed below the ordinary cylinder numbers.

W182 =SG 819		Mint	Used
5d.	black, yellow-olive, blue, emerald, greenish yellow, rose-red, gold and orange-red	10	10
a.	Gold (Queen's head) omitted	£3500	
b.	Emerald omitted	£475	
c.	Phosphor omitted	£375	
d.	White flaw in desk (R. 2/6)	30·00	
e.	White spot in hem (R. 5/5)	30·00	
f.	Missing portions of desk and foot (R. 20/4)	30·00	

W183 =SG 820			
9d.	ochre, deep blue, carmine, black, blue-green, yellow-olive, gold and blue	10	10
a.	Ochre omitted	£475	
b.	Embossing omitted	15·00	
c.	Phosphor omitted	5·00	

W184 =SG 821			
1s.	green, greenish yellow, brown, black, cerise, gold and light blue	15	15
a.	Gold (Queen's head) omitted	90·00	
b.	Green and embossing omitted	£150	
c.	Green omitted	£150	
d.	Brown and phosphor omitted	£300	
e.	Brown omitted	£300	
f.	Embossing and phosphor omitted	22·00	
g.	Embossing omitted	12·00	
h.	Phosphor omitted	5·00	
i.	Imperf through left margin	£100	

W185 =SG 822			
1s.6d.	greenish yellow, carmine, deep yellow-olive, emerald, black, blue, gold and sage-green	20	20
a.	Gold (Queen's head) omitted	£300	
b.	Emerald omitted	£150	
c.	Embossing omitted	6·00	
d.	Phosphor omitted	5·00	
e.	Flag flaw (R. 20/5)	30·00	

W186 =SG 823			
1s.9d.	black, slate, lemon, gold and bright purple	20	20
a.	Lemon (trousers and document) omitted	£10000	£6000
b.	Phosphor omitted	5·00	
c.	Embossing omitted	75·00	
d.	Error. One broad band	10·00	

First Day Cover (W182/W186)	95
Presentation Pack (W182/W186)	4·00

Pack also exists With a Dutch, German or Japanese insert card.

The 5d. is known with the gold partly omitted, possibly due to under-inking. Of a complete sheet seen, the cylinder number did not show, the traffic lights appeared smaller and the back of the Queen's head on every stamp was rounded with no ribbons.

No. W184i is believed to come from a single sheet which was fed into the perforator upside down.

The 1s.9d. (No. W186a) is also known used on first day cover postmarked London WC.

Nos. W182/W186 were pre-released at Dorking on 25 March. Two dies were used to emboss the presentation pack Coat of Arms. The designer's name was spelt as "Majorie" instead of "Marjorie", used on the later version.

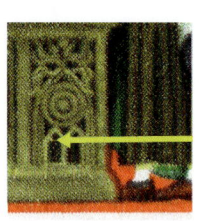

W182d

W182e
Amount of white varies with the registration of colours

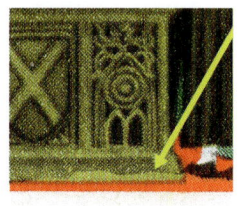

W182f
Large part of base of desk and front of shoe missing

All the above are multipositive flaws which appear on no dot and dot panes

W185e
Portion of blue in bottom right-hand corner of Union Jack is missing

Cylinder Numbers (Blocks of Eight (5d., 9d., 1s., 1s.6d.) or Six (1s.9d.))

		Perforation Types		
	A (T) (E/P)		F (P/E)	F(L) (I/E)
Cylinder Nos.	No dot	Dot	No dot	No dot
5d. 1A (black)–1B (gold)–1C (blue)–1D (emerald)–IE (olive)–1F (rose-red)–1G (yellow)–1H (orange-red)– P1 (phosphor)	1·50	1·50	†	†
9d. 2A (blue)–1B (ochre)–1C (deep blue)–1D (green)–1E (gold)–2F (black)–1G (olive)–1H (carmine)–P2 (phosphor)	†	†	1·50	†

General Anniversaries. **1970** **W**

1s.	1A (black)–1B (blue)–1C (yellow)–1D (brown)–IE (gold)–2F (cerise)–1G (green)–P2 (phosphor)	†	†	1·75	£300
1s.6d.	1A (black)–1B (sage-green)–1C (yellow)–1D (carmine)–1E (gold)–2F (blue)–1G (deep yellow-olive)–1H (emerald)–P2 (phosphor)	†		2·00	†
1s.9d.	1A (black)–1E (gold)–1B (slate)–1C (lemon)–2D (bright purple)–P2 (phosphor)	†		2·00	†

The phosphor cylinder numbers appear below the ordinary cylinder numbers opposite R. 20/1.

In the 5d. the P1 is indented into the phosphor band but in the other values the P2 is to the left of the phosphor band.

In the 5d. the 1 of 1C and the bar below it are sometimes missing. The 9d. is known without phosphor cylinder number.

In the 1s.9d. the cylinder numbers are always out of sequence.

Minor Constant Flaws

5d. Cyls. 1A–1B–1C–1D–1E–1F–1G–1H–P1 no dot
- 2/1 Weak patches in background below "r" and "t" of "Declaration"
- 6/1 Vertical scratch in background, through and below "th" of "Arbroath" (Th. A10 to C11)
- 7/1 As 6/1

9d. Cyls. 2A–1B–1C–1D–1E–2F–1G–1H–P2 no dot
- 8/6 Pale area surrounds final "e" of "Florence"
- 19/4 Dark patch in background below second "g" of "Nightingale"

1s. Cyls. 1A–1B–1C–1D–1E–2F–1G–P2 no dot
- 3/4 Missing top to "t" in "Co-operative"
- 8/3 Dark flaw by top of first "l" of "Alliance"

1s.6d. Cyls. 1A–1B–1C–1D–1E–2F–1G–1H–P2 no dot
- 8/3 Letters "flo" of "Mayflower" have hazy appearance

1s.9d. Cyls 1A–1E–1B–1C–2D–P2 no dot
- 2/3 Pale patch in background above "on" of "Astronomical"
- 2/6 Small break in "t" of "Astronomical"
- 19/1 Dark patch on left leg of figure at right (Th. F6)
- 19/5 Bright purple coloured flaw on left sleeve of man at left due to lack of screening dots on black cylinder (Th. D3)
- 20/4 Black dot on "e" of "Society"

Sheet Details

Sheet sizes: 120 (6×20).
- **5d.** double-pane reel-fed with no dot pane above dot pane
- **Others:** single-pane sheet-fed

Sheet markings:

Cylinder numbers:
- **1s.9d.** Opposite rows 18/19, left margin, boxed.
- **Others:** Opposite rows 17/19, left margin, boxed.

Guide holes:
- **5d.** Opposite rows 6/7 (boxed), at both sides.
- **Others:** None

Marginal arrows (photo-etched):
"W" shaped, at top, bottom and sides

Marginal rule: None

Colour register marks:
- **5d.** Opposite rows 9/12 at right (no dot) or left (dot).
- **Others:** Above and below vertical rows 1 and 6

Coloured crosses:
- **5d.** None.
- **Others:** Above and below vertical rows 3/4

Autotron marks (solid):
- **5d.** Gold, black, blue, emerald, olive, rose-red, yellow, orange-red above left margin and above vertical rows 1/4.
- **Others:** None

Colour designations: None

Sheet values:
- **1s.** Opposite rows 5/6 and 15/16 reading upwards in left margin and downwards in right margin
- **Others:** Opposite rows 4/7 and 14/17 reading upwards in left margin and downwards in right margin

Traffic lights (boxed):
- **5d.** Embossing, gold, black, blue, emerald, olive, rose-red, yellow and orange-red opposite rows 16/18, right margin; also in same order reading left to right above vertical rows 4/5
- **9d.** Blue, ochre, deep blue, green, gold, embossing, black, olive and carmine opposite rows 17/19, right margin; also in reverse order reading left to right above vertical rows 4/5
- **1s.** Green, black, cerise, gold, embossing, brown, yellow and blue opposite rows 18/19, right margin; also blue, yellow, embossing, gold, brown, cerise, black and green reading left to right above vertical rows 4/5
- **1s.6d.** Sage-green, yellow, carmine, blue, gold, embossing, deep yellow-olive, black and emerald opposite rows 17/19, right margin; also in reverse order reading left to right above vertical rows 4/5
- **1s.9d.** Black, gold, embossing, slate, lemon and bright purple opposite rows 18/19, right margin; also embossing, gold, black, slate, lemon and bright purple reading left to right above vertical row 5

Imprimaturs from the NPM or BPMA
Nos. W182/W186 imperforate

No watermark (set of 5)	£5000
5d. cylinder 1A, 1B, 1C, 1D, 1E, 1F, 1G, 1H P1 block of eight	£9000
9d. cylinder 2A, 1B, 1C, 1D, 1E, 2F, 1G, 1H, P2 block of eight	£9000
1s. cylinder 1A, 1B, 1C, 1D, 1E, 2F, 1G, P2 block of eight	£9000
1s.6d. "Flag flaw" R. 20/5 block of eight	£1500
1s.6d. cylinder 1A, 1B, 1C, 1D, 1E, 2F, 1G, 1H, P2 block of eight	£9000
1s.9d. cylinder 1A, 1B, 1C, 2D, 1E, P2 block of six	£7000

Quantities Sold

5d.	71,259,000
9d.	10,590,120
1s.	10,287,840
1s.6d.	11,388,960
1s.9d.	6,120,600;
Pack	120,564

Withdrawn: 31.3.71

W 1970 Literary Anniversaries.

Type W187. Mr. Pickwick and Sam Weller (*Pickwick Papers*)

Type W188. Mr. and Mrs. Micawber (*David Copperfield*)

Type W189. David Copperfield and Betsy Trotwood (*David Copperfield*)

Type W190. Oliver asking for more (*Oliver Twist*)

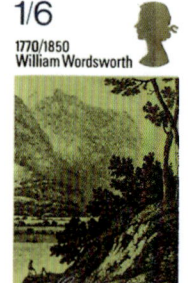

Type W191. Grasmere (from engraving by J. Farington, R.A.)

(Des. Rosalind Dease. 5d. based on etchings by Phiz and George Cruickshank)

(Printed in photogravure with the Queen's head embossed in gold)

1970 (3 June). **Literary Anniversaries.** Two phosphor bands. Types **W187/W191**

The four 5d. stamps, commemorating the death centenary of Charles Dickens, feature popular characters from his novels.

The 1s.6d. stamp commemorates the birth bicentenary of Lakeland poet William Wordsworth.

The 5d. values were issued together *se-tenant* in blocks of four throughout the sheet.

W187 = S.G.824	Mint	Used
5d. black, orange, silver, gold and magenta	10	10
a. Block of 4. Nos. W187/W190	40	60
ab. Imperf. (block of four)	£2250	
ac. Silver (inscr) omitted (block of four)	—	
ad. Error. One broad band (block of four)	35·00	

W188 =SG 825		
5d. black, magenta, silver, gold and orange	10	10
W189 =SG 826		
5d. black, light greenish blue, silver, gold and yellow-bistre	10	10
b. Yellow-bistre (value) omitted	£8000	
W190 =SG 827		
5d. black, yellow-bistre, silver, gold and light greenish blue	10	10
b. Yellow-bistre (background) omitted	£22000	
c. Light greenish blue (value) omitted*	£775	
d. Light-greenish blue and silver (inscription at foot) omitted	£32000	
W191 =SG 828		
1s.6d. light yellow-olive, black, silver, gold and bright blue	15	20
a. Gold (Queen's head) omitted	£10000	
b. Silver ("Grasmere") omitted	£250	
c. Bright blue (value) omitted	£20000	
d. Embossing and phosphor omitted	22·00	
e. Embossing omitted	6·00	
f. Phosphor omitted	5·00	
g. Retouch in slope (R. 1/18)	30·00	
h. Extra road (R. 6/8)	30·00	
i. Bright blue and silver omitted	£25000	
First Day Cover (W187/W191)		90
Presentation Pack (W187/W191)	4·00	

Pack also exists with a Dutch, German or Japanese insert card

* No. W190c (unlike No. W189b) results from a partial missing colour. Although it is completely missing on No. W190, it is only partially omitted on No. W189.

5d. Prices for missing colour errors in blocks of four:

Yellow-bistre	£30000
Light greenish blue	£775
Light greenish blue and silver	£32000

The light greenish blue and silver error in block of four is unique.

W191g Retouch consists of diagonal black lines over triangular green patch N.E. of "Grasmere".

Normal — Green line gives the impression of an extra road leading up the foothill

W191h

254

Cylinder Numbers (Blocks of Eight (5d.) or Four (1s.6d.))

	Perforation Types	
	A (P/E)	F (E/P)
Cylinder Nos.	No dot	Dot No dot
5d. 1A (orange)–1B (magenta)–3C (bistre)–1D (blue)–1E (black)–1F (silver)–1G (gold)–P4 (phosphor)	1·75	1·75 †
1s.6d. 1A (blue)–1B (gold)–1C (silver)–1D (black)–1E (olive)–P3 (phosphor)	†	† 1·50

Perforation Type A on 5d. have the sheets orientated showing head to right.

In the 5d. the 1F is printed over a figure 2 in both panes.

Minor Constant Flaws
5d. Cyls. 1A–1B–3C–1D–1E–1F–1G dot

5/17 Extra button on Sam's coat under armpit (Th. B6)

5/19 Dot by "7" of "1870" level with centre of "8"

Sheet Details
Sheet size: 120 (20×6)

5d. In *se-tenant* blocks of four, double-pane reel-fed with no dot pane above dot pane

1s.6d. Single-pane sheet-fed

Sheet markings:
Cylinder numbers:

5d. above vertical rows 1/3, boxed

1s.6d. Opposite row 5, left margin, boxed

Guide holes:

5d. In single box above and below vertical rows 14/15

1s.6d. None

Marginal arrows (photo-etched):
"W" shaped, at top, bottom and sides

Marginal rule: None

Colour register marks:

5d. None

1s.6d. Opposite rows 1 and 6 at both sides

Coloured crosses:

5d. None

1s.6d. Opposite rows 3/4 at both sides

Autotron marks (solid):

5d. Opposite rows 1/4 at right on no dot pane only

1s.6d. None

Sheet values: Above and below vertical rows 4/7 and 14/17

Traffic lights (boxed):

5d. Embossing, gold, silver. blue, bistre, magenta, orange and black opposite rows 5/6, right margin; also in reverse order below vertical rows 3/4

1s.6d. Embossing, gold, silver, blue, black and olive opposite row 5, right margin; also in same order above vertical rows 18/19

Essays. Nos. W187/W190 exist as a block of four, each design 22½×38½ mm. (larger than issued). The Queen's head is printed in silver and the Copperfield stamps are in olive-green. The four inscriptions read: Mr. Pickwick & Sam, Mr. & Mrs. Micawber, David Copperfield & Aunt Trotwood and Oliver asks for more.

Encapsulated Stamp Card: On black card 4¼ × 6 in, encapsulated in perspex

Imprimaturs from the NPM or BPA
Imperforate, no watermark

Nos. W187/W190 *se-tenant* block of four	£4000
5d. cylinder 1A, 1B, 3C, 1D, 1E, 1F, 1G, P4 block of eight	£9000
Nos. W191 single	£1000
1s.6d. "Retouch in slope" R. 1/18	£1500
1s.6d. "Extra road" variety R. 6/8	£1500
1s.6d. cylinder 1A, 1B, 1C, 1D, 1E, P3 block of four	£5000

Quantities Sold
5d.	83,472,440
1s.6d.	10,913,360
Pack	113,770

Withdrawn: 3.6.71

W 1970 British Commonwealth Games.

Type **W192**. Runners

Type **W193**. Swimmers

Type **W194**. Cyclists

(Des. Andrew Restall)

(Lithography by De La Rue)

1970 (15 July). **British Commonwealth Games.** Comb perforation 13½×14. Two phosphor bands applied by letterpress. Type **W192/W194**

These were issued on the eve of the Ninth British Commonwealth Games which were held in Edinburgh. Like the Post Office Technology issue these were printed in lithography by De La Rue.

W192 =S.G 832		Mint	Used
5d.	pink, emerald, greenish yellow and deep yellow-green	10	10
a.	Greenish yellow omitted	—	
b.	Phosphor omitted	£200	
c.	Error. One diagonal broad band at right	55·00	
W193 =SG 833			
1s.6d.	light greenish blue, lilac, bistre-brown and Prussian blue	15	15
a.	Phosphor omitted	60·00	
W194 =SG 834			
1s.9d.	yellow-orange, lilac, salmon and deep red-brown	15	15
First Day Cover (W192/W194)			75
Presentation Pack (W192/W194)		3·00	

Pack also exists with a Dutch, German or Japanese insert card

Plate Numbers (Blocks of Four)

		Perforation Type F (L) (I/E)	
Plate Nos.		No dot	Dot
5d.	1A (yellow)–1B (emerald)–1C (pink)–1D (green)	1·00	1·00
	2A–1B–1C–1D	1·00	1·00
1s.6d.	1A (bistre-brown)–1B (greenish blue)–1C (lilac)–1D (indigo)	1·25	1·25
	2A–2B–2C–2D	1·25	1·25

		Perforation Type F (L) (I/E)	
Plate Nos.		No dot	Dot
1s.9d.	1A (salmon)–1B (lilac)–1C (yellow-orange)1D (red brown)	1·25	1·25
	1A–2B–1C–1D	1·25	1·25

Minor Constant Flaws
The notes relating to minor flaws in lithographed stamps under the 1969 Post Office Technology issue also apply here.

Sheet Details
  Sheet size: 120 (10×12). Double-pane sheet-fed with no dot pane at top and dot pane below

Sheet markings:
Plate numbers: Opposite rows 1/2, left margin, unboxed
Guide holes: Above and below vertical row 4 in crossed box on no dot pane and below vertical row 4 in crossed box on dot pane; the reserve box in top margin was not used. In addition reserve guide-hole boxes appear above and below vertical row 6 in both panes but these were not used
Marginal arrows (solid): "W" shaped, at top, bottom and sides
Marginal rule: None
Colour register marks: Below vertical rows 1 and 12 and in right-hand margin opposite rows 1 and 12 in both panes; in addition, they occur in the left-hand margin opposite row 12 in the no dot pane
Coloured crosses, Autotron marks, Colour designations: None
Sheet values: Above and below vertical rows 2/4 and 7/9 reading left to right in top margin and right to left (upside down) in bottom margin
Traffic lights (unboxed): Opposite rows 9/10, right margin in same order as plate numbers
Encapsulated Stamp Card: On black card 4¼×6 in, encapsulated in perspex

Imprimaturs from the NPM or BPMA
Nos. W192/W194 imperforate

No watermark (set of 3)	£3000
5d. cylinder 1A, 1B, 1C, 1D (dot) block of four	£5000
1s.6d. cylinder 1A, 1B, 1C, 1D (no dot) block of four	£5000
1s.9d. cylinder 1A, 1B, 1C, 1D (dot) block of four	£5000

Quantities Sold:

5d.	75,255,440
1s.6d.	10,909,760
1s.9d.	6,303,800
Pack	114,209

Withdrawn: 15.7.71

1970 (14 September). **Collectors Pack 1970**

WCP3	Comprises Nos. W171/W194	15·00

This pack also exists with a German or Japanese insert card.

Quantity Sold: 54,768

Withdrawn: 13.9.71

Philympia 70 Stamp Exhibition. 1970

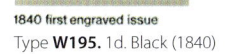

Type W195. 1d. Black (1840)

Type W196. 1s. Green (1847)

Type W197. 4d. Carmine (1855)

(Des. David Gentleman)

1970 *(18 September).* **Philympia 70 Stamp Exhibition.** Two phosphor bands. Types W195/W197

Issued for the opening of the International Philatelic Exhibition held at the Olympia Exhibition Hall, London. The 5d. depicts the first adhesive postage stamp ever issued, the famous Penny Black. This is shown with the check letters "P" and "L" for Philympia and London. The 9d. and 1s.6d. show the first Great Britain stamps using the embossed and surface-printed processes respectively.

W195 =SG 835		Mint	Used
5d.	grey-black, brownish bistre, black and dull purple	10	10
a.	Dull purple (Queen's head) omitted	—	
b.	Phosphor omitted*	5·00	
c.	Error. One broad phosphor band	25·00	
d.	White blob (No dot, R. 5/6)	30·00	
e.	Weak entry (Dot, R. 1/2)	25·00	
W196 =SG 836			
9d.	light drab, bluish green, stone, black and dull purple	15	15
a.	Phosphor omitted	12·00	
W197 =SG 837			
1s.6d.	carmine, light drab, black and dull purple	20	20
a.	Phosphor omitted	4·00	
b.	Missing dot over i (R. 6/12)	30·00	
First Day Cover (W195/W197)			75
Presentation Pack (W195/W197)		3·00	

Pack also exists with a Dutch, German or Japanese insert card

The 5d. is known postmarked at Boughton, King's Lynn on 17 September.

* The phosphor is sometimes difficult to see on the 5d. due to dry prints so care is needed in identifying true missing phosphors.

W195d Large white blob between "OS" of "POSTAGE" (later retouched)

W195e Weak entry of frameline in top left corner

In No. W197b the dot is missing over the "i" of "printed"

Cylinder Numbers (Blocks of Four)

		Perforation Types		
		A (T)	(I/E)	A (P/E)
Cylinder Nos.		No dot	Dot	No dot
5d.	1A (black)–1B (dull purple)–1C (brownish bistre)–1D (grey-black)–P6 (phosphor)	1·00	1·00	†
9d.	1A (black)–1B (stone)–2C (bluish green)–1D (dull purple)–1E (light drab)–P10 (phosphor)		†	1·25
1s.6d.	1A (black)–1B (light drab)–1C (dull purple)–1D (carmine)–P5 (phosphor)		†	1·50

Perforation Types A and A (T) of the above are with sheets orientated showing head to right.

Minor Constant Flaw
1s.6d Cyls. 1A–1B–1C–1D–P5 no dot
  1/1 Frame flaw below "N" of "PENCE"

Sheet Details
  Sheet size: 120 (12×10).
    5d. double-pane reel-fed with no dot pane above dot pane
    Others: Single-pane sheet-fed

Sheet markings:

Cylinder numbers: Opposite row 9, left margin, boxed but the phosphor number is opposite row 10, left margin

Guide holes:
    5d. Above and below vertical row 6 (boxed).
    Others: None

Marginal arrows (photo-etched):
"W" shaped, at top, bottom and sides

Marginal rule: None

Colour register marks:
    5d. None.
    Others: Above and below vertical rows 1 and 10/11

Coloured crosses:
    5d. None.
    Others: Above and below vertical rows 3/4

Autotron marks and Colour designations: None

Sheet values: Opposite rows 2/4 and 7/9 at both sides, reading up at left and down at right

Traffic lights (boxed):
    5d. Dull purple, black, brownish bistre, grey-black opposite row 10 right margin; also in same order reading from left to right above vertical rows 11/12
    9d. Bluish green, stone, dull purple, black, light drab opposite row 10 right margin; also in same order reading from left to right above vertical rows 11/12

W 1970 *Christmas.*

1s.6d. Light drab, dull purple; carmine, black opposite 9/10 right margin; also in reverse order reading from left to right above vertical row 12

Encapsulated Stamp Card: On black card 3⁷/₈ × 5¾ in, encapsulated in perspex

Imprimaturs from the NPM or BPMA
Nos. W195/W197 imperforate

No watermark (*set of* 3)	£3000
5d. "Weak entry" R. 1/2	£1500
5d. cylinder 1A, 1B, 1C, 1D, P6 (dot) block of four	£5000
9d. cylinder 1A, 1B, 2C, 1D, 1E, P10 block of four	£5000
1s.6d. cylinder 1A, 1B, 1C, 1D, P5 block of four	£5000

Quantities Sold:

5d.	72,211,000
9d.	16,330,000
1s.6d.	15,203,836

Withdrawn: 18.9.71

Type **W198**. Shepherds and Apparition of the Angel

Type **W199**. Mary, Joseph and Christ in the Manger

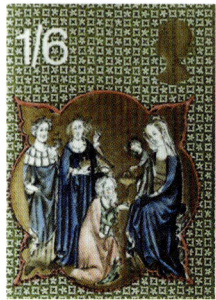

Type **W200**. The Wise Men bearing Gifts

(Des. Sally Stiff)

(Printed in photogravure with the Queen's head in gold and then embossed)

1970 (25 November). **Christmas.** One central 4 mm. phosphor band (4d.) or two phosphor bands (others). Types **W198/W200**

The designs depict traditional Nativity scenes taken from the De Lisle Psalter in the Arundel Collection at the British Museum.

The 4d. stamps were printed by the Wood machine which has a capacity for ten cylinders. Eight were used for the colours and the others for simultaneous application of the embossing and phosphor bands.

W198 =SG 838		Mint	Used
4d	brown-red, blue, turquoise-green, pale chestnut, brown, grey-black, gold and vermilion	10	10
a.	Embossing omitted	50·00	
b.	Phosphor omitted	60·00	
c.	Error. Two side bands	30·00	
ca	Error. Band at left or right	20·00	
d.	Imperf, between stamp and left margin	£375	
e.	Thinned frame (No dot, R. 4/6)	28·00	
W199 =SG 839			
5d.	emerald, gold, blue, brown-red, ochre, grey-black and violet	10	10
a.	Gold (Queen's head) omitted	†	£3500
b.	Emerald omitted	£140	
c.	Imperforate (pair)	£400	
d.	Embossing omitted	15·00	
e.	Phosphor omitted	5·00	
f.	Ochre omitted	£5500	†

Christmas. **1970**

W200 =SG 840

1s.6d.	gold, grey-black, pale turquoise-green, salmon, ultramarine, ochre, red and yellow-green	15	15
a.	Salmon omitted	£220	
b.	Ochre omitted	£140	
c.	Embossing and phosphor omitted	60.00	
d.	Embossing omitted	35.00	
e.	Phosphor omitted	5.00	
f.	Error. One broad band	40.00	

First Day Cover (W199/W200)	40
Presentation Pack (W199/W200)	4.00

Pack also exists with a Dutch, German or Japanese insert card

A red slip-in wallet bearing the Royal Arms and inscribed "Christmas 1970" was issued with the "Scandinavia 71" special pack produced for sale during a visit to six cities in Denmark, Sweden and Norway by a mobile display unit between 15 April and 20 May 1971. Due to the moratorium on commemoratives at the time of the introduction of decimal issues, these 1970 £.s.d. Christmas stamps were the only recent commemoratives on sale at special counters etc. which could be offered for sale in Scandinavia alongside the decimal definitives.

W198e
Gold frame at right by shepherd's arm is thinned and has been strengthened by two parallel chestnut lines

Cylinder Numbers (4d. Blocks of Ten; Others Blocks of Six)

		Perforation Type A (P/E)	
	Cylinder Nos.	No dot	Dot
4d.	1A (vermilion)–1B (grey-black)–1C (brown)–1D (brown-red)–1E (turquoise-green)–1F (blue)–1G (pale chestnut)–1J (gold)–P9 (phosphor)	1·75	1·75
5d.	1A (violet)–1B (brown-red)–1C (blue)–1D (ochre)–3E (grey-black)–1F (emerald)–1G (gold)–P7 (phosphor)	1·25	†
1s.6d.	1A (yellow-green)–1B (grey-black)–1D (red)–1E (salmon)–1F (pale turquoise-green)–1G (gold)–1J (ochre)–1C (ultramarine)–P7 (phosphor)	1·75	†

Perforation Type A on the above are with sheets orientated showing head to right.
On some sheets of the 4d. the J is completely omitted.

Minor Constant Flaws
4d. Cyls. 1A–1B–1C–1D–1E–1F–1G–1J–P9 no dot
  5/5 Dotted line across central shepherd's temple and through hair (Th. G6–7)
5d. Cyls. 1A–1B–1C–1D–3E–1F–1G–P7 no dot
  8/8 Diagonal line over Mary's left hand (Th. J3)
1s.6d. Cyls. 1A–1B–1D–1E–1F–1G–1J–1C–P7 no dot
  1/12 Horizontal scratch across cloaks of Three Wise Men (Th. K2–6)

The Thirkell Position Finder readings are taken with the finder over the perforations.

Sheet Details
  Sheet size: 120 (12×10).
    4d. double-pane reel-fed with no dot pane above dot pane
    Others: Single-pane sheet-fed
Sheet markings:
Cylinder numbers:
    4d. Bottom margin, unboxed, reading down below vertical rows 5/2
    5d. Opposite rows 8/9, left margin, boxed but the phosphor number is opposite row 10, left margin
  1s.6d. Opposite rows 8/10, left margin, boxed. The 1C was added at the bottom opposite row 10
Guide holes:
    4d. Above and below vertical row 6 (boxed).
    Others: None
Marginal arrows (photo-etched):
"W" shaped, at top, bottom and sides
Marginal rule: None
Colour register marks:
    4d. Above and below vertical rows 2/5.
    Others: Above and below vertical rows 1/2 and 12
Autotron marks and Colour designations: None
Coloured crosses:
    4d. None.
    Others: Above and below vertical rows 3/4
Sheet values: Opposite rows 2/4 at both sides and rows 7/8 at left and 7/9 at right, reading up at left and down at right
Traffic lights (boxed):
    4d. Vermilion, grey-black, brown, brown-red, turquoise-green, blue, pale chestnut, gold, embossing* opposite rows 9/10 right margin; also in same order reading from left to right above vertical rows 11/12
    5d. Violet, brown-red, blue, ochre, grey-black, emerald, gold, embossing opposite rows 9/10 right margin; also in same order reading from left to right above vertical rows 10/11
  1s.6d. Yellow-green, grey-black, ultramarine; red, salmon, pale turquoise-green, gold, ochre, embossing; also in same order reading from left to right above vertical rows 9/11
* The embossing is usually very faint on the 4d. traffic lights.

Encapsulated stamp card: On black card 4×5¼ in, encapsulated in perspex
Imprimaturs from the NPM or BPMA
Nos. W198/W200 imperforate

No watermark (set of 3)	£3000
5d. cylinder 1A, 1B, 1C, 1D, 3E, 1F, 1G, P7 block of four	£5000
1s.6d. cylinder 1A, 1B, 1C, 1D, 1E, 1F, 1G, 1J, P7 block of four	£5000

Quantities Sold:
	4d.	360,016,216
	5d.	181,161,720
	1s.6d	22,598,520

Withdrawn: 25.11.71

Section XA
Regional £.s.d. Issues
1958–1970. Photogravure

General Notes

Introduction. On 18 August 1958 the first Great Britain Regional issues were put on sale for use in Northern Ireland, Scotland and Wales (including Monmouthshire) and in the islands of Guernsey, Jersey and the Isle of Man. The ordinary postage stamps of Great Britain in the same values were not on sale at post offices in these regions except at the Philatelic Counters in Belfast, Cardiff, Edinburgh and Glasgow, apart from Monmouthshire where the Welsh Regionals and Great Britain postage stamps were on sale concurrently.

Although specifically issued for regional use, these issues were initially valid for use throughout Great Britain. However, they ceased to be valid in Guernsey and Jersey from 1 October 1969 when these islands each established their own independent postal administrations and introduced their own stamps. Guernsey and Jersey Regionals were withdrawn locally on 30 September 1969 but remained on sale at British Philatelic Counters until 30 September 1970.

Following the practice set by Great Britain, these issues do not bear the names of the regions, these being indicated by various devices and symbols which relate to them. The three island issues are inscribed Postage only and had no usage as revenue stamps as they have their own Parliaments.

The portrait used is by Dorothy Wilding, Ltd.

Printers. All the £.s.d. Regional issues were printed in photogravure by Harrison & Sons on continuous reels of paper on the web. The 3d., 4d. and 5d. values of Northern Ireland, Scotland and Wales and Monmouthshire were printed in double pane width, i.e. 480 stamps consisting of two panes (no dot and dot) each of 240 stamps arranged in 20 rows of 12 stamps, the panes being guillotined before issue. All the island issues and the 6d., 9d., 1s.3d. and 1s.6d. values from the other regions were made from single cylinders printing sheets of 240 stamps (i.e. no dot panes only).

Paper and watermark. As with the Wilding definitives, for the first few years the Regional issues were printed on a creamy paper but starting in February 1962 a whiter paper was gradually introduced as new printings were made. See the General Notes for Section S for further information. Exceptionally, a chalk-surfaced paper was used for a printing of the Isle of Man 3d. in 1963.

Crowns
W.**24**

Only the Crowns watermark, type W.**24** was used for the Regional issues. From 1967 new printings of a number of values were on the chalk-surfaced paper without watermark, as used for the Machin definitives.

Gum. Gum arabic was used from 1958 to 1968 after which PVA gum was introduced. The distinction between gum arabic and PVA gum is explained in the General Notes to Section U. It is worth noting that gum arabic was used on the creamy, white and unwatermarked chalk-surfaced papers but that PVA gum exists only on the last of these.

Perforation. Harrisons used the same 15×14 comb perforation as for the Wilding definitives. A number of different perforators were used and these are described and illustrated in Appendix G. The following listings include abbreviations for the side and horizontal margins of the listed block so that the first letter refers to the left margin and the second to the bottom margin. See page 2 under Notes in Section S.

Phosphor bands. See the General Notes for Section S for a detailed description of these. In the Regional issues it is sufficient to state that these were applied as follows:

Blue 8 mm bands: 1963–1964
Violet 8 mm bands: 1965–1966
Violet 9·5 mm bands: 1967–1970

The one centre band stamps in the violet period were always 4 mm bands.

Phosphor omitted. A number of values have appeared with the phosphor bands omitted in error and these are listed separately. All values are believed to have had the bands applied in photogravure.

Misplaced Bands. The instances of misplaced bands in the regionals is unusual. One broad (9·5mm) instead of two bands are listed and one (No. XG8b) with horizontal band is recorded under Guernsey.

Dates of issue. Conflicting dates of issue have been announced for some of the issues, partly explained by their being released on different dates by the Philatelic Bureau in Edinburgh or the Philatelic Counter in London and in the regions. We give the earliest date, since once released the stamps could have been used anywhere in the UK

First Day Covers. Prices for these are now quoted, whether or not there was a specific service provided by the Post Office. These are listed at the end of each region.

Presentation Packs. The pack containing stamps from the six regions is listed after Wales and Monmouthshire. The other packs are listed at the end of each region.

Sheet Markings. Reference should be made to the descriptions of sheet markings given in the General Notes for Sections S and U, as most of them apply to this Section and the information given there is not repeated here. Additional information is given below.

Cylinder Numbers. In the Regional issues these appear in the left-hand margin opposite Row 18 No. 1 (R. 18/1) in the style as illustrated in Section S.

Phosphor Cylinder Numbers. The notes in the General Notes for Section U £.s.d. Low Values also apply here but they are only found on the Scottish 5d. No. XS15 and Welsh 5d. No. XW10.

Marginal Arrows. In the Regional issues these are "W" shaped (photo-etched) at top, bottom and sides, except for the Jersey and Isle of Man 3d. and the Northern Ireland, Scotland and Wales and Monmouthshire 3d., 6d. and 1s.3d. which are all "V" shaped (hand-engraved) at top and bottom of the sheet and "W" shaped (photo-etched) at both sides (only cyl. 4 Scotland 1s.3d.).

Perforation Guide Holes. Perforation guide holes which relate to the perforator employed appear in the sheet margins. Refer to the descriptions given for Section U at the end of the General Notes where an illustration of the box associated with perforator type F(L)* appears. Perforator types are given under

Cylinder Block listings and further details will be found under Appendix G.

Cancelled Overprint. No. XW5 exists overprinted "CANCELLED" as part of the test programme carried out by the Forensic Department of the Post Office.

Withdrawal Dates. All £.s.d. Regional issues, not previously withdrawn, were taken off sale at the Post Office Philatelic Counters on 25 November 1971 and were invalidated as from 1 March 1972.

*Prices for Cylinder Blocks with Asterisks
These denote cylinder blocks containing a listed variety and the price includes the variety.

XA GUERNSEY

GUERNSEY

Type **XG1**
(Des. E. A. Piprell)

Type **XG2**

2½d. Type XG1 (1964)

1964 (8 June). **2½d.** Watermark Crowns

XG1 =SG 6		Mint	Used
2½d.	(1) Pale rose-red (Cyl. 1)	1·00	1·00
	(2) Rose-red (Cyl. 3)	40	40

Cylinder Numbers (Blocks of Six)
Single-pane cylinders. Perforation Type F (L) (I/E)

Cylinder No.	No Dot
1	12·00
3	4·00

Minor Constant Flaws

Cyl. 1	1/4	Small retouch over "TA"
	1/5	White patch over left part of diadem to left of central cross (Th.A3)
	17/12	Background disturbance in top loop of left-hand ribboning (Th.B1)
	19/2	White patch below left leg of "R"
Cyl. 3	17/5	Dark spot under topmost tip of ribboning at right (Th.B6)
	17/12	and 19/2. As on cyl. 1 (multipositive flaws)

Quantity Sold: 3,485,760 including 10,100 on First Day Covers
Withdrawn: 31.8.66

3d. Type XG2 (1958–1962)

1958 (18 August). **3d.** Watermark Crowns

A. Cream Paper

XG2		Mint	Used
3d.	Deep lilac	1·00	50

B. White Paper (5 July 1962)

XG3 =SG 7		Mint	Used
3d.	Deep lilac	30	30

Cylinder Numbers (Blocks of Six)

Cream Paper (No XG2) — Perforation Types

Cylinder No. (No Dot)	B(I/P)	C (E/P)
4	15·00	15·00

Whiter Paper (No XG3) — Perforation Types

Cylinder No. (No Dot)	B(I/P)	C (E/P)	F(L)(I/E)
4	5·00	5·00	5·00
5	†	†	4·75

Minor Constant Flaws

Cyl. 5	4/1	Background scratch above right-hand petal (Th.C–D2)
	7/10	Dark spot in left-hand margin (opposite Th.C1)
	9/10	Pale scratch in background from petal at far right down to Queen's chin (Th.D–E3)
	11/11	Diagonal background scratch from base of lily's stem to base of Queen's neck (Th.F3–E4)
	13/1	Flaw in background above centre stamen of lily (Th.C2)
	18/6	Smudge in background near Queen's mouth (Th.D3)

Quantity Sold: 25,812,360
Sold Out: 6.3.68

1967 (24 May). **3d.** One centre phosphor band reacting violet. Watermark Crowns

XG4 =SG 7p		Mint	Used
3d.	(1) Deep lilac	30	30
	(2) Deep reddish lilac	60	40

Cylinder Number (Block of Six)
Single-pane cylinder. Perforation Type F (L) (I/E)

Cylinder No.	No Dot
5	4·75

Minor Constant Flaws
As for flaws on Cyl. 5 of No. XG3

Sold Out: 11.68

4d. Type XG2 (1966–1969)

1966 (7 February). **4d.** Watermark Crowns

XG5 =SG 8		Mint	Used
4d.	Ultramarine	40	40
a.	Stem flaw (R. 12/8)	25·00	

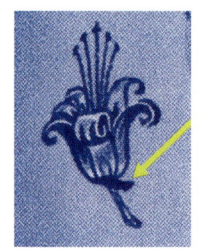

Coloured line across top of stem

XG5a, XG6a, XG7b, XG8c

Cylinder Number (Block of Six)
Single-pane cylinder. Perforation Type F (L) (I/E)

Cylinder No.	No Dot
1	5·00

Minor Constant Flaws

Cyl. 1	1/1	Small spot above centre stamen of lily (Th.C2)
	9/5	White dot between two stamens on left-hand side (Th.D2)
	13/4	White spot on right-hand petal (Th.D3)
	20/12	Pale flaw in background to right of central diadem (Th.A5)

These are generally more marked on later issues from this cylinder.

Quantity Sold: 4,415,040 including 12,350 on First Day Covers
Sold Out: 6.3.68

262

GUERNSEY XA

1967 *(2 October).* **4d.** Two 9·5 mm. phosphor bands reacting violet. Watermark Crowns

XG6 =SG 8p	Mint	Used
4d. Ultramarine	20	20
a. Stem flaw (R. 12/8)	25·00	

For illustration of No. XG6a, see No. XG5a.

Cylinder Number (Block of Six)
Single-pane cylinder. Perforation Type F (L) (I/E)

Cylinder No.	No Dot
1	4·50

Minor Constant Flaws
Cyl. 1	5/10	Circular background retouch below Queen's chin (Th.E4)
	16/12	Break in centre stamen (Th.C–D2)
	17/10	Break in second stamen from left (Th.C2)

Others: As on No. XG5

Sold Out: 10.68

1968 *(16 April*).* **4d.** No watermark. Chalk-surfaced paper. PVA Gum. Two 9·5 mm phosphor bands reacting violet

XG7 =SG 9	Mint	Used
4d. Pale ultramarine	20	20
a. Phosphor omitted	50·00	
b. Stem flaw (R. 12/8)	25·00	

* This was not issued in Guernsey until 22 April.
For illustration of No. XG7b, see No. XG5a.

Cylinder Number (Block of Six)
Single-pane cylinder. Perforation Type F (L) (I/E)

Cylinder No.	No Dot
1	4·00

Minor Constant Flaws
| Cyl. 1 | 2/8 | Weak patch in background at upper left (Th.A1) |
| | 19/6 | Small retouch between "A" and "G" |

Others: As on Nos. XG5 and XG6

Sold Out: 3.69

1968 *(4 September).* **4d.** Change of colour. No watermark. Chalk-surfaced paper. PVA Gum. One centre phosphor band reacting violet

XG8 =SG 10	Mint	Used
4d. Olive-sepia	20	20
a. Phosphor omitted	50·00	
b. Error. Phosphor horizontal	£150	
c. Stem flaw (R. 12/8)	25·00	
d. Retouched "4" (R. 16/10)	25·00	

For illustration of No. XG8c, see No. XG5a.

XG8d

Spot over "4" has been retouched
Corrected on No. XG9

Cylinder Number (Block of Six)
Single-pane cylinder. Perforation Type F (L) (I/E)

Cylinder No.	No Dot
1	4·00

Minor Constant Flaws
As for No. XG7 except that flaw on R. 5/10 does not show

Withdrawn: 30.9.70

1969 *(26 February).* **4d.** Further change of colour. No watermark. Chalk-surfaced paper. PVA gum. One centre phosphor band reacting violet

XG9 =SG 11	Mint	Used
4d. Bright vermilion	20	20
a. Stem flaw retouched (R. 12/8)	25·00	

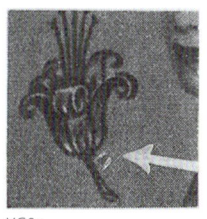

XG9a

The stem flaw has been retouched but still shows as a smudge to right of stem

Cylinder Number (Block of Six)
Single-pane cylinder. Perforation Type F (L) (I/E)

Cylinder No.	No Dot
1	4·00

Minor Constant Flaws: As for No. XG8

Withdrawn: 30.9.70

5d. Type XG2 (1968)

1968 *(4 September).* **5d.** No watermark. Chalk-surfaced paper. PVA gum. Two 9·5 mm phosphor bands reacting violet

XG10 =SG 12	Mint	Used
5d. Royal blue	30	30
a. Stamen flaw (R. 12/1)	25·00	
b. Retouched	25·00	

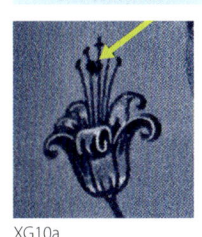

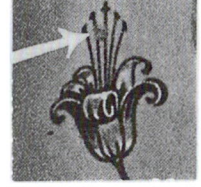

XG10a

XG10b
Still visible after retouch on late printing

Cylinder Number (Block of Six)
Single-pane cylinder. Perforation Type F (L) (I/E)

Cylinder No.	No Dot
1	4·75

Minor Constant Flaw
| Cyl. 1 | 12/6 | Small white flaw to left of Queen's mouth (Th.D3) |

Withdrawn: 30.9.70

XA GUERNSEY, ISLE OF MAN

First Day Covers
(Guernsey)

18.8.58	3d.	20·00
8.6.64	2½d.	30·00
7.2.66	4d. ultramarine	8·00
4.9.68	4d. olive-sepia, 5d.	3·00

INVALIDATION. The regional issues for Guernsey were invalidated for use in Guernsey and Jersey on 30 September 1969 but remained valid for use in the rest of the United Kingdom. Those still current remained on sale at philatelic sales counters until 30 September 1970.

Imprimaturs from the NPM or BPMA
Imperforate, watermark Type W.24

2½d	£800
2½d. cylinder 1 block of six	£5500
3d. (cream paper)	£800
3d. (cream paper) cylinder 4 block of six	£5500
3d. (whiter paper)	£800
3d. (whiter paper) cylinder 4 block of six	£5500

ISLE OF MAN

Type **XM1**

Type **XM2**

(Des. J. H. Nicholson)

2½d. Type XM1 (1964)

1964 (8 June). **2½d.** Watermark Crowns

XM1 =SG 1	Mint	Used
2½d. Carmine-red	70	70

Cylinder Number (Block of Six)
Single-pane cylinder. Perforation Type F (L) (I/E)

Cylinder No.		No Dot
1		10·00

Minor Constant Flaw
Cyl. 1   11/1   Red dot to right of lower cross of crown (Th.C5)

Quantity Sold: 4,298,160 including 9,237 on First Day Covers

Withdrawn: 31.8.66

3d. Type XM2 (1958–1968)

1958 (18 August). **3d.** Watermark Crowns

A. Cream Paper

XM2	Mint	Used
3d. Deep lilac	1·00	50

B. Chalk-surfaced Paper (17 May 1963)

XM3 =SG 2a

3d. Deep lilac	6·50	6·50

C. Whiter Paper (1963)

XM4 =SG 2

3d. Deep lilac	50	50

No. XM3 was released in London sometime after 17 May 1963.
 The paper used for No. XM3 was the residue of the heavy chalk-surfaced paper remaining from the 1961 Post Office Savings Bank Centenary issue.

Cylinder Numbers (Blocks of Six)

Cream paper No. XM2   Perforation Types

Cylinder No. (No Dot)	B(I/P)	C (E/P)
1	10·00	10·00

Chalk-surfaced paper No. XM3

Cylinder No. (No Dot)	J(I/P)
1	£100

Whiter paper No. XM4

Cylinder No. (No Dot)	F (L) (I/E)
1	7·50

Minor Constant Flaw
Cyl. 1   19/6   Fine curved line to right of second link from bottom at left (Th.G1)

ISLE OF MAN XA

Quantity Sold: 35,959,420 up to 31.3.68 and including 1,080,000 on chalk-surfaced paper (No. XM3)

Sold Out: 12.68

1968 (27 June). **3d.** One centre phosphor band reacting violet. Watermark Crowns

XM5 =SG 2p	Mint	Used
3d. Deep lilac	20	20

This issue is known postmarked at Douglas, Isle of Man, on 19 June 1968.

Cylinder Number (Block of Six)
Single-pane cylinder. Perforation Type F (L) (I/E)

Cylinder No.	No Dot
1	4·00

Minor Constant Flaws: As for Nos. XM2/4

Sold Out: 4.69

4d. Type XM2 (1966–1969)

1966 (7 February). **4d.** Watermark Crowns

XM6 =SG 3	Mint	Used
4d. Ultramarine	1·00	1·00

Cylinder Number (Block of Six)
Single-pane cylinder. Perforation Type F (L) (I/E)

Cylinder No.	No Dot
1	10·00

Minor Constant Flaws

Cyl. 1	7/12	Fine line from top of diadem to inner frame at right (Th.B–35)
	8/7	Coloured dot left of inner frame line at right (Th.C5–6)
	17/1	Coloured scratches below Queen's left eye (Th.D3–4)
	19/1	Coloured scratch behind Queen's neck (Th.F5)

Quantity Sold: 4,353,840 including 7,553 on First Day Covers

Sold Out: 11.67

1967 (5 July). **4d.** Two 9·5 mm phosphor bands reacting violet. Watermark Crowns

XM7 =SG 3p	Mint	Used
4d. Ultramarine	30	30

Cylinder Number (Block of Six)
Single-pane cylinder. Perforation Type F (L) (I/E)

Cylinder No.	No Dot
1	4·50

Minor Constant Flaws: As for No. XM6

Sold Out: 12.68

1968 (24 June). **4d.** No watermark. Chalk-surfaced paper. PVA gum. Two 9·5 mm phosphor bands reacting violet

XM8 =SG 4	Mint	Used
4d. Blue	25	25

Cylinder Number (Block of Six)
Single-pane cylinder Perforation Type F (L) (I/E)

Cylinder No.	No Dot
1	4·25

Minor Constant Flaws

| Cyl. 1 | 6/7 | Flaw behind lower cross of diadem (Th.D5) |
| | 14/2 | White background spot just above Queen's right eye (Th.C–D2) |

Others as for No. XM6

Sold Out: 16.7.69

1968 (4 September). **4d.** Change of colour. No watermark. Chalk-surfaced paper. PVA Gum. One centre phosphor band reacting violet

XM9 =SG 5	Mint	Used
4d. Olive-sepia	30	30
a. Phosphor omitted	25·00	

Cylinder Number (Block of Six)
Single-pane cylinder. Perforation Type F (L) (I/E)

Cylinder No.	No Dot
1	4·25

Minor Constant Flaws: As for No. XM8

1969 (26 February). **4d.** Further change of colour. No watermark. Chalk-surfaced paper. PVA gum. One centre phosphor band reacting violet

XM10 =SG 6	Mint	Used
4d. Bright vermilion	45	45

Cylinder Number (Block of Six)
Single-pane cylinder. Perforation Type F (L) (I/E)

Cylinder No.	No Dot
1	5·50

Minor Constant Flaws
As for No. XM8

5d. Type XM2 (1968)

1968 (4 September). **5d.** No watermark. Chalk-surfaced paper. PVA gum. Two 9·5 mm phosphor bands reacting violet

XM11 =SG 7	Mint	Used
5d. Royal blue	45	45
a. Phosphor omitted	£175	
b. Error. Single broad band	50·00	
c. Frame flaw (top right) (R. 20/1)	25·00	
d. Frame flaw (bottom left) (R. 20/12)	25·00	

XA ISLE OF MAN, JERSEY

XM11c

XM11d

Cylinder Number (Block of Six)
Single-pane cylinder. Perforation Type F (L) (I/E)

Cylinder No.	No Dot
1	28·00

First Day Covers
(Isle of Man)

18.8.58	3d.	32·00
8.6.64	2½d.	45·00
7.2.66	4d. ultramarine	15·00
4.9.68	4d. olive-sepia, 5d.	4·00

Imprimaturs from the NPM or BPMA
Imperforate, watermark Type W.24

3d. (cream paper)	£800
3d. (cream paper) cylinder 1 block of six	£5500
3d. (whiter paper)	£800
3d. (whiter paper) cylinder 1 block of six	£5500

JERSEY

Type **XJ1**

(Des. Edmund Blampied)

Type **XJ2**

(Des. William M. Gardner)

2½d. Type XJ1 (1964)

1964 *(8 June).* **2½d.** Watermark Crowns

XJ1 =SG 9	Mint	Used
2½d Carmine-red	45	45
a. Imperf. three sides (pair)	£3250	
b. Thin "POSTAGE" (R. 18/1)	25·00	

Normal   XJ1b

Letters of "POSTAGE" are thinner, resulting in more white showing in the "O" and "G"

Cylinder Number (Block of Six)
Single-pane cylinder. Perforation Type F (L) (I/E)

Cylinder No.	No Dot
1	28·00*

Minor Constant Flaws
| Cyl. 1 | 11/1 | Two tiny dots on Queen's nose |
| | 18/2 | Spot to right of mace level with "O" of "POSTAGE" |

Quantity Sold: 4,770,000 including 12,800 on First Day Covers

Withdrawn: 31.8.66

3d. Type XJ2 (1958–1967)

1958 *(18 August).* **3d.** Watermark Crowns

A. Cream Paper

XJ2	Mint	Used
3d. Deep lilac	1·00	50
a. Joined tomato (Cyl. 1, R. 19/9)	25·00	
b. Halberd flaw (Cyl. 1, R. 20/3)	25·00	

B. Whiter Paper *(23 September 1962)*

XJ3 =SG 10		
3d. Deep lilac	30	30
a. Scratched collar (Cyl. 2, R. 9/8)	25·00	

266

JERSEY XA

XJ2a **XJ2b**

Both these varieties were later retouched to normal

XJ3a, XJ4a

Cylinder Numbers (Blocks of Six)

Cream Paper (No XJ2)

Cylinder No. (No Dot)	Perforation Types	
	B(I/P)	C (E/P)
1	10·00	10·00

Whiter Paper (No XJ3)

Cylinder No. (No Dot)	Perforation Types		
	B(I/P)	C (E/P)	F(L)(I/E)
1	4·75	4·75	4·75
2	†	†	30·00

Minor Constant Flaws

Cyl. 1	20/4	Short white line extends below left of "D"
Cyl. 2	3/7	Weak background below left-hand berry of middle pair on right-hand plant (Th.E5)
	14/12	Dot in left-hand margin (Opposite Th.D1)
	16/1	Dot on top left leaf of right-hand plant (Th.C5–6)
	16/12	Dot in top margin (Above Th.A4)
	20/3	Dot in top margin (Above Th.A4)

Quantity Sold: 35,169,720

Sold Out: 10.67

1967 (9 June). **3d.** One centre phosphor band reacting violet. Watermark Crowns

XJ4 =SG 10p	Mint	Used
3d. (1) Deep lilac	20	20
(2) Dull reddish lilac	45	30
a. Scratched collar (Cyl. 2, R. 9/8)	25·00	

For illustration of No. XJ4a, see No. XJ3a.

Cylinder Numbers (Blocks of Six)
Single-pane cylinder. Perforation Type F (L) (I/E)

Deep Lilac No XJ4 (1)

Cylinder No.	No Dot
2	4·75

Dull reddish lilac No. XJ4 (2)

2	7·00

Minor Constant Flaws: As for flaws on Cyl. 2 of No. XJ3

Sold Out: 10.68

4d. Type XJ2 (1966–1969)

1966 (7 February). **4d.** Watermark Crowns

XJ5 =SG 11	Mint	Used
4d. Ultramarine	25	25
a. Leaf flaw (R. 3/6)	25·00	
b. Neck flaw (R. 18/9)	25·00	

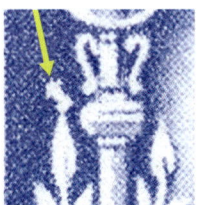

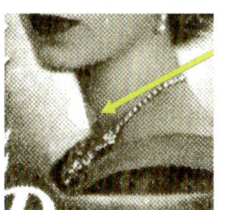

XJ5a
Arrow-like flaw over top leaf at left. Later retouched and only exists retouched on phosphor issues

XJ5b, XJ6a, XJ7b, XJ8a

Cylinder Number (Block of Six)
Single-pane cylinder. Perforation Type F (L) (I/E)

Cylinder No.	No Dot
1	4·25

Minor Constant Flaws

Cyl. 1	3/4	Diagonal scratch under Queen's chin (Th.E2–3)
	3/11	Spot in top margin (close to perf. hole) (Above Th.A4)
	9/10	Slight dent in left-hand frame line (Opposite Th.D–E1)
	11/10	White flaw in background behind Queen's hair (Th.C5)
	15/1	Dark patch in background to left of top leaf on left-hand side of sceptre (Th.D1). This varies in intensity and is particularly strong on No. XJ7.
	15/12	Two small white flaws in front of Queen's collar (Th.F2–3)
	18/8	Break in top frame line (Above Th.A5)
	20/8	Diagonal scratch to right of Queen's left eye (Th.C3–4)

Quantity Sold: 6,623,040 including 14,487 on First Day Covers

Sold Out: 11.67

1967 (5 September). **4d.** Two 9·5 mm phosphor bands reacting violet. Watermark Crowns

XJ6 =SG 11p	Mint	Used
4d. Ultramarine	20	20
a. Neck flaw (R. 18/9)	25·00	

For illustration of No. XJ6a, see No. XJ5b.

Cylinder Number (Block of Six)
Single-pane cylinder. Perforation Type F (L) (I/E)

Cylinder No.	No Dot
1	4·00

Minor Constant Flaws: As for No. XJ5

Sold Out: 10.68

267

XA JERSEY

1968 *(4 September).* **4d.** Change of colour. No watermark. Chalk-surfaced paper. PVA Gum. One centre phosphor band reacting violet

XJ7 =SG 12	Mint	Used
4d. Olive-sepia	20	20
a. Phosphor omitted	£1100	
b. Neck flaw (R. 18/9)	25·00	

For illustration of No. XJ7b, see No. XJ5b.

Cylinder Number (Block of Six)
Single-pane cylinder. Perforation Type F (L) (I/E)

Cylinder No.	No Dot
1	4·00

Minor Constant Flaws: As for No. XJ5

Withdrawn: 30.9.70

1969 *(26 February).* **4d.** Further change of colour. No watermark. Chalk-surfaced paper. PVA Gum. One centre phosphor band reacting violet

XJ8 =SG 13	Mint	Used
4d. Bright vermilion	20	20
a. Neck flaw (R. 18/9)	25·00	

For illustration of No. XJ8a, see No. XJ5b.

Cylinder Number (Block of Six)
Single-pane cylinder. Perforation Type F (L) (I/E)

Cylinder No.	No Dot
1	4·00

Minor Constant Flaws: As for No. XJ5

Withdrawn: 30.9.70

5d. Type XJ2 (1968)

1968 *(4 September).* **5d.** No watermark. Chalk-surfaced paper. PVA Gum. Two 9·5 mm phosphor bands reacting violet

XJ9 =SG 14	Mint	Used
5d. Royal blue	20	20
a. Leaf dot (R. 16/6)	25·00	
b. Shield flaw (R. 19/12)	25·00	

XJ9a
White dot above lowest leaf

XJ9b
Leaf joined to shield

Cylinder Number (Block of Six)
Single-pane cylinder. Perforation Type F (L) (I/E)

Cylinder No.	No Dot
1	4·00

Minor Constant Flaws

Cyl. 1	5/1	Dot in top margin (Above Th.A2)
	6/5	White scratch from back of Queen's collar to back of neck (Th.E–F4)
	9/11	Flaw in background above middle right-hand jewel of sceptre (Th.A2)
	10/4	White scratch extending from Queen's chin to top of "P"
	11/1	Tiny break in left-hand frame line (Th.C1)
	14/12	Small white flaw on Queen's collar (Th.F3–4)
	17/12	Dotted line extending from right of top leaf below flower at right of sceptre across Queen's face and plant at right (Th.E2–6)

Withdrawn: 30.9.70

First Day Covers
(Jersey)

18.8.58	3d.		20·00
8.6.64	2½d.		30·00
7.2.66	4d. ultramarine		10·00
4.9.68	4d. olive-sepia, 5d.		3·00

Invalidation. The regional issues for Jersey were invalidated for use in Jersey or Guernsey on 30 September 1969 but remained valid for use in the rest of the United Kingdom. Those still current remained on sale at philatelic sales counters until 30 September 1970.

Imprimaturs from the NPM or BPMA
Imperforate, watermark Type W.24

2½d.	£800
2½d. cylinder 1. block of six	£5500
3d. (cream paper)	£800
3d. (cream paper) cylinder 1. block of six	£5500
3d. (whiter paper)	£800
3d. (whiter paper) cylinder 1. block of six	£5500

NORTHERN IRELAND

XN1 (Des. W. Hollywood)
XN2 (Des. L. Pilton)
XN3 (Des. T. Collins)

3d. Type XN1 (1958–67)

1958 (18 August). **3d.** Watermark Crowns

A. Cream paper

XN1		Mint	Used
3d.	Deep lilac	1·00	25

B. Whiter Paper (21 May 1962)

XN2 =SG NI1		Mint	Used
3d.	Deep lilac	15	15

Cylinder Numbers (Blocks of Six)

Cream Paper No. XN1
Perforation Type A (E/I)

Cylinder No.	No Dot	Dot
3	10·00	10·00

Whiter Paper No. XN2
Perforation Type A (E/I)

Cylinder No.	No Dot	Dot
3	3·75	3·75

Perforation Type F (L)*

Cylinder No.	No Dot (I/E)	Dot (P/E)
3**	—	—

** This is probably No XN3 with the phosphor omitted.

Minor Constant Flaw

Cyl. 3   4/9   White flaw on edge of lowest flax flower (Th.G2)

Quantity Sold: 375,417,400

Sold Out: 10.67

1967 (9 June). **3d.** One centre phosphor band reacting violet. Watermark Crowns

XN3 =SG NI1p		Mint	Used
3d.	Deep lilac	25	25

Cylinder Numbers (Blocks of Six)

Perforation Type A (E/I)

Cylinder No.	No Dot	Dot
3	4·25	4·25

Perforation Type F (L)*

Cylinder No.	No Dot (I/E)	Dot (P/E)
3	4·25	4·25

Minor Constant Flaw: As for flaw on Nos. XN1/2

4d. Type XN1 (1966–1969)

1966 (7 February). **4d.** Watermark Crowns

XN4 =SG NI2		Mint	Used
4d.	Ultramarine	15	15
a.	Dot on leaf (No dot, R. 3/12)	25·00	
b.	Flower flaw (No dot, R. 7/7)	25·00	
c.	Dot under "S" of "POSTAGE" (Dot R. 2/4)	25·00	

XN4a, XN5a, XN6a, XN7a, XN8b
White dot on leaf of plant. Retouched on No. XN9

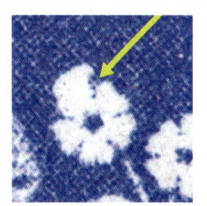

XN4b
White spot on top flower. The above only exists on No. XN4. It was retouched and shows as a dark patch on Nos. XN5b, XN6b, XN7b, XN8c and XN9b

XN4c
White dot under "S" of "POSTAGE". Retouched on No. XN5.

Cylinder Numbers (Blocks of Six)

Perforation Type A (E/I)

Cylinder No.	No Dot	Dot
1	3·75	3·75

Cylinder number: Opposite R.18/1. In addition, early printings of both no dot and dot panes bore a trace of cylinder numbers reading 1A and 1A. with two sides of a box opposite R.19/1. These had been inserted in error. Attempts to remove them were only partially successful, so that they exist in varying degrees of faintness.

Minor Constant Flaws

Cyl. 1	16/5	Small white spot to right of second leaf down on upright flax plant (Th.B6)
Cyl. 1.	2/1	Small coloured projection above upper frame line (Th.A2)
	3/12	Small white dot below lower right leaf of flax plant (Th.G4)
	10/6	Coloured flaw in lower left of badge (Th.E1)
	12/1	Pale patch below "P" of "POSTAGE" (Th.F1)

Quantity Sold: 61,449,360

Sold Out: 11.7.68

269

XA NORTHERN IRELAND

1967 (2 October). **4d.** Two 9·5 mm phosphor bands reacting violet. Watermark Crowns

XN5	=SG NI2p		Mint	Used
4d.	Ultramarine		15	15
	a.	Dot on leaf (No dot, R. 3/12)	25·00	
	b.	Flower flaw retouch (No dot, R. 7/7)	25·00	
	c.	Dot under "s" of "POSTAGE" retouched (Dot R 2/4)	20·00	

For illustration of No. XN5a see No. XN4a.

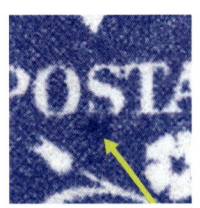

XN5c

Cylinder Numbers (Blocks of Six)
Perforation Type F (L)*

Cylinder No.	No Dot (I/E)	Dot (P/E)
1	3·75	3·75

Minor Constant Flaws
Cyl. 1	16/5	Small white spot to right of second leaf down on upright flax plant (Th.B6)
Cyl. 1.	2/1	Small coloured projection above upper frame line (Th.A2)
	2/4	Dark patch below "S" of "POSTAGE" where former white dot, No. XN4a, existed (Th.F2)
	3/12	Small white dot below lower right leaf of flax plant (Th.G4)
	10/6	Coloured flaw in lower left of badge (Th.E1)
	12/1	Pale patch below "P" of "POSTAGE" (Th.F1)

Sold Out: 1.70

1968 (27 June). **4d.** No watermark. Chalk-surfaced paper. Two 9·5 mm phosphor bands reacting violet

A. Gum Arabic

XN6	=SG NI7		Mint	Used
4d.	Ultramarine		25	25
	a.	Dot on leaf (No dot, R. 3/12)	25·00	
	b.	Flower flaw retouch (No dot, R. 7/7)	25·00	

B. PVA Gum* (23 October 1968)

XN7	=SG NI7Ev			
4d.	Ultramarine		30·00	
	a.	Dot on leaf (No dot, R. 3/12)	50·00	
	b.	Flower flaw retouch (No dot, R. 7/7)	50·00	

For illustration of Nos. XN6a and XN7a and for description of Nos. XN6b and XN7b, see Nos. XN4a/XN4 respectively.

* No. XN7 was never issued in Northern Ireland. After No. XN6 (gum arabic) had been withdrawn from Northern Ireland but whilst still on sale at the philatelic counters elsewhere, about 50 sheets with PVA gum were sold over the London Philatelic counter on 23 October 1968, and some were also on sale at the British Philatelic Exhibition post office.

Cylinder Numbers (Blocks of Six)
Gum Arabic No XN6
Perforation Type A (E/I)

Cylinder No.	No Dot	Dot
1	4·00	4·00

PVA Gum No XN7
Perforation Type A (E/I)

Cylinder No.	No Dot	Dot
1	£175	†

Minor Constant Flaws
Cyl. 1	16/5	Small white spot to right of second leaf down on upright flax plant (Th.B6)
Cyl. 1.	2/1	Small coloured projection above upper frame line (Th.A2)
	2/4	Dark patch below "S" of "POSTAGE" where former white dot, No. XN4a, existed (Th.F2)
	3/12	Small white dot below lower right leaf of flax plant (Th.G4)
	6/12	Small coloured flaws on leaf above NU of REVENUE
	10/6	Coloured flaw in lower left of badge (Th.E1)
	12/1	Pale patch below "P" of "POSTAGE" (Th.F1)

Sold Out: No. XN6, 4.70

Withdrawn: No. XN7 on the same day as released

1968 (4 September). **4d.** Change of colour. No watermark. Chalk-surfaced paper. PVA gum. One centre phosphor band reacting violet

XN8	=SG NI8		Mint	Used
4d.	Olive-sepia		25	25
	a.	Phosphor omitted		
	b.	Dot on leaf (No dot, R. 3/12)	25·00	
	c.	Flower flaw retouch (No dot, R. 7/7)	25·00	

For illustration of No. XN8b and for description of No. XN8c, see Nos. XN4a/XN4 respectively.

Cylinder Numbers (Blocks of Six)
Perforation Type A (E/I)

Cylinder No.	No Dot	Dot
1	4·00	4·00

Cylinder number: Opposite R.18/1. In addition both no dot and dot panes bear traces of cylinder numbers reading 1A and 1A. with two sides of a box opposite R. 19/1. These exist in varying degrees of faintness.

Minor Constant Flaws: As for Nos. XN6/XN7

1969 (26 February). **4d.** Further change of colour. No watermark. Chalk-surfaced paper. PVA gum. One centre phosphor band reacting+ violet

XN9	=SG NI9		Mint	Used
4d.	Bright vermilion		30	30
	a.	Phosphor omitted	4·50	
	b.	Flower flaw retouch (No dot, R. 7/7)	25·00	

For description of No. XN9b, see No. XN4b.

Cylinder Numbers (Blocks of Six)
Perforation Type A (E/I)

Cylinder No.	No Dot	Dot
1	4·50	4·50

Cylinder number: Opposite R. 18/1. In addition both no dot and dot panes bear traces of cylinder numbers reading 1A and 1A. with two sides of a box opposite R. 19/1. These exist in varying degrees of faintness.

NORTHERN IRELAND XA

Minor Constant Flaws

Cyl. 1.	2/4	Dark patch below "S" of "POSTAGE" where former white dot, No. XN4a, existed (Th.F2)
	6/12	Small coloured flaws on leaf above "NU" of "REVENUE"
	10/6	Coloured flaw in lower left of badge (Th.E1)
	12/1	Pale patch below "P" of "POSTAGE" (Th.F1)

5d. Type XN1 (1968)

1968 (4 September). **5d.** No watermark. Chalk-surfaced paper. PVA gum. Two 9·5 mm phosphor bands reacting violet

XN10 =SG NI10	Mint	Used
5d. Royal blue	40	40
a. Phosphor omitted	25·00	
b. Extra leaf (No dot, R. 13/2)	25·00	

XN10b

Cylinder Numbers (Blocks of Six)
Perforation Type A (E/I)

Cylinder No.	No Dot	Dot
1	4·75	4·75

6d. Type XN2 (1958–1962)

1958 (29 September). **6d.** Watermark Crowns

A. Cream Paper

XN11	Mint	Used
6d. Deep claret	1·50	50

B. Whiter Paper (4 June 1962)

XN12 =SG NI3		
6d. Deep claret	50	50

Cylinder Numbers (Blocks of Six)

Cream Paper (No XN11) — Perforation Types

Cylinder No. (No Dot)	B(I/P)	C (E/P)
1	20·00	20·00

Whiter Paper (No XN12) — Perforation Types

Cylinder No. (No Dot)	B(I/P)	C (E/P)	F(L)(I/E)
1	6·00	6·00	4·50

Minor Constant Flaws

Cyl. 1	1/12	Flaw in background to right of diadem (Th.A4)
	2/11	White coloured spur on lowest leaf of left flax plant (Th.F1)
	3/9	Dot in diamond to right of 6D (Th.F4); also similar dot in diamond to right of Queen's collar (Th.E–F5)
	3/10	Ring on little finger of hand at left (Th.F2)
	3/12	Dark spot in centre of central cross of diadem (Th.B3)
	4/2	Coloured line in background to right of 6D (Th.G4)
	10/2	White bulge half way down stalk at left (Th.D1)
	12/2	Coloured spot in background to right of Queen's hair (Th.D5)

Quantity Sold: 28,531,180 up to 31.3.68

Sold Out: 11.68

9d. Type XN2 (1967)

1967 (1 March). **9d.** Watermark Crowns. Two 9·5 mm phosphor bands reacting violet

XN13 =SG NI4	Mint	Used
9d. Bronze-green	40	40

Cylinder Number (Block of Six)
Single-pane cylinder. Perforation Type F (L) (I/E)

Cylinder No.	No Dot
1	5·00

1s.3d. Type XN3 (1958–1962)

1958 (29 September). **1s.3d.** Watermark Crowns

A. Cream Paper

XN14	Mint	Used
1s.3d. Green	5·00	1·25

B. Whiter Paper (9 November 1962)

XN15 =SG NI5		
1s.3d. Green	50	50

Cylinder Numbers (Blocks of Six)

Cream Paper (No XN14) — Perforation Types

Cylinder No. (No Dot)	B(I/P)	C (E/P)
1	30·00	30·00

Whiter Paper (No XN15) — Perforation Types

Cylinder No. (No Dot)	B(I/P)	C (E/P)	F(L)(I/E)
1	6·50	6·50	5·00

Minor Constant Flaws

Cyl. 1	1/1	White dot in upper loop of "S" of "POSTAGE"; also small area of retouching above emblems in diadem (Th.A4)
	3/7	White spur to "O" of "POSTAGE" (Th.E1)

Quantity Sold: 14,060,520 up to 31.3.68

1s.6d. Type XN3 (1967–1969)

1967 (1 March). **1s.6d.** Watermark Crowns. Two 9·5 mm phosphor bands reacting violet

XN16 =SG NI6	Mint	Used
1s.6d. Grey-blue	40	40
a. Phosphor omitted	£225	

Cylinder Number (Block of Six)
Single-pane cylinder. Perforation Type F (L) (I/E)

Cylinder No.	No Dot
1	4·75

271

XA NORTHERN IRELAND

Minor Constant Flaws

Cyl. 1	4/12	Small area of retouching behind Queen's head. Consists of several small dark coloured dots (Th.E5)
	14/1	Dark coloured spot on Queen's cheek (Th.D4)
	15/12	A multitude of tiny coloured spots over the Queen's face, neck and collar, and in the background behind her neck
	17/8	Coloured spot to right of Queen's left eye (Th.D3–4)

●────────────●

1969 *(20 May).* **1s.6d.** No watermark. Chalk-surfaced paper. PVA Gum. Two 9·5 mm phosphor bands reacting violet

XN17 =SG NI11		Mint	Used
1s.6d. Grey-blue		1·50	1·50
a. Phosphor omitted		£500	

It is believed that only three examples exist of No. XN17a.

Cylinder Number (Block of Six)
Single-pane cylinder. Perforation Type F (L) (I/E)

Cylinder No.	No Dot
1	20·00

Minor Constant Flaws

Cyl. 1	4/12	Small area of retouching behind Queen's head. Consists of several small dark coloured dots (Th.E5)
	11/12	Small dark coloured flaw on Queen's neck, just above necklace (Th.E4)
	14/1	Small dark coloured flaw on Queen's cheek (Th.D4)
	15/12	A multitude of tiny dark coloured spots over the Queen's face, neck and collar, and in the background behind her neck
	17/8	Area of retouching to right of Queen's left eye (Th.D3–4)

Presentation Pack
XNPP1 (9.12.70) Seven stamps 3·50

Comprises Nos. XN3, XN8/XN10, XN13, and XN15/XN16

Quantity Sold: 28,944

Withdrawn: 25.11.71

First Day Covers
(Northern Ireland)

18.8.58	3d.	30·00
29.9.58	6d., 1s.3d.	35·00
7.2.66	4d. ultramarine	7·00
1.3.67	9d., 1s.6d.	4·00
4.9.68	4d. olive-sepia, 5d.	3·00

Imprimaturs from the NPM or BPMA
Imperforate, watermark Type W.**24**

3d. (cream paper)	£800
3d. (cream paper) cylinder 3 (no dot) block of six	£5500
3d. (whiter paper)	£800
3d. (whiter paper) cylinder 3 (no dot) block of six	£5500
6d. (cream paper)	£800
6d. (cream paper) cylinder 1 block of six	£5500
6d. (whiter paper)	£800
6d. (whiter paper) cylinder 1 block of six	£5500
9d. (cream paper)	£800
9d. (cream paper) cylinder 1 block of six	£5500
1s.3d. (cream paper)	£800
1s.3d. (cream paper) cylinder 1 block of six	£5500
1s.3d. (whiter paper)	£800
1s.3d. (whiter paper) cylinder 1 block of six	£5500
1s.6d. (cream paper)	£800
1s.6d. (cream paper) cylinder 1 block of six	£5500
Imperforate, no watermark	
1s.6d. (chalk-surfaced paper)	£800
1s.6d. (chalk-surfaced paper) cylinder 1 block of six	£5500

●────────────

SCOTLAND

Type **XS1**
(Des. Gordon F. Huntly)

Type **XS2**
(Des. J. B. Fleming)

Type **XS3**
(Des. A. B. Imrie)

3d.   Type XS1 (1958–1968)

1958 (18 August). **3d.** Watermark Crowns

A. Cream Paper

XS1		Mint	Used
	3d. Deep lilac	1·00	50
a.	Spot on "U" of "REVENUE" (Cyl. 3 No dot, R. 19/8)	25·00	
b.	Dot in "d" of "3d" (Cyl. 3 Dot, R. 20/12)	25·00	

B. Whiter Paper (9 July 1962)

XS2 =SG S1

	3d. Deep lilac	15	15
a.	Spot after last "E" of "REVENUE" (Cyl. 5 No dot, R. 20/2)	25·00	

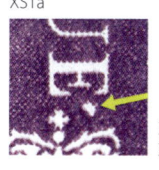

XS1a

XS1b Later retouched

XS2a, XS3a, XS4b, XS5b, XS7b XS8b

Cylinder Numbers (Blocks of Six)

Cream Paper (No XS1)
Perforation Type A (E/I)

Cylinder No.	No Dot	Dot
3	12·00	12·00
4	12·00	12·00

Whiter Paper (No XS2)
Perforation Type A (E/I)

Cylinder No.	No Dot	Dot
4	4·00	4·00
5	4·00	7·00

Quantity Sold: 1,487,481,480
Sold Out: 18.3.68

1962 Miniature Sheet. On the occasion of "Scotex" the 1962 Scottish Stamp Exhibition, a miniature sheet, size 105 × 60 mm, was produced comprising Types XS1/XS3 printed *se-tenant* in black, imperforate and surrounded by a decorative frame and inscription in blue on white chalk-surfaced gummed paper watermarked HARRISON AND SONS LTD sideways. The sheet was printed by Harrison & Sons with the use of actual stamp positives. It had no franking value. 15,000 printed.

1963 (29 January). **3d.** phosphor bands reacting blue. Watermark Crowns

A. Two 8 mm Bands

XS3 =SG S1p		Mint	Used
	3d. Deep lilac	7·50	6·00
a.	Spot after last "E" of "REVENUE" (Cyl. 5 Dot, R. 20/2)	40·00	

B. One Side Band* (30 April 1965)

XS4

	3d. Deep lilac (band at left)	6·00	3·00
a.	Band at right	6·00	3·00
ab.	Nos. XS4/XS4a (horiz. pair)	12·00	12·00
b.	Spot after last "E" of "REVENUE" (Cyl. 5 Dot, R. 20/2)	25·00	

* The one side band stamps were produced by an 8 mm band applied down alternate vertical rows of the sheets over the perforations so that alternate stamps have the band at left (No. XS4) or right (No. XS4a). In theory the width of the band on a single stamp should be 4 mm but this will vary if the bands have not been perfectly positioned.
For illustration of Nos. XS3a and XS4b, see No. XS2a.

Cylinder Numbers (Blocks of Six)

Two Bands No. XS3
Perforation Type A (E/I)

Cylinder No.	No Dot	Dot
4	75·00	75·00
5	75·00	£110

One Side Band No. XS4
Perforation Type A (E/I)

5	45·00	60·00*

Sold Out: No. XS3, 1968

1965 (December 16). **3d.** phosphor bands reacting violet. Watermark Crowns

A. One Side Band*

XS5 =SG S1pb		Mint	Used
	3d. Deep lilac (band at left)	25	25
a.	Band at right	25	25
ab.	Nos. XS5/XS5a (horiz. pair)	60	75
b.	Spot after last "E" of "REVENUE" (Cyl. 5 Dot, R. 20/2)	25	

B. One 4 mm Centre Band (9 November 1967)

XS6 =SG S1pd

	3d. Deep lilac	15	15

* The note regarding one side band stamps after No. XS4b also applies here.
For illustration of No. XS5b, see No. XS2a.

Cylinder Numbers (Blocks of Six)

One Side Band No. XS5
Perforation Type A (E/I)

Cylinder No.	No Dot	Dot
5	4·25	28·00

One Centre Band No. XS6
Perforation Type A (E/I)

Cylinder No.	No Dot	Dot
4	4·25	4·25

Sold Out: No. XS5, 15.7.68; No. XS6, 11.68

XA SCOTLAND

1968 (16 May). **3d.** No watermark. Chalk-surfaced paper. One centre phosphor band reacting violet

A. Gum Arabic

XS7 =SG S7	Mint	Used
3d. Deep lilac	15	15
a. Phosphor omitted	7·00	
b. Spot after last "E" of "REVENUE" (Cyl. 5 Dot, R. 20/2)	20·00	

B. PVA Gum (11 July 1968)

XS8 =SG S7Ev		
3d. Deep lilac	10	
a. Phosphor omitted	4·00	
b. Spot after last "E" of "REVENUE" (Cyl. 5 Dot, R. 20/2)	20·00	

For illustration of Nos. XS7b and XS8b, see No. XS2a.

Cylinder Numbers (Blocks of Six)

Gum Arabic No. XS7
Perforation Type F (LI)*

Cylinder No.	No Dot (I/E)	Dot (P/E)
5	3·25	22·00*

PVA Gum No. XS8
Perforation Type F (LI)*

Cylinder No.	No Dot (I/E)	Dot (P/E)
5	3·25	22·00*

Minor Constant Flaws

Cyl. 5	8/6	Retouching on Queen's forehead, nose and around lips (Th.B–D3)
	13/3	Pale patch on Queen's collar (Th.E–F4)
	15/3	Small dark flaw surrounded by white area on right side of thistle (Th.G6)
	17/7	Area of retouching on Queen's neck (Th.E4–5)
	18/1	Horizontal coloured line through "G" of "POSTAGE"

4d. Type XS1 (1966–1969)

1966 (7 February). **4d.** Watermark Crowns

XS9 = SG S2	Mint	Used
4d. Ultramarine	20	20
a. Dot before second "E" of "REVENUE" (Dot, R.10/9)	25·00	
b. Spot on "T" (Dot, R. 4/4)	25·00	

XS9a, XS10a
Later retouched on No. XS10

XS9b, XS10b

Cylinder Numbers (Blocks of Six)
Perforation Type A (E/I)

Cylinder No.	No Dot	Dot
2	4·00	4·00

Minor Constant Flaws

Cyl. 2	7/11	White spot to left of crown at right (Th.F5)
	8/6	Small blue flaw on top left-hand leaf of thistle (Th.F5)
	20/5	Small dark flaw in background to right of "d" of "4d" (Th.F4–5)
Cyl. 2.	8/12	Blue spot below Queen's left eye (Th.C3)
	11/7	Small blue spot on Queen's forehead (Th.B2)
	12/8	Small dark flaw in background to left of "EV" of "REVENUE" (Th.B5); also retouching on Queen's temple and cheek (Th.C3–4)
	20/3	Small coloured flaw above Queen's left eye (Th.B3); also small blue spot on top left-hand leaf of thistle (Th.F5)

Sold Out: 7.70.

1966 (7 February). **4d.** Two 8 mm phosphor bands reacting violet. Watermark Crowns

XS10 =SG S2p	Mint	Used
4d. Ultramarine	20	20
a. Dot before second "E" of "REVENUE" (Dot, R.10/9)	25·00	
b. Spot on T (Dot, R. 4/4)	25·00	

For illustrations of Nos. XS10a/XS10b, see Nos. XS9a/XS9b.

Cylinder Numbers (Blocks of Six)
Perforation Type A (E/I)

Cylinder No.	No Dot	Dot
2	4·00	4·00

Minor Constant Flaws

Cyl. 2   As for flaws on No. XS9 except that flaw on R. 20/5 was later retouched

Cyl. 2.   As for flaws on No. XS9

Sold Out: 7.70.

1967 (28 November). **4d.** No watermark. Chalk-surfaced paper. Two 9·5 mm phosphor bands reacting violet

A. Gum Arabic

XS11 =SG S8	Mint	Used
4d. Ultramarine	30	30
a. Phosphor omitted	10·00	

B. PVA Gum (25 July 1968)

XS12 = SG S8Ev		
4d. Ultramarine	10	

SCOTLAND XA

Cylinder Numbers (Blocks of Six)
Gum Arabic No. XS11

Perforation Type F (L)*	No Dot	Dot
Cylinder No.	(I/E)	(P/E)
2	3·00	3·00

PVA Gum No. XS12

Perforation Type A (E/I)	No Dot	Dot
Cylinder No.	(I/E)	(P/E)
2	3·00	3·00

Minor Constant Flaws

Cyl. 2	1/7	Retouch on Queen's forehead (Th.B3). PVA only
	3/7	Retouch on Queen's collar (Th.E4–5). PVA only
	5/10	White patches on Queen's nose and forehead
	8/6	Small blue flaw on top left-hand leaf of thistle (Th.F5)
	10/11	Retouch to right of Queen's mouth (Th.D3). PVA only
	12/12	White spot at rear tip of diadem (Th.C5)
	14/10	Retouch on Queen's forehead (Th.B3). Less pronounced on PVA
	15/4	Retouch on Queen's cheek (Th.C–D3)
	19/7	White spot on Queen's cheek (Th.C3). Retouched on PVA where it shows as three dark spots
	20/5	Small dark flaw in background to right of "d" of "4d" (Th.F4–5). Less pronounced on PVA but can be confirmed by additional retouches on Queen's nose and forehead (Th.C2 and B3)
	20/6	Small blue flaw on Queen's cheek (Th.C3). On PVA there is an additional white flaw on Queen's right cheek (Th.C2)
Cyl. 2.	1/5	Coloured spot above Queen's left eye (Th.B3).
	2/6	Retouch on Queen's collar (Th.E4)
	6/11	White spot on Queen's cheek (Th.C–D3). Retouched on PVA where it shows as a dark spot
	8/12	White spot below Queen's left eye where former blue spot appeared (Th.C3). Further retouched on PVA
	11/7	Small blue spot on Queen's forehead (Th.B2)
	12/8	Small dark flaw in background to left of "EV" of "REVENUE" (Th.B5); also retouching on Queen's temple and cheek, the latter much more pronounced on PVA (Th.C3–4)
	15/1	Small retouch on Queen's temple (Th.C3–4). PVA only
	15/2	Small retouch on Queen's forehead (Th.B2). PVA only
	18/4	Weak patches on Queen's chin (Th.D2–3).
	18/6	Blue spot on Queen's collar (Th.E4). Retouched on PVA but a scratch now appears across Queen's neck and collar (Th.E4)
	19/3	White spot on Queen's left cheek (Th.D3). Shows larger on PVA
	20/3	Small coloured flaw above Queen's left eye (Th.B3); also small blue spot on top left-hand leaf of thistle (Th.F5)
	20/4	Coloured spots around Queen's eyes and nose (Th.C2–3)

1968 (4 September). **4d.** Change of colour. No watermark. Chalk-surfaced paper. PVA gum. One centre phosphor band reacting violet

XS13 =SG S9	Mint	Used
4d. olive-sepia	15	15
a. Phosphor omitted	3·00	

Cylinder Numbers (Blocks of Six)
Perforation Type A (E/I)

Cylinder No.	No Dot	Dot
2	3·00	3·00

Minor Constant Flaws

Cyl. 2	12/12	White spot at rear tip of diadem (Th.C5)
Cyl. 2.	1/5	Coloured spot above Queen's left eye (Th.B3)
	2/6	Retouch on Queen's collar (Th.E4)
	6/11	Retouch on Queen's cheek (Th.C–D3)
	8/12	Retouch below Queen's left eye (Th.C3)
	11/7	Coloured spot on Queen's forehead (Th.B2)
	12/8	Small dark flaw in background to left of "EV" of "REVENUE" (Th.B5); also retouching on Queen's temple and cheek (Th.C3–4)
	15/1	Small retouch on Queen's temple (Th.C3–4)
	15/2	Small retouch on Queen's forehead (Th.B2)
	18/4	Weak patches on Queen's chin (Th.D2–4)
	18/6	Retouch on Queen's collar and also scratch across her neck and collar (Th.E4)
	19/3	Large white spot on Queen's left cheek (Th.D3)
	20/3	Small coloured flaw above Queen's left eye (Th.B3); also small coloured spot on top left-hand leaf of thistle (Th.F5)
	20/4	Coloured spots around Queen's eyes and nose (Th.C2–3)

1969 (26 February). **4d.** Further change of colour. No watermark. Chalk-surfaced paper. PVA gum. One centre phosphor band reacting violet

XS14 =SG S10	Mint	Used
4d. Bright vermilion	15	15
a. Phosphor omitted	2·50	

Cylinder Numbers (Blocks of Six)
Perforation Type A (E/I)

Cylinder No.	No Dot	Dot
2	3·00	3·00
4	3·00	3·00

Minor Constant Flaws

Cyl. 2	1/7	Retouch on Queen's forehead (Th.B3)
	3/7	Retouch on Queen's collar (Th.E4–5)
	5/10	Retouching on Queen's nose and forehead where former white patches appeared
	8/11	Retouch by Queen's ear (Th.C–D4)
	12/12	White spot at rear tip of diadem (Th.C5)
	10/11	Retouch to right of Queen's mouth (Th.D3)
	14/10	Heavy retouching on Queen's forehead (Th.B3)
	15/4	Retouch on Queen's cheek (Th.C–D3)
	19/7	Retouch on Queen's cheek where former white spot appeared (Th.C3)
	20/5	Retouches on Queen's nose and forehead (Th.C2 and B3). Small dark flaw in background to right of "d" of "4d" now hardly shows (Th.F4–5)
	20/6	Retouches on both of the Queen's cheeks where former flaws appeared (Th.C2–3)

275

XA SCOTLAND

Cyl. 2.	1/5	Coloured spot above Queen's left eye (Th.B3)
	2/6	Retouch on Queen's collar (Th.E4)
	6/11	Heavy area of retouching on Queen's cheek (Th.C–D3)
	8/12	Retouch below Queen's left eye (Th.C3)
	10/5	Extensive area of retouching on Queen's temple and cheek (Th.B3 and C3–4)
	11/7	Area of retouching on Queen's forehead where former coloured spot appeared (Th.B2)
	12/8	Small dark flaw in background to left of "EV" of "REVENUE" (Th.B5) is now less noticeable but retouches on Queen's temple and cheek remain (Th.C34)
	15/1	Small retouch on Queen's temple (Th.C3–4)
	15/2	Small retouch on Queen's forehead (Th.B2)
	18/4	Weak patches on Queen's chin (Th.D–24)
	18/6	Retouch on Queen's collar and also scratch across her neck and collar (Th.E4)
	20/3	Small coloured flaw above Queen's left eye (Th.B3); also small coloured spot on top left-hand leaf of thistle (Th.F5)
	20/4	Coloured spots around Queen's eyes and nose (Th.C2–3)

5d. Type XS1 (1968)

1968 (4 September). **5d.** No watermark. Chalk-surfaced paper. PVA gum. Two 9·5 mm phosphor bands reacting violet

XS15 =SG S11		Mint	Used
5d. Royal blue		25	25
a. Phosphor omitted		55·00	
b. Shoulder retouch (Cyl. 2., R. 16/6)		25·00	

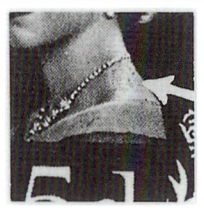

XS15b
Large retouch on Queen's shoulder

Cylinder Numbers (Blocks of Six)
Perforation Type A (E/I)

Cylinder No.	No Dot	Dot
2	4·00	4·00
3	12·00	12·00

Phosphor Cylinder number: Ph 1 found on cyl. 3 dot, right margin

6d. Type XS2 (1958–1966)

1958 (29 September). **6d.** Watermark Crowns

A. Cream Paper

XS16		Mint	Used
6d. Reddish purple		1·50	70
a. Broken "V" of "REVENUE" (Cyl. 1, R. 11/12)		25·00	
ab. Retouched		20·00	
b. Curled leaf (Cyl. 1, R. 7/7)		25·00	

B. Whiter Paper (28 May 1962)

XS17 =SG S3			
6d. Deep reddish purple		25	25
a. Broken "V" of "REVENUE" (Cyl. 1, R. 11/12)		25·00	
ab. Retouched		20·00	
b. Curled leaf (Cyl. 1, R. 7/7)		25·00	
c. Cut leaf (Cyl. 4, R. 2/10)		25·00	

XS16a, XS17a
This is a multipositive flaw. It was later retouched on Cyl 1. On Cyls. 2 and 4 it is only known retouched

XS16b, XS17b
Later reouched

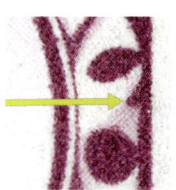

XS17c, XS18a Leaf half-way down at right has V-shaped cut in solid colour

XS16ab, XS17ab
Retouched "V"
Cyls 1, 2 and 4

Cylinder Numbers (Blocks of Six)

Cream Paper (No XS16)

		Perforation Types	
Cylinder No.	No Dot	B(I/P)	C (E/P)
1		25·00	25·00

Whiter Paper (No XS17)

		Perforation Types		
Cylinder No.	No Dot	B(I/P)	C (E/P)	F(L)(I/E)
2		4·00	4·00	†
4		†	†	4·00

Marginal rule:

Cylinder 1: Instead of the usual stamp width rule below each stamp in the bottom row the rules on this cylinder are shorter (approx. 17 mm) and are arranged alternately with a 1 mm wide rectangular rule, the latter being perforated through. The rules below vertical rows 9/12 are damaged.

Cylinders 2 and 4: As given in General Notes

Minor Constant Flaws

Cyl. 1	5/8	Small white flaw by left thistle just outside oval frame (Th.B2)

SCOTLAND XA

1963 (29 January). **6d.** Two 8 mm phosphor bands reacting blue. Watermark Crowns

XS18		Mint	Used
6d.	Deep reddish purple	3·25	1·00
	a. Cut leaf (Cyl. 4, R. 2/10)	30·00	

Cylinder Number (Block of Six)
Single-pane cylinder. Perforation Type F (L) (I/E)

Cylinder No.	No Dot
4	30·00

1966 (2 February). **6d.** Two 8mm phosphor bands reacting violet. Watermark Crowns

XS19 =SG S3p	Mint	Used
6d. Deep reddish purple	25	25

Cylinder Number (Block of Six)
Single-pane cylinder. Perforation Type F (L) (I/E)

Cylinder No.	No Dot
4	4·50

Quantity Sold: 26,758,320 (including No. XS18) up to 31.3.68
Sold Out: 10.68

9d. Type XS2 (1967–1970)

1967 (1 March). **9d.** Watermark Crowns. Two 9·5 mm phosphor bands reacting violet

XS20 =SG S4	Mint	Used
9d. Bronze-green	40	40

Cylinder Number (Block of Six)
Single-pane cylinder. Perforation Type F (L) (I/E)

Cylinder No.	No Dot
1	5·50

1970 (28 September). **9d.** No watermark. Chalk-surfaced paper. PVA gum. Two 9·5 mm phosphor bands reacting violet

XS21 = S.G. S12		Mint	Used
9d.	bronze-green	4·00	4·00
	a. Phosphor omitted	£275	

Cylinder Number (Block of Six)
Single-pane cylinder. Perforation Type F (L) (I/E)

Cylinder No.	No Dot
1	35·00

1s.3d. Type XS3 (1958–1965)

1958 (29 September). **1s.3d.** Watermark Crowns

A. Cream Paper

XS22		Mint	Used
1s.3d.	Green	2·00	90
	a. Broken oblique in value (Cyl. 4, R. 15/2)	30·00	
	b. Broken hinge (Cyl. 4, R. 19/2)	25·00	

B. Whiter Paper (31 July 1962)

XS23 =SG S5		Mint	Used
1s.3d.	Green	40	40
	a. Broken oblique in value (Cyl. 4, R. 15/2)	25·00	
	b. Broken hinge (Cyl. 4, R. 19/2)	22·00	

XS22a, XS23a, XS24a, XS25a

XS22b, XS23b, XS24b, XS25b
Lowest "hinge" of the flag is incomplete. A multipositive flaw, (Cyls 4 and 8, R.19/2

Cylinder Numbers (Blocks of Six)

Cream Paper (No XS22) — *Perforation Types*

Cylinder No. (No Dot)	B(I/P)	C (E/P)
4	35·00*	35·00*

Whiter Paper (No XS23) — *Perforation Types*

Cylinder No. (No Dot)	B(I/P)	C (E/P)	F(L)(I/E)
4	24·00*	24·00*	24·00*

Marginal arrows: "V" shaped, hand-engraved at top and bottom; "W" shaped, photo-etched at both sides. Early printings have the arrows omitted from the top and bottom of the sheet. *Price for marginal strip of 7 stamps £60.*

Minor Constant Flaws

Cyl. 4	3/7	Green spot on shoulder of right-hand unicorn (Th.D6)
	11/12	Small break in inner frame line at right of value tablet (Th.G4)
	15/2	Hind leg of lion on standard is severed (Th.B1)

1963 (29 January). **1s.3d**. Two 8mm phosphor bands reacting blue. Watermark Crowns

XS24		Mint	Used
1s.3d.	Green	8·00	2·50
	a. Broken oblique in value (Cyl. 4. R. 15/2)	40·00	
	b. Broken hinge (Cyl. 4, R. 19/2)	25·00	

277

XA SCOTLAND

For illustration of Nos. XS24a/XS24b, see Nos. XS22a/XS22b.

Cylinder Number (Block of Six)
Single-pane cylinder. Perforation Type F (L) (I/E)

Cylinder No.	No Dot
4	70·00*

Minor Constant Flaws
As for Nos. XS22/XS23

1965 (26 November). **1s.3d.** Two 8mm phosphor bands reacting violet. Watermark Crowns

XS25 =SG S5p	Mint	Used
1s.3d. Green	50	50
a. Broken oblique in value (Cyl. 4, R. 15/2)	25·00	
b. Broken hinge (Cyls. 4, 8, R. 19/2)	22·00	

For illustration of Nos. XS25a/XS25b, see Nos. XS22a/XS22b.

Cylinder Numbers (Blocks of Six)
Single-pane cylinders. Perforation Type F (L) (I/E)

Cylinder No.	No Dot
4	25·00*
8	32·00*

Minor Constant Flaws: Cyl. 4 As for Nos. XS22/XS23

1s.6d. Type XS3 (1967–1968)

1967 (1 March). **1s.6d.** Watermark Crowns. Two 9·5 mm phosphor bands reacting violet

XS26 =SG S6	Mint	Used
1s.6d. Grey-blue	60	60

Cylinder Number (Block of Six)
Single-pane cylinder. Perforation Type F (L) (I/E)

Cylinder No.	No Dot
1	8·00

Minor Constant Flaw
Cyl. 1 1/11 Coloured spot in background to right of Queen's neck, below her hair (Th.E4)

1968 (12 December). **1s.6d.** No watermark. Chalk-surfaced paper. PVA gum. Two 9·5 mm phosphor bands reacting violet

XS27 =SG S13	Mint	Used
1s.6d. Grey-blue	1·25	1·25
a. Phosphor omitted	£125	

Cylinder Number (Block of Six)
Single-pane cylinder. Perforation Type F (L) (I/E)

Cylinder No.	No Dot
1	18·00

Minor Constant Flaw: As for No. XS26

Presentation Pack
XSPP1	(9.12.70)	Eight stamps	8·00

Comprises Nos. XS8, XS13/XS15, XS17, XS21, XS25 and XS27.

Quantity Sold: 31,476

Withdrawn: 25.11.71

First Day Covers
(Scotland)

18.8.58	3d.	17·00
29.9.58	6d., 1s.3d.	25·00
7.2.66	4d. ultramarine	7·00
1.3.67	9d., 1s.6d.	6·00
4.9.68	4d. olive-sepia, 5d.	3·00

Imprimaturs from the NPM or BPMA
Imperforate, watermark Type W.**24**

3d. (cream paper)	£800
3d. (cream paper) cylinder 3 (no dot) block of six	£5500
3d. (whiter paper)	£800
3d. (whiter paper) cylinder 4 (no dot) block of six	£5500
3d. (2 bands, blue phosphor)	£800
3d. (2 bands, blue phosphor) cylinder 4 (dot) block of six	£5500
6d. (cream paper)	£800
6d. (cream paper) cylinder 1 block of six	£5500
6d. (whiter paper)	£800
6d. (whiter paper) cylinder 2 block of six	£5500
6d. (2 bands, blue phosphor)	£800
6d. (2 bands, blue phosphor) cylinder 4 block of six	£5500
9d. (2 bands, violet phosphor)	£800
9d. (2 bands, violet phosphor) cylinder 1 block of six	£5500
1s.3d. (cream paper)	£800
1s.3d. (cream paper) cylinder 4 block of six	£5750*
1s.3d. (whiter paper)	£800
1s.3d. (whiter paper) cylinder 4 block of six	£5750*
1s.3d. (2 bands, blue phosphor)	£800
1s.3d. (2 bands, blue phosphor) cylinder 4 block of six	£5750*
1s.6d. (2 bands, violet phosphor)	£800
1s.6d. (2 bands, violet phosphor) cylinder 1 block of six	£5500

Imperforate, no watermark

9d. (chalky paper)	£800
9d. (chalky paper) cylinder 1 block of six	£5500
1s.6d. (chalky paper)	£800
1s.6d. (chalky paper) cylinder 1 block of six	£5500

* Contains positional variety.

WALES AND MONMOUTHSHIRE

Type **XW1**   Type **XW2**   Type **XW3**

(Des. Reynolds Stone)

3d. Type **XW1** (1958–1967)

1958 (18 August). **3d.** Watermark Crowns
A. Cream Paper

XW1		Mint	Used
3d.	Deep lilac	1·00	50
a.	Bulge on oval value tablet (Cyl. 1 No dot, R.6/3)	25·00	
b.	Wing-tail flaw (Cyl. 2 No dot, R. 16/1)	25·00	

B. Whiter Paper (30 April 1962)

XW2 =SG W1			
3d.	Deep lilac	15	15
a.	Wing-tail flaw (Cyl. 2, No dot, R. 16/1)	25·00	

XW1a
Later retouched

XW1b, XW2a
White flaw joins spine of dragon's wing to its tail

Cylinder Numbers (Blocks of Six)
Cream Paper (No XW1)
Perforation Type A (E/I)

Cylinder No.	No Dot	Dot
1	35·00	35·00
2	10·00	10·00

Whiter Paper (No XW2)
Perforation Type A (E/I)

Cylinder No.	No Dot	Dot
2	4·50	4·50
3	4·50	4·50

Minor Constant Flaws
Multipositive flaws

Cyl. 1, 2 and 3	1/12	Small coloured flaw on dragon's neck (Th.F–G3)
	17/10	Known in three states: Cyl. 1 Two pale coloured dots on back of Queen's neck just below hair (Th.D4) Cyl. 2 Cylinder retouched to almost normal Cyl. 3 Cylinder retouched but still leaving one coloured dot on back of neck
Cyl. 1	15/7	White flaw in middle of central cross of diadem (Th.A3)
Cyl. 2	6/11	White spot on end of top horizontal bar of first "E" of "REVENUE"

Quantity Sold: 902,289,240
Sold Out: 12.67

1967 (16 May). **3d.** One centre phosphor band reacting violet. Watermark Crowns

XW3 =SG W1p	Mint	Used
3d. Deep lilac	20	15

Cylinder Numbers (Blocks of Six)
Perforation Type A (E/I)

Cylinder No.	No Dot	Dot
3	4·00	4·00

Minor Constant Flaws
Multipositive flaws

Cyl. 3	1/7	Coloured spot on oval frame line opposite "R" of "REVENUE" (Th.A5)
	1/8	Small coloured flaw just inside oval frame opposite "G" of "POSTAGE" (Th.E2)
	1/12	Small coloured flaw on dragons neck (Th.FG3)
	7/11	Small coloured flaw on Queen's collar (Th.E5)
	10/11	Small dot on leaf to right of final "E" of "REVENUE" (Th.E6)
	11/10	Small dot on leaf to left of second "E" of "REVENUE" (Th.C6)
	17/10	Pale coloured dot on back of Queen's neck just below hair (Th.D4)
Cyl. 3.	1/6	Small retouch to right of Queen's mouth (Th.D3)
	1/8	Retouch on Queen's cheek (Th.C–D4)
	3/5	Small dot on leaf above "E" of "POSTAGE" (Th.E1)
	3/9	Coloured flaw on Queen's neck just above collar (Th.E4)
	4/9	Coloured diagonal flaw in front of Queen's neck (Th.E3)
	5/9	Coloured spot inside lower loop of 3 of right-hand 3d
	8/1	Two white flaws on dragon's front left foot (Th.G–H2)
	10/2	Coloured spot on Queen's collar (Th.E4)
	11/6	Small retouch on back of Queen's collar (Th.E4–5)
	18/10	Retouch to background within oval to right of O of POSTAGE (Th.A–B2)
	18/11	Small dot on leaf to right of "T" of "POSTAGE" (Th.C1–2)
	20/6	Pale patch on Queen's shoulder (Th.E4)

Sold Out :1.68

1967 (6 December). **3d.** No watermark. Chalk-surfaced paper. One centre phosphor band reacting violet

XW4 =SG W7	Mint	Used
3d. Deep lilac	15	15
a. Phosphor omitted	70·00	

Cylinder Numbers (Blocks of Six)
Perforation Type F (L)*

Cylinder No.	No Dot (I/E)	Dot (P/E)
3	3·75	3·75

Minor Constant Flaws
As for multipositive and cylinder flaws on No. XW3 with the addition of the following cylinder flaws:

Cyl. 3	5/9	Retouch on Queen's cheek (Th.D3–4)
Cyl. 3.	5/8	Retouch on Queen's chin (Th.D3)
	14/1	Retouch on Queen's cheek (Th.D4)
	20/5	Retouch on Queen's chin (Th.D3–4) and several dark spots on her forehead, cheek and neck

XA WALES AND MONMOUTHSHIRE

4d. Type XW1 (1966–1969)

1966 (7 February). **4d.** Watermark Crowns

XW5 =SG W2	Mint	Used
4d. Ultramarine	20	20

Cylinder Numbers (Blocks of Six)
Perforation Type A (E/I)

Cylinder No.	No Dot	Dot
1	4·00	4·00

Quantity Sold: 148,137,600

Sold Out: 7.2.68

1967 (October). **4d.** Two 9·5 mm phosphor bands reacting violet. Watermark Crowns

XW6 =SG W2p	Mint	Used
4d. Ultramarine	20	20

Cylinder Numbers (Blocks of Six)
Perforation Type F (L)*

Cylinder No.	No Dot (I/E)	Dot (P/E)
1	4·00	4·00

Sold Out: 4.70

1968 (June 21). **4d.** No watermark. Chalk-surfaced paper. PVA Gum. Two 9·5 mm phosphor bands reacting violet

XW7 =SG W8	Mint	Used
4d. Ultramarine	15	15
a. White spot before "E" of "POSTAGE" (No dot, R. 17/12)	25·00	
b. White spot after "E" of "POSTAGE" (No dot, R. 18/10)	25·00	
c. Bump on dragon's head (No dot, R. 19/2)	22·00	
d. White spot above dragon's hind leg (No dot, R. 20/1)	22·00	

XW7, XW7a, XW8a
Later retouched on No. XW8

XW7b, XW8b
Later retouched on No. XW8

XW7c, XW8c, XW9b

XW7d, XW8c
Retouched on No. XW9

Cylinder Numbers (Blocks of Six)
Perforation Type A (E/I)

Cylinder No.	No Dot	Dot
2	25·00*	4·00

Minor Constant Flaws

Cyl. 2	6/9	Small dot on leaf to left of second "E" of "REVENUE" (Th.C6)
	12/6	Coloured flaw on Queen's left eye-brow (Th.C4)
	13/2	Small dot on leaf above "U" of "REVENUE" (Th.D6)
	18/5	Coloured spots over Queen's face and background
	20/12	Coloured flaw over "d" of left-hand "4d."
Cyl. 2•	1/6	Small dot on leaf above "U" of "REVENUE" (Th.D6)
	3/12	Small dot on leaf to left of "N" of "REVENUE" (Th.D6)
	4/3	Small dot on leaf to right of "T" of "POSTAGE" (Th.C1–2)
	4/6	White spot in background of oval frame opposite "R" of "REVENUE" (Th.A4)
	4/9	White spot on right-hand frame line by first "E" of "REVENUE" (Th.B67)
	7/2	Small dot on leaf to right of "E" of "POSTAGE" (Th.E2)
	7/11	Small coloured flaw in background of oval frame opposite "VE" of "REVENUE" (Th.C5)
	8/6	Small white flaw to right of dragon's left hind foot (Th.H5)
	11/7	Coloured spot in left-hand margin opposite "P" of "POSTAGE" (opposite Th.A1)
	12/2	Retouch on Queen's chin (Th.D3)
	12/6	White flaw over Queen's upper lip (Th.D3)
	16/10	Small coloured flaw on Queen's shoulder just above collar (Th.E4)

Sold Out: 4.70

1968 (4 September). **4d.** Change of colour. No watermark. Chalk-surfaced paper. PVA gum. One centre phosphor band reacting violet

XW8 =SG W9	Mint	Used
4d. Olive-sepia	15	15
a. White spot before "E" of "POSTAGE" (No dot, R. 17/12)	25·00	
b. White spot after "E" of "POSTAGE" (No dot, R. 18/10)	25·00	
c. Bump on dragon's head (No dot, R. 19/2)	22·00	
d. White spot above dragon's hind leg (No dot, R. 20/1)	22·00	

For illustrations of Nos. XW8a/XW8d, see Nos. XW7a/XW7d.
Note. Varieties XW8a/XW8b were later retouched.

Cylinder Numbers (Blocks of Six)
Perforation Type A (E/I)

Cylinder No.	No Dot	Dot
2	25·00*	4·00

Minor Constant Flaws: As for No. XW7

WALES AND MONMOUTHSHIRE XA

1969 (26 February). **4d.** Further change of colour. No watermark. Chalk-surfaced paper. PVA Gum. One centre phosphor band reacting violet

XW9 =SG W10	Mint	Used
4d. Bright vermilion	15	15
a. Phosphor omitted	2·00	
b. Bump on dragon's head (No dot, R. 19/2)	22·00	

Cylinder Numbers (Blocks of Six)
Perforation Type A (E/I)

Cylinder No.	No Dot	Dot
2	25·00*	4·00

Minor Constant Flaws

Cyl. 2	As for flaws on No. XW7 except that flaw on R. 13/2 has been retouched
Cyl. 2.	As for flaws on No. XW7 except that the following were retouched, R. 7/2, 8/6 and 12/6

5d. Type XW1 (1968)

1968 (4 September). **5d.** No watermark. Chalk-surfaced paper. PVA Gum. Two 9·5 mm phosphor bands reacting violet

XW10 =SG W11	Mint	Used
5d. Royal blue	15	15
a. Phosphor omitted	3·00	

Cylinder Numbers (Blocks of Six)
Perforation Type A (E/I)

Cylinder No.	No Dot	Dot
2	4·00	4·00

Phosphor Cylinder number: Ph 1 found on cyl. 2 dot, right margin

Minor Constant Flaws

Cyl. 2	2/3	Coloured spot in background of oval frame just above central cross of diadem (Th.A3)
	16/5	Coloured flaws in background of oval frame to left of Queen's nose (Th.C–D2)
	20/4	White flaw on bottom frame line below dragon's left hind foot (Th.H4)

6d. Type XW2 (1958–62)

1958 (29 September). **6d.** Watermark Crowns

A. Cream Paper

XW11	Mint	Used
6d. Deep claret	1·50	80

B. Whiter Paper (18 July 1962)

XW12 =SG W3	Mint	Used
6d. Reddish purple	35	35

Cylinder Numbers (Blocks of Six)

Cream Paper (No XW11)

	Perforation Types	
Cylinder No. (No Dot)	B(I/P)	C (E/P)
2	16·00	16·00

Whiter Paper (No XW12)

	Perforation Types		
Cylinder No. (No Dot)	B(I/P)	C (E/P)	F(L)(I/E)
3	6·50	6·50	6·50

Minor Constant Flaw
Cyl. 3 16/4 Coloured spot on dragon's tail (Th.F5)
Quantity Sold: 66,754,200

Sold Out: 3.68

9d. Type XW2 (1967)

1967 (1 March). **9d.** Watermark Crowns. Two 9·5 mm phosphor bands reacting violet

XW13 =SG W4	Mint	Used
9d. Bronze-green	35	35
a. Phosphor omitted	£375	

Cylinder Number (Block of Six)
Single-pane cylinder. Perforation Type F (L) (I/E)

Cylinder No.		No Dot
1		6·50

1s.3d. Type XW3 (1958–1964)

1958 (29 September). **1s.3d.** Watermark Crowns

A. Cream Paper

XW15	Mint	Used
1s.3d. Green	4·00	2·00

B. Whiter Paper (11 May 1964)

XW15 =SG W5	Mint	Used
1s.3d. (1) Myrtle-green	5·00	90
(2) Deep dull green	40	40
(3) Deep myrtle-green	2·00	75

Cylinder Numbers (Blocks of Six)

Cream Paper (No XW14)

	Perforation Types	
Cylinder No. (No Dot)	B(I/P)	C (E/P)
2	32·00	32·00

Whiter Paper (No XW15)
Single pane cylinder. Perforation Type F (L) (I/E)

Cylinder No.	No Dot
2	15·00
3	6·50

Sold Out: 7.70.

XA WALES AND MONMOUTHSHIRE

1s.6d. Type XW3 (1967–1969)

1967 *(1 March).* **1s.6d.** Watermark Crowns. Two 9·5 mm phosphor bands reacting violet

XW16 =SG W6	Mint	Used
1s.6d. Grey-blue	40	40
a. Phosphor omitted	50·00	

Cylinder Number (Block of Six)
Single-pane cylinder. Perforation Type F (L) (I/E)

Cylinder No.		No Dot
1		6·50

Minor Constant Flaws

Cyl. 1	3/11	Small dot in top of left fork of "V" of "REVENUE"
	6/7	Coloured flaw in base of second "E" of "REVENUE"
	10/1	Small dot on upper right-hand leaf of leek (Th.F6)
	10/3	Small coloured flaw on Queen's neck (Th.D4)
	15/9	Retouch on Queen's shoulder just above collar (Th.E4)

1969 *(August 1).* **1s.6d.** No Watermark. Chalk-surfaced paper. PVA Gum. Two 9·5 mm phosphor bands reacting violet

XW17 =SG W12	Mint	Used
1s.6d. Grey-blue	2·00	2·00

Cylinder Number (Block of Six)
Single-pane cylinder. Perforation Type F (L) (1/E)

Cylinder No.		No Dot
1		40·00

Minor Constant Flaws: As for No. XW16

Presentation Pack

XWPP1	(9.12.70)	Six stamps	5·50

Comprises Nos. XW4, XW8/XW10, XW13 and XW16.

Quantity Sold: 32,964

Withdrawn: 25.11.71

First Day Covers
(Wales)

18.8.58	3d.	12·00
29.9.58	6d., 1.3d.	25·00
7.2.66	4d. ultramarine	7·00
1.3.67	9d., 1s.6d.	4·00
4.9.68	4d. olive-sepia, 5d.	3·00

Presentation Pack (Six Regions)

XPP1	(Issued 1960) Twelve values	£100

The issued pack contained one each of the ordinary 3d., 6d. and 1s.3d. stamps from Northern Ireland, Scotland and Wales and Monmouthshire and one each of the ordinary 3d. stamps from Guernsey, Jersey and the Isle of Man together with a 6-page printed leaflet describing the stamps.
Two forms of the pack exist:
(a) Inscribed 7s.3d. for sale in the UK and
(b) Inscribed $1.20 for sale in the USA

Imprimaturs from the NPM or BPMA
Imperforate, watermark Type W.**24**

3d. (cream paper)	£800
3d. (cream paper) cylinder 1 (no dot) block of six	£5500
3d. (whiter paper)	£800
3d. (whiter paper) cylinder 2 (no dot) block of six	£5500
6d. (cream paper)	£800
6d. (cream paper) cylinder 2 block of six	£5500
6d. (whiter paper)	£800
6d. (whiter paper) cylinder 3 block of six	£5500
9d. (2 band, violet phosphor)	£800
9d. (2 band, violet phosphor) cylinder 1 block of six	£5500
1s.3d. (cream paper)	£800
1s.3d. (cream paper) cylinder 2 block of six	£5500
1s.3d. (whiter paper)	£800
1s.3d. (whiter paper) cylinder 2 block of six	£5500
1s.6d. (2 bands, violet phosphor)	£800
1s.6d. (2 bands, violet phosphor) cylinder 1 block of six	£5500

Imperforate, no watermark

1s.6d. (chalky paper)	£800
1s.6d. (chalky paper) cylinder 1 block of six	£5500

Section ZA
Postage Due Stamps
1954–1969 Letterpress and
1968–1971 Photogravure

General Notes

Introduction. These stamps generally fulfilled two functions: the lower values, inscribed POSTAGE DUE, were affixed to understamped and unstamped correspondence by the Post Office, to indicate to the postman and to the addressee the amount which was to be collected on delivery (usually twice the excess). The higher values, inscribed TO PAY, were affixed to mail from abroad for the collection of customs charges. The same basic stamp design was in continual use from 1914 until 1971.

Printers. All the Postage Due stamps were printed letterpress by Harrison & Sons with the exception of the 4d. and 8d. values of 1969 and 1968, respectively, which were printed in photogravure.

They were printed on sheet-fed machines in single panes of 240 each arranged in 12 rows of 20 stamps and this applies to both printing processes.

Paper. As with the Wilding definitives, for about the first ten years the Postage Due stamps were printed on a creamy paper but starting in 1964 a whiter paper was gradually introduced as new printings were made. See the General Notes for Section S for further information. Exceptionally, the 2s.6d. to £1 values were always printed on a yellow paper which did not change its appearance.

From 1968 unwatermarked chalk-surfaced paper, as used for the Machin definitives, was introduced for a number of values.

Watermarks. These were used as follows:
W.**22** Tudor Crown   Nos. Z1/Z6 (1954–1955)
W.**23** St Edward's Crown Nos. Z7/Z16 (1955–1957)
W.**24** Crowns   Nos. Z17/Z37 (1959–1964)
No watermark   No. Z38 onwards (1968–1969)
See the General Notes for Section S for illustrations of these.

The watermarks are *always* sideways and *when seen from the back of the stamp* the normal watermark has the top of the Crowns pointing to right. In cases where the sheets were fed into the press the wrong way round (sideways inverted), the watermark appears as sideways with the Crowns pointing to left *when seen from the back of the stamp*.

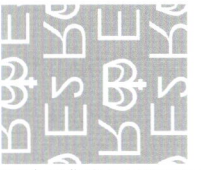

St Edward's Crown Watermark   Multiple Crowns Watermark
Sideways watermarks *as viewed from the back of the stamp*

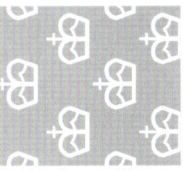

St Edward's Crown Watermark   Multiple Crowns Watermark
Sideways inverted watermarks *as viewed from the back of the stamp*

Gum. This was used as follows:
Gum Arabic   Nos. Z1/Z39 (1954–1968)
PVA Gum   No. Z40 onwards (1968–1969)
The distinction between gum arabic and PVA gum is explained in the General Notes relating to Section UA.

Perforation. All values are comb perforated 14×15. The perforation types used are given following each issue, and are described and illustrated in Appendix G. In the photogravure-printed values the cylinder numbers are listed and priced according to the type of perforator used. The letterpress issues do not have plate numbers.

Date of issue. The dates given are those on which the stamps were first issued by the Supplies Dept. to postmasters except in the case of dates for changes to chalky paper or to PVA gum when we have usually quoted dates of release by the Philatelic Bureau.

Sheet markings. Compared with other stamps the Postage Due stamps show very few markings.

Cylinder Numbers. These only occur on the photogravure-printed stamps, opposite Row 11 No. 1 (4d.) or opposite Row 10 No. 1 (8d.). They are similar in style to the illustration in Section S.

Marginal Arrows. These are "W" shaped at top and bottom of the sheet only. They appear solid (letterpress issues) or photo-etched (photogravure issues) as illustrated in Section S.

Marginal Rule. This occurs on all four sheet margins in the letterpress issues only. It is similar in style to the Narrow Rule illustration in Section S. In the 1½d., 6d., 5s., 10s. and £1 values an additional 1 mm. square appears at each corner of the sheet thus giving a neater appearance.

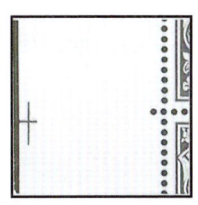

Morse Code marking   Cross

Other Markings. On the letterpress issues Morse Code markings as illustrated appear opposite rows 6/7 at both sides of the sheet. These are possibly allied to the way in which the printing plate was fixed to the press.

In photogravure issues the Morse Code markings are replaced by a cross as illustrated. These are often trimmed off.

ZA Postage Due Stamps

Watermarks. The normal sideways watermark *when seen from the back of the stamp* has the top of the Crowns pointing to right.

Type **Z1**. POSTAGE DUE

Type **Z2**. TO PAY

1954–55. *Letterpress.* **Watermark Tudor Crown, Type W.22**, sideways. Types **Z1** and **Z2** (2s.6d.).

			Mint	Used
Z1	=SG D40			
	½d.	Bright Orange (8.6.55)	7·00	5·25
	a.	Wmk. sideways inverted	£150	£150
Z2	=SG D41			
	2d.	Agate (28.7.55)	26·00	23·00
	a.	Wmk. sideways inverted		
Z3	=SG D42			
	3d.	Violet (4.5.55)	75·00	60·00
Z4	=SG D43			
	4d.	Blue (14.7.55)	26·00	32·00
	a.	Imperf. (pair)	£175	
Z5	=SG D44			
	5d.	Yellow-brown (19.5.55)	20·00	20·00
Z6	=SG D45			
	2s.6d.	Purple/yellow (11.54)	£150	5·75
	a.	Wmk. sideways inverted		

Perforation Type
Type A, all values

Imprimaturs from the NPM or BPMA

Imperforate, watermark Type W.**22** (sideways) ½d., 2d., 3d., 4d., 5d.	£750 each
Perf. 14 × 15, watermark Type W.**22** (sideways) 2s.6d.	—

1955–57. *Letterpress, Watermark St Edward's Crown, Type W.23, sideways.* Types **Z1** and **Z2** (2s.6d., 5s.).

			Mint	Used
Z7	=SG D46			
	½d.	Orange (16.7.56)	2·75	3·25
	a.	Wmk. sideways inverted	£100	
Z8	=SG D47			
	1d.	Violet-blue (7.6.56)	5·00	1·50
Z9	=SG D48			
	1½d.	Green (13.2.56)	8·50	7·00
	a.	Wmk. sideways inverted	£100	
	b.	Stop after "THREE" (Row 1)	20·00	
Z10	=SG D49			
	2d.	Agate (22.5.56)	45·00	3·50
Z11	=SG D50			
	3d.	Violet (5.3.56)	6·00	1·50
	a.	Wmk. sideways inverted	£125	
Z12	=SG D51			
	4d.	Blue (24.4.56)	25·00	6·00
	a.	Wmk. sideways inverted	£200	
Z13	=SG D52			
	5d.	Brown-ochre (23.3.56)	26·00	20·00
Z14	=SG D53			
	1s.	Ochre (22.11.55)	65·00	2·25
	a.	Wmk. sideways inverted		
Z15	=SG D54			
	2s.6d.	Purple/yellow (28.6.57)	£200	8·25
	a.	Wmk. sideways inverted		
Z16	=SG D55			
	5s.	Scarlet/yellow (25.11.55)	£150	32·00
	a.	Wmk. sideways inverted		£375

Stamps from the above issue are known bisected and used for half their face value at the following sorting offices:

1d. Huddersfield (1956), London SEDO (1957), Beswick, Manchester (1958)
2d. Eynsham, Oxford (1956), Garelochhead, Helensburgh (1956), Harpenden (1956), Hull (1956), Kingston on Thames (1956), Leicester Square, London WC (1956), London WC (1956)
3d. London SE (1957)
4d. Poplar, London E (1958)

Z9b Z19a
Stop after "THREE". Occurs on most stamps in Row 1

Perforation Types
Type A, all values, except that in the case of the 5s. the left-hand sheet margin is perforated through, possibly due to the use of a wider comb-head

Imprimaturs from the NPM or BPMA

Imperforate, watermark Type W.**23** (sideways) ½d., 1d., 1½d., 2d., 3d., 4d., 5d., 1s., 2s.6d., 5s.	£750 each

1959–70. *Letterpress.* **Watermark Crowns, Type W.24**, sideways. Types **Z1** and **Z2** (2s.6d. to £1).

A. Cream Paper

			Mint	Used
Z17	=SG D56			
	½d.	Orange (18.10.61)	50	1·25
Z18	=SG D57			
	1d.	Violet-blue (9.5.60)	50	20
Z19	=SG D58			
	1½d.	Green (5.10.60)	2·50	2·50
	a.	Stop after "THREE" (Row 1)	15·00	
Z20	=SG D59			
	2d.	Agate (14.9.59)	2·75	1·00
Z21	=SG D60			
	3d.	Violet (24.3.59)	75	25
Z22	=SG D61			
	4d.	Blue (17.12.59)	75	30
Z23	=SG D62			
	5d.	Yellow-brown (6.11.61)	90	60
	a.	Wmk. sideways inverted	28·00	
Z24	=SG D63			
	6d.	Purple (29.3.62)	1·00	1·25
Z25	=SG D64			
	1s.	Ochre (11.4.60)	3·00	50
Z26	=SG D65			
	2s.6d.	Purple/*yellow* (11.5.61)	3·00	50
	a.	Wmk. sideways inverted	15·00	15·00
Z27	=SG D66			
	5s.	Scarlet/*yellow* (8.5.61)	8·25	1·00
	a.	Wmk. sideways inverted	25·00	25·00

Z28 =SG D67

10s.	Blue/*yellow* (2.9.63)	11·00	5·75
a.	Wmk. sideways inverted (4.70)	40·00	25·00

Z29 =SG D68

£1	Black/*yellow* (2.9.63)	45·00	8·25

Whilst the 2s.6d. and 5s. already existed with watermark Crown to right further printings were issued in 1970, as also of the 10s., on highly fluorescent paper and with watermark Crown to right. These can only be distinguished by the use of a uv lamp and so are not listed separately.

B. Whiter Paper

Z30 =SG D56

½d.	Orange (22.9.64)	15	1·25
a.	Wmk. sideways inverted	2·00	

Z31 =SG D57

1d.	Violet-blue (1.3.65)	15	50
a.	Wmk. sideways inverted	£150	

Z32 =SG D59

2d.	Agate (1.3.65)	1·10	50
a.	Wmk. sideways inverted	£200	

Z33 =SG D60

3d.	Violet (1.6.64)	30	30
a.	Wmk. sideways inverted	£100	

Z34 =SG D61

4d.	Blue (3.3.64)	30	30
a.	Wmk. sideways inverted	£300	

Z35 =SG D62

5d.	Yellow-brown (9.6.64)	45	60
a.	Wmk. sideways inverted	5·00	6·00

Z36 =SG D63

6d.	Purple (30.1.64)	50	30
a.	Wmk. sideways inverted	£400	£400

Z37 =SG D64

1s.	Ochre (28.8.64)	90	30
a.	Wmk. sideways inverted	75·00	75·00

Stamps from the above issue are known bisected and used for half their face value at the following sorting offices:

- **1d.** Chieveley, Newbury (December 1962, March 1963), Henlan, Llandyssil (1961), Mayfield (1962), St Albans (1964)
- **2d.** Doncaster (?)

For illustration of No. Z19a, see No. Z9b.

Perforation Types
Type A, all values; 2s.6d. also Type A (T)

Imprimaturs from the NPM or BPMA

Imperforate, watermark Type W.**24** (sideways)	
Cream paper ½d., 1d., 1½d., 2d., 3d., 4d., 5d., 6d., 1s., 2s.6d., 5s., 10s., £1	£750 each
Whiter paper ½d., 1d., 2d., 3d., 4d., 5d., 6d., 1s.	£750 each

Sold Out: 1s. 11.68; 2d. 1.69; 4d. 11.69; 3d. 9.71; 6d. 10.71

Withdrawn: The 1½d. was withdrawn from sale to the public on 26.4.65. It had ceased to be issued on 31.1.65 but post offices continued to use existing stocks until exhausted.

1968–69. Letterpress. No Watermark. Chalk-surfaced paper. Type **Z1**

A. Gum Arabic

Z38 =SG D69

		Mint	*Used*
2d.	Agate (11.4.68)	75	1·00

Z39 =SG D71

4d.	Blue (25.4.68)	1·00	1·00

B. PVA Gum

Z40 =SG D69Ev

2d.	Agate (26.11.68)	75	

Z41 =SG D70

3d.	Violet (5.9.68)	1·00	1·00

Z42 =SG D71Ev

4d.	Blue (See footnote)	£2250	

Z43 =SG D72

5d.	Orange-brown (3.1.69)	8·00	11·00

Z44 =SG D73

6d.	Purple (5.9.68)	2·25	1·75

Z45 =SG D74

1s.	Ochre (19.11.68)	4·00	2·50

A copy of No. Z42 has been confirmed using infra-red attenuated total reflection spectroscopy, there is no date of issue.

Perforation Types
4d., 6d. Type A; other values Type A (T), except that in the case of the 2d. the right-hand sheet margin is perforated through and in the 4d. the left-hand sheet margin is perforated through, both possibly due to the use of a wider comb-head

1968–69. Smaller format. 21½×17½ mm. Photogravure. No watermark. Chalk-surfaced paper. PVA gum. Type **Z1**

Z46 =SG D75

4d.	Blue (12.6.69)	7·00	6·75

Z47 =SG D76

8d.	Red (3.10.68)	50	1·00

Cylinder Numbers (Block of Four (4d.) or Six (8d.))

		Perforation Type A (T) (E/P)
	Cyl. No.	*No dot*
4d.	1	35·00
8d.	1	5·00

On the 8d. the cylinder number appears as I.

Imprimaturs from the NPM or BPMA

Chalk-surfaced paper, imperforate. No watermark	
2d., 3d., 4d., 5d., 6d., 8d., 1s.	£750 each
8d. cylinder 1 block of six	£5250

Stamps from the above issue are known bisected and used for half their face value at the following sorting offices:

- **4d.** Northampton (1970)
- **6d.** Kilburn, London NW (1968)

Appendix G
Perforators

General Notes

Introduction. Two kinds of perforating machines were used for British stamps listed in this catalogue, 1952–70: sheet-fed and reel-fed. The sheet-fed machines employ a single-row or two-row comb and the reel-fed machines a three-row or four-row comb. Other than the single-row sheet-fed, both kinds are full width, i.e. they are able to perforate two panes side by side.

In sections 1 to 3, types A to H and J are the different sheet perforation types recorded in this catalogue, produced either by the sheet-fed or the reel-fed machines but they should not be regarded as representing the use of different machines, rather they are different sheet perforation types produced by various perforating machines.

At the beginning of the reign of Queen Elizabeth, the same perforaters were used as previously. Accordingly, in section 1, Type A with the sheet-fed, two-row horizontal comb is the same perforator as Type 5, described under "Perforators" in Volume 2 of this catalogue. Similarly, Types B and C are the same as Types 6 and 6B, Type E is the same as Type 5AE (extension hole at the bottom of even number stap rows) and Type F(L) is the same as Type 2 in Volume 2.

In section 4, Types E, E (½v) (from sheets), I, Ie, I (½v), AP, AP(2E) and P relate to booklet panes.

Guide Holes. Perforation guide holes can be an indication of the type of perforator used and these are recorded, where known, following the sheet perforation characteristics for each type. For reasons unknown these may not always appear in the sheet margins.

ORDER. This Appendix is divided into four sections:
1. Low Value Definitive Stamps
   (including Regionals and Postage Due Stamps)
2. High Value Definitive Stamps
3. Special Issues
4. Booklet Panes

Illustrations. The illustrations are all from definitive stamps but they are equally representative of the High Value and Special issues where the same types occur.

Table of Perforation Types. The useful tabulated list of Perforation Types at the end of section 3 is primarily designed to be used for Special issues, although, the first part may also be used in conjunction with the Low and High Value definitive stamps for Types A, A (T), B, C, E (no dot panes only).

1. Low Value Definitive Stamps

This section deals with the small-size Wilding and Machin definitives, the Regionals and the Postage Due Stamps.

Type A. Horizontal two-row comb. Sheet-fed.

No dot and dot panes		
	Top margin	Perforated through
	Bottom margin	Imperforate
	Left margin	A single extension hole
	Right margin	A single extension hole
	Guide holes	Opposite rows 14/15, at left (no dot panes) or right (dot panes)

In this machine an appropriate number of sheets (usually six to eight) are impaled through the guide holes and they go forward together under the comb. The imperf. margin (at the bottom) indicates the point of entry.

Type A (T). Horizontal two-row comb. Sheet-fed.

Single-pane printing		
	Top margin	Imperforate
	Bottom margin	Perforated through
	Left margin	A single extension hole
	Right margin	A single extension hole
	Guide holes	None

This is simply a top (T) instead of a bottom feed of Type A. In the definitive stamps it only occurs in the Postage Due Stamps. Cylinder blocks are identical in appearance with Type C.

Types B and C. Horizontal three-row comb. Reel-fed.

Type B. No dot panes		
	Top margin	Perforated through
	Bottom margin	Perforated through
	Left margin	Imperforate
	Right margin	A single extension hole
	Guide holes	Usually opposite rows 1, 7/8 and 14/15 at both sides of pane
Type C. No dot and dot panes		
	Top margin	Perforated through
	Bottom margin	Perforated through
	Left margin	A single extension hole
	Right margin	Imperforate
	Guide holes	As Type B, above

Type B is the left and Type C the right halves of the same reel-fed perforator. The outer ends of the comb are without extension pins, there being only single extension pins in the interpane margin. In this machine the continuous web of paper advances under the comb in a single thickness and without interruption, hence both top and bottom margins are perforated through.

It often happened that two narrow reels were perforated together by placing them side by side on the machine so that single-pane printings (i.e. no dot panes only) occur perforated with Type B and also Type C. It is only when double-pane printings are perforated on this machine that no dot panes will always be Type B and dot panes will always be Type C, except that in the Special issues, the 4d. Scout Jamboree stamp from Cyl. 1 dot is known with perforation Type B and Type C.

Type E. Horizontal two-row comb. Sheet-fed.

No dot panes	Top margin	Perforated through
	Bottom margin	Imperforate
	Left margin	A single extension hole on alternate rows only
	Right margin	A single extension hole
	Guide hole	Opposite rows 14/15, at left
Dot panes	Top margin	Perforated through
	Bottom margin	Imperforate
	Left margin	A single extension hole
	Right margin	A single extension hole on alternate rows only
	Guide hole	Opposite rows 14/15, at right

This is a simple variation of Type A (q.v.) that may result from the removal of a perforating pin or a repair to a comb-head. Therefore, no dot cylinder blocks are as Type A but left margin has the single extension hole missing on alternate rows.

Cylinder blocks from the dot pane would be indistinguishable from Type A, hence only no dot cylinder blocks are recorded with Type E.

Type F (L). Vertical single-row comb. Sheet-fed.

No dot panes	Top margin	Perforated through
	Bottom margin	A single extension hole
	Left margin	Imperforate
	Right margin	Perforated through
	Guide holes	Through marginal arrow above vertical rows 6/7 and below vertical row 10

This perforates from the left (L) through to the right side of the sheet. In this catalogue it has been used only on 6d. Single-pane printings (i.e. no dot panes only), S104 and S106.

Type F (L)*. Vertical two-row comb. Sheet-fed.

No dot panes	Top margin	A single extension hole
	Bottom margin	A single extension hole
	Left margin	Imperforate
	Right margin	Perforated through
	Guide holes	Above and below eighth vertical row
Dot panes	Top margin	A single extension hole
	Bottom margin	A single extension hole
	Left margin	Perforated through
	Right margin	Perforated through
	Guide holes	None (occur on no dot panes only)

This is similar to Type F (L) but is used when double-pane printings (i.e. no dot and dot panes) have been perforated together prior to their being guillotined into single sheets. This gives no dot cylinder blocks exactly as Type F (L) but because the vertical comb has perforated horizontally from left to right across both panes the interpane margin is also perforated and, therefore, the dot cylinder blocks are perforated through the left margin.

Type H. Horizontal two-row comb. Sheet-fed.

No dot panes	Top margin	Perforated through
	Bottom margin	Imperforate
	Left margin	A single extension hole
	Right margin	Perforated through
	Guide hole	Opposite rows 14/15, at left
Dot panes	Top margin	Perforated through
	Bottom margin	Imperforate
	Left margin	Perforated through
	Right margin	A single extension hole
	Guide hole	Opposite rows 14/15, at right

This is a further variation of Type A (q.v.) differing by the fact that the interpane margin is perforated through instead of there being single extension holes at the end of every row at right on the no dot pane and at the end of every row at left on the dot pane. Therefore, dot cylinder blocks are as Type A but left margin is perforated through. Cylinder blocks from the no dot pane would be indistinguishable from Type A, hence only dot cylinder blocks are recorded with Type H.

Type J. Vertical two-row comb. Sheet-fed.

Single pane printing	Top margin	A single extension hole
	Bottom margin	Perforated through
	Left margin	Imperforate
	Right margin	Perforated through
	Guide holes	Through marginal arrow above vertical rows 6/7 and below vertical row 10

This is similar to Type F (L) (q.v.), except that the top and bottom perforations are reversed. Accordingly, the bottom sheet margin is perforated through instead of there being only a single extension hole at the bottom of every column. Cylinder blocks are identical in appearance with Type B.

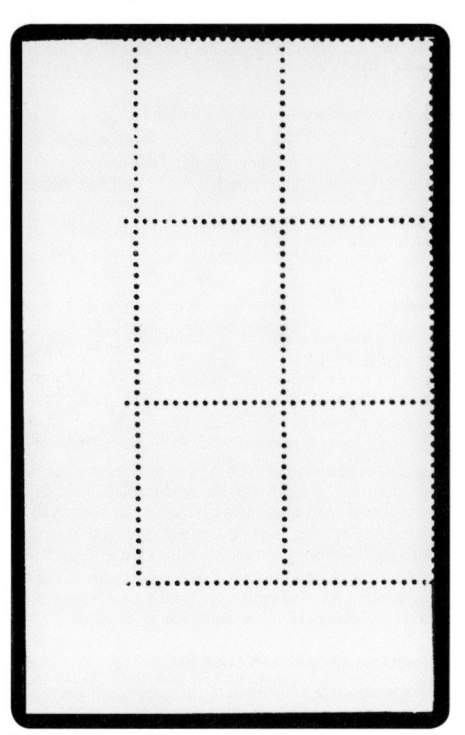

Appendix G *Perforators*

Type A No Dot and Dot panes

Types C and A (T) Right or Dot pane

Types B and J Left or No Dot pane

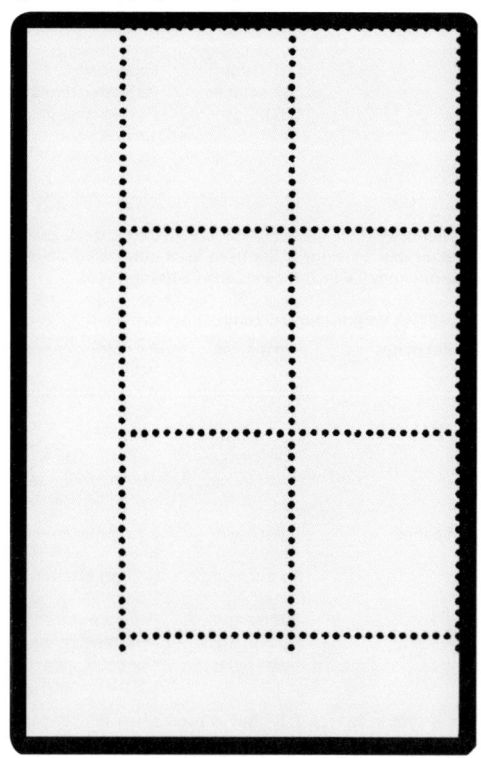

Types F(L) and F(L)* (no dot panes)

Perforators   Appendix G   **G**

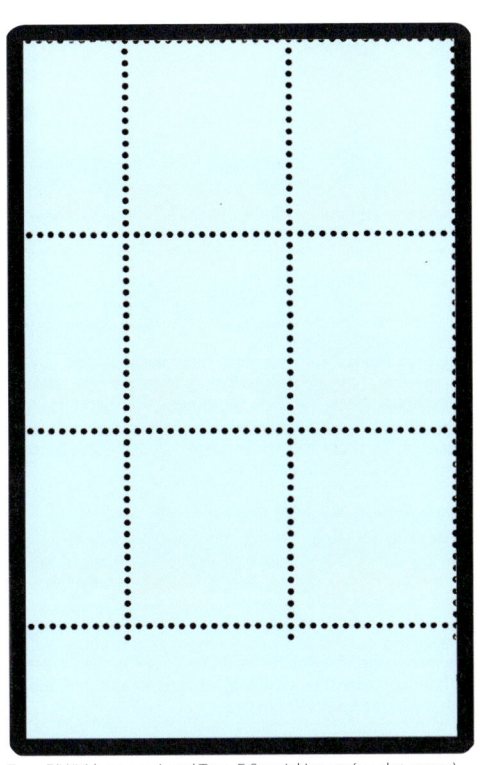

Type F(L)* (dot panes) and Type F Special Issues (no dot panes)

2. High Value Definitive Stamps

This section deals with the Wilding and Machin High Value stamps.

Wilding High Values

Perforation Type A, as described at the beginning of this Appendix, was used exclusively for these stamps. Waterlow and De La Rue both used a single-row comb and Bradbury, Wilkinson a two-row comb.

The guide holes appear opposite row 6, at left on left-hand panes and at right on right-hand panes.

For diagram showing printers guide marks see the General Notes for Section T.

Machin £.s.d. High Values

The printer's sheet was perforated with Type A prior to being guillotined into four panes, so that the characteristics of each individual Post Office pane are different and this has, therefore, been described as perforation Type A*. The description of Type A, given at the beginning of this Appendix, applies equally to Type A*, except that Bradbury, Wilkinson used a single-row comb.

For diagram showing the printer's sheet, the method of perforation and the position of plate numbers and guide holes see the General Notes for Section UC.

G Appendix G Perforators

3. Special Issues

Type A. In the special issues this type is exactly as described at the beginning of this Appendix except that with single-pane printings (i.e. no dot panes only) the guide holes are opposite rows 14/15, at both sides of the sheet.

Type A (T). In the special issues this type is exactly as described at the beginning of this Appendix and it applies equally to both no dot and dot panes. Guide holes very rarely appear in the sheet margins but where they do this is given under Sheet Details in Section W.

Types B and C. In the special issues these types are exactly as described in the first part of this Appendix.

Type E. Horizontal two-row comb. Sheet-fed.

Right-hand panes	Top margin	Perforated through
	Bottom margin	Imperforate
	Left margin	A single extension hole on alternate rows only
	Right margin	A single extension hole
	Guide hole	Opposite rows 14/15, at right

This is a variation of Type A that may result from the removal of a perforating pin or a repair to a comb-head. Therefore, cylinder blocks are as Type A but left margin has the single extension hole missing on alternate rows.

This type is only known on the 1s.3d. Freedom from Hunger and the 3d. Red Cross on the right-hand panes only (i.e. dot cylinder pane of 3d. Red Cross). The left-hand panes in both cases are believed to be Type A.

Perforation Type E did not affect the cylinder blocks of the 1s.3d. Freedom from Hunger issue as the cylinder numbers were placed at bottom right corner of each pane, at the opposite side of the left margin perforated with alternate extension holes.

Types F and F (L). Vertical single-row comb. Sheet-fed. Single pane printings.

Type F. Right feed	Top margin	A single extension hole
	Bottom margin	A single extension hole
	Left margin	Perforated through
	Right margin	Imperforate
Type F (L). Left feed	Top margin	A single extension hole
	Bottom margin	A single extension hole
	Left margin	Imperforate
	Right margin	Perforated through

Type F perforates from the right through to the left side of the sheet and Type F (L) perforates from the left through to the right side of the sheet. Both types are used for single pane printings (i.e. no dot panes only). Guide holes very rarely appear in the sheet margins but where they do this is given under Sheet Details in Section W.

Type G. Vertical single-row comb. Sheet-fed.

No dot and dot panes	Top margin	Perforated through
	Bottom margin	Perforated through
	Left margin	Perforated through
	Right margin	Imperforate
	Guide holes	None

This was a special perforator used exclusively for the 6d. Battle of Hastings issue. The cylinder block is perforated through in both the bottom and left margins.

Table of Special Issue Perforation Types

The table below combines a list of the different sheet perforation types recorded in Section W, together with the characteristics of the four sheet margins. Following the basic perforation type the characteristics given relate to the sheet viewed with the stamps the right way up.

The identification of a particular perforation type from a cylinder block (or any corner block) can easily be established by referring to this table in conjunction with the recorded types under Cylinder Numbers in Section W.

Whilst this table is mainly designed to be used for the special stamps, the first part may also be used in conjunction with the Low and High Value definitive stamps for Types A, A (T), B, C, E (no dot panes only) and F (L).

I. Horizontal Format Stamps

Perforation Type	Top margin	Bottom margin	Left margin	Right margin
Type A (bottom feed)	Perforated through	Imperforate	Single extension hole	Single extension hole
Type A (T) (top feed)	Imperforate	Perforated through	Single extension hole	Single extension hole
Type B	Perforated through	Perforated through	Imperforate	Single extension hole
Type C	Perforated through	Perforated through	Single extension hole	Imperforate
Type E	Perforated through	Imperforate	Single extension hole alternate rows only	Single extension hole
Type F (right feed)	Single extension hole	Single extension hole	Perforated through	Imperforate
Type F (L) (left feed)	Single extension hole	Single extension hole	Imperforate	Perforated through
Type G	Perforated through	Perforated through	Perforated through	Imperforate

II. Vertical Format Stamps*

Perforation Type	Top margin	Bottom margin	Left margin	Right margin
Type A (head to right)	Single extension hole	Single extension hole	Perforated through	Imperforate
Type A (head to left)	Single extension hole	Single extension hole	Imperforate	Perforated through
Type A (T) (head to right)	Single extension hole	Single extension hole	Imperforate	Perforated through
Type A (T) (head to left)	Single extension hole	Single extension hole	Perforated through	Imperforate
Type B (head to right)	Single extension hole	Imperforate	Perforated through	Perforated through
Type C (head to right)	Imperforate	Single extension hole	Perforated through	Perforated through
Type F (head to right)	Imperforate	Perforated through	Single extension hole	Single extension hole

* The position of the head on vertical format stamps is determined by viewing the sheet with the marginal rule (normally on a short side) at the bottom. In most instances the head (or top of the stamp) is to the right; the head to the left occurring on the 3d. Post Office Tower, 4d. Football World Cup, 4d. World Cup Victory and the 3d. and 1s.6d. 1966 Christmas issue, although the latter does not in fact bear marginal rules but it should be regarded as being head to left.

From the 1966 Christmas issue onwards many sheets did not bear marginal rules. Where this is the case with vertical format designs the correct orientation of the sheets to determine the perforation type is given below the Cylinder Numbers in the listings.

Exceptionally, the 1967 British Paintings 4d. and the British Discovery and Inventions 1s.9d. show the marginal rule on a long side and this should be orientated to the left-hand side to show perforation Types A (T) (head to right) and F (head to right), respectively.

G Appendix G *Perforators*

4. Booklet Panes

(a) Panes of Four

Type I

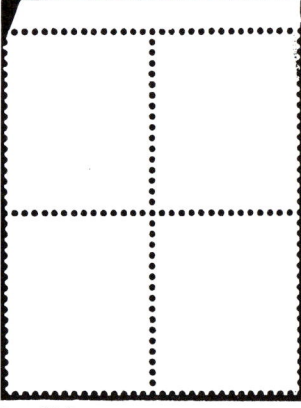

Type I(½v)

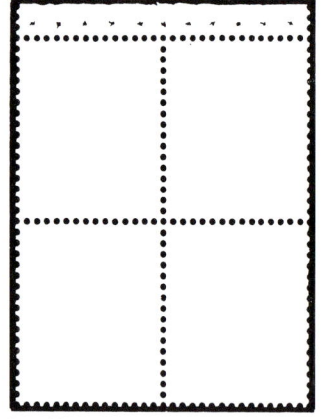

Type AP

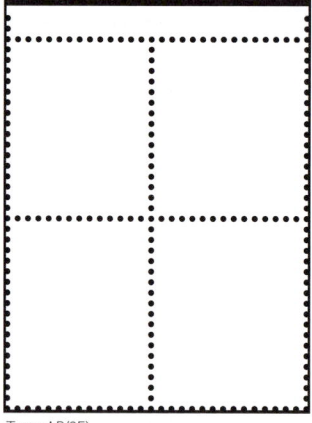

Type AP(2E)

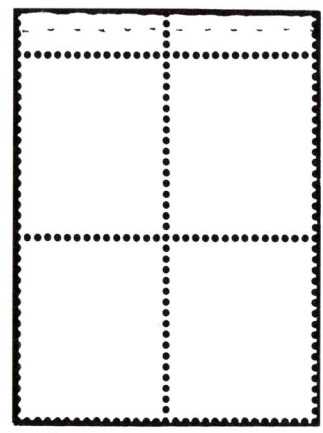

Type P

Type I. Margin imperforate
Type I(½v). Ditto but with slanting cut at left or right (left illustrated)
Type AP. Margin perforated through alternate rows
Type AP(2E) Margin perforated alternate rows, but two extension holes only
Type P. Margin fully perforated through every row

In order to facilitate access to the bottom selvedge of sheets with sideways watermark panes (and a side selvedge for Holiday Booklet (NR1/NR1a), which was torn off by hand, a slanting scissor cut was made in the imperforate trimmed margin. This pane is termed I(½v). The vertical perforations below the cut must be torn, and not guillotined, for the pane to be authentic. Occasionally, a scissored cut was not used, so the I (½v) pane can exist with a torn selvedge and torn adjacent perforations.

Panes of four with Type AP(2E) occur in the majority of issues with sideways watermark. This was caused by the main perforator having a pin missing from the bottom line of the comb in the margin adjacent to stamps in column 12 of the sheet, resulting in Type AP(2E) perforations on 12 panes in each sheet.

Appendix G

(b) Panes of Six

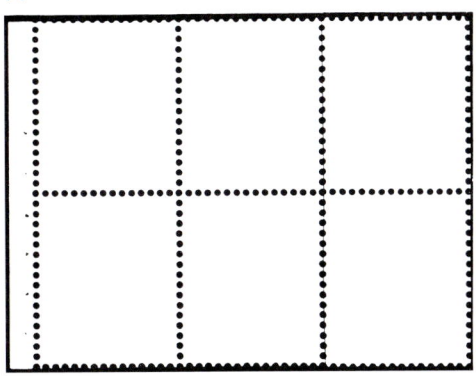

Type I

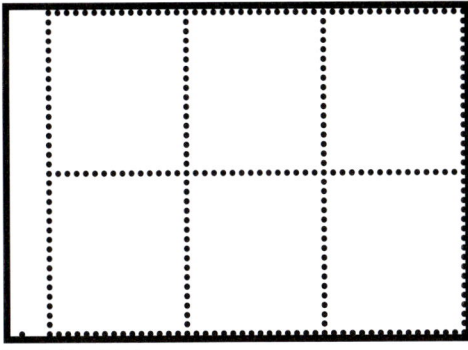

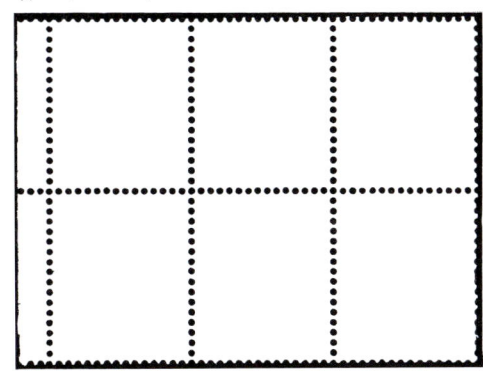

Type Ie (at bottom)

Type P

Type I. Margin imperforate
Type Ie. Margin with extension hole set wide
Type P. Margin every row perforated through

Generally, all panes of six were rotary printed in double sheets and perforated in the web, resulting in Type I and Ie. Exceptionally, UB3 and UB4 were printed in single sheets and sheet perforated, UB3 in Type I, later changed to Type P, and UB4 in Type P only.

Both the 20-row and the 21-row sheets perforated with Type I come with extension holes in the margin between the no dot and dot sheets. The 20-row sheets, giving rise to Type Ie. were perforated with a three-row comb, so that panes can be found with traces of the inter-pane extension hole at the top, in the middle or at the bottom of the binding margin. After the change to 21-row sheets a four-row comb was used and on these panes the extension hole can be found at the top or at the bottom of the margin only. As an aid to identification, all dot cylinder panes should have traces of the extension hole.

On 21-row sheets the perforated web is cut at every 20th row to make sheets of 480 (two panes of 240 (20×12)). Consequently on successive sheets the cylinder number appears one row lower so that a pane can have it adjoining the top or bottom row. In the listing of cylinder panes the letter "T" after the cylinder number indicates that it is a pane with the cylinder number adjoining the top row.

For a short period during March/April 1954, the bottom selvedge of some panes for label panes SB23 and SB24 was torn off using a scissor cut, resulting in Type I(½v) perforation, described under section (a) of these notes. These are rare and are known on a few cylinder panes.

(c) Panes of Fifteen

These come from the £1 Stamps for Cooks booklet and are all perforated Type I.

(d) Panes of Two

Type E(½v)

Type E. Extension hole in the margin in each row
Type E(½v). Ditto but with slanting cut at top or bottom (bottom illustrated)
Type I. Margin imperforate
Type I(½v). Ditto but with slanting cut at top or bottom

The panes of two stamps were made up from columns 1 and 2 of counter sheets. The vertical sheet margin was guillotined leaving a narrow binding margin which was either imperforate or showed an extension hole at the top and bottom of the binding margin. In addition, both types exist with the slanting scissor cut already described under section (a) of these notes. Panes with this form of separation show torn and not guillotined perforations below the cut. As mentioned above, occasionally a scissor cut was not used, resulting in a torn imperforate selvedge.

Appendix HB
Postage Rates

Postage rates from 1635 have been researched from official records and the following extract is reproduced with kind permission of the Post Office. The rates given apply only to the period covered by this Catalogue.

Letter Post

The Treasury was empowered to regulate rates of postage, and subsequent changes were made by Treasury Warrant

Date	Rates of Charge	
1 May 1952	2oz.	2½d.
	4oz.	3d.
	Then 1d. for each additional 2oz.	
1 January 1956	2oz.	2½d.
	Then 1½d. for each additional 2oz.	
1 October 1957	1oz.	3d.
	2oz.	4½d.
	Then 1½d. for each additional 2oz.	
17 May 1965	2oz.	4d.
	Each additional 2oz. up to 1lb. 2d.	
	Each additional 2oz. thereafter 3d.	
3 October 1966	2oz.	4d.
	Each additional 2oz. up to 1lb. 2d.	
	Each additional 2oz. up to 1lb. 8oz. 3d.	
	Over 1lb. 8oz. up to 2lb. 3s.6d.	
	Each additional 1lb. 2s.	

Introduction of the first and second class services for letters and cards.

Date	Weight not exceeding	First Class	Second Class
16 September 1968	4oz.	5d.	4d.
	6oz.	9d.	6d.
	8oz.	1s. 0d.	8d.
	10oz.	1s. 3d.	10d.
	12oz.	1s. 6d.	1s. 0d.
	14oz.	1s. 9d.	1s. 2d.
	1lb 0oz.	2s. 0d.	1s. 4d.
	1lb 2oz.	2s. 3d.	1s. 6d.
	1lb 4oz.	2s. 6d.	1s. 7d.
	1lb 6oz.	2s. 9d.	1s. 8d.
	1lb 8oz.	3s. 0d.	1s. 9d.
	2lb 0oz.	4s. 0d.	Not admissible over 1½lbs.
	Each additional 1lb. 2s.		

Postcards

From 1925 the maximum size allowed was 5⅞ × 4⅛in and the minimum size was 4 × 2¾in.

Date	Charge
1 May 1940	2d.
1 October 1957	2½d.
17 May 1965	3d.

Printed Papers

Date	Rates of Charge	
1 June 1951	4oz.	1½d.
	Then ½d. for each additional 2oz. up to 2lb.	
1 January 1956	2oz.	1½d.
	Then 1d. for each additional 2oz.	
1 June 1956	4oz.	2d.
	Then 1d. for each additional 2oz.	
1 October 1957	2oz.	2d.
	4oz.	4d.
	Then 1d. for each additional 2oz.	
1 October 1961	2oz.	2½d.
	4oz.	4d.
17 May 1965	Not over 2oz.	3d.
	Not over 4oz.	5d.
	Each additional 2oz.	1d.

Newspaper Post

From 1870 the charge had been ½d. per copy irrespective of weight, but from 1 November 1915 the maximum weight permitted was 2lb.

Date	Charge Per Copy not exceeding	
1 July 1940	4oz.	1½d.
	Then ½d. for each additional 4oz.	
1 June 1956	6oz.	2d.
	Then 1d for each additional 6oz.	
1 October 1957	6oz.	2½d.
	Then 1½d. for each additional 6oz.	
1 October 1961	6oz.	3d.
	Then 1½d. for each 6oz.	
17 May 1965	2oz.	3d.
	4oz.	5d.
	Then 1d. for each additional 2oz. Per copy regulation abolished	

Articles for the Blind

This service was made free of charge from 17 May 1965 (maximum weight 15lb.).

Date		Rates of Charge
1 July 1940	2lb.	½d.
	5lb.	1d.
	8lb.	1½d.
	11lb.	2d.
	15lb.	2½d.
12 April 1954	2lb.	½d.
	5lb	1d.
	8lb.	1½d.
	11lb.	2d.
	15lb.	2½d.

Note that the rates were unchanged in 1954 but certain details of the regulations were amended, including the fact that the rates were extended to mail to the Irish Republic.

Registration Rates for Inland and Overseas Mail

During the period covered by this catalogue the registration fee on overseas letters (including airmail) was generally the same as the inland fee, with the exception of a few short periods noted below.

Date	Cover	Fee
1 May 1949	£5	4d.
	£20	5d.
	£40	6d.
	£60	7d.
	Each additional £20 up to £400 – 1d. Maximum fee 2s.	
1 May 1952	£5	6d.
	£20	7d.
	£40	8d.
	£60	9d.
	Each additional £20 up to £400 – 1d. Maximum fee 2s. 2d.	
1 June 1956	£10	1s.
	£20	1s. 1d.
	£40	1s. 2d.
	£60	1s. 3d.
	Each additional £20 up to £400 – 1d. Maximum fee 2s. 8d. The registration fee on overseas mail remained 6d. until 1 October 1957.	
1 February 1961	£20	1s. 6d.
	£40	1s. 7d.
	£40	1s. 8d.
	£60	1s. 9d.
	Each additional £20 up to £400 – 1d. Maximum fee 3s.1d.	
25 April 1963	£20	1s. 9d.
	£40	1s. 10d.
	£60	1s. 11d.
	£80	2s.
	Each additional £20 up to £400 – 1d. Maximim fee 3s. 4d. The registration fee on overseas mail remained 1s. 6d until 1 July 1963.	

Recorded Delivery

This service was introduced on 1 February 1961 for letters that contained no valuables but for which the sender required a signature on delivery. It was available for any class of inland mail. The fee charged was 6d. per item, rising to 9d. on 3 October 1966.

Express Service

Service 1. Express by special messenger all the way.

Date	Charges	Notes
1934	6d. per mile plus cost of special conveyance if used. Weight fee (for packets over 1lb.) 3d.	Charge for additional articles 1d. per article after the first. Waiting fee 2d. for each 10 minutes after the first 10 minutes
1 January 1956	1s. per mile plus cost of special conveyance if used	Additional articles 2½d. for each item beyond the first. Waiting fee 4d. for each 10 minutes after the first 10 minutes
1 October 1957	As above	Additional articles 3d. for each item beyond the first
17 May 1965	3s. per mile plus cost of special conveyance if used	Each additional article 4d. for each item beyond the first. Waiting fee 1s. for each 10 minutes after the first 10 minutes

Service 2. Special Delivery at the request of the sender. Post Office messenger from the delivery office after transmission by post.

Date	Charges	Notes
1 January 1956	Full postage plus special fee of 1s. (from 1934 6d.).	If a special conveyance was used the actual cost, or if that was unknown, 1s. per mile
17 May 1965	Full postage plus special fee of 3s.	As above but 6s. per mile
16 September 1968	As above but only for first class service.	

There was also a Limited Sunday Special Delivery Service. Charges were as for Service 2 except the special fee was 1s.6d. in 1934; 3s. from 1 January 1956 and 9s. from 17 May 1965 in addition to full postage.

The service providing for the express delivery of a message received by telephone was withdrawn on 30 December 1955.

Service 3. Express delivery all the way at the request of the addressee. Charges were the same as for Service 1. Additional articles 2d. for every ten beyond the first (from 1934 1d.). From 17 May 1965 this charge was increased to 6d. for every ten after the first.

Railex

This service was introduced on 1 January 1934. It provided for the conveyance of a postal packet to a railway station by Post Office messenger for despatch on the first available train, and for its immediate delivery by Post Office messenger from the station of destination.

Date	Charge	
1 July 1940	Not exceeding 2oz.	3s. 0d.
	Over 2oz. and up to 1lb	3s. 6d.
1 January 1956	Not over 2oz.	6s. 0d.
	Not over 1lb	7s. 0d.
17 May 1965	Charge per packet (irrespective of weight but not exceeding 1lb.)	20s. 0d.

Appendix HB   Postage Rates

Official Parcel Post
This service had first been introduced on 1 August 1883.

Date		Rates of Postage
31 March 1952	2lb.	11d.
	3lb.	1s. 1d.
	4lb.	1s. 3d.
	5lb.	1s. 5d.
	6lb.	1s. 7d.
	7lb.	1s. 9d.
	8lb.	1s. 10d.
	11lb.	1s. 11d.
	15lb.	2s.
7 April 1953	2lb.	1s.
	3lb.	1s. 2d.
	4lb.	1s. 4d.
	5lb.	1s. 6d.
	6lb.	1s. 8d.
	7lb.	1s. 10d.
	8lb.	1s. 11d.
	11lb.	2s.
	15lb.	2s. 1d.
12 April 1954	2lb.	1s. 1d.
	3lb.	1s. 3d.
	4lb.	1s. 6d.
	5lb.	1s. 8d.
	6lb.	1s. 10d.
	7lb.	2s.
	8lb.	2s. 1d.
	11lb.	2s. 3d.
	15lb.	2s. 4d.
1 January 1956	2lb.	1s. 3d.
	3lb.	1s. 5d.
	4lb.	1s. 8d.
	5lb.	1s. 11d.
	6lb.	2s. 1d.
	7lb.	2s. 3d.
	8lb.	2s. 6d.
	11lb.	2s. 8d.
	15lb.	2s. 9d.
1 June 1956.	2lb.	1s. 4d.
	3lb.	1s. 6d.
	4lb.	1s. 9d.
	5lb.	2s.
	6lb.	2s. 3d.
	7lb.	2s. 6d.
	8lb.	2s. 9d.
	15lb.	3s.
1 October 1957	2lb.	1s. 6d.
	3lb.	1s. 9d.
	4lb.	2s.
	5lb.	2s. 3d.
	6lb.	2s. 6d.
	7lb.	2s. 9d.
	8lb.	3s.
	11lb.	3s. 3d.
	15lb.	3s. 6d.
1 October 1961	2lb.	2s.
	3lb.	2s. 3d.
	4lb.	2s. 6d.
	5lb.	2s. 9d.
	6lb.	3s.
	7lb.	3s. 3d.
	8lb.	3s. 6d.
	11lb.	3s. 9d.

Date		Rates of Postage
	15lb.	4s.
29 April 1963.	2lb.	2s.
	3lb.	2s. 3d.
	4lb.	2s. 6d.
	5lb.	2s. 9d.
	6lb.	3s.
	8lb.	3s. 6d.
	10lb.	4s.
	12lb.	4s. 6d.
	15lb.	5s.
	18lb.	5s. 9d.
	22lb.	6s. 6d.

Increased weight limit of 22 lbs. introduced 18 February 1963

17 May 1965	2lb.	2s. 9d.
	3lb.	3s.
	4lb.	3s. 3d.
	6lb.	3s. 6d.
	8lb.	4s.
	10lb.	4s. 6d.
	14lb.	5s. 6d.
	18lb.	6s. 6d.
	22lb.	7s. 6d.
3 October 1966 (Ordinary Rate)	1½lb.	2s. 6d.
	2lb.	3s.
	6lb.	4s. 6d.
	10lb.	6s.
	14lb.	7s. 6d.
	18lb.	9s.
	22lb.	10s. 6d.

(Local delivery) As for ordinary less 1s.0d. at each step.
The Local Parcel Delivery comprised all places which had, in their local address, the same post town name as that of the office of posting.

Overseas Letter Rates (Surface Mail)
From 1 July 1948 mail to European destinations was sent by airmail at surface mail rates.

Date	Weight	Foreign Fee	Empire Fee
1 October 1951	1oz	4d.	2½d.
	2oz	6½d.	3½d.
	3oz	9d.	4½d.
	4oz	11½d.	5½d.
	Each additional oz	2½d.	1d.
1 October 1957	1oz	6d.	3d.
	2oz	10d.	4½d.
	3oz	1s. 2d.	6d.
	4oz	1s. 6d.	7½d.
	Each additional oz	4d.	1½d.
17 May 1965	1oz	6d.	4d.
	2oz	10d.	5½d.
	3oz	1s. 2d.	7d.
	4oz	1s. 6d.	8½d.
	Each additional oz	4d.	1½d.

Postage Rates Appendix HB

Date	Weight	Foreign Fee	Empire Fee
3 October 1966	1oz	9d.	4d.
	2oz	1s. 2d.	5½d.
	3oz	1s. 7d.	7d.
	4oz	2s.	8½d.
	Each additional oz	5d.	1½d.
16 September 1968	1oz	9d.	5d.
	2oz	1s. 2d.	7d.
	3oz	1s. 7d.	9d.
	4oz	2s.	11d.
	Each additional oz	5d.	2d.

Postcard Rates (Surface Mail)

Date	Foreign rate	Empire rate
1 October 1950	2½d.	2d.
1 October 1957	4d.	2½d.
17 May 1965	4d.	3d.
3 October 1966	5d.	5d.

Small Packet Rates (Surface Mail)

The small packet service allowed for small articles of merchandise to a maximum weight of 2lb to be sent with letter mail. Letters could not be included, but packets could contain dutiable items as long as they complied with postal and customs regulations and a green Customs label was attached.

Date	Weight	Fee
1 October 1950	10oz	7½d.
	12oz	9d.
	14oz	10½d.
	1lb	1s.
	Each additional 2oz	1½d. (Maximum 2s.)
1 October 1957	10oz	10d.
	12oz	1s.
	14oz	1s. 2d.
	1lb	1s. 4d.
	Each additional 2oz	2d. (Maximum 2s.8d.)
1 July 1963	10oz	1s. 0½d.
	12oz	1s. 3d.
	14oz	1s. 5½d.
	1lb	1s. 8d.
	Each additional 2oz	2½d. (Maximum 3s.4d.)
3 October 1966	8oz	1s. 6d.
	10oz	1s. 8d.
	12oz	2s.
	14oz	2s. 4d.
	Each additional 2oz	4d. (Maximum 5s.4d.)

Printed Paper Rates (Surface Mail)

From 1950 a 'reduced rate' was introduced for printed papers, not of a 'commercial character', including pamphlets, maps, books and sheet music.

Date	Weight	Full Rate	Reduced Rate
1 October 1950	2oz	1½d.	1d.
	4oz	2d.	1½d.
	6oz	2½d.	2d.
	8oz	3d.	2½d.
	Each additional 2oz	½d.	½d.
1 October 1957	2oz	2d.	1½d.
	4oz	3d.	2½d.
	6oz	4d.	3½d.
	8oz	5d.	4½d.
	Each additional 2oz	1d.	1d.
1 July 1963	2oz	2½d.	2d.
	4oz	4d.	3½d.
	6oz	5½d.	5d.
	8oz	7d.	6½d.
	Each additional 2oz	½d.	1½d.
3 October 1966	2oz	4d.	2d.
	4oz	6d.	3½d.
	6oz	8d.	5d.
	8oz	10d.	6½d.
	Each additional 2oz	2d.	1½d.
16 September 1968	2oz	4d.	2d.
	4oz	6d.	3d.
	6oz	8d.	6d.
	8oz	10d.	9d.
	Each additional 2oz	2d.	3d.

Airmail Rates

From 17 January 1947 the countries of the world were grouped into zones:
Zone A North Africa and the Middle East
Zone B The Americas, most of Africa and the Indian subcontinent.
Zone C East and South-East Asia, Australasia and Oceania.
Mail to Europe was normally sent by air at surface mail rates.

Date	Weight	Zone A	Zone B	Zone C
17 January 1947	½oz	6d.	1s.	1s. 3d.
	1oz	1s.	2s.	2s. 6d.
	1½oz	1s. 6d.	3s.	3s. 9d.
	2oz	2s.	4s.	5s.
	Each additional ½oz	6d.	1s.	1s. 3d.
1 May 1952	½oz	9d.	1s. 3d.	1s. 6d.
	1oz	1s. 6d	2s. 6d.	3s.
	1½oz	2s. 3d.	3s. 9d.	4s. 6d.
	2oz	3s.	5s.	6s.
	Each additional ½oz	9d.	1s. 3d.	1s. 6d.
3 October 1966	½oz	1s.	1s. 6d.	1s. 9d.
	1oz	2s.	3s.	3s. 6d.
	1½oz	3s.	4s. 6d.	5s. 3d.
	2oz	4s.	6s.	7s.
	Each additional ½oz	1s.	1s. 6d.	1s. 9d.

Postcard Rates (Airmail)

Date	Zone A	Zone B	Zone C
17 January 1947	3d.	6d.	7d.
1 May 1952	5d.	8d.	9d.
3 October 1966	6d.	9d.	10d.

Appendix HB Postage Rates

Small Packet Rates (Airmail)
The maximum weight was 2lb

Date	Weight	Zone A	Zone B	Zone C
1 October 1950	½oz	7½d.	7½d.	7½d.
	1oz	7½d.	8d.	10d.
	1½oz	9d.	1s.	1s. 3d.
	2oz	1s.	1s. 4d.	1s. 8d.
	Each additional ½oz Minimum rate 7½d.	3d.	4d.	5d.
1 May 1952	½oz	7½d.	7½d.	7½d.
	1oz	10d.	1s.	1s. 2d.
	1½oz	1s. 3d.	1s. 6d.	1s. 9d.
	2oz	1s. 8d.	2s.	2s. 4d.
	Each additional ½oz Minimum rate 7½d.	5d.	6d.	7d.
1 October 1957	½oz	10d.	10d.	10d.
	1oz	1s. 3d.	1s.	1s. 2d.
	1½oz	1s. 8d.	1s. 6d.	1s. 9d.
	2oz	2s. 1d.	2s.	2s. 4d.
	Each additional ½oz Minimum rate 10d.	5d.	6d.	7d.
1 June 1963	½oz	1s. 0½d.	1s. 0½d.	1s. 0½d.
	1oz	1s. 0½d.	1s. 0½d.	1s. 2d.
	1½oz	1s. 3d.	1s. 6d.	1s. 9d.
	2oz	1s. 8d.	2s.	2s. 4d.
	Each additional ½oz Minimum rate 1s. 0½d.	5d.	6d.	7d.
3 October 1966	1oz	1s. 6d.	1s. 6d.	1s. 6d.
	1½oz	1s. 6d.	1s. 9d.	2s.
	2oz	2s.	2s. 4d.	2s. 8d.
	2½oz	2s. 6d.	2s. 11d.	3s. 4d.
	Each additional ½oz Minimum rate 1s. 6d.	6d.	7d.	8d.

Printed Paper Rates (Airmail)

Date	Weight	Zone A	Zone B	Zone C
1 February 1948	½oz	3d.	4d.	5d.
	1oz	6d.	8d.	10d.
	1½oz	9d.	1s.	1s. 3d.
	2oz	1s.	1s. 4d.	1s. 8d.
	Each additional ½oz	3d.	4d.	5d.
1 May 1952	½oz	5d.	6d.	7d.
	1oz	10d.	1s.	1s. 2d.
	1½oz	1s. 3d.	1s. 6d.	1s. 9d.
	2oz	1s. 8d.	2s.	2s. 4d.
	Each additional ½oz	5d.	6d.	7d.
3 October 1966	½oz	6d.	7d.	8d.
	1oz	1s.	1s. 2d.	1s. 4d.
	1½oz	1s. 6d.	1s. 9d.	2s.
	2oz	2s.	2s. 4d.	2s. 8d.
	Each additional ½oz	6d.	7d.	8d.

Further Reading

The following list is representative of the major works relating to Queen Elizabeth II pre-decimal issues, stamp booklets, postmarks and postal history. Originally culled in part from *A List of Books on the Postal History, and Adhesive Postage and Revenue Stamps of Great Britain*, compiled by Arnold M. Strange (2nd edition, 1971, Great Britain Philatelic Society, London). Later publications have been included.

GENERAL

Alderfer, David and Rosenblum, Larry. *Introduction to the Stamps of Great Britain.* (2004, Amos Press, Sidney, Ohio, USA)

Allen, Giles. *Special Stamp History: 1953 Coronation Issue* (1997, National Postal Museum, London.)

Allen, Giles. *The Wildings: The First Elizabeth II Definitives* (2002, British Philatelic Bulletin Publication No 9, Royal Mail, London)

Allen, Giles. *The First Elizabeth II Castle High Value Definitives* (2005, British Philatelic Bulletin Publication No 11, Royal Mail, London)

Bater, Gerry and The Lord Spens. *The Queen Elizabeth II Waterlow Castle High Values, 1955–1958.* (1990. The GB Overprints Society.)

Furfie, Michael. *British Postage Due Mail, 1914–1971.* (1993. The Author, Middx.)

Gentleman, David. *Artwork* (2002, Ebury Press, London)

Hine, I. S. and Loveland, R. A. *Great Britain, Queen Elizabeth II. Check List of Photogravure Cylinder Numbers, 1952–1963.* (1964, A. L. Bert.)

J. L. Shelley *Simplified Catalogue of Varieties on Queen Elizabeth II Postage Stamps.* (11th Edn. 1968. Shelley Stamps, London. Supplement 1969/1970.)

Klempka, Edward. *The Dollis Hill Find, Mechanisation of the mail and phosphor trials on Wilding portrait stamps. 1958–1972.* (2013, GB Philatelic Publications Ltd)

Langston, Colin M. *Catalogue of Flaws on Q.E. GB Sheet Stamps.* (1966. The Author, London.)

Langston, Colin M. *A Priced Catalogue and Guide to Collecting Queen Elizabeth Great Britain Stamp Booklets. March 1953 to December 1963.* (1964. The Author, London.)

Langston, Colin M. *The Complete List of Flaws on Queen Elizabeth Great Britain (1st Design) Stamps from Booklets and Coils.* (1969. The Author, London.)

Langston, Colin M. and Corliss, H. C. *Stamps of Great Britain Issued in Rolls and the Machines which Use Them. An Historical Survey including a Check List of the Rolls issued since 1938.* (1961. The Authors, London.)

Mackay, James A. *British Stamps.* (1985. Longman Group Ltd., London.)

Machin, Arnold. *Artist of an Icon: The Memoirs of Arnold Machin* (2002, Frontier Publishing, Kirstead, Norfolk)

Morgan, Glenn H. *British Stamp Exhibitions* (1995, The Author, London.)

Myall, D. G. A. *The Deegam Se-tenant Catalogue of GB Elizabethan Definitives.* (1979. The Author, Bridport, Dorset.)

Myall, D. G. A. *The Deegam Catalogue of Elizabethan Coil Leaders.* (1987. The Author, Bridport, Dorset.)

Myall, D.G.A. *The Complete Deegam Machin Handbook* (2003, 3rd edition, The Author, Bridport, Dorset. Published in printed & electronic versions. Supplement published 2005)

Pierron, Tom. *The Catalogue of Great Britain Errors & Varieties* (Published in and electronic version)

Potter, David. *British Elizabethan Stamps.* (1971. B.T. Batsford, London.)

Rigo de Righi, A. G. *The Stamps of Royalty; British Commemorative Issues for Royal Occasions, 1935–1972.* (1973. The National Postal Museum, London.)

Rose, Stuart. *Royal Mail Stamps.* A Survey of British Stamp Design. (1980. Phaidon Press, Oxford.)

The Shalan Catalogue. *A Guide to the Missing Phosphor Lines Issues of Queen Elizabeth II Great Britain.* (3rd. Edn. 1971. Shelley Stamps, and B. Alan Ltd., London.)

Sweet, Fay. *Queen Elizabeth II: A Jubilee Portrait in Stamps* (2002, Royal Mail & The British Library, London).

West, Richard and Muir, Douglas N. *The Story of Definitive Stamps* (1993, Royal Mail, London).

Wijman, J. J. *Postage Stamps of Great Britain and their History.* (1986. The Author, Netherlands.)

Williams, L. N. and M. *Commemorative Postage Stamps of Great Britain.* (1967. Arco Publications, London.)

Woodstock Catalogue, 5th edition, 1970

POST OFFICE BOOKLETS OF STAMPS

Alexander, Jean and Newbery, Leonard F. *British Stamp Booklets.* Part 1, Series 1: Part 2, Series 1/2; Part 3, Series 3/5; Part 4, Series 6: Part 5, Series 7; Part 6, Series 8/9: Part 7, Series 10/11, Part 8, Appendix A and B, Part 9, Appendix C, Addenda & Corrigenda and Index (1987–97 in nine parts. The Great Britain Philatelic Society, London.) Parts 4/7 contain information on booklets issued from 1951/1970.

POSTAL HISTORY AND POSTMARKS

Awcock, P. G. *Automatic Letter Sorting in the United Kingdom.* (7th. Edn. 1985. The Author, Haywards Heath.)

Bennett, J. Bruce, Parsons, Cyril, R. H., and Pearson, G. R. *Current Machine Postmarks of the United Kingdom.* (1963. British Postmark Society, London.)

Dagnall, H. *The Mechanised Sorting of Mail.* (1976. The Author, Leicester.)

Daunton, M. J. *Royal Mail: The Post Office since 1840.* (1985. The Athlone Press, London.)

Farrugia, Jean. *A Guide to Post Office Archives.* (1986. The Post Office, London.)

Holland, F. C. *Introduction to British Postmark Collecting.* (1971.)

Langston, Colin M. *Surcharge and Explanatory Dies of Great Britain.* (1964. The Author.)

Mackay, James A. *The Parcel Post of the British Isles.* (1982. The Author, Dumfries.)

Mackay, James A. *Registered Mail of the British Isles.* (1983. The Author, Dumfries.)

Mackay James A. *Scottish Postmarks 1693–1978.* (1978. The Author, Dumfries.)

Mackay James A. *English and Welsh Postmarks since 1840.* (1980. The Author, Dumfries.)

Mackay, James A. *British Post Office Numbers 1924–1969.* (1981. The Author, Dumfries.)

Mackay, James A. *Surcharged Mail of the British Isles.* (1984. The Author, Dumfries.)

Mackay, James A. *Official Mail of the British Isles.* (1983. The Author, Dumfries.)

Further Reading

Mackay, James A. *Machine Cancellations of Scotland*. (1986. The Author, Dumfries.)
Mackay, James A. *Postal History Annual*. (From 1979. The Author, Dumfries.)
Mackay, James A. *Scotland's Posts* (2000. The Author, Glasgow)
Muir, Douglas N. and Robinson Martin. *An Introduction to British Postal Mechanisation*. (1980. Postal Mechanisation Study Circle, Henley-on-Thames, Oxon. Supplements 1981, 1983 and 1992.)
Parsons, Cyril R. H., Peachey, Colin G. and Pearson, George R. *Local Publicity Slogan Postmarks 1963–1969*. (1981. 2nd edn. The Authors, Herts.)
Parsons, Cyril R. H., Peachey, Colin G. and Pearson, George R. *Slogan Postmarks of the Seventies*. (1980. The Authors, London.)
Parsons, Cyril R.H., Peachey, Colin G. and Pearson, George. *Collecting Slogan Postmarks 1917–69*. (1986. The Authors, Aylesbury.)
Pask, Brian and Peachey, Colin, G. *Twenty Years of First Day Postmarks*. (1983. British Postmark Society, Herts.)
Peach, Jack. *UK Machine Marks*. (1982. 2nd Edn. Vera Trinder Ltd., London.)
Peachey, Colin G. *In-depth U.K. Slogan Postmark Listings*: Details of All Towns Using Multi-Town Slogan Postmarks in the UK Over Four Decades 1960–1999. (1996. The Author, Hemel Hempstead.)
Pearson, George R. *Special Event Postmarks of the United Kingdom, Vol. II 1963–1983*. (1996. British Postmark Society, Hemel Hempstead, Herts.)
Pearson, George R. *Special Event Postmarks of the United Kingdom. Vol. I The Early Years 1851–1962* (1991 4th. Edn. British Postmark Society, Hemel Hempstead, Herts.)
Pipe, W. (Ed). *Collect British Postmarks*. (2013 9th Edition. Stanley Gibbons Ltd.)
Reynolds, Paul. *The Machine Cancellations of Wales 1905–1985*. (1985. Welsh Philatelic Society, Swansea.)
Swan, V. *British Slogan Cancellations, 1917–1960*. (1960. The Author, Alton.)
Wellsted, Hilary. *Express Service 1891–1971*. (1986. Postal History Society, Tonbridge.)

POSTAL RATES
Johnson, Robert and Peet, Gordon. *British Postal Rates 1937 to 2000*. (2000)

PHILATELIC PERIODICALS DEVOTED TO GREAT BRITAIN
The GB Journal (From 1956) (The Great Britain Philatelic Society, London.)
The GB Philatelist (1961–65) (The Regent Stamp Co., Ltd., London.)
Gibbons Stamp Monthly (*British Stamps* supplement from October 1981, January, April and July 1982, monthly since October 1982.)
British Philatelic Bulletin (From 1963) (title was *Philatelic Bulletin*, 1963–83). (Royal Mail, London.)
The Philatelist/Philatelic Journal of Great Britain (1981–83) (The P.J.G.B., 1891–1980, was then merged with *The Philatelist*, after March 1966 the former was wholly devoted to Great Britain (Robson Lowe Ltd., London.)
The Philatelic Review (1977–82) (Candlish, McCleery Ltd., Bristol.)
Cross Post. Published by Friends of the British Postal Museum and Archive (formerly Association of Friends of the National Postal Museum).
GBCC Chronicle. Published by Great Britain Collectors Club in USA.
Rundbrief. Published by GB collectors society in Germany, Forschungsgemeinschaft Grossbritannien e.V (FgGB).

Gibbons Stamp Monthly

FIRST CHOICE FOR STAMP COLLECTORS SINCE 1890

SUBSCRIBE TO RECEIVE 10% OFF NEW STANLEY GIBBONS CATALOGUES AND GAIN ACCESS TO EXCLUSIVE SG OFFERS EVERY MONTH
(print subscribers only)

SUBSCRIBE & **SAVE MONEY**
ON THE COVER PRICE*

3 EASY WAYS TO READ...
Print, Online and iTunes App

PRINT SUBSCRIPTION	APP	WEB
12-Month Print Subscription	Available to download from iTunes	GSM ONLINE SUBSCRIPTION
UK £46.20	Per issue £2.99	12 months £24.95
Europe (airmail) £90	6 months £16.99	**GSM** WINNER OF A LARGE VERMEIL AT PRAGA 2018
ROW (airmail) £95	12 months £31.99	

*UK print subscription only

SUBSCRIBE TODAY

Visit **stanleygibbons.com/gsm**
or call **+44 (0)1425 472 363**

BY APPOINTMENT TO
HER MAJESTY THE QUEEN
PHILATELISTS
STANLEY GIBBONS LTD
LONDON

STANLEY GIBBONS
LONDON 1856

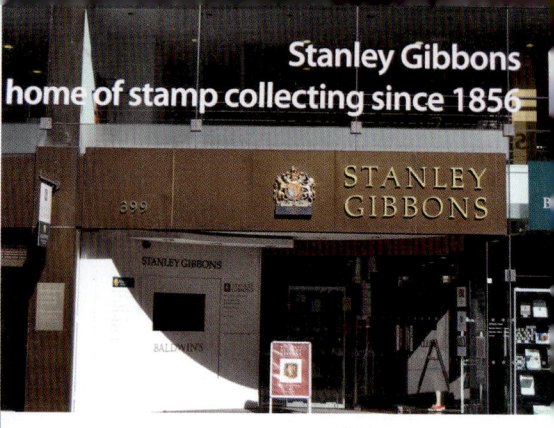

STANLEY GIBBONS - THE HOME OF STAMP COLLECTING FOR OVER 160 YEARS.

Visit our store at 399 Strand for all your philatelic needs.

EVERYTHING FOR THE STAMP COLLECTOR.

- Great Britain Stamps
- Commonwealth Stamps
- Publications and Accessories
- Auctions

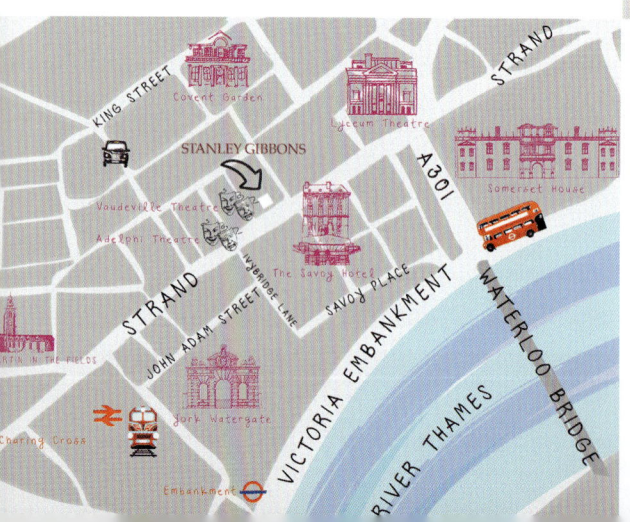

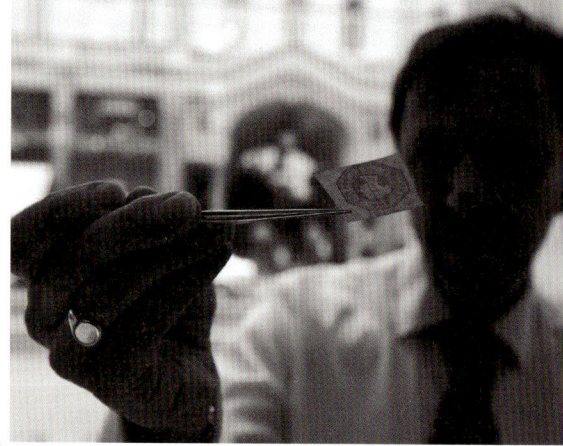

WHERE TO FIND US

STANLEY GIBBONS
399 STRAND
LONDON, WC2R 0LX
UNITED KINGDOM

0207 557 4436

SHOP@STANLEYGIBBONS.COM

OPENING HOURS

Mon - Fri: 9am - 5:30pm | Sat: 9:30 - 5:30pm | Sun: Close

BY APPOINTMENT TO
HER MAJESTY THE QUEEN
PHILATELISTS
STANLEY GIBBONS LTD
LONDON

STANLEY GIBBONS
LONDON 1856

Stanley Gibbons has been the home of stamp collecting since 1856 and is today's market leader for all your philatelic needs.

For the best quality in stamps, catalogues, albums and all other accessories, visit our website today and explore our unrivalled range of products, all available at the touch of a button.

WWW.STANLEYGIBBONS.COM

Looking for that Elusive Stamp?

Get in touch with our team

Great Britain Department: email **gb@stanleygibbons.com** or phone 020 7557 4413
Commonwealth Department: email **amansi@stanleygibbons.com** or phone 020 7557 4415

BY APPOINTMENT TO
HER MAJESTY THE QUEEN
PHILATELISTS
STANLEY GIBBONS LTD
LONDON

STANLEY GIBBONS
LONDON 1856

STANLEY GIBBONS 399 STRAND LONDON WC2R 0LX | WWW.STANLEYGIBBONS.COM

Mint G.B. Stamps Ltd

Unit 2 Lok 'n' Store, 1-4 Carousel Way, Riverside, Northampton, NN3 9HG
Tel: **01604 406371**   Mobile: **07851576398**

Part Perf/Imperf Booklet Panes

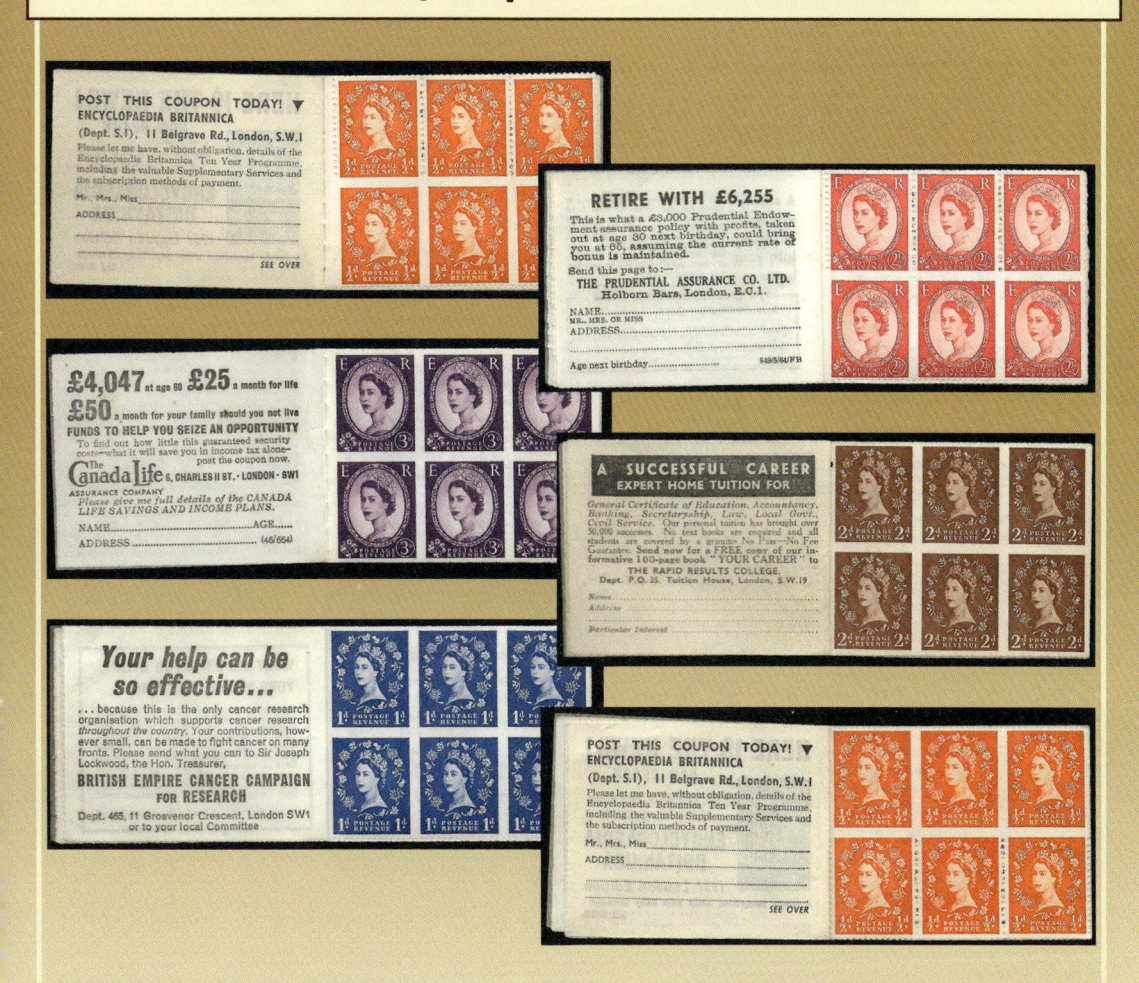

Please request a free copy of our comprehensive Wilding price list.

www.mintgbstamps.co.uk
email: sales@mintgbstamps.co.uk

Mint G.B. Stamps Ltd

Unit 2 Lok 'n' Store, 1-4 Carousel Way, Riverside, Northampton, NN3 9HG
Tel: **01604 406371**   Mobile: **07851576398**

Please request a free copy of our comprehensive Wilding price list.

www.mintgbstamps.co.uk
email: sales@mintgbstamps.co.uk